THE NEW
AMERICAN
COMMENTARY

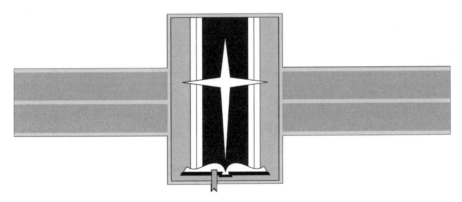

An Exegetical and Theological
Exposition of Holy Scripture

THE NEW
AMERICAN
COMMENTARY

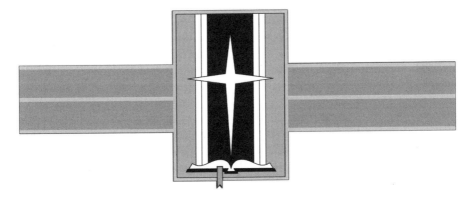

Volume
29

2 CORINTHIANS

David E. Garland

PUBLISHING GROUP

Brentwood, Tennessee

© 1999 • B&H Publishing Group
All rights reserved
ISBN: 978–0-8054–0129–5
Dewey Decimal Classification: 227.30
Subject Heading: Bible. N.T. Corinthians
Library of Congress Catalog Number: 99-045166
Printed in China
12 13 14 15 16 • 28 27 26 25 24

Library of Congress Cataloging-in-Publication Data

Garland, David E.
    2 Corinthians / David E. Garland
        p. cm — (New American commentary ; v. 29)
    Includes bibliographical references and indexes.
    ISBN 0-8054-0129-6
        1. Bible N.T. Corinthians, 2nd—Commentaries. I. Title. II. Title: Second Corinthians. III. Series.

    BS2675.3G37 1999
    227'.3077 21—dc21

To

Ministers of Reconciliation Everywhere

Editors' Preface

God's Word does not change. God's world, however, changes in every generation. These changes, in addition to new findings by scholars and a new variety of challenges to the gospel message, call for the church in each generation to interpret and apply God's Word for God's people. Thus, THE NEW AMERICAN COMMENTARY is introduced to bridge the twentieth and twenty-first centuries. This new series has been designed primarily to enable pastors, teachers, and students to read the Bible with clarity and proclaim it with power.

In one sense THE NEW AMERICAN COMMENTARY is not new, for it represents the continuation of a heritage rich in biblical and theological exposition. The title of this forty-volume set points to the continuity of this series with an important commentary project published at the end of the nineteenth century called AN AMERICAN COMMENTARY, edited by Alvah Hovey. The older series included, among other significant contributions, the outstanding volume on Matthew by John A. Broadus, from whom the publisher of the new series, Broadman Press, partly derives its name. The former series was authored and edited by scholars committed to the infallibility of Scripture, making it a solid foundation for the present project. In line with this heritage, all NAC authors affirm the divine inspiration, inerrancy, complete truthfulness, and full authority of the Bible. The perspective of the NAC is unapologetically confessional and rooted in the evangelical tradition.

Since a commentary is a fundamental tool for the expositor or teacher who seeks to interpret and apply Scripture in the church or classroom, the NAC focuses on communicating the theological structure and content of each biblical book. The writers seek to illuminate both the historical meaning and contemporary significance of Holy Scripture.

In its attempt to make a unique contribution to the Christian community, the NAC focuses on two concerns. First, the commentary emphasizes how each section of a book fits together so that the reader becomes aware of the theological unity of each book and of Scripture as a whole. The writers, however, remain aware of the Bible's inherently rich variety. Second, the NAC is produced with the conviction that the Bible primarily belongs to the church. We believe that scholarship and the academy provide an indispensable foundation for biblical understanding and the service of Christ, but the editors and authors of this series have attempted to communicate the findings of their research in a manner that will build up the whole body of Christ. Thus, the commentary concentrates on theological exegesis while providing practical, applicable exposition.

THE NEW AMERICAN COMMENTARY's theological focus enables

the reader to see the parts as well as the whole of Scripture. The biblical books vary in content, context, literary type, and style. In addition to this rich variety, the editors and authors recognize that the doctrinal emphasis and use of the biblical books differs in various places, contexts, and cultures among God's people. These factors, as well as other concerns, have led the editors to give freedom to the writers to wrestle with the issues raised by the scholarly community surrounding each book and to determine the appropriate shape and length of the introductory materials. Moreover, each writer has developed the structure of the commentary in a way best suited for expounding the basic structure and the meaning of the biblical books for our day. Generally, discussions relating to contemporary scholarship and technical points of grammar and syntax appear in the footnotes and not in the text of the commentary. This format allows pastors and interested laypersons, scholars and teachers, and serious college and seminary students to profit from the commentary at various levels. This approach has been employed because we believe that all Christians have the privilege and responsibility to read and seek to understand the Bible for themselves.

Consistent with the desire to produce a readable, up-to-date commentary, the editors selected the *New International Version* as the standard translation for the commentary series. The selection was made primarily because of the NIV's faithfulness to the original languages and its beautiful and readable style. The authors, however, have been given the liberty to differ at places from the NIV as they develop their own translations from the Greek and Hebrew texts.

The NAC reflects the vision and leadership of those who provide oversight for Broadman Press, who in 1987 called for a new commentary series that would evidence a commitment to the inerrancy of Scripture and a faithfulness to the classic Christian tradition. While the commentary adopts an "American" name, it should be noted some writers represent countries outside the United States, giving the commentary an international perspective. The diverse group of writers includes scholars, teachers, and administrators from almost twenty different colleges and seminaries, as well as pastors, missionaries, and a layperson.

The editors and writers hope that THE NEW AMERICAN COMMENTARY will be helpful and instructive for pastors and teachers, scholars and students, for men and women in the churches who study and teach God's Word in various settings. We trust that for editors, authors, and readers alike, the commentary will be used to build up the church, encourage obedience, and bring renewal to God's people. Above all, we pray that the NAC will bring glory and honor to our Lord who has graciously redeemed us and faithfully revealed himself to us in his Holy Word.

SOLI DEO GLORIA
The Editors

Author Preface

I would like to thank F. Matthew Schobert, my student assistant at George W. Truett Theological Seminary, Baylor University, for offering invaluable help in the preparation of this commentary. I also wish to thank the editors at Broadman and Holman and especially Ray Clendenen for offering encouragement during the project. I also thank Paul House and Linda Scott for their careful editing. I also am grateful to the many students of Paul who have written on the Corinthian correspondence.

—David E. Garland
Professor of Christian Scriptures
George W. Truett Theological Seminary
Baylor University

Abbreviations

Bible Books

Gen
Exod
Lev
Num
Deut
Josh
Judg
Ruth
1, 2 Sam
1, 2 Kgs
1, 2 Chr
Ezra
Neh
Esth
Job
Ps (pl. Pss)
Prov
Eccl
Song

Isa
Jer
Lam
Ezek
Dan
Hos
Joel
Amos
Obad
Jonah
Mic
Nah
Hab
Zeph
Hag
Zech
Mal
Matt
Mark

Luke
John
Acts
Rom
1, 2 Cor
Gal
Eph
Phil
Col
1, 2 Thess
1, 2 Tim
Titus
Phlm
Heb
Jas
1, 2 Pet
1, 2, 3 John
Jude
Rev

Apocrypha

Add Esth	*The Additions to the Book of Esther*
Bar	*Baruch*
Bel	*Bel and the Dragon*
1,2 Esdr	*1, 2 Esdras*
4 Ezra	*4 Ezra*
Jdt	*Judith*
Ep Jer	*Epistle of Jeremiah*
1,2,3,4 Mac	*1, 2, 3, 4 Maccabees*
Pr Azar	*Prayer of Azariah and the Song of the Three Jews*
Pr Man	*Prayer of Manasseh*
Sir	*Sirach, Ecclesiasticus*
Sus	*Susanna*
Tob	*Tobit*
Wis	*The Wisdom of Solomon*

Commonly Used Sources for New Testament Volumes

AB	Anchor Bible
ACNT	Augsburg Commentary on the New Testament
AGJU	Arbeiten zur Geschichte des antiken Judentums und des Urchristentums
AJBI	Annual of the Japanese Biblical Institute
AJT	*American Journal of Theology*
AJTh	*Asia Journal of Theology*
ANF	Ante-Nicene Fathers
ANQ	*Andover Newton Quarterly*
ANRW	*Aufstieg und Niedergang der römischen Welt*
ATANT	Abhandlungen zur Theologie des Alten and Neuen Testaments
ATR	*Anglican Theological Review*
ATRSup	*Anglican Theological Review Supplemental Series*
AusBR	*Australian Biblical Review*
AUSS	*Andrews University Seminary Studies*
BAGD	W. Bauer, W. F. Arndt, F. W. Gingrich, and F. Danker, *Greek-English Lexicon of the New Testament*
BARev	*Biblical Archaeology Review*
BBC	Broadman Bible Commentary
BBR	*Bulletin for Biblical Research*
BDF	F. Blass, A. Debrunner, R. W. Funk, *A Greek Grammar of the New Testament*
BETL	Bibliotheca ephemeridum theologicarum lovaniensium
BETS	*Bulletin of the Evangelical Theological Society*
BEvT	Beiträge zur evangelischen Theologie
Bib	*Biblica*
BJRL	*Bulletin of the John Rylands Library*
BK	*Bibel und Kirche*
BLit	*Bibel und Liturgie*
BR	*Biblical Research*
BSac	*Bibliotheca Sacra*
BT	*The Bible Translator*
BTB	*Biblical Theology Bulletin*
BVC	*Bible et vie chrétienne*
BZ	*Biblische Zeitschrift*
BZNW	Beihefte zur *ZAW*
CBC	Cambridge Bible Commentary
CBQ	*Catholic Biblical Quarterly*
CCWJCW	Cambridge Commentaries on Writings of the Jewish and Christian World
CNTC	Calvin's New Testament Commentaries

CO	W. Baur, E. Cuntiz, and E. Reuss, *Ioannis Calvini opera quae supereunt omnia,* ed.
ConBNT	Coniectanea biblica, New Testament
Conybeare	W. J. Conybeare and J. S. Howson, *The Life and Epistles of St. Paul*
CJT	*Canadian Journal of Theology*
CSR	*Christian Scholars' Review*
CTM	*Concordia Theologial Monthly*
CTQ	*Concordia Theological Quarterly*
CTR	*Criswell Theological Review*
Did.	*Didache*
DJD	Discoveries in the Judaean Desert
DNTT	*Dictionary of New Testament Theology*
DownRev	*Downside Review*
DSB	Daily Study Bible
EBC	Expositor's Bible Commentary
EDNT	*Exegetical Dictionary of the New Testament*
EGT	*The Expositor's Greek Testament*
EGNT	*Exegetical Greek New Testament*
EKKNT	Evangelisch-katholischer Kommentar zum Neuen Testament
ETC	English Translation and Commentary
ETL	*Ephemerides theologicae lovanienses*
ETR	*Etudes théologiques et religieuses*
ETS	Evangelical Theological Society
EvT	*Evangelische Theologie*
EvQ	*Evangelical Quarterly*
Exp	*Expositor*
ExpTim	*Expository Times*
FNT	*Filologia Neotestamentaria*
FRLANT	Forschungen zur Religion und Literatur des Alten und Neuen Testaments
GAGNT	M. Zerwick and M. Grosvenor, *A Grammatical Analysis of the Greek New Testament*
GNB	Good News Bible
GNBC	Good News Bible Commentary
GSC	Griechischen christlichen Schriftsteller
GTJ	*Grace Theological Journal*
HBD	*Holman Bible Dictionary*
HBT	*Horizons in Biblical Theology*
HDB	J. Hastings, *Dictionary of the Bible*
Her	Hermeneia
HNT	Handbuch zum Neuen Testament
HNTC	Harper's New Testament Commentaries

HeyJ	*Heythrop Journal*
HTKNT	Herders theologischer Kommentar zum Neuen Testament
HTR	*Harvard Theological Review*
HUCA	*Hebrew Union College Annual*
IB	*The Interpreter's Bible*
IBS	*Irish Biblical Studies*
ICC	International Critical Commentary
IDB	*Interpreter's Dictionary of the Bible*
IDBSup	Supplementary Volume to *IDB*
Int	*Interpretation*
INT	Interpretation: A Bible Commentary for Preaching and Teaching
ISBE	*International Standard Bible Encyclopedia*
IVP	InterVarsity Press
IVPNTC	IVP New Testament Commentary
JAAR	*Journal of the American Academy of Religion*
JANES	*Journal of Ancient Near Eastern Studies*
JAOS	*Journal of the American Oriental Society*
JBL	*Journal of Biblical Literature*
JES	*Journal of Ecumenical Studies*
JETS	*Journal of the Evangelical Theological Society*
JJS	*Journal of Jewish Studies*
JR	*Journal of Religion*
JRE	*Journal of Religious Ethics*
JRH	*Journal of Religious History*
JRS	*Journal of Roman Studies*
JSNT	*Journal for the Study of the New Testament*
JSOT	*Journal for the Study of the Old Testament*
JSS	*Journal of Semitic Studies*
JTS	*Journal of Theological Studies*
LB	*Linguistica Biblica*
LEC	Library of Early Christianity
LouvSt	*Louvain Studies*
LS	Liddel and Scott, *Greek-English Lexicon*
LTJ	*Lutheran Theological Journal*
LTP	*Laval théologique et philosophique*
LTQ	*Lexington Theological Quarterly*
LW	Luther's Works
LXX	Septuagint
MCNT	Meyer's Commentary on the New Testament
MDB	*Mercer Dictionary of the Bible*
MM	J. H. Moulton and G. Milligan, *The Vocabulary of the Greek Testament*
MNTC	Moffatt NT Commentary

MQR	*Mennonite Quarterly Review*
MT	Masoretic Text
NAB	New American Bible
NAC	New American Commentary
NASB	New American Standard Bible
NBD	*New Bible Dictionary*
NCB	New Century Bible
NEB	New English Bible
Neot	*Neotestamentica*
NICNT	New International Commentary on the New Testament
NIDNTT	*New International Dictionary of New Testament Theology*
NIGTC	New International Greek Testament Commentary
NIV	New International Version
NIVAC	NIV Application Commentary
NJB	New Jerusalem Bible
NorTT	*Norsk Teologisk Tidsskrift*
NovT	*Novum Testamentum*
NovTSup	Novum Testamentum, Supplements
NPNF	Nicene and Post-Nicene Fathers
NRSV	New Revised Standard Version
NRT	*La nouvelle revue théologique*
NTD	Das Neue Testament Deutsch
NTI	D. Guthrie, *New Testament Introduction*
NTM	*The New Testament Message*
NTS	*New Testament Studies*
PC	Proclamation Commentaries
PEQ	*Palestine Exploration Quarterly*
PRS	*Perspectives in Religious Studies*
PSB	*Princeton Seminary Bulletin*
RB	*Revue biblique*
RelSRev	*Religious Studies Review*
ResQ	*Restoration Quarterly*
RevExp	*Review and Expositor*
RevQ	*Revue de Qumran*
RevThom	*Revue thomiste*
RHPR	*Revue d'histoire et de philosophie religieuses*
RSPT	*Revue des sciences philosophiques et théologiques*
RSR	*Recherches de science religieuse*
RSV	Revised Standard Version
RTP	*Revue de théologie et de philosophie*
RTR	*Reformed Theological Review*
SAB	*Sitzungsbericht der Preussischen Akademie der Wissenschaft zu Berlin*

SBLDS	SBL Dissertation Series
SBLMS	SBL Monograph Series
SBLSP	SBL Seminar Papers
SE	*Studia Evangelica*
SEÅ	*Svensk exegetisk årsbok*
SEAJT	*Southeast Asia Journal of Theology*
Sem	*Semitica*
SJT	*Scottish Journal of Theology*
SNTSMS	Society for New Testament Studies Monograph Series
SNTU	*Studien zum Neuen Testament und seiner Umwelt*
SO	Symbolae osloenses
SPCK	Society for the Promotion of Christian Knowledge
ST	*Studia theologica*
Str-B	H. Strack and P. Billerbeck, *Kommentar zum Neuen Testament*
StudBib	Studia Biblica
SWJT	*Southwestern Journal of Theology*
TB	*Tyndale Bulletin*
TBC	Torch Bible Commentaries
TBT	*The Bible Today*
TDNT	G. Kittel and G. Friedrich, eds., *Theological Dictionary of the New Testament*
Theol	*Theology*
THKNT	Theologischer Handkommentar zum Neuen Testament
ThT	*Theology Today*
TLZ	*Theologische Literaturzeitung*
TNTC	Tyndale New Testament Commentaries
TRE	*Theologische Realenzyklopädie*
TrinJ	*Trinity Journal*
TRu	*Theologische Rundschau*
TS	*Theological Studies*
TSK	*Theologische Studien und Kritiken*
TTZ	*Trierer theologische Zeitschrift*
TU	Texte und Untersuchungen
TynBul	*Tyndale Bulletin*
TZ	*Theologische Zeitschrift*
UBS	United Bible Societies
UBSGNT	United Bible Societies *Greek New Testament*
USQR	*Union Seminary Quarterly Review*
VC	*Vigiliae christianae*
VD	*Verbum Domini*
VE	*Vox Evangelica*
WBC	Word Biblical Commentary
WEC	Wycliffe Exegetical Commentary

WP	Word Pictures in the New Testament, A. T. Robertson
WTJ	*Westminster Theological Journal*
WUNT	Wissenschaftliche Untersuchungen zum Neuen Testament
ZDPV	*Zeitschrift des deutschen Palästina-Vereins*
ZNW	*Zeitschrift für die neutestamentliche Wissenschaft*
ZRGG	*Zeitschrift für Religions- und Geistesgeschichte*
ZST	*Zeitschrift für systematische Theologie*
ZTK	*Zeitschrift für Theologie und Kirche*

Contents

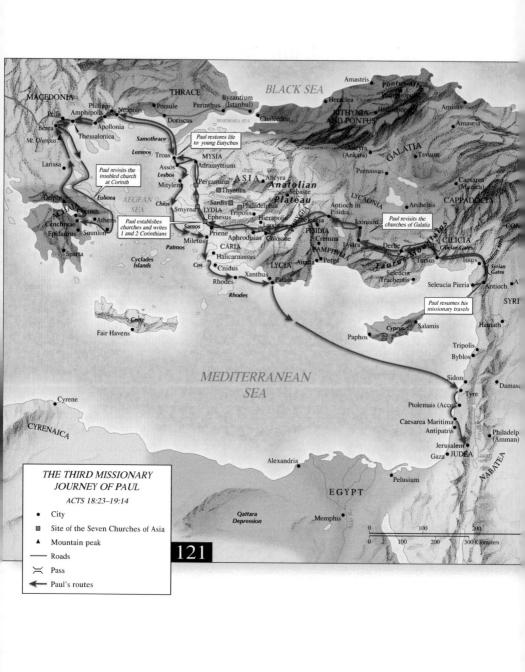

BLACK SEA

Amastris
Pontus Mts.
Heraclea
BITHYNIA
AND PONTUS
Amisus

THRACE
Byzantium
(Istanbul)
Chalcedon

MACEDONIA
Philippi
Pella
Amphipolis Neapolis
Berea
Apollonia
Thessalonica
Mt. Olympus
Larissa

Porsule
Perinthus
Doriscus
MARMARA SEA

Ancyra
(Ankara)
GALATIA
Tavium

Parnassus

Amaseia

Caesarea
(Mazaca)
CAPPADOCIA

Samothrace

*Paul restores life
to young Eutychus*

Lemnos
Troas
Assos
Lesbos
Mitylene

MYSIA
Adramyttium
Pergamum
Thyatira

ASIA
Ancyra
Anatolian
Plateau

Archelais

Delphi
Euboea
ACHAIA Corinth
Cenchreae Athens
Epidaurus Sounion
Sparta

*Paul revisits the
troubled church
at Corinth*

AEGEAN
SEA

Chios

Smyrna
Sardis
LYDIA
Ephesus

Philadelphia
Tripolis
Hierapolis
Laodicea
Colossae

LYCAONIA
Antioch in
Pisidia
Iconium

Cremna
PISIDIA

*Paul revisits the
churches of Galatia*

CILICIA
Tarsus
Issus

Cibian Gates

Syrian
Gates

*Paul establishes
churches and writes
1 and 2 Corinthians*

Samos
Priene
Aphrodisias
Miletus
CARIA
Halicarnassus
Patmos
Cos
Cnidus

Derbe

Lystra

PAMPHYLIA
Attalia
Perga

Seleucia
Tracheotis

Seleucia Pieria
Antioch

SYRI

LYCIA
Xanthus
Rhodes
Patara

Rhodes

*Paul resumes his
missionary travels*

Cyclades
Islands

Crete

Fair Havens

MEDITERRANEAN
SEA

Cyprus
Salamis
Paphos

Hamath

Tripolis
Byblos

Sidon
Tyre

Damasc

Cyrene

CYRENAICA

Alexandria

Ptolemais (Acco)
Caesarea Maritima
Antipatris
Jerusalem
Gaza JUDEA

Philadelp
(Amman)

NABATEA

EGYPT

Pelusium

Qattara
Depression

Memphis

0   100   200
0   100   200   300 Kilometers

121

THE THIRD MISSIONARY
JOURNEY OF PAUL

ACTS 18:23–19:14

- ● City
- ■ Site of the Seven Churches of Asia
- ▲ Mountain peak
- — Roads
- ⤫ Pass
- ← Paul's routes

2 Corinthians

─────────────── **INTRODUCTION** ───────────────

1. Political History of Corinth

The Roman consul Lucius Mummius destroyed Corinth in 146 B.C., killing most of the Greek male population and selling the women and children into slavery. The site then lay desolate, although not totally deserted, for one hundred and two years. Its grand old shrines became a curiosity for tourists, and the ruins provided shelter to visitors to the Isthmian games (held in Sicyon). In 44 B.C., shortly before his assassination, Julius Caesar decided to establish a Roman colony on the site. Corinth's location near the land bridge between the Peloponnesos and mainland Greece and its two nearby ports, Cenchreae, six miles east on the Saronic Gulf, and Lechaeum, two miles north on the Corinthian Gulf, ensured its prosperity.

Corinth's resettlement, however, gave the city a decidedly Roman character. It was geographically in Greece but culturally in Rome. Stansbury notes, "The Greek Corinth of old would live on in folk memory and literature, reinforced by the traditions of the Isthmian festival."[1] But the city's status as a

---

[1] H. Stansbury, "Corinthians Honor, Corinthian Conflict: A Social History of Early Roman Corinth and Its Pauline Community" (Ph.D. diss., University of Michigan, 1990) 116. W. Willis argues that we should not de-emphasize the Greek past of Corinth and stress its Roman character in studying the Corinthian correspondence. He makes the case for the continuation of the Hellenistic character of Corinth ("Corinthusne deletus ist?" *BZ* 35 [1991] 233–41). D. W. J. Gill effectively disputes his conclusions and contends that scholarship should continue to read the correspondence against the background of a Roman city ("Corinth: A Roman Colony in Achaea," *BZ* 37 [1993] 259–64). See also B. W. Winter, "The Achaean Federal Imperial Cult II: The Corinthian Church," *TynBul* 46 (1995) 169–78.

Roman colony made it dependent on Rome's power and goodwill. Roman colonies were established to foster the majesty of Roman culture, religion, and values. Aulus Gellius claimed that Roman colonies were "miniatures" of Rome.[2] The city adopted Roman laws, political organizations, and institutions. The official language of Latin is predominant in the extant inscriptions. Eight of seventeen names in the New Testament of persons connected to Corinth are Latin: Fortunatus (1 Cor 16:17); Lucius (Rom 16:21); Tertius (Rom 16:22) Gaius and Quartus (Rom 16:23); Aquila and Priscilla (Acts 18:2); Titus Justus (Acts 18:7).[3] The city also took on a quite different appearance from its Greek period. Although the Romans utilized many existing Greek buildings in the design of their own city, the organization and city plan differed from its Greek predecessor.[4] The imposing mass of the Acrocorinth, however, continued to overshadow the city. At its summit, the many shrines and temples remained dominated by the Temple of Aphrodite.

According to Strabo, Caesar colonized the city with persons belonging predominately to the "freedman class" and with some soldiers.[5] As a result the city had a mixed ethnic population that included descendants from the original Greek population, as well as former slaves from everywhere in the world—Egypt, Syria, Judea, and elsewhere. Furnish cites the lament of a Greek poet over this situation:

> What inhabitants, O luckless city, hast thou received, and in place of whom? Alas for the great calamity of Greece! Would Corinth, thou didst lie lower than the ground and more desert than the Libyan sands, rather than that wholly abandoned to such a crowd of scoundrelly slaves, thou shouldst vex the bones of the ancient Bacchiadae![6]

---

[2] Aulus Gellius, *Attic Nights* 16.13.9.

[3] T. B. Savage, *Power through Weakness: Paul's Understanding of the Christian Ministry in 2 Corinthians,* SNTSMS 86 (Cambridge: University Press, 1996) 35.

[4] For a general discussion of the history of Corinth during this time period, see J. Wiseman, "Corinth and Rome I: 228 B.C.–A.D. 267," *ANRW* II, 7.1 (Berlin: 1979) 438–548. See also O. Broneer, "Corinth: Center of St. Paul's Missionary Work in Greece," *BA* 14 (1951) 78–96; J. Murphy-O'Connor, *St. Paul's Corinth: Texts and Archaeology* (Wilmington: Michael Glazier, 1983); V. P. Furnish, "Corinth in Paul's Time," *BAR* 15 (1988) 14–27; and D. W. J. Gill, "Achaia," in *The Book of Acts in Its First Century Setting: Volume 2: Greco-Roman Setting,* ed. D. W. J. Gill and C. Gempf (Grand Rapids: Eerdmans, 1994) 433–53. The Corinth Computer Project seeks to reconstruct the city plan and landscape of Roman Corinth. See D. G. Romano and B. C. Schoenbrun, "A Computerized Architectural and Topographical Survey of Ancient Corinth," *Journal of Field Archaeology* 29 (1993) 177–90; D. G. Romano and O. Tolba, "Remote Sensing, GIS and Electronic Surveying: Reconstructing the City Plan and Landscape of Roman Corinth," in *Computer Applications and Quantitative Methods in Archaeology 1994,* ed. J. Huggett and N. Ryan, *BAR* International Series 600 (1995) 163–74.

[5] Strabo, *Geography* 8.6.23; 17.3.15.

[6] Crinagoras, *Greek Anthology* 9.284, cited by V. P. Furnish, *II Corinthians* AB (Garden City: Doubleday, 1984) 7.

In the time of Paul, one third of the population consisted of slaves, and Corinth was a main depot for the slave trade in the Aegean.

Because it was a Roman colony, Corinth was posh. Stansbury observes, "The city's position in relation to the sea made it comparable to an advantageously located island. Its attachment to the mainland made it viable as an administrative center."[7] It had the longest Stoa in the world, and a building boom between the reigns of Augustus and Nero made it one of the most splendid and modern of the Greek cities. Corinth also presided over the Isthmian games, having taken over control from Sicyon. It was a major festival honoring the sea god Poseidon and attracted hosts of people every other spring. Dio Chrysostom relates how the philosopher Diogenes, who had moved to Corinth, observed the vast crowds attending the Isthmian games. His description of that visit is probably strongly influenced by Dio's own experiences there:

> That was the time, too, when one could hear crowds of wretched sophists around Poseidon's temple shouting and reviling one another, and their disciples, as they were called, fighting with one another, many writers reading aloud their stupid works, many poets reciting their poems while others applauded them, many jugglers showing their tricks, many fortune-tellers interpreting fortunes, lawyers innumerable perverting judgment, and peddlers not a few peddling whatever they happened to have.[8]

Many inhabitants of Corinth were prosperous, and "wealth and ostentatious display became the hallmark of Corinth."[9] Many other inhabitants were also impoverished. A writer from the second century explained why he did not go to Corinth: "I learned in a short time the nauseating behavior of the rich and the misery of the poor."[10] Because the city was relatively new, its aristocracy was fluid. Since it was refounded largely as a freedman's city, upward social mobility was more attainable than in other more established cities of the empire with their entrenched aristocracies. Socially ambitious Corinthians could seize the opportunity to advance themselves. As a result, there was an even greater preoccupation with the symbols of social status in this city.[11] The citizens were obsessed with their status and their ascent up the ladder of honor. Savage asks, "What kind of people created such a city?" His answer: people "impressed with material splendour and intent on raising their standing in the world."[12] In this

---

[7] Stansbury, *Corinthian Honor, Corinthian Conflict*, 22.

[8] Dio Chrysostom, *Orations* 8.9.

[9] H. D. Betz, *2 Corinthians 8 and 9: A Commentary on Two Administrative Letters of the Apostle Paul*, Her (Philadelphia: Fortress, 1985) 53.

[10] Alciphron, *Epistles* 3.60.

[11] Stansbury describes it as a commercial city, but "Corinth's political oligarchy … [was] a rather rigid elite with a typical zeal to promote its own honor and perpetuate its own power" (*Corinthian Honor, Corinthian Conflict*, 87).

[12] Savage, *Power through Weakness*, 35.

society one can only rise via a "combination of patronage, marriage, wealth, and patient cultivation of connections."[13]

But the commodity of honor is always scarce, and not everyone could rise to the pinnacle of society, even with incredible wealth. Petronius's bawdy novel, *Satyricon,* contains the famous account of a lavish dinner given by the freedman Trimalchio, who has since attained fabulous wealth as a merchant.[14] The story reveals Trimalchio's pitiful craving for higher status and honor. No matter how wealthy he had become, a glass ceiling (or to make a pun, a class ceiling) prevents the fulfillment of his social aspirations. Since the satire was written by one of the nobility and a member of Nero's court (his minister of culture), it reflects an upper class contempt for freedmen like Trimalchio. He can never attain what he craves—honor from those above him in rank—and he will always be regarded by them as a crass bumpkin.

People compensated for this situation by seeking honor wherever they could get it. Stansbury observes:

> The shortage of reasonable avenues of honor at the top of the political structure meant many well-to-do sought it elsewhere by somewhat similar methods. The options included endeavors such as private entertainment, games and festivals, patronage of new cults or collegia, demonstration of rhetorical skill or philosophical acumen, sponsorship or receipt of an approved honorary statue with appropriate epigraph, and socially conspicuous displays of a private retinue of slaves and freedmen.[15]

For some in Corinth the church may have been attractive as another forum to compete for status according to the norms of society. It may have offered more promise of success in winning influence and honor in the small gathering of Christians. The Corinthian correspondence reveals that Paul had to deal with a church overcome by vanity and rent asunder by an overweening desire for honor and distinction.

2. Paul's Mission in Corinth

Given the strategic location of Corinth, we can understand why Paul spent so much time there. The following reasons are given by Engels:

1. "As a major destination for traders, travelers, and tourists in the eastern

---

[13] Stansbury, *Corinthian Honor, Corinthian Conflict,* 87.

[14] A prominent citizen in Corinth according to inscriptions was Gnaeus Babbius Philenus, a freed slave who attained his wealth from shipping and served in prominent offices as *aedile,* city commissioner, *duovir,* one of two magistrates, and *pontifex,* the foremost religious office (Furnish, *II Corinthians,* 11–12).

[15] Stansbury, *Corinthian Honor, Corinthian Conflict,* 278.

Mediterranean, Corinth was an ideal location from which to spread word of a new religion."

2. The city would also have provided Paul with "an opportunity to practice his own trade as tentmaker since there was probably a high demand for his products: tents for sheltering visitors to the spring games, awnings for the retailers in the forum, and perhaps sails for merchant ships." It also gave him the opportunity for some measure of economic independence. We should remember that Paul did not separate working from preaching. He tells the Thessalonians, "We worked night and day in order not to be a burden to anyone while we preached the gospel of God to you" (1 Thess 2:9). His workshop became a public place from which he could preach the gospel to passersby (see Acts 17:17; 19:11–12).

3. Throughout the first century A. D. Corinth's economy was a magnet for immigrants from all over the eastern Mediterranean who came to work in its flourishing manufacturing, marketing, and service sectors.[16] This influx of people provided increased opportunities to preach the gospel to those who would perhaps carry it further into the world as they traveled elsewhere. Engels cites a modern sociological assessment of those who live in cities: "A population concentrated in cities was more accessible to the influence of new ideological trends than a population scattered throughout the countryside. The man who had severed his traditional local ties to live in the impersonal and anonymous city searched for something he could identify with, for new loyalties and attachments."[17] A city like Corinth provided many persons who might be open to hearing and believing the gospel of the crucified Lord.

According to Acts 18:1–8, Paul spent his first visit to Corinth trying to convince Jews attending the synagogue to believe that Jesus was the Messiah. He instructed the household of Gentiles who lived next to the synagogue, and Jewish anger over his preaching and perhaps his encroaching on the pool of Gentiles attracted to Judaism led to a riotous brush with the Roman governor, Gallio. The result of this first mission was that some Jews and Gentiles (see 1 Cor 12:2) responded to the gospel. Many things would have attracted both Jews and Gentiles to become Christian, namely, signs, wonders, and mighty works (2 Cor 12:12); Paul's persuasive interpretation of the Scripture (see 2 Cor 3:12–18); the community's care for one another; open acceptance of Gentile members, greater than they received in the synagogue; the theoretical absence of social boundaries (1 Cor 12:13; Gal 3:27–28); and the personal transformation worked by the Spirit (2 Cor 5:17). The result was a thriving and brilliant congregation composed of persons from

---

[16] D. Engels, *Roman Corinth: An Alternative Model for the Classical City* (Chicago: University of Chicago, 1990) 112–13.

[17] Ibid., 231, n. 82, citing N. Rich, *The Age of Nationalism and Reform: 1850–1890* (New York: W. W. Norton, 1977) 26.

mixed backgrounds and social standings. It was an explosive mix that led to dissension and rivalry that caused Paul much anguish and concern.

3. Chronology of Events

Second Corinthians contains significant biographical information about Paul's varied hardships and revelatory visions that we otherwise would not know. But reconstructing the events leading up to this letter is difficult because one's conclusions about the literary unity of the letter have a direct bearing on the sequence of what happened. The following outline of what happened after Paul left Corinth assumes that 2 Corinthians is a unity.

1. Paul's physical absence from Corinth apparently created a theological and administrative vacuum that others moved to fill.[18] Paul may not have appointed specific leaders in the church since the Christians met in the houses of individuals who naturally tended to exert influence over others because of their wealth and social prominence. Paul argues that though they have a myriad of guardians in Christ, they have only one father in the gospel (1 Cor 4:15). This statement suggests that the church was inundated with would-be guides even before any interlopers arrived.

2. In two letters, a previous letter now lost (1 Cor 5:9–13) and 1 Corinthians, Paul challenged important persons in the community for their ethical misbehavior and their association with idolatry. Paul sent Timothy to Corinth from Ephesus with 1 Corinthians (1 Cor 4:17; 16:10–11). The guilty parties did not accept his discipline passively. His bold rebukes caused them to lose face and sparked deep resentment. They counterattacked by impugning his motives, methods, and person to undermine his authority in the church. The result: some members continue as avid supporters of Paul, some waver, and some comprise a determined element of resistance to his leadership.[19] Anyone who has held a leadership position in a church can probably identify with this scenario.

3. Paul has changed his plans from what he sketched out in 1 Cor 16:5–9. He intended to come to them after passing through Macedonia and perhaps spend the winter with them. Later, he says he wanted to go to Macedonia via

[18] S. J. Hafemann conjectures from 1 Cor 4:18–21 that some were objecting that while Paul may have been the founder of the church "his absence now meant that his authority was no longer valid for the entire church, but only for those whom he personally won to the Lord. As for the rest, they owed their allegiance to their own particular guides" (*Suffering and Ministry in the Spirit: Paul's Defense of His Ministry in II Corinthians 2:14–3:3* [Grand Rapids: Eerdmans, 1990] 60).

[19] J. Murphy-O'Connor contends, correctly in our view, that Paul's treatment of them in 1 Corinthians was so "harsh and unsympathetic that it can only have antagonized them even more. It would be extremely unrealistic to think that their anger and frustration has dissipated in the twelve months that separates 1 Cor from 2 Cor 1–9. They remained a focus of opposition to Paul at Corinth" ("Philo and 2 Cor 6:14–7:1," *RB* 95 [1988] 65–66).

Corinth and then return before setting sail for Jerusalem (2 Cor 1:15–16). Instead, Timothy may have returned from Corinth with bad news that caused Paul to make an emergency visit.[20]

4. The visit turned out to be bitter and distressing for Paul (1:23; 2:1; 12:14; 13:1). He was the object of an attack by someone in the community (2:5–8; 7:11–12), and no one from the Corinthian congregation took up his defense.

5. Paul beat a hasty retreat and apparently returned to Ephesus and did not go on to Macedonia as previously planned.

6. He then wrote the sorrowful letter from Ephesus in lieu of another visit (1:23; 2:3–4; 7:8,12) in which he sought to test their obedience (2:6). The letter apparently called on them to take action against the offender and to demonstrate their innocence in the matter and their zeal for him before God (7:12).[21]

7. After this letter was written, Paul's life became so endangered in Asia that he attributes his survival to God's miraculous deliverance.

8. Titus probably delivered this severe letter to the Corinthians. He stayed to insure their repentance, to cement their renewed commitment to Paul, and to rejuvenate their dedication to the collection for the poor of the saints in Jerusalem. Paul had assured Titus of his confidence in the Corinthians' positive response to the letter (7:14) and expected to hear some word from Titus about the Corinthians' response to his letter.

---

[20] J. B. Lightfoot argues that Timothy was detained by circumstances in Macedonia (Acts 19:22) and never made it to Corinth. Paul speaks of his coming with uncertainty in 1 Cor 16:10, and he is not mentioned in 2 Cor 12:17–18. Instead, Lightfoot believes the mission was carried out by Titus, one of the "other brothers" mentioned in 1 Cor 16:11–12 ("The Mission of Titus to the Corinthians," in *Biblical Essays* [London: Macmillan, 1893] 276–80).

[21] D. H. Liebert helpfully describes the dynamic of the group letter ("The 'Apostolic Form of Writing' Group Letters before and after 1 Corinthians," in *The Corinthian Correspondence*, ed. R. Bieringer [Leuven: University Press, 1996] 433–40):

1. There must be multiple addressees who know each other well.

2. There must be at least some minimal identifiable diversity in the audience that becomes a conscious focus of the communication.

3. The author must know the kinds of people intimately enough to address their differences.

4. The communication must be designed to be delivered to the group orally.

5. The author intends to adjust the relationships between the people in the audience.

Liebert says that the public reading of a will is a good analogy, "The potential beneficiaries are gathered together to hear the words of the absent one." What is read will affect the way the people gathered see each other. "Someone who had received very little recognition in the community could suddenly receive much attention" (p. 437). He contends, "The best way to write to friends who disagree is to write them in a group letter, especially if you want them to *adjust* the way they look at each other" (p. 438). In 1 Corinthians Paul writes about the "low and despised" (1:28), the "weak" (12:22), those married to non-Christians (7:12–15), the uncircumcised (7:18–19), slaves (7:21–22), those who have nothing (11:22), etc. in front of people who may well look down on them. In 2 Corinthians he talks about himself in front of people who do look down on him.

9. Apparently, Paul planned to meet Titus in Troas (2:12–13). He had an evangelistic opportunity there, but his nagging worries about the situation in Corinth (see 11:28) caused him to leave this work. Presumably, when Paul realized that Titus was not on the last boat of the season (now autumn), he assumed that Titus would now have to travel by land through Macedonia. He left for Macedonia in hopes of meeting Titus there (2:12–13).

10. Titus's arrival with good news about the repentance of the majority (2:6) and their zeal for Paul greatly comforted him (7:6–7,9,11,13,15). His expression of joy in chap. 7 indicates that the severe letter and Titus's visit had repaired the breach.

11. Healing a broken relationship takes time, as does complete ethical reformation. Paul responded by writing 2 Corinthians and sending Titus back with two brothers to complete the collection (8:6,17–18,22). Murphy-O'Connor writes, "Ministry has two facets, the activity of the apostle and the receptivity of the community."[22] Paul is concerned about both in this letter. He defends his activity as an apostle and makes a fervent appeal for the Corinthians to be receptive to him again. Their affection for him, however, has been alienated by the presence of boastful rivals, and he is still concerned that their former openness to him has diminished.

12. At some point during this time, these interlopers arrived in Corinth. They apparently came off as "superapostles" who were more spiritual, eloquent, and compelling than Paul (11:5,23; 12:11). It is likely that when they came to Corinth they made inroads with the group in Corinth already at odds with Paul and most receptive to alternative views. Murphy-O'Connor believes that they would have captured the interest particularly of the spiritual ones *(pneumatikoi)* and "flattered their sensibilities" with "themes developed at some length and with a spice of mystery."[23] These rivals sought to capitalize on the disaffection with Paul and undermined his influence further to enhance their own status. The boastful rivals also embraced the prevailing self-assertive demeanor of the age, which may explain why some gladly welcomed them. They confirmed the Corinthians' own prejudices. Throughout his correspondence with them Paul asserts repeatedly that glory, ease, and exaltation were yet to come. Now was the time for self-emptying, not self-exaltation, suffering, not contentment, humiliation, not advancement. The presence of rivals forces Paul to address the issue of how they can discern a true apostle from a huckster, a true witness from an imposter, and true speech from foolishness.

In 2 Corinthians Paul explains why he changed his travel plans and why he wrote them the severe letter instead of coming himself (1:15–2:1; 2:3–4;

---

[22] Murphy-O'Connor, "Philo and 2 Cor 6:14–7:1," 65.
[23] Id., *"Pneumatikoi* and Judaizers in 2 Cor 2:14–4:6," *AusBR* 34 (1986) 49.

7:8–12). He justifies his frank criticism in that letter of tears and his suffering and seeming weakness as an apostle. He then addresses the arrangements for the collection, castigates them for their flirting with boastful rivals, and warns them that they should not mistake his meekness and gentleness in person for impotency. If they have not broken off their flirtation with the superapostles, completely dissociated themselves from idolatry, rectified the moral problems, and stopped all their bickering and dissension, he will discipline them on his anticipated visit. He does not relish a confrontation and writes in hopes that the letter will motivate them to amend their ways.

Paul has been comforted by God with the Corinthians' positive response to his severe letter and to Titus, but this letter betrays that he continues to suffer some measure of distress from what has happened in Corinth. He has experienced turbulent times in the two places where he concentrated his ministry efforts, Corinth and Ephesus. In Asia his life was seriously threatened; in Corinth his relationship with the church was seriously threatened. Paul has to deal with difficult external circumstances and a difficult church. Feeling imperiled in Ephesus and unwelcome in Corinth, he went to Troas and later to Macedonia where he writes this letter. We, however, are the ones blessed and comforted by this crisis as much as the original readers of this letter. Brown comments that the Corinthian crisis "wrings out of Paul passages of remarkable oratorical power."[24]

The letter appears to have resolved some issues. Paul spent three months in Greece (Acts 20:2–3) before leaving for Jerusalem with the collection, and, presumably, most of that time was spent in Corinth. The letter to the Romans was therefore probably written from Corinth on the eve of his departure. He notes that the Achaians contributed to the fund (Rom 15:26), but his warning in Rom 16:17–18 fits the situation he has faced in Corinth: "I urge you, brothers, to watch out for those who cause divisions and put obstacles in your way that are contrary to the teaching you have learned. Keep away from them. For such people are not serving our Lord Christ, but their own appetites. By smooth talk and flattery they deceive the minds of naive people." This reference to people who cause divisions, who do not serve the Lord but use smooth talk and flattery to deceive people, leads us next to the question of the perpetrators of the problems between Paul and the Corinthians and the roots of the dispute.

The problems encountering Paul as he writes this letter are complex. He must do more than provide rebuttals to various charges. He must restore his relationship with the church so that he might continue to guide it in spiritual matters. How does he prove that he does not make his decisions according to

---

[24] R. E. Brown, *An Introduction to the New Testament* (New York: Doubleday, 1997) 544–45.

the self-centered wisdom of this world but that he always has their best interests at heart? How does he defend his sufficiency as Christ's apostle when he appears to be so weak and afflicted? How does he change their attitudes toward his afflictions and suffering as an apostle? How does he convince them to give generously to the collection for Jerusalem and assure them that he has no intention of profiting from it? He must also quash the deleterious influence of the superapostles. How does he counter their boasts without boasting in the same way they have? He must curb the continued immorality and association with idolatry. How does he get them to accept his frank criticism so that they will not take offense but will amend their ways? If they do not appreciate his sincerity as an apostle and accept his correction, they will not contribute to the important project for Jerusalem and, worse, will fall further away from the true gospel under the toxic influence of false apostles.

4. The Corinthians' Displeasure with Paul and the Letter's Purpose

The breach between Paul and the Corinthians was not simply over theological issues but had its roots in Corinthian cultural values that clashed with Christian values he wanted them to adopt. Savage asks:

> What would have prevented the recently converted Corinthians from approaching their new life in Christ with the same set of expectations with which they once approached their pagan worship? They were recent initiates into a religion of surpassing glory and power, the very things which people of their day cherished. How reasonable, then, to expect to share in that glory. How natural to regard Christ as the source of all blessing. How plausible to view his lordship as the fountain of the individual wealth and his exalted position as the source of personal honour and esteem.[25]

The problem was that as Christians they now lived under the sign of the cross that revolutionizes worldly values and expectations. The Corinthian correspondence reveals that they were not yet comfortable in living out the scandal of the cross, but Paul kept calling them back to Christ crucified. First Corinthians was a public rebuke of their worldly aspirations, and some did not welcome his reproof or accept his advice as authoritative. They may have chafed at his adamant refusal to humor their pretensions to glory.

Marshall notes that Paul does not use "the language of friendship to describe patronal relationships but instead he refers to his patrons as 'fellow-workers.'" He surmises that those who thought themselves his patrons in Corinth probably understood their relationship with Paul in terms of friendship with its incumbent duties and prescribed protocol. He

---

[25] Savage, *Power through Weakness*, 160.

suggests that "it must have been startling for them to be addressed in servile terms." Paul refers to "positions of leadership or authority as 'slaves' and 'ministers' instead of using the regular vocabulary of leadership."[26] He claims that Paul does not use the language of friendship because he is conscious of its connotations of status and discrimination

> and that he is deliberately countering them by rejecting status as a distinguishing element. ... I suggest we find in Paul's writings the idea of unity based on the notions of servitude and subordination to Christ and to each other. Where Paul is in conflict with those of rank and influence, the idea is expressed more sharply, polemically and personally.[27]

Paul consistently attempts to reverse the honor/shame value system that corrupts the Corinthians' grasp of the gospel so as to root out arrogance and power mongering.

Today, we may revere Paul for his determined hard work for the gospel that endured the suffering of imprisonments, beatings, shipwrecks, poverty, and fatigue to further its reach into the world. These things did not sap his love for God or his commitment to the cause of Christ. Rather, they only whetted his zeal to do more. Some Corinthians apparently did not share the same appreciation for this selfless suffering. To them Paul cut a shabby figure. Religion, in their mind, is supposed to lift people up, not weigh them down with suffering. They may well have asked how someone so frail, so afflicted, so stumbling in his speech and visibly afflicted with a thorn in the flesh could be a sufficient agent for the power of God's glorious gospel. Paul writes an impressive letter, but his physical presence is disappointingly unimpressive. He is too reticent to boast and to act forcefully. His refusal to

---

[26] P. Marshall, *Enmity in Corinth: Social Conventions and Paul's Relations to the Corinthians*, WUNT 2/23 (Tübingen: Mohr [Siebeck], 1987) 134–35. See E. A. Judge, "Paul as Radical Critic of Society," *Interchange* 16 (1974) 196–97. Marshall points out that Paul refers to himself and to those with whom he works and has a long relationship using servile language or of the household:
- "slaves," δοῦλοι (Rom 16:1; 2 Cor 4:5; Gal 1:10; Phil 1:1; 2:22; Col 4:12); "fellow slaves," σύνδουλοι (Col 1:7; 4:7); "to slave," δουλεύω (1 Cor 9:19)
- "servants," διάκονοι (1 Cor 3:5; 2 Cor 6:4; Eph 3:7; 6:21; Col 1:7,23,25; 4:7; see 1 Cor 16:15; 2 Cor 6:3)
- "servants," ὑπηρέται (1 Cor 4:1)
- "yokefellows," σύζυγοι (Phil 4:3)
- "steward," οἰκονόμος (1 Cor 4:1, 2; 9:17); "stewardship," οἰκονομία (Eph 3:1)
- "necessity," ἀνάγκη (1 Cor 9:16)
- "unwilling [service]," ἄκων (1 Cor 9:17)
- "laborers," οἱ κοπιῶτες (Rom 16:12; 1 Cor 16:16; 1 Thess 5:12; see Rom 16:6)
- "labor," κόπος (2 Cor 6:5; 11:23); "toil and moil," κόπος καὶ μόχθος (1 Thess 2:9; 2 Thess 3:8).
This servile language has lost its sting over the centuries.
[27] Marshall, *Enmity in Corinth*, 135.

accept their financial support and allowing himself to be demeaned as a poor laborer reflected badly on them as well. Such unconventional behavior betrays a lack of dignity appropriate for an apostle. He insists, however, that his refusal to accept their support does not mean that he does not love them or that he intends to slight them in some way. It does reveal that his practice has become a sore spot. His sardonic riposte, "Have I committed a sin by preaching the gospel to you without charge?" (11:7) and "Forgive me this wrong!" (12:7) reflects the tension. Paul's catalog of hardships in 6:8–10 may sum up the Corinthians' complaints about him:

> Through glory and dishonor, bad report and good report; genuine, yet regarded as impostors; known, yet regarded as unknown; dying, and yet we live on; beaten, and yet not killed; sorrowful, yet always rejoicing; poor, yet making many rich; having nothing, and yet possessing everything.

The Corinthian situation caused Paul intense worry, distress, and frustration. The Corinthians readily accepted his boastful rivals. A less persistent minister might think it prudent to compromise to avoid any further rancor or to concede defeat and wash his hands of the Corinthians completely. Why keep up the battle? Why keep defending yourself against personal insults and slander? In the litigious American culture many might be tempted to sue the slanderers for defamation of character. In the biblical context he does in effect bring a lawsuit against them before God. The epistle is about Paul's ministry, which the Corinthians fail to understand (not about the legitimacy of his apostleship, which is not in question). They understand him only in part (1:14) because they still evaluate things from the perspective of the flesh.

Paul makes his case, defending his ministry in this letter; but, more importantly, he clarifies the implications of the gospel that they have failed to grasp. He hopes that on reading this letter they not only will become proud of him again (5:12) but that they will revive their interest in the ministry for the poor in Jerusalem, contribute generously, and understand the countercultural nature of the gospel. The Corinthians are dumbfounded by Paul because they do not understand this basic paradox that expresses the very heart of the gospel of the cross that he has preached to them. If they cannot understand and appreciate his cross-centered life and ministry as demonstrated by weakness and suffering, how can they understand the cross and the weakness and suffering of Christ and apply it to their own lives? Paul tries to show them that God's power exhibits itself in his ministry "in the same way in which it was expressed in Jesus: in cross-shaped humility."[28] The world, especially the world of first-century Corinth, abominates

---

[28] Savage, *Power through Weakness*, 189.

this kind of humility and ridicules it because it so threatens its own self-seeking outlook. Paul's argument throughout the letter is that "only in cruciform sufferings like his" can the Lord "perform his powerful work, introducing glory into an age of darkness, salvation into a world of despair, a new age with the old life and power to more and more people."[29] Those who cannot see the glory in the cross of Christ because they are captured by the wisdom of this world will hardly see it in his suffering apostle. If they do see it, however, they will see how exceedingly glorious Paul's ministry is. This letter is not just a personal defense; it is a restatement of the basic doctrine of the cross which Paul preached to them (1 Cor 2:2).

5. The Unity of 2 Corinthians

In 1776, J. Semler first conjectured that 2 Corinthians was composed of different fragments of letters that Paul wrote to Corinth and challenged "the final perfection of Scripture" as we have it in the canon.[30] Although no textual evidence exists for 2 Corinthians being anything but a unity, his work opened a floodgate of speculation about the integrity of 2 Corinthians.[31] Scholars have since raised questions about whether 2:14–7:3 (7:4) was originally connected to 1:1–2:13, whether 6:14–7:1 is an interpolation from another letter, whether chaps. 8 and 9 are of a piece and fit in the epistle, and whether chaps. 10–13 belong as part of chaps. 1–7 (8–9). Commentators on 2 Corinthians can no longer assume the unity of the letter but must wrestle with the various arguments that it is a mosaic of different letters joined together.

1. Some have argued that 1:1–2:13 and 7:5–16 form a separate letter of reconciliation. As proof, Weiss claimed that "2:13 and 7:5 fit onto each other as neatly as the broken piece of a ring."[32] Murphy-O'Connor summarizes the argument: "Since 7.5 *appears* to be the logical continuation of 2.13,

---

[29] Ibid.

[30] J. S. Semler, *Paraphrasis II. epistulae ad Corinthos. Accessit Latina Vetus translatio et lectionum varietas* (Halle-Magdeburg, 1776).

[31] For a history of partitioning theories, see R. Bieringer, "Teilungshypothesen zum 2. Korintherbrief. Ein Forschungsüberblick," in *Studies on 2 Corinthians*, ed. R. Bieringer and J. Lambrecht, BETL 112 (Leuven: University Press, 1994) 67–105.

[32] J. Weiss, *The History of Primitive Christianity*, ed. F. C. Grant (New York: Wilson-Erickson, 1937) 1:349. D. Georgi claimed: "The seams in 2:13–14 and 7:4–5 are the best examples in the entire New Testament of one fragment secondarily inserted into another text. The splits are so basic, and the connections so obvious, that the burden of proof now lies with those who defend the integrity of the canonical text" (*The Opponents of Paul in Second Corinthians* [Philadelphia: Fortress, 1986] 335). See also A. Loisy, "Les épîtres de Paul," *Revue d'histoire et de littérature religieuses* 7 (1921) 213; and L. L. Welborn, "Like Broken Pieces of a Ring: 2 Cor 1:1–2:13; 7:5–16 and Ancient Theories of Literary Unity," *NTS* 42 (1996) 559–84 = *Politics and Rhetoric in the Corinthians Epistles,* 95–131.

there *must* be a break between 7.4 and 7.5." He concludes: "Just to state the argument in this way explains why it fails to convince; the reasoning is entirely subjective."[33]

Not only is the reasoning fallacious, but 2:13 and 7:5 do not splice together seamlessly. In 2:12–13 we have the first person singular; in 7:5 we have the first person plural. The passage in 2:12–13 refers to Paul's spirit having no rest; in 7:5 it refers to his flesh having no rest. Furthermore, a close connection can also be discerned between 7:4 and 7:5. Barnett claims that 7:4 serves as an "overlap verse" that provides a bridge from one section to the remainder of the letter.[34] Thrall disdains the argument from some that a redactor composed 7:4 to achieve a smooth transition from one letter to another as "a counsel of desperation."[35] The supposed editor has only deleted sections and not created bridging passages elsewhere; why would he do it only here? The argument is circular. When a smoother transition appears between hypothetically joined letters, the hand of a redactor is cited as the explanation. If the transition is not smooth, it is taken as evidence that a redactor has joined two separate letters.

Clear connections do emerge between 1:15–2:12 and 7:4–16. Paul is restless in Troas (2:12–13) and restless in Macedonia (7:5). He leaves for Macedonia to look for Titus (2:12–13), and when in Macedonia, he experiences more afflictions yet also receives comfort from the safe return and the good report from Titus. But these connections should not be viewed as signs of a splice. Instead they point to Paul's familiar A B A' construction in his letters. The reference to the painful letter and the dispatch of Titus in 1:15–2:13 and his return with a report of the letter's effect in 7:4–16 brackets the discussion of the grounds for his frank criticism in 2:14–7:3. Otherwise, 2:14–7:3 becomes a kind of orphan as an independent letter. What was its purpose? Why would a redactor insert it between two parts of the so-called letter of reconciliation? Failure to offer reasonable answers to such questions should make such speculative partition theories suspect.[36]

---

[33] J. Murphy-O'Connor, "Paul and Macedonia: The Connection between 2 Corinthians 2.13 and 2.14," *JSNT* 25 (1985) 99. F. W. Hughes claims to find an exordium (1:1–11), partitio (1:12–14), narratio and probatio (1:15–2:13; 7:5–13a), peroratio (7:13b–16) and exhortation (8:1–24) making 1:1–2:13 and 7:5–8:24 a deliberative letter ("The Rhetoric of Reconciliation: 2 Corinthians 1.1–2.13 and 7.5–8.24," in *Persuasive Artistry*, ed. D. F. Watson, JSNTSS 50 [Sheffield: JSOT, 1991] 246–61). But the discovery of rhetorical phenomena in the text is purely subjective and subject to quite different verdicts.

[34] P. Barnett, *The Second Epistle to the Corinthians*, NICNT (Grand Rapids: Eerdmans, 1997) 362–63, 365.

[35] See M. Thrall, "A Second Thanksgiving Period in II Corinthians," *JSNT* 16 (1982) 109–10.

[36] Possibly in the exchange of letters among the churches only the most important parts were copied and kept together. Would Paul have authorized the circulation of bowdlerized versions of his letters? In Col 4:16 he expects that they will read the entire letters and not some mutation.

2. The abrupt contrast between 6:14–7:1 and its context has also suggested to some scholars that it must be an independent fragment of a letter. Rather than repeat the lengthy arguments for its original inclusion in the text here, we will deal with it in the commentary on this passage where it can be more clearly shown how it fits into Paul's argument. We need only quote here Scott's observation that all hypotheses on this passage, including interpolation theories, must account for how it relates to its context.

But it is precisely at this point that the interpolation theories often plead ignorance, without realizing that an interpolation would have had a detectable reason for being placed in context, whereas an irrelevant digression should more probably be traced to Paul himself. In the case of a well-formed text like 2 Cor 6:14–7:1, such a digression might represent catechectical material from the classroom of the apostle. Very likely, however, the passage is neither an interpolation nor a digression, but rather an integral part of Paul's argument in context.[37]

3. Using epistolary and rhetorical theory, Betz attempts to show that chaps. 8 and 9 and are two independent, administrative letters, one sent to Corinth, the other to churches in Achaia.[38] Murphy-O'Connor questions the logic behind such a conclusion. He contends that this thesis only shows that the two chapters can be *thought* of as independent letters. "All that his analyses *prove*, however, is that when at the end of a letter of reconciliation Paul came to deal with an administrative matter he did so in a businesslike way."[39]

Paul mentions his trip to Judea and their "sending him on," a technical term for financial assistance, in 1:16. The Judea trip is very much on his mind, and his plans for it have been temporarily derailed by his affliction in Asia and by the growing rift with the Corinthians. The collection for the saints is still on, and we should expect in a letter that mentions the trip to Judea that Paul will somewhere offer further encouragement to spur their generosity for the collection. That is precisely what we find in chaps. 8–9. His appeal in these two chapters capitalizes on the renewed goodwill of the community toward him that he recounts in 7:5–16 and heartens him to raise again the issue of their generous participation in the collection. Olson contends that Paul's expression of confidence is part of his persuasive technique.[40] We would not go as far as to say that this is only a manipulative technique that is not also a genuine reflection of how

---

[37] J. M. Scott, *Adoption as Sons of God*, WUNT 2/48 (Tübingen: Mohr [Siebeck] 1992) 217–18.

[38] H. D. Betz, *2 Corinthians 8 and 9: A Commentary on Two Administrative Letters of the Apostle Paul*, Her (Philadelphia: Fortress, 1985).

[39] J. Murphy-O'Connor, *The Theology of the Second Letter to the Corinthians* (Cambridge: University Press, 1991) 78, n. 55.

[40] S. N. Olson, "Pauline Expressions of Confidence in his Addressees," *CBQ* 47 (1985) 282–95.

Paul feels about their response. But we would agree that Paul expresses his confidence in 7:2,14–16 as a prelude to his request for them to renew their commitment to the project and to fulfill their pledges. His praise would create in them a sense of obligation.

Paul's authority is reestablished through the visit of Titus (2:17; 7:2–3), but he still steps gingerly in making his requests for their contributions. He does not peremptorily order them as he did in two verses in his previous letter (1 Cor 16:1–2). Instead, he takes two chapters to try to convince them to do the right thing. Verbrugge concludes that Paul "can no longer simply give orders and expect them to be honored."[41] In these two chapters he uses only one verb in the imperative mood. He gives the example of the poverty-stricken Macedonians who gave generously and of Christ who gave his life for all, outlines the character and competence of those who will accompany him with the gifts, and provides a theological motivation for giving. He also appeals to their sense of shame: they had said yes; were they going back on their word and now saying no? Through it all he insists that their gift be voluntary. He asks them to give whatever they can afford. God will bless what may seem to be only a negligible amount. Further arguments for the integrity of these chapters will be presented in the commentary.

4. While most scholars believe that chaps. 1–9 are a unity, a majority also believe that the dramatic change in tone in chaps. 10–13 suggests that it must be part of another letter sent earlier as the letter of tears or later after interlopers had caused further erosion in the relationship between Paul and the Corinthians. The warm, heartfelt relief expressed in chap. 7 followed by the confidence that the Corinthians will complete their pledge for the collection in chaps. 8 and 9 abruptly changes to a more strident temper in chaps. 10–13. Paul is on the defensive, and his self-defense as a "fool" constitutes a bitter reproach of the Corinthians. Does one castigate people immediately after asking them to contribute to a fund?

a. Some therefore argue that the sarcastic tone of chaps. 10–13 and torrent of reproaches in 12:20–21 sounds more like the sorrowful letter Paul spoke about in 2:3–4 and 7:8.[42] If the sorrowful letter was more reproachful

---

[41] V. D. Verbrugge, *Paul's Style of Church Leadership Illustrated by His Instructions to the Corinthians on the Collection* (San Francisco: Mellen Research University Press, 1992) 336.

[42] So A. Hausrath, *Der Vier-Capitel-Brief des Paulus an die Korinther* (Heidelberg: Basserman, 1870); J. H. Kennedy, *The Second and Third Epistles of St. Paul to the Corinthians* (London: Methuen, 1900); K. Lake, *The Earlier Epistles of St. Paul: Their Motive and Origin* (London: Rivingtons, 1914) 151–60; A. Plummer, *A Critical and Exegetical Commentary on the Second Epistle of St. Paul to the Corinthians*, ICC (New York: Scribner's, 1915); R. H. Strachan, *The Second Epistle of Paul to the Corinthians*, MNTC (London: Hodder and Stoughton, 1935); T. W. Manson, "The Corinthian Correspondence (2)," in *Studies in the Gospels and Epistles*, ed. M. Black (Manchester: University Press, 1962) 210–24; and F. Watson, "2 Cor x–xiii and Paul's Painful Letter to the Corinthians," *JTS* 35 (1984) 324–46.

than this, it must have been a scorcher. Paul's explanation in 13:4 that he writes this letter so that he may not have to be severe in his use of authority when he comes seems to match his description of the painful letter in 2:9: "The reason I wrote you was to see if you would stand the test and be obedient in everything." According to 10:16, Paul intends to preach in "lands beyond" Corinth. If chaps. 1–9 were written in Macedonia, this reference to "lands beyond" is said to be unintelligible. If the origin of the sorrowful letter were Ephesus, however, then the reference becomes more comprehensible as Paul looks westward.[43] If chaps. 10–13 were the sorrowful letter, it might also explain the supposed change in Paul's attitude toward self-boasting. In 3:1–3 Paul seems to refute his need to commend himself again; in chaps. 10–13 Paul takes great pains to commend himself. In 5:12 he states that we do not commend ourselves again! Perhaps Paul was chastened by the bitter conflict and amended his view of boasting.[44]

Several arguments can be mustered against this view. No specific mention of the offense (2:5; 7:12) that prompted the letter of tears appears in chaps. 10–13, while Paul's defense of his apostleship in comparison to interlopers in these chapters does not appear in chaps. 2 and 7 as an issue. How could Paul fail to mention the offense and the offender who caused the strife in the letter of tears when he is mentioned specifically in the so-called letter of reconciliation? The arguments that chaps. 10–13 contain only the concluding part of the letter and omit the part referring to the wrongdoer (perhaps removed by the redactor) or that the opponents as itinerant apostles had already left Corinth by the time Paul wrote the letter of reconciliation beg the question and argue from silence.[45] Arguments that claim that Paul implicates the church in the offense against him (2:5–11; 7:12) and alludes to the opponents and their attack on him in chaps. 1–7 and that he alludes to the offense and the offender in chaps. 10–13 make the case as much for the unity of the epistle as for the identity of chaps. 10–13 with the letter of tears.[46] In 12:18 Titus, the presumed bearer of the tearful letter, had gone to Corinth and returned ("I urged Titus to go to you and I sent our brother with him. Titus did not exploit you, did he?"). What Paul writes in chaps. 10–13 therefore must be after Titus's visit, and these chapters could not comprise

---

[43] Such arguments are anachronistic for a premap culture and carry no weight.

[44] We will deal with the meaning of "self-commendation" and "commending myself again" in the commentary on 3:1.

[45] G. Bornkamm, *Die Vorgeschichte des sogenannten Zweiten Korintherbriefes* (Heidelberg: Winter, 1961) 19.

[46] Wellborn's argument that a letter of reconciliation (1:1–2:13; 7:5–16; 13:11–13) would purposefully omit any reference to the cause of strife tries to remove the objection that this letter fails to agree at crucial points with the letter of tears. His hypothesis creates more problems than it solves.

the tearful letter. More significantly, the letter of tears was written because Paul did not want to visit them (2:1–4), while chaps. 10–13 prepare for an upcoming visit (12:20–13:1–2).

b. Others argue more plausibly that chaps. 10–13 comprise a later letter and assume that Paul rejoiced prematurely over the Corinthians' response to Titus or that his praise of them was only a tactical ploy to soften them for the appeal for money. The conflict was not resolved. After Paul wrote chaps. 1–9, interlopers arrived, rose to prominence, and stirred up dissension against Paul. He became informed about their illegitimate boasting and under-handed tactics and wrote another forceful letter to check the growing crisis.

Hurd's explanation is the simplest: the letters to the Corinthians were arranged in order of descending length: 1 Corinthians; 2 Corinthians 1–9; 2 Corinthians 10–13. But the letters were not simply attached to one another. The missing conclusion of chaps. 1–9, and the missing salutation and thanksgiving section of chaps. 10–13, requires a deliberate editing by some-one who cropped off the original opening formulas and closing benedic-tions. The greetings and thanksgiving section in Paul's letters, however, were never perfunctory but an essential lead-in to the themes discussed in the body of the letter. Such theories assume that a redactor ignored their function to make a composite letter. The questions of who did this and why are frequently ignored or given only perfunctory explanations that strain cre-dulity.[47]

(1) General Considerations for the Unity of the Letter

Most hypothetical reconstructions of the various letters making up 2 Corinthians completely neglect the physical difficulty involved in such a procedure. A. Steward-Sykes argues that the criterion of "physical pos-sibility" should factor into any evaluation of division hypotheses.[48] He assumes that Paul's letters "were originally written and subsequently pre-served on rolls. Complicated partition theories completely overlook ancient practice and the difficulty involved that working with rolls would have created for undertaking the sort of complex editorial work the theo-ries require.[49] Classical sources imply that when a letter consisted of

---

[47] This is especially true of more complex theories that presume that a redactor edited the text extensively to produce a medley of Paul's letters to the Corinthians that was wholly different from Paul's original intention. E.g., G. Bornkamm argues that 2 Corinthians was rearranged after Paul's death as his last testament and chaps. 10–13 placed at the end as a warning against false apostles to come ("The History of the Origin of the So-called Second Letter to the Corinthians," *NTS* 8 [1961–62] 258–64).

[48] A. Steward-Sykes, "Ancient Editors and Copyists and Modern Partition Theories: The Case of the Corinthian Correspondence," *JSNT* 61 (1996) 53–64.

[49] Ibid., 55.

more than one sheet they were glued together in rolls.[50] In some elaborate theories the redactor would have had to work with four rolls simultaneously, and such a complicated process would have required the services of several assistants keeping their fingers in various places to be excerpted or excised.

In addition to the physical difficulty involved, the motivation for undertaking such a difficult procedure is also usually ignored.[51] For example, the hypothetical letter fragment of 6:4–7:1 would have taken up "approximately one narrow column." Much of the letter it supposedly came from would have had to be deleted, and this column would have been inserted in the middle of another letter. Why was this done? Copying one letter at a time would make more sense because it was more "scribally feasible," but it also would have been "editorially unusual." Steward-Sykes concludes that if we are to adopt a complex theory, "it should be possible to explain in detail the redactional process that has been undergone to produce the canonical epistles that we currently possess."[52] But Duff points out that "any suggestion that proposes a credible rationale for a redactor's putting several letters together in a particular way also eliminates the need for a redactor."[53] If we can make sense of what was in the mind of some imaginary redactor, then we can also make sense of the text as it stands from Paul's own hand. Paul frequently switches from one topic to another, although it is not done arbitrarily.

The serious nature of the Corinthian problem also argues for the unity of

---

[50] Ibid., 56–57; see G. Milligan, *Saint Paul's Epistles to the Thessalonians* (London: Macmillan, 1908) 121–30; F. W. Beare, "Books and Publication in the Ancient World," *University of Toronto Quarterly* 14 (1945) 165; and F. G. Kenyon, *Books and Readers in Ancient Greece and Rome*, 2d ed. (Oxford: Clarendon, 1951).

[51] Steward-Sykes, "Ancient Editors and Copyists and Modern Partition Theories," 59. He argues that what would have to have been done in some theories was "difficult and unusual." (p. 60). W. Schmithals develops a complex partition theory and refers to the skill of the redactor ("Dei Korintherbriefe als Briefsammlung," *ZNW* 64 [1973] 263–88). One wonders if he does not admire even more the skill of the one who discovered the complex partition theory. Steward-Sykes responds: "So much skill is employed in such an unusual manner that it raises acutely the question of the motivation of the redactor in undertaking such a difficult process" (p. 61). Would it have been employed, e.g., only to fashion the Pauline corpus into an ideal number of seven letters?

[52] Steward-Sykes, "Ancient Editors and Copyists and Modern Partition Theories," 64. Citing W. Schenk's division of the two letters to the Corinthians into nearly thirty different fragments belonging to seven different letters ("Korintherbriefe," *TRE* 19 [1990] 620–32), M. Hengel asks whether this is probable. "How do we know that these letters were all sent to Corinth, and that these fragments all derive from Paul? And what fool of a redactor are we to think perpetrated all this?" ("Tasks of New Testament Scholarship," *BBR* 6 (1996) 75.

[53] P. B. Duff, "2 Corinthians 1–7: Sidestepping the Division Hypothesis Dilemma," in *BTB* 24 (1994) 21.

this letter.[54] The Corinthian situation is complex. Like adolescent children, they are a source of great pride and an enormous heartache for Paul. They have been put off by his frank criticism of them and misled by boastful rivals when he is wanting to launch a major project of collecting funds for Jerusalem as a token of Gentile Christian and Jewish Christian unity. In such a major crisis, would Paul dash off only short notes? M. Sternberg makes the point:

> As persuader, the rhetorician seeks not just to affect but to affect with a view of establishing consensus in the face of possible demur and opposition. Success has only one meaning and one measure to him: bringing the audience's viewpoint into alignment with his own.[55]

To accomplish this goal should we not expect from Paul a lengthy, carefully nuanced approach to the problems in such a delicate situation?

The position taken in this commentary is that the sorrowful letter is lost and 2 Corinthians is a unity. How do we explain the change in tone in chaps. 10–13? We should not resort to imaginary fancies that Paul awoke in the morning in a grumpy mood after one of his sleepless nights or that he received a fresh news bulletin announcing that interlopers were making dangerous inroads to explain the change in mood.[56] He explains the joy he felt when Titus relayed such good news (7:13–14). If he suddenly received bad news, why would he not mention it to explain his changed humor (see 1 Cor 1:11)? If this were a later letter, it is also surprising that he does not explain more fully what news precipitated such a radical shift in his attitude toward them from the earlier, happier epistle.

Arguing that Paul aims chaps. 10–13 at a minority opposition (although the whole church is implicated) and chaps. 1–9 at the majority (see 2:6) not opposed to Paul is unconvincing. Allusions to the Corinthians' criticism of Paul appear in 1:17; 2:17; 3:1–3; 4:2–5,12; 5:12; and 6:3. His complaints about their failure to reciprocate his love in 6:11–13; 7:2–3 and his call for them to be reconciled to God (5:20) suggest that he does not assume that all is well in Corinth. If one accepts 6:14–7:1 as part of the original letter, then

---

[54] For a history of arguments for the original integrity of the letter, see R. Bieringer, "Der 2. Korintherbrief als Ursprüngliche Einheit. Ein Forschungsüberblick," in *Studies on 2 Corinthians*, ed. R. Bieringer and J. Lambrecht, BETL 112 (Leuven: University Press, 1994) 107–30. For a thorough defense of the letter's unity in the same volume, see Bieringer, "Plädoyer für die Einheitlichkeit des 2. Korintherbriefes: Literarkritische und Inhaltliche Argumente," 131–79.

[55] M. Sternberg, *The Poetics of Biblical Narrative: Ideological Literature and the Drama of Reading* (Bloomington: Indiana University Press, 1985) 482.

[56] J. Murphy-O'Connor is right that this approach basically "redefines the concept of literary unity in such a way to make it meaningless. If chs. 10–13 were written after a certain interval, and motivated by a concern other than that animating chaps. 1–9, it is a separate letter by normal standards" (*Paul: A Critical Life* [Oxford/New York: Oxford University Press, 1997] 254).

it reveals that Paul does not assume that the Corinthians are obedient in everything and makes his admonishments in chaps. 10–13 less jarring. In this section Paul's mood also shifts dramatically within only a few verses. He rues their unreciprocated affection (6:12), asks them to open their hearts to him as he has his to them (6:13; 7:2). He then rejoices over their longing, mourning, and renewed zeal for him and his helpers (7:7,12). While some regard this seeming resolution as a sign that 6:14–7:1 is a foreign object inserted into the letter by a later redactor, one is hard pressed to explain why the redactor would have done this. If 6:14–7:1 is accepted as integral to the letter, then it shows that the swing in the mood of chaps. 10–13 is not as exceptional as sometimes imagined.

Arguments can also be made from Paul's rhetorical strategy in the letter. It is not implausible that the apostle reserved his strong condemnation for the end of his letter.[57] Witherington, for example, claims that Paul is using forensic rhetoric in this letter. A sudden change in tone and atmosphere was not unusual in such a document, "especially when the case was difficult and a firm appeal to the stronger emotions (*pathos*) near the end was required to win the audience."[58] In the earlier sections of the argument, "it was considered important to win the audience over and thus gain a hearing."[59] He contends: "In a delicate case such as Paul is dealing with here, it was important to establish rapport and *ethos* first, and not deal with contentious matters at the outset lest the audience be alienated from the start."[60] It is critical for Paul to reestablish good relations with this church. He does not fly off the handle and immediately go into the attack mode. He woos them first. Witherington argues that "Paul's approach in the first nine chapters is to urge or persuade, not command." Paul uses milder forms of the art of persuasion in these chapters because he "does not wish to control his audience in their faith. Rather, he wants them to respond voluntarily to his discourse."[61] Paul expresses both joy

---

[57] Paul demonstrates in 1 Corinthians that he deals with topics seriatim. Brown remarks, "To understand what Paul wants to communicate, it will suffice for most readers to recognize that II Cor contains different topics expressed with different rhetorical emphases" (*Introduction to the New Testament*, 551).

[58] B. Witherington III, *Conflict and Community in Corinth: A Socio-Rhetorical Commentary on 1 and 2 Corinthians* (Grand Rapids: Eerdmans, 1994) 431.

[59] Ibid., 356.

[60] Ibid., citing Quintilian *Inst. Or.* 4.1.23, 27, 33. Witherington (429) argues that Paul is using *insinuatio*, the indirect approach to all the problems in Corinth. "In this rhetorical move one only alludes to the major issue that is under dispute in the early stages of the rhetorical discourse, reserving the real discussion of the major bone of contention for the end of the discourse, where it is attacked, using much *pathos*, in a more direct fashion." He cites Aristotle *Rhetoric* 1419b that in the closing stages of a forensic argument one must include "both praise of one's self and blame of one's opponent."

and relief and also warning and worry in the letter. Only after he has established his love for them, explained the grounds for his frank speech, and affirmed their zeal for him after the visit from Titus does he raise the issues that presently worry him.

The remarks of Dio Chrysostom on the ideal cynic are relevant. He tries to lead all men to virtue and sobriety "partly by persuading and exhorting, partly by abusing and reproaching, in the hope that he may thereby rescue somebody from folly." He then quotes Homer: "With gentle words at times, at others harsh."[62] Danker cites Demosthenes' justification for his "closing histrionics" in *De Corona*. Demosthenes asks: "But under what circumstances ought the politician and orator be vehement? Of course, when the city is in any way imperiled and when the public is faced by adversaries. Such is the obligation of a noble and patriotic citizen."[63] Harvey also notes that since "an orator would tend to reserve the more impassioned part of his appeal to the end of his speech, we should perhaps not be surprised if Paul adopted the same strategy in his writing."[64]

(2) Specific Evidence Arguing for the Unity of the Letter

Besides these arguments about Paul's rhetorical tactics that might explain shifts in subject and tone in the letter, there is a consistency of themes running through the letter that argues for its unity. This fact becomes clear in the thematic statement of the letter in 1:12–14:

> Now this is our boast: Our conscience testifies that we have conducted ourselves in the world, and especially in our relations with you, in the holiness and sincerity that are from God. We have done so not according to worldly wisdom but according to God's grace. For we do not write you anything you cannot read or understand. And I hope that, as you have understood us in part, you will come to understand fully that you can boast of us just as we will boast of you in the day of the Lord Jesus.

---

[61] Witherington, *Conflict and Community in Corinth*, 358.

[62] Dio Chrysostom, *Orations* 77/78.38 (Homer, *The Iliad* 12.267).

[63] F. W. Danker, "Paul's Debt to the *De Corona* of Demosthenes: A Study of Rhetorical Techniques in Second Corinthians," in *Persuasive Artistry: Studies in NT Rhetoric in Honor of George A. Kennedy*, ed. D. F. Watson (Sheffield: Sheffield Academic Press, 1991) 278.

[64] A. E. Harvey, *Renewal through Suffering: A Study of 2 Corinthians*, Studies of the New Testament and Its World (Edinburgh: T & T Clark, 1996) 93. Witherington notes that the thanksgiving in 9:12–15 followed by the stern exhortation in chap. 10 matches the same pattern found in 1 Thessalonians, where the exhortation in chap. 4 is preceded by a thanksgiving in 3:11–13, and Romans, where the exhortation in chap. 12 is preceded by a thanksgiving in 11:33–36 (*Conflict and Community in Corinth*, 432).

This statement announces that Paul will be writing about himself (see 3:1; 4:2; 5:12; 6:3; 10:8,12–18; 11:10,16–18,30; 12:1,5–6,9,11).[65] Paul's hope is that the Corinthians will pray for him in his sufferings, give thanks for his deliverance (1:11), and embrace him as their boast. He wants them to recognize his complete straightforwardness and sincerity in carrying out his apostolic commission.

1. The subject of boasting (1:12,14) appears as a central theme in the letter (see 5:12; 10:8,13,15–16,18; 11:10,12,16–18, 30; 12:1,5–6,9). His boast about them is also prominent in 7:4,14; 8:24; 9:2–3.[66]

2. The sincerity or uprightness of his apostolic conduct appears in 1:17; 2:17; 4:2; 6:3–10; 7:2 (defraud); 10:2; 12:16–18 (defraud). In 8:20–21; 11:7–8; 12:13–18, Paul implies that some in Corinth may have raised suspicions that Paul was trying to dupe them in the matter of collection. If they are going to make any contribution to the collection that was so vital to him—he calls it *"my* service" in Rom 15:31—Paul must assure them of his credibility and honesty. They must recognize that in all of his relations with them he is open, scrupulous, and noble. He will not abscond with their money; he will not siphon it off for other purposes; he will not profit from it himself except as it brings glory to God and helps to foster unity in the church and lead Jewish Christians to bless his circumcision-free mission to the Gentiles. In 6:5–7 the list moves from ministerial afflictions to ethical qualities ("purity," "insight," "patience") and then takes a polemical turn by defining his "love" as being "sincere" (lit., "unhypocritical"), his "word" as "of truth," his "power" as "of God," and his "weapons" as "of righteousness." The implication is that others may feign love, use words that are not the word of truth, exercise a power that is not from God but from Satan, and employ weapons that are unrighteous (see 11:4).

3. Paul does not use the phrase "fleshly wisdom" again in the letter, but he does mention again about how he made his plans versus acting "according to the flesh" *(kata sarka)* in 1:17; 4:2; 5:16; 10:2–4; 12:16.

4. The grace of God as the controlling factor in his life appears in 2:14; 3:5; 4:7–11; 11:23–33; 12:9.

5. The topic of Paul's writing or his letters appears throughout the letter (2:3–4,9; 7:8,12; 10:1,9–11; 13:10).

6. The problem of only knowing him in part resurfaces in 2:5; 4:2,16–18; 5:11–12 and throughout chaps. 10–13.

7. The day of the Lord Jesus implies the time when all will be judged, and

---

[65] Only four references to self-commendation occur in Paul's other letters. R. Bauckham calls it a "rambling *apologia* for his life and work" ("Weakness—Paul's and Ours," *Themelios* 4 [1982] 4).

[66] The verb καυχάομαι ("boast") occurs twenty times, the nouns καύχημα ("boast," "object of boasting") three times and καύχησις ("boasting") six times.

this theme appears in 5:10; 7:1; 13:5–10.

Starting from chaps. 10–13 we find connections with earlier parts of the letter, which suggests the letter's original unity.[67]

1. The verb *parakalō* (I beg, exhort, comfort) in 10:1 appears at key junctures throughout the letter (1:4,6; 2:7–8; 5:20; 6:1; 7:6–7,13; 8:6; 9:5; 12:8; 13:11).

2. Paul's bodily weakness (10:10) is a key theme of the letter that seems to mystify the Corinthians utterly when they evaluate Paul from the standards of their culture. After Jesus' death on the cross, the suffering of his followers takes on new meaning. Their suffering is not simply that of the righteous but also bears the imprint of Jesus' suffering on the cross. It is becoming like him in his death (4:10–11) which prepares them for the matchless eternal glory that awaits them (4:17). One last attempt to dispel their bafflement over his apparent weakness comes in 13:4: "For to be sure, he was crucified in weakness, yet he lives by God's power. Likewise, we are weak in him, yet by God's power we will live with him to serve you." To be weak means not to strive for oneself, not to vie with others to gain superiority, and not to exalt oneself.

3. The lists of hardships in 4:8–10; 6:4–7 prepares readers for the list in 11:24–29, which recapitulates these difficulties.

4. Allusions to the false apostles may also appear, although they are not primarily in view, in Paul's references to peddlers (2:17) and those who need letters of recommendation (3:1). His renunciation of disgraceful and cunning ways prefigures his suggestion that the Corinthians have been taken in by guile (4:2; see 11:3,13–15). His assertion that he does not preach himself (4:5) implies that others do and prepares for his attack on the rivals as given to unrestrained boasting (10:12; 11:18).

The ultimate decision about the unity of this letter cannot be made simply from listing arguments pro and con. It must be made from a contextual analysis of Paul's argument. Murphy-O'Connor argues that deciding the integrity of a letter is based on the following "litmus test": "are the internal tensions so great as to destroy the methodological assumption of literary unity?"[68] We will show in the commentary that the tensions in the letter do not require some kind of partition theory to account for them but that they can be explained by assuming the letter's unity.[69]

---

[67] Similar vocabulary appears in earlier portions of the letter, but this linkage is not conclusive for proving the letter's unity: "obedience" (ὑπακοή) 10:5–6; 2:9; knowledge of God (γνῶσις τοῦ θεοῦ) 10:5; 2:14; see 4:6; "to punish" (ἐκδικῆσαι) 10:6; 7:11; "approved" (δόκιμος) 10:18; 2:9; "zeal," "earnestness" (ζηλόω, ζῆλος) 11:2, 7:7,11; chaste, guiltless (ἁγνός) 11:2; 7:11; repent / repentance (μετανοιέω / μετάνοια) 12:21; 7:9.

[68] Murphy-O'Connor, *Paul: A Critical Life,* 253.

[69] See further the Appendix to this commentary.

─────── *OUTLINE OF THE BOOK* ───────

I. GREETING AND BLESSING (1:1–7)

1. The Greeting (1:1–2)

**¹Paul, an apostle of Christ Jesus by the will of God, and Timothy our brother,
To the church of God in Corinth, together with all the saints throughout
Achaia:
²Grace and peace to you from God our Father and the Lord Jesus Christ.**

1:1 Ancient letters normally began by naming the sender, his rank or
profession, and the recipients, which was followed by a greeting and wish
for good health.[1] Paul follows that pattern with notable differences. (1)
The author is no ordinary person but one who writes with apostolic
authority from God. He has been chosen by God, and he addresses the
congregation as God's representative. (2) The recipients are not ordinary
people but a consecrated society established by God. They too have been
chosen by God and set apart. (3) The greetings are not ordinary good
wishes but blessings that have become a spiritual reality through the death
and resurrection of Christ.

Paul identifies himself as an apostle by the will of God (see 10:8; 13:10).
This statement clarifies three things.

1. He is not an apostle because he decided to enter apostolic ministry or
because he nominated himself to be an apostle. God's sovereign will called
him to be what he is (Gal 1:15–16).[2] Paul did not choose his career as an
apostle; God chose him. Acts testifies to this basic conviction so central to
Paul's self understanding: "This man is my chosen instrument to carry my
name before the Gentiles and their kings and before the people of Israel. I

---

[1] See J. L. White, *Light from Ancient Letters, Foundations and Facets: New Testament* (Philadelphia: Fortress, 1986).

[2] S. J. Hafemann, "The Comfort and Power of the Gospel: The Argument of 2 Corinthians 1–3," *RevExp* 86 (1989) 326.

will show him how much he must suffer for my name" (Acts 9:15–16). In Gal 1:15–16 Paul describes himself as having been set apart from his mother's womb, which reveals that he understands his ministry to be a prophetic calling like that of Isaiah (Isa 49:1,5) and Jeremiah (Jer 1:5).

2. As an apostle he knows himself to be sent by God to speak God's word. He therefore contrasts himself with the horde of street preachers: "Unlike so many, we do not peddle the word of God for profit. On the contrary, in Christ we speak before God with sincerity, like men sent from God" (2:17). His authority derives from the one who has commissioned him as his agent. Rejecting his authority as God's apostle and Christ's envoy is serious and tantamount to rejecting God.

3. As God's apostle, "God is the ultimate arbiter of all that he does."[3] God is therefore the one who will judge him, not they. Some called apostles in the New Testament are delegates of individual congregations commissioned for a particular task (Phil 2:25 Epaphroditus; 2 Cor 8:23 our brethren, the apostles of the churches who were to deliver the collection to Jerusalem). As an apostle chosen by God, Paul is not tied to any one congregation but understands himself as uniquely commissioned to carry the gospel to the Gentiles (Gal 1:16; 2:7; see also Rom 11:13; 2 Cor 10:13–16; Eph 3:1–2). This may refer both to the direction of his ministry, "from Jerusalem to Illyricum" (Rom 15:20), and the recipients of his ministry (Gal 2:7–8).

Some have claimed that Paul's status as an apostle is in doubt in Corinth, and most regard him to be overly defensive and prickly about his special status.[4] We are mistaken to read this letter in light of the situation in Galatians, where his apostleship is definitely challenged. We should not automatically assume that the Corinthians are suspicious of Paul's eligibility as an apostle simply because he asserts here that he is an apostle by the will of God.[5] They may have questioned his adequacy and his style, but they do not question that he is an apostle. Otherwise, they would not

---

[3] F. W. Danker, *II Corinthians,* ACNT (Minneapolis: Augsburg, 1989) 29.

[4] C. H. Dodd writes, "There is a touchiness about his dignity which sorts ill with the selflessness of one who had died with Christ" (*New Testament Studies* [Manchester: University Press, 1953] 79).

[5] Paul did not fare well according to the criteria set forth in Acts for the replacement of Judas among the Twelve. According to Acts 1:21–25, the one who would replace Judas as an apostle was required: (1) to have been with Jesus from the beginning; (2) to have been a witness of the resurrection; and (3) to have been chosen for the purpose by Christ (in this case through the casting of lots). But Corinth did not have a copy of Acts from which to derive these criteria to challenge Paul's eligibility on this score.

have read past this first line.[6] Even Paul's rivals must have acknowledged that Paul was an apostle because 11:12 makes clear that they have tried to claim for themselves the same apostolic status.

Paul identifies himself as an apostle here not to rebut critics or to establish his high office but because that was who he was. He understood himself to be one set apart and sent by God (see Rom 1:1; 1 Cor 1:7; 9:16–18). The one who knows himself to be sent as an apostle knows himself to be sent for the purpose of preaching the gospel (1 Cor 1:17).

Timothy is identified as "the brother" and the cosender of the letter.[7] Sosthenes was listed as the cosender of 1 Corinthians, but Timothy is the cosender of 1 and 2 Thessalonians, Philippians, Colossians, and Philemon. According to Acts 16:1–2, Paul met him during his ministry in Derbe or Lystra. Since Timothy's mother was Jewish, Paul made his status as a Jew official by circumcising him (Acts 16:3). In various letters Paul lauded Timothy as a devoted son (1 Cor 4:17; Phil 2:22) and entrusted him with sundry mission assignments when he himself was unable to go (1 Cor 4:17; Phil 2:19; 1 Thess 3:2,6). Although Timothy is not an apostle, Paul attests that he carries on the same work (1 Cor 16:10) and has the same preaching task (2 Cor 1:19) that he does. Timothy had visited Corinth (Acts 18:5; 1 Cor 4:17; 16:10; 2 Cor 1:19) and may have given Paul the bad news that precipitated the sudden visit that turned out so painfully.

Is Timothy named as a coauthor in the sense that he assisted Paul in the letter's composition?[8] Or does he function as a scribe transcribing Paul's dictation? It is difficult to know. The scribe (amanuensis) is not always named in Paul's letters. When he is, as with Tertius, he names himself at the end of the letter (Rom 16:22). Possibly Paul mentions Timothy because he serves as a second witness to Paul's directing and exhorting the community

---

[6] Paul was conscious that he was the least of the apostles as an ἐκτρώμα (1 Cor 15:8). Nevertheless, he confirms that it was the risen Lord who gave him his special commission, and he was the last to receive it (1 Cor 9:1; 15:3–11). This word ἐκτρώμα has been interpreted to refer to the timing of Paul's call, "as to one untimely born" (KJV, RSV, Phillips). Christ appeared to him "last of all," but the word would more appropriately refer to one who was born early, prematurely (REB "like sudden abnormal birth"). It also may refer to the violent nature of his birth (NEB "though this birth of mine was monstrous"). The best option understands this word to mean "embryonic," something that needed to be formed. Paul had been set apart by God in his mother's womb (Gal 1:15), but because his persecution of the church opposed the purpose of his election by God, he was still in an embryonic stage. The appearance of Christ made him what God intended him to be from the womb (G. W. E. Nickelsburg, "An Ἐκτρώμα, Though Appointed from the Womb: Paul's Apostolic Self-Description in 1 Corinthians and Galatians 1," in *Christians among Jews and Gentiles,* ed. G. W. Nickelsburg and G. W. MacRae [Philadelphia: Fortress: 1986] 198–205).

[7] V. P. Furnish renders it "brother Timothy" (*II Corinthians,* AB [Garden City: Doubleday, 1984] 100).

[8] See M. Prior, *Paul the Letter-Writer and the Second Letter to Timothy,* JSNTSup 23 (Sheffield: Sheffield Academic Press, 1987) 42–43.

(Deut 17:6; 19:15; 2 Cor 13:1). By citing his colleagues as cosenders, he makes it clear that he does not stand alone on these issues (in Gal 1:2, he cites "all the brethren with me"). He is not a maverick apostle, and his letters do not contain his peculiar opinion that stands apart from the consensus of the church. They reflect the consensus of those who are with him.

Paul identifies the recipients as the church of God in Corinth. The word *ekklēsia* would have been readily familiar in the Greek world as an assembly of citizens "in which the people's voice was heard."[9] Identifying the Corinthians as the church of God (see also 1 Cor 1:2; 10:32; 11:22; 15:9) distinguishes them from other assemblies: this is the assembly in which God's voice is heard. It also distinguishes them from other associations. They are not a gathering "of like-minded individuals with a religious bent" but people who are God's possession (1 Cor 1:2; 10:32; 11:16,22; 15:9; 1 Thess 1:4; 2:14). They are not their own but God's, bought with a price (1 Cor 6:19–20). Identifying them as the church of God also serves to designate them as "the plenary assembly of believers—as opposed to the constituent house meetings."[10] It would reinforce the idea of their unity from God's perspective. This idea may be reinforced by the phrase "together with all the saints throughout Achaia."

Why does Paul refer to the Achaians since 1 Corinthians is addressed only to the Corinthians?[11] This letter is not intended as a circular letter as is Galatians, which is addressed to the *churches* of Galatia (Gal 1:2). Possibly Paul mentions the Achaians in anticipation of his instructions on the collection that will be taken up throughout Achaia (9:2). Another possibility is that Paul intends to let the Corinthians know that "they are not the whole church even in Achaia."[12] The Corinthians are given to arrogance and self-sufficiency and may think that the spiritual world revolves around them. An unholy grandiosity may have caused them to look down on neighboring churches in the outlying region. Such an attitude would have been reinforced by the economic and social disparity between the two. Betz writes:

---

[9] Danker, *II Corinthians,* 31. For a thorough discussion of the term, see M. E. Thrall, *A Critical and Exegetical Commentary on the Second Epistle to the Corinthians,* ICC (Edinburgh: T & T Clark, 1994) 1:89–93.

[10] P. Barnett, *The Second Epistle to the Corinthians,* NICNT (Grand Rapids: Eerdmans, 1997) 59–60.

[11] Augustus had divided Greece into two provinces: Achaia and Macedonia in 27 B.C. Gallio's presence in Corinth (Acts 18:11–12) implies that it was the capitol of Achaia. Paul identifies Stephanus as the first convert of Achaia (1 Cor 16:15–18), and converts were made in Athens (Acts 17:34). Phoebe comes from Cenchreae, the eastern seaport of Corinth on the Saronic Gulf (Rom 16:1–2).

[12] A. Plummer, *A Critical and Exegetical Commentary on the Second Epistle of St. Paul to the Corinthians,* ICC (New York: Scribner's, 1915) 4.

While Achaia as a whole suffered poverty and neglect, Corinth enjoyed prosperity; while Achaia led a quiet life remote from the noise and the press of the city and its politics, Corinth teemed with commerce and intrigue. While the Greeks tried as best they could to preserve their traditional culture, the Corinthians indulged new attitudes and ways of life fueled by the new wealth and unbridled by ancestral tradition. Thus, the province and its capital were in many respects worlds apart.[13]

Possibly, Paul seeks to bridge that gap, reminding the Corinthians that he does not see them apart from but *together with* the saints of Achaia.

Paul calls them "saints"; and since he does not see any need to explain what it means, he must presume that they understand the terminology. Many today, however, do need instruction on what "saints" means. A. Bierce defined a saint as "a dead sinner, revised and edited." Benito Mussolini said that they were "mainly ... insane people." Others think in terms of those who are morally and spiritually perfect or canonized by a church body.

The term "saints" signifies those who are set apart, and they are called out from the ranks of sinners. God is the Holy One (Isa 6:1–4), and those set apart to God become holy.[14] Saints are called to be separated from the world but then are called to go back into the world to flood it with God's light and reconciliation. Schelkle comments, "Holiness is a dignity attributed to them, but it is at the same time a duty which they must discharge by making the gift a reality in their lives."[15] From the world's point of view they may be insane because ideally they give themselves to God, their fellow believers, and to humankind without thought to themselves.

1:2 Many contend that Paul made a minor alteration of the normal epistolary greeting from *chairein* ("hail," "good luck") to *charis* ("grace"), which "Christianizes" it, and that he combined it with the normal Jewish greeting of peace *(shalom)*. But the greeting "grace and peace" is found, for example, in a letter in *2 Apocalypse Baruch* 78:2.[16] Paul therefore may not have originated the greeting, but he would have understood it from a Christian theological perspective. "Grace" is the foundation of their Christian existence and most clearly expresses Paul's understanding of Christ's work of salvation which presents us

---

[13] H. D. Betz, *2 Corinthians 8 and 9: A Commentary on Two Administrative Letters of the Apostle Paul,* Her (Philadelphia: Fortress, 1985) 53.

[14] Plummer writes, "All Christians are 'holy' in virtue, not of their lives, but of their calling; they are set apart in a holy Society as servants and sons of the Holy God" (*The Second Epistle of St. Paul to the Corinthians,* 3).

[15] K. Schelkle, *The Second Epistle to the Corinthians,* New Testament for Spiritual Reading (New York: Herder & Herder, 1969) 7.

[16] See E. Lohmeyer, "Probleme paulinischer Theologie. I. Briefliche Grussüberschriften," *ZNW* 26 (1927) 158–73; G. Friedrich, "Lohmeyer's These über das paulinische Briefpräskript kritisch beleuchtet," *TLZ* 81 (1956) 343–46; K. Berger, "Apostelbrief und apostolische Rede/Zum Formular frühchristlicher Briefe," *ZNW* 65 (1974) 191–207; and Furnish, *II Corinthians,* 106–7.

with the undeserved forgiveness of our sins and our unearned acceptance by God (Rom 3:23–24). "Peace" is the effect of God's action in Christ. It is not simply the absence of hostility under the Pax Romana but peace that God won through Christ's death, defeating the supernatural enemies and bringing about reconciliation (Rom 5:1; Eph 2:17; Col 1:20). It covers a person's physical and spiritual well-being and wholeness, which can only be given by God (see Isa 48:18; Ps 85:10). Furnish makes the important observation that Paul assumes the authority of an apostle of Christ in this salutation by imparting God's grace and peace to the congregation.[17]

We should note that Paul does not introduce God as some remote ruler of the universe but as the God who acts in history and has acted specifically in the life, death, and resurrection of his beloved Son. We can see his acts in history, hear his words speaking to us in Scripture and through his Spirit, and know him as Father through Jesus Christ. Schelkle notes, "In no other religion is God called Father with such a sense of intimacy and assurance as in the New Testament."[18]

2. Praise to the God of Comfort (1:3–7)

[3]Praise be to the God and Father of our Lord Jesus Christ, the Father of compassion and the God of all comfort, [4]who comforts us in all our troubles, so that we can comfort those in any trouble with the comfort we ourselves have received from God. [5]For just as the sufferings of Christ flow over into our lives, so also through Christ our comfort overflows. [6]If we are distressed, it is for your comfort and salvation; if we are comforted, it is for your comfort, which produces in you patient endurance of the same sufferings we suffer. [7]And our hope for you is firm, because we know that just as you share in our sufferings, so also you share in our comfort.

Second Corinthians differs from all of Paul's other letters by opening with a blessing ("Blessed be *[eulogētos]* the God and Father of our Lord Jesus Christ"). Comparing this exordium with those in Paul's other letters offers some clues about the chief concern of this letter.[19] Three differences emerge.

1. Paul usually begins his letters with a congratulatory thanksgiving that allows him to tell his readers how he is pleased with them and to identify issues for their spiritual growth.[20] In 2 Corinthians he uses the

---

[17] Furnish, *II Corinthians,* 106.

[18] Schelkle, *The Second Epistle to the Corinthians,* 8.

[19] The term *exordium* is the Latin word found in rhetorical handbooks referring to the introduction of a speech that introduces the central issue to be addressed.

[20] The exception in his letter to the Galatians, which omits a thanksgiving, results from his astonished dismay over his opponents' rapid success in winning them over (Gal 1:6–7) or, as Paul later expresses it in the letter, by "bewitching" them; Gal 3:1).

language of blessing, encouragement, and comfort instead of thanksgiving. Although blessing and thanksgiving are comparable ideas, Paul's switch to a blessing should not go unnoticed since it offers a clue to Paul's purposes in this letter.[21]

2. Paul normally gives thanks for his readers because of what God has accomplished for and through them. For example, he begins 1 Corinthians by writing, "I always thank God for you because of his grace given you in Christ Jesus" (1 Cor 1:4). In these opening thanksgiving segments Paul usually focuses on the particular situation of the church, their faithfulness to the gospel, and their fruitfulness. His thanksgiving to God normally reminds his readers that whatever is praiseworthy about their faith and life comes entirely from God, not from their own feeble efforts. In 2 Corinthians, however, Paul does not give thanks for what God has accomplished for and through the church but offers praise to God for what God has accomplished for and through *him*.[22] He focuses on *himself*, not his addressees. At the conclusion of this blessing period he asks them to join in giving prayers and thanks on his behalf for the blessing granted to him (1:11). Instead of giving thanks for the Corinthians, he hopes *they* will be giving thanks for him.

3. Paul regularly mentions his prayers for the church at the beginning of the letter (see Rom 1:8–15; 1 Cor 4–9; Phil 1:3–11; Col 1:3–8; 1 Thess 1:2–10; 2 Thess 1:3–12; 2 Tim 1:3–7; Phlm 4–7), and a request for prayers for himself usually occurs toward the end (see Rom 15:30–32; Col 4:3–4; 1 Thess 5:25; Phlm 22; see Phil 1:19). Here his request for their prayers for him occurs at the start of the letter.

Why the change in a pattern? Several explanations are possible and not mutually exclusive. Paul may rejoice because God has so recently delivered him from a grave peril in Asia. This recent trauma brought him to the edge of despair as he felt unbearably crushed with all hope for life draining away (1:8). A break in the clouds of this unrelenting suffering and the ray of hope afforded by the comforting news from Titus about the Corinthians' response to his "severe letter" (7:5–11) evokes his praise

---

[21] Thrall, *Second Epistle to the Corinthians,* 1:98–99. P. Barnett observes that it matches a Jewish convention (see Eph 1:3–14; 1 Pet 1:3), but the variation from Paul's pattern in other letters, especially 1 Corinthians, is significant (*The Message of 2 Corinthians,* The Bible Speaks Today [Leicester/Downers Grove: IVP, 1988] 28).

[22] P. T. O'Brien argues that Paul uses the thanksgiving formula (εὐχαριστέω) to express gratitude for what God has done in the lives of the addressees and the blessing formula (εὐλογητός) for what he has participated in himself (see Rom 9:5; Eph 1:3–4; *Introductory Thanksgivings in the Letters of Paul,* NovTSup 49 [Leiden: Brill, 1977] 239). Paul does offer thanks to God in 2:14, but his gratitude is for what God has done for him and through him. Paul again directs all the attention to himself (see S. J. Hafemann, *Suffering and Ministry in the Spirit: Paul's Defense of His Ministry in II Corinthians 2:14–3:3* [Grand Rapids: Eerdmans, 1990] 12).

for God's unexpected grace.[23] Although this explanation for Paul's use of blessing and comfort language instead of a thanksgiving language makes good sense, the variation may be attributed instead to the letter's rhetorical purpose.

He begins this letter differently because of its apologetic nature.[24] The switch from his normal thanksgiving pattern hints that the rift between Paul and everyone in the church has not yet been completely mended. He recognizes that healing after a bitter altercation takes time, and the signs of reconciliation must be expressed in concrete ways. Not until they can offer up prayers and thanksgiving to God for their apostle who experiences abundant sufferings for Christ and abundant comfort will his unshakable hope for them be fulfilled. Consequently, Paul will not express his thanksgiving for the church until the quarrel has been fully resolved after his next visit (see 12:20–21). Just as the circumstances in Galatia did not warrant a thanksgiving (see Gal 1:6–10), so the current situation in Corinth did not warrant one either.

Paul is encouraged by the Corinthians' genuine repentance after receiving the "severe letter" (7:5–12), but all is still not well. Interlopers continue to lurk in the wings, endangering Paul's relationship with the church. An opposing faction, perhaps a recalcitrant house church, still exists within the community. Paul therefore continues to defend his integrity and authority in this letter, and he focuses the blessing period on himself as part of his tactics to win back their full confidence and support. How one interprets this blessing period therefore has an impact on the view of the letter's integrity.

Although Paul lambasted the Galatians for abandoning the truth of the gospel, the situation with the Corinthians is far more ticklish. He writes to the Galatians as an aggrieved parent who feels that he has to give birth to them again (Gal 4:19). He did not believe that his good relationship with them would be irretrievably broken simply by telling the truth. The

---

[23] Furnish contends: "It is probably this, perhaps recent, deliverance from a situation Paul had himself considered hopeless that is chiefly responsible for the form as well as for the content of the opening verses" (*II Corinthians*, 117). A letter recorded in *2 Macc* 1:10–2:18 purportedly by Judas Maccabeus to Aristobulus, a priest and respected teacher of the Jews of Egypt, explains the origins of Hanukkah and urges them to celebrate it. It also begins with a thanksgiving to God for deliverance from grave dangers. Barnett argues that Paul's opening benediction follows the pattern of the nineteen synagogue benedictions that supposedly arose in the NT era (*The Second Epistle to the Corinthians*, 65–68).

[24] C. J. Bjerkelund, *PARAKALŌ. Form, Funktion, und Sinn der Parakalō-Sätze in den paulinischen Briefen* (Oslo: Universitetsforlaget, 1967) 150. B. Witherington III (*Conflict and Community in Corinth: A Socio-Rhetorical Commentary on 1 and 2 Corinthians* [Grand Rapids: Eerdmans, 1995] 356) argues that the exordium of forensic rhetoric is directed to the judge, not the audience or the jury. God, not the Corinthians, will judge him (1 Cor 4:4–5; see 2 Cor 12:9; 13:3–7).

Galatians, he says, would have been willing to pluck out their eyes for him (4:16). He therefore could be more forthright with the Galatians; not so with the Corinthians. The Corinthian correspondence reveals that some have not accepted his rebukes well. Some have questioned his motives and put the worst possible spin on his actions. Consequently, he begins this letter more gingerly. Although the relationship is on the mend, Paul saves the rebuke and warning for the end after he has established his case. The quarrel-filled visit that ended when Paul beat a hasty retreat had not helped matters, but the bitter scolding he fired off in the "letter of tears" did bring a change of heart.

Paul implies in this letter that he could resort to force and domination to exercise his rightful authority (2 Cor 10:6; see 1 Cor 4:20–21), but he prefers that the Corinthians respond willingly.[25] His rhetorical strategy seeks first to win the readers' sympathy and support before shifting into the attack mode against those outsiders who have sabotaged his relationship with the church and those few who continue in their defiance.[26] At one time, this church may have appreciated their father in the faith, but they have now "shifted their affections, love offerings, and devotion to traveling missionaries instead."[27] When they began to compare him unfavorably with the visiting superapostles (12:11,16–17), it led some to question a range of issues concerning Paul. Those disgruntled with Paul belittled his apostolic gifts, claiming that "his letters are weighty and strong, but his bodily presence is weak, and his speech is of no account" (10:10). They also distrusted his motives (11:7–11) and accused him of unreliability, duplicity, and cowardice. They even began to call into question his gospel. Roetzel summarizes the situation well: "Suspicious and contemptuous of Paul, the Corinthians followed instead the more glamorous gospel of the new apostles and preferred their spirituality and radiant personalities to Paul."[28]

Paul's need to defend himself and commend himself best explains the shift from his usual pattern of opening with a thanksgiving for the church to whom he is writing. Rather than giving thanks for what God is doing through this church, Paul needs *them* to give thanks for him and what God is

[25] See J.-N. Aletti, "L'Authoritaté apostolique de Paul: Théorie et practique," in *L'Apôtre Paul: Personalité, style et conception du ministère,* ed. A. Vanhoye (Leuven: University Press, 1986) 230–33; and V. D. Verbrugge, who contends that Paul's tentative relationship with the church effects his show of authority (*Paul's Style of Church Leadership Illustrated by His Instructions to the Corinthians on the Collection* [San Francisco: Mellen Research University Press, 1992]).

[26] J. H. Bernard, "The Second Epistle to the Corinthians," *EGT* (Grand Rapids: Eerdmans 1979) 3:38.

[27] C. J. Roetzel, "As Dying, and Behold We Live," *Int* 46 (1992) 3–18.

[28] Ibid.

doing in and through him.[29] He anticipates that thanksgiving will follow if they are reconciled enough to him to pray for him (1:11). When that happens, they will also recognize how God works in mighty ways through the affliction of God's servants.

Paul refuses to surrender this church to unscrupulous interlopers or allow the disaffection of some in the church to force him to relinquish his connection to them as their apostle. He therefore begins the letter with an indirectly self-congratulatory benediction. He is grateful for them and proud of them (6:11; 7:4,14,16; 9:2) and wants them to be grateful and proud of him in return. His joy will be overflowing when they understand him more completely and give thanks for what God has done and will continue to do through him.

The introductory sections of Paul's letters contain an outline of the major concerns the letter will address, and 2 Corinthians is no exception.[30] Key vocabulary and motifs in the letter appear in this opening blessing.

1. The first motif relates to affliction and suffering. The noun and verb form of affliction *(thlipsis, thlibō)* occur three times in this opening period (1:4,6,8), suffering *(pathēma)* appears three times (1:5,6,7), and the sentence of death appears once (1:9). Paul's own suffering, which reveals even more clearly his weakness and God's strength, is a motif that runs through the entire letter (2:4; 4:8–10,17; 6:4–5; 7:4; 11:23–29; 12:7–9; see 8:2). Some in Corinth have misconstrued the significance of Paul's suffering, and he begins his rejoinder here. Paul does not cite Ps 34:19, "A righteous man may have many troubles, but the LORD delivers him from them all," but this principle underlies his self-defense.

2. The second motif deals with comfort. The noun and verb form of consolation *(parakēlsis, parakaleō)* occur ten times in the opening period (1:3,4,5,6,7). It sets the tone for chaps. 1–9. The letter opens with Paul's exulting in the comfort he has received from God, and the first section of the letter (1:1–7:16) ends with Paul returning to this theme. Both Paul and Titus were comforted by the Corinthians' godly grief, longing for Paul,

---

[29] J. T. Fitzgerald, *Cracks in an Earthen Vessel: An Examination of the Catalogue of Hardships in the Corinthian Correspondence,* SBLDS 99 (Atlanta: Scholars Press, 1988) 156.

[30] O'Brien (*Introductory Thanksgivings in the Letters of Paul,* 233–40) notes that it performs a threefold function in Paul's letters: epistolary, didactic, and parenetic. Hafemann puts it well. These verses "introduce the main themes of the letter, express Paul's key perspective on them, and contain an implicit appeal to his readers to join him in his outlook" ("The Comfort and Power of the Gospel," *RevExp* 86 [1989] 327). On the Pauline thanksgiving see further P. Schubert, *Form and Function of the Pauline Thanksgivings,* BZNW 20 (Berlin: Töpelmann, 1939); J. L. White, *Form and Function of the Greek Letter: A Study of the Letter Body in the Non-Literary Papyri and in Paul the Apostle,* SBLDS 2 (Missoula, Mont.: Scholars Press, 1972); and G. P. Wiles, *Paul's Intercessory Prayers: The Significance of the Intercessory Prayer Passages in the Letters of Paul,* SNTSMS 24 (Cambridge: University Press, 1974).

and zeal (7:4–16).[31]

3. Life and death comprise the third motif (1:8,9,10).[32] Paul acknowledges that to "one, we are the smell of death unto death; to the other, the fragrance of life unto life" (2:16). This theme comes out most clearly in 4:10–12:

> We always carry around in our body the death of Jesus, so that the life of Jesus may also be revealed in our body. For we who are alive are always being given over to death for Jesus' sake, so that his life may be revealed in our mortal body. So then, death is at work in us, but life is at work in you (see also 5:4).

The picture one gets from reading between the lines is that Paul has been exposed to so much suffering that he looks like death. Some Corinthians doubted that the reign of Christ could ever triumph through such a weak and perishable apostle whose life always seemed to be at risk. His mission seemed to be filled with nothing but mishap. Where was the evidence of God's power? For some who evaluated him from a worldly perspective, Paul's unending suffering cast doubt on his apostolic power, and the shame that some attached to this travail subverted his authority in the church. They may have thought that God would do a better job of watching over him if he were doing what God wanted.

In response to such doubts, Paul asserts that he shares the same divinely ordained paradox that "constituted" the life and destiny of Jesus Christ: comfort from suffering, life from death, strength from weakness, and wisdom from foolishness (see 11:30; 12:5,8–10; 13:2–9).[33] His apostleship conforms to the death and resurrection of Christ (see Phil 3:10–11), not the expectations of worldly wisdom. As Christ lives by God's power, who raised him from the dead, so does Paul. Consequently, Paul can dismiss his afflictions as "light and momentary." They become particularly light when one views them from the perspective of eternity; they achieve "for us an eternal glory that far outweighs them all" (4:17). Paul refers to his suffering surpassing his strength in 1:8 ("far beyond our ability to endure"). He uses the same term *(hyperbolē)*, however, to refer to the "all-surpassing" power from God (4:7) and to refer to the eternal glory "that far outweighs" the suffering. The divine glory that fills his heart surpasses his imagination to believe. It lifts this lethal load of suffering so that it not only becomes bearable, but it

---

[31] The noun and verb (παράκλησις, παρακαλέω) occur six times (7:4,6,7,13). They do not appear in the last three chapters, but this absence does not necessarily mean they are fragments from a different letter when Paul did not experience this comfort.

[32] The noun "life" occurs six times; the verb "to live," nine times in 2 Corinthians (1:8; 3:3; 4:11; 5:15; 6:9,16; 13:4). The noun "death" occurs nine times (1:9,10; 2:16; 3:7; 4:11,12; 7:10; 11:23). The verb "to put to death" (θανατόω) occurs once (6:9); the verb "to die" (ἀποθνήσκω), five times (5:14,15; 6:9).

[33] R. P. C. Hanson, *II Corinthians,* TBC (London: SPCK, 1954) 32.

also becomes meaningful as a part of God's purposes for him.[34] Therefore Paul does not fix his eyes on the suffering (4:17) but on what cannot be seen, his inner glory (4:18); not on the external crumbling but his inner renewal; not on his daily dying but his future resurrection; not on this present evil age but the new age; not on what is momentary and inconsequential (4:17) but what is eternal; not on the earthly but the heavenly (5:1–2).

The Corinthians have not adjusted their eyes to be able to see what is still invisible (5:7). They have fixed their eyes instead on the wrong things, on temporary realities. This spiritual myopia results in a failure to see how God is working though Paul's afflictions. What distresses Paul even more is the arrival of braggart outsiders who confirm the Corinthians in this grave spiritual error. He reserves discussion of these interlopers and their dangerous delusions about the nature of apostleship until the end of the letter.

4. The fourth motif that emerges in this section is the interconnectedness between Paul and the Corinthians. What happens to him directly affects them. As Paul sees it, his affliction leads to consolation from God for consolation of others. Therefore when he experiences affliction, it is for their benefit. When he experiences God's comfort, it is to comfort them (1:6). They endure the same hardships (1:7).[35] This motif is expressed most clearly in 4:14: "We know that the one who raised the Lord Jesus from the dead will also raise us with Jesus and present us *with you* in his presence" (cf. 1 Thess 2:19; Phil 4:1). He is not a freelance apostle who is detachable from the churches he founded. He is intimately yoked to them in the cause of Christ.

1:3 Paul launches his letter with a classic Jewish liturgical formula that praises God for his benefits: "Blessed be the God and Father of our Lord Jesus Christ."[36] Had Paul not identified God as the Father of Jesus Christ, this benediction would have had a familiar ring in the synagogue but would also have been jarring. The synagogue blessed the God of our fathers, who revealed himself to Moses as "I AM WHO I AM" (or "I WILL BE WHO I WILL BE"; Exod 3:14). For Christians, God is now revealed as the God and Father of our Lord Jesus Christ.[37] This affirmation has two implications. First, as the Father of Jesus Christ, God is no longer to be known simply as the Father of Israel. Through Jesus Christ all, both Jew

---

[34] Barnett notes that suffering brings matching comfort, offers encouragement, and intensifies hope (*The Second Epistle to the Corinthians,* 56).

[35] See Paul's emphasis on their interrelatedness in 1:24; 2:2–3,10; 3:2; 6:12–13; 7:3,12; 13:9; see 1 Cor 12:5.

[36] See Gen 24:26–27; 1 Kgs 8:15; Pss 41:13; 72:18–19; 89:52; 106:48; *2 Macc* 1:17; and Luke 1:68. The first tractate in the *Mishna, Berakot,* has to do with blessings. The verb "to be" is not present in the text, and the NIV translation supplies an optative form of the verb. Furnish argues that a simple indicative is better, blessed is God (see 11:31: he who is blessed [*II Corinthians,* 108]).

[37] See also 11:31; Rom 1:7; 15:6; Eph 1:3,17; Col 1:3; 1 Pet 1:3; and Rev 1:6.

and Greek, have access to the Father (Eph 2:18). One can only truly know God as Father as the Father of Jesus Christ. Second, it declares that Jesus is the foremost blessing God has bestowed on humankind (see Col 1:12).[38]

Elsewhere Paul exults that God the Father has given Jesus the name "Lord" that is above every name (Phil 2:11) and that denotes his special status and supreme authority. That Jesus is *our Lord* is central to all that Paul believes and also sums up his preaching (4:5; see Col 2:6).[39] Unfortunately, this lofty title has lost its impact in our era and, according to one, "has become one of the most lifeless words in the Christian vocabulary."[40] It means that those who call him Lord belong absolutely to him and owe him, and no other so-called lords (1 Cor 8:5–6), absolute obedience (see Luke 6:46). Since God has given Jesus this status, to reject Jesus as Lord is "to repudiate God as Father."[41] To confess Jesus as Lord brings glory to God (Phil 2:11).

Paul identifies God as the God of love and peace (2 Cor 13:11), the God of endurance and comfort (Rom 15:5), the God of hope (Rom 15:13), the God of peace (Rom 16:20; 1 Thess 5:23; 2 Thess 3:16), the God who gives endurance and encouragement (Rom 15:5). Here he identifies him as the Father of all mercies and God of all comfort and implies that mercies and comfort are brought to realization through Christ (1:5).[42] Bernard says that God is not called the Father of judgments or vengeances but the Father of *all* mercies and comfort.[43] The threefold repetition of *all* "intensifies the idea of abundance."[44]

The God to whom Paul offers up praise is not known only through theological theorems and creeds but through his direct action of comforting and showing mercy (see Ps 103:13–14). Hofius has shown from the usage of the word "comfort" in the Old Testament that it refers to God's concrete inter-

---

[38] Danker, *II Corinthians*, 33. The sentence has a chiastic structure: The God and Father of Jesus Christ : the Father of mercies and God of all comfort.

[39] Paul refers to Christ as "Lord" over two hundred times in his letters. For the phrase "our Lord" in Paul see Rom 1:4; 4:24; 5:1,11,21; 6:23; 7:25; 8:39; 15:6,30; 16:18,20; 1 Cor 1:2,7–10; 5:4; 9:1; 15:31,57; 2 Cor 8:9; Gal 1:3; 6:14,18; Eph 1:3,17; 3:11; 5:20; 6:24; Col 1:3; 1 Thess 1:3; 2:19; 3:11,13; 5:9,23,28; 2 Thess 1:8; 2:1,14,16; 3:18; 1 Tim 1:2,12,14; 6:3,14; and 2 Tim 1:2,8.

[40] Plummer, *The Second Epistle of St. Paul to the Corinthians*, 8.

[41] Barnett, *The Message of 2 Corinthians*, 29.

[42] C. M. Proudfoot, "Imitation or Realistic Participation? A Study of Paul's Concept of 'Suffering with Christ,'" *Int* 17 (1963) 143. C. Kruse notes that Paul uses the expression "the mercies of God" in Rom 12:1 "to denote the great saving acts of God in Christ as described in Rom 1–11," *2 Corinthians*, TNTC (Grand Rapids: Eerdmans, 1987) 59.

[43] Bernard (Serm. 5 de Natali Dom) cited by C. à Lapide, *The Great Commentary of Cornelius à Lapide: II Corinthians and Galatians*, trans. and ed. W. F. Cobb (London: John Hodges, 1897) 3.

[44] Plummer, *The Second Epistle of St. Paul to the Corinthians*, 9.

vention.[45] The divine commission that the prophet Isaiah overhears, "Comfort ye, my people" (Isa 40:1), does not have as its end simply consoling the people in their affliction. God intends to intervene and deliver them out of their affliction. The loud lament for God to wake up and do something (Isa 51:9),

> Awake, awake! Clothe yourself with strength,
>   O arm of the LORD;
> awake, as in days gone by,
>   as in generations of old.
> Was it not you who cut Rahab to pieces,
>   who pierced that monster through?

receives its answer in Isa 51:12: "I, even I, am he who comforts you."[46]

Paul's use of the *paraklēsis* word group ("comfort," "consolation," "appeal") predominates in 2 Corinthians (twenty-nine out of fifty-nine instances in the New Testament). The noun form (*paraklēsis*) appears six times in these five verses and the verb form (*parakaleō*) appears four times. The verb had a variety of usages in the New Testament. It was used for making an earnest appeal, for consoling or comforting someone who is distraught, for admonishing another (to abjure), or for making amends (to apologize).

For us, the word "comfort" may connote emotional relief and a sense of well-being, physical ease, satisfaction, and freedom from pain and anxiety. Many in our culture worship at the cult of comfort in a self-centered search for ease, but it lasts for only a moment and never fully satisfies. Watson comments that the word "comfort" "has gone soft" in modern English. In the time of Wycliffe the word was "closely connected with its root, the Latin *fortis*, which means brave, strong, courageous."[47] The comfort that Paul has in mind has nothing to do with a languorous feeling of contentment. It is not some tranquilizing dose of grace that only dulls pains but a stiffening agent that fortifies one in heart, mind, and soul. Comfort relates to encouragement, help, exhortation. God's comfort strengthens weak knees and sustains sagging spirits so that one faces the troubles of life with unbending resolve and unending assurance.

We know God's promises best when we are in the direst need of them, when we are, as Paul says, "harassed at every turn" with "conflicts on the

[45] O. Hofius, "'Der Gott allen Trostes.' Παράκλήσις und παρακαλεῖν in 2 Kor 1, 3–7," *Theologische Beiträge* 14 (1983) 217–27. Hafemann comments that it refers to "God's decisive intervention to rescue and relieve his people in times of distress and affliction" ("The Comfort and Power of the Gospel," 327).

[46] See Isa 49:13; 51:3; 52:9; 61:2; and 63:7; see also *Bar* 4:21,29–30.

[47] N. Watson, *The Second Epistle to the Corinthians*, Epworth Commentaries (London: Epworth, 1993) 3.

outside, fears within" (7:5). We learn in such circumstances that God's comfort is sufficient to overcome the slings and arrows that cut us to the quick and the sorrows that break hearts. The same power that raised Christ from the dead is available to comfort us. Christians also learn that, unlike the Greek pantheon of gods who are quite unconcerned about human anguish, their God cares for them. Pliny the Elder, a first-century Roman naturalist and Stoic, wrote "that [a] supreme being, whatever it be, pays heed to human affairs is a ridiculous notion."[48] He also asserted that suicide was the "supreme boon" that God bestowed on man.[49] Israel's God, by contrast, is one who sees the misery of the people, hears them crying out, and is concerned about their suffering so that he comes down to rescue them (Exod 3:7–8; see Neh 9:9). Paul is keenly aware that God has acted decisively in Christ to deliver humankind from the bondage of sin and that in God's saving action Christ also revealed to him how God delivers—even through death. That God is the Father of the one who was crucified reveals that God intimately knows our suffering. God may not always remove the afflictions that come our way, but God always comforts by giving the fortitude to face them. This comfort is a foretaste of the final consolation to come.[50] Paul therefore begins with praise to God because he knows "sufferers are in the hands of a loving Father, and this assurance they can pass on to others in all their afflictions."[51]

1:4   Paul gives the reasons for his blessing God in the first half of this verse: "God comforts in all our troubles." In the second half he gives the purpose behind the comfort he receives: "in order that we can comfort others in every affliction."[52] Paul does not theorize in general terms about God's comfort. He has in mind specific incidences in which he experienced God's deliverance from affliction.[53]

Paul uses the word "affliction" to refer both to external distress (4:8; Rom 8:35) and inner torment (7:5; Phil 1:17). Both may be involved here, though he does not detail what exactly these afflictions were. We can only guess what they were from the hardship catalogs in this letter (4:7–12; 6:4–10; 11:23–29) and from the accounts of his persecution in Acts: plots, riots, and

---

[48] Pliny, *Natural History* 2.5.20.

[49] Ibid., 2.5.27.

[50] Kruse, *2 Corinthians*, 60.

[51] Plummer, *The Second Epistle of St. Paul to the Corinthians*, 11.

[52] C. Talbert, *Reading Corinthians: A Literary and Theological Commentary on 1 and 2 Corinthians* (New York: Crossroad, 1987) 134. The NIV chooses to translate the phrase εἰς τὸ δύνασθαι ἡμᾶς as a result clause, "so that we can comfort those in any trouble." It can also express purpose, and "in order that we can comfort those in any trouble" seems to capture the sense best.

[53] Πᾶς with the definite article in the first phrase suggests "in all the affliction we have faced," and πᾶς without the definite article in the second phrase means "in any affliction." See N. Turner, *A Grammar of New Testament Greek, Vol. III, Syntax* (Edinburgh: T & T Clark, 1963) 199–200.

mob violence (Acts 9:23–25; 14:19–20; 17:5–9; 19:28–41; and 21:27–36), false accusations (Acts 16:20–22; 17:6–7; 18:13; 19:26–27; 21:20–21; 21:28; and 24:5–6), imprisonments (Acts 16:16–40), and stoning (Acts 14:19). So far, God has delivered him from every peril. But when God delivers Paul from one distress, the apostle tumbles into another.

Paul's response to these afflictions teaches us several things. First, he does not view this affliction as something alien to faithful commitment to Christ. These are not chance happenings that occasionally arise and catch the unlucky. God promised Paul suffering when he was called (Acts 9:16), so persecution is normal (see Mark 4:17; Acts 11:19; 14:22; 1 Thess 1:6; 3:3). These are also not the average troubles that hit Christian and non-Christian alike, such as worries about money, relationships, or illnesses. Nor are they the disasters that seemingly strike persons at random. These are afflictions that come from serving Christ. Caird describes the changes when he writes:

> The cross has demonstrated that reconciliation is a costly business. Wherever the gospel of reconciliation is preached there is a price to be paid in suffering.[54]

Suffering comes for anyone who preaches the gospel in a world twisted by sin and roused by hostility to God. If God's apostle experienced so much distress in carrying out his commission, then we can see that God does not promise prosperity or instant gratification even to the most devoted of Christ's followers. This effect runs counter to the Roman utilitarian attitude toward religion. Most adherents expected their service to the gods to profit them in some way. Cicero typifies this outlook when he says that one only thanks the gods "because he was rich, because he was honored, because he was safe and sound. They call Jupiter Best and Greatest because of these things: not because he makes us just, temperate and wise, but safe, secure, opulent, and well-supplied."[55]

Second, Paul makes clear that the comfort comes from God. Thomas à Kempis wrote, "All human comfort is vain and short." Not so with God's comfort; it takes many forms but can always match the suffering. God can deliver us *"out of* affliction" or encourage us *"in* affliction" so that we can endure it.[56] For example, Paul wrote to the Philippians that their minister to his need, Epaphroditus, was so sick that he almost died. But, he said, "God had mercy on him, and not on him only but also on me, to spare me sorrow upon sorrow" (Phil 2:27). Acts reports the Lord speaking to Paul in a vision:

---

[54] G. B. Caird, *Paul's Letters from Prison,* New Clarendon Bible (Oxford: Clarendon, 1976) 183.

[55] Cicero, *De Natura Deorum* 3.36.87.

[56] Kruse, *2 Corinthians,* 62.

"Do not be afraid; keep on speaking, do not be silent. For I am with you, and no one is going to attack and harm you, because I have many people in this city" (Acts 18:9–10).

Third, the afflictions serve to deepen Paul's faith in God's power rather than to weaken it. Hanson cites S. Weil that Christianity did not profess to cure suffering but did profess to use it.

> Christianity faces it [suffering] by making suffering the means by which healing and rescue were brought to the world, and the very stock-in-trade and accustomed diet of Christians. Yet to Christians suffering is not a deliberately contrived instrument for atonement as it is to the Indian fanatic who tortures himself in order to gain the peace of detachment, but an evil force in the world which yet by Christ's atonement can be used for redemption and healing, even in the individual's personal life.[57]

This conviction helps explain why Paul never tried to explain the problem of suffering as many try to do today. He did not welcome it, but he never asked why bad things happen to good people. He does not try to flee from it or shield himself from it but instead embraces it. He never becomes resentful or embittered because of the tribulations he endured as an apostle for Christ. Nouwen's observation on pruning is a fitting commentary on Paul's attitude toward his suffering.

> Pruning means cutting, reshaping, and removing what diminishes vitality. When we look at a pruned vineyard, we can hardly believe it will bear fruit. But when harvest time comes we realize that the pruning enabled the vine to concentrate its energy and produce more grapes than it could have had it remained unpruned. Grateful people are those who can celebrate even the pains of life because they trust that when harvest time comes the fruit will show that the pruning was not punishment but purification.[58]

Severe adversity can cause one to be frightened about the future and bitter because others do not seem to care or because they add to their woes. Paul's suffering did not cause him to doubt his faith in God but served only to confirm it. He needs to convey this lesson to the Corinthians who use false standards and false hopes to evaluate his sufferings.

We also learn from Paul who the true source of comfort is. Affliction can come from many sources, but real comfort in every affliction can only come from God alone. Abandoning Christ might seem to offer an escape from suffering, but suffering comes also to unbelievers, and abandoning Christ means that one has also abandoned the only source of comfort. Lapide observes that "the sufferings of the world are vinegar without honey, and as

---

[57] Hanson, *II Corinthians,* 34.
[58] H. J. M. Nouwen, "All Is Grace," *Weavings* 7 (1992) 40.

they increase, so do desolation and mourning and woe." God's comfort does not always remove the affliction, but God gives us the grace to face it through.[59]

Fourth, and most important, Paul's experience has taught him that God comforts him so that he can be a comfort to others. God's comfort is not intended to stop with us.[60] God always gives a surplus, and God intends it to overflow to others. It is given not just to make us feel better but to bolster us for the task of fortifying others to face suffering. Jowett has observed that God does not comfort us to make us comfortable but to make us comforters.[61]

Some in Corinth may have cast doubt on Paul's sufficiency as an apostle because he was a victim of such great suffering (2:16). One thing is clear. Paul's inordinate suffering is met by a superabundance of God's comfort that makes him more than sufficient to shower divine comfort upon others. On his own, Paul cannot comfort anyone. The comfort is God's, and it merely flows through him. Paul is not the source of comfort for the Corinthians, but, as Christ's apostle, he is the relay station.[62] A. Bierce's cynical definition of "comfort" in *The Devil's Dictionary,* "A state of mind produced by contemplation of a neighbor's uneasiness," starkly reveals how radically different the Christian perspective is from its secular counterpart. God's comfort is intended to be used to comfort others in every kind of affliction so that others in turn can comfort us.[63]

We experience God's comfort in various ways. Since Christians are united to Christ, they are also bound together. Christianity is not a religion of the alone communing with the alone. Paul identifies with all those who suffer: "Who is weak, and I do not feel weak? Who is led into sin, and I do not inwardly burn?" (11:29). We therefore experience God's comfort when other Christians express their care for us. Suffering becomes an unbearable burden when we feel alone and abandoned. His sense that the Corinthians were on the verge of deserting him, coupled with the terrible affliction he experienced in Asia, acted like a pincer movement to make him almost

---

[59] Paul learns that the thorn in the flesh will not be removed but also that grace is sufficient for him to bear it.

[60] See n. 52.

[61] Schelkle comments, "In the communion of faith, no one is alone in distress, no one receives consolation for himself alone" (*The Second Epistle to the Corinthians,* 13).

[62] God is the source of the comfort (1:4); Christ is the channel (1:5); and that comfort multiplies through our comforting others (Barnett, *The Message of 2 Corinthians,* 30).

[63] The church is a fellowship of the broken who are held together by God's love and love for one another. It therefore is to become a transmitter station for comfort, which means that no Christian can expect to enjoy the benefits that come from being in Christ without being a benefit to the church or others.

despair of life. Paul will relate later in the letter that God comforted him with the news from Titus that the Corinthians felt a deep longing and ardent concern for him (7:6–7).

We also experience God's comfort by caring for others even when we are in the midst of suffering. Sometimes the sudden onslaught of affliction may tempt one to retreat into a shell, to shut oneself off from others. The suffering, however, then becomes purposeless. Those who focus only on themselves are the most miserable of people. The persons who turn their pain to helping others can redirect and conquer that pain. Paul knew how to encourage because he knew what it was like to be discouraged. He knew how to comfort because he knew what it was like to feel unbearably crushed. He knew how to console others because he knew what it was like to be at the end of his tether. The difference is that he knows who holds the other end of the tether—God. He set his hope on God who delivered Christ Jesus from death and has faithfully delivered him in the past and will deliver him in the future. He shared this hope with others.

We can also experience God's comfort by witnessing its power in the lives of others. Kruse reminds us, "The testimony of God's grace in one's life is a forceful reminder to others of God's ability and willingness to provide the grace and strength they need."[64] It is a comfort to see those undergoing trouble reaching out to comfort others. Their valiant example emboldens others (see Phil 1:14).

1:5 Paul offers an explanation ("because," *hoti*) of how he is able to comfort others through his affliction (1:3). The verb translated "flow" and "overflow" *(perisseuei)* belongs to a family of words that in commercial contexts expresses profit or surplus.[65] In describing his sufferings in Christ, Paul pictures a balance sheet of two columns: sufferings of Christ versus comfort through Christ. Ministering in this present evil age brings him a surplus of suffering that becomes almost unbearable. But the consolation column also shows a surplus, and it more than balances the suffering. Paul's hope of our final deliverance melts the pain away: "I consider that our present sufferings are not worth comparing with the glory that will be revealed in us" (Rom 8:18). The future governs his understanding of everything in the present.

What are "the sufferings of Christ"? One view understands them to be sufferings on account of Christ. Paul refers to the suffering that comes to him as a loyal apostle to Christ who preaches a message that sparks violent

---

[64] Kruse, *2 Corinthians*, 61.

[65] Danker, *II Corinthians*, 34. Περισσεύειν εἰς plus a personal object means "to be abundant" (see Rom 5:15; 2 Cor 9:8; Eph 1:8). Paul uses the same verb to describe how the Macedonians' severe ordeal of affliction overflowed in a wealth of generosity for the ministry to the saints in Jerusalem (8:2).

reactions from those who remain savagely hostile to God in this world (see 4:10–12). Those who preach the gospel in this fallen world will be especially exposed to dangers and suffering. The question arises, however, whether the genitive case alone can express this concept.

A second view takes the phrase as a genitive of source. In other words, Paul refers to sufferings ordained by Christ for believers (see Acts 9:15–16).

A third view interprets the phrase to mean sufferings associated with the Messiah, that is, Messianic sufferings. Paul may have in mind the birth pangs of the Messiah that God's people must undergo prior to the coming of the kingdom.[66] Jewish apocalyptic writings foretell disasters coming upon the world as a prelude to the end time ushering in the new age, which may be labeled the birth-pangs of the Messiah.[67]

A fourth view understands Paul to be referring to sufferings Christ himself endured.[68] This interpretation would mean that the solidarity between Christ and his followers applies also to his sufferings.[69] Christians are baptized into Christ's death (Rom 6:3) and are called to endure the same sufferings, to go to dark Gethsemane with Christ (see Mark 10:38–39). Paul speaks of being "heirs of God and co-heirs with Christ, if indeed we share in *his sufferings* in order that we may also share in his glory" (Rom 8:17). He tells the Philippians that he wants to know "Christ and the power of his resurrection and the fellowship of sharing in his sufferings, becoming like him in his death, and so, somehow, to attain to the resurrection from the dead" (Phil 3:10–11). He also tells the Galatians that he bears the marks of Jesus in his body (Gal 6:17).

The passage in 2 Cor 4:10–11 should tip the scales toward this last view. Paul says he carries about in his body "the dying of Jesus." He "continually

---

[66] Thrall cites Isa 26:17; 66:8; Jer 22:23; Hos 13:13; and Mic 4:9–10 as evidence (*Second Epistle to the Corinthians,* 1:108).

[67] See Dan 7:21–22,25–27; 12:1; *Jub.* 23:13; *4 Ezra* 13:16–19; *2 Apoc. Bar.* 25–30; Mark 13:20; and Rev 7:14; 12:13–17. Later rabbinic texts refer to the woes of the Messiah (*Mek. Vayassa* 5 to Exod 16:25; *b. Šabb.* 118a; *b. Pesaḥ.* 118a; *b. Sanh.* 97a). E. Best comments:

It would be only natural that Paul when he was won over to Jesus the suffering Messiah should take up this conception of 'the woes of the Messiah,' which, of course, were woes that the generation of the Messiah suffered, and not he himself. The Messiah suffered, and his Church would continue his sufferings until he should return again. Hence the sufferings of the Messiah abound unto his redeemed. Consolation would also abound in the time of the Messiah, when he should come. But he has already come, so consolation abounds at the same time as suffering, both together and not one without the other (*One Body in Christ: A Study in the Relationship of the Church to Christ in the Epistles of the Apostle Paul* [London: SPCK, 1955] 133–34).

[68] This interpretation best fits the way the expression is used in 1 Pet 1:11; 4:13; and 5:1.

[69] Barnett remarks: "Just as Christ suffered in his ministry and death from forces hostile to God, so, too, the apostle, in continuity with Christ, suffered in the course of his ministry and proclamation" (*The Second Epistle to the Corinthians,* 75).

and physically experiences the sufferings of the cross," and he interprets it as the continuation of Jesus' suffering in the flesh. Therefore he believes that his apostolic ministry extends Christ's earthly ministry, which included suffering and hardship.[70] His vocation as an apostle of Christ demands suffering if he is to confront the same evil forces that sentenced Christ to the cross so that in his suffering he joins in the suffering and death of Christ.[71] He not only preaches Christ crucified, but he lives it. And his suffering brings him joy because he recognizes it to be an irrefutable confirmation of his close tie to his Lord. Hanson's comments are on the mark:

> ... because Christians do not merely imitate, follow or feel inspired by Christ, but actually live in him, are part of him, dwell supernaturally in a new world where the air they breathe is his Spirit, then for them henceforward suffering accepted in Christ must bring comfort, death accepted in Christ must bring life, weakness accepted in Christ must bring strength, foolishness accepted in Christ must bring wisdom.[72]

The opposites are transformed from one to the other by the divine power.

1:6 This verse explains how he can comfort those in any affliction (1:4b). "If we are distressed" ("afflicted," *thlibometha*) may allude to one of the Corinthian complaints; some think that he is too much afflicted. Paul turns it around and argues that his affliction is for their "comfort and salvation."[73] He came to them in suffering but brought them the gospel. How can they disdain what brought them their new life in Christ? Paul has suffered much, but he has been comforted much and passes it along to them.[74] His comfort therefore becomes their comfort.

We might ask, however, How does his suffering affect their salvation? First, his afflictions come from his proclaiming the gospel by which they are saved. If Paul had chosen to shrink from the dangers he faced and to retreat unscathed to safer places, many in the Gentile world would not have heard the saving word of the gospel. As Christ endured suffering to bring salvation to the world, Paul endured it to bring the message of salvation to the world.[75] As a result, he is comforted by God and a comforter of others.

---

[70] L. Belleville, *2 Corinthians,* IVPNTC (Downers Grove/Leicester: IVP, 1995) 56–57.

[71] R. C. Tannehill, *Dying and Rising with Christ,* BZNWKAK (Berlin: Alfred Töpelmann, 1966) 91.

[72] Hanson, *II Corinthians,* 32.

[73] On the textual variant "and salvation" see Thrall, *Second Epistle to the Corinthians,* 1:113.

[74] Paul's love for his churches is revealed by his rejoicing that he suffers for them (Col 1:24–29).

[75] The "for" (ὑπέρ) does not suggest that Paul's suffering for them has any vicarious effect as Christ's death for us does (5:14–15,21). Paul's sufferings simply became a channel through which God's salvation and comfort reached them. In 4:12 he states that death in him becomes life in the Corinthians.

Paul clearly implies that he benefits the Corinthians at great cost to him-self, and therefore they are indebted to him. The problem was that the Corin-thians did not appreciate the significance of his suffering. They considered that all this suffering cast doubt on the power of his apostleship. His life seemed to be filled with suffering, not with the Spirit. As Hafemann puts it, some of them thought, "Surely God's redemption in Christ was meant to free us from such effects of this evil age!"[76]

He argues, however, that his comfort produces endurance in them to suf-fer the same sufferings.[77] We should not understand endurance as some human power that can last through hard times. Plato, for example, used the word in connection with courage that faces difficulties "without expecting help or putting one's confidence in others."[78] Spicq shows that the word *hypomonē* has a different set of connotations in the Greek Old Testament and for the first time takes on religious meaning. It translates the Hebrew terms (*qāwâ* [in the *piel*], *tiqwā, miqweh*) that signify "expectant waiting, intense desire," and this intense desire is usually directed toward God (see Pss 39:7; 71:5; Jer 14:8; 17:13). In contrast to Plato it attributes this virtue to one "who is counting on help from someone else."[79] Spicq concludes that "endurance" is a "constancy in desire that overcomes the trial of waiting, a soul attitude that must struggle to persevere, a waiting that is determined and victorious because it trusts in God."[80] This understanding of endurance as something that comes from God and is focused on God (see Rom 15:5) runs counter to a do-it-yourself religion. If Christians endure without complain-ing or growing weary or despondent (see Matt 10:22; 24:13; Mark 13:13; Luke 21:19), it is because God enables it, not because they are extraordinar-ily heroic.

The "same sufferings" refer to "the sufferings of Christ (1:5). Paul believes that all those connected to Christ crucified will experience suffer-ing, and he implies that they should therefore not disparage Paul for his suf-

---

[76] Hafemann, "The Comfort and Power of the Gospel," 325–26. One might guess that they wanted to know the power of Christ's resurrection independently from participating in his suffer-ings (Phil 3:10). For Paul, "the two go together hand-in-glove" (G. D. Fee, *Paul's Letter to the Phil-ippians,* NICNT [Grand Rapids: Eerdmans, 1995] 331).

[77] See Rom 5:3; 15:5. The participle τῆς ἐνεργουμένης (translated "produces") could be taken as a middle voice (NIV; see also NASB; REB); or it could be taken as a passive voice and translated "your comfort which is worked by endurance" (NRSV).

[78] Plato, *Laches* 192b–d.

[79] C. Spicq, *Theological Lexicon of the New Testament,* trans. and ed. J. D. Ernest (Peabody, Mass.: Hendrickson, 1994) 3:414–15, 418. Furnish comments, "As Paul uses it, 'endurance' refers not just to the human virtue of fortitude by which one bears up under adversity; it designates, rather, the obedient faith of those who can rejoice, precisely in the midst of adversity, in the confidence that God's love will not only perdure but will indeed prevail (Rom 5:1–5) ..." (*II Corinthians,* 111).

[80] Spicq, *Theological Lexicon of the New Testament,* 3:418.

fering. They share these sufferings because they share Christ and because they live in a fallen world, ruled temporarily by malevolent powers that have pitted themselves against God. Those who do not simply try to understate the gospel and soothe the opposition but proclaim the gospel boldly and stand up against all God's adversaries should anticipate suffering.

1:7 Paul gives a dire picture of the Corinthians' disobedience in this letter, but he never loses confidence in them (see 2:3; 7:4; 9:3) because his hope for them centers on what God has done and will do in them. Paul repeats that they share in the sufferings. The NIV inserts "our" before "sufferings," but it is not present in the text. The sufferings refer to the sufferings of Christ. Since the sufferings are connected to Christ, they will receive the same wealth of consolation that Paul has received. Since they share Christ, they share Christ's sufferings. Since they share Christ's sufferings, they also share Christ's comfort.

Plummer contends that Paul shares the intensity of his suffering with the Corinthians so "they will regard their own sufferings more patiently, and will also appreciate his own present comfort and derive comfort from it."[81] But Paul's correspondence with the Corinthians does not suggest that they were undergoing any particular persecution. On the contrary, Barclay notes a stark contrast between the issues dealt with in 1 Thessalonians and those in 1 Corinthians. Though these two churches were founded by Paul within months of each other, he argues that "these sibling communities developed remarkably different interpretations of the Christian faith."[82] He isolates social relations with outsiders as one neglected factor that may explain this phenomenon. Paul's letter to the Thessalonians betrays evidence of conflict with outsiders (1 Thess 1:6; 2:2,14–16; 3:3) and a sense of alienation from society and hostility toward it (1 Thess 4:5,13; 5:7). The letters to the Corinthians, by contrast, contain no hint of conflict between the church and outsiders. Instead, Paul contrasts his situation of affliction and dishonor with their relative tranquility (1 Cor 4:9–13; 15:30–32; 16:9). The Corinthians therefore appear to be getting on quite well in their community and do not seem to experience much, if any, social ostracism. They manifest little evidence of any countercultural impact so central to the preaching of the cross (1:18–25). Their faith did not create any significant social and moral realignment of their lives. Leaders ("a man of knowledge") participate in feasts in dining rooms of pagan temples (8:10). Some are invited to share meals in the homes of nonbelievers (10:27). Nonbelievers drop into the house church (14:24–25).

---

[81] Plummer, *The Second Epistle of St. Paul to the Corinthians,* 15.

[82] J. M. G. Barclay, "Thessalonica and Corinth: Social Contrasts in Pauline Christianity," *JSNT* 47 (1992) 50.

One wonders if the Corinthians actually share these sufferings. Perhaps, as Thrall argues, they are the objects of the same Jewish scorn that Paul received when he was in the city (Acts 18:15–17).[83] But it is more likely that this concluding line of this opening period has a rhetorical purpose. He seeks to dispel mistrust by naming them partners in his suffering. Partners in suffering become partners in comfort. If they do not share his sufferings, then they will not share his consolation. They should not, then, look upon his suffering with such a jaundiced eye.

But far more important to Paul's argument throughout the letter is his conviction that "only in cruciform sufferings like his" can the Lord "perform his powerful work, introducing glory into an age of darkness, salvation into a world of despair, a new age with the old life and power to more and more people."[84] If they continue to disparage his sufferings as something that afflicts only a frail and ineffective apostle, then they will not understand the wisdom of the cross (1 Cor 1:18–25). If they do not see that the power of God works most powerfully through weakness and affliction and even when the sentence of death hangs over mortal flesh, then they will not truly experience God's power in their lives—only vaporous, momentary, spiritual ecstasies (see 1 Cor 12:1–2). They will also vainly rely on themselves, a fatal decision that brings its own sentence of death and repudiates the only power that can raise persons from death.

---

[83] Thrall, *Second Epistle to the Corinthians,* 1:113.

[84] T. B. Savage, *Power through Weakness: Paul's Understanding of the Christian Ministry in 2 Corinthians,* SNTSMS 86 (Cambridge: University Press, 1996) 189.

II. THE PAINFUL VISIT AND TEARFUL LETTER: PAUL'S
DEFENSE OF HIS EXCEPTIONAL CANDOR (1:8–7:16)
1. The Issue of Paul's Love for the Church and His Dependability
(1:8–2:13)
   (1) Paul's Afflictions in Asia (1:8–11)
   (2) The Theme Statement of the Letter: Rightly Understanding
   Paul's Ministry (1:12–14)
   (3) Paul's Changes in Travel Plans and the Faithfulness of God
   (1:15–22)
   (4) The Sorrowful Visit and the Explanation for His Decision Not
   to Return (1:23–2:4)
   (5) Forgiveness of the Offender (2:5–11)
   (6) Paul's Afflictions in Macedonia and Waiting for Titus (2:12–13)
2. Paul's Defense of His Frank Criticism (2:14–7:3)
   (1) The Nature of Apostolic Ministry (2:14–3:6)
   Paul's Sufficiency for a Ministry That Results in Life or Death
   (2:14–17)
   The Corinthians as Paul's Letter (3:1–3)
   Paul's Sufficiency as Minister of the New Covenant (3:4–6)
   (2) The Old and the New Ministries (3:7–18)
   The Glory of the Ministry Now Set Aside (3:7–9)
   The Greater Glory of the New Eclipses the Old (3:10)
   The Glory of the Ministry Now Set Aside (3:11)
   The Unveiled Paul (We, Apostles) (3:12–13)
   Veiled Israel (They, Israelites) (3:14–17)
   Unveiled Christians (We, Christians) (3:18)
   (3) Christian Ministry (4:1–6)
   Commending Himself through the Open Statement of the
   Truth (4:1–2)
   The Spiritual Condition of Those Blinded to the Glory of
   Christ in "Our Gospel" (4:3–4)
   The Basic Thrust of Paul's Preaching: Christ as Lord;
   Ourselves as Your Slaves (4:5–6)
   (4) Self-Defense: Catalog of Afflictions: Always Being Given over
   to Death (4:7–15)
   (5) The Resurrection Hope (4:16–5:10)
   Our Inner Nature Prepared by God for an Eternal Weight of
   Glory (4:16–18)
   The Eternal Building from God (5:1–5)

Our Eternal Destiny before the Judgment Seat of Christ
(5:6–10)
(6) Persuading Others to Be Reconciled to God (5:11–21)
Self-Defense: Reiteration of the Letter's Theme Statement
(5:11–13)
An Emissary of Christ for Reconciliation (5:14–21)
(7) Self-Defense: Catalog of Afflictions: Why the Corinthians
Should Honor His Appeals (6:1–10)
(8) Plea for Them to Open Their Hearts (6:11–13)
(9) Frank Appeal: Separate Yourselves (6:14–7:1)
(10) Plea for Them to Open Their Hearts (7:2–3)
3. The Report from Titus (7:4–16)
(1) Paul's Boldness toward the Corinthians Brings Joy (7:4)
(2) Titus's Arrival Comforts Paul in His Affliction (7:5–7)
(3) The Purpose and Effect of the Tearful Letter (7:8–13a)
(4) Titus's Report Proved Paul's Boast (7:13b–15)
(5) Paul's Boldness toward the Corinthians Brings Joy (7:16)

1. The Issue of Paul's Love for the Church and His Dependability (1:8–2:13)

(1) Paul's Afflictions in Asia (1:8–11)

[8]We do not want you to be uninformed, brothers, about the hardships we suffered in the province of Asia. We were under great pressure, far beyond our ability to endure, so that we despaired even of life. [9]Indeed, in our hearts we felt the sentence of death. But this happened that we might not rely on ourselves but on God, who raises the dead. [10]He has delivered us from such a deadly peril, and he will deliver us. On him we have set our hope that he will continue to deliver us, [11]as you help us by your prayers. Then many will give thanks on our behalf for the gracious favor granted us in answer to the prayers of many.

1:8 Paul does not present theological speculation divorced from his own real life experience.[1] He begins the body of the letter with a recent example of his experience of affliction and God's comfort.[2] He can quote the evidence when time and again God has been faithful to deliver him.[3]

---

[1] N. Watson, "'… To make us rely not on ourselves but God who raises the dead': 2 Cor. 1,9b as the Heart of Paul's Theology," in *Die Mitte des Neuen Testaments,* ed. U. Luz and H. Weder (Göttingen: Vandenhoeck & Ruprecht, 1983) 389.

[2] See Rom 1:13 with a negative formula. In Phil 1:12 the body of the letter begins with a positive formula.

[3] His catalog of afflictions and deliverances in 4:7–15 more concretely expresses what he has reference to here in 1:8–11.

"All our afflictions" (1:4) are narrowed down to a specific affliction that took place in Asia. "Asia" refers to the Roman senatorial province that included most of the western part of Asia Minor and its coastal islands in the Aegean Sea. As a senatorial province it was ruled by a governor appointed by the Senate, and Ephesus had become the provincial capital.

Paul gives no details about what this affliction in Asia precisely was. Was he tormented by the onset of a stubborn and life-threatening ailment, menaced by particularly dangerous persecution, struck down by an accident of some kind, or stricken with some psychological distress? He does not say. He only explains that the depth of the great danger he faced in Asia was matched by the depth of his gratitude to God for his deliverance. He also says as little about the recovery as he does about the grievous circumstances. The emphasis falls entirely on giving thanks to God for his rescue, on learning again to depend entirely on God, and on the confidence that his friends would offer more thanksgiving to God for his deliverance.[4]

It is unlikely that Paul simply wants to inform the Corinthians about his most recent troubles, which may explain the lack of any clear details. He wants to tell them what his affliction and deliverance means theologically in hopes that it will deepen their relationship with him and increase their thanksgiving for the grace bestowed on him by God (1:11).[5] The experience accents his own suffering and weakness, which brings an overflow of God's comfort. We find many signs in Paul's correspondence with the Corinthians that some in the church deplored all his suffering and belittled his ministerial power because of them. They regarded all this affliction to be unseemly and an embarrassment to their interpretation of the gospel's power, which was supposed to lift one above all deadly perils to a higher spiritual plane. Some questioned how God's power could result in such abundant frailty. Does God's power truly energize Paul? If these are questions that some Corinthians are asking, he must give some

---

[4] We may attribute the lack of any specific details to Paul following the pattern of the sufferer in the Psalms (e.g., Ps 115:1,4–7,18). A. E. Harvey observes, "All the emphasis is on prayer, the 'rescue' afforded by God, and the thanksgiving this evokes" (*Renewal through Suffering: A Study of 2 Corinthians, Studies of the New Testament and Its World* [Edinburgh: T & T Clark, 1996] 32).

[5] Paul begins the body of the letter to the Philippians by describing his imprisonment, which so concerned them (1:12–26). Again, Paul provides no details about where he is, what the conditions are like, and only focuses on what it means. Rather than being a setback to the gospel, his circumstances have served to advance the gospel.

explanation for his afflictions.[6]

Paul omits the particulars of his affliction to focus on the divine purpose behind the experience.[7] He has no interest in chatting about himself or sharing personal information, no matter how gripping it might be.[8] Nevertheless, we want to know what happened. The Corinthians had the advantage of being able to ask the one who delivered the letter; we can only guess.

1. One possibility is that Paul refers to the riot in Ephesus led by the silversmith, Demetrius, described in Acts 19:23–20:1.[9] Paul's preaching con-

---

[6] Does the reference to "our affliction," "what we suffered," also include Timothy (1:1), or is it a literary "we"? J. B. Lightfoot contended that Paul never used the "epistolary" plural to refer to himself alone (*Saint Paul's Epistles to the Colossians and to Philemon* [1879; rev. ed., Grand Rapids: Zondervan, 1959] 229). But this judgment is unduly strict, and the evidence reveals that Paul could switch back and forth from the singular to the authorial (epistolary or literary) plural. Paul uses the first person plural 108 times in 2 Corinthians and not infrequently switches back and forth from plural to the first person singular, which appears sixty-four times (for the shifting, see 1:13; 5:11; 7:2,3,4,5,6,7,12,14; 9:4; 10:2,8,11:21; 12:19–20; 13:6–10). M. Carrez ("Le 'Nous' en 2 Corinthiens. Paul parle-t-il au nom de toute la communauté," *NTS* 26 [1980] 474–86) helpfully distinguishes four usages of the first person plural pronoun: (1) The "we" that refers to something true of all Christians (see 3:18; 5:10, the presence of "all" makes this clear). (2) The "we" that refers to Paul and his fellow workers (1:19). (3) The "we" that applies to the category of true apostles or preachers of the gospel (see 5:18,20). (4) The "we" that refers to his personal solidarity with the Corinthians. In addition, (5) Paul also uses the authorial "we" that refers only to himself (1 Thess 3:1, "we were left alone in Athens"; see 2 Cor 1:13,16; 10:2,7,11,15; 11:21). For further discussion see also J. J. Klijne, "We, Us and Our in I and II Corinthians," *NovT* 8 (1966) 171–79; N. Baumert, *Täglich sterben und auferstehen. Der Literalsinn von 2 Kor 4,12–5,10,* SANT 34 (Munich: Kösel, 1973) 25–36; C. E. B. Cranfield, "Changes of Person and Number in Paul's Epistles," in *Paul and Paulinism,* ed. M. D. Hooker and S. G. Wilson (London: SPCK, 1982) 280–89; and E. Verhoef, "The Senders of the Letters to the Corinthians and the Use of 'I' and 'We,'" in *The Corinthian Correspondence,* ed. R. Bieringer (Leuven: University Press, 1996) 423. Ultimately, "each case must be judged by its context" (A. Plummer, *A Critical and Exegetical Commentary on the Second Epistle of St. Paul to the Corinthians,* ICC [New York: Scribner's, 1915], 10). Verhoef challenges the theory of J. Murphy-O'Connor ("Co-authorship in the Corinthian Correspondence," *RB* 100 [1993] 562–79), who divided the we sections where Timothy is the coauthor. He claimed, e.g., that Paul wrote 1:15–17 while Timothy wrote 1:18–22. Verhoef concludes that Paul uses the singular so frequently because he is the author of the letter despite there being a cosender: "When he uses the plural, it usually can be interpreted as relating to a group of people including himself" ("The Senders of the Letters to the Corinthians," 425).

[7] Harvey makes the case that in Paul's time they would be more interested in asking, Who has done this to me? and What does this mean? than What is wrong with me? or What happened to me? (*Renewal through Suffering,* 11–14).

[8] Watson comments, "The proclamation of the gospel, for Paul, does not consist in a continual retelling of his own religious experiences of God" (*The Second Epistle to the Corinthians,* 389). E.g., Paul gives only tantalizing details about his call and conversion in Gal 1:16 because he only wants to reveal the divine purpose behind it: "God revealed his son in me in order that I might preach him among the Gentiles."

[9] The riot may be connected to the time after the assassination of M. Junius Silanus and the anarchy that ensued (G. S. Duncan, *St. Paul's Ephesian Ministry* [London: Hodder & Stoughton, 1929] 100–107). See also A. J. Malherbe, "The Beasts at Ephesus," *JBL* 87 (1968) 71–80.

cerning "the Way" and his denunciation of idolatry provoked antagonism. The city's extreme devotion to the goddess Artemis coupled with the economic loss connected to the dramatic drop in the trade of cult artifacts provoked a mob uprising against Paul and his coworkers. In 1 Corinthians Paul hinted at the adversity he faced by referring to fighting "wild beasts" in Ephesus (1 Cor 15:32). His comment in 2 Cor 1:8 and 2:13 that he left Asia for Macedonia also matches the sequence recorded in Acts 19:23–20:1 and makes the connection to this event more plausible.

The problem with this view is that the danger seems to have passed when the town clerk took control of the situation and asserted that no formal charges had been made (Acts 19:35–41). Paul and his companions were roughed up by the militant crowds and barely escaped being lynched, but the tumult, according to Acts, was soon over. He was not under any death sentence, and he quickly departed from the city. It is possible that Luke toned down the severity of the peril when he reflected back on the events from a later time. Acts does tell us that when Paul was journeying to Jerusalem, he decided to sail past Ephesus and sent for the leaders of the church there to meet him in the port of Miletus (Acts 20:16–17). Paul was in a hurry to reach Jerusalem before Pentecost, but Ephesus may also have been too dangerous a place for him to return. He may have thought it inadvisable to stop off there because of past trouble.

Although this episode in Acts may be the most obvious candidate for the event Paul alludes to, some doubt whether it fits his description of it as "a burden too heavy to bear." This phrase implies something that seems to have menaced Paul for some time. Why also would he refer to this episode as something that happened in Asia? Why not write "in Ephesus," since he refers to the city by name in 1 Cor 15:32, and then tells them that he wants "to stay on at Ephesus until Pentecost, because a great door for effective work has opened to me, and there are many who oppose me" (1 Cor 16:8–9)? These earlier references to Ephesus suggest that some new calamity has befallen him that the Corinthians did not know about. Such objections do not rule out the possibility that Paul refers to the event narrated in Acts, but other options have been proposed.

2. A second proposal identifies the affliction as a flare-up of some illness that was nearly fatal.[10] The perfect tense in 1:9, "we had" (eschēkamen, trans. "we felt" NIV) would be well suited to describe a recurrent illness that persists, such as the thorn in the flesh (12:7). The malady did not vanish but

---

[10] The verb ἐβαρήθημεν appears in the papyri to refer to sickness (H. Windisch, *Der zweite Korintherbrief, MeyerK*, 9th ed. [Göttingen: Vandenhoeck & Ruprecht, 1924] 45, n. 4); but it can be used in the context of dissipation and sadness (Luke 21:34), misfortune and injustice, financial burdens (1 Thess 2:9; 2 Thess 3:8; 1 Tim 5:16; Ignatius, *Phld.* 6:3), and social burdens.

continued to hang over him.[11] Thrall points out that Old Testament writers refer to God as the one who raises the dead (1:9) in a context of divine help in serious illness.[12] The problem with this view is that the word "affliction" is not the usual term for an illness. Paul normally uses "afflictions" to refer to persecutions (Gal 6:17; Col 1:24). How would an illness fit under the category of "sufferings of Christ" (1:5), and how do the Corinthians share in it (1:7)? He also uses the plural to refer to our afflictions: "we were burdened"; we had the sentence of death "in ourselves." If Paul is not using an authorial *we*, then he is talking about something that happened to others with him, which makes it unlikely that he has in mind some sickness he suffered.

3. A third option suggests that Paul refers to a time of imprisonment when he faced possible execution that is not recorded in Acts. Acts does not pretend to catalog all the perils that Paul faced, and an imprisonment that threatened his life would fall into the category of afflictions of Christ.[13] The problems with this view are also significant. Hemer shows that the reference to a "death sentence" was not a judicial metaphor from the law court but has a neutral connotation.[14]

4. A fourth possibility is that Paul refers to intense opposition from his fellow Jews. Not only would his rejection of the works of the law have created intense hostility—five times, he says, he submitted to synagogue discipline and received the maximum lashes (11:24)—by siphoning off potential proselytes attracted to the synagogue he would have provoked a hostile rivalry. His kindred Jews continued to plot against him (Acts 20:3,19; 21:11), and "the Jews from Asia" instigated his arrest in Jerusalem (Acts 21:27).[15] The metaphorical fighting with wild beasts (1 Cor 15:32) may have continued and intensified.

5. A fifth view contends that Paul may not refer to some life-threatening experience but is using a vivid metaphor for how he felt about what was

---

[11] Paul's discussion of the thorn in the flesh develops in a similar way (12:7–10). Paul repeatedly petitioned God to take away a thorn in the flesh. God's answer was that Paul must live with it and that God's power is made perfect in his weakness.

[12] Thrall, *The Second Epistle to the Corinthians,* 1:115.

[13] Some argue that such an imprisonment might fit the provenance of Philippians. He wrote the Philippians of his possible execution (Phil 1:19–30). Timothy was with him at the time (Phil 2:19–23), which may account for the plural. He speaks about having grief upon grief (Phil 2:27). Titus had been sent on to Corinth (2 Cor 2:13; 7:6–7), which may explain why Paul says he had no one other than Timothy (Phil 2:20). He states his intention to come to Philippi if and when he is released (Phil 2:24). V. P. Furnish notes, "That Timothy is named as a co-sender of a letter from Macedonia (2 Cor 1:1) agrees with the plan of Phil 2:19–24 that Paul would follow his associate to Philippi as soon as he could" (*II Corinthians,* AB [Garden City: Doubleday, 1984] 123).

[14] C. J. Hemer, "A Note on 2 Corinthians 1:9," *TynBul* 23 (1972) 103–7.

[15] One Alexander attempted to dissociate the Jewish community from Paul (Acts 19:33; see 1 Tim 1:20; 2 Tim 4:14–17, which refers to an Alexander the coppersmith who had done him great harm).

going on between him and the church. He has in mind the psychological anguish caused by the Corinthian situation. The deterioration of their relationship was like a sentence of death to him. This view might explain why he refers to something happening "in ourselves" (1:9; but see Phil 1:29 "in us"). Paul specifically speaks about his affliction (2:4; 7:5) when he had to write the letter of tears and how he was tormented and unable to rest over worry about Titus and how the letter would be received (2:13; 7:5).[16] Nevertheless, why specify the location of his grief, particularly if the comfort he received from God refers to the renewal of their commitment to him? Paul's distress continued in Macedonia (7:5). The absence of rest for our bodies is hardly equivalent to a sentence of death. Psychological distress over the Corinthians' defiance would be taxing but not life threatening, and the aorist participle "what happened" (*tes genomenes*, rendered "we suffered" by the NIV) "indicates an event rather than a state of mind."[17]

In the final analysis we cannot know precisely what affliction Paul had in mind because he does not tell us. He only describes its severity. The string of superlatives conveys the intensity of his suffering. It was something that left his life hanging by a thread. Paul does not pass himself off as some kind of superhero immune to all adversity. He is keenly aware of his defects and weaknesses and confesses that he bordered on absolute despair.[18]

We might surmise that Paul's despair was not related to any fear of death, but the premature end to his Gentile mission would be another story.[19] Since he is the apostle to the Gentiles, who would continue that apostolic mission? That work would be left uncompleted and perhaps, with false and unscrupulous rivals making inroads into his churches, negated. His gospel was in danger of being swept away by persecution or "amended by libertines and legalists."[20] His project to bring about reconciliation between Jewish and Gentile Christians through the collection for the poor saints of Jerusalem had just gotten off the ground. Who would continue it? Besides these concerns, his relationship with the strategic Corinthian congregation was steadily worsening. But God delivered him from this deadly peril. Paul gives thanks to God for the miracle of grace

---

[16] C. Talbert, *Reading Corinthians: A Literary and Theological Commentary on 1 and 2 Corinthians* (New York: Crossroad, 1987) 135.

[17] M. E. Thrall, *A Critical and Exegetical Commentary on the Second Epistle to the Corinthians,* ICC (Edinburgh: T & T Clark, 1994) 1:115. Other guesses from the list of hardships in the letter, such as drowning (2 Cor 11:25) or danger from robbers, are just that, pure guesswork.

[18] He says he despaired of life (ὥστε ἐξαπορηθῆναι ἡμᾶς καὶ τοῦ ζῆν), which parallels one of his hardships listed in 4:8, "perplexed" (ἀπορούμενοι), "but not driven to despair" (ἐξαπορούμενοι).

[19] J. Héring, *The Second Epistle of Saint Paul to the Corinthians* (London: Epworth, 1967) 3.

[20] R. Yates, "Paul's Affliction in Asia: 2 Corinthians 1:8," *EvQ* 53 (1981) 245.

that allows him to continue his work. It served once again to reinforce his view that "the Gospel was effective in weakness as well as in strength."[21]

How does this account function in Paul's appeal to the Corinthians? He may bring up his recent affliction as the excuse for his change of plans that so upset them. In learning of his near-death experience, they may be shamed for criticizing him for altering his travel plans and accusing him of lacking concern for them (1:16–17).[22] But Paul is not offering this information as an excuse for failing to follow through on previous plans. The emphasis in this paragraph is on God's deliverance. He was burdened in Asia beyond his power to endure the load of sorrow, but God rescued him. It was beyond his strength to endure but not beyond God's grace to fortify him or God's power to deliver him. He relates this incident to unveil a theme that runs throughout chaps. 1–7. It has three components: his suffering as an apostle (2:14–17; 6:4–10; see also 11:23–29); how this suffering has driven him to rely completely on God and not himself (4:7–12; see also 12:7–10); and how this suffering will eventually result in his divine vindication (3:18; 4:14; 4:16–5:10; see 13:4).[23]

1:9 Paul continues his description of the affliction in Asia by saying that "we [emphatic with *autoi*] had the sentence of death in ourselves" (literal translation).[24] Does he refer here to a judicial sentence handed down by some court? Calvin thought so and rendered it, "I thought my death fixed and decided."[25] But Paul may not have intended for the phrase to be taken literally.[26] The verb *eschēkamen* (translated "felt" in the NIV) is in the perfect tense, and it may convey the traditional idea of completed action with

---

[21] Ibid.

[22] F. W. Hughes goes too far in claiming that Paul exaggerates his sufferings as a rhetorical ploy to engage the sympathy of the addressees ("The Rhetoric of Reconciliation: 2 Cor. 1:1–2:13 and 7:5–8:24," in *Persuasive Artistry*, ed. D. F. Watson, JSNTSS 50 [Sheffield: JSOT, 1991] 246–61).

[23] See P. B. Duff, "2 Corinthians 1–7: Sidestepping the Division Hypothesis Dilemma," in *BTB* 24 (1994) 24.

[24] The ἀλλὰ ("but") beginning the clause means "moreover," or, as the NIV translates it, "indeed."

[25] J. Calvin, *The Second Epistle of Paul the Apostle to the Corinthians and the Epistles to Timothy, Titus and Philemon*, CNTC, trans. T. A. Small, ed. D. W. Torrence and T. F. Torrance (Grand Rapids: Eerdmans, 1964) 12.

[26] *Sir* 41:1–4 refers to the "sentence" or "decree" (τὸ κρίμα) of death in a metaphorical sense: O death, how bitter is the reminder of you to one who lives at peace among his possessions, to a man without distractions, who is prosperous in everything, and who still has the vigor to enjoy his food! O death, how welcome is your sentence to one who is in need and is failing in strength, very old and distracted over everything; to one who is contrary, and has lost his patience! Do not fear the sentence of death; remember your former days and the end of life; this is the decree from the Lord for all flesh, and how can you reject the good pleasure of the Most High? Whether life is for ten or a hundred or a thousand years, there is no inquiry about it in Hades. (NRSV)

continuing results or consequences. The perfect periphrastic in the next clause, "that we might not rely" (*hina mē pepoithotes ōmen*), certainly suggests some "ongoing awareness of a 'death sentence,'" which does not fit a judicial condemnation from which he has received a reprieve.[27] Paul also uses similar imagery in 1 Cor 4:9. He says that in comparison to the Corinthians he has been made a spectacle "like men condemned to die in the arena." He clearly does not intend this statement literally. According to Roman law, those who were condemned to death lost whatever civil rights they had; and Acts records Paul continuing to exercise his rights as a Roman citizen (Acts 22:25–29; 23:27; 25:11–12).[28] By saying that he received this "sentence" "within ourselves" *(en heautois),* he implies that it was some subjective experience, not a verdict passed by a magistrate. It was something that he came to understand.

Hemer demonstrates that the word translated "sentence" *(apokrima)* does not refer to a judicial sentence but was used in the official language of the early empire for an answer or decision that settles a petition or inquiry from an embassy. Paul therefore does not refer to a judgment handed down by some magistrate but to an answer he received for a petition he made to God.[29] We may not be certain precisely what "the answer of death" was, but Paul makes clear what God's decision meant.

1. He received it "in order that" *(hina)* he might rely solely upon God, who raises the dead. Calvin commented that Paul was no different from other human beings in being tempted to place his confidence on his own powers rather than on God.[30] The roots of human pride grow deep, like those of the Acacia trees in the Serengeti desert, and they are not easily dislodged. And Calvin reflects that "we are not brought to real submission until we have been laid low by the crushing hand of God."[31] We frequently need a good dose of helplessness when we are reduced to extrem-

---

[27] P. Barnett, *The Second Epistle to the Corinthians,* NICNT (Grand Rapids: Eerdmans, 1997) 86, n. 32.

[28] Yates, "Paul's Affliction in Asia," 242, noting Justinian, *Digests* 28.1.8.4.

[29] Hemer, "A Note on 2 Corinthians 1:9," 103–7. See also F. Büchsel, "κρίνω ...," *TDNT* 3:945–46: "By human judgment Paul could only reckon that his position was like that of a man condemned to death who had made a petition for mercy and received the answer that he must die." See also Furnish, *II Corinthians,* 113. Hemer wrongly connects this answer to Paul's expectation to survive until the parousia (1 Thess 4:15,17). He assumes that 2 Cor 5:1–10 has a different perspective on the resurrection than 1 Corinthians 15 and that Paul shifted his views. The change was caused by Paul's extreme circumstances and his petitioning God. He received the answer that no one could claim any exemption from death until the Lord came—the sentence of death. A different interpretation of Paul's expectation concerning the Parousia and his death will be presented in the discussion of 5:1–10, but this explanation fails to take into account Paul's statement in 1:10. Paul fully expected God to deliver him yet again in the future.

[30] Calvin, *The Second Epistle of Paul the Apostle to the Corinthians,* 12.

[31] Ibid.

ities and stripped of all false self-confidence before we learn humility and open ourselves up to God's power.[32] Deep certainty of death for Paul led to a deeper trust in God.[33]

This brush with death and God's deliverance taught him again that all we have comes from God and we cannot rely on our own puny strength but on the God who raises the dead (1:9). Those who rely on themselves for their strength, their righteousness (Rom 10:3; Phil 3), and their wisdom (1 Cor 1:30) cannot rely entirely on God and thus doom themselves to failure. Those who rely on God may appear to be weak and even to be failures, but God does not fail to deliver them. This statement undermines the self-confident rivals who boast of their virtuosity and seem sufficient unto themselves. Paul is the first to acknowledge his own insufficiency (3:5); what sufficiency he has comes entirely from God. What power he has comes from God, not from himself (4:7).

2. The affliction was so great that it required the direct intervention of God to overrule it in favor of life, and this divine intervention led him to recognize God's great power even more. When things are at their worst and all human resources are exhausted, then one is most receptive to learning about the power of God. Watson observes that in both letters to the Corinthians, "Paul speaks of the insufficiency of man as the means to the revelation of the all-sufficiency of God."[34] Paul describes his affliction as causing him to be weighed down exceedingly (1:8; *kath' hyperbolēn. ... ebarēthēmen*). He uses the adjective "great," "exceeding" *(hyperbolē)* later in the letter to describe the surpassing nature of God's power (4:7), the exceeding eternal weight of glory (4:17; see 12:7, the exceeding greatness of the revelations he has received).

Paul characterizes God in this verse as the one who raises the dead. The use of the present participle means that he understands this to be a permanent attribute of God (see Rom 4:17). His basic conviction is that in Christ God "has destroyed death and has brought life and immortality to light through the gospel" (2 Tim 1:10; see 1 Cor 15:21,26,54–57). God is the one who comforts (1:4) and the one who raises the dead, a familiar confession in Judaism. The second benediction of the eighteen benedictions *(Shemone Esre)* addresses God as the one

---

[32] This is not to say that Paul was not already humble and needed such an experience to take him down a peg or two, as some have argued. C. H. Dodd, e.g., contended that this experience was some psychological watershed, which he labeled "a sort of second conversion" for Paul. A more mellow Paul emerged from this ordeal. His theory assumes that chaps. 10–13 were written prior to 1–9, which we have argued is wrong. But Paul's reflections here on the lesson he learned comports well with that of a saint. Saints, more than others, recognize how far short they fall from the mark and how much they need to learn and grow. Paul recognized that he had not attained everything and that he needed to press on toward the goal (Phil 3:12–14).

[33] Barnett, *The Message of 2 Corinthians*, 34.

[34] Watson, "2 Cor. 1,9b as the Heart of Paul's Theology," 388.

"who revives the dead." For Paul, however, this Jewish confession has a more specific content that has become the heartbeat of his faith; God is the one who raised the crucified Jesus from the dead (Rom 8:1; 10:9; Gal 1:1; Col 2:12; 1 Thess 1:10). Paul does not trust himself to just any god in general but to the one God who raised Jesus from the dead.[35] He therefore does not take the abundant suffering that comes his way with a gloomy stoicism but with a sense of triumph because of the power of Christ's resurrection. That resurrection insures his own, and he now interprets all that happens to him in life from that perspective. In the midst of suffering he experienced God's empowering presence and became convinced that it created an even more intimate bond with Christ, who had suffered and died for him. That is why he boasts in his afflictions (11:30; 12:5) and continues to expose himself to unrelenting danger and incessant hardships.

Not all of Paul's Corinthian converts have grasped the truth that one can only experience God's power when one has become utterly weak and despairing of any human solution. God raises those who are dead, not those who are already exalted. God's power is made perfect in the weakness of the cross of his Son, and that divine pattern of working in the world continues in the cruciform ministry of his apostle. This wonderful affirmation of faith is Paul's opening salvo for deconstructing the Corinthians' worldly mind-set.

1:10 Paul is no less ambiguous about the nature of his deliverance than he is about the nature of the affliction.[36] But again he only wishes to stress its theological consequence. He has received a temporary reprieve from such a menacing peril. This is not the first time he has been in trouble, nor will it be the last if he continues his ministry.[37] When God has rescued you once

---

[35] C. Wolff, *Der zweite Brief des Paulus an die Korinther,* THKNT (Berlin: Evangelische Verlaganstalt, 1989) 26–27.

[36] This verse contains three problematic textual variants. The first, τηλικούτου θανάτου ("such a deadly peril") in the singular, is supported by the vast majority of witnesses (א A B C D^{gr} G^{gr} K P Ψ 33 88 614). But a plural reading also exists, τηλικούτων θανάτων ("such deadly perils," in $\mathfrak{P}^{46}$ 81 630 1739 it^{d,e} sy^{p,h} goth Ambrosiaster). In 11:23 Paul uses the plural ἐν θανάτοις πολλάκις ("in danger of many deaths") to refer to the various threats he has faced, and he could be referring to repeated scrapes with death in which God delivered him. Most, however, yield to the preponderance of witnesses and accept the singular reading, which would refer to a particular recent event. The second variant, καὶ ῥύσεται ("and will deliver"), is omitted in some texts (A D* Ψ it^{d,61} syr^{p} eth^{pp}). Perhaps some scribes thought that the repetition of the verb "will deliver" in the sentence was superfluous and omitted it; others, however, changed it to the present tense, so that Paul referred to deliverance in the past, present, and future. Despite its redundance, the strong support for the reading "and will deliver" ($\mathfrak{P}^{46}$ א B C P 0209 33 81 365 1175). The alliance of $\mathfrak{P}^{46}$ B D^{gr} for the ἔτι ("continue," NIV) argues for regarding it as the original reading, and the awkward sequence of particles ὅτι καὶ ἔτι probably caused scribes to drop one of them.

[37] See 2 Tim 4:17–18: "But the Lord stood at my side and gave me strength, so that through me the message might be fully proclaimed and all the Gentiles might hear it. And I was delivered from the lion's mouth. The Lord will rescue me from every evil attack and will bring me safely to his heavenly kingdom. To him be glory for ever and ever. Amen."

from great danger, you are confident that God can and will rescue you again.

Paul is not simply expressing wishful thinking as one would if one says, "I hope that God will deliver me." He voices his fundamental confidence that God will deliver him. The prayers of the Bible that praise God as a deliverer have clearly influenced Paul's language here (1 Sam 22:2; see Pss 18:2–6; 40:17; 70:5; 72:12; 91:15; 140:7; 144:2; see also Pss 32; 38; 116). He is confident that God will continue to deliver him, but the verdict of death has not been removed. His hope is set on God's final deliverance from death.[38]

1:11 Paul believes that deliverance comes through intercessory prayer. The verb *synypourgeō* means "to work together with" or "cooperate" by means of something, in this case, by means of their prayers on his behalf.[39] Does this statement, which basically means "with your help," take for granted that they pray for him or does he imply that they should be praying for him? One gets the impression that they have not been faithful in their petitions to God on Paul's behalf. Paul does not hide behind the facade of a superman who pretends that he can survive quite well on his own without help from anyone else. He has no qualms about expressing his desperate need for their prayers. Paul is firmly convinced of prayer's power because he knows that God listens, responds, and delivers.

The next clause is difficult, but Paul seems to be saying that God's gracious favor *(charisma)*, which, in this context, would refer to his recent deliverance,[40] was bestowed on him through the many faces uplifted in prayer on his behalf.[41] But the emphasis is on giving thanks on our behalf. Paul's personal deliverance is not the sole goal of the prayer but the giving of thanks to God for his joyous deliverance.[42] United thanksgiving to God is one of his great aims. After listing the hardships he has suffered in 4:7–12, he declares in 4:15, "All this is for your benefit, so that the grace that is

---

[38] The perfect tense of εἰς ὃν ἠλπίκαμεν, "in whom we have hoped," places the emphasis on the continuing effects of his confidence in God. Barnett comments: "We should remember ... that God's 'deliverances' in this life are always partial. We may recover from an illness, but there is no way to sidestep our last enemy, death. We are inextricably tangled in the sorrow and suffering of the world, whose form is passing away. Only in the resurrection of the dead is there perfect deliverance" (*The Message of 2 Corinthians,* 34).

[39] BAGD, 793.

[40] G. D. Fee argues that the word *charisma* here refers "to some concrete expression of grace received," some specific event in Paul's life, perhaps "the gift of life itself," when he recovered from his distress (*God's Empowering Presence: The Holy Spirit in Letters of Paul* [Peabody, Mass.: Hendrickson, 1994] 286, 32–35. In Rom 5:15–16 the gift *(charisma)* refers to "God's gracious intervention through Christ" (Thrall, *Second Epistle to the Corinthians,* 1:123).

[41] The reference to many faces does not refer figuratively to persons. The word "face" appears ten times in the letter and does not mean "person" (see 2:10; 3:7,13,18; 4:6; 8:24; 10:1,7; 11:20). Paul seems to imagine many faces upturned to God in prayer.

[42] Wolff, *Der zweite Brief des Paulus an die Korinther,* 27.

reaching ever more people may cause thanksgiving to overflow to the glory of God" (see 9:11–12). Paul is not soliciting their prayers for his benefit alone. The surplus of suffering brings a greater surplus of comfort that overflows into the lives of others. This enrichment leads to prayers of thanksgiving that redound to the glory of God. Paul's ultimate concern is not his rescue from danger but that God will be honored more and more. The pattern of suffering and deliverance drives him further into the arms of God, who alone has the power to raise the dead, and increases the volume of prayer. Paul's vision is never confined to himself and his own little world; it stretches to the entire world and its response to God.

But Paul writes this letter because the relationship with the church has gone through some rocky times. Besides the danger Paul faced in Asia, the growing rift between him and the Corinthians probably added to his feeling unbearably crushed. He makes it clear that he has given his life to a great and powerful God who supports and comforts him in all things, but he also needs them.[43] It is equally true that they need him. If they earnestly join in praying for his deliverance, then they cannot disparage his suffering. Joyously giving thanks to God for God's intervention in Paul's life becomes the surest sign of the reconciliation between them. Consequently, Paul does not begin this letter by offering thanksgiving for what God has done in their lives but with hope that they will give thanks for what God has done in his life through his affliction.

(2) The Theme Statement of the Letter (1:12–14)

[12]**Now this is our boast: Our conscience testifies that we have conducted ourselves in the world, and especially in our relations with you, in the holiness and sincerity that are from God. We have done so not according to worldly wisdom but according to God's grace. [13]For we do not write you anything you cannot read or understand. And I hope that, [14]as you have understood us in part, you will come to understand fully that you can boast of us just as we will boast of you in the day of the Lord Jesus.**

This passage contains the theme statement for the letter (cp. Rom 1:16–17).[44] Paul hopes the Corinthians will understand that he is their boast in the Lord and will see that they can and should be proud of him instead of deni-

---

[43] Talbert (*Reading Corinthians,* 135) cites Epictetus: "There is nothing more effective in the style for exhortation than when the speaker makes clear to his audience that he has need of them" (*Dissertations* III.23.37).

[44] So J. T. Fitzgerald, *Cracks in Earthen Vessels: An Examination of the Catalogues of Hardship in the Corinthian Correspondence,* SBLDS 99 (Atlanta: Scholars Press, 1988) 232–34, 247–48; Wolff, *Der zweite Brief des Paulus an die Korinther,* 29. Furnish thinks that these verses only introduce the first theme of the letter (*II Corinthians,* 129).

grating him. This theme is restated in 5:11b–12: "What we are is plain to God, and I hope it is also plain to your conscience. We are not trying to commend ourselves to you again, but are giving you an opportunity to take pride in us, so that you can answer those who take pride in what is seen rather than in what is in the heart." His object is to get them to evaluate him properly so they can speak of him with pride, in spite of his afflictions, and will defend him against those who denigrate his ministry. His hope is that they will pray for him in his sufferings and give thanks for his deliverance rather than belittle him (1:11), that they will embrace him as their boast (1:13–14), and that they will come to acknowledge his complete straightforwardness and sincerity in carrying out his apostolic commission (1:13).

Paul's deprivation and the unexpected shifts in his fortunes, his ministry style, and his frank criticism of the Corinthians have apparently offended some Corinthians. Those displeased with Paul have raised doubts about his sufficiency as an apostle. They also have cast suspicions on his integrity, scoffed at his rhetorical skills, and challenged his authority. While Paul claimed that his suffering deepened his solidarity with Christ and authenticated further his message, most in the ancient world would have assumed exactly the opposite. Such suffering would have refuted his claims.

Most assumed that the philosopher's responsibility was to teach others the way to the good life and to exemplify it. Paul's near-death experiences suggested that he was leading anything but the good life and that all this suffering was the result of God's displeasure. He should no longer be trusted. As Harvey puts it:

> Such reactions would come to a head when the sufferer actually made an appearance: he would bear the humiliating marks of the condition from which he was only just beginning to recover; his activities would be limited by the weakness of his "flesh." And he would have lost the ability to do that by which he had always set particular store, namely to support himself during his visits and to lay no burden of care and hospitality upon his hosts.[45]

He reminded the Galatians that he first preached the gospel to them because of some illness ("weakness of the flesh"). He rejoiced that though his illness would normally have been a trial to them, they did not despise him but received him as if he were an angel from God (Gal 4:13–14). Some Corinthians apparently did belittle him because of his abundant afflictions. He looked too much like a loser—battered, bruised, and sick—too close a companion to death for their comfort.

If the messenger is discredited, then so is his message. This discrediting of his message is Paul's primary concern. He therefore argues throughout this letter that he has not brought discredit to his ministry and hopes that the

---

[45] Harvey, *Renewal through Suffering,* 94.

Corinthians will affirm this fact (see 6:3). He hopes that they will see how God works powerfully through his weaknesses as God worked powerfully through Christ's sufferings. He may seem to be weak and of no account (1 Cor 2:1–5; 2 Cor 10:10), but appearances are deceiving. Just as the cross appears to be proof of God's weakness and foolishness but is really evidence of God's power and wisdom, so Paul's sufferings and humiliations confirm him as an apostle (see 1 Cor 1:17; 2:3–5; 4:7–11). They reveal that he is conforming to the divine paradigm of Christ crucified.

1:12 The word "boast" *(kauchēsis)* frames this thematic statement (1:12,14). Paul begins by presenting his grounds for boasting (1:12) and ends by expressing the hope that they will realize that he will be their grounds for boasting at the day of the Lord (1:14).

References to boasting occur more frequently in this letter than in all of Paul's other writings combined (twenty-nine times out of fifty-five occurrences).[46] "Boasting," however, has a negative connotation for most people today. It smacks of vanity, arrogance, and audacity and is synonymous with bragging, vaunting ourselves, gloating, and showing off. Therefore we assume that it should be shunned by Christians who should be properly humble. Paul told the Corinthians that no one can boast in the presence of God (1 Cor 1:29; see Rom 3:27) and that they should not boast in men (the different leaders; 1 Cor 3:21). He himself was not a boastful apostle (1 Cor 9:15–16; 2 Cor 10:13–15), and he criticizes his rivals for their foolish boasting, which only reveals them to be false apostles and deceitful workers (12:13). In Phil 3:3–8 he catalogs his former grounds for boasting and confidence in the flesh but says that he disdains it all now as rubbish in comparison to knowing Christ as Lord. He tells the Galatians that he only boasts in the cross of Christ that has saved him not only from his sin but from a false trust in his own righteousness (Gal 6:14). Heralding his boast and hoping that the Corinthians will come to take pride in him as their boast may therefore seem inconsistent to the modern reader.[47]

First Corinthians indicates that boasting was a problem in Corinth long before the braggart rivals appeared on the scene. Savage attributes it to the secular values and attitudes that had infected the Corinthian Christians.[48] They were little different from their pagan fellow citizens who were

---

[46] The verb "to boast" (καυχάομαι) occurs twenty times (5:12; 7:14; 9:2; 10:8,13,15,16, 17(2x); 11:12,16,18(2x),30(2x); 12:1,5(2x),6,9). The noun (καύχησις) referring to the act of boasting occurs six times (1:12; 7:4,14; 8:24; 11:10,17). The noun (καύχημα) referring to the grounds for boasting occurs three times (1:14; 5:12; 9:3).

[47] See 5:12: "We are not trying to commend ourselves to you again, but are giving you an opportunity to take pride in us, so that you can answer those who take pride in what is seen rather than in what is in the heart."

[48] Savage, *Power through Weakness,* 64.

obsessed with exalting themselves and trying to leap over one another to attain honor and prominence. Boasting, arrogance, and contempt for others of lesser status were common in the Corinthian environment and were gaining a secure place in the church as well. Some in the congregation used boasting to gain greater prominence among their peers (1 Cor 1:12; 3:21; 4:7). They even looked down on Paul. They took offense that he worked with his hands and derided his humble condition (1 Cor 4:8–13).

It is only human nature to want others to appreciate us, even admire us. We normally become angry or hurt when they ignore us or pour contempt upon us. Some Corinthians had not properly appreciated Paul's worth. Still, Paul is not venting his hurt feelings in this letter for being scorned. The problem is that they do not appreciate his work as an apostle because they have adopted a false means by which to measure apostles and spirituality.

Paul wants them to understand him better, to understand his ministry— how it is that a minister of the glorious gospel must withstand such dishonor and indignity—to esteem his motives behind his actions—how he had done all things without guile and with their best interests at heart. They have renewed their zeal for Paul (7:7,11), but the statement in 1:14a implies that they have only a partial understanding of him, something he may have concluded from his discussion with Titus about his visit. He knows himself and wants them to know him fully. What may still confound them about Paul is how one so weak, so humble, so impoverished, and so afflicted "rightly claim to be a minister of the glorious gospel of Jesus Christ."[49] Paul does not desire to gain personal vindication or to rehabilitate his reputation for personal integrity as if he were only a discredited politician. Rather, he believes that if they understand him and his sufficiency as God's apostle, then they will also understand better the nature of the cross and how it should be lived out in the lives of all followers of Christ.

Therefore he commends his behavior as Christ's apostle and wants them to commend him because it will reveal their spiritual maturity. It will show that they can recognize that God's power works most powerfully through weakness. By criticizing his wretched afflictions the Corinthians betray an ignorance of his gospel (4:3). He needs to reacquaint them with the gospel that he preaches: Jesus Christ as Lord and ourselves as your servants (4:5). One letter or two will not provide an immediate cure for their fleshly outlook. He will need to visit them again. That is why he concludes in 13:5–6 by asking them to examine themselves to see if indeed they are in the faith.

A boastful group of rivals has compounded the problem for Paul. They arrived on the scene, wormed their way into the congregation's affections, and exalted themselves by portraying him in a negative light. His pride may have

---

[49] Ibid., 103.

been hurt by the Corinthians' rejection, but he disdains this shameless contest for honor. He does not want to be adored by them, and he does not need an ego boost. Yet he also does not want to be ignored by them. He wants to instill their confidence in him again because if he does not, he will lose the congregation to false apostles. He wants to preserve his relationship with the church. He does not want them to doubt his integrity and then be taken in by whatever false gospel his opponents champion. What he wants to do in this letter is to restore the relationship between the two of them. Paul therefore speaks of the mutuality of pride: we are your boast as you also are ours.

It is a delicate situation. How do you boast inoffensively and in accordance with the gospel? Yet boasting is not always wrong. It all depends on the basis for boasting. Boasting is related to confidence, and confidence is good if one places it in the right things. Paul's understanding of boasting derives from Jer 9:23–24, which he partially cites in 10:17 and 1 Cor 1:24: "'Let not the wise man boast of his wisdom or the strong man boast of his strength or the rich man boast of his riches, but let him who boasts boast about this: that he understands and knows me, that I am the LORD, who exercises kindness, justice and righteousness on earth, for in these I delight,' declares the LORD." If one boasts in human achievements, then it is sinful. If one boasts (or glories) in what God has done, then it is good.

We will return to the issue of boasting later in the letter, but we should note three things about Paul's boast in this verse. First, Paul's boasting is done with God as his witness (1:12; 2:17; 4:2; 5:11). Second, if he boasts that he has dealt with them and all the world in sincerity and trustworthiness, then he also confesses that these virtues came from God, not from himself.[50] He boasts only in the Lord (10:17), in God's grace that delivered him from deadly peril (1:12), and in his weaknesses (12:9), not in his stellar abilities. He can take no credit at all for anything in his ministry but being trustworthy in carrying out the task (1 Cor 4:2). His boasting therefore does not glory in anything about himself but in Christ, who makes him sufficient (2:16) and whose power is made perfect in weakness (12:9). Third, Paul's does not boast to gain any personal advantage. His boasting is related to his apostolic ministry, which has been misunderstood by the Corinthians. Again, his boasting is in God, who called him and empowered him even in his weakness.

Paul does not want the Corinthians to boast about all that he has accomplished but to boast about what Christ has done in their midst through him (see Rom 15:18; 1 Cor 15:10). His aim is not simply to get back into their

---

[50] The NIV translates the genitive τοῦ θεοῦ as a genitive of source, "from God." It could also be a qualitative genitive "godly sincerity." The first option is best since Paul takes no credit for anything but attributes all that is good in him to God's grace (see 1 Cor 15:10).

good graces again but to edify them (12:19; 13:9).[51] If they cannot understand the paradox of God's power manifesting itself in his own weakness
and suffering, how will they comprehend the death of Jesus that saves them?
If they understand the cross, then they will see its "glorious imprint" on his
ministry.[52] The boast will not be in "our great apostle, Saint Paul," but in
God, who mightily uses our humble, thorn-afflicted, suffering Paul to convince, convert, and console others.

The witness of his own conscience, which only God can judge, bears testimony to his honorable motives and behavior.[53] The word "conscience" should
not be understood as some inner voice that urges us to do what is right or nags
us when we do wrong.[54] It refers to "the human faculty whereby a person either
approves or disproves his or her actions (whether already performed or only
intended) and those of others."[55] It denotes the human faculty of critical self-
evaluation.[56] Paul argues that the inner tribunal of his conscience has assessed
whether or not he conducted himself according to the norms of holiness and
godly sincerity. The verdict of his conscience is yes, he did.[57] Later in the letter

[51] Clearly chaps. 10–13 belong to chaps. 1–9 since 12:19 and 13:9 explain Paul's self-commendation.

[52] Savage, *Power through Weakness,* 163.

[53] For his appeal to the judgment of his conscience see Rom 9:1; Acts 23:1; 24:16; see also Heb
13:18.

[54] R. Wall, "Conscience," *ABD* 1:1128–30. The OT does not have a word for conscience
because it resisted an "an introspective and autonomous anthropology" (p. 1129). Hellenistic Judaism appropriated the term from Stoicism. Wall did not restrict it to a person's past acts (usually the
bad ones) citing P. Sevenster, *Paul and Seneca* (Leiden: Brill, 1961) 84–102.

[55] M. E. Thrall, "The Pauline Use of συνείδησις," *NTS* 14 (1967–68) 118–25. Conscience
"denotes a neutral inward faculty of judgment possessed by all humanity, which evaluates conduct
in an objective way in accordance with given and recognized norms. For Christian believers these
criteria will be Christian. In 2 Cor 1:12 the norms are those of integrity (or moral purity) and sincerity. The function of conscience is not to provide these norms, but to judge whether or not Paul's
behavior has conformed to them" (id., *The Second Epistle to the Corinthians,* 1:132). See also H.-J.
Eckstein, *Der Begriff Syneidēsus bei Paulus: Eine neutestamentlich-exegetische Untersuchung
zum Gewissensbegriff,* WUNT 2/10 (Tübingen: Mohr [Siebeck], 1983) 311–14.

[56] Furnish, *II Corinthians,* 127. Since Paul uses the term most frequently in the Corinthian correspondence, C. A. Pierce contends that conscience was a fashionable term in Corinth. They
appealed to conscience to justify their behavior, and Paul took it over from them (*Conscience in
the New Testament,* SBT 15 [Naperville: Allenson, 1955] 60–65). R. P. Martin argues that conscience is not the sole arbiter; it must be subordinated "to a wider network of issues that bear on a
person's relationship to God and his or her neighbor's well-being" (*2 Corinthians,* WBC [Waco:
Word, 1986] 20). Thrall counters that "conscience" is not a negative term here: it can bear witness
to holiness (*The Second Epistle to the Corinthians,* 1:131–32).

[57] F. W. Danker draws an interesting contrast between Paul and other benefactors in the ancient
world. The latter went to great expense to broadcast on monuments or tombs their benefactions for
the public welfare or that they had behaved in an honorable manner. Danker comments: "Paul does
not require such letters. His own conscience and the perceptiveness of his addressees are all the
witnesses he needs" (*II Corinthians,* ACNT [Minneapolis: Augsburg, 1989] 38).

he trusts that their consciences will reach the same decision (see 4:2; 5:11).

Such a defense, however, contains a potential danger for those church leaders who may use it to cloak their selfish motives and intimidate any who would challenge them. "My conscience is clear." Best warns that "many of those who have misled others in religion have been most sure they themselves were led by God." He then asks the crucial question: "How can we be sure of acting sincerely? It is not sufficient to say that our conscience will tell us. Our conscience is largely formed by the culture in which we live so that we may miss what God is saying to us."[58] Many have done evil in good conscience. For example, Paul was sure that he was doing God's will before his conversion when he violently persecuted the church (Phil 3:6). In 1 Cor 4:4 Paul says that even a clear conscience does not clear him before God: "My conscience is clear, but that does not make me innocent. It is the Lord who judges me." The judgment of our conscience is only right if it accords with God's norms. The apostle Paul was so attuned to God's calling and so imbued with Christian values that his conscience was now a reliable judge of his conduct.

The phrase "especially in our relations with you" reveals, perhaps unintentionally, that dealing with the Corinthians was like walking on eggshells. Paul may only mean that "they had more opportunity than others (Acts 18:11) of knowing how scrupulous he was."[59] Nevertheless, relations with this congregation were exceptionally touchy, which is why Paul refused their offer of financial support; and his actions were readily misinterpreted. It is not that Paul had to be particularly honest with them but he had to be especially cautious, and we see this caution emerging in his long discussion about the collection in chaps. 8–9.

Paul appears to be defending himself in 1:12b against charges that have been leveled against him. His threats in his letters and his failure to follow through when present have raised suspicions about his integrity. He passes himself off as strong in his letters but comes off as weak in person (10:1–11; 13:2,10). He threatens the rod (1 Cor 4:21) but runs away when discipline is necessary (2:1–4). He pretends to be one thing in his letters and deceives them into thinking that he is bold and strong. He tries to conceal this weakness behind a barrage of threatening words. When he shows up in person, they witness his true weakness and timidity. Breaking his commitment to come to the Corinthians as he promised (1:15–17) only confirmed their hunch that he has something to hide.[60] Hints emerge in the letter that some Corinthians were suspicious that the apostle was guilty of trying to cheat them in some way (7:2; 8:20–21; 11:7–

---

[58] E. Best, *Second Corinthians,* INT (Atlanta: John Knox, 1987) 16.

[59] R. Bultmann, *The Second Letter to the Corinthians,* ed. E. Dinkler, trans. R. A. Harrisville (Minneapolis: Augsburg, 1976) 35.

[60] Savage, *Power through Weakness,* 67.

8; 12:13–18). Paul defends his integrity against any doubters by insisting, "What we are in our letters when we are absent, we will be in our actions when we are present" (10:11). Paul begins his defense with three verdicts from his conscience about his conduct.

1. He has acted with sincerity. The reading "with holiness" in the NIV has strong manuscript support. The variant reading "with sincerity," "simplicity," "frankness" *(en aplotēti)* possibly makes more sense in the context if Paul is countering charges about his integrity (see 4:2).[61] He affirms that he has held nothing back from them.[62]

He always acted with sincerity and integrity. Integrity prompts one to act on what is right even if it is risky, unpopular, or unpleasant and to do so steadfastly when the hail of criticism falls. L. Smedes says: "When a person makes a promise, he stretches himself out into circumstances that no one can control and controls at least one thing: he will be there no matter what the circumstances turn out to be." Paul was such a person.

2. The root meaning of the word translated "sincerity" *(eilikrineia)* refers to something "examined by the light of the sun and found pure."[63] Paul is found to be truthful, honest, and transparent (in contrast to the peddlers of the word, 2:17). Spicq contends that the word does not connote "so much an absence of duplicity or hypocrisy as a fundamental integrity and transparency; it can be compared to innocence."[64] Paul knows, however, that he will be judged by the light of the Son of God and will be found pure because he is being transformed into his likeness (3:18).

3. He does not make his plans or conduct his life according to ordinary, worldly standards (lit. "fleshly wisdom," see 1:17).[65] "Fleshly wisdom" is the opposite of "true wisdom," which comes only from God (1 Cor 1:18–25,30). Most people in the ancient world, as in ours today, regarded "wisdom" to be "wholly good" no matter what form it took.[66] Wisdom by defini-

---

[61] Thrall argues for ἁγιότητι ("holiness") as the original reading ("2 Corinthians 1:12: ΑΓΙΟΤΗΤΙ or ΑΠΛΟΤΗΤΙ?" in *Studies in New Testament Language and Text,* ed. J. K. Elliott, *NovT-Sup* 44 [Leiden: 1976] 366–72). She thinks it is preferable because holiness is a characteristic of God. But Paul does not use this form of the word elsewhere in his letters (the noun form ἁγιωσύνη appears in 7:1; Rom 1:4; 1 Thess 3:13; see ἁγνότητι, "purity," in 6:6) and the word ἁπλότης appears four other times in the letter (8:2; 9:11, 13; 11:3). It is easy to understand how a scribe might have confused one word for another when they are written in uncial script ΑΠΛΟΤΗΤΙ — ΑΓΙΟΤΗΤΙ.

[62] Furnish, *II Corinthians,* 127.

[63] R. H. Strachan, *The Second Epistle of Paul to the Corinthians,* MNTC (London: Hodder & Stoughton, 1935) 54.

[64] C. Spicq, *Theological Lexicon of the New Testament,* trans. and ed. J. D. Ernest (Peabody: Hendrickson, 1994) 1:423. See also F. Büchsel, "εἰλικρινής ...," *TDNT* 2:397.

[65] "Wisdom," which is so prominent in 1 Corinthians (see 1 Cor 1:20; 2:5–6; 3:19), occurs only here in 2 Corinthians.

[66] Harvey, *Renewal through Suffering,* 34.

tion was an understanding of what was true, right, or lasting and was manifest in behavior marked by common sense and good judgment. But Paul did not believe that Christ simply offered a greater wisdom that could be added to the wisdom of this world. He thought the wisdom of Christ *invalidated* the wisdom of this world. Christ offered the only true wisdom, and the world offered only a false, fleshly wisdom.

Those directed by fleshly wisdom allow expediency to dictate their conduct and beliefs. Fickleness reigns as they are blown about by each new wind of teaching. They give promises that they never intend to fulfill (1:17–18). They want to lord it over the faith of others (1:23). They delight in causing pain to others to demonstrate their superiority and want to glory in routing their enemies (2:1–4,5–11). They twist the truth for their own ends and resort to cunning and duplicity to win over others (4:2). They therefore prize rhetorical eloquence to allure and sway others (see 1 Cor 1:17–25; 2:1–5). Those directed by worldly wisdom will use their philosophy to get rich and care nothing about making others poor (2:17; 6:10). They consider the moral defilement of body and spirit to be a matter of indifference (7:1). They boast in the things of the flesh (11:18).

Such calculating, egocentric behavior infused the whole cultural scene of Corinth, and it despised the divine wisdom of the cross that accepts weakness and suffering and refrains from trying to take advantage of others but rather giving one's life freely to serve others. If Paul were driven by such motives, then their complaints would be justified. Paul insists, however, that his motives are controlled by God's grace. Paul has never relied on highflown grandiloquence but on the power of God's word to persuade others. He has never resorted to rhetorical tricks to garnish a weak case to deceive others. His message was true and straightforward; his sincerity, unpretentious and unfeigned.

Paul's defense makes clear that his exemplary conduct is guided by God's grace. Comparing this statement ("we have not done so according to worldly wisdom but according to God's grace") with a parallel statement in 1 Cor 2:5, "so that your faith might not rest on men's wisdom, but on God's power," we see that Paul also understands grace as an expression of God's power (2 Cor 12:9). Grace here refers to the power God grants to live according to God's will and is the driving force behind his work as an apostle (see 1 Cor 3:10; 15:10).

1:13 Paul's assertion that he does not write them anything they cannot read or understand contains a play on the words "to read" *(anaginōskein)* and "to know" or "to recognize" *(epiginōskein)* that is impossible to capture in English. He appears to be reacting to some complaint about his letters, perhaps that they were obscure.[67] If that is the concern, then Paul does little

---

[67] Plummer takes it to mean Paul defends himself against the charge of writing ambiguous and deliberately obscure letters (*The Second Epistle of St. Paul to the Corinthians*, 26); 2 Pet 3:15–16 would seem to confirm such a criticism: "His letters contain some things that are hard to understand, which ignorant and unstable people distort, as they do the other Scriptures, to their own destruction."

in this letter to improve matters. Hanson comments that Paul answers this odd charge by writing "a letter which is obscurer and more ambiguous than any of his surviving ones."[68]

But Paul may be alluding instead to what he perceives to be deliberate misinterpretations of what he wrote.[69] Some have accused him of intending exactly the opposite of what he said. Furnish correctly directs us to Paul's sensitivity to how his letters will be received and interpreted. He argues that Paul is conscious that "someone or some group in Corinth was deliberately trying to turn Paul's letters to the apostle's own disadvantage."[70] The Corinthians have a penchant for misreading his letters (see 1 Cor 5:9–11), hence Paul's anxiety over how they would receive the letter of tears. Therefore he "begs them to pay attention to what he actually says and not to impose their own interpretation on his words."[71] There is no discrepancy between his letters and his conduct. Let them have a "fair hearing."[72]

Paul affirms the straightforward character of his letters. His teaching is not veiled, equivocal, or mercurial. They do not need to ask, What did he really mean by what he said? He has no hidden agenda. He is transparent in all that he does and all that he writes. If they comprehend his letters, then they will also understand his purposes and will not impugn his motives.

Some Corinthians may also presume that Paul somehow veils the gospel (4:3). It is not that it is unclear or garbled. What makes his gospel obscure is his own suffering. Such affliction does not comport well with a message supposed to be good news. He is unimpressive in person, which also makes his gospel unattractive. To this charge Paul responds vigorously later in the letter:

> We have renounced secret and shameful ways; we do not use deception, nor do we distort the word of God. On the contrary, by setting forth the truth plainly we commend ourselves to every man's conscience in the sight of God. And even if our gospel is veiled, it is veiled to those who are perishing (4:2–3).

1:14 Paul now claims that they understand him only in part, not fully. Although he has reason to rejoice over the good news from Titus that the church has repented and wants to patch things up with him (7:7,9,12–13,16), he has no intention of turning a blind eye to the underlying issues that caused the dissension. They do not understand or appreciate the cruciform

---

[68] Hanson, *II Corinthians*, 31.

[69] Calvin observes that "some men do in fact treat Christ in this way, making a game of their teaching like people tossing a ball from hand to hand merely to show off their dexterity" (*The Second Epistle of Paul the Apostle to the Corinthians*, 21).

[70] Furnish, *II Corinthians*, 130.

[71] J. Murphy-O'Connor, *The Theology of the Second Letter to the Corinthians* (Cambridge: University Press, 1991) 24.

[72] Furnish, *II Corinthians*, 130.

nature of his ministry (5:11; 6:11–13; 7:2; 10:1–11; 12:11; 13:3,5–6). They may have shown a zeal for him by renouncing the so-called "offender" (cf. 7:5–13a), but Savage contends that "it was merely a superficial response to the forcefulness of his letter. As pertains to his meekness and humility, they remain disturbed and unimpressed (10:1)."[73] If they do not understand that the meekness and gentleness of Christ guides his dealings with them, then they do not understand what it means to be a Christian.

Paul's appeal, shifting to the first person singular, "I hope," is that they understand fully that "we are your boast" (see 5:12).[74] He boasts in the Corinthians (1 Cor 15:31; 2 Cor 7:4,14; 8:24; 9:2–3). After reading his correspondence with them, one might wonder why. But he boasts in three things: how God has given growth from the planting and watering of his apostles, how the Spirit has bestowed gifts upon them, and how God provides them with every blessing so that they may share abundantly in every good work. Paul hopes that both he and they can boast in one another at the judgment, saying, Here is my church; here is our apostle.

"The day of the Lord Jesus" refers to the Parousia, which Christians associated with the day of judgment found in the Old Testament (see Isa 13:6,9; Ezek 13:5; Amos 5:18; Joel 2:1; Obad 1:15; Zeph 1:14). Paul identifies it as the time when God judges an individual's motives (1 Cor 4:3–5). Boasts can only be fully realized on the day of the Lord, when God's judgment reveals who we are and what our work was (see 1 Cor 3:12–15).[75] The curtain will rise on all deceptions. He trusts that in that day they will fully recognize how God has worked through him. He hopes that he does not have to wait until then, however, but that they can see it now and will vouch for their apostle. It is better for the Corinthians to find out now rather than later how mistaken they were and how they were taken in by frauds.

This theme statement makes clear that Paul will be writing about himself in this letter, and we have already discussed in the introduction how these verses point to the unity of the letter. The subject of boasting is a central theme in the letter (see 5:12; 10:8,13,15–16,18; 11:10,12,16–18,30; 12:1,5–6,9) and his boast about them is also prominent (7:4,14; 8:24; 9:2–3). His sincerity and uprightness as an apostle recurs throughout the letter (1:17;

---

[73] Savage, *Power through Weakness,* 68.

[74] "Until the end" (ἕως τέλους) in 1:13 is translated as "fully" in 1:14.

[75] Paul tells the Thessalonians that they are his hope, joy, and crown of boasting (1 Thess 2:19–20; see Phil 2:16). Paul's hope is fixed on the return of the Lord when his work will be appraised, and he expects that appraisal to produce joy. The crown that Paul looks forward to is the fact that the Thessalonian Christians will be ready at the Parousia, blameless in Christ (see also Phil 4:1). Paul has a corporate understanding of salvation. He is not interested in insuring his own personal victory and his private triumphant entrance into the pearly gates of heaven. That would be only a hollow victory if he were the only one there. He therefore links his destiny at the judgment to his church's fidelity to the gospel. His reward will be that his churches will be saved with him.

2:17; 4:2; 6:3–10; 7:2; 10:2; 12:16–18). Paul does not use the phrase "fleshly wisdom" again in the letter, but he does mention again about making his plans or acting "according to the flesh" (*kata sarka;* 1:17; 4:2; 5:16; 10:2–4; 12:16). Paul asserts in the letter that the grace of God is the controlling factor in his life (2:14; 3:5; 4:7–11; 11:23–33; 12:9). Mention of Paul's writing or his letters appear throughout the letter (2:3–4,9; 7:8,12; 10:1,9–11; 13:10). The problem of only knowing him in part resurfaces in 2:5; 4:2,16–18; 5:11–12 and throughout chaps. 10–13. He makes clear that God knows what he is (5:11) even if he is not fully known to the Corinthians. Being known by God also implies that one will be judged at the day of the Lord Jesus, and this idea recurs in 5:10; 7:1; 13:5–10.

(3) Paul's Changes in Plans (1:15–22)

¹⁵Because I was confident of this, I planned to visit you first so that you might benefit twice. ¹⁶I planned to visit you on my way to Macedonia and to come back to you from Macedonia, and then to have you send me on my way to Judea. ¹⁷When I planned this, did I do it lightly? Or do I make my plans in a worldly manner so that in the same breath I say, "Yes, yes" and "No, no"?

¹⁸But as surely as God is faithful, our message to you is not "Yes" and "No." ¹⁹For the Son of God, Jesus Christ, who was preached among you by me and Silas and Timothy, was not "Yes" and "No," but in him it has always been "Yes." ²⁰For no matter how many promises God has made, they are "Yes" in Christ. And so through him the "Amen" is spoken by us to the glory of God. ²¹Now it is God who makes both us and you stand firm in Christ. He anointed us, ²²set his seal of ownership on us, and put his Spirit in our hearts as a deposit, guaranteeing what is to come.

Paul's changes in his travel plans have cast suspicions on his sincerity, so he tries to lay the matter to rest in these verses.[76] In 1 Cor 16:5–9 he told them that he would come to them after he went through Macedonia and perhaps even spend the winter. He specifically says that he did not want to make only a passing visit but wanted to spend time with them. Because a "great door for effective work" had opened for him in Ephesus, he intended to stay there until Pentecost. He does qualify his own announced plans by saying "if the Lord permits" (1 Cor 16:7). As for the collection for the saints in Judea, he told them to put aside something every week and save whatever extra they earn so that he

---

[76] References to his travel plans appear in 1 Cor 4:18–21; 11:34; 16:3–9; 2 Cor 9:4; 12:14; 13:1. He has also changed his mind about the collection. He now has decided that he should go to Jerusalem with the churches' representatives, probably to interpret its significance (Rom 15:25). If it were just a matter of sending money, any group of trustworthy persons would do. The collection, however, is not just an offering; it is a token of the unity between Gentile and Jewish Christians. Paul apparently worried about how it would be received (Rom 15:31) and believed he must help clarify its significance (see Rom 15:27).

need not take up an offering when he comes (1 Cor 16:1–3). He apparently did not plan to go to Jerusalem himself since he tells the Corinthians that he will send letters of recommendation for any whom they approve to take the gift (1 Cor 16:3). He then writes that he expects them to send him on his way *(propempō)* "wherever I go" (1 Cor 16:6). Meanwhile, Paul sent Timothy to visit them. If the verb in 1 Cor 4:17 is an epistolary aorist, which is most likely, then Timothy delivered 1 Corinthians. Paul's interesting request—"see to it that he has nothing to fear while he is with you, … let no one treat him with contempt" (1 Cor 16:10–11; NIV, "See to it that he has nothing to fear while he is with you. … No one, then, should refuse him")—suggests that he had some forebodings about their reception of him.

For some unknown reason, Paul modified his original plan and made a crisis visit to Corinth (1:15–16). Perhaps he had received news from Timothy, who had since returned to Ephesus, that the situation had taken a turn for the worse.[77] This emergency visit was cut short because of some painful confrontation (2:1). The superapostles may already have begun their meddling in the church, but the defining event was the abuse poured upon him by someone in the congregation and less likely from someone outside. His pain was intensified when the church either supported this individual or stood by silently and did not come to his defense (2:5; 7:12). The dispute does not seem to be over some theological deviation (see 1:24) but over some affront directed either at Paul's person, ministry style, attempted discipline, or all of the above (see 7:12). Acts is silent about this painful visit (Acts 18:1–7; 20:3) and generally presents a congenial relationship between the Corinthian church and Paul. Paul's letters, however, clearly show that his relationship with the church had some rocky moments.

This unpleasant event forced Paul to make "a passing visit," something he said he wanted to avoid (1 Cor 16:7). Then, Paul withdrew as suddenly as he appeared, vexed and humiliated; and he did not return (1:23). Sometimes retreating is better than staying and fighting. By withdrawing, Paul attempts to defuse an explosive situation and let things cool down. He apparently did not want to risk another rebuff and have his authority undermined any further. His visit to Corinth seems to have exacerbated rather than corrected the problem, and he decided that a return visit so soon after this embarrassing showdown would do little good. Unlike some leaders who try to hide their insecurity behind a blustering facade that projects their mastery of everyone and every situation, Paul is not afraid to let his frailty show. Even now, in this letter, he is still apprehensive about returning to Corinth and openly

[77] P. Marshall suggests that Paul wished to bring the conflict with the boastful opponents to a head before taking care of the preparations for the collection (*Enmity in Corinth: Social Conventions and Paul's Relations to the Corinthians,* WUNT 2/23 [Tübingen: Mohr[Siebeck] 1987] 261).

shares his uneasiness with them: "I am afraid that when I come again my God will humble me before you, and I will be grieved over many who have sinned earlier and have not repented of the impurity, sexual sin and debauchery in which they have indulged" (12:21). He confesses that he is not sure how to manage the situation since this person's posture toward him poisoned his relationship with the Corinthians.

Paul wrote the sorrowful letter, now lost (2:1–4), and dispatched Titus, not Timothy, to deliver it (cf. 1 Thess 3:1–3) rather than return himself to Corinth. Titus was an uncircumcised Greek (Gal 2:1–3) and may have been harder to intimidate than Timothy, or he may have possessed tougher skin and therefore was better suited to deal with stubborn opposition. The disaffected faction may have been only a small minority, but Paul wanted to test the obedience of the entire congregation to see if they would take it upon themselves to discipline the individual (2:9).

Paul had since gone to Troas and did not find Titus there as he expected. He was too preoccupied with worry about what was happening in Corinth to take advantage of another opened door for evangelism (2:12–13). Consequently, he headed on to Macedonia (2:12). The events in Corinth still burdened him (7:5) as he waited anxiously for Titus's status report (2:13–14). When Titus finally arrived in Macedonia, Paul rejoiced over the good news that confirmed his confidence in them. The sorrowful letter apparently released some of the tension by heightening it, that is, by confronting the issues directly (7:5–6).

Paul, however, had not won over the whole church (see 7:6–13). Pockets of resistance still existed. Perhaps members meeting in different house churches continued to oppose Paul and to champion the rival superapostles. Nevertheless, matters had been sufficiently settled for Paul to plan to visit them again. Second Corinthians was written to prepare for this next visit (see Acts 20:2). Paul sent Titus on ahead with this letter to solidify the support for him and to stimulate their preparations for the collection (8:1–7; 9:1–4). His return prompted this letter.

1:15–16 Paul probably learned from Titus how disturbed the Corinthians were over his failure to follow through on his plans and not return. He was confident (lit., "in this confidence") that his communication with them was not influenced by fleshly wisdom but by the grace of God and that it was transparent, sincere, and plainspoken (1:12–14); therefore he explains that he had planned to come to them first. This statement reveals how important Achaia was to him. Less clear is what he means when he says "that you might have a second grace" (NIV "that you might benefit twice").[78] The "second grace" might be something he confers on them or something they confer on him.

---

[78] The emphasis on confidence appears again with a different word (*pepoithēsis,* instead of the *kauchēsis*) in 1:12.

1. Some interpret the "second grace" to be an apostolic blessing accorded them by Paul's presence. This interpretation assumes that "grace" has its normal theological meaning here. Because he was a bearer of divine grace (see Rom 1:11), fellowship with Paul, even a passing visit, conveys grace. Schelkle comments: "The apostle is not only a teacher and preacher, but he is also mediator of grace between God and man. His presence in the community opens up the floodgates of God's mercy."[79] Paul therefore would be intimating that his two apostolic visits would bring a double spiritual blessing to the Corinthians.[80]

Modern readers may think that Paul seems too full of himself in thinking that he bestows such a divine blessing by his very presence. Paul believes, however, that a visit brings mutual encouragement, both to himself and to the community, as they share their faith and spiritual gifts (Rom 1:11–12). In 2:3 he talks about having grief if he came. He therefore understands his coming as bringing either grace or grief (see 12:20–21). He avoided returning to Corinth when it was sure to result only in grief.

2. Another view opts for a textual variant, "joy." This reading would mitigate the seeming arrogance behind Paul calling his visit a grace and have him refer to it as a shared joy.[81] The textual evidence, however, supports "grace" as the original reading.[82]

3. A third alternative interprets the double grace as some grace conferred by the Corinthians on Paul. Fee contends that Paul is not saying that they will receive grace twice because of his presence "but that they will experience it twice *as they help him along the way.*" He places the emphasis on his being sent on *by them* to Macedonia *(di' hymōn dielthein eis Makedonian)* and then on to Judea *(hyph' hymōn propemphthēnai eis tēn Ioudian)* in the next verse. He interprets the "double grace" to be a double opportunity for kindness as they help send him on to Macedonia and then after he returns as they send him on his way to Judea.[83] The

---

[79] Schelkle, *The Second Epistle to the Corinthians*, 24.

[80] Furnish compares this verse to Rom 1:11, where Paul hopes to take "a spiritual gift" to the Roman church, and Rom 15:29, where he says he will come to Rome with "the blessing of Christ." In Phil 1:25–26 he believes his coming will bring "joy in the faith" and enable them to glory in Christ Jesus. He is therefore fully conscious of "the grace of God operative in and through his apostolic ministry to them" (*II Corinthians,* 142). But, we should note, the Philippians rejoice over his reprieve from death and his release from prison.

[81] Héring translates it "a second opportunity for rejoicing" (*The Second Epistle of Saint Paul to the Corinthians*, 9); the Moffatt translation has "a double delight."

[82] The words "grace" (χάριν) and "joy" (χαράν) in the accusative cases are similar in Greek, but the reading "joy" probably was introduced by scribes who assimilated it to the mention of joy in 2:3.

[83] G. Fee, "ΧΑΡΙΣ in II Corinthians I.15: Apostolic Parousia and Paul—Corinth Chronology," *NTS* 24 (1978) 533–38. See also Marshall, *Enmity in Corinth*, 261, n. 7. Thrall argues to the contrary that the order of the words suggests that the grace is connected to the fact of the visit rather than what the Corinthians will do on the occasion of it. She says that one would expect 1:16 to begin with "that is" rather than "and" (*The Second Epistle to the Corinthians,* 1:138).

grace then refers to their hospitality and gracious help in assisting him for his two journeys.

Several arguments support this interpretation. First, Paul uses the word "grace" to refer to the collection in 1 Cor 16:3 and 2 Cor 8:4,6–7,19 (translated as "generous undertaking" in NRSV and "grace of giving" in NIV). In 2 Cor 8:7 Paul emphasizes how they experience grace "by service toward others (in this case, Paul and his companions)."[84] Paul does not say that they might "receive a second grace" but that they might *have* a second grace. They have grace when they give service to others.

Second, the emphasis in 1 Cor 16:6–7 is not on benefits that Paul will bring to them but on benefits they will give to him. Third, the verb "to send on" *(propempein)* in 1:17 entails providing someone resources, such as money, supplies, and companions, for a journey (see 1 Cor 16:6).[85] Although Paul did not receive support from a congregation while he was working among them, he did allow them to equip him for his travel to other cities.[86] Since the Corinthians have taken umbrage over Paul's refusal to receive support from them (11:7–11; 12:14–18), he notifies them at the very beginning of the letter that he had intended to allow them to help him in his travels to gather up the collection and to deliver it.

Choosing between the first and last options is difficult, but the last interpretation seems best. It fits the meaning of the verb to "send on," Paul's theology about giving, and the value he places on the partnership of his churches in his mission enterprise.

1:17 Someone in Corinth seized on his postponed visit and blew it out of proportion in much the way politicians use negative campaigning to embarrass and defeat their rivals. They recast his failure to come into a breach of promise, giving it the worst possible interpretation. Paul cannot deny that he changed his plans but rejects the negative construction given to it. He did say one thing and do another, but that does not mean that he is indifferent to them, that he makes his plans without thinking, or that he is irresponsible.[87] Rather, what he wanted to do he was unable to do.

Paul asks them two questions which are both governed by the particle *mēti,* expecting a negative answer. "You do not think then that I treat my

---

[84] Fee, "ΧΑΡΙΣ in II Corinthians I.15," 536.

[85] Furnish points out that "sending him on his way" became "a technical missionary term (Acts 15:3; 1 Cor 16:6,11; Titus 3:13; 3 John 6)" that involved providing escorts and supplies for the journey (*II Corinthians*, 134). See also Rom 15:24.

[86] See the discussion on 11:7–9 concerning Paul's policy on support from churches on 11:7–9.

[87] Barrett thinks that Paul may be accused of "writing one thing, saying another, and doing a third" (*The Second Epistle to the Corinthians,* 70). If true, this would explain the enmity of the Corinthians.

relationship to you lightly, do you?"[88] They are not accusing him of being fickle but of being blasé about his relationship to them. We all may have experienced the disappointment when a loved one promises to visit and then fails to do it. They may have the best reasons in the world, but we may still interpret their actions to mean that they do not love us. Paul insists that his failure to follow through does not mean that he does not care for them.[89]

He also insists that the motivations behind his failure to return as promised were not selfish. He makes this point by asking them, "I do not make my plans according to the flesh, do I?" "Surely you do not think that I made my plans in a frivolous way, do you?" Self-centered concerns—What's best for me? or What's in it for me?—direct the decisions made by "worldly men." But Paul chose not to return because he wanted *to spare them* another painful visit (1:23), not because he was serving his own needs.

The double affirmation "so that from me might be the yes, yes; the no, no" (literal translation) continues the thought of making plans "according to the flesh"; but its meaning is unclear. The NIV translation assumes, with most commentators, that Paul alludes to some charge of duplicity or vacillation against him—the readiness to say yes and no at the same time (so also NRSV). A yes and no man talks out of both sides of his mouth and says whatever he thinks will serve his best interests.

This interpretation makes sense but reads too much into the text. It assumes that Paul meant to say, without saying it, that he says yes and no "at the same time." The words "in the same breath" in the NIV translation do not appear in the Greek; but if this interpretation is correct, it requires introducing some such phrase into the text or arguing that it is somehow implied.[90] It also assumes that Paul repeats the particles "Yes, yes, no, no"

---

[88] Harvey argues that Paul's response is "entirely devoted to his original wishes and intentions—I wanted to come to you ... when I *wanted* this was I being 'fickle?'" He takes this to mean that Paul was judged before he changed his plans and that "it was the original project that aroused suspicion." He understands the "second favor" to be a reference to a visit Paul had already made. The word ἐλαφρία is rare and means "stupidity" or "irresponsibility," not "fickleness" as Jerome translated it. The definite article with it would make it mean "my well-known" "foolish irresponsibility." He argues that the one thing Paul was well-known for was his refusal to accept money from the local church to support him during his stay and concludes that Paul is really talking about money. Paul's real anxiety has to do with his recent inability, which would make him unable to fend for himself and to go back on his policy of refusing support (*Renewal through Suffering*, 38–39). The whole paragraph, however, has to do with making plans. Therefore Paul's answer in 1:18 that God is faithful implies that someone is claiming that Paul is not. They have questioned his plans and his motives for changing them.

[89] The Corinthians were extremely sensitive to slights in receiving honor. They would not accept second place in Paul's heart. Some may accuse him of showing partiality to the churches of Macedonia (see 11:8–9; so Furnish, *II Corinthians*, 144). If so, Paul only stokes that jealousy with his lavish praise of the Macedonians (8:1–7; 9:1–5).

[90] Barrett, *The Second Epistle to the Corinthians*, 75.

only for emphasis.

Others contend that the phrase is a stock description of the flatterer who agrees with whatever is said—a yes-man.[91] The flatterer, however, responds to what someone else says.[92] In this instance Paul is responding to *his own* yes and no. This view fails to explain why the particles are doubled, "Yes, yes; No, no." The doubled particles are reminiscent of Jesus' teaching on oaths: "Let your word be 'Yes, yes' and 'No, no'" (see Matt 5:37; Jas 5:12).[93] To stop the abuse of real oaths and substitute oaths, Jesus rejected swearing oaths altogether, for they diminish the demand for absolute truthfulness at all times. Their use implies either that one is normally untruthful or that one need only be truthful when swearing an oath. The doubling of the words intensifies the yes into a real yes and the no into a real no. Jesus teaches that a plain yes or no is as wholly binding upon a person as the most intricate and ceremonious oath. A misunderstanding of this teaching that construes the "Yes, yes and No, no" as substitute oaths may have been known to the Corinthians and would provide the backdrop for Paul's response.[94] The rep-

---

[91] Marshall, *Enmity in Corinth*, 70–90, 317–25. Talbert concurs (*Reading Corinthians,* 136), citing Plutarch's observation that the flatterer "is not simple, not one, but variable and many in one, and like water that is poured into one receptacle after another, he … changes his shape to fit his receiver" (*How to Tell the Flatterer from a Friend,* 52b–53d). C. E. Glad elaborates: "The flatterer, in the judgment of his critics, has only his personal advantage in view. In an attempt to secure his advantage he consents to everything, speaks in order to please, is charming, affable, and witty. In rendering his services he accommodates himself to those he flatters, and is, like the friend of many and the polyp, cunning in his affable, versatile, and all-adaptable approach. As such, his behavior is seen as 'soft' and servile" ("Frank Speech, Flattery, and Friendship in Philodemus," in *Friendship, Flattery and Frankness of Speech: Studies on Friendship in the New Testament World,* ed. J. T. Fitzgerald, NovTSup 82 [Leiden: Brill, 1996] 26).

[92] Cicero's citation of Gnatho (*Amicitae* 25.93) in Terence's play *The Eunuch* (251–53) sounds similar to what Paul is saying, "Whatever they say I praise; if again they say the opposite I praise that too. If one says no, I say no; if one says yes. I say yes" (cited by Marshall, *Enmity in Corinth,* 81–82). But this is a response to what someone else says and does not genuinely match Paul's statement, "the Yes, Yes and the No, No."

[93] A small minority of witnesses (p[46] 424 Vg and Pelagius) omit the doubled yes and no. This shorter reading is probably to be attributed to a scribe or scribes not understanding its significance and assimilating it to the single yes and no in the next verse.

[94] D. Wenham, "2 Corinthians 1:17, 18: Echo of a Dominical Logion," *NovT* 28 (1986) 271–79. Wellborn contends that "The doubling of the particles was one of several ways of seeking to establish the truth of one's statement by employing what amounts to an oath." (L. L. Welborn, "The Dangerous Double Affirmation: Character and Truth in 2 Cor 1,17," *ZNW* 86 [1995] 42). This view is supported by *2 Enoch* 49:1 (in the longer recension J) even if it is a Christian gloss. Enoch teaches his sons not to use oaths:

> For I am swearing to you, my children—But look! I am not swearing by any oath at all, neither by heaven nor by earth nor by any other creature which the Lord created. For [the Lord] said, "There is no oath in me, nor any unrighteousness, but only truth." So, if there is no truth in human beings, then let them make an oath by means of the words, "Yes, Yes!" or, if it should be the other way around, "No, No!"

Later rabbis argued that when one repeated the yes or the no they became oaths (*b. Sanh.* 36a).

etition of the yes and no "serves to establish the truth of what is said."[95] This interpretation makes the best sense of the text as it stands.

Paul refers to this ersatz oath formula to express dramatically the difficult situation in which he finds himself. He wants to convince the Corinthians that in all his dealings with them he has been wholly sincere and that only one principle has guided him: the promotion of their joy (1:24).[96] As Wellborn puts it, "Paul says: 'You suspect me of acting insincerely; you accuse me of vacillation and self-interestedness; you deem me untrustworthy. As a result, I am like a man who must continually seek to establish the truth of his statements by employing what amounts to an oath.'"[97] Paul was reluctant to take an oath since it was "weak, artificial proof, by definition an unprovable statement." Human promises and oaths only mirror human fallibility. Having to take some kind of oath to prop up the truthfulness of his assertions would also give evidence that the relationship with the Corinthians was still broken, "still troubled by suspicion." Paul wants to remove the grounds for their suspicion, but if he has to swear oaths to get them to believe him, then something is terribly wrong between them.

This interpretation has the advantage of not having to add the words "at the same time" or "in the same breath" to the text. It also best explains what follows in 1:18–19. These verses do not clarify what Paul says in 1:17 but continue the argument with an adversative, "but" *(de)*. He contrasts "the apostolic word about Jesus the Messiah" that is "unequivocal" (1:19) with human promises that are precarious and uncertain.[98]

1:18   Although Paul may have changed his plans, he affirms that God is faithful and has faithfully worked through him in all his dealings with the Corinthians (1:18–22). He will explain that his failure to return to them as planned was to spare them another painful visit and a rebuke (1:23–2:2). But he will not swear an oath to confirm the truthfulness of what he says. Instead, before giving his "excuse," he makes a theological affirmation about God's faithfulness. One could easily accuse the Olympian gods, for example, of being mercurial and capricious, but one could not accuse the God of Scripture of being so. Balaam asserts that God "is not a man that he should lie, nor a son of man that he should change his mind: Does he speak and then not act? Does he promise and not fulfill?" (Num 23:19; see Deut 7:9). Paul's argument runs as follows: God is faithful (1:18a), and God's faithfulness guarantees Paul's word to them (1:18b). That word involves far more than his travel plans. It encompasses Paul's preaching of Christ among them (1:19). Paul's trustworthiness does not come from himself or from any fee-

[95] Welborn, "The Dangerous Double Affirmation," 45.
[96] Ibid., 48–49.
[97] Ibid.
[98] Ibid., 37.

ble oath he might make; it comes from the faithfulness of God's word. The theological insight that his sincerity (1:12), competency (3:5), and power (4:12) comes entirely from God pervades this whole epistle.

Paul therefore does not respond to doubts about his character by saying: " 'Trust me! I know what I'm doing and it's for your good.' Rather, he is saying in effect, 'Trust God, His promises have been fulfilled in Christ, and our faithfulness in dealing with you had been assured by our preaching Christ to you.' "[99] Paul defends himself with a theological argument. Meeks notes: "The stability of God's promises provides the necessary context for moral action, particularly when the action itself is defined as *faithful*, that is, action befitting the pattern of God's action, which may defy the customary and commonsensical."[100] Since God is faithful (see 1 Cor 1:9; 10:13; see 1 Thess 5:24; 2 Thess 3:3; see also Heb 10:23; 1 John 1:9), and God has commissioned him to preach the gospel, his message from God is faithful and his actions to proclaim that message are faithful. God's faithfulness also stands behind those whom he has commissioned to preach Christ (see 3:4–6). That word is unequivocal and does not fluctuate with the market or change with the tide.

We are aware, however, that unreliable, capricious, and impetuous ministers can lead others to regard the gospel they preach as untrustworthy and not worth serious consideration. Paul argues that the Corinthians know the gospel he preached to be trustworthy, and that attests to his trustworthiness. They should infer therefore that God prevented his coming because it was for their greater good. Without saying so explicitly, he insinuates that he failed to come as announced because his plans were overruled by God.

1:19 Paul reminds them that he and his coworkers Silvanus (NIV, "Silas") and Timothy delivered the message to them about Jesus as the Son of God (see 1 Cor 2:2). The Corinthians became Christians through their preaching (1 Cor 3:10; 4:15).[101] Paul rarely uses the full Christological title, "Son of God, Jesus Christ"; and its appearance here may be intended to refer to Jesus as the Messiah and fulfillment of God's promise.[102] However opaque God's purposes may sometimes seem to humans, God has directed the course of history to this positive goal. The mention of both Timothy and Silvanus provides the two or three witnesses required to verify the truth of something (see 13:1; Deut 19:15). But Paul always mentions one or more of his coworkers when he writes to his churches. He does not stand alone on

---

[99] Furnish, *II Corinthians*, 145.

[100] W. A. Meeks, *The Origins of Christian Morality: The First Two Centuries* (New Haven/London: Yale University Press, 1993) 160.

[101] Others who came later apparently became the Corinthians' favorites. Among them was Apollos, who apparently was not part of Paul's team when he first evangelized the city.

[102] Thrall, *The Second Epistle to the Corinthians,* 1:146.

these issues, for he is bound up in community and expresses solidarity with his associates.

"Silvanus" is the Latinized form of the Aramaic "Silas," a form of the Hebrew "Saul." He is mentioned in Acts 15:22,32 as a prominent member, prophet, and emissary of the Jerusalem church, one who risked his life for the gospel (Acts 15:26). Silas served as Paul's travel companion on his second missionary journey, suffering imprisonment and beatings together with him (Acts 15:40–18:22). He appears in the salutation as a cosender of the letters to the Thessalonians (1 Thess 1:1; 2 Thess 1:1; see 1 Pet 5:12). Here Paul recognizes him along with Timothy as one of the first to preach the gospel to the Corinthians.

1:20 The faithfulness of God's word is most clearly manifested in the coming of his Son (1:20a). All of God's promises to Israel find their yes in him.[103] Christ is God's yes to the promise to Abraham that by his seed all the nations of the earth will gain blessing[104] and to David to raise up David's offspring and to establish his throne forever.[105] In Christ we not only see all God's promises coming to fruition but also God's unqualified yes to humankind.

The yes is *in* him; our yes in response is *through* him. The only way we can clearly hear God's yes is in Christ, and the only way we can respond fully to God is through Christ. No other way exists. The gospel is not yes, today one finds salvation in Christ, and no, tomorrow one finds salvation in someone or something else.[106] Strachan comments correctly, "There is no hope for any civilization apart from acceptance of the Person and obedience to the teaching of Jesus Christ."[107]

Christ is God's yes to all meaningful human hopes. Christ is God's yes to human longing for life, wisdom, righteousness, sanctification (1 Cor 1:30). But we should be mindful that God also speaks a no "to every selfish and perverted longing of humanity, to every desire to 'get rich quick,' to dominate others, or to organize society for selfish advantage."[108]

Paul recalls for the Corinthians how they affirm their faith in God's faithfulness through the "Amen" response in corporate worship. Most people today may understand the "amen" only as the last word one says in a prayer. They mouth it without giving any thought to its rich background. "Amen" is a transliteration of the Hebrew word *ʿāmēn,* which means "surely," and it

---

[103] The plural "promises" recurs in 7:1; see also Rom 9:4; 15:8; and Gal 3:16,21.

[104] Gen 12:3; 18:18; Gal 3:16; and Eph 1:13; 3:6.

[105] 2 Sam 7:12–16; 1 Chr 17:11–14; Pss 89:3; 132:11; Isa 11:1–5,10; Jer 23:5–6; 30:9; 33:14–18; Ezek 34:23–24; 37:24; and Rom 1:4.

[106] Best, *Second Corinthians,* 17.

[107] Strachan, *The Second Epistle of Paul to the Corinthians,* 58.

[108] Best, *Second Corinthians,* 18.

was a community response found in the Old Testament in which the congregation spoke their assent to a curse (Deut 27:15–16; or individuals in Num 5:5; Jer 11:5) or to the praise of God (1 Chr 16:36; Neh 8:6; Pss 41:13; 72:19; 89:52; 106:48; and *1 Esdr* 9:47). In his letters Paul placed an "Amen" after benedictions (Rom 15:33; 16:27; 1 Cor 16:24; Gal 6:18; Phlm 25) and expressions of praise (Rom 1:25; 9:5; 11:36; [16:27]; Gal 1:5; Eph 3:21; Phil 4:20; 1 Tim 1:17; 6:16; 2 Tim 4:18).[109] We can assume that the Corinthian congregation spoke it as the response to prayer and thanksgiving in their corporate worship (see 1 Cor 14:16), but Paul interprets it to be their affirmation of faith that God's promises have been fulfilled in Christ. Their chorus of amens in worship proclaims God's faithfulness in making salvation possible for them through Christ. Proclaiming God's faithfulness in worship brings glory to God, the very goal of human existence.

The implication is that if they affirm that the message about Christ is trustworthy, then they should also be able to affirm that the messengers are trustworthy too. How can they say yes to God while saying no to God's apostle?[110] Since they believed God endorsed the trustworthiness of the messengers in the proclamation of the gospel, then God will also vouch for their trustworthiness in the less serious business of making travel plans.[111]

1:21 Paul next reminds them that this same trustworthy God has caused us to stand firm in Christ.[112] He uses the same verb "confirm" (*bebaioō*, "makes us stand firm") twice in his thanksgiving section in 1 Corinthians. He gives thanks that his testimony about Christ was confirmed in them (1:6) and that Christ will confirm them ("keep you strong," NIV) until the end, blameless on the day of our Lord Jesus Christ.

We do not stand firm by dint of our own courage, strength, or faith. God who is faithful calls us and establishes us firmly in the faith and gives us whatever constancy we have. When we fulfill promises, God is the one who must receive the credit.[113] We also do not stand alone. The Greek reads, "The one who establishes us *with you* in Christ ... God."[114] "In Christ" is

---

[109] See also Heb 13:21; 1 Pet 4:11; 5:11; 2 Pet 3:18; Jude 25; Rev 1:6; 7:12.

[110] Best, *Second Corinthians*, 18.

[111] W. C. van Unnik, "Reisepläne und Amen-Sagen ...," in *Sparsa Collecta I*, NovTSup 29 (Leiden: Brill, 1973) 144–59.

[112] The NIV correctly supplies the verb "to be" before "God": "The one who confirms us along with you in Christ and anointed us [is] God."

[113] The word βεβαιόω had a legal connotation that signified a seller's guarantee to honor certain commitments. The contract will be carried out (see 1 Cor 1:8; Col 2:7). L. L. Belleville comments that it is "a technical word for the legal guarantee that a seller would give a buyer to ensure the validity of the sale against any possible third-party claims. Applied to the Spirit, it refers to his activity in confirming the ongoing validity of God's relationship to his people (present participle)" ("Paul's Polemic and Theology of the Spirit in Second Corinthians," *CBQ* 58 [1996] 284–85).

[114] ὁ δὲ βεβαιῶν ἡμᾶς σὺν ὑμῖν εἰς Χριστὸν ... θεός.

literally "into Christ" *(eis Christon)* and may be associated with baptism (Rom 6:3; Gal 3:27). The "with us" makes clear that Paul does not *stand over against* the Corinthians; both he and the Corinthians *stand firm together* in Christ. Through Christ he is connected to them and they to him. This means that Paul cannot cut his ties to them; they cannot cut their ties to him without weakening in some way their establishment in Christ (see Eph 4:15–16).

The use of the present participle, "who makes us stand firm" ("confirm," *bebaiōn),* when all the other participles in this sentence are in the aorist suggests that God continually confirms us. The following aorist participles, "anointed" *(chrisas)* "set his seal" *(sphragisamenos)* and "put" *(dous)* also suggest antecedent action to the main verb. "Having anointed, sealed and given us the deposit of the Spirit," Paul says, "God is now in the process of establishing us together with you."[115] This reading implies that the anointing, sealing, and giving of the Spirit must apply to the Corinthians and not just Paul. "God's continuing activity in the church is dependent on his past work through the deposit of the Spirit in the human heart."

This verse is the only place where the verb "anointed" *(chriō)* appears in Paul. Some have argued that he has only himself in view.[116] He would be making the amazing assertion that he is related to God's Anointed *(Christos)* as one who is also anointed *(chrisas).* God has made him another christ. The implication would be that God "grants him the grace to be as totally reliable as Christ was."[117]

But the other metaphors in 1:22 apply to all Christians, and the metaphor of anointing should also apply to other Christians and not just Paul. The four participles divide into two separate groups governed by one definite article:

"the one who confirms ... and anoints"

"the one who seals (stamps) ... and gives."

Paul speaks about God as the one who establishes believers in Christ and in the community that responds with the Amen to God's yes and gives them the Spirit. All Christians are related to God's Anointed and are also anointed as a consequence. The anointing would be related to the Spirit (see 1 John 2:20,27).

In the Old Testament the verb is used for commissioning to a particular office, but in Isa 61:1–4 it appears as a metaphor for the Spirit's equipping for mission or service. Belleville contends, "In the context of 2 Cor 1:21–22 it refers to the Spirit's equipping the church to carry forth Christ's mis-

---

[115] Belleville, "Paul's Polemic," 284.

[116] Plummer, *The Second Epistle of St. Paul to the Corinthians*, 39; and Strachan, *The Second Epistle of Paul to the Corinthians*, 59.

[117] Murphy-O'Connor, *The Theology of the Second Letter to the Corinthians*, 24–25.

sion in the world."[118]

1:22   The sealing metaphor draws on ancient custom in Paul's every-day world and could have a variety of meanings.[119] Something was sealed or stamped to indicate ownership. The Spirit has stamped us as belonging to God as opposed to the principalities and powers (Eph 1:13). In Eph 4:30 the sealing of the Spirit refers to the believer being marked as God's possession and kept secure for the day of redemption. We were bought with a price (1 Cor 6:20); therefore we do not belong to ourselves but to God. Seals were also used to attest to truthfulness as a legal guarantee, to guarantee the security of something (see Rom 15:28), to guarantee the quality of goods, or to provide proof of identity (see Rom 4:11).[120] Paul has told the Corinthians that they are the seal of his apostleship (1 Cor 9:2), that they validate him as an apostle. But the meaning of sealing in this text is controlled by the idea of marking ownership. They belong to God as God's possession.[121] Thus "sealing" marks the beginning of God's work in believers.

The second metaphor, "the deposit *[arrabōn]* of the Spirit," comes from the world of legal documents and may also be rendered "first install-ment."[122] It was a down payment that created obligations and guaranteed that more would be forthcoming. Kerr notes that the word was used in contracts for the hire of services and in contracts of sale and argues that the contract for services is the best source for the metaphor. In such a contract, the person who gives the *arrabōn* is engaging another to do work. The person who receives the *arrabōn* obligates himself to do the

---

[118] Belleville, "Paul's Polemic," 285.

[119] Fee writes: "The imagery derives from a wide variety of transactions in the Greco-Roman world, most often in the form of a stamped imprint in wax bearing the 'seal' of the owner or sender. Primarily such a seal denoted ownership and authenticity; this thereby guaranteed the protection of the owner. Paul uses it metaphorically seven times in all, with seven different nuances. In this case, as in Eph 1:13 and 4:30, it metaphorically refers to the Spirit as the 'seal' of God's ownership and therefore the guarantee of the believer's final inheritance" (*God's Empowering Presence*, 292–93).

[120] Cp. Jesus' declaration that God has set his seal of authority on the Son of Man (John 6:27).

[121] See 2 Tim 2:19; and Rev 7:3–5,8. See further G. Fitzer, "σφραγίς ...," *TDNT* 7:939–953.

[122] The phrase translated "put his Spirit in our hearts as a deposit" reads lit. "gave the deposit of the Spirit in our hearts." "Deposit of the Spirit" is a genitive of apposition (epexegetical) that means "the deposit, namely, the Spirit." A. J. Kerr shows that translations that render the word ἀρ-ραβών as "pledge" or one of its synonyms are misleading ("᾽APPABΩN," *JTS* 39 (1988) 91–97). A pledge was something handed over as collateral for some promise and could be reclaimed at a later date when the promise was fulfilled. It also focuses on a promise of a gift yet to come. But the term is used in contracts "in which both parties have obligations," which is different from a gift in which the recipient has no obligation.

work.[123] The *arrabōn* is a portion of the payment the worker will receive in full when he fulfills his task.

In the context of Paul's argument, he is saying that both he and the Corinthians have received the same Spirit from God as a first installment that guarantees their common destiny with God. But the Spirit who guarantees their common destiny also guarantees his integrity. Having anointed us, that is, having "sealed" us by giving us the Holy Spirit as down payment on our secure future, God continues to confirm him with them.[124] The Spirit, not human oaths, therefore verifies Paul's integrity. Compared with the testimony of God's Spirit, human oaths are hollow and worthless. If the Corinthians doubt his integrity, then they also cast doubts on the Spirit's work in their own lives.[125] As God establishes the trustworthiness of the message, God also establishes the trustworthiness of the messengers. If they doubt Paul's trustworthiness, then they also cast doubts on the message he and his team preached to them.

We can also see theological significance of this metaphor beyond Paul's use of it in the context to defend his integrity.[126] God gives the Spirit as a first installment to those who believe in and serve him.

1. It guarantees that our relationship with God is not something ephemeral but permanent and will continue beyond our death. The believers' future destiny is assured in Christ. Having the deposit of the Spirit insures that we belong to the age to come. It provides surety that God will fulfill his promises and that believers in Christ will pass through the judgment unscathed.

2. What is given is part of the whole. Fee observes: "For Paul, the gift of the Spirit is the first part of the redemption of the whole person, the beginning of the process that will end when believers assume their 'spiritual' bodies (= enter into a mode of existence determined solely by the Spirit; see 1 Cor 15:44)."[127] Believers therefore receive the Spirit at the time of their

---

[123] Ibid., 95. See also J. B. Lightfoot, *Notes on the Epistles of St. Paul from Unpublished Commentaries* (London: Macmillan, 1904) 323–24.

[124] Fee, *God's Empowering Presence*, 288–89.

[125] Belleville, "Paul's Polemic," 284.

[126] Many have connected the imagery of confirming, anointing, sealing, and giving a deposit with Christian baptism (see e.g., E. Dinkler, "Die Taufterminologie in 2 Kor. 1, 21 f," in *Neotestamentica et Patristica*, NovTSup 6 [Leiden: Brill, 1962] 173–91; G. R. Beasley-Murray, *Baptism in the New Testament* [Grand Rapids: Eerdmans, 1963] 171–77). Paul may be alluding to baptism, but it is not the focal issue. Furnish correctly sees that Paul's "concern is to document and describe God's faithfulness, and not to detail the steps by which the Corinthians have come into the believing community" (*II Corinthians*, 149). Fee points out that none of the metaphors in these verses is used in the NT to refer to baptism. The evidence for the connection for such imagery comes from the mid to late second century and then is read into Paul's words (*God's Empowering Presence*, 294–95).

[127] Fee, *God's Empowering Presence*, 294.

conversion (Gal 3:2–3). It brings what Christ has accomplished for them on the cross to fruition in believers' lives and conveys into their lives God's power that raised Christ from the dead.

3. Believers do not receive a portion of the Spirit, but the Spirit is the installment that gives a foretaste and assures the glory that is to come. The Spirit makes present God's future blessing.[128] It helps believers to evaluate the present suffering in light of the glorious future (see Rom 8:9–27).

4. The final inheritance the Spirit guarantees is yet to be realized. Believers have not yet arrived at the heavenly goal.

5. The deposit of the Spirit does not come without any strings attached. The metaphor of a deposit implies that those who receive the first installment obligate themselves to fulfill their part of the contract. Believers should understand that God gives the Spirit to empower them for service.

We can now summarize Paul's defense so far. He was not content simply to give them reassurances of his integrity; he spells out a theological basis for his integrity.[129] Paul uses theologically rich terms in this paragraph for the Spirit's activity in believers' lives to confirm his reliability. He does not make the conclusion explicit but leaves it for his readers to infer. What he does is completely governed by the Spirit, not worldly standards or self interest. It is the same Spirit that empowers their lives and guarantees their salvation. Therefore he had good spiritual grounds for changing his plans.[130] His motives were God honoring, not frivolous. They cannot attribute his changes in plans to his capriciousness. His personal whimsy does not propel his apostolic work.

(4) The Sorrowful Visit (1:23–2:4)

[23]**I call God as my witness that it was in order to spare you that I did not return to Corinth. [24]Not that we lord it over your faith, but we work with you for your joy, because it is by faith you stand firm.**

[1]**So I made up my mind that I would not make another painful visit to you. [2]For if I grieve you, who is left to make me glad but you whom I have grieved?**

[3]**I wrote as I did so that when I came I should not be distressed by those who ought to make me rejoice. I had confidence in all of you, that you would all share my joy. [4]For I wrote you out of great distress and anguish of heart and with many tears, not to grieve you but to let you know the depth of my love for you.**

---

[128] J. D. G. Dunn, *Jesus and the Spirit* (Philadelphia: Westminster, 1975) 311.

[129] Most modern readers are impatient with such a long theological explanation and may want him to get directly to the point. Furnish calls it a "somewhat ponderous excursus" (*II Corinthians*, 141). But Paul's mission vision and calling from God controls all that he does; and it is natural for him to explain his actions in light of the theological underpinnings of his life.

[130] F. F. Bruce, *I & II Corinthians*, NCB (Grand Rapids: Eerdmans, 1971) 182.

Paul has given them the theological basis for his reliability and now reveals the reason for his failure to make the double visit that he promised: It was to spare them.

1:23 Paul does not first provide his excuse for changing his plans but first reconfirms his integrity by establishing that a true apostle of Christ could not be guilty of untrustworthiness. He now gives the reasons behind his changed plans. Paul sees himself as on trial before the Corinthians and has called for his defense the witness of his own conscience (1:12). He now calls God as a witness since only God can know and reveal the truth about his conscience.[131] God not only attests to his truthfulness but will condemn him if he is lying.[132] He says that he did not return as announced out of consideration for them because he wanted to spare them.

He does not spell out what he wanted to spare them from, but we can safely assume that he has in mind some kind of severe chastisement. He had warned them earlier about those who had become arrogant as if he were not coming back to them and notifies them:

> But I will come to you very soon, if the Lord is willing, and then I will find out not only how these arrogant people are talking, but what power they have. For the kingdom of God is not a matter of talk but of power. What do you prefer? Shall I come to you with a whip [lit., "rod"], or in love and with a gentle spirit? (1 Cor 4:19–21).

At the conclusion of this letter he forewarns them when he comes he will show no leniency to those who continue defiantly in their sin (13:2). These persons include those who have not repented of their unclean lives, those who have not withdrawn from their associations with idolatry, and those who have been stirring up the dissension. His reasons for not returning had nothing to do with any wavering in his purpose or fear of being humiliated again. He wanted to spare them from being humiliated and the severe discipline that might forever alienate them from him and even from the faith.

If he had come, he would have had to rebuke a certain member, and it could have been quite a nasty confrontation that may have undermined any chance for reconciliation. What he believes to be the most redemptive action governs his decisions. He is not interested in asserting his power over others or defending the integrity of his office. Under the Spirit's guidance, he takes necessary steps to bring genuine repentance. The false image, popular today, of a dour and sour Paul who regularly thrashes his congregation and bulldozes opponents needs correcting. Paul's bitter battle with the Judaizers in

---

[131] See Rom 1:9; Phil 1:8; and 1 Thess 2:5,10. Early Christians believed that falsifying the Holy Spirit would have dire consequences and certainly would not have appealed lightly to the Spirit or to God as a witness (Acts 5:1–11).

[132] The NIV translation omits the phrase "against my soul" (ἐπὶ τὴν ἐμὴν ψυχήν).

Galatians is mistakenly projected onto all his letters. He takes no joy in frightening, berating, or punishing congregations. Nor is he fond of wrangling or blasting his opponents off the theological map.[133] He understands himself to be their father, and as a father he expects obedience. Paul advises fathers in Col 3:21 not to embitter their children lest they become discouraged, and he practices what he preaches with his spiritual children. He believes that a father's discipline should be tempered by love, compassion, kindness, and patience (see Col 3:12). That does not mean that he condones or ignores their theological error or ethical lapses, but he sees his primary task as facilitating the blessings of salvation in their lives.

1:24 The statement that he wanted to spare them touches upon two issues in this letter, his love for them and his authority over them. Some in Corinth may have protested that Paul did not love them (2:4; see 6:11–13; 7:2–3; 11:11; 12:15). From his perspective, however, it was an act of love to refrain from coming to Corinth to dish out punishment. Also, stating in this way that he wanted to spare them assumes that he has authority over the community. If he could spare, he also has the authority to punish. But he is sensitive to how they perceive him exercising this authority. He has intimated that had he come he would have been forced to exercise his authority and punish the guilty parties. He backtracks, however, to make it clear that he has no desire to dominate them, to tell them what to think or do, or to control their faith. Apostles (and certainly pastors) are not lords over their churches. Only Jesus is Lord over their faith. Paul has no business and no intention of arrogating that role for himself.

Christians have been sealed with the Spirit and set free in the Spirit (Gal 5:1), and Paul has no desire to make them his theological serfs (1 Cor 7:23). He does not seek to control their thinking except to bring it in line with the cross or to make them his devotees except to make them recognize how God works through his weakness and give glory to God (see 1 Cor 1:12–17). He

---

[133] See the discussion of the Eurocentric view of Paul in R. Jewett, *Paul: The Apostle to America: Cultural Trends and Pauline Scholarship* (Louisville: W/JKP, 1994) 3–12. Jewett argues that our picture of Paul has come from a dominant European legacy which has projected its eristic style (love of wrangling) on to Paul. This perspective tends to interpret all of Paul's letters as "expressions of theological combat" (p. 5). It assumes that Paul adopts a take-no-prisoners style that diminishes or ignores clear evidence in Paul where he tries to find common ground, is tolerant of differing points of view, and is gentle as a nurse (1 Thess 2). But many have made him over in the mold of Luther, a bull in a theological china shop, blistering his opponents with invective. Paul is perceived as prickly and defensive, and many fail to appreciate that Paul looks for common ground with his churches and is always intent on building them up rather than tearing them down (2 Cor 10:8). Jewett comments that this eristic legacy shaped not only the picture of Paul but the style of scholarly discourse: "The Paul who struggled against the competitive and divisive spirit in his church has been presented in such divisive, harsh tones, with such severe rhetoric directed against alternative views, that the truth has sometimes seemed smothered by eristic controversy" (p. 6).

wants to win their consensus and develop the church's sense of responsibility. Consequently, Paul does not browbeat his churches like an unbending dictator or manage their lives like a meddling parent. He believes in persuasion, not coercion, which is why he writes letters. How he uses his authority over the community's faith is one of the things that distinguishes him from the interlopers who do act as overlords (11:19–20). He exercises considerable restraint because he wants to work "with" them, not "on" them.[134] He understands the role of apostle as being a servant (4:5) and facilitator who brings joy, not pain, who builds up rather than tears down (see 10:8; 13:10).[135] We frequently forget that one of the true marks of Christ's church is joy. "If it was lacking, then the message of Jesus had either not been received or it had been given up; if it wavered, then faith also wavered."[136]

Paul's goal in this letter is to help the Corinthians make the necessary corrections themselves. He does not want to destroy the congregation's responsibility.[137] They must share in the exercise of authority (see 1 Cor 5:3–5; 2 Cor 2:6–8).[138] They must learn to stand on their own faith. Sometimes it may seem easier to force compliance, but Paul knows that real faith cannot be force fed nor should it be spoon fed. Calvin's comments on this passage are apt:

> Faith should be completely free of any bondage to men. We should note well who it is that says this, for, if ever any mortal man had a right to claim such lordship, Paul was he. Thus we conclude that faith should have no master but

---

[134] He designates them coworkers (συνεργοί). Coworkers are a select group that, in Paul's letters, includes Prisca and Aquila, and Urbanus (Rom 16:3,9); Timothy (Rom 16:21; 1 Thess 3:2); Apollos (1 Cor 3:9); Titus (2 Cor 8:23); Epaphroditus (Phil 2:25); Euodia, Syntyche, and Clement (Phil 4:3); Aristarchus, Mark, and Jesus Justus (Col 4:11); Philemon (Phlm 1); and Luke (Phlm 24).

[135] Furnish's keen eye for the crucial issue deserves citing. Paul is not "contrasting two different objectives of the ministerial service, the tyrannical and the co-operative. He would be contrasting two different objectives of the ministerial office: the enhancement of one's own position by the self-serving exercise of one's authority versus the enhancement of the *joy* of those who, by God's power, *stand firm in the faith*" (*II Corinthians*, 152).

[136] G. R. Beasley-Murray, "2 Corinthians," in *The Broadman Bible Commentary* (Nashville: Broadman, 1971) 14, citing A. Schlatter, *Paulus: Der Bote Jesu: Eine Deutung Seiner Briefe an die Korinther*, 2d ed. (Stuttgart: Calwer, 1956) 485.

[137] The classic example of Paul's refusal to lord over another's faith and decisions is his letter to Philemon. He does not order Philemon but exercises extraordinary tact and restraint in his effort to persuade Philemon to do what is right. He could command, but instead he appeals to him on account of love (Phlm 8–9). "But I did not want to do anything without your consent, so that any favor you do will be spontaneous and not forced" (Phlm 14). See further D. E. Garland, *Colossians Philemon*, NIVAC (Grand Rapidos: Zondervan, 1998).

[138] H. von Campenhausen contended that in Paul's appeal "to the congregation's own judgment and sense of responsibility he takes their freedom seriously, possibly indeed more seriously than they themselves had expected" (*Ecclesiastical Authority and Spiritual Power in the Church of the First Three Centuries* [London: A & C Black, 1969] 50).

the Word of God and is not subject to human control. ... spiritual lordship belongs to none but God alone. This is always a settled principle—that pastors have no special lordship over men's consciences because they are ministers and helpers and not lords.[139]

He cites the castigation of the wicked shepherds in Ezekiel: "You have not strengthened the weak or healed the sick or bound up the injured. You have not brought back the strays or searched for the lost. You have ruled them harshly and brutally" (Ezek 34:4).

Some translations have Paul affirming that they stand firm in the faith, "because you stand firm in the faith" (NRSV). The NIV interprets this statement more as a general principle, "because it is by faith you stand firm." In this translation Paul is telling them how to stand firm. They do not stand firm because of Paul's control as lord over their faith but by the faith they exercise in Christ as Lord. As Barrett understands it, Paul is saying, "You have your existence as Christians by faith, and your Christian existence in faith is determined by no man, but by God only." Barrett concludes, "The apostolic proclamation evokes faith, but there is no apostolic domination that can command it."[140] An apostle can only work together with them for their joy.

The rendering of this verse in the NIV is the most likely, "it is by faith you stand firm." But if this text should be interpreted instead as an affirmation of where they stand, "you stand firm in the faith," it poses a difficulty. In 13:5 Paul writes, "Examine yourselves to see whether you are in the faith; test yourselves. Do you not realize that Christ Jesus is in you—unless, of course, you fail the test?" Could he write both these lines in the same letter? Some contend that chaps. 10–13 are a separate letter written at a different time when he did not believe that the Corinthians did not stand firm in the faith.

An affirmation of their faith does not fit the context of his argument. But if this rendering is correct, it does not mean that this statement does not belong in the same letter as the challenge in 13:5. Paul knows that he is dealing with an audience alienated from him, and he does not wish to antagonize them from the outset before they have heard his argument to the end. It was extremely important to affirm the rapprochement between them and to establish their goodwill toward him first. The contentious issues over which he must chastise them are reserved for the conclusion of the letter. There we learn that the faith of some in Corinth may not be as secure. But Paul's combination of the indicative and the imperative is well known.[141]

2:1 Paul now explains why he judged it best not to make another pain-

---

[139] Calvin, *The Second Epistle of Paul the Apostle to the Corinthians*, 26.

[140] Barrett, *The Second Epistle to the Corinthians*, 84.

[141] See 1 Cor 16:13, where he uses the imperative, "stand firm in the faith."

ful visit, which implies that he experienced an unpleasant confrontation the last time he was there (2:5–11; 7:9,12; 10:10).[142] We infer from this statement that Paul paid them an unannounced visit after writing 1 Corinthians.[143] Because it was so disagreeable (see 2:5–11; 7:9,12; 10:10), he abandoned plans for a double visit, and Paul explains that he did not want another scene.[144]

A high concentration of pain language dominates 2:1–5. The noun "pain" *(lupē)* appears twice (2:1,3), and the verb form appears five times *(lypeō,* 2:2 [2x],4,5[2x]) in 2:1–5.[145] Paul may have in mind being humiliated by them, but he did not simply want to avoid another humiliation by this upstart church. After all, the Corinthians' failure to live according to their Christian calling or their deserting the true gospel of the cross and resurrection for a false, but more glittering, gospel of success dispensed by false apostles would have caused him the greatest pain.

2:2 Paul faced a dilemma. To come to Corinth might intensify the problems and the pain; to stay away would allow the problems to fester and make reconciliation even more difficult.[146] Again, Paul's affection for the church comes out. They are a source of joy to him, and when their relationship is out of sorts, his pain is multiplied. The "I" in the Greek is emphatic, "if *I* am the one who causes you pain."[147] If he adds to the sadness in some way, they can hardly cheer him. Paul's solution for reconciling the situation was to write a painful letter of rebuke.

2:3 Paul sent a letter—probably the weighty letter mentioned in

---

[142] The reading γὰρ (NIV "so") is to be preferred over δέ because Paul is not making a supplementary or adversative comment but giving the reason for postponing his visit.

[143] He implies that his next visit will be his third in 12:14; 13:1.

[144] Barrett comments: "They had thus been promised a visit, and had received one, earlier than they had been led to expect; what right had they to complain if the treatment Paul had experienced prevented them from receiving an additional visit—especially in the circumstances this must have been a visit painful alike for him and for them?" (*The Second Epistle to the Corinthians*, 86).

[145] The noun λύπη ("grief") also appears in 7:10 (2x) and 9:7, and therefore six out of the nine usages of the word in Paul's letters occur in 2 Corinthians. The verb λυπέω ("to grieve") also appears in 6:10; 7:8(2x),9(3x),11, and therefore twelve out of the fifteen usages of the word in Paul's letters occur in 2 Corinthians. If Philippians is known for the predominance of the word "joy" in the letter, 2 Corinthians should be known for the predominance of the word "pain." The Corinthians were his problem children.

[146] Héring divides the sentence in two: "For if I make you sad, who then will make me glad? Certainly not the one who has been plunged into sorrow by me!" (*The Second Epistle to the Corinthians*, 14). See the critique by Furnish, *II Corinthians*, 140–41.

[147] Barrett contends that the use of the preposition ἐκ ("out of") instead of ὑπό ("by") "might suggest not 'sorrow caused directly by my agency,' but 'sorrow that arises from me, on my account, sorrow that is occasioned rather than caused by my presence'" (*The Second Epistle to the Corinthians*, 87). He takes this to imply that the one who injured Paul was a visitor, not a native Corinthian. But the ἐκ here refers to the effective cause; see BAGD, 235.

10:10—in lieu of a visit. The phrase "I wrote as I did" *(egrapsa touto auto)* could be translated adverbially: "I wrote for precisely this reason," "namely in order that I might not come" (so NRSV).[148] Another option takes it as referring to a quotation from the letter. I wrote this very thing (NEB, "This is precisely the point in my letter"). The quotation could be 1:23, "It was in order to spare you that I did not return to Corinth," or 2:1, "So I made up my mind that I would not make another painful visit to you," or 2:3, "I am writing so that I may not come and be caused sorrow." But all of these possible quotes are more appropriate as Paul's explanation for his failure to return.

The most likely option takes the phrase as a summary of the contents of the painful letter. The surrounding verses then "repeat the main drift."[149] Paul did not write to them to vent his anger and to inflict on them the same pain they had dealt him (see Phil 1:17).[150] We learn from 2 Corinthians that Paul had four motives in writing his letter.

1. He wrote so that his next visit would bring joy instead of pain (2:3). In 13:10 he says he writes these things in 2 Corinthians while he is away from them so that he will not have to use a heavy hand when he is present. If they respond obediently, his visit will bring joy. This joy is more than good cheer over a happy reunion. Joy for Paul is related to the submission of the community to God's will, which in turn advances the gospel and brings glory to God.

2. He wanted them to know ultimately of his love (2:4; see 3:2; 12:15; 1 Cor 16:24).

3. He wanted to test their obedience (2:9).

4. He wanted to reveal to them their real earnestness for Paul (7:11–12).

The many attempts to discover the painful letter preserved somewhere within the Corinthian correspondence have not been successful. The letter has disappeared, and we can only guess its contents. Certainly it contained some blunt and serious rebuke (7:8–9). It apparently instructed them on what they should do and probably required them to take Paul's side and to discipline his nemesis. But we should not think that the letter was overly harsh. Lambasting others may make us feel better for a while and may even rouse cheers from observers. But fierce denunciations rarely help. In dealing with his problem children, Paul chose the way of the cross, which in this case was through weeping. Ministers who have given long years of service

---

[148] BDF § 290(4).

[149] Barrett, *The Second Epistle to the Corinthians*, 87; and Thrall, *The Second Epistle to the Corinthians*, 1:168.

[150] The textual variant which reads "grief upon grief" is probably an assimilation to Phil 2:27, although T. W. Manson argues that it refers to making a second painful visit ("St. Paul in Ephesus (3) and (4): The Corinthian Correspondence," in *Studies in the Gospels and Epistles*, ed. M. Black [Philadelphia: Westminster, 1962] 213–14).

to their churches and have become targets of sniping by a vocal minority or casualties of callous treatment can understand and sympathize with the bitter anguish Paul must have felt in dealing with the Corinthians. In spite of receiving a serious and humiliating rebuff from the Corinthians, Paul refused to forget the church. He confronted them in a letter. Sometimes confrontation is the clearest proof of love. It is easier to gloss over the problems with others, to cover them up, to pretend that they do not exist, or to write problem people off and terminate the relationship. Paul refused to do any of these things and tenaciously tried to restore the bond by confronting the problems directly. One needs wisdom, however, to know what is worth a showdown and when airing the differences will yield the most fruitful resolution. Confronting others to solve problems rather than simply forcing our opinions on them requires real love because it costs enormous emotional energy. It certainly caused Paul mental anguish as he worried that the letter might exacerbate the problem rather than assuage it.

Mentioning joy and pain (NIV "distress") picks up the earlier contrasts between affliction and consolation. As God provides consolation in the midst of affliction, Paul is sure that God will bring joy out of a painful relationship. Therefore, Paul expresses his supreme confidence in them despite the seriousness of the problems. He wrote the earlier letter with confidence that it would have its intended effect and can now write with even greater confidence after hearing from Titus about their remorse and repentance (7:9). As they share his sufferings and consolation (1:7), he expects them also to share his joy (7:7). The assumption behind this statement is that joy in Christ is something shared with others, and when it is shared, it is multiplied.

2:4 Paul is not stoical about the pain the dispute caused him. He does not try to hide his emotion but expresses it boldly. He had felt deeply their affection for him, and the apparent withdrawal of that affection had wounded him all the more deeply. He wrote from great psychological affliction and anguish and through many tears. It was not simply personal hurt that caused the tears. He wept over those who were ethically impure (Phil 3:18) and over those who have veered from God's will.

Discipline is never painless—for the one who delivers it or the one who receives it. Calvin points out that godly pastors weep within themselves before making others weep.[151] Paul is neither ironhearted nor ironhanded. His love for them motivated his actions entirely. If they were grieved, he leaves no doubt that he was grieved more.

Paul insists that the grief he caused them was the surest sign of his love. He gives them direction and rebukes them as a loving father would (see also

---

[151] Calvin, *The Second Epistle of Paul the Apostle to the Corinthians*, 28.

7:8–10; 10:6; 1 Cor 4:14–16,21).[152] In the Jewish tradition about paternal discipline, chastisement is proof of love.

> My son, do not despise the LORD's discipline
> and do not resent his rebuke,
> because the LORD disciplines those he loves,
> as a father the son he delights in. (Prov 3:11–12).[153]

In spite of being the object of the Corinthians' abuse, Paul, like a good father, continues to seek their best interests and responds to impudence with sacrificial love. A good parent may have a nasty argument with an adolescent child but will not terminate the relationship because of it. Instead, the parent seeks both to correct the child and to bring about reconciliation. The determination and tenacity it requires to straighten out the child and to remedy the hurt is one of the clearest signs of love.

Paul gives three reasons why he did not return to Corinth. He has mentioned his near-death affliction in Asia (1:8–10) which would have prevented him from coming. He implies that the sovereignty of God controls his agenda (1:12) and that he responds to the will of God for the glory of God (1:20). He now explains that he was anxious to avoid another painful visit that would only worsen the situation and make reconciliation all the more difficult (1:23–2:4).

(5) Forgiveness of the Offender (2:5–13)

⁵If anyone has caused grief, he has not so much grieved me as he has grieved all of you, to some extent—not to put it too severely. ⁶The punishment inflicted on him by the majority is sufficient for him. ⁷Now instead, you ought to forgive and comfort him, so that he will not be overwhelmed by excessive sorrow. ⁸I urge you, therefore, to reaffirm your love for him. ⁹The reason I wrote you was to see if you would stand the test and be obedient in everything. ¹⁰If you forgive anyone, I also forgive him. And what I have forgiven—if there was anything to forgive—I have forgiven in the sight of Christ for your sake, ¹¹in order that Satan might not outwit us. For we are not unaware of his schemes.

¹²Now when I went to Troas to preach the gospel of Christ and found that the Lord had opened a door for me, ¹³I still had no peace of mind, because I did not find my brother Titus there. So I said good-by to them and went on to Macedonia.

---

[152] The letter to the Galatians offers a parallel in which Paul mixes harsh reproof, "You foolish Galatians! Who has bewitched you? Before your very eyes Jesus Christ was clearly portrayed as crucified" (Gal 3:1), with expressions of love and pain, "My dear children, for whom I am again in the pains of childbirth until Christ is formed in you, how I wish I could be with you now and change my tone, because I am perplexed about you!" (Gal 4:19–20).

[153] A. A. Myrick, "'Father' Imagery in 2 Corinthians 1–9 and Jewish Paternal Tradition," *TynBul* 47 (1996) 163–71. See also Prov 10:13,17; 13:1,24; 15:5; 22:15; 23:13–14; 27:5; 29:15; *Sir* 30:1–2,13; and *Wis* 11:9–10.

Paul now turns to the specific incident that provoked his grief and sudden departure without rehashing what happened. The Corinthians obviously do not need Paul to tell them what happened, and dredging up the unhappy details might awaken the old feelings of anger again. The wounds are still healing, and rehearsing the events that caused them serves no purpose. Unfortunately, the lack of particulars leaves us later readers, far removed from the situation, in the dark.

2:5 Paul's tact leads him to speak about a specific situation in ambiguous generalities as he avoids naming the person or describing the nature of the indignity. The anonymous person had repented, and now Paul only identifies the transgression euphemistically, "if anyone has caused grief," and identifies the person in a veiled way as "the one who did the wrong" (7:12). Naming names and specifying the crimes and punishment would only unleash more grief by bringing more shame on the one who has now repented and has been sufficiently punished.[154] Paul apparently would concur with the rhetorical advice found in Pseudo-Libanius that letters of conciliation should avoid the cause of the strife as much as possible.[155] His goal is to bring healing, not to recount the events to prove how right he was. Instead of criticizing the culprit, he describes his own grief, what happened to him, and how this plays out in his sufferings for the gospel. But modern readers would like to know who the offender was and what his offense was.[156]

To ascertain who this miscreant was, we must first compile the evidence available.[157]

1. The offense does not seem to be some theological error since Paul does not mention doctrinal issues. Nevertheless, some kind of theological misconception may have been at the root of the problem. Paul's lengthy discussions of his afflictions throughout the letter and his statement that they only

---

[154] The same delicacy emerges in the way Paul refers to Onesimus in his letter to Philemon. He avoids mentioning the unmentionable—Onesimus's desertion. He uses a pun to describe Onesimus's (a name that means "useful") former "uselessness" (v. 11). Instead of plainly saying that Onesimus ran away, Paul describes his absence with a passive voice, suggesting that God's hand was involved, "He was separated from you for a little while" (v. 15). He broaches the subject of Onesimus's past misdeeds with a conditional sentence, "If he has done you any wrong or owes you anything" (v. 18). Paul does not explicitly ask Philemon to forgive his slave, but the general tone of the letter assumes that he should adopt a forgiving attitude (Garland, *Colossians and Philemon*, 300–301).

[155] A. Malherbe, *Ancient Epistolary Theorists* (Atlanta: Scholars Press, 1988) 68–69.

[156] On this issue, see further the discussions in C. K. Barrett, "Ο ΑΔΙΚΗΣΑΣ (2 Cor 7.12)," in *Essays on Paul* (Philadelphia: Westminster, 1982) 108–17; C. G. Kruse, "The Offender and the Offense in 2 Corinthians 2:5 and 7:12," *EvQ* 60 (1988) 129–39; and Thrall, *A Critical and Exegetical Commentary on the Second Epistle to the Corinthians*, 1:61–69.

[157] What follows is adapted from Barrett, "Ο ΑΔΙΚΗΣΑΣ (2 Cor 7.12)," 109.

understand him in part (1:14) suggests that the individual and others in the community failed to appreciate the path of suffering Paul follows as the apostle who preaches Christ crucified. This misunderstanding may have fed the conflict.

2. A single individual committed the offense, but somehow the Corinthians were implicated (2:5).

3. We can infer from Paul's insistence that he was not hurt as much as the Corinthians were (2:5), that he had already forgiven the offender (2:10), and that the man's action was a direct slap at Paul. It was serious enough to force Paul to leave and to dispatch the letter of tears.[158]

4. The offense affected the whole community in some way. Originally, the Corinthians may not have recognized the full gravity of what had happened, or they may have cowered in silence. Like many bystanders in conflict situations, they may have wanted to melt into the background or bury their heads in the sand and wish that it would all go away.

5. Paul's statement in 2:10, "If there is anything to forgive," may imply, as Bultmann argues, that the issue concerned principles.[159] It is not simply a matter of Paul receiving personal satisfaction for an offense against him but of the community understanding correctly the principles involved in the offense and taking appropriate action to correct them.

Paul's theological response suggests that the offence was more serious than simply a personal verbal affront such as name calling. This person rejected Paul's authority.[160] His rebellion against the apostle makes it likely that he belonged to the minority of members who were socially advantaged and financially better off. He apparently wielded some power in the community and misused it in a cutthroat attempt to wrest a following from those loyal to Paul by shaming him in some way. It is also likely that he may have spiraled free from moral constraints in arrogantly exercising the freedom he assumed for himself in the name of Christ.

The majority of ancient commentators identified the offender as the man guilty of living with his father's wife (1 Cor 5:1–5). Paul insisted that the Corinthians discipline the man by evicting him from their fellowship because he was a corrupting influence. He previously had instructed them not to associate with those who were immoral, but the Corinthians apparently ignored his instructions for some reason (1 Cor 5:9–11). Paul's belief that this man's sin gave the whole community a bad reputation (1 Cor 5:2) may explain why he says that he caused pain to all of you (2:5). Paul refers

---

[158] F. Bleek first identified this letter as one written after 1 Corinthians and now lost ("Erörterungen in Beziehung auf die Briefe Pauli an die Korinther," *TSK* 3 [1830] 614–32).

[159] Bultmann, *The Second Letter to the Corinthians,* 49.

[160] This person may also have resisted Paul by treating his coworker Timothy with contempt and may have tried to stir up resistance against him during his absence.

to the involvement of the whole church in disciplining and restoring the one who did wrong (2:9; 7:12), which conforms to his admonition for them to discipline the man in 1 Cor 5:4–5. Satan is also mentioned in both texts. In 1 Corinthians they are to exercise discipline by delivering the offender to Satan; in 2 Corinthians they are to keep Satan from gaining an advantage over them by forgiving the offender, by accepting him back into their fellowship.[161] A reference to Christ also appears in both texts: "In the name of the Lord Jesus" (5:4); "in the face of Christ" (2:10).

The majority of modern commentators emphatically reject identifying the offender with the man guilty of incest in 1 Corinthians 5.[162] Barrett says that this view "is now almost universally, and rightly, abandoned," and Bultmann argues that "under no circumstances" can it be right.[163] Several matters challenge this view. First, Tertullian, in the heat of the Montanist controversy, refuted this connection because he could not accept that such a short disciplinary period was adequate for the particularly abhorrent sin of incest (*On Modesty,* 13–15). The gentleness and reserve with which Paul treats the offender does not seem to match the offense, even if he had repented.

Second, deliverance for the destruction of the flesh (1 Cor 5:5) would seem to involve something more drastic than a brief suspension from the church gatherings. If Paul relented and reversed himself on the stern punishment, it might add to the impression that he vacillates or is too meek when dealing with sin. Would Paul have insisted on such profound chastisement only to test whether they would obey him in all things?[164]

Third, Paul says he forgives him before they have (2:10). This statement suggests that the man committed some personal injury against Paul, but there is no indication from 1 Corinthians 5 that the incestuous man directed any insults Paul's way.

---

[161] The offender is identified as "such a one" (τοιοῦτος; 1 Cor 5:5; 2 Cor 2:6). Paul customarily refrains from identifying his opposition (see "some," 1 Cor 4:18; 2 Cor 3:1; 10:10; "many who," 2 Cor 2:17; 12:21; "those who," 5:12; "someone," 11:4; "such people," 11:13). Plummer counters that in every single matter (7:11) there is a τις and a τοιοῦτος with Satan at work (*The Second Epistle of St. Paul to the Corinthians,* 55).

[162] The exceptions are S. Cox, "That Wicked Person," *Expositor,* 1st ser. 3 (1875) 355–68; P. E. Hughes, *The Second Epistle to the Corinthians,* NICNT (Grand Rapids: Eerdmans, 1961) 59–65; A. M. G. Stephenson, "A Defense of the Integrity of 2 Corinthians," in *The Authorship and Integrity of the New Testament* (London: SPCK, 1965), 96; G. W. H. Lampe, "Church Discipline and the Interpretation of the Epistles to the Corinthians," in *Christian History and Interpretation,* ed. W. R. Farmer, C. F. D. Moule, R. R. Niebuhr (Cambridge: University Press, 1967) 353–54; D. R. Hall, "Pauline Church Discipline," *TynBul* 20 (1969) 3–26; N. Hyldahl, "Die Frage nach der literarischen Einheit des zweiten Korintherbriefes," *ZNW* 64 (1973) 305–06; and Kruse, "The Offender and the Offense."

[163] Barrett, "Ὁ ΑΔΙΚΗΣΑΣ (2 Cor 7.12)," 111; Bultmann, *The Second Letter to the Corinthians,* 48.

[164] Plummer, *The Second Epistle of St. Paul to the Corinthians,* 55.

Fourth, how could Paul say that he had forgiven someone who sank to such depths that even pagans considered his behavior abhorrent? How could Paul say "if there was anything to forgive" (2:10) if he has in mind such a sin?[165]

Fifth, critics of this view point to the inconsistent references to Satan. In 1 Cor 5:5 Satan is the means of chastisement; in 2 Cor 2:11, he is a crafty enemy to guard against. Finally, Héring argues that the incident concerning the incest happened long ago and was settled by an anathema.[166]

Interpreters have therefore proposed other candidates for the offender. Windisch claimed it was the man who was taking legal action against another (1 Cor 6:1–8).[167] But this view places too much weight on the verb *adikeō* (7:12). Barrett argues that it was an outsider, one of the pseudo-apostles who had been meddling in the church's affairs.[168] The visitor "claimed superior rights for himself, challenged the apostle's position, belittled his authority."[169] Since Paul shows greater concern for the church than the individual (2:9), he reasons that the individual was an outsider. That the Corinthians demonstrated their innocence to Titus and punished the offender suggests to Barrett that they did not fully share in the guilt. If they were pure in the matter (7:9), he argues, then the offender must have been an outsider.[170]

Barrett's argument fails to convince because it is predicated on chaps. 10–13 being written after chaps. 1–9 when more intruders had arrived. More importantly, Paul's call to restore the offender would make no sense if he were an outsider. Nor would it be likely for an outsider to be overwhelmed by grief and to desert the faith if the Corinthians were to reject him in some way. It is also hard to explain why Paul would feel such compassion for an intruder who has caused the congregation such harm.

Thrall makes the intriguing suggestion that the offender was someone who stole money designated for the collection.[171] The individual denied the charges, and Paul was somehow implicated. The Corinthians did not entirely believe Paul's side of the story, resulting in the embarrassing confrontation. Although this view is possible, it is not entirely plausible. If chaps. 8–9 and 12:17–18 were written after this event, it seems likely that Paul would have

---

[165] Belleville, *2 Corinthians*, 202.

[166] Héring, *The Second Epistle of Saint Paul to the Corinthians*, 15.

[167] Windisch, *Der zweite Korintherbrief*, 237–39; The verb ἀδικεῖν has its full legal force.

[168] Barrett, *The Second Epistle to the Corinthians*, 91; "Ο ΑΔΙΚΗΣΑΣ (2 Cor 7.12)," 108–17; followed by Martin, *2 Corinthians*, 34.

[169] Barrett, *The Second Epistle to the Corinthians*, 113.

[170] He claims that Paul was not certain how much the Corinthians were implicated in the matter and learned from Titus that they had taken the letter in the right way and had been quite innocent. (ibid., 114–15). They now zealously take Paul's part.

[171] Thrall, *Second Epistle to the Corinthians*, 1:68–69.

made some direct reference to some previous dishonesty related to the col-lection.

The majority of commentators assume that the guilty party was some unknown person who led a revolt against Paul. Barnett suggests that he may have supported the practice of attending the temples in the city (6:14–7:1) despite Paul's warnings (1 Cor 10:14–22).[172] He thinks it more probable that the man was a recent member who joined the church after Paul founded it, and Paul must overturn his harmful influence. The offense occurred dur-ing Paul's visit, and he wrote the severe letter testing to see if they would discipline the offender.

Modern readers can only guess what happened and how this anonymous "certain one" has grieved Paul and the church, but scholars may have been too quick to dismiss the man mentioned in 1 Corinthians 5 as the prime can-didate for the one who caused the rift. Paul's call in 1 Cor 5:5 for a church to carry out such extreme disciplinary measures is unique in his letters. It would be strange if Paul never broached the subject again or failed to com-mend the Corinthians for obeying his instructions regarding this grievous offense had they done so. Since Paul never specifically mentions this person in 2 Corinthians, commentators must assume that he was expelled, never to be heard from again, thus resolving the matter for good. This scenario seems highly unlikely.

Paul had warned the Corinthians that he was prepared to come to them "with a rod" if they did not heed what he said (1 Cor 4:21). This threat occurs immediately before his insistence that they discipline the man who is living with his father's wife (1 Cor 5:1–5). It is possible that Paul attempted to follow through on his threat and was rebuffed by the church either overtly or, more probably, by their inaction. Paul's exercise of authority apparently caused resentment. When Paul made his infelicitous visit, an individual acted in such a way to abuse Paul (2:5; 7:7–8,10,12).

There is no way to know the whole story behind the incestuous man's behavior, but it is probable that one who defied the mores even of pagans and sinned so terribly would not have submitted meekly to the discipline urged by Paul. He had somehow gained the community's support so that they apparently took some twisted pride in his sin ("you are puffed up," 5:2) instead of grieving over the immorality. It is unlikely that the offender would surrender that support without a fight. This man is also the most likely candi-date to hold a grudge against Paul and to chafe over his interference. He may have resisted Paul's efforts to get the church to take action against him by engaging in a campaign to undermine Paul's authority and mocking him to his face when he visited. He would have been likely to resort to the Roman

---

[172] Barnett, *The Second Epistle to the Corinthians,* 124, 125, n. 13.

custom of publicly ridiculing enemies with invective to humiliate them and divest them of their friends.[173] He also would have the most to gain from courting the attentions of the false apostles. The church's failure to take up for their apostle in this acrimonious confrontation suggests that this man probably wielded some influence. It is quite likely that he was wealthy and influential and possibly was the host of a house church. Naturally, the church would be reluctant to discipline such a man whatever his sin.

If the incestuous man was indeed the one who brought grief to the church, Paul's letter apparently steeled their nerve and gave them the theological discernment to take action. Paul had asked them to hand him over to Satan "so that the sinful nature [lit., "flesh"] may be destroyed and his spirit saved on the day of the Lord" (1 Cor 5:5). "To deliver to Satan" means simply to put the man out of the church and into the world where Satan reigns (2 Cor 4:4; see also 2 Thess 3:14; Titus 3:10–11). Paul's warning in 1 Cor 11:29–30 reveals how seriously the Corinthian Christians believed that the power of Christ worked in the community. Both 1 Cor 5:5 and 2 Cor 2:11 reflect a belief that the church, if successful in fending off Satan's wiles, is a bastion against Satan—a place where Satan does not rule. Although the implications of being expelled from a church community may not be as significant today when someone can join another group quite easily, in the first century it would have had a serious impact.

Furnish argues that in 1 Cor 5:1–5 "there is not the slightest intimation that the man might repent and thereby be reconciled to his Christian brothers and sisters; in fact, the character and permanence of the punishment left no room for that."[174] He assumes that the punishment was intended to be permanent and irrevocable.[175] But such discipline, like the wrath of God in Rom 1:18–32, is intended to cause people to snap out of their sinfulness and come to their senses. The purpose is to bring the offender to repentance and to protect the community from the corruption of brazen sinners. The view that this punishment was to be immutable does not permit gentleness when a sinner repents and implies that certain sins are unforgivable.

Paul does not believe that discipline should be meted out for discipline's sake. The purpose of handing him over to Satan was to destroy his fleshly orientation and to save his soul (1 Cor 5:5). It was not, as Furnish contends,

---

[173] See Marshall, *Enmity in Corinth,* 67. He comments that the fear of public humiliation ran deep in Roman and Greek society. In a society generally unsympathetic to losers, there was no middle ground, no benefit of doubt. Failure almost always meant the destruction of a man's status and reputation in public estimation, sometimes temporarily, often permanently. Paul's call for punishment of this man would have devastated the man's honor in the congregation.

[174] Furnish, *II Corinthians,* 166.

[175] See C. J. Roetzel, *Judgment in the Community: A Study of the Relationship between Eschatology and Ecclesiology in Paul,* NovTSup (Leiden: Brill, 1972) 120–21.

so that he is "totally cut off from the community and left to the ultimately destructive powers of Satan—that is, physical death, the same order of judgment involved for those who profane Christ's body at the Lord's Supper (1 Cor 11:29–30, illness and death)."[176] The "flesh" in this passage refers to an orientation to life characterized by "self-sufficiency" (see Gal 3:3; 5:24; 2 Cor 10:13; Rom 8:5–8; 1 Cor 3:3). The Spirit refers to an orientation characterized by absolute reliance on God (see Gal 5:16–17,25; Rom 8:4,9).[177]

Paul wants him expelled from the fellowship in hopes that the shock would force him to change his fleshly orientation. Now that the individual has repented, Paul worries that they not allow Satan to gain advantage (2 Cor 2:11). Satan has had him long enough; Paul wants him forgiven and restored or excessive sorrow might overwhelm the man. Paul knows that Satan will try to undermine the reconciliation and forgiveness.[178]

Although the sin of incest did not wrong Paul, he identifies himself so closely with the church that any wrong directed against it directly affects him. He writes in 11:29: "Who is weak, and I do not feel weak? Who is led into sin, and I do not inwardly burn?" (see also 1 Cor 12:26: "If one part suffers, every part suffers with it; if one part is honored, every part rejoices with it"). Paul takes it personally when sin shakes the Christian community. But an additional offense occurred after Paul wrote 1 Corinthians when he made the personal visit. The man apparently publicly rebuked him and attacked his teaching, which caused Paul to cut short his time in Corinth.[179]

While a case can still be made for the incestuous man as Paul's nemesis, final certainty eludes us. We simply cannot know and must therefore examine the text, not to establish what happened but to discern its enduring theological and ethical implications.

---

[176] Furnish, *II Corinthians*, 165.

[177] Talbert, *Reading Corinthians*, 16.

[178] The encouragement to forgive the offender fits the general instructions in Eph 4:25–32, where Paul admonishes his readers to speak the truth to neighbors. This command has to do with more than simply being honest but refers to confronting the neighbor honestly with the truth, even when it hurts. It alludes to Zech 8:16, "Speak the truth to each other, and render true and sound judgment in your courts," which refers to maintaining the covenant community through upright behavior. When confronting wrong, anger must be handled constructively, or "it will make room for the devil" and ruin community. Therefore, Paul urges that they "get rid of all bitterness, rage and anger, brawling and slander, along with every form of malice. Be kind and compassionate to one another, forgiving each other, just as in Christ God forgave you" (Eph 4:31–32).

[179] Paul mentions the one who was offended in 7:12. Most assume that if the offender was the man guilty of incest, then the one who was wronged was his father although he is not mentioned in 1 Cor 5:1–5. But it is more likely that the one wronged was Paul, and this connection is hard to square with the original offense of incest. Paul may not be referring in 7:12 to the original wrong but a subsequent event. Instead, he may have in mind an incident that occurred when he made his painful visit and provoked the severe letter. Ultimately, his primary concern was not this offense but the breakdown in his relationship with the church.

The Greek phrase *apo merous* lends itself to different interpretations.[180] Paul could mean "to some extent" (NIV) or "in some measure" and refer to the extent of pain that his action caused the church. If this phrase refers to part of the congregation, to a section of "you," it would mean that not all have been grieved in the same measure. Bultmann believes that the offense "was not at all felt or construed as such by one part of the community. Only the other part really suffered from it"—the majority in 2:6.[181] Furnish allows for both meanings.[182] In referring to the incident, however, Paul claims that he was not hurt as much as the congregation. In doing so, he makes clear that this dispute was not simply the result of personal animosity between Paul and the offender.[183] If this person offended him, Paul makes it plain that he has already forgiven him. The problem for the Corinthians, however, still needed to be resolved.

It is frequently difficult for those who are not directly involved in personal disputes in churches to see how they also are directly affected. Church disputes affect everyone whether or not they are personally involved. They damage the entire congregation. In this instance the dispute had repercussions even on people in Troas. If the offender was the incestuous man, his very presence in the congregation exposed them to his spiritual contagion. Paul understands the offender's mistreatment of him also injured the entire community. But Paul steps gingerly to avoid overstating the case with the phrase "not to put it too severely" and incite afresh the person's resentment.[184]

At the heart of the conflict was the offender's self-interested behavior, which apparently clashed with Christian morality and the spiritual welfare of the community. When Paul learned of the offense, he protested loudly. His protest inflamed the offender's resentment, and he in turn protested against Paul. When Paul arrived in person, the offender took the initiative to make his feelings known publicly to try to shame Paul in some way. Paul had communicated that this offense was not a private matter but something that involved the entire community. The dispute therefore reached the point of critical mass with this public confrontation. It would either escalate or be defused. Escalation could lead to an explosion that might permanently

---

[180] On the various ways of constructing the Greek phrase, see Thrall, *Second Epistle to the Corinthians,* 1:171–73.

[181] Bultmann, *The Second Letter to the Corinthians,* 48.

[182] Furnish, *II Corinthians,* 154–55.

[183] Furnish, *II Corinthians,* 160; Thrall, *Second Epistle to the Corinthians,* 1:171.

[184] If the phrase ἵνα μὴ ἐπιβαρῶ is transitive, it would mean "not to be too severe on him." It is more likely that it is intransitive and should be translated "not to put it too severely" (NIV) or "not to labor the point" (NEB). The phrase may be an allusion to his "heavy" (βαρεῖαι) letters (10:10).

destroy the relationship between Paul and the church. Paul had no intention of coercing the Corinthians to fall into line because that would defeat his purpose to develop churches capable of making mature Christian decisions on their own without constant supervision (see 1 Cor 6:1–6). To keep the situation from creating an irreconcilable rupture, he retreated.

Paul had no intention of sacrificing core Christian values, however, for the sake of an uneasy peace. Nor would he ever give up on the church. A letter—even a stinging letter—was better than open confrontation because it gave him an opportunity to lay out the issues from a theological perspective. The ultimate goal was to bring about a peaceful resolution, not an unholy compromise. The final outcome had to be one fitting for those who were baptized into Christ and bore his name. Paul's wisdom in taking this tack was vindicated by the Corinthians' positive response. They rallied to Paul's defense and chastised the guilty person. Paul's seeming defensiveness in this letter leaves readers unprepared for the Corinthians' apparent positive response to the severe letter that we meet in chap. 7. There Paul's defense of his use of frank criticism reveals his ultimate love for the congregation.

2:6 Paul's concern about the punishment of the offender presents the picture that church members presided as judges over the person involved and pronounced a sentence (see 1 Cor 6:1–11).[185] Paul does not specify what the punishment was.[186] In the majority of the uses of the word *epitimia* in the New Testament it means "rebuke" or "reproof." Barrett therefore argues for translating it "reproof" here instead of "punishment."[187] Furnish counters, however, that Barrett's attempt to identify the offender as someone outside the congregation not subject to its discipline drives his analysis. He argues, "It could not have been a simple reprimand, because the wording here shows that it has some enduring aspect or consequences, which can—and, Paul believes, ought to—be now discontinued." The "majority" *(pleiones)* does not refer to the "main body of persons concerned in any matter without the necessary implication of a minority, though the main body are sometimes distinguished from their leaders" as Barrett contends.[188] When Paul uses this word, it nearly always refers to the majority (see 1 Cor 9:19; 10:5; 15:6; 2 Cor 9:2; Phil 1:14; with the possible exception

---

[185] Paul's command to the brothers in general in 1 Thess 5:14 assumes that each member has the responsibility to admonish other members when they are in the wrong. Such a practice may have sparked tension if members from a lower strata of society took it upon themselves to admonish those with higher status (see C. E. Glad, *Paul and Philodemus: Adaptability in Epicurean and Early Christian Psychagogy,* NovTSup 81 [Leiden: Brill, 1995] 209).

[186] The verb "inflicted" does not appear in the Greek; lit., the text reads "this punishment." See Jude 9.

[187] Barrett, *The Second Epistle to the Corinthians,* 90. He argues that the cognate verb ἐπι-τιμᾶν has the meaning "to rebuke" in its thirty (twenty-nine) appearances in the NT. The one exception is Jude 9, where it can mean "to impose a punishment."

of 2 Cor 4:15). The reference to the majority therefore implies that not all concurred with the action and may reveal that the church is split, perhaps around different house churches.

Either a minority still rejects Paul's authority,[189] or they may think that this is a personal matter between Paul and the individual that should not involve the church. Possibly "ultra-Paulinists" might regard the penalty as inadequate and want to take even stronger measures.[190] Thrall may be correct that the phrase is only an innocuous reference to a congregational vote "without any emphasis on those who might have dissented from the decision, whether they supported a harsher sentence or a more lenient one."[191] The majority rules. Paul says that he has confidence in "all" of them (2:3), not just his supporters. But Paul would never have left Troas to go to Macedonia and anxiously await Titus if he had full confidence in all of them. The later challenge in chaps. 10–13 suggests that Paul knows that some resistance still exists in the church.

Paul has no interest in retribution and does not want them to be punitive. The goal was reached when the man repented, and consequently the punishment need not continue. This passage should disabuse people of the image that Paul was rigid, combative, and harsh in dealing with his churches. Vincent voices the impression that many have about Paul: "We are accustomed to conceive of the apostle as always armed for warfare, sheathed in logic, and bristling with arguments."[192] We meet here a Paul who is humble, irenic, tolerant, forgiving, and full of pastoral tenderness. In fact, his forbearance may be one of the Corinthians' criticisms of Paul. In person he is too humble, too irenic, too meek. They misinterpret these traits as weakness (2 Cor 10:10). His encouragement to forgive may be taken by them as another of Paul's shortcomings. Someone in Corinth who believed, as most did in this Roman culture, that one proved one's mettle by completely demolishing any opposition, might accuse Paul of feeble vacillation by shifting from the role of prosecutor to the role of defender with a tender plea for clemency. If it is a sign of weakness, it is the weakness that comes from living out the cross. Paul has no desire to overwhelm his opponents, not even those who may have grievously injured him. When his antagonist is down,

---

[188] Barrett, *The Second Epistle to the Corinthians*, 91. He argues that it may parallel the use of "the many" *(ha-rabbim)* in the Dead Sea Scrolls to refer to the main body. The word οἱ πλείονες, however, needs to be distinguished from οἱ πολλοί (so Furnish, *II Corinthians*, 155).

[189] So Bultmann, *The Second Letter to the Corinthians*, 49; Belleville, *2 Corinthians*, 74.

[190] M. J. Harris, "2 Corinthians," EBC (Grand Rapids: Zondervan, 1976) 10:329. J. Munck comments, "Paul ... will not allow the church now to push off all the guilt on the individual" *(Paul and the Salvation of Mankind* [Richmond: John Knox, 1959] 188).

[191] Thrall, *Second Epistle to the Corinthians*, 1:176.

[192] M. R. Vincent, *A Critical and Exegetical Commentary on the Epistles to the Philippians and to Philemon*, ICC (Edinburgh: T & T Clark, 1897) 169.

he asks everyone to join together in helping him up. He never wishes to rout those who are guilty of sin but always wants to edify (see 13:10).

Paul therefore tries to prevent the affair from deteriorating into a win-lose situation. Paul asserts that the punishment has been sufficient, and it is now fitting that they forgive and restore the individual. His call for forgiveness changes an "I win, you lose" situation to one where brothers in Christ win and Satan loses. The brother is won back to Christ and not lost to Satan.

2:7–8 Inflexibility does not secure Paul's standing in the community. The honor of his office as apostle is not sabotaged if he reverses himself on how to treat the offender. On the contrary, it is confirmed. Paul is a minister of reconciliation (5:18–6:2) and preaches a gospel of forgiveness. Someone has hurt Paul and people he considers his children. Nevertheless, he does not gloat over the fact that this one has received his comeuppance and is weighed down by sorrow. He does not say, "I am glad that this one got what he deserves." Instead, he says, "Take him back." "Reaffirm your love for him." "Grant him pardon and comfort him." The "you ought" in the NIV is not in the Greek, although it may be implied. Plummer notes that Paul does not tell them "what they *must* do." In 2:8, "He does not invoke his Apostolic authority and command forgiveness; as an equal he entreats them to grant it."[193]

We can draw several insights from Paul's approach to this conflict.

1. He emphasizes forgiveness. C. S. Lewis has said, "We all agree that forgiveness is a beautiful idea until we have to practice it."[194] In urging forgiveness and forgiving the offender himself, Paul would seem to be putting into practice what Jesus taught in the Lord's Prayer and in the admonition recorded in Luke 17:3–4: "If your brother sins, rebuke him, and if he repents, forgive him. If he sins against you seven times in a day, and seven times comes back to you and says, 'I repent,' forgive him" (see also John 20:22; Matt 18:15–18). True forgiveness neither excuses the sin nor ignores what happened. It means that you still relate to that person in spite of what happened but also in light of what happened. Forgiveness, however, does not require that the church reinstate the person into a position of authority again but does require his reinstatement into their fellowship.

2. Paul also instructs them to comfort the offender. The verb "comfort" *(parakaleō)* includes many different kinds of activities. They should deal benevolently with him, support him, and encourage him (see Gal 6:1–5). In 1 Thess 2:11–12 Paul uses the verb to describe his dealing with them as a father deals with his own children, "encouraging, comforting and urging you to live lives worthy of God, who calls you into his kingdom and glory."

---

[193] Plummer, *The Second Epistle of St. Paul to the Corinthians,* 58.
[194] C. S. Lewis, *Reflections on the Psalms* (London: Geoffrey Bles, 1958) 27.

"Comforting" is therefore not unrelated to spurring others to live worthily of the gospel. It does not mean making others feel comfortable about their past sin but leading them to godly sorrow where they find God's forgiveness.

3. Paul also underscores their need to show love. He tells the Colossians:

> As God's chosen people, holy and dearly loved, clothe yourselves with compassion, kindness, humility, gentleness and patience. Bear with each other and forgive whatever grievances you may have against one another. Forgive as the Lord forgave you. And over all these virtues put on love, which binds them all together in perfect unity (Col 3:12–14).

The reaffirmation of love requires some public, concrete expression rather than just mouthing expressions of love.[195]

Paul knows what it is to be burdened by sorrow (2:3,13) and does not want to inflict such a state on anyone else unnecessarily. He worries that the man might be overwhelmed (lit. "drowned," "swallowed up") by excessive sorrow (see Ps 69:1). Christians are to live triumphantly, knowing that their sins have been forgiven by God; and living under an excessive, all-consuming guilt can only destroy life, not bring life. The past disgrace may continue to burden the offender, but now he will not need to carry the load alone but will have his fellow Christians to bear him up.

The issue of church discipline is a difficult one, and the danger is that we will go to one extreme or the other. On the one hand, we may not want to do anything when someone is guilty of an offense that brings disgrace upon or disrupts the community. We will bury our heads in the sand and hope that all the unpleasantness will soon go away. Or we may try to substitute cheap grace for real grace by letting bygones be bygones without signs of genuine repentance.

On the other hand, we may be tempted to go too far in discipline so that it becomes destructive rather than constructive. We may try to turn the one who is condemned into a scapegoat and inappropriately cover up our own hidden sins by taking out our anger on this victim. Hughes correctly recognizes that it is "no less a scandal" to ban a penitent sinner forever from the redeemed and reconciled community as it is to wink at flagrant wickedness.[196]

Calvin gives sage advice: "Severity is required in order that wicked men may not be made more bold by being allowed to go unpunished—for this is

---

[195] κυρῶσαι means to "confirm" or "ratify" and has a legal connotation in Gal 3:15. Thrall argues that Paul expects "a congregational resolution" that would be regarded within the church "as having a kind of legal validity" (*Second Epistle to the Corinthians*, 1:177). This suggestion would make sense if the punishment was pronounced by a formal decision by the church. But Plummer argues that no formal resolution is implied "any more than 'ratify' would imply that in English" (*The Second Epistle of St. Paul to the Corinthians*, 60).

[196] Hughes, *The Second Epistle to the Corinthians*, 66–67.

rightly said to be an enticement to sin. But on the other hand there is a danger that a man who is disciplined will fall into despair so that the Church must practice moderation and be ready to pardon anyone as soon as it is sure that he has sincerely repented."[197] Sinners must pass through a period of despair, but the danger comes when they become permanently mired in gloom and lose all hope of forgiveness. Feeling that there is no way out can present an even worse danger to the soul. Along these lines, John Chrysostom cites the grief of Judas, which resulted in his suicide (Matt 27:3–5).[198]

2:9   Paul explains that the reason he wrote to them instead of coming in person and taking the disciplinary matters into his own hands was that he wanted them to accept responsibility and act. He therefore does not vacillate, first, demanding stern punishment, then relenting and demanding forgiveness. This was his purpose all along. He acted the way fathers were expected to act by disciplining his children and testing their character. In 13:3 Paul states that they wanted to test his character. The word translated "proof" *(dokimē)* in 13:3 is the same word translated "character" in 2:9 (see "approved," *dokimos* in 10:18). But Paul turns things around: They are to test themselves, lest he come and find that they have not met the test (13:5–7).

All worldly criteria that attest to character are invalid; one can only be attested if one is in Christ. Paul gives several criteria in this letter for confirming Christian character. It reveals itself when they discipline wrongdoers and forgive them after they repent (2:6–9); when they maintain the joy of Christian faith in the midst of affliction (8:2); when they demonstrate love (8:8) and respond with generosity to those in need (9:13); and when they do what is right (13:5–7).[199] But the primary characteristic is being "obedient in everything." Paul does not say to whom they are to be obedient, but in 10:5–6 he makes it clear that they must be obedient to Christ. He does not want to bring the Corinthians to heel so that they obey him. He is not the Lord of their faith, Christ is (1:24).

2:10   The NIV translation implies a condition, "If you forgive," but the "if" does not appear in the Greek text. Paul says, "Whom you forgive anything [with the dative of the person and accusative of the thing], I also." Surprisingly, Paul makes no mention of divine forgiveness, which implies that the community's forgiveness conveys it (see Matt 18:18).

Paul continues his tactful approach by saying "if there was anything to

---

[197] Calvin, *The Second Epistle of Paul the Apostle to the Corinthians,* 29.

[198] John Chrysostom, *Homilies on Second Corinthians IV.4; Saint Chrysostom: Homilies on the Epistles of Paul to the Corinthians,* NPNF 1st ser. XII [Grand Rapids: Eerdmans, 1969; the Oxford trans. revised by T. W. Chambers] 297.

[199] Other positive criteria emerge in other letters, such as discerning the truth and slaving for the gospel (Phil 2:22). A negative criterion is splintering into different factions governed by worldly concerns and standards (1 Cor 11:19).

forgive." If the offender were the one guilty of incest, Paul could not mean that sin. He must refer to the insult he received during his aborted visit. This comment shows his magnanimity. He did not hold personal grudges (see Phil 1:15–18). Paul's spirit matches the best wisdom of pagan philosophers, who recognized that forgiving is more important than reveling in the defeat of an associate. Dionysius of Halicarnassus said, "Wise people overcome hostilities with displays of friendship; fools and uncivilized people destroy their friends along with their enemies."[200] But his charitable response is more than a stratagem to keep friends. Paul recognizes that it would have been no victory if he triumphed personally in the dispute and left a church riddled with dissension. As for him, it is not a matter that a wrong directed against him be redressed but that the community understand correctly the principles involved in the offense and act responsibly. By submitting to their judgment, he places the burden of responsibility squarely on them—whatever they decide.[201] Paul always wants to stimulate his congregations to grow in Christian maturity, and he is pleased because they have accepted responsibility in the matter (7:8–12). This comment again shows that he has no intention of lording over them.

"I have forgiven in the sight of Christ for your sake" literally reads "in the face of Christ" and could have a variety of possible meanings. It may mean in "the light of the forgiveness which they had all received through Christ (cf. Col 3:13; Eph 4:32)."[202] But it is more likely that Paul refers to "in the presence of Christ"[203] or perhaps as Christ looked on with approval and as a witness.[204] It is comparable to the way the father of the prodigal son would have looked on with approval had his eldest son rejoiced at the repentance of his younger brother and received him with welcoming forgiveness. With this expression Paul also reminds them that forgiveness cannot be unmindful or indulgent. Christ is our judge (1 Cor 11:32), who assesses what we forgive too easily and what we refuse to forgive.

Since the punishment was for their sake, the forgiveness also is for their sake. Paul's concern is always for the whole group and not for himself or even the offender. The forgiveness mends the differences between Paul and

---

[200] Dionysius of Halicarnassus, *Roman Antiquities* 5.4.3, cited by Danker, *II Corinthians,* 45. See also Plutarch, *Fraternal Love,* 488a.

[201] In 1 Cor 5:3–4 Paul stresses his spiritual presence in the community. This presence gives him the right to speak as he does without destroying the responsibility of the congregation. The punishment he stipulated therefore was not simply Pauline fiat. He works with the community, not on them.

[202] So Bruce, *I & II Corinthians,* 185–86.

[203] Barrett, *The Second Epistle to the Corinthians,* 93; Furnish, *II Corinthians,* 157–58; Martin, *2 Corinthians,* 39.

[204] Harris, "2 Corinthians," 10:329; Thrall, *A Critical and Exegetical Commentary on the Second Epistle to the Corinthians,* 1:180–81.

the individual, the individual and the church, and, most important, between Paul and the church.

2:11   Paul's final comments about the dispute puts it in the context of the cosmic battle between God and Satan. Satan is mentioned here and also in 11:14 and 12:7. He is identified as the god of this age in 4:4, Beliar in 6:15, and the serpent in 11:3.

The verb *pleonekteō* (passive voice) can mean "gain advantage" or "outwit" (see 7:2; 12:17; 1 Thess 4:6). It could also mean "rob." Satan will rob the community of a member of their group.[205] If Paul refers to the man in 1 Corinthians 5, they may have turned him over to Satan, but Satan cannot keep him if he repents. If the community does not forgive and accept the contrite offender, however, Satan may cheat them of another soul. For Paul, Christians experience salvation as a part of a community, not as isolated free agents. If the community stubbornly blacklists persons who have sinned and genuinely repented, they bear responsibility if they drive them away from Christ and back into the clutches of Satan. We can only ponder, for example, what might have happened in Jesus' parable had the returning prodigal son run into his elder brother first rather than the outstretched arms of his forgiving father. Throughout the Corinthian correspondence Paul seeks to build up community (see 1 Cor 12:12–26), and that requires taking responsibility for one another, disciplining when necessary, forgiving when appropriate, and never doing anything that might lead to another's eternal ruin (1 Cor 8:7–13).

This passage and 1 Cor 5:1–5 reveal how important it is for the Christian community to balance the exercise of firm discipline with compassionate charity toward those who repent. Failure to do either plays into the hands of Satan. In this passage Paul reveals that showing forgiveness is one way for the church to close the door on Satan's evil designs to destroy it.[206] Satan's realm is one where immorality, the thirst for revenge, ruthlessness, heartlessness, and deadly rancor hold sway. Those who are in Christ have received God's free pardon, and they are transferred into a realm where faith, hope, love, and tender mercies rule. Satan is powerless before a united community filled with love and humble forgiveness.

Satan's goal is always to foil God's work of reconciliation. Note how the wiles of Satan work in the Gospel narratives. Satan induces one disciple, Peter, to try to dissuade Jesus from obeying God's will in going to

---

[205] BAGD, 667.

[206] See Eph 6:11, the "methods" of Satan; and 2 Cor 11:14; 12:7. Satan also seeks to devour people (1 Pet 5:8) and frequently allows them to stew in the juices of their own spitefulness and bitterness.

his death (Mark 8:31–33). When that fails, Satan coaxes another disciple, Judas, to help ensure Jesus' death by handing him over to the enemy (Luke 22:3; John 13:27). Satan can be behind both moral laxity—anything goes—and a callous inflexibility—everyone goes who does not toe the line. Satan can use the church's permissiveness in failing to chastise sinners in their midst to bring it to ruin, and he can use the church's rigidity in failing to forgive chastened sinners to bring it to ruin. All too often, "efforts to remove evil may lead to the ultimate triumph of evil."[207] Therefore we should be wary because Satan can be at work even in attempts to purify the church. A situation that requires forgiveness is the time when Satan can work his worst and is the most dangerous. Satan fans the flames of hurt into an inferno of hostility. The next verses demonstrate how Satan schemes through the conflict between fellow Christians to undermine their preaching in the world.

Paul's concluding greetings in Rom 16:20, "The God of peace will soon crush Satan under your feet," may seem ironic—a God of peace crushing an enemy. But Satan is the enemy of peace. He is defeated by reconciliation. Christian love and charity neutralize all of Satan's powers over us and serves as an invisible, protective shield.

2:12 These next two verses serve as a transition from his defense for failing to come as planned and his defense of his boldness and afflictions as an apostle of Christ. Paul does not complete the story of the relief he felt when he finally saw Titus in Macedonia and received the good news about their godly sorrow and renewed zeal for him (7:5–16). Instead, he returns to the theme of the grief he suffered from his visit (2:3). On the one hand, harking back to his aborted mission to Troas reinforces his point that his failure to visit them as planned was not because he did not care for them but because he was overwhelmed with sorrow regarding them. It also makes clear that he does not make changes in his plans lightly; he was weighed down by anguish. On the other hand, it provides a transition for the discussion of his many afflictions which have caused some in Corinthians to question his suitability and qualifications as an apostle.

The full name of Troas was Alexandria the Troas, which distinguished it from other cities named Alexandria. "The Troad" with the definite article may refer to the region of the Troad and not just the city of Troas; but since the city was a seaport on the Aegean, it would have been the most likely rendezvous point for Paul to await for the return of Titus.[208]

Paul may have traveled to Troas to wait for Titus and, as in Athens, could

---

[207] Strachan, *The Second Epistle to the Corinthians*, 72.
[208] See C. J. Hemer, "Alexandria Troas," *TynBul* 26 (1975) 79–112.

not resist the urge to proclaim the gospel (Acts 17:16–17). Troas was one of the few Roman colonies in Asia Minor and therefore had the status of a Roman city, as did Corinth, Ephesus, and Philippi. Its strategic location at the entrance of the Dardanelles would fit Paul's policy of working in strategic centers. It is more likely, then, that he went there, as he says, to preach the gospel of Christ.[209] The gospel of Christ is the catalyst that controls all that Paul does as an apostle.[210] His purpose was to take the gospel to places where Christ has not been named (Rom 15:20), and he reports that "a door was opened in the Lord." "In the Lord" may express both the means by which the door was opened and the sphere in which the opportunity presented itself.[211] He stormed through it to seize the opportunity but then quickly exited.

2:13 Paul candidly shares his anxiety, "my spirit could not rest," because he wants to convey how devastating his conflict with the Corinthians was. It sends the message to them how deeply he cares for them. Paul was burdened by worry because he did not know how they would respond to his letter, and that worry was compounded when days passed with no word from Titus. The unexplained delay may signify that all was not well at Corinth. Paul's worst fears may have been realized, and the situation had worsened. With no high speed communications system in the ancient world, waiting anxiously for news could be excruciating. Paul was therefore torn between Troas and Corinth, between putting out a brush fire in a church conflict as a pastor and kindling the embers of new faith as an evangelist. Most ministers know firsthand that the demands and pressures of the ministry can pull them in different directions. Thus they may sympathize with Paul, who could not put his distress about Titus and the Corinthians out of his mind. This spiritual unrest so distracted him that it inhibited his work in Troas, so he was forced to make "a reluctant and solemn farewell."[212] That good-bye does imply, however, that all was not lost; some converts were won (see Acts 20:6–12).

These verses explain to the Corinthians why Paul was writing to them from Macedonia. He left for Macedonia perhaps after he realized that Titus was not on the last boat of the season (now autumn) and would now

---

[209] Barnett, *The Second Epistle to the Corinthians,* 135. The verb "to preach" does not appear in the text, but the phrase εἰς τὸ εὐαγγέλιον τοῦ Χριστοῦ, "for the gospel of Christ," basically means to preach the gospel about Christ (objective genitive).

[210] The gospel will reappear in 4:3–4; 8:18; 10:14; 11:4,7.

[211] Furnish, *II Corinthians,* 169. The image of an opened door appears also in 1 Cor 16:9; Col 4:3; see also 1 Thess 1:9, εἴσοδος, "entrance," "access," "reception," "welcome"; and Rev 3:8.

[212] Harris, "2 Corinthians," 10:331.

have to travel by land through Macedonia.[213] This sad account reveals how interconnected Christians are. We cannot hurt one another without also hurting the work of God in the world. Paul does not discuss whether it was the right thing to do to abandon a place where God had made an opportunity. His uneasiness over the Corinthians, however, made it impossible for him to continue his work there. The implication is that Paul's change in plans was caused by the Corinthians and that they also were behind his failure to pursue fully a golden opportunity for evangelism. Again we can see Satan's designs at work! The conflict with Corinth agitated Paul so much that it sabotaged a mission opportunity. His grief undermined his effectiveness and led him to exit doors that God may have wanted him to enter.

Paul suffered from the same kinds of problems that any of us do. Every reader of this text can probably identify some time in their Christian lives when they felt that they could not minister to others or that they only went through the motions because they were consumed by anxiety caused by a church conflict—the threat of dismissal, backbiting, slanderous rumors. It is even more devastating when disloyalty and back stabbing come from within our own congregation, from those whom we have personally served and loved. Preoccupation with such things and the depression and worry they create hinders evangelism. Church strife never speeds the gospel's advance.

We learn later in the letter that God's plan overrules, and Paul's anxiety was transformed into joy. But Paul breaks off this account about Titus and does not pick it up again until 7:5, where he exults over the good news that Titus bore from Corinth. In 7:5–16 Paul rejoices that they have renewed their longing for Paul and their bond with him (7:6–7), that they had repented (7:8–13a), and that his boast to Titus about the church proved true (7:13b–15). This reaction to the letter of tears reaffirms Paul's confidence in the church (7:16). I would argue that what follows in the intervening sections is Paul's defense for his apostolic boldness in that letter and for his manifold afflictions, which seem to make such boldness incongruous if not completely inappropriate and groundless. The theological grandeur and complexity of what follows in chaps. 3 and 5 have so occupied readers of 2 Corinthians that they have tended to eclipse the issue of the dispute, which almost ruined his relationship with the community. For this reason some readers may be surprised that Paul comes back to the issue in 7:4–16 since they may assume that it is not as

---

[213] W. L. Knox, *St. Paul and the Church of the Gentiles* (Cambridge: University Press, 1939) 144. The sea voyage from Corinth to Ephesus covered 250 miles. The land route passing through Macedonia was, of course, much further, around nine hundred miles.

important as his theological affirmations preceding it. But the matters of Paul's confidence (2:15; 7:16), his integrity and apostolic boldness (2:17–24; 7:4,16), the painful visit that precipitated the painful letter (2:1–11; 7:8–13a), and Titus's return (2:12–13; 7:5–7) frame Paul's arguments in 2:14–7:3.

2. Paul's Defense of His Frank Criticism (2:14–7:3)

The transition in 2:14 from the previous verse is abrupt. Since 7:5 seems to continue the thought of 2:13, some have theorized that 2:14–7:4 is a separate letter. If, as I have argued, 2 Corinthians is a unity, it is necessary to ask how this sudden shift in Paul's train of thought fits his argument as a whole. His outpouring of thanks to God (see 8:16; 9:15; Rom 6:17; 7:25; 1 Cor 15:57) may anticipate his joy over the happy result from the letter and Titus's visit (7:5–16), but Paul specifically gives thanks for all that God has done in his ministry.[214] He thanks God because God's designs are wiser and more powerful than Satan's (2:11) and because, in spite of failures here and there, the knowledge of God spreads everywhere through the apostolic preaching like an aroma. The preaching generates differing responses—both rejection which leads to death and acceptance which leads to life. The life-and-death impact of Paul's apostolic ministry causes him to ask who is adequate to shoulder the responsibility for proclaiming such a potent word from God.

---

[214] M. E. Thrall, "A Second Thanksgiving Period in 2 Corinthians," *JSNT* 16 (1982) 101–24. She argues that 2:14 is a second introductory period. The verb εὐχαριστῶ is not used, but she contends that this verb may be associated in Paul's mind with giving thanks for the readers. Therefore, Paul uses χάρις here instead. S. J. Hafemann argues that as a thanksgiving formula it becomes the thesis statement for 2:14–4:6 [–7:4], which "also contains an implicit paraenetic appeal to his readers" (*Suffering and Ministry in the Spirit: Paul's Defense of His Ministry in II Corinthians 2:14–3:3* [Grand Rapids: Eerdmans, 1990] 10–11). J. Murphy-O'Connor maintains that the reference to the Macedonians spurred Paul's discussion about his apostolate as he was reminded of the resonances between their reception of the gospel and his own ministry ("Paul and Macedonia: The Connection Between 2 Corinthians 2.13 and 2.14," *JSNT* 25 [1985] 100–103). The Macedonians embraced the gospel despite fierce opposition (1 Thess 1:6–8). The circumstances surrounding their acceptance of the gospel matches two themes in 2:14–17: the gospel as a manifestation of God's power and "the tragic division between those who accept and those who refuse the gospel." The Macedonians were models of obedience, an inspiration to other Christians, and offered "life" to non-Christians.

What follows in 2:14–7:3 (4) is a long explanation that establishes Paul's justification for his boldness in his severe letter, in which he must have frankly confronted them for their moral failures. In this section he does not explicitly take on his rivals. Instead he defends himself against the complaints raised by some Corinthians that he overstepped the bonds of friendship by challenging their moral failures so directly and provocatively.[215] He had to speak to them severely to bring them back into line, but he also had to be careful so they did not feel that he crossed the line of propriety by being too severe. They would then break off relations with him completely. Paul therefore justifies his license to be so frank with them in this letter while assuring them that he meant it for their own good.

The key text in this unit is 3:12. Paul declares that we have much boldness because we have been given a glorious ministry that leads to life and righteousness. "Boldness" *(parrēsia)* has to do with boldness of speech.[216] It was particularly important for confronting spiritual failures and disorders. The distinguished philosopher and orator, Dio Chrysostom, claimed, "Reformation of the human condition requires truth and bold speech" (*Orations* 33.7). But Paul's outspokenness contributed to the mounting tensions. Some Corinthians were distressed, and "the wise" may have regarded his reprimands as brazen audacity.[217] His imprisonments and many afflictions were, from their point of view, a cause for shame and silence and hardly made him fit to scold them in any way. But his authority in the community was based on his ability to comfort and to admonish others.

Paul shows in this section that he is not capriciously or imperiously going off on his own tangent; he has a divine commission in which God has charged their spiritual care to him. He claims, "In Christ we speak as persons of sincerity, as persons sent from God and standing in his presence" (2:17). He does not try to manipulate people through underhanded means. Rather, he states that "by open statement of the truth we commend ourselves

---

[215] Martin asks the vital question, "What led him to this extended 'diversion' (if that is the right word) in this letter?" (*2 Corinthians*, 136). We would argue that "diversion" or "digression" are not the right words. W. J. Webb postulates that "the apostle deliberately crafts 2.14–7.4 to be read in suspense, drawing his readers into the suffering he feels (as he waits for a reply to his sorrowful letter) through the words 'not finding Titus …' echoing in the background" (*Returning Home: New Covenant and Second Exodus as the Context for 2 Corinthians 6.14–7.1*, JSNTSup 85 [Sheffield: JSOT, 1993] 73–74.

[216] D. E. Fredrickson, "ΠΑΡΡΗΣΙΑ in the Pauline Epistles," in *Friendship, Flattery and Frankness of Speech: Studies on Friendship in the New Testament World*, ed. J. T. Fitzgerald, NovTSup 82 (Leiden: Brill, 1996) 163–64. In Phlm 8–9 Paul says he deliberately restrains himself from using bold free speech. Instead he uses an extraordinarily deft touch in dealing with a highly sensitive matter (see Garland, *Colossians Philemon*, 301–2, 333, 336, 340–41.

[217] We need not posit external rivals as the instigators of the complaints that Paul is too presumptuous and brazen in dealing with the Corinthians.

to the conscience of everyone in the sight of God" (4:2). He adds that God makes his appeal through us, as ambassadors for Christ (5:20). Paul's boast is in the church (7:4,14), and consequently their repentance is no casual matter for him. His stinging words are a sign of his love. Like a father correcting a child, he did it for their own good. Therefore he says his mouth is open to them ("we speak freely to you"), and his heart is likewise open wide. He wants them to open their hearts once more to him (6:11–13). Paul's defense of his boldness is therefore couched in love and concern for them.[218] His concern is not simply that they resisted his chastisement but also that they rejected reasons behind that resistance. Still, some are unable to see the glory of God manifest in the sufferings of Paul.

Observing the A B A′ pattern in 2:14–4:6 makes it possible to see the section's coherence and to follow movement of Paul's thought from 2:14–4:6. The following outline is adapted from Lambrecht.[219]

A 2:14–3:6 Christian Ministry
  A 2:14–17 Paul's Sufficiency for a Ministry That Results in Life or Death
  B 3:1–3 The Corinthians as Paul's Letter
  A′ 3:4–6 Paul's Sufficiency as Minister of the New Covenant
  B 3:7–18 The Old and the New Ministries
    A 3:7–9 The Glory of the Ministry Now Set Aside
    B 3:10 The Greater Glory of the New Eclipses the Old
    A′ 3:11 The Glory of the Ministry Now Set Aside (3:7–8 and 3:11
      form an inclusion)
    A 3:12–13 The Unveiled Paul (We, Apostles)
    B 3:14–17 The Veiled Israel (They, Israelites)
    A′ 3:18 Unveiled Christians (We, Christians)
A′ 4:1–6 Christian Ministry

---

[218] Allusions to this boldness appear in 2:17, where the metaphor for the merchant is used to affirm that he does not use adulterated, deceptive speech but speaks the truth. In 3:4, his confidence forms the basis of boldness. In 3:17 his boldness is grounded in freedom granted by the Spirit. In 4:2 he says he makes manifest the truth, which implies an inherent boldness. In 6:6–7
  he speaks unhypocritical love in words of truth. In 7:4 a hinge text leading to the next section, Paul reaffirms his boldness (παρρησία) toward them; and in 7:14, he again says that he speaks the truth always to them. The entire section concludes with a final statement about his boldness (θαρρέω) in 7:16.
[219] J. Lambrecht, "Structure and Line of Thought in 2 Cor 2,14–4:6," *Bib* 64 (1983) 344–80, in R. Bieringer and J. Lambrecht, *Studies on 2 Corinthians,* BETL 112 (Leuven: University Press, 1994) 257–94. Lambrecht makes the important point that the following pattern is not something Paul carefully outlined in advance but may be instead the result of the cyclic sequence of thought, his composing habit, or his way of reasoning and writing (p. 278). He comments, "We should recognize that Paul easily and frequently interrupts himself and afterwards comes back to the idea which had been forgotten for a moment, and using then elements derived from his interruption" (p. 292). See also Thrall, *Second Epistle to the Corinthians,* 1:189.

A 4:1–2 Commending Himself through the Open Statement of the Truth
B 4:3–4 The Spiritual Condition of Those Blinded to the Glory of Christ
    in "Our Gospel"
A′ 4:5–6 The basic thrust of Paul's preaching: Christ as Lord; ourselves
    as your slaves

The first unit (2:14–3:6) is framed by the life and death antithesis in 2:16 ("the smell of death," "the fragrance of life") and 3:6 ("the letter kills, but the Spirit gives life") and by the key idea of his sufficiency or competency (2:16; 3:5–6).[220] The focus falls on the qualities of apostolic ministry and Paul's qualifications for it.[221] Paul uses the first person plural throughout 2:14–3:6 to refer to himself because he is "conscious that he represented the apostolic office."[222] The emphasis is therefore more on "the nature of apostolic ministry" than on Paul's qualification to be an apostle.[223]

The next unit (3:7–18) divides into two parts. The theme of glory frames the first part (3:7,11).[224] It develops the comment in 3:6 on the differences between the two Covenants by stressing the negative character of the Old as transitory, past, and leading to death and condemnation. The glory the Old Covenant possessed pales beside the glory of the New. The second unit is framed by the reference to veils. The "unveiled face" in 3:18 is the opposite of the veil covering the face in 3:13. The idea of being transformed from one glory to another in 3:18 reflects the "hope" in 3:12.[225] In 3:12–18 Paul deals with persons, "we" (Christians) and "they" (Jews) and their differing attitudes toward Christ. It contrasts the two ministries of Moses and Paul and the two destinies of Christians and Jews. The ministry of Moses was veiled because of the hardened minds of its hearers; the ministry of Paul is bold and unveiled and transforms persons into Christ's likeness with ever-increasing glory.

In the third unit (4:1–6) Paul returns to the theme of the apostolic ministry raised in 2:14–3:6. Lambrecht detects the parallel terms and themes shared by the two units.[226]

---

[220] The key words are ἱκανός (2:16, NIV "who is equal to such a task?"; 3:5, "not that we are competent in ourselves"), ἱκανότης (3:5, NIV "our competence comes from God"), and ἱκανοῦν (3:6, NIV "He has made us competent as ministers of a new covenant").

[221] Hafemann, *Suffering and Ministry in the Spirit,* 15.

[222] Ibid.

[223] Barnett calls it an "apostolic plural" (*The Second Epistle to the Corinthians,* 140–41). It does not include Timothy or Silvanus or Apollos.

[224] "Glory" (δόξα) appears eight times (3:7 [twice],8,9,10,11 [twice]; see also 3:18 [twice]) and as a verb (δοξάζω) twice (3:10).

[225] Lambrecht, "Structure," 271. In 3:12–18 the keywords "veil" (κάλυμμα, 3:13–16) and "unveil" (ἀνακαλυπτόμενον, 3:14; and ἀνακεκαλυμμένῳ, 3:18) dominate.

[226] Ibid., 263.

4:1 ministry *(diakonia)*	3:6 ministers *(diakonoi)* 3:3 "the result of our ministry" *(diakonēotheisa)*

4:1 "we do not lose heart" (better
   translated "we are not cowardly,"
   or "we do not shrink back")
	3:4 "We have such confidence"

4:1 "Just as he mercied us"	3:4 "through Christ"

4:2 "we have renounced secret and
   shameful ways; we do not use
   deception, nor do we
   distort the word of God"
	2:17 "we do not peddle the word of
	   God for profit"

4:2 "setting forth the truth plainly" *(phaneroō)*	2:14 "spreads" *(phaneroō)* 3:3 "show" *(phaneroō)*

4:2 "we commend ourselves"
   "to every man's conscience"
	3:1 "to commend ourselves"
	   "by everybody"

4:3 "to those who are perishing"	2:15 "those who are perishing"

4:5 "ourselves"
   "your servants" *(douloi)*
   "we preach"
	3:1 "ourselves"
	 3:6 "ministers" *(diakonoi)*
	 2:17 "we speak"

4:6 "in our hearts"
   "to give us the light of the
   knowledge ... of God"
	3:2 "on our hearts"
	 2:17 "the knowledge of him"

Recognizing this A B A′ pattern helps us better understand the function of 3:7–18. It provides the theological basis for the affirmations in 2:14–3:6 and 4:1–6.

(1) The Nature of Apostolic Ministry (2:14–3:6)

[14]But thanks be to God, who always leads us in triumphal procession in Christ and through us spreads everywhere the fragrance of the knowledge of him. [15]For we are to God the aroma of Christ among those who are being saved and those who are perishing. [16]To the one we are the smell of death; to the other, the fragrance of life. And who is equal to such a task? [17]Unlike so many, we do not peddle the word of God for profit. On the contrary, in Christ we speak before God with sincerity, like men sent from God.

[1]Are we beginning to commend ourselves again? Or do we need, like some people, letters of recommendation to you or from you? [2]You yourselves are our letter, written on our hearts, known and read by everybody. [3]You show that you are a letter from Christ, the result of our ministry, written not with ink but with the Spirit of the living God, not on tablets of stone but on tablets of human hearts.

4Such confidence as this is ours through Christ before God. **5**Not that we are competent in ourselves to claim anything for ourselves, but our competence comes from God. **6**He has made us competent as ministers of a new covenant— not of the letter but of the Spirit; for the letter kills, but the Spirit gives life.

PAUL'S SUFFICIENCY FOR A MINISTRY THAT RESULTS IN LIFE OR DEATH (2:14–17)   **2:14**   The verb *thriambeuomai,* which the NIV translates "leads us in a triumphal procession," is a Latinism (from *triumphare*) that has long puzzled interpreters. Metaphors speak powerfully, but not always clearly. The life setting of this metaphor is the elaborate celebration of victory for the conquering Roman general parading through the streets of Rome. Normally, the verb is used intransitively with the meaning "to celebrate a victory by means of a triumph." But in the rare cases when the verb is used transitively, it means to lead captives in a triumphal procession.[227] Many interpreters, however, could not understand why Paul would picture himself as a defeated captive. Consequently they have tried to make the meaning of the verb fit an interpretation more in keeping with the triumphal sweep of the gospel. Calvin, for example, knew the common of meaning of the phrase but contended that it did not fit his understanding of what Paul could have meant. He asked: How could Paul praise God for leading him as a vanquished and dishonored prisoner? How could he liken himself as an apostle to one chained and marched in disgrace to his death before the conqueror? Such incongruity led Calvin to argue on theological rather than lexical grounds that Paul must have meant "to triumph with." Paul praised God because God graciously allowed him to share in this triumph.[228] Paul pictures himself as joining the procession as a soldier in God's victorious army.[229]

At first glance, this interpretation may seem to make better sense of the text, but we must allow the first century meaning of the word to guide our interpretation before trying to make it match what we think Paul ought to

---

[227] The NEB captures this meaning in its translation: "But thanks be to God, who continually leads us about, captives in Christ's triumphal procession."

[228] Calvin, *The Second Epistle of Paul the Apostle to the Corinthians,* 33. In modern times Strachan states that such an interpretation presents a "logical difficulty that a captive in such circumstances is only a spectacle of humiliation and defeat" (*The Second Epistle of Paul,* 73). Watson expresses the same sentiment: "Any suggestion that the relationship of the messengers to God is like that of conquered prisoners or that they are constantly exposed to shame and humiliation hardly fits the setting of thanksgiving" (*The Second Epistle to the Corinthians,* 22.

[229] Windisch, *Der zweite Korintherbrief,* 97; and Barrett, *The Second Epistle to the Corinthians,* 98.

be saying.[230] We should point out that Theophylact did understand how this meaning might fit. Those things that seem to be suffering and shame are our glory and triumph.[231]

Williamson's evaluation of the evidence leads him to conclude: "When followed by a direct personal object, *thriambeuo* means 'to lead as a conquered enemy in a victory parade.'"[232] It was not used to refer to those who participated in the procession as members of the army. If Paul's use of the verb accords with its common meaning, he does not represent himself as a garlanded, victorious general nor as a foot soldier in God's army who shares in the glory of Christ's triumph. Quite the opposite; he portrays himself as a conquered prisoner being put on display. He was previously God's enemy but is now defeated (Rom 5:10; see Phil 3:18) and being led to death in a display that reveals the majesty and power of God and effectively proclaims the gospel.[233]

---

[230] C. Breytenbach concludes from all the lexical evidence that this meaning of the verb θριαμβεύω should be excluded ("Paul's Proclamation and God's 'Thriambos' [Notes on 2 Corinthians 2:14–16b]," *Neot* 24 [1990] 265). Other attempts have been made to make meaning of the verb θριαμβεύω fit preconceived notions of what Paul intends in the context. The KJV translates the verb to mean "to cause to triumph"; but this interpretation must be dismissed because, as Thrall puts it, "the linguistic evidence for this meaning is weak ... or nonexistent" (*Second Epistle to the Corinthians,* 1:192). Belleville interprets the verb to mean "to triumph over" and thinks that Paul has in mind that God overcomes "ministerial weaknesses and ineffectiveness" (*2 Corinthians,* 81–82). But this interpretation hardly explains the crowd's mixed response to the supposed conqueror. R. B. Egan interprets the verb to mean "to noise abroad," "to display" and translates it "God who is always making us known ... " (Egan, "Lexical Evidence on Two Pauline Passages," *NovT* 19 [1977] 34–62). So also C. Wolff, who claims that Paul has no intention of portraying himself as a captive (*Der zweite Brief des Paulus an die Korinther,* THKNT, 54–55). But Hafemann challenges Egan's lexical evidence from BGU 1061, which uses ἐκθριαμβίζω which is not necessarily a synonym to θριαμβεύω (*Suffering and Ministry in the Spirit,* 33).

[231] C. Lapide, *The Great Commentary of Cornelius à Lapide: II Corinthians and Galatians,* trans. and ed. W. F. Cobb (London: John Hodges, 1897) 19.

[232] L. Williamson, "Led in Triumph: Paul's Use of *Thriambeuo,*" *Int* 22 (1968) 319. So G. G. Findlay, "St. Paul's Use of ΘΡΙΑΜΒΕΥΩ," Expositor 1st series 10 (1897) 403–2; and Breytenbach, "Paul's Proclamation and God's 'Thriambos,'" 257–71. G. Delling argues that Paul "regards it as a grace that in his fetters he can accompany God always and everywhere ... in the divine triumphal march through the world, even though it be only as the δοῦλος Χριστοῦ" ("θριαμβεύω," *TDNT* 3:160). P. Marshall argues that it is a metaphor of shame ("A Metaphor of Social Shame: ΘΡΙΑΜΒΕΥΕΙΝ in 2 Cor 2:14," *NovT* 25 [1983] 302–17). Seneca used the Latin equivalent in a metaphorical way in criticizing the person who continually harps about the wonderful benefits he has bestowed on another. It crushes his spirit and makes him want to cry out in frustration:

> I owe nothing to you if you saved me in order that you might have someone to exhibit. How long will you refuse to let me forget my misfortune? In a triumph, I should have had to march but once! (*On Benefits* 2.11.1)

[233] Hafemann, *Suffering and Ministry in the Spirit,* 31. He contends that this "grim reality" was not appreciated by biblical scholars (p. 25). See also Furnish, *II Corinthians,* 175.

The metaphor refers to the celebration after a major military victory in which the spoils of war, rolling stages presenting battle scenes, and pictures of the cities that were sacked were paraded on chariots through the city of Rome to the Capitoline hill and the Temple of Jupiter. Most relevant for Paul's use of the image is the train of eminent captives who were marched in chains through the streets to their execution at the end of the route.[234] Plutarch describes a triumphal procession devoted to Aemilius that lasted for three days. The people erected scaffolding around the city to witness the parade while clothed in white garments. "Every temple was open and filled with garlands and incense, while numerous servitors and lictors restrained the thronging crowds and kept the streets open and clear."

> On the third day, as soon as it was morning, trumpeters led the way, sounding out no marching or processional strain, but such as the Romans use to rouse themselves to battle. After these there were led along a hundred and twenty stall-fed oxen with gilded horns, bedecked with fillets and garlands. Those who led these victims to the sacrifice were young men wearing aprons with handsome borders, and boys attended them carrying gold and silver vessels of libation.

Then came the arms and diadem of the captured king, Perseus, in a chariot followed by his children led as slaves,

> and with them a throng of foster-parents, teachers, and tutors, all in tears, stretching out their own hands to the spectators and teaching the children to beg and supplicate. ... Behind the children and their train of attendants walked Perseus himself, clad in a dark robe and wearing the high boots of his country, but the magnitude of his evils made him resemble one who is utterly dumbfounded and bewildered. He, too, was followed by a company of friends and intimates, whose faces were heavy with grief.

The victorious general, Aemilius, came "mounted on a chariot of magnificent adornment wearing 'marks of power.'" He wore "a purple robe interwoven in gold, and held in his right hand a spray of laurel. He was followed by his army singing hymns in praise of the achievements of Aemilius."[235]

---

[234] Seneca refers to being "placed upon a foreign barrow to grace the procession of a proud and brutal victor" (*On the Happy Life* 25.4).

[235] Plutarch, *Lives (Aemilius Paulus)* 6.441–47 (32–34). See also Appian, *Punic Wars 66* 8.66. Dionysius of Halicarnassus describes a triumph: "He accordingly drove into the city with the spoils, the prisoners, and the army that had fought under him, he himself riding in a chariot drawn by horses with golden bridles and being arrayed in the royal robes, as is the custom of the greater triumphs" (VIII.67.9–10; see also IX.36.3, 71.4; and Horace, *Odes* IV.2.50–52). The Arch of Titus, which is still standing, commemorates his triumph over the Jews in A.D. 70. Josephus reports that "the tallest and most handsome of the youth" were selected for the "triumph" (*Wars* 6.9.2 § 41) and that one of the rebel leaders, Simon, son of Gioras, was "reserved for execution at the triumph" (*Wars* 6.9.2 § 433). He then describes the elaborate pageant of victory in Rome, where "not a soul among that countless host in the city was left at home" (*Wars* 7.5.2–6 §§ 122–57).

The image of the triumph was widely known and would have been particularly evocative in a Roman city like Corinth.[236] But how could Paul see himself as a conquered prisoner (now a slave) who is exposed to public ridicule?[237] Writers choose metaphors to stir the imaginations of audiences and to awaken new insight and inspire new wisdom.[238] Paul was a master word painter, using metaphors in creative and arresting ways, as in 3:2, where he pictures the Corinthians themselves as his letter of recommendation written on his heart. The metaphor of the triumph can convey several things at the same time.

1. The imagery presupposes God's prior victory and fits well with Paul's theology that before becoming followers of Christ we were all "enemies of God" (Rom 5:10). Paul himself bemoans his past as a persecutor of the church of God who sought to destroy it (1 Cor 15:9; Gal 1:13). Christ had to conquer him and did.

The purpose of the Roman triumph was to flaunt the power of the victorious army and nation and gods.[239] The celebration reinforced the mythology of "the ruler as the invulnerable victor and guarantor of the world order." The victory was "'proof' of the unique and godlike nature of the ruler" and

---

[236] Marshall points out that "the triumphal procession must have been a familiar institution to Greeks and Romans" since "approximately 350 triumphs are recorded in their literature" and triumphal motifs appear on "arches, reliefs, statues, columns, coins, cups, cameos, medallions, and in paintings and the theatre" ("Metaphor," 304).

[237] Paul uses the verb θριαμβεύω in Col 2:15 to envision God's supernatural enemies stripped, exposed, and led captive by Christ.

[238] K. A. Plank's comment on Paul's ironic metaphors is apropos:

Through the use of symbolic speech a writer taps the potential of language to estrange ordinary images and notions from their expected contexts, thereby jolting readers out of familiar continuities. Arrested by the novelty of symbolic speech, its readers are diverted from their well-defended patterns of thinking and may find their perception of new insight now blocks any retreat into the familiar system of values (*Paul and the Irony of Affliction,* SBLSS [Atlanta: Scholars Press, 1987] 77).

[239] P. Zanker, *The Power of Images in the Age of Augustus,* trans. A. Shapiro (Ann Arbor: University of Michigan Press, 1988) 184–85. H. S. Versnel drew these conclusions from his study of the Roman triumph:

The entire history of Rome has thus been marked by a ceremony which testified to the power of Rome, its mission of conquest and domination, and to the courage of the soldiers. Primarily, however, the triumph characterized the greatness of Rome as being due, on the one hand, to the excellence of the victorious general, and, on the other, to the favor of the supreme God, who, optimus maximus, ensured the continuance and the prosperity of the Roman empire. (*Triumphus: An Inquiry into the Origin, Development and Meaning of the Roman Triumph* [Leiden: Brill, 1970] 1)

Hafemann, who cites this comment, emphasizes that the triumph had a religious dimension in that it was intended to give thanks to the God or gods who granted victory in battle as well as to honor the victorious general or consul. It was therefore an act of worship (*Suffering and Ministry in the Spirit,* 21, 29–30).

reaffirmed for one and all that the gods were on their side.[240] Captured prisoners were exhibited to exalt the might of the triumphant general and bring glory to the gods who won for him the victory. By applying this image to God, Paul asserts that the Roman ruler is *not* the invulnerable victor and guarantor of world order. That role belongs only to the God who is fully revealed in the death and resurrection of Jesus Christ and proclaimed by the apostles. The image points to God's absolute sovereignty over the world. Later in his argument, Paul will say that we have this treasure, the knowledge of God's glory, "in jars of clay to show that this all-surpassing power is from God and not from us" (4:7) and that the purpose of "the grace that is reaching more and more people" is to "cause thanksgiving to overflow to the glory of God" (4:15). Paul pictures himself as a previously defeated enemy of God being led in a triumph that reveals and heralds God's majesty and power.

2. This interpretation also interjects the idea of Paul's suffering and fits the immediate context in which he wishes to justify to the Corinthians his own perils and afflictions, most recently, in Asia and Macedonia. Some Corinthians were overly enamored with power, success, and triumphalism; and to them Paul's suffering exposed his impotence which, in turn, cast doubt on his power as an apostle. This metaphor fits the wider context of his dealings with the Corinthians, who regarded him as a figure of shame, regularly exposed to ridicule. In 1 Cor 4:9–13 he directly confronts their disapproving attitude toward him:

> For it seems to me that God has put us apostles on display at the end of the procession, like men condemned to die in the arena. We have been made a spectacle to the whole universe, to angels as well as to men. We are fools for Christ, but you are so wise in Christ! We are weak, but you are strong! You are honored, we are dishonored! To this very hour we go hungry and thirsty, we are in rags, we are brutally treated, we are homeless. We work hard with our own hands. When we are cursed, we bless; when we are persecuted, we endure it; when we are slandered, we answer kindly. Up to this moment we have become the scum of the earth, the refuse of the world.

He is "always" being led to death (see 4:10); and some in Corinth have asked, How can divine power be revealed in such human adversity and misfortune? They apparently have a myriad of guides (1 Cor 4:17), and the Corinthian dissidents do not see any need to listen to an absent Paul, who did not baptize them, appears so flawed in comparison to others, and seems

---

[240] Josephus concludes his record of the Roman triumph after the defeat of the Jews in A.D. 70 with these words: "The triumphal ceremonies being concluded and the empire of the Romans established on the firmest foundation" (*Wars* 7.5.7 § 158). The ceremony was intended to reassure the populace that Roman rule was rock solid and impregnable.

so handicapped by unrelenting suffering.

Witherington points out the irony that Paul's humble view of himself as God's captured prisoner and slave probably lies at the root of the Corinthians' alienation from him. He contends, "They were looking for a leader powerful in speech, deeds, and personal presence, that is, one who exudes the self-confidence of an agent of God."[241] I would argue, instead, that the Corinthians disputed whether someone who suffered as much as Paul should assert the authority he did in his letters.[242] It is not that they want a more forceful apostle; they question whether one so forceful and bold as Paul is in his letters has the right to be so. Where does he get such authority and boldness to tell them what they must do?

Paul insists that his suffering does not nullify his power as an apostle but that it reveals more clearly the power of God. The central argument in this section is how God's glory is manifest in him through his suffering, and the theme of power through weakness emerges in 4:7–5:10; 6:3–10. Paul asserts through this image of being led in a triumph that God does not make Christ's followers winners, as the world defines winners, but instead captures them and leads them as prisoners in humiliation.[243] But he would rather be God's prisoner and slave than Satan's vice regent in a promenade leading to eternal damnation.

God's gracious and sovereign reign wrests victory from seeming defeat and bestows life instead of death. As Christ triumphed by dying a humiliating death on a cross, Paul triumphs with God as one who has been defeated. With this metaphor, Paul subtly refutes any criticism of his ministry by turning it into a cause for thanks to God. Paul's critics regard him as inferior and weak. He concedes his weakness but will not concede that he is inferior. As God takes the captive Paul in tow in the grand pageant showcasing God's power throughout the world, the knowledge of God emits a distinctive aroma that spreads everywhere. Being set aside as a minister of the new covenant who preaches the gospel gives him his boldness and confidence in wielding his authority (1:9; 3:4,12; 5:11; 7:4,16; 10:1–2,7–8; 13:10).

This striking image of being led as a prisoner "highlights the ambiguity of power and weakness in this world and in so doing deconstructs the trium-

---

[241] Witherington III, *Conflict and Community in Corinth*, 367.

[242] See 1 Cor 4:18–21: "Some of you have become arrogant, as if I were not coming to you. But I will come to you very soon, if the Lord is willing, and then I will find out not only how these arrogant people are talking, but what power they have. For the kingdom of God is not a matter of talk but of power. What do you prefer? Shall I come to you with a whip, or in love and with a gentle spirit?"

[243] Williamson presents a brief history of interpretation of the passage and draws an interesting conclusion that the historical situation of the interpreter—whether they lived in a time when they perceive the gospel clearly triumphing over foes or in a time of persecution or a perceived decline—determines the conclusion ("Led in Triumph," 327–32).

phalistic glorification of success of the 'super apostles.' "[244] Paul has incarnated his apostolic message of the cross of Christ. The cross determines both his message and his style of ministry, and those who preach Christ crucified cannot expect to be crowned with glory by the world which crucified him.

3. The metaphor also fits Paul's self-identification as a slave of Christ.[245] Being captured makes a man a slave, says Dio Chrysostom (*Orations* 15.27).[246] In 5:14 Paul says the love of Christ "constrains" me. The verb *synechō* could also mean "to take or hold captive,"[247] but the striking combination of words makes clear that "Paul is not 'led in triumph' by a vengeful deity." He has been captured by love.[248] That love revealed to him that deliverance can only come from the defeat of the old life. God rescues us by shattering the fortified walls of our own strength, wisdom, and rectitude and making us slaves to Christ. Paul's image therefore accords with what those captured by Christ have recognized through the ages. Martin Luther said: "God creates out of nothing. Therefore until a man is nothing, God can make nothing out of him."

In commenting on 1 Cor 9:16–18, Martin contends that Paul depicts his leadership as slavery and that his authority derives from his association with his master, Christ. This claim to authority differs markedly from the ideas of "the strong" in Corinth who "think of Christian leadership as modeled on the benevolent, free, high-status *sophos*." He rejects their idea of the ideal leader as demagogue and benevolent patriarch who exercises authority from above. Paul exercises his authority from below, which makes it "a more subtle, ambiguous authority that is not based on normal social position and normal status hierarchy."[249]

4. The metaphor may also fit Paul's assurance of God's final rescue. The prisoners of war being exhibited before the crowds knew that they were being led to their execution, which would come when the cavalcade reached

---

[244] C. J. Roetzel, "As Dying, and Behold We Live," *Int* 46 (1992) 11–12. E. Schweizer comments that "the exalted one's victorious march through the world takes place not in a triumphal advance (such that those who belong to him appear as those who hold possession, and give generously from the riches of their power) but in suffering and this fact belongs to the essence of the Lord who is proclaimed in this epistle (2 Cor. 13:3)" (*The Letter to the Colossians,* trans. A. Chester [Minneapolis: Augsburg, 1982] 101).

[245] Rom 1:1; 1 Cor 9:16–23; Gal 1:10; Phil 1:1; Titus 1:1; see 1 Cor 7:22; Eph 6:6; Col 4:12; 2 Tim 2:24.

[246] Paul identifies himself specifically as Christ's captive (Eph 3:1; 4:1; 2 Tim 1:8; Phlm 1, 9; see also "fellow prisoner [of war]," Rom 16:17; Col 4:10; Phlm 23) and as an ambassador in chains (Eph 6:20).

[247] H. Koester, "συνέχω ..." *TDNT* 7:87–89.

[248] P. B. Duff, "The Mind of the Redactor: 2 Cor. 6:14–7:1 in Its Secondary Context," *NovT* 35 (1993) 166.

[249] D. B. Martin, *Slavery as Salvation: The Metaphor of Slavery in Pauline Christianity* (New Haven: Yale University Press, 1990) 135.

its destination. Some were spared, however, in an act of grace by the one celebrating the triumph. Paul knows God as his deliverer and comforter (1:3–7). God has rescued him from death and will rescue him from ultimate death (1:9–10; 11:23). He has been put on display as prime evidence of God's mercy. Consequently, he is not downcast or defeated but gives exuberant thanks to God. His defeat and submission to God does not result in his annihilation but his salvation. He is treated as one who is dying, and yet he lives; as punished, and yet he is not killed (6:9).

Paul's joyous thanks to God derives from his understanding of the paradox of victory in Christ (see 1 Cor 15:57). The image of the conquered slave exhibited as a showpiece of God's triumph matches his assertion in 12:10: "I delight in weaknesses, in insults, in hardships, in persecutions, in difficulties. For when I am weak, then I am strong." His conquest by God actually allows him to take part in God's triumphant march as one now reconciled to God. Paul's theology is remarkable for its sense of paradox.[250] He suffers with Christ in order to be glorified with him (Rom 8:17,37). Victory comes in defeat; glory, in humiliation; and joy, in suffering (Col 1:24). The wise must become fools to become truly wise (1 Cor 3:18); the rich one becomes poor so that the poor might become rich (2 Cor 8:9).

Paul chooses another metaphor in referring to the effects of his being paraded before others. The aroma of the knowledge of him spreads everywhere. The "him" could refer to God or Christ; but since the metaphor of light is used for knowledge of God in 4:6 in the last verse of this section, it is more likely that he refers to knowledge about God.[251] Thrall comments, "Just as perfume spreads everywhere into the atmosphere, so the divine revelation is all-pervading and irresistible."[252] But as in Jesus' parable of the sower, the sower scattered the seed widely, but the soils where it lands are not equally productive. In some soils the seed is destroyed before it can even begin to take root; in others it is destroyed eventually. In Paul's metaphor the gospel's piquant aroma permeates everything so that persons are forced to take notice. But what some find to be a sweet aroma, others regard as a stench.

2:15–16 In 2:14 Paul uses a metaphor that pictures himself being carried around as God's display of Christ to the world. In 2:15 he switches metaphors to affirm that he carries around the aroma of Christ pleasing to God.[253] The noun changes from "fragrance" *(osmē),* a neutral term referring

---

[250] Williamson, "Led in Triumph," 325.

[251] The genitive is more likely an objective genitive, "knowledge about him," than a genitive of source, "an aroma which comes from knowing him," or a genitive of apposition, "fragrance which is knowing him" (see 1:22).

[252] Thrall, *Second Epistle to the Corinthians,* 1:197.

[253] Savage, *Power through Weakness,* 104.

to a smell of any kind, in 2:14, to "aroma" *(euōdia)* which refers to a sweet savor aromatic, in 2:15, and back to "fragrance" *(osmē)* in 2:16. Paul is not the source of the aroma. It comes from his message about the cross of Christ.

This image most probably derives from Paul's adaptation of the cultic language of the Old Testament.[254] After the flood, the pleasing aroma of Noah's sacrifice aroused in God a benevolent disposition toward humankind (Gen 8:20–22). But it is the self-offering of Christ on the cross that Paul believes has replaced all sacrifices: "Christ loved us and gave himself up for us as a fragrant offering and sacrifice to God" (Eph 5:2; see 2 Cor 5:21). This sacrifice that shows God's love for us is the sum and substance of Paul's preaching. The smell of death therefore permeates Paul's preaching and ministry.[255] What was seen in Jesus can now be seen in Paul—namely the suffering that gives his ministry divine confirmation. The key phrase is "to God." Paul only cares that all he does is well-pleasing to God.

The image of a sweet aroma could have other associations in Paul's culture, and his first readers would have made the connections. In ancient religious ceremonies, fragrances conveyed the ethereal yet keenly sensed presence of the deity. During religious festivals when the image and accouterments associated with a deity were carted through cities in processionals, cult personnel would spread incense or other aromatic substances along the way to announce the approach of the deity.[256] Duff suggests that as "the pleasing fragrance of Christ" Paul "depicts himself as the harbinger of the deity's presence because it is through him that 'the knowledge of God' is made known" (see 4:6).[257] Paul will write later that God is making his appeal through us as ambassadors of Christ (5:20).

---

[254] Among the eighty appearances of the noun ὀσμή in the LXX, see Lev 1:9,13,17; 2:9,12; 3:5,16; 4:31; 6:15,21; 8:21,28; 17:6; 23:13,18; 26:31. The OT is more likely as the foreground for understanding this term than the use of incense bearers along the Roman victor's route (see Appian, *Punic Wars* 66), though such an allusion would accord with the picture of the triumph (so Breytenbach, "Paul's Proclamation," 265–69). Hafemann argues that the terms "aroma" and "sweet fragrance" (εὐωδία) have been merged in meaning and function together as a metonymy for the idea of sacrifice (*Suffering and Ministry in the Spirit,* 40). Thrall points out that there is a complex web of associations behind the image drawing "from ideas of sacrifice, Torah, and Wisdom, and combining motifs from each" (*Second Epistle to the Corinthians,* 1:207). Nevertheless, the idea of "sacrifice is primary."

[255] He sees himself in the priestly service of the gospel of God and hopes that the Gentiles whom he wins might be "an offering acceptable to God, sanctified by the Holy Spirit" (Rom 15:16). He conceives his own possible death as a sacrifice to God (Phil 2:17–18), but he does not use the same terminology, ὀσμή εὐωδίας, as he does for Christ's death in Eph 5:2.

[256] Apuleius, *Metamorphosis (The Golden Ass)* 11.9 provides a good description of such a procession.

[257] Duff, "The Mind of the Redactor," 168–69.

Paul expresses his thought in 2:15–16 with a chiasm:[258]

among those being saved	among those being destroyed
to the one the smell *(osmē)* of death	to the other the smell *(osmē)* of life

The message of the gospel creates a crisis of decision that does not allow anyone to remain neutral or to take a wait-and-see attitude. In 1 Cor 1:18 he makes a similar appraisal: to some who are being destroyed the word of the cross is foolishness, but to others who are being saved it is the power of God. How persons respond to the gospel determines whether their final fate is eternal life or eternal death. The use of the present participles, "those who are being saved" *(tois sōzomenois)* and "those who are perishing" *(tois apollumenois)* would argue against any idea that they have been predestined for one or the other.[259] They are being saved or destroyed because they choose to accept or reject the message.

We do not normally think about an odor producing death or life, but such an idea did conform to ancient perceptions.[260] We are aware that smells may warn of something deadly or attract us in some way. Paul says that to some we reek of death. It is not surprising, since his message is Christ crucified and he himself is always being given up to death for Jesus's sake (4:11).

The NIV perhaps misses a nuance of meaning by translating the phrases that read literally "the smell from death to death" *(osmē ek thanatou eis thanaton)* and "the smell from life to life" *(osmē ek zōēs eis zōēn)* as simply "the smell of death" and "the fragrance of life." Paul may have more in mind than simply a deadly odor or life-giving fragrance. The preposition *ek* refers to the source or nature of the apostolic message; the preposition *eis* refers to the results. Clement of Alexandria interpreted the phrases to mean that unbelievers regard the preaching of Christ's death on a cross as foolishness or a stumbling block (1 Cor 1:18,23) and that this response results in their own death. Believers, on the other hand, do not view the cross as merely death but as something that offers them life, and this response leads to greater life.[261] Paul

---

[258] M. Carrez does not see a chiasm in 2:15–16. He contends that the phrases are parallel and that the smell has positive results for both groups. One is converted by the power of Christ's death; the other by the power of Christ's life (*La Deuxième Épitre de Saint Paul aux Corinthiens, Commentaire du Nouveau Testament*, 2d ed. [Geneva: Labor et Fides, 1986] 79–80).

[259] F. Filson states: "Paul does not say how this happens, but only states the fact" ("II Corinthians," *IB* [Nashville: Abingdon, 1953] 10:301).

[260] See G. Delling, "ὀσμή," *TDNT* 5:493–94.

[261] Lapide, *The Great Commentary of Cornelius à Lapide,* 22. Some argue that the idiom reflects a Semitic superlative: "the stench of ultimate death" (so Furnish, *II Corinthians,* 177). Cp. 3:18; 4:17; and Rom 1:17. Belleville contends that the emphasis is on a progression: it goes from bad to worse or from good to better. "To those who are on the road to destruction the gospel is like a noxious fume that relentlessly carries the unwary to their death. To those on the road to salvation it is comparable to a compelling fragrance that invigorates all who come in contact with it" (*2 Corinthians,* 84).

concedes that many already have and will continue to disdain him, recoiling at the acrid stench of death that seems to hang over his ministry. But Lapide cites an epigram from Martial: "He smells not sweet who always smells sweet." The aphorism implies that the person who smells sweet all the time is trying to cover up some shameful foulness with some artificial scent.

Paul does not smell sweet to everyone, and he cautions his readers not to dismiss him. He always carries around the death of Jesus (4:10), and only those who are perishing are repelled by his message and by the messenger. To God, however, his ministry emits the sweet aroma of Christ's loving sacrifice. To those who are being saved, it is redolent of the life assured them by God (see 5:4; Rom 5:21; 6:23).[262] If any in Corinth disdain his apostolic suffering, weakness, or close acquaintance with death, then perhaps they have not fully understood the gospel or the significance of Christ's death.

The awesome responsibility of preaching a message that has such eternal consequences for others is a heavy burden to bear. For some, the word about Christ opens up the way of life; for others, the same word causes them to become even more hardened in their resistance to God and destines them for destruction. Harvey recognizes that "to speak of oneself in terms of being an agent of God for life or death, a kind of litmus paper to distinguish between good and evil, is to make an enormous claim—that one's motives are perfectly clear, that one is totally transparent to the purposes of God."[263] Paul asks, Who is equal to it? The noun "equal" *(hikanos)* means "to be sufficient, large enough, or large in number or quantity, and also more generally to be fit, appropriate, competent, qualified, able or worthy."[264] Paul does not give a direct answer to the question because it may seem obvious. No human could ever hope to be sufficient in himself for such a trust. Nevertheless, Paul implies that he is fully sufficient for these things, but only by the grace of God. His own afflictions in God's service have taught him that he cannot rely on himself but only on God, who raises the dead. His confidence therefore rests in faith that God gave him his ministry in the *new* covenant (see 1 Cor 15:9; Col 1:12), and when God gives one such a ministry, God also bestows the necessary sufficiency to discharge it.

Since Paul compares himself with Moses in what follows, he may be alluding to the qualms voiced by Moses when God called him to lead Israel out of bondage. In the interpretive translation of the LXX, Moses says, "I am not worthy" *(hikanos* or sufficient; Exod 4:10). God responds by assuring him that the "one who gave a mouth to man" will "open your

---

[262] The rabbis viewed the law as an odor of life (*b. Taʿan.* 7a; *b. Yoma* 72b; *b. Šabb.* 88b; *b. ʿErub.* 54a), but Paul argues that the law, when it is misread, can only be associated with death.

[263] Harvey, *Renewal through Suffering,* 46.

[264] See K. H. Rengstorf, "ἱκανός," *TDNT* 3:293–96; F. T. Fallon, "Self-Sufficiency or God's Sufficiency," *HTR* 76 (1983) 369–74.

mouth" and will "teach you what you are to say" (Exod 4:11–12).[265] In Paul's case God does much the same (see 12:9). God chooses him despite his personal insufficiency and gives him a divine sufficiency to fulfill the task assigned him. But Paul will go on to say that God works through him in a far more glorious way than God ever did through Moses because the ministry of the Spirit is far more glorious. As he did with Moses, God supplies the sufficiency, and it applies to the persuasion of his words and the power of his actions. The comparison, however, breaks down, and Paul will argue for a stark contrast between himself and Moses that derives primarily from his service in the new and greater ministry of the Spirit.

Many have concluded that Paul is defending himself against Corinthian opponents who question his competence as an apostle. But the Corinthians do not question that he is a legitimate apostle.[266] It is his style and his behavior as an apostle that they challenge. The question that he answers in this section (2:14–7:3) is: "What is the source of his boldness?" (3:4,12; see 10:10), not, "Is he a legitimate apostle compared with others?"

He gives the following answers to this question. He addresses them boldly because:

1. He speaks the truth as one commissioned by God who ministers in the fear of God (2:17; 3:5; 4:1–2; 5:9–10).

2. He brought the church into existence, and they are therefore his letter of recommendation written on his heart (3:2). They are his beloved children, and he has the right to admonish them as such (see 6:13; 1 Cor 4:14–15).

3. God has made him sufficient because his ministry comes through Christ toward God. It has an even greater glory than that of Moses because it is a ministry of the Spirit (3:4–18). His "boldness" does not derive from empty pride, megalomania, or a false sense of self-importance but from the splendor of the ministry he serves.

4. He does not proclaim himself but Jesus Christ as Lord (4:5–6), and the love of Christ compels him in what he does (5:14).

5. He speaks boldly because of his confidence that God works through all deadly experiences in his own life to bring life and glory to others (4:7–18; 6:2–10).

6. His sole aim is to please God (5:9–10), and he knows that God makes

---

[265] See further S. J. Hafemann, *Paul, Moses, and the History of Israel: The Letter/Spirit Contrast and the Argument from Scripture in 2 Corinthians 3* (Peabody: Hendrickson, 1996) 42–47.

[266] There is no reason to believe that the interlopers introduced such terminology, as is argued by D. Georgi, *The Opponents of Paul in Second Corinthians* (Philadelphia: Fortress, 1986). Paul says he is not "worthy" (ἱκανός) to be called an apostle in 1 Cor 15:9 long before the opponents appeared on the scene (see Matt 3:11; 8:8; Luke 7:6). Furnish points to the presence of similar terminology in Hellenistic Judaism (*II Corinthians*, 196).

his appeal to them through him (5:20) and that he works together with God in making his entreaties to them (6:1).

2:17 The word translated "peddle" (*kapēleuō*) by the NIV does not mean "to corrupt," "to water down," "to falsify," or as the REB renders it: "We are not adulterating the word of God for profit as so many do."[267] Hafemann's reexamination of the primary evidence shows that Paul refers to "selling the Word of God as a retail dealer sells his wares in the market."[268] Paul avows that he does not treat his apostolic calling as a trade, and his refusal to accept material gain from his preaching the gospel was well known to the Corinthians and a sore spot with them (1 Cor 9:3–18; 2 Cor 11:7–11). He was not simply in "the business of preaching ... without any ultimate concern."[269] His ministry has ultimate significance both for himself and the world. He does not "market" the gospel with an eye for the bottom line. To survive in the marketplace the peddler must adapt to the market either by making sure that he has what people want to buy or by tricking them into thinking that they want to buy what the peddler has to sell.

Paul also may be contrasting himself with the professional rhetorician. In Petronius's *Satyricon* a teacher of rhetoric tries to defend his means of earning his bread:

> When spongers are trying to get a dinner out of their rich friends, their main object is to find out what they would most like to hear. The only way they will get what they are after is by winning over their audience. It is the same with a tutor of rhetoric. Like a fisherman he has to bait his hook with what he knows the little fishes will rise for; otherwise he's left on the rocks without a hope of their biting.[270]

Although the verb "to peddle" means simply "to engage in retail business," it was associated with deceptiveness and greedy motives. Isaiah

---

[267] So Windisch, *Der zweite Korintherbrief,* 100. T. E. Provence writes: "The 'watered' down gospel of the 'many' was neither offensive enough to lead to destruction nor powerful enough to lead to salvation (cf. I Cor. i 18). Paul's gospel was such a word, however, since it was a pure gospel from God" ("'Who Is Sufficient for These Things?' An Exegesis of 2 Corinthians ii 15–iii 18," *NovT* 24 [1982] 59).

[268] Hafemann, *Suffering and Ministry in the Spirit,* 106–25 (p. 124). He argues that Paul does not take aim at opponents with this statement but instead is making a positive assertion about his own ministry. It prepares for his opposing practice of supporting himself and not charging for his preaching (p. 161). There is nothing wrong with receiving payment for teaching in principle (1 Cor 9:6–12), but Paul may have believed that the very nature of the gospel he received freely from God required that it be given without pay to unbelievers (Matt 10:8).

[269] J. I. H. McDonald, "Paul and the Preaching Ministry: A Reconsideration of 2 Cor 2:14–17 in Its Context," *JSNT* 17 (1983) 42.

[270] Petronius, *Satyricon* 3, cited from J. P. Sullivan, trans., *Petronius, the Satyricon, and Seneca, the Apocolocyntosis* (New York: Penguin, 1965) 30.

decries the sellers who dilute wine with water (Isa 1:22, LXX).[271] Sirach cynically expresses the view that

> A merchant can hardly keep from wrongdoing,
> nor is a tradesman innocent of sin. (*Sir* 26:29).

Paul may have intended the image of peddling to evoke connotations of fleecing unsuspecting buyers in some way by charging too much, misrepresenting what is sold, or tampering with the wares in some way.[272] In 4:2 Paul insists that he has "renounced disgraceful, underhanded ways." Paul's ministry is not driven by an eye for the bottom line; he does not "do deals." The gospel he preaches is the unvarnished truth. He commends himself as a man of sincerity, who, before God, speaks in Christ with confidence (3:4) and boldness (3:12). If, as we believe, Paul is defending his bold speech to the Corinthians, then he implies that he is not some vendor trying only to move the merchandise while compromising ethical principles just to make a sale. He can be honest, blunt, and forthright because he is not concerned for profit margins or market share. He does not water down his directives to make them more palatable or comfortable for the disobedient in Corinth.

"The many" need not be a reference to some particular group but may be a contemptuous reference to "the mob of teachers."[273] The description can apply to both Christian or pagan teachers. Concern for money undermines their sincerity as they tailor their teaching to the audience. It causes them to cultivate those with money and leads them to be preoccupied with success. By contrast (1) Paul speaks as one who is sincere (see 1:12). His manner and methods are determined entirely by God's grace in his life,

---

[271] Fredrickson cites T. Kleberg (*Hôtels, restaurants et cabarets dans l'antiquité romaine: Études historique et philologique, Bibliotheca Ekmaniana Universitatis Regiae Upsaliensis 61* [Upssala: Almqvist & Wiksell, 1957] 1–6) for evidence that the word κάπηλος (merchant) was used to designate innkeepers who were notorious for adulterating wine. Thus the word had become a cliché for deception ("ΠΑΡΡΗΣΙΑ," 174).

[272] Thrall contends that "the verb conjures up the image of the petty trader who was suspected of dishonest dealing, and a stock form of dishonesty was the adulteration of the product, self-evidently from motives of greed" (*Second Epistle to the Corinthians*, 1:214). Furnish makes the same argument: "The ancient stereotype of the merchant was of a person concerned only for profit and quite willing to adulterate the product or give short measure for the sake of it" (*II Corinthians*, 178). B. W. Winter provides a helpful portrait of sophists in Alexandria and Corinth that reveals "their insatiable appetite for wealth." From the time of Plato, their greed was proverbial. Plato asked (*Protagoras* 313 c–d): "Can it be … that the sophist is really a sort of merchant or dealer in provisions on which the soul is nourished … ? And in the same way, those who take their doctrines round of the cities, hawking them about to any odd purchaser who desires them" (*Philo and Paul Among the Sophists*, SNTSMS 96 [Cambridge: University Press, 1997] 163–64).

[273] Plummer, *Second Epistle of St. Paul to the Corinthians*, 73.

not by worldly cunning.[274] (2) He speaks as one whose message comes "from God." (3) He speaks before God (4:2; 12:19) knowing that he will be judged by God. (4) He speaks as one who is "in Christ." Speaking in Christ (12:19; 13:3) is synonymous with being taught by the Spirit (1 Cor 2:13; 7:40; 12:3; 2 Cor 4:13). What follows is Paul's bid to establish in his converts' minds not only the sufficiency of his ministry but its superiority. This ministry is centered on Christ and is bold in its open proclamation of Christ.

THE CORINTHIANS AS PAUL'S LETTER (3:1–3). When others may criticize one's ministry, one needs a clear measuring rod by which to appraise oneself before God. The critics will try to impose their own measuring rods to gauge the minister. If the minister is to remain faithful to God's calling, then only God's standards matter. In the face of the Corinthians' challenge, Paul shows that he has a keen understanding of his place in God's scheme of things. He knows *whose* he is, and consequently he knows *who* he is, a minister of the new covenant whom God made sufficient for his task.

3:1 In 3:1 Paul broaches the topic of commendation that reappears throughout the letter.[275] At first glance "commending oneself" would seem to point to some kind of self-boasting. The "again" would suggest that someone in Corinth has already accused Paul of being too boastful and that his protest that he is not commending himself betrays his touchiness about the subject. Thus he wants to check any possible criticism that he might be reverting to his so-called penchant to vaunt his own authority.[276] But the verb "to commend" *(synistanein)* does not mean "to boast," "to extol," or "to exalt." "Commendation" needs to be understood in the context of friendship and recommendation in the ancient world. Paul does not use self-commendation in a negative sense to mean self-applause. Marshall shows that it refers to a recognized way of establishing friendships:

> ... self-commendation was an accepted and common convention which differs little from written commendation by third parties. Praise or complimentary phraseology is a traditional though not essential element of both third party and self-commendation and was acceptable if done inoffensively; even extravagant

---

[274] Plutarch, *Precepts of Statecraft* (*Moralia* 802F–803A) says that the speech of a statesman must be full of unaffected character, true high mindedness, a "father's frankness, foresight, and thoughtful concern for others" (cited by S. B. Marrow, "*Parrhsia* in the New Testament," *CBQ* 44 [1982] 443–44).

[275] The verb συνιστάνειν and the adjective συστάτικος appear in 3:1; 4:2; 5:12; 6:4; 7:11; 10:12,18; and 12:11.

[276] P. E. Hughes contends that Paul is ironically and sarcastically referring to the intruders with this question (*Paul's Second Epistle to the Corinthians,* NICNT [Grand Rapids: Eerdmans, 1962] 85). Many conclude that the Corinthians have accused Paul of recommending himself (so, e.g., Furnish, *II Corinthians,* 245).

praise by a recommender was acceptable, especially if the recommended proved himself to be worthy of it.[277]

Self-commendation is therefore equivalent to self-introduction. The REB comes closer to this technical sense of the verb with its translation: "Are we beginning all over again to produce our credentials?" Marshall shows that "self-commendation was a common form of recommendation in which a person committed himself to another, with or without the aid of mutual connections, with the intention of forming a reciprocal relationship based on trust."[278] In self-commendation the person does more than simply introduce himself; he entrusts himself to the other. The practice of commendation is therefore not a moral issue but a social one.[279] The "again" in 3:1 refers to Paul's initial visit to Corinth, when he "entrusted himself to his first converts or Christian contacts."[280] When Paul sought out hosts in the various places where he established his ministry, he probably followed the normal convention of self-commendation, which established bonds of trust.[281] In his first visit he solidified his friendship with them by entrusting himself in person rather than presenting them with written letters from third parties.

Recent dissension has buffeted the original relationship between Paul and the Corinthians, and some in Corinth may have blamed him for the breach. If he were to commend himself to them again, he would be admitting that he had done something to jeopardize the friendship and must do something now to regain their trust.[282] Rather than Paul's having to reestablish the ties of friend-

---

[277] Marshall, *Enmity in Corinth,* 266–67. On the practice of commendation in the ancient world, see pp. 268–71. Romans is Paul's letter of self-introduction to the Roman congregation. When he writes to Rome to lay the groundwork for a mission to Spain, he recognizes that he will be going to an established church outside of his orbit of influence. But he does not gather kudos from others; instead, he lays out the gospel that he preaches so they can see for themselves his insight into the mysteries of God.

[278] Ibid., 268.

[279] Recognition of this social context for commendation obviates any need to try to explain Paul's apparent contradictions regarding his statements about self-commendation in this letter by arguing that he has in mind egotistical self-applause in one instance and legitimate self-recommendation in another. Some have argued that ἑαυτὸν συνιστάνειν (3:1; 5:12; 10:12,18) with the pronoun placed before the verb is egotistical commendation, but when it is placed after the verb, it is legitimate commendation (so J. H. Bernard, "The Second Epistle to the Corinthians," in *The Expositors Greek Testament,* ed. W. R. Nicoll (Grand Rapids: Eerdmans, 1967) 53; see also Plummer, *The Second Epistle of St. Paul to the Corinthians,* 77.

[280] Marshall, *Enmity in Corinth,* 271.

[281] Ibid., 271–72.

[282] Ibid., 272–73. Thrall agrees that Paul rejects the idea of having to repeat the process of self-introduction all over again let alone the necessity of bringing in testimonials from third parties (*Second Epistle to the Corinthians,* 1:218). This interpretation means that Paul is not taking aim at rivals; his purpose in these verses is not polemical but apologetic (Thrall, *Second Epistle to the Corinthians,* 1:221). She correctly dismisses Georgi's contention that this section is polemical as "purely speculative: he is not able to produce any examples of the kind of letter he has in mind."

ship by commending himself to them again (3:1; 5:12), the Corinthians should have commended him as their apostle because they have witnessed and have been the beneficiaries of his apostolic work (3:2–3; 12:11). His life and work are an open book, and he has always acted with godly sincerity and love toward them (1:12; 2:17). He never transferred his affections for them to someone else (2:4; 6:11–13; 7:2–4; 11:11; 12:15). He will make the point, however, that God is the one who ultimately knows him best and commends apostles (5:11–12; 10:12,18). Human endorsements do not make apostles. Consequently, Paul seeks only God's commendation (10:18) and evaluates his apostleship according to the measure God assigned to him ("measured him"; 10:13). He firmly believes that "God's recommendation of him was indelibly written by the Spirit and, with regard to them, could not be withdrawn (3:3)."[283] That explains why he does not try to conceal his humiliations, afflictions, hardships, or faults (1 Cor 4:9–13; 2 Cor 4:8–9; 6:4–10; 11:23–33) as others might. Instead, he boasts of his deficiencies (11:30; 12:9) because they show most clearly how the power of God works in and through him.

This background explains why Paul frames his question, "We do not need letters of recommendation to you or from you as certain ones do, do we?" to expect the answer no. Paul does not disdain letters of recommendation.[284] They were an essential part of initiating and fostering friendship in the ancient world. Letters were the usual means to introduce fellow Christians to one another as they traveled around the world.[285] Paul is therefore not engaged in a polemic against those who flaunt their own laudatory letters of recommendation.[286] But the whole issue causes him some pain. In a rueful

---

[283] Marshall, *Enmity in Corinth,* 273.

[284] On letters of recommendation, see Marshall, *Enmity in Corinth,* 90–129; and C. H. Kim, *Form and Structure of the Familiar Greek Letter of Recommendation,* SBLDS 4 (Missoula: Scholars Press, 1972).

[285] It is noteworthy that Apollos was sent to Achaia with a letter of recommendation (Acts 18:27) and that Paul includes a recommendation of others in this letter (8:16–24). Other examples of letters of recommendation in the NT are Acts 9:2; 15:23–29; 18:27; 21:25; 22:5; Rom 16:1–2; 1 Cor 16:3,10; Phil 2:19–23; Col 4:7–9; and Phlm.

[286] In 10:12 the interlopers are referred to with the same indefinite plural pronoun, "certain ones" (τινες). If the "certain ones" mentioned in 3:1 is an allusion to his rivals who brought letters from others to establish their relationship with the Corinthians, Paul does not object to the practice but to the nature of the relationship resulting from their letters. They sought by their friendship to oppose and exclude him (Marshall, *Enmity in Corinth,* 128). Belleville maintains that Paul did not use letters "because the only letter of reference that a preacher of the gospel can bring to an unevangelized field like Corinth is the presence and power of the Spirit working to convince the listener of the truths of the gospel message (v. 3)" ("Paul's Polemic and Theology of the Spirit in Second Corinthians," *CBQ* 58 [1996] 290). The key word is "unevangelized field." A letter of recommendation from another Christian would hardly have any influence on those who were not Christians. This does not mean that he looked askance at the practice of letters of commendation or self-commendation.

tone he basically asks them: "Has our relationship sunk to such a low that I must now call upon outside parties to vouch for me?"

3:2 Paul contends that he needs no letters with them because they are his letter of commendation. The imagery again is striking. Instead of something written on paper with pen and ink, he pictures a divine letter inscribed on human hearts by the Spirit of the living God.[287] The Corinthians are Paul's letter to the world, having been engraved on his heart, known and read by everyone. Moule aptly comments that Paul's credentials "are not on paper but in persons."[288] Today most people in churches recognize that it is not the degrees earned that truly commend a minister but rather the degree of concern for the lives of others and the willingness to sacrifice for them.

It may seem unusual that Paul refers to a letter written on "our hearts" rather than on the Corinthians' heart.[289] But the one who was recommended frequently carried the letter of recommendation with him.[290] Paul carries around in his heart the memory of their response to his preaching. This metaphor expresses his love for the community while providing unequivocal proof of his legitimacy at the same time. Paul appeals to the results of his preaching in Corinth. God alone can provide the validation of his ministry. Indeed, God wrote a letter for him in the sense that God's power, through the

---

[287] The metaphor excludes some natural force at work (J. Murphy-O'Connor, *Paul on Preaching* [New York: Sheed & Ward, 1963] 78.

[288] C. F. D. Moule, "2 Cor 3:18b," in *Neues Testament und Geschichte,* ed. H. Baltensweiler and B. Reicke (Tübingen: Mohr [Siebeck], 1972) 232.

[289] A textual variant reads "your hearts." This reading is more weakly attested (א 33 88 436 1175 1881). But some scholars make a case for it by arguing that it fits the context better. If the Corinthians want a letter (see "to you," 3:1), they already have it on their hearts. Harvey, e.g., argues: "If a letter of commendation had been written in the Corinthians' hearts as a result of his work among them, and if this could be described in terms of the 'new covenant' prophesied by Jeremiah as written on human hearts, then Paul himself could be regarded as an agent in the process of moving people on from laws in stone to spontaneous obedience: he was a 'minister of the new covenant'" (*Renewal through Suffering,* 47–48; see also Bultmann, *The Second Letter to the Corinthians;* Barrett, *The Second Epistle to the Corinthians,* 96; J. Murphy-O'Connor, *The Theology of the Second Letter to the Corinthians* (Cambridge: University Press, 1991) 32, n. 23; and Thrall, *Second Epistle to the Corinthians,* 1:224). But R. B. Sloan, Jr. argues that the passage from Jeremiah affirming that God will write the law on the people's hearts should not determine the meaning of 2 Cor 3:2–3. He insists that Paul refers to something written on his own heart, not the Corinthians' ("2 Corinthians 2:14–4:6 and 'New Covenant Hermeneutics'—A Response to Richard Hays," *BBR* 5 [1995] 135–36). The reading "our hearts" has early textual support with a wide geographical distribution (p46 A B C D G K P Ψ 614 1739 it vg syrᵖ ʰ cop). Some have asked how a letter written on Paul's heart could be read by others. This question would seem to make "our hearts" the hardest reading, and a scribe may have changed it in an attempt to clarify the text. On the other hand, it may have been an accidental change since both words "ours" (ἡμῶν) and "yours" (ὑμῶν) were pronounced the same.

[290] Wolff, *Der zweite Brief des Paulus an die Korinther,* 58, n. 44; citing C. W. Keyes, "The Greek Letter of Introduction," *American Journal of Philology* 56 (1935) 28–44.

Spirit, founded the church when they responded to Paul's preaching of the gospel (see 1 Cor 3:6). He does have a letter, so to speak, in the Corinthians themselves; their very existence is divine testimony to power of his apostleship. Hays writes, "They cannot question the legitimacy of his ministry without simultaneously questioning the legitimacy of their own origins as a community."[291] Consequently, Paul regards the Corinthians as his "workmanship in the Lord" and "the seal of his apostleship in the Lord" (1 Cor 9:1–2). Such language shows that Paul was never satisfied to make quick converts and then quit the scene. His life became intertwined with theirs.

A letter written in pen and ink is visible to only a few; this letter is visible to all. Paul's use of the perfect participle, *eggegramenē* ("having been inscribed"), suggests that this letter differs significantly from "ephemeral human recommendations."[292] The switch to participles in the present tense "being known and read" implies that this letter is being known and read by all who encounter him in his itinerant service for the gospel.[293] Only those who are not looking for marvelous spiritual exploits, however, will be able to read and understand this letter.

3:3 Paul gives four characteristics of the letter in this verse. First, it is a letter from Christ.[294] Others may have letters, but these letters have a human author. Since the Corinthians are his letter and they were created in Christ, Paul has a letter written by the highest authority.

Second, this letter is related to Paul's ministry. The phrase translated "the result of our ministry" reads literally "being ministered by us" (*diakonētheisa hyph' hymōn*). The variety of translations of this phrase show that this image can be taken in different ways. (1) Some interpret it to mean that Paul "delivered" the letter (RSV, REB). He is not the letter's writer or recipient, only its courier.[295] The letter written by Christ recommends its bearer as an authorized minister of the gospel. But it is unlikely that Paul would understand himself to be the substance of the letter. (2) This image is also taken to imply that the apostle was Christ's amanuensis ("prepared by us," NRSV),

---

[291] R. B. Hays, *Echoes of Scripture in the Letters of Paul* (New Haven: Yale University Press, 1989) 127.

[292] E. Richard, "Polemics, Old Testament, and Theology: A Study of II Cor. III,1–IV,6," *RB* 88 (1981) 346.

[293] In the Greek text the words translated "know" and "read" in English are cognates, γινώσκω, ἀναγινώσκω. "To read" means "to know again."

[294] The NIV translates the verb φανερούμενοι as a middle voice, "you show that," but it could also be taken as passive, "you are shown to be." The NIV also interprets ἐπιστολὴ Χριστοῦ as a genitive of origin, "letter from Christ." Less likely options interpret the phrase as a possessive, a letter belonging to Christ, which would seem to mean that they are Christians, or as an objective genitive, "a letter that tells of Christ."

[295] W. Baird, "Letters of Recommendation: A Study of II Cor 3:1–3," *JBL* 80 (1961) 166–72. See the criticism of Baird's thesis in Hafemann, *Suffering and Ministry in the Spirit,* 200–205.

but Paul explicitly states that the letter is written by the Spirit. (3) The translation "ministered by us" is to be preferred because it implies that Paul is instrumental in producing and delivering the letter without specifying how.[296] The verb "to minister" and the nouns "minister" and "ministry" refer to Paul's work for the gospel.[297] In context it refers to Paul's founding of the Corinthian church. He fulfilled the task entrusted to him.[298] The expression "ministered" anticipates Paul's arguments in what follows about his role as a minister of the new covenant (3:6, *diakonos*) and the ministry of the Spirit and of righteousness (3:8–9, *diakonia*).

Third, Paul says that this letter was inscribed by the Spirit of the living God. Fourth, he draws a contrast between what is written with ink and what is written by the Spirit. It is implanted into hearts made receptive by the Spirit. When ink is written on a page of paper, the page receives the image but makes no response. The letters remain only lifeless squiggles unless there is something to make sense of them and to respond to them.[299] A response comes only from human hearts in which the words are sown, take root, and produce fruit. As letters of Christ, they are to communicate to the world what God has done in Christ and what God's purposes are for humanity and this world.

Paul goes on to draw a contrast between fleshy hearts and stone tablets. Papyrus or parchment would seem to be a more appropriate comparison at this point, since letters of recommendation would hardly have been etched in stone. But Paul chooses stones because he will draw a comparison between his ministry for Christ and Moses' ministry for the law. His primary concern is to give the grounds for "the confidence we have through Christ before God" (3:4), and he wants to contrast the giving of the law that was engraved on stones (Exod 24:12; 31:18; 32:15–16; 34:1; Deut 9:10) with the promise of the new covenant that will be inscribed on hearts. God prefers living hearts to dead stones because they can better communicate what the purposes of the living God are for humanity and what the presence of the life-giving Spirit can do. In composing 3:3, Paul appears to have drawn on more than one Old Testament text in which he interprets Scripture by Scripture.

---

[296] Thrall, *Second Epistle to the Corinthians*, 1:225.

[297] διακονέω (3:3; 8:19–20); διακονία (3:7–9; 4:1; 5:18; 6:3; 8:4; 9:1,12–13; 11:8) (see Rom 11:13); διάκονος (3:6; 6:4; 11:15,23; see also 1 Cor 3:5; Eph 3:7; Col 1:23,25). Sloan argues that "by his apostolic ministry, his preaching of the gospel, Paul "writes" the letter, which is the Corinthians. He, as the founder of the church and God's διάκονος—the real author after all is Christ and/or the Spirit—brings them as a "letter" into existence" ("New Covenant Hermeneutics," 136).

[298] Hafemann, *Suffering and Ministry in the Spirit,* 204.

[299] Hays writes, "The script ... remains abstract and dead because it is not embodied" (*Echoes of Scripture in the Letters of Paul*, 131).

"When the LORD finished speaking to Moses on Mount Sinai, he gave him the two tablets of the Testimony, the tablets of stone inscribed by the finger of God." Exod 31:18

"I will give them an undivided heart and put a new spirit in them; I will remove from them their heart of stone and give them a heart of flesh." Ezek 11:19

"I will give you a new heart and put a new spirit in you; I will remove from you your heart of stone and give you a heart of flesh." Ezek 36:26

"This is the covenant which I will make with the house of Israel after those days, says the LORD: I will put my law within them, and I will write it upon their hearts; and I will be their God and they will be my people." Jer 31:33[300]

Hafemann contends that the contrast between stones and hearts is not, as is so often argued, one between the external and the internal, between ritualism and spirituality, or between law and gospel. We should not automatically assume that the reference to stone tablets is a negative image. "Written on stone tablets" was the standard expression used to describe the revelation given to Moses on Mount Sinai and stemmed from the biblical account of the giving of the law. In a Jewish context it was a hallmark of the law's glory, underscoring its divine origin and "its everlasting permanence and certainty."[301] Paul may not use the phrase with the same honorific sense it has in rabbinic literature, but it would fit his assertion that the law came in glory (3:7,9,11).

Thrall counters that in some contexts "literal inscriptions and actual writing were regarded as inferior means of communicating knowledge, ensuring memory, and the like. What counted was the inward memorial, and the inward understanding of virtue in the heart and mind."[302] She thinks "it scarcely seems possible to deny that the phrase 'stone tablets' in the present

---

[300] See also Exod 32:15: "Moses turned and went down the mountain with the two tablets of the Testimony in his hands. They were inscribed on both sides, front and back." According to Deut 9:10–11: "The LORD gave me two stone tablets inscribed by the finger of God. On them were all the commandments the LORD proclaimed to you on the mountain out of the fire, on the day of the assembly. At the end of the forty days and forty nights, the LORD gave me the two stone tablets, the tablets of the covenant." See also Prov 3:3; 7:3: "Bind them on your fingers; write them on the tablet of your heart."

[301] Hafemann, *Suffering and Ministry in the Spirit,* 215. See *Jub.* 1:1, 26; 2:1; 6:23; 15:25–26; 16:30; 32:10–11,15; 49:8; *1 Enoch* 81:1–2; 103:2–4; *2 Apoc. Bar.* 6:7–9; *Tg. Ps.–J.* to Exod 31:18; *b. Ned.* 38a; *Exod Rab.* 41:6; 46:2; *Lev. Rab.* 32:2; 35:5; *Cant. Rab.* 5.14 § 3. The later rabbis believed that since humans had stony hearts God ordained that stone should watch over stone (see H. Räisänen, *Paul and the Law,* WUNT 29 [Tübingen: Mohr [Siebeck], 1983] 244).

[302] Thrall, *Second Epistle to the Corinthians,* 1:227. In support of this view, Josephus praises the average man from his nation for being able to repeat the laws "more readily than his own name. The result, then, of our thorough grounding in the laws from the first dawn of intelligence is that we have them, as it were, engraven on our souls" (*Ag. Ap.* 2.18 §178).

verse has a negative ring." In Gal 3:19 Paul uses the phrase "ordained through angels" (NIV, "put into effect through angels"), which was used in Judaism to glorify the law, and turns it to negative effect.[303] It is not likely, therefore, that a positive connotation lies behind Paul's use of the term "stone tablets" nor that the Corinthians would have taken it in a positive sense.

What prompted this imagery? Georgi contends that the opponents used the Decalogue as their introductory letter.[304] Thrall correctly disputes this view and makes the case that the simplest explanation infers that Paul himself "combined the thought of the metaphorical letter of introduction with Christ as its author, with that of the Decalogue, written 'by the finger of God,' and has used it as a subordinate motif to underline the superiority of the new order."[305] If God has put a new spirit in them removing the heart of stone and replacing it with a heart of flesh as Ezekiel foretold, then the new age has dawned.

Hafemann has his finger on the pulse of Paul's argument: "While in the 'old age' the locus of God's activity and revelation was the law, in the 'new age' according to Ezekiel, God will be at work in the heart."[306] Paul therefore draws a contrast "between the law as it usually functioned in the old covenant, in its impotency to change one's heart, and the potency of the Spirit in its work in the heart within the new covenant, the result of which is that the law itself is not able to be kept." He concludes:

> ... Paul is not merely pointing to the fact that the eschatological promise of Ezekiel is now being fulfilled. He is also asserting that it is being fulfilled through his own ministry, since Paul is the one through whom the Spirit came to the Corinthians."[307]

The upshot is that Paul understands himself "to be an eschatological agent of revelation through whom the Spirit is now being poured out in the gospel."[308] Paul confidently declares that the prophecies about God writing on hearts have come to pass through his ministry in the church at Corinth.

What is the significance of such a declaration? (1) The "age characterized by the law as the locus of God's revelatory activity is over." Their relationship to God does not come through the revelation of God in the law but through the heart-changing work of the Spirit. The reason is that the law

---

[303] See Deut 33:2 (LXX); Acts 7:38,53; Heb 2:2; *Jub.* 1:27; 2:1; and Josephus, *Ant.* 15.5.3 § 136.

[304] Georgi, *The Opponents of Paul in Second Corinthians.*

[305] Thrall, *Second Epistle to the Corinthians,* 1:228.

[306] Hafemann, *Suffering and Ministry in the Spirit,* 221.

[307] Ibid., 222.

[308] Ibid., 224.

demanded obedience but could not engender obedience. The Spirit makes the letter obsolete, "since what the Law requires is now written on the heart."[309] (2) Their conversion through the Spirit is evidence of the arrival of the new age prophesied by Ezekiel. (3) The old covenant is no longer in force because it has been replaced by a new covenant where conduct is guided by God's Spirit. The gospel is more than "some new religious advice—an improved spirituality, a better code of morals, or a freshly crafted theology." The gospel proclaims that "in the unique life, death and resurrection of Jesus the whole cosmos had turned the corner from darkness to light."[310] It initiated the new covenant of the Spirit, which is what enables the old man to become new (see Eph 4:22,24; Col 3:9–10).

PAUL'S SUFFICIENCY AS MINISTER OF THE NEW COVENANT (3:4–6). **3:4** The Spirit's work in his ministry justifies and explains his confidence as an apostle. It is not an illusory feeling of self-confidence based on his own abilities and strengths or on the plaudits of others who cheer his religious powers. Paul refers to the content of his confidence, namely Christ.[311] His confidence is based on his calling through Christ; but since it is also "before God" (see 2:17), he is constantly reminded of his proper place. What sufficiency he has to fulfill this ministry assigned to him comes only by God's grace through Christ (see 1 Cor 15:9–10). We see more clearly human limitations when face to face with "divine omnipotence."[312] But we also see more clearly God's power that can work mightily through human imperfections and frailties.

3:5 God has demolished Paul's former confidence in himself as a Hebrew of Hebrews, a zealous Pharisee who was blameless when it came to righteousness under the law (Phil 3:3:5–6). He no longer places any trust in his own heritage, devotion, or natural powers and now knows that the only resource from which he can draw is the infinite reservoir of grace provided by God's empowering Spirit. In saying that he does not reckon that we have any sufficiency from ourselves, Paul is not resorting to false humility. He would argue that he is fully sufficient to exercise his ministry, yet at the same time he fully admits that his sufficiency comes entirely from God's Spirit, who works in and through him. In interpreting God's call of Moses, Theodoret asks, "When the God of all things used Moses as His minister, why did He choose for himself a man of stammering speech and slow of tongue?" His answer: "Because this displayed all the more his divine power. For just as He chose fishermen and tax-gatherers to be preachers of truth and

---

[309] Fee, *God's Empowering Presence,* 306.

[310] N. T. Wright, "Thy Kingdom Come: Living the Lord's Prayer," *Christian Century* 114 (Mar 12, 1997) 268.

[311] See Hafemann, *Paul, Moses, and the History of Israel,* 94.

[312] Thrall, *Second Epistle to the Corinthians,* 1:229.

teachers of piety, it is by means of a weak voice and slow tongue that He put to shame the wise men of Egypt." Paul would have agreed that the same applies to God's choice of him to be a minister of the gospel.

3:6 Paul concludes this unit by giving the answer to the question raised in 2:16b, "Who is sufficient for these things?" The answer is, We are—through the empowerment of God. Paul uses the verb "to make us sufficient" instead of "to call" (Gal 1:15) to make the point that God makes fit for service those who are manifestly unfit (1 Cor 15:9).[313] Worldly rulers might bestow positions of responsibility on individuals, but such appointments can never give the competence to exercise authority effectively. God bestows both the authority and the competence.

The word *diakonos* does not simply connote humble service. In this context it refers to an agent's charge to transmit messages, and Paul consistently uses the term in relation to the charge laid upon him to preach the word of God.[314] It conveys Paul's conviction that he is God's intermediary to them charged with a message from God.[315] This idea moves beyond the issue of commendatory letters and leads to Jeremiah's prophecy of the new covenant written in the hearts (Jer 31:33). He also invites the contrast between the old Mosaic covenant written on stone tablets and the new covenant that is taken up in 3:7–18.

The phrase the "letter kills" has passed into everyday speech and has been invoked to assail everything from reading Scripture literally to any kind of moral constraints. Paul probably used the antithesis between letter and Spirit as "a handy formula expressing central convictions." But since it appears only in three texts (Rom 2:29; 7:6; 2 Cor 3:6), what he meant by it is not immediately evident.[316]

"Letter" cannot refer to the law itself since Paul affirms that the law is "spiritual" (Rom 7:14), yet it clearly is connected to the law in some way and must refer to some aspect of it.[317] Origen argued that "letter" referred to the literal, external sense of Scripture and that "Spirit" referred to the spiri-

[313] J. Lambrecht states, "That Paul is God's minister is not questioned, only the way he behaves as a minister" ("The Favorable Time: A Study of 2 Corinthians 6,2a in its Context," in *Studies on 2 Corinthians,* ed J. Lambrecht and R. Bieringer, BETL 112 [Leuven: University Press, 1994] 523). R. P. Martin aptly comments: "He was not out to prove he was a servant; rather, because he is a servant, he can put forth what he does as an example of the power of God (12:9)" (*2 Corinthians,* WBC [Waco: Word, 1986] 172).

[314] See 1 Cor 3:5; 2 Cor 6:4; Eph 3:7; Col 1:23,25.

[315] See the analysis of the term in J. N. Collins, *Diakonia: Re-interpreting the Ancient Sources* (New York/Oxford: Oxford University Press, 1990) 73–191. The interlopers also understand themselves as "servants of Christ" (11:23).

[316] S. Westerholm, "Letter and Spirit: The Foundation of Pauline Ethics," *NTS* 30 (1984) 229.

[317] The Greek word for "letter" (γράμμα) in 3:6 is different from the word for "letter" (ἐπιστολή) used in 3:1–3 and is connected to the written law.

tual, internal sense of Scripture. This passage then became the support for the allegorical interpretation of Scripture which he championed and which dominated biblical exegesis for centuries.[318] Few make the same distinction between two levels of meaning in the text, but some still argue that Paul contrasts two different ways of understanding the text, the literal and the spiritual.[319] The Spirit is understood to be the hermeneutical key for understanding Scripture. Although this principle may be true, it is not what Paul had in mind when he distinguished letter and Spirit. The Spirit denotes a divine power that gives life rather than a divine inspiration that opens the true meaning of Scripture. The Spirit implies God's new action in Christ that enables believers to do what they could not otherwise do—obey the letter.[320]

A comparable view interprets the "letter" to mean a legalistic interpretation of the law. This interpretation relates the letter to the veil that hardens the minds of those in Israel who hear the reading of the old covenant (3:14). Cranfield's comment, " 'Letter' is rather what the legalist is left with as a result of his misunderstanding and misuse of the law," is often quoted.[321] The "letter and Spirit" are therefore regarded as a contrast between what

---

[318] Westerholm, "Letter and Spirit," 229. For a history of the interpretation of the letter and the Spirit in seven representative figures—Origen, Theodore of Mopsuestia, Augustine, the authors of the Glossa Ordinaria, Thomas Aquinas, Nicholas of Lyra, and Martin Luther, see W.-S. Chau, *The Letter and the Spirit: A History of Interpretation from Origen to Luther,* American University Studies, Series VII, Theology and Religion, 167 (New York: Peter Lang, 1995).

[319] Héring argues that after the opposition between letter and spirit, Paul "describes two ways of reading the Law of Moses: a literal way ... and a spiritual way" (*The Second Epistle of Saint Paul to the Corinthians,* 23). Provence (" 'Who Is Sufficient for These Things?' " 63) cites K. Barth's position: "In II Cor. 3 everything depends upon the fact that without the work of the Spirit Scripture is veiled, however great its glory and whatever its origin" (*Church Dogmatics* I/2 ed. G. W. Bromiley and T. F. Torrance [Edinburgh: T & T Clark, 1956] 515). Provence points out, however, that when Paul refers to a veil that lies upon the reading of the old covenant in 3:14, "the veil is a veil of hard-heartedness which hides not the meaning of the Bible, but the glory of God" (" 'Who Is Sufficient for These Things?' " 63–64). The veil is removed when an individual is spiritually transformed and can see the glory of the Lord (3:18).

[320] In 1:22 Paul reminds the Corinthians that God sealed them and placed the down payment of the Holy Spirit in their hearts. Paul affirms that the promise of Ezek 39:29 has been fulfilled: " 'I will no longer hide my face from them, for I will pour out my Spirit on the house of Israel,' declares the Sovereign LORD."

[321] C. E. B. Cranfield, *A Critical and Exegetical Commentary on the Epistle to the Romans,* ICC (Edinburgh: T & T Clark, 1975) 1:339. Barrett understands "the letter" to refer to the misuse of the law. "Letter thus points to the way in which (in Paul's view) many of his Jewish contemporaries understood the law on which their religion was based, and through this to man-made religion in general, whether legalistic, antinomian, or mystical" (*The Second Epistle to the Corinthians,* 113). Years before, E. Käsemann argued in a scintillating and influential essay that God's original, sacred intention in the law was perverted by humans resulting in "the letter," which confused God's demand for obedience as a demand for works ("The Spirit and the Letter," in *Perspectives on Paul* [Philadelphia: Fortress, 1971] 138–66). See also Provence, " 'Who is Sufficient for These Things?' " 65–67.

humans do and what God does. The law, which is holy, just, and good (Rom 7:12), cannot penetrate the heart and can easily be twisted by unspiritual minds so that it leads to death. This analysis of what humans do with the law is certainly true. All too frequently we turn God's revelation into a rigid, death-dealing code or into a set of rules that establishes or confirms our own righteousness. But is this what Paul meant by the antithesis between letter and Spirit? Misunderstanding or misapplying the law is not at issue in 3:6. This interpretation ignores that Paul specifically contrasts God's inscribing the law on stones with God's inscribing it on human hearts through the Spirit (3:3).

Interpreting "letter" to mean some warped perception or misuse of the law also does not fit well the contexts of the other passages where it occurs. In Rom 2:27 "letter" does not refer to a perverted understanding of God's law but to the possession of the law in written form. In Rom 2:29 "letter" refers simply to the external rite of circumcision in the flesh which Paul contrasts with spiritual circumcision.[322] Possessing the written code and being circumcised can lead to a false sense of security.[323] It is false because it is the security of a prison that ultimately puts everyone on death row. In Rom 7:6 "oldness of letter" and "newness of Spirit" denote different ways of serving under the old and new dispensations respectively. "Letter" refers to the concrete demands of the Old Testament law which God's people were duty bound to obey but which in fact resulted in a bondage to sin and death. The "letter" denotes what is merely written, and when Paul contrasts it with Spirit, he is contrasting an external code with an indwelling power that can transform believers into the image of God (3:18).[324]

Paul argues in Gal 3:10–14 that the law pronounces a curse on all who fail to obey it. Since no one is able to obey it in every respect,[325] all stand under this curse.[326] The law's curse is removed only through Christ's death,

---

[322] Westerholm, "Letter and Spirit," 233–36.

[323] Furnish comments, "*What is written kills* because it enslaves one to the presumption that righteousness inheres in one's doing of the law, when it is actually the case that true righteousness comes only as a gift from God (cf. 'a righteousness of my own'/'the righteousness from God'— Phil 3:9, RSV)" (*II Corinthians,* 201).

[324] As C. Hodge put it: "A covenant is simply a promise suspended upon a condition. The covenant of works, therefore, is nothing more than the promise of life suspended on the condition of perfect obedience" (*Commentary on the Second Epistle to the Corinthians* [Grand Rapids: Eerdmans, 1950] 57).

[325] A similar assumption is found in *4 Ezra* 9:26–10:58; though the law is sown in us, we cannot keep it.

[326] The reality of the law's curse may have been branded on Paul's mind by the lashings he submitted to in the synagogue (2 Cor 11:24). During the lashing, the curses prescribed in the law (Deut 28:58–59) were to be read aloud (A. Deissmann, *Paul: A Study in Social and Religious History* [1927; reprint, New York: Harper & Row, 1957] 62, citing *m. Mak.* 3:10–14).

which also bestows the promised Spirit on all who believe (Gal 3:13–14). "Spirit" refers to the Spirit of God. The Spirit's power to direct the Christian's conduct from within not only has replaced all feeble and vain attempts to heed the laws of the Torah on our own but it also has resulted in righteousness and life instead of condemnation and death.[327] We therefore should not attach an unduly negative connotation to the "letter" since it played a divinely given but specific role in salvation history. The letter was to be obeyed, but humans failed to obey it. The problem is with humans and with the letter's inability to create obedience. Even the most valiant attempts to obey the letter are doomed. Since the letter only specifies God's demand and the punishment for failing to obey, it ends up only condemning the disobedient to death and never giving life or righteousness (Gal 3:21). The Spirit is the power that enables the moral life and sets people free. The Spirit therefore completes God's action in giving the law because it gives obedience, life, and the potential for the old to become new (5:17; Eph 4:22,24; Col 3:9–10).[328]

In 3:6 Paul is talking about "ministry" or rendering service to God. The letter and Spirit refer to the two different ways of rendering service to God under the two different covenants.[329] The one is carved in letters on stone tablets which require obedience, while the other is written on human hearts and impels obedience through divine agency. S. H. Hooke astutely observed: "A vine does not produce grapes by Act of Parliament; they are the fruit of the vine's own life; so the conduct which conforms to the standard of the Kingdom is not produced by any demand, not even God's, but it is the fruit of that divine nature that God gives as the result of what he has done in and by Christ."[330] For Paul the letter is part of the old covenant now transcended by the new covenant inaugurated by the age of the Spirit.

Paul more fully lays out the contrasts in Rom 8:1–7. Those under the law must live with condemnation (8:1), the law of sin and death (8:2), slavery (8:3), the impotency of the flesh (8:3), an existence determined by the things of the flesh (8:4–5), death (8:6), and hostility (8:7). Those in the Spirit experience no condemnation (8:1), the freedom created by the law of the Spirit of life in Christ (8:2), the potency of God (8:3), an existence determined by the things of the Spirit (8:4–5), and life and peace (8:6).

We would argue that Paul is not engaging in polemics against opponents in this section, as so many contend, but seeking instead to remind the Corinthians that he serves as a minister of the new covenant directed by the power of the Spirit. Next, he will compare himself with Moses, a minister of the

---

[327] Furnish, *II Corinthians*, 239.
[328] Paul maintains that his ministry among the Corinthians has demonstrated Spirit and power (1 Cor 2:3–5) and that it results in life in them (2 Cor 4:12).
[329] Furnish, *II Corinthians*, 240.
[330] S. H. Hooke, "What Is Christianity?" 264.

old covenant (3:7–18). If Moses' ministry under the old covenant was marked by glory, so his ministry in the new covenant is marked by glory to an "incomparably greater degree." As Hafemann aptly describes it:

> Moses was called to mediate the Law to a stiff-necked people under the Law who could not obey it. Paul is called to mediate the Spirit now being poured out as a result of the cross of Christ to a people whose hearts are being transformed to obey the covenant stipulations of the Law.[331]

(2) The Old and New Ministries (3:7–18)

[7]Now if the ministry that brought death, which was engraved in letters on stone, came with glory, so that the Israelites could not look steadily at the face of Moses because of its glory, fading though it was, [8]will not the ministry of the Spirit be even more glorious? [9]If the ministry that condemns men is glorious, how much more glorious is the ministry that brings righteousness! [10]For what was glorious has no glory now in comparison with the surpassing glory. [11]And if what was fading away came with glory, how much greater is the glory of that which lasts!

[12]Therefore, since we have such a hope, we are very bold. [13]We are not like Moses, who would put a veil over his face to keep the Israelites from gazing at it while the radiance was fading away. [14]But their minds were made dull, for to this day the same veil remains when the old covenant is read. It has not been removed, because only in Christ is it taken away. [15]Even to this day when Moses is read, a veil covers their hearts. [16]But whenever anyone turns to the Lord, the veil is taken away. [17]Now the Lord is the Spirit, and where the Spirit of the Lord is, there is freedom. [18]And we, who with unveiled faces all reflect the Lord's glory, are being transformed into his likeness with ever-increasing glory, which comes from the Lord, who is the Spirit.

The profusion of scholarly works trying to unpack the meaning of 3:7–18 attests to its difficulty. In this segment of his argument Paul contrasts the ministry of Moses and the glory associated with the giving of the law with his own ministry and the glory associated with the gospel. He is not concerned that rivals "have overstressed the Old Testament and understressed the newness of Christ."[332] Paul is not arguing against false apostles who have invaded his territory and supposedly have appealed to Exodus 34 to undermine Paul and advance their agenda. He is defending his bold speech in correcting the Corinthians. He argues from premises that the Corinthians would readily accept about the glory of the old ministry—that it is a ministry that yields only death and that

---

[331] Hafemann, *Paul, Moses, and the History of Israel,* 173

[332] As E. Best, e.g., contends (*2 Corinthians,* INT [Atlanta: John Knox, 1987] 28, 30, 32, 33). Beasley-Murray also argues that Paul introduces the idea of the new covenant at this point because "the opponents at Corinth were Jewish teachers, boasting in their Jewish heritage" ("2 Corinthians," BBC [Nashville: Broadman, 1971] 11:22). Plummer cites John Chrysostom, who says that the argument cuts "the ground out from under the Judaistic point of view" (*The Second Epistle of St. Paul to the Corinthians,* 89). Although that may be true, that is not Paul's purpose here. He is not trying to muster support for the new covenant over against the old.

the glory of new ministry in Christ far surpasses the old ministry's glory—to make a case about his role as an agent of this new ministry. Glory, not the contrast between law and grace, is the key theme of this unit.[333] Paul makes the incredible assertion that his ministry is far more glorious than that of Moses, the most illustrious figure in Scripture. It is this glorious ministry that is the grounds for his frank speech in the letter written in tears.

Some interpreters, however, insist that Paul's opponents in Corinth have already made a negative comparison between Paul and Moses; and Paul seeks to put things straight. These opponents supposedly claim that Paul lacks the splendor of the mediator of the Sinai covenant. Thrall contends that had Paul brought up the comparison himself, the Corinthians would have rejected it.[334] If that were true, why would they be any more convinced

---

[333] Hafemann contends that "Paul's point is not to demonstrate the superiority of the new covenant over the old per se, though this is the implied basis of his argument, but to demonstrate his own qualifications to be a minister of the new covenant." ("Paul's Argument from the Old Testament and Christology in 2 Cor 1–9," in *The Corinthian Correspondence,* ed. R. Bieringer, BETL 125 [Leuven: University Press, 1996] 290–91).

[334] Thrall, *Second Epistle to the Corinthians,* 1:246. Some have argued that Paul inserts here a pre-existing "midrash" on Exod 34 (Windisch, *Die zweite Korintherbrief,* 105, 112–13). Just because Paul's argument remains coherent if these verses are removed from the text does not mean that it is tangential to his argument or that it is an independent interpretation of the text that he inserts parenthetically. It is the nature of A B A' structure for the B section to appear as a kind of digression. W. C. Van Unnik baldly asserts that "there is not a shred of evidence that the apostle is commenting upon a previously existing document or teaching nor is it clear why Paul himself should have been unable to make this application of the Exodus story" ("'With an Unveiled Face,' An Exegesis of 2 Corinthians iii 12–18," *NovT* 6 [1963] 262. The views of S. Schulz, that the opponents used this text to exalt Moses and the law ("Die Decke Moses. Untersuchungen zu einer vorpaulinischen Überlieferung in 2 Kor. 3:17–18," *ZNW* 49 [1958] 1–30), and Georgi, that Paul rewrites the rival's exegesis of the passage (*Opponents,* 264–71), should also be rejected as groundless conjecture. Georgi asserts that the adversaries used Exod 34 to exalt Moses as a divine man and that they were divine men themselves who have deeper insight into the Scripture (chap. 3). The text does not support such an assumption. How would Paul have gained access to his opponents writings? (so J.–F. Collange, *Énigmes de la deuxième épître de Paul aux Corinthiens: étude exégetique de II Cor 2:14–7:4,* SNTSMS 18 [Cambridge: University Press, 1972] 68). It is not impossible that Paul taught on this passage in a synagogue at some other time and maybe even in the church at Corinth. He drew on the same section of Scripture, Exod 32:1–34:35, in 1 Cor 10:1–22. See C. J. A. Hickling, "Paul's Use of Exodus in the Corinthian Correspondence," in *The Corinthian Correspondence,* ed. R. Bieringer, BETL 125 (Leuven: University Press, 1996) 367–68. W. J. Dumbrell makes the case that Paul has faithfully captured the flow of thought of Exod 34 ("Paul's Use of Exodus 34 in 2 Corinthians 3," in *God Who is Rich in Mercy,* ed. P. T. O'Brien and D. G. Peterson [Homebush, Australia: Lancer Books, 1986] 179–94). Hafemann's exhaustive study makes the point more forcefully (*Paul, Moses, and the History of Israel* [Peabody: Hendrickson, 1996] 189–254 = *Paul, Moses, and the History of Israel: The Letter/Spirit Contrast and the Argument from Scripture in 2 Corinthians,* WUNT 81 [Tübingen: Mohr [Siebeck], 1995]). Paul does not engage in arbitrary midrash in his interpretation of Exod 32–34. The key word is arbitrary, which means interpreting the text with total disregard for its original meaning. It remains an interpretation, but Paul did not intentionally misinterpret the OT passage through additions that contradicted the text whether to support his position over against opponents or to make his case about his own ministry.

by these so-called counterarguments? Nothing in the text suggests that anyone in Corinth took Moses as an exemplar or compared Paul unfavorably to Moses.[335] This is another case of "mirror reading," which does mischief to the text. The conclusion in 3:12 is not, "Therefore we have a glorious apostleship" but, "Therefore we have boldness."

At this point in his defense, Paul is not countering the false teaching of those stirring up the congregation against him but justifying his own boldness (3:12) and confidence (3:4) as a worthy apostle of the new covenant (3:6) by contrasting his ministry, a ministry of the Spirit, with that of Moses, a ministry of the letter. He draws a parallel between his sufficiency and Moses' sufficiency because both serve as intermediaries between God and the people despite their own insufficiencies.[336] He is not interested in establishing the glory of his own ministry so much as establishing the basis for his plainspokenness. Since this text is not an overtly polemical section which castigates opponents, the best procedure for understanding it is to try to grasp its internal logic within its own context. Interpreting what Paul says against some contrived, hypothetical scenario regarding a prior background for the exegesis of Exodus 34 or the reconstruction of the teaching of imagined opponents will only lead us far afield.[337]

Structure

Paul expands on his statement that the letter kills through an exposition of Exod 34:29–35, which recounts Moses' shining face when he came down from Mount Sinai with the two tablets of the covenant. In the first part, 3:7–11, Paul uses three conditional sentences to compare the glory associated with the old ministry served by Moses with that of the new. He begins with what he considers to be an undeniable fact that glory accompanied the old covenant. "Glory" *(doxa)* is a key word that occurs eight times in 3:7–11 and three times in 3:18 (see also 4:4,6). The verb form *(doxazō)* appears twice in 3:10. The phrases "how much more" in 3:7 and "much more" in 3:9,11 highlight the contrasts between the glory of the old and the glory of the new.

protasis (3:7)	apodosis (3:8)
protasis (3:9a)	apodosis (3:9b) with an explanation (3:10)
protasis (3:11a)	apodosis (3:11b)

With each comparison the glory associated with the two ministries becomes increasingly disparate. The refrain "but if … how much more" pulses through

---

[335] What Paul says about himself applies to all ministers of the gospel.

[336] Hafemann, *Paul, Moses, and the History of Israel,* 34.

[337] See the discussion in Furnish, *II Corinthians,* 242–44; see also M. Hooker, "Beyond the Things That Are Written? St. Paul's Use of Scripture," *NTS* 27 (1981) 295–309.

these verses as Paul contrasts "the ministry of death" with "the ministry of the Spirit" (3:7), "the splendor of the ministry of condemnation" with "the splendor" of "the ministry of righteousness" (3:9), and that which is "annulled" with that which is "permanent" (3:11).

He adopts a commonly used logical argument, from the lesser case to the greater, to make his point.[338] If splendor attended a ministry that was chiseled in stone, temporary, and resulted in condemnation, how much more must glory attend the ministry of the Spirit, which is inscribed on hearts, is abiding, and leads to acquittal. The comparison of the differing effects of the two ministries reveals that what formerly had glory is now so eclipsed by the surpassing glory of the new that it has no glory (3:11). The glorious ministry of the Spirit results in bold speech (3:12).[339]

Paul continues his argument in 3:12–18 with an enigmatic explanation of why Moses veiled himself before the sons of Israel whereby he contrasts his own boldness with Moses' cautious reserve. His interpretation of Exodus 34 shows that the boldness (3:12), freedom (3:17), and glory (3:18) that he lays claim to has nothing to do with his personal characteristics but has everything to do with the intrinsic splendor of the ministry he serves. He knows himself to be a flawed vessel yet one that contains a perfect treasure (4:7). The glory he claims is not the empty glory *(kenodoxia)* bestowed by self-applause or the acclamation of others. It is the glory that God bestows on all those who serve in the ministry of the Spirit.

THE GLORY OF THE MINISTRY NOW SET ASIDE (3:7–9). **3:7–8** Israel's idolatry with the golden calf violated the commandment to make no idol or bow down to a form of anything in heaven above or on the earth below (Exod 20:4–5). It caused Moses to smash the two tablets of the covenant (Exod 32:1–35). Moses castigates the people for sinning a great sin and returns to the presence of the Lord on Mount Sinai in hopes that he can make atonement for their sin (Exod 32:30). The Lord will not relent, however, saying: "Whoever has sinned against me I will blot out of my book" (Exod 32:33). A plague ravages the people because they made the calf (Exod 32:35). Moses successfully intervenes with God on behalf of the people (Exod 33:12–17) and is shown the glory of the Lord (Exod 33:18–23). When Moses descended a second time with the tablets of the covenant, his face shone from being in the presence of God (Exod 34:29). His radiance evoked fear, so after delivering to the people all that the Lord had spoken to him, he covered his face with a veil. From then on when Moses approached the Isra-

---

[338] The term for this form of argument in the rabbis is *qal wāhômer* (lit., light and heavy); in modern logic it is called *a fortiori*. It appears in Rom 5:9–10,15,17; 11:12,24 and frequently in the teaching of Jesus (Matt 6:30; 7:11; 10:25) and particularly in his parables (Luke 11:5–8; 15:1–7,8–10; 18:1–8). See also Heb 9:13–14; 10:28–29; 12:9.

[339] Fredrickson, "ΠΑΡΡΗΣΙΑ," 177.

elites to reveal God's commands, he wore a veil to cover his face.

Paul takes for granted that the giving of the law was a glorious moment, and that glory was etched on Moses' face as he emitted a luminous glow from his divine encounter. He does not intend to denigrate Moses and his glory but wants to stress it so he can show how much greater is the glory attached to his ministry. He does identify the ministry associated with Moses as a ministry of death. The NIV translation that the ministry "brought death" is misleading.[340] Paul states in Rom 5:12–14 that death entered the world through sin and "death reigned from the time of Adam to the time of Moses" (see 1 Cor 15:21). But in Rom 7:11–14 he argues that "sin seizing the opportunity afforded by the commandment, deceived me, and through the commandment put me to death." Sin "produced death in me through what was good, so that through the commandment sin might become utterly sinful." The NEB's translation "dispensed death" is therefore more nuanced. It means that the law deals out death to those guilty of sinning against it.

To identify the Sinai experience as a ministry of death (3:7) is an astounding assertion for any Jew to make. Jews proclaimed that just the opposite occurred; the law gave life. A later rabbi expressed it this way: "While Israel stood below engraving idols to provoke their Creator to anger …, God sat on high engraving tablets which would give them life."[341] As a Pharisee, Paul was no different from any other devout Jew who searched the Law and the prophets because he believed he had life in them (see John 5:39). But after his encounter with the risen Lord (4:6), he came to realize that the Law bore witness to Christ (see John 5:47). He also became convinced that the righteousness of God had been manifested in Jesus Christ apart from Law (see Rom 3:22; 1 Cor 1:30; 2 Cor 5:21). It followed that if salvation comes only through Christ, then salvation could not come through the written law. If the law does not lead to life, then it must lead to death, which in turn gives the chance for life (Rom 7:10; Gal 3:21; 1 Cor 15:56). Because of his faith in Christ, Paul came to view the law—holy, righteous, and good as it was (Rom 7:12)—as a ministry of death. To say that it was engraved in letters on stones (3:7) is simply another way of saying that the letter kills (3:6).

Paul can say that the ministry of Moses metes out death for those whose hearts have not been changed for four reasons. First, the law prescribes death as the penalty for sin (Rom 5:12–21). It places the disobedient under a curse: "Cursed is the man who does not uphold the words of this law by car-

---

[340] It correctly renders "ministry of death" (ἡ διακονία τοῦ θανάτου), however, as an objective genitive.

[341] *Exod. Rab.* 41:1. See also *Ep. Arist.* 31, 127; *2 Apoc. Bar.* 38:2; 46:4–5; 48:22; *Ps. Sol.* 14:2. According to *Sir* 17:13: "Their eyes saw his glorious majesty, / and their ears heard the glory of his voice" (NRSV; see also 45:5).

rying them out" (Deut 27:26).[342]

Second, the law specifies transgressions. One can sin in ignorance, "for the law brings about wrath, but where there is no law there is no transgression" (Rom 4:15; see 5:13). Transgression requires a recognized standard of what is right and wrong, and the law makes sin to be known as sin (Rom 3:20; 7:7,13; see the JB translation of Gal 3:18: "The law was added to specify crimes"). Transgression is a willful violation of that standard and is consequently more serious than sin. The law clarified the moral and religious situation of the world by revealing that sin is a conscious and deliberate transgression. Sinners not only violate God's will, but they now know that what they do is a violation of God's will and defiantly continue in their sin. The law exposes the sinful character of wrongdoing by revealing it to be conscious, active rebellion against God. Its effect is to increase transgression which leads to death (Rom 5:20).

Third, the law provides an opportunity for sinful people to garble God's commands with legalistic casuistry and to delude themselves into thinking that they have done what God requires. They then rely on their own inadequate achievements and racial and religious heritage rather than placing their trust in God (Rom 3:19–31). Their legalism may even foster an inner rebellion so that they are ruled by the rule book rather than God.

Fourth, the law cannot give life because it has no power to do so (see Rom 7:10; 8:1–11). The law does not offer assistance to obey it and does not grade on a curve. It only announces the penalty of death for those who fail. Even a 99.99 percent obedience rate earns a failing grade.

In spite of its deadly consequences, this ministry of death came with an evident splendor reflecting God's glory. The glory of the Lord is described as a fiery divine radiance (Exod 24:16–17; 40:34–35 [which the LXX renders "glory"]; 16:10; 32:22–23; 34:29–35). When Moses came down from Sinai with the tablets of the law, his face radiated the residual rays of the divine glory.

Paul says that the Israelites were unable to look at the face of Moses *because of the glory of his face (dia tēn doxēn tou prosōpou).* Consequently, Moses had to veil this glory from the gaze of the Israelites.[343] What was it about the glory that demanded this practice? The Exodus narrative makes clear that viewing the glory of a righteous and holy God can be extremely hazardous for iniquitous humans. Moses had asked to see God's glory (Exod 33:18), but God warned him that gazing directly into the face of God was fatal (Exod 33:20). Moses hid his face at the burning

---

[342] See also Deut 30:17–18a: "But if your heart turns away and you are not obedient, and if you are drawn away to bow down to other gods and worship them, I declare to you this day that you will certainly be destroyed."

[343] The ὥστε expresses result.

bush because he was afraid to look at God (Exod 3:6). When God placed Moses safely in the cleft of a rock, covered him with his hand, and revealed only his back (Exod 33:21–23), Moses' face still shone from his encounter with God. Moses alone caught a fleeting glimpse of God's frightening majesty and splendor and lived to tell about it (Exod 33:17–23).[344] By contrast the Israelites had continuously grumbled against God, mutinied against Moses, and bowed down to a golden calf. Their sinful condition put them in jeopardy to look even at this glimmer of God's glory reflected in Moses' face. Provence summarizes Paul's idea well:

> For those who have already determined to be rebellious, God's truth only causes them to be more rebellious against it. Paul's intention, then, is to illustrate the hardening effect that the glory of God may have upon those whose hearts have not been changed by the Spirit.[345]

God's holiness would have consumed the people had not Moses veiled himself.

The verb translated by the NIV "fading as it was" is Paul's editorial comment on the text and is difficult to interpret.[346] If the verb *katargeō* is taken to mean "to fade," then Paul must have conjectured that the glory on Moses' face faded. This waning glory might then betray that the glory of the law's ministry was to fade away (3:11) with the coming of Christ. The covenant of the letter was only transitory (see Gal 3:19–25; Rom 10:4) and can now be identified as "old" (3:14; see Rom 7:6). The present tense of the participle lends itself to the idea of something "fading." Bruce argues that Paul could have inferred that the radiance on Moses' face receded from the account in Exod 34:33–35, which might suggest that Moses' face was "re-charged" with glory every time he went before God

---

[344] The noun "glory" *(doxa)* occurs twenty times in 2 Corinthians, thirteen times in 3:7–4:6 and two more times in 4:15,17. On the history of its meaning, see J. Jervell, *Imago Dei. Gen. 1,26f im Spätjudentum, in der Gnosis und in den paulinischen Briefen,* FRLANT 76 (Göttingen: Vandenhoeck & Ruprecht, 1960) 176–80; G. H. Boobyer, *Thanksgiving and Glory of God in Paul* (Borna-Leipzig: Noske, 1929); and C. C. Newman, *Paul's Glory-Christology,* NovTSup 69 (Leiden: Brill, 1992). The term "glory" in Paul can refer to the visible manifestation of God in creation (Rom 1:20–23; see Ps 19:1), to God's presence (Rom 9:4; see Exod 40:34–35; 1 Kgs 8:10–11; Ps 26:8), and to the future glory that will be revealed to Christians (Rom 8:18; Col 3:4). It can also denote God's present transforming power (Rom 8:30). Glory can refer to God's power that raised Christ from the dead (Rom 6:4), that strengthens Christians (Col 1:11; see Eph 1:19), and that transforms Christians (2 Cor 3:18).

[345] Provence, "Who Is Sufficient for These Things?" 71. God's glory always brings into sharp relief human sin (Isa 6:1–7; Rom 3:23).

[346] Twenty-five of the twenty-seven uses of the verb καταργεῖν in the NT appear in Paul. Four appear in this unit (3:7,11,13,14).

in the tent of meeting.[347] The major problem with this interpretation is that *katargeō* does not have this meaning in other passages in Paul and reads too much into the text.[348] It also runs counter to Jewish tradition that assumed that Moses' radiance did not diminish.[349]

Paul normally uses the word *katargeō* to mean "to nullify," "to make of no effect," "to make powerless," "to pass away," or "to be abolished" (the KJV renders it "which [glory] was to be done away," and the NRSV renders it "now set aside").[350] This meaning best fits 3:11 where the verb is used as an antonym for "abide" *(menō)*. It also fits a basic premise of Paul's argument: the ministry of the Spirit replaces the ministry of the letter. The present tense would imply that "the glory was in process of abolition" from the time of its beginning.[351] The passive voice would point to God as the agent.

Hafemann argues that the verb has an eschatological significance in Paul's letters that express the discontinuity between this age and the age to come.

> Its context is consistently eschatological and its meaning is best translated, 'to render (something) inoperative, ineffective, powerless', or 'to nullify (something) in terms of its effects. Indeed, Paul's use of καταργέω *[katargeō]* warrants its consideration as a Pauline *terminus technicus* to express the significance of the coming and return of Christ for the structures of this world.[352]

---

[347] F. F. Bruce, *I & II Corinthians,* NCB (Grand Rapids: Eerdmans, 1971) 191. Harvey tries to support this view by arguing that in Greek philosophical tradition the word δόξα meant "'opinion,' as opposed to knowledge, a perception that might often be proved false, being based on the appearances of things and not their real nature." He suggests that a possible explanation for why such an ambivalent word as *doxa* was used to translate *kabod* "lies deep in the psychology of Hebrew religion." No human being can ever see God. "All that could ever be experienced of God was something like him, some appearance." Moses saw God's glory, the intense presence of God, but the Greek word *doxa* "implied some distance from reality." Paul may suggest that what Moses saw "was such an imperfect 'likeness' that it was bound to fade even from Moses' features. What was promised to the Christian minister was of another order: it was permanent (τὸ μένον 3:11)" *(Renewal through Suffering,* 51–52). But it is questionable if Paul is engaging in such subtlety here.

[348] Hafemann argues that it never refers to the "gradual 'fading away' of some aspect of reality" *(Paul, Moses, and the History of Israel,* 309; see his entire discussion, 301–9).

[349] L. L. Belleville's interpretation of conflicting evidence that the shining of Moses' face was a passing phenomenon is open to a different interpretation *(Reflections of Glory: Paul's Polemical Use of the Moses-Doxa Tradition in 2 Cor 3, 1–18,* JSNTSup 53 [Sheffield: JSOT Press, 1991] 41–42, 67). See Hafemann's critique *(Paul, Moses, and the History of Israel,* 287–98).

[350] See Rom 3:3, 31; 4:14; 1 Cor 13:8 (2x),10,11; Gal 3:17; 5:4,11. The verb has the meaning "perish" or "destroy" in 1 Cor 2:6; 6:13; 15:24,26; 2 Thess 2:8; 2 Tim 1:10 (see Heb 2:14).

[351] Barrett; *The Second Epistle to the Corinthians,* 116; Barnett, *The Second Epistle to the Corinthians,* 183, n.23.

[352] Hafemann, "Paul's Argument," 288; see further Hafemann, *Paul, Moses, and the History of Israel,* 301–13.

He translates it "so that the sons of Israel were not able to gaze intently into the face of Moses because of the glory of his face, which was being rendered inoperative."[353] "Rendered inoperative" fits well the usage of the verb in Rom 6:6; 7:6; and 1 Cor 1:28.

Hafemann vigorously contends that the glory associated with the ministry of the Spirit is not more glorious because the glory associated with the ministry of the death was in some way inferior in quality or quantity. He states: "It is not as if the glory of God in the new covenant is better or stronger, or more brilliant than the revelation of the glory of God on Mount Sinai or that associated with the Law through the ministry of Moses."[354] He interprets the verb *katargeō* to mean that "the glory on Moses' face was continuously being brought to an end or cut off in regard to its effects."[355] He insists that Paul does not compare the inferior with the superior but argues from the similarity of the two glories. The difference is that the one is connected to death and condemnation.[356] Hafemann makes the important point that Paul's ministry of the Spirit differed from Moses' ministry of death because it allows others "to encounter the glory of God without being destroyed."[357] But implicit in this comparison of ministries is the inferiority of one compared with the other. One has greater glory because it has life-giving effects.[358]

Not knowing precisely what Paul meant by the verb *katargeō* does not mean that we cannot grasp the sense of Paul's argument. The giving of the law on Mount Sinai and the ministry of Moses came with a magnificent glory despite all its deficiencies, which we now recognize more clearly after Christ's coming. In some way it was a transient glory. Paul's point: if glory accompanied something that leads to death (see 1 Cor 10:1–12), how much more glory will accompany the ministry of the Spirit that leads to life (3:8).[359] The glory of God revealed in the face of Christ that shines in our

---

[353] Id., "Paul's Argument," 288.

[354] Id., *Paul, Moses, and the History of Israel,* 323.

[355] Id., "Paul's Argument," 288.

[356] Id., *Paul, Moses, and the History of Israel,* 271.

[357] Ibid., 313.

[358] The rabbis believed that blessedness comprised contemplating the glory of God (*b. Ber.* 34a). Paul's conviction is that without the transforming power of the Spirit that comes through faith in Christ, such contemplation will bring only destruction, not blessing.

[359] The verb ἔσται in 3:8 is future. If we understand it as future from Paul's perspective as he writes, the glory would then refer to an end-time glory revealed at the consummation (Rom 6:5; 8:18). But in 3:9 the ministry of righteousness abounds in glory now. It is therefore more likely that the future tense refers to logical sequence (so Plummer, *The Second Epistle of St. Paul to the Corinthians,* 91; Bultmann, *The Second Letter to the Corinthians,* 81; Thrall, *Second Epistle to the Corinthians,* 1:245). It means that the ministry of the Spirit will reflect even greater glory. Furnish argues for both a chronological and a logical meaning for the verb (*II Corinthians,* 228).

hearts (4:6) is far greater. It will never be abolished, and looking at it does not lead to death but allows believers to begin the transformation into that perfect glory (3:18).

Paul's point is that if the ministry of Moses had glory and power whether it was fading, being annulled, or covered up, then how much more glory and power will the gospel ministry have that does not fade, has eternal effects (see Rev 14:6), and does not need to be shrouded to guard sinners from God's majestic holiness that might otherwise destroy them. The contrast is between the effects of the two ministries. The law's edicts bring death to those who cannot obey them; the gospel brings life through God's Spirit. Hafemann helpfully stresses that Paul does not discredit the law "because of some theological inadequacy in the Law itself" but because it "can no longer be the means of preparing for the final consummation." The new covenant promised in Jeremiah 31 and Ezekiel 36 has been inaugurated with the coming of Christ, and God's people can only be made fit for the day of judgment if they are in Christ and transformed by the Spirit.[360] The difference between the old and new ministry is "the activity, or lack of activity, of the Holy Spirit within the human heart."[361]

3:9 In 3:9 the contrast is restated in different terms: the ministry of condemnation versus the ministry of righteousness.[362] Righteousness must be the opposite of condemnation and refer in this instance to acquittal (see also 1 Cor 1:30; 4:4; 6:11; 2 Cor 5:21).[363] God's character of righteousness leads to his righteous action in being faithful to the covenant with Abraham. Its effect in the lives of believers is their right standing before God and their right living. For this reason the new ministry is even more glorious. When the people of Israel sinned, Moses could valiantly attempt to intercede on their behalf but was helpless to remove either their guilt (Exod 32:31–33) or his own. He could not make them righteous. He was entrusted only with a ministry of the letter that specified crimes and stipulated the punishment. The law he gave Israel only results in curse and condemnation, since Paul believed none could fully obey it. In this sense the law was transitory because God's purpose was not to condemn but to save (Rom 3:21–26). God does not intend to bring the judgment of death but righteousness that leads to life. The new ministry of the Spirit makes this clear. The Spirit converts

---

[360] Hafemann, *Paul, Moses, and the History of Israel,* 343.

[361] Provence, "Who Is Sufficient for These Things?" 77.

[362] A textual variant has the nominative ἡ διακονία instead of the dative τῇ διακονία. It is more likely that the nominative was assimilated to the nominative in the previous verse. The dative would be translated "if there was glory in the ministry of condemnation."

[363] Both "ministry of condemnation" and "ministry of righteousness" are subjective genitives: the ministry that condemns and the ministry that makes righteous. In 11:15 Paul refers derisively to the interlopers as ministers of Satan who disguise themselves as ministers of righteousness.

hearts of stone into hearts that are receptive to God's righteousness. The previous allusions to Ezek 11:19; 36:26 and Jer 31:33 in 3:3 make clear that the new covenant does not completely jettison the law but offers a new way to keep the law through this transformed heart.

The Spirit acquits (Rom 5:16,18; 8:1) because Christ not only intercedes for the condemned (Rom 8:26,34), but his death effectively atones for their sins (Rom 3:25; 2 Cor 5:21).[364] The law demands obedience; the Spirit gives it (Rom 8:3). The law would eliminate sinners by sentencing them to death; the Spirit would illuminate them by revealing the glory of the Lord (3:18), the truth of God (4:2), and the promise of the resurrection (4:13–14). The Spirit's work is therefore the key difference that distinguishes the new covenant from the old (3:17–18). This distinction leads him to argue: If a ministry that could lead only to condemnation possessed glory, how much more glory must the ministry that leads to righteousness possess?

We should note that this ministry of righteousness can still lead to death for those who remain stubbornly unrepentant (see 2:15–16). The difference is that now there is a remedy for hardened hearts—the Spirit. The revelation of God's glory in Christ does not lead unswervingly to destruction for those who view it. For those whose hearts have been transformed by the Spirit so that they surrender to God's righteousness, it leads to life.

THE GREATER GLORY OF THE NEW ECLIPSES THE OLD (3:10). **3:10** Paul offers an explanation for the previous assertion: "For what had been glorified has no glory now."[365] The effects of the glory associated with the giving of the law do not endure when one compares it with the glory associated with the ministry of righteousness.[366] Paul believes that the law is therefore no longer the touchstone for the revelation of God's glory to the

---

[364] The translation of the verb προτίθημι in Rom 3:25 is much debated, but "purposed" seems better than "set forth" (NRSV) or "presented" (NIV). Paul uses the verb in 1:13 to tell the Romans how many times he intended to come to them. The noun form appears in 8:28 and 9:11 and refers to the purpose of election. Therefore, Paul believes that the cross reflects God's eternal purpose. In this passage he is not concerned with the issue of the publication of Christ's death but with explaining the apparent theological problem of God passing over sins. Simply letting sins go would be incompatible with God's faithfulness because it would imply that God condones evil. But Paul explains that God has passed over the sins without compromising righteousness because God intended all along to deal with sin decisively and once and for all through the cross. Sin demands death, and death it got on a cross, in darkness and agony. Jesus' death was God's long intended solution to atone for human sins.

[365] Paul uses a neuter participle in the perfect tense τὸ δεδοξασμένον. It cannot refer to the law (masculine) or the covenant (feminine) or the ministry of glory (feminine) but refers instead to "the ministry of the old covenant as a whole, especially its theological purpose (v. 9a) and results (v. 7)" (Hafemann, "Paul's Argument," 291).

[366] The phrase ἐν τούτῳ τῷ μέρει means "in this respect," "in this case" (see 9:3). In this case the ministry of condemnation does not seem to have any glory at all.

world after Christ's arrival.[367] The breathtaking glory of the new so out-shines the old that it makes its glory seem nonexistent.[368] The coming of the new also makes the Sinai covenant old. Theodoret insightfully commented, "As the light of a lantern shines at night, but at noonday is overpowered by the sun, so was the glory of Moses overshadowed by Christ."[369] One splendor outshines the other.

THE GLORY OF THE MINISTRY NOW SET ASIDE (3:11).   **3:11**   In the third *qal wāhômer* comparison, Paul applies the term used to describe the glory on Moses' face to the old covenant in general. He contrasts what is being annulled with what abides.[370] The old covenant was impermanent because it did not represent God's ultimate purpose to save both Jew and Greek through faith (see Gal 3:19–25; Rom 10:4). From the outset, then, it was destined to pass away. When Christ came, the old had run its course. The gospel, with its forgiveness based on free grace and direct access to God, is God's last word and is permanent. The gospel, like God's righteousness, abides forever (see 9:9, citing Ps 112:9).

THE UNVEILED PAUL (WE, APOSTLES) (3:12–13).   This next stage in the argument interprets Exod 34:29–35, which recounts how Moses veiled himself before the people of Israel and unveiled himself when he went in before the Lord to speak with him.[371] Paul's exposition of the passage may be outlined as follows:[372]

---

[367] Hafemann, "Paul's Argument," 292.

[368] The noun form of the verb "surpassing" (ὑπερβάλλω) appears in 4:17: "For our light and momentary troubles are achieving for us an eternal glory that far outweighs them all" (see also 9:14).

[369] Cited by Lapide, *The Great Commentary of Cornelius à Lapide,* 32. Variations of this statement have appeared in many commentaries. E.g., Plummer writes: "When the sun is risen, lamps cease to be of use" (*The Second Epistle of St. Paul to the Corinthians,* 91).

[370] No exegetical significance is to be attached to Paul's change in prepositions, "What was being annulled came through glory" (διὰ δόξης), "what abides comes in glory" (ἐν δόξῃ). Both ministries are said to come "in glory" (ἐν δόξῃ) in 3:7–8. The same change in prepositions appears in 1 Cor 12:8–9 (see also Rom 5:10; 3:30; Gal 2:16).

[371] Scholars will frequently refer to this passage as a "midrash," which may lead readers to think of it as something arbitrary and capricious, without any regard for its original context or meaning. J. Neusner opines that the term "midrash" has become essentially meaningless because it can be applied to anything. It "presently stands for pretty much anything any Jew in antiquity did in reading and interpreting the Scripture" (*What Is Midrash?* [Philadelphia: Fortress, 1987]). Midrash may be defined quite simply as "biblical exegesis by ancient Judaic authorities." It does not imply that the exegesis is fanciful or frivolous.

[372] Adapted from Belleville, *Reflections of Glory,* 177; Hafemann, *Paul, Moses, and the History of Israel,* 336–62, and N. T. Wright, "Reflected Glory: 2 Corinthians 3," in *The Climax of the Covenant: Christ and the Law in Pauline Theology* [Minneapolis: Fortress, 1992] 184. Belleville believes that 3:13b–14a contain the text from Exod 34:33 and the commentary on it begins in 3:14b, but Hafemann makes a better case that Paul's commentary begins in 3:13b. See also the structure offered by Richard, "Polemics, Old Testament, and Theology," 358–59.

3:12 opening statement	"We use great boldness"
3:13a text from Exod 34:33	Contrast with Moses' custom of veiling himself before the people
3:13b–15 commentary	Explanation for Moses' custom and its continuing implications for Israel
3:16 text from Exod 34:34	Moses' removal of the veil when he returned to the Lord and its current implications
3:17 commentary	Explanation of the meaning of the term "the Lord" and the assertion of freedom
3:18 text from Exod 34:35 combined with commentary	Moses' unveiling before the glory of the Lord resulted in his transformation; the Christian's unveiling results in an even greater transformation

3:12 Paul draws the conclusion from his assertions in 3:7–11, "Therefore, having such a hope we are very bold," which serves as the opening statement for his interpretation of the veil passage in Exodus. He now will contrast his ministry with that of Moses to make the point that if the ministry of the Spirit has a greater splendor, then its ministers can have a greater boldness.

They also have a greater hope. "Hope" does not refer, as it generally does in our culture, to some wistful daydream or airy optimism that may have little foundation in reality. Paul is not saying, "I hope this is true." "Hope" denotes for him a supreme confidence grounded in divine realities (see 3:4).[373] The hope is so sure that it transforms how one understands and reacts to everything in the present. In this context Paul's hope, his confidence, is that he serves in the ministry of the Spirit that makes hearts receptive to God. He serves in the ministry of righteousness that justifies sinners and in the ministry that abides forever.[374] Consequently, his ministry is far more glorious than even that of Moses, since he is an instrument that makes the glory of God known to the world. This solid assurance gives him his boldness.

---

[373] Hafemann comments that hope "refers to a solid confidence concerning the future because of the promises and acts of God in the past" (*Paul, Moses, and the History of Israel*, 337). And Belleville asserts that Paul calls it a hope "because its full splendor is yet to be seen" (*2 Corinthians*, 102). But it is not simply hope for the future. Paul has an unshakable confidence (hope) in the Corinthians (1:7; see 1:24; 7:4,14,16; 8:7) and confidence (hope) that as their faith "continues to grow, our area of activity among you will greatly expand" (10:15).

[374] See Hughes for other options (*Paul's Second Epistle to the Corinthians*, 107).

If by "very bold" Paul means "audacious," that "audacity" becomes immediately evident as he moves from comparing the ministry of death and the ministry of the Spirit to comparing himself directly with Moses. Moses ministered with a veil covering the glory reflected in his face; Paul is unveiled, along with all Christians, beholding the glory of the Lord and being transformed from one degree of glory to another (3:18). But the word "bold" *(parrēsia)* does not mean "brazen" or "presumptuous" here.

The verb *chraomai* is left untranslated in the NIV and may mean "to act or proceed" or "to make use of or exercise."[375] Most commentators assume that Paul has reference to a certain kind of behavior or a state of mind. Paul's behavior is open and public as opposed to obscure and hidden, or he is intrepid in carrying out his commission as an apostle.[376] Furnish, for example, comments: "It describes the courage with which he is emboldened, as an apostle, to exercise his ministry openly and without fear."[377] Hafemann concurs that it refers to his courage and openness in proclaiming the gospel.[378] The word "boldness" is certainly used in the New Testament to refer to a fearless, clear testimony. In Acts the coming of the Spirit resulted in the transformation of the disciples from fainthearted weaklings cowering in the darkness to stout heroes dauntlessly proclaiming the word.[379] Hafemann

---

[375] BAGD, 884. See 1:17 "to act with levity."

[376] Belleville calls it "conduct befitting a minister of the new covenant" and, using a colloquial expression, comments, "Unlike Moses, who veiled his faced to prevent public scrutiny of the fading character of his ministry, the new covenant minister is very up-front" (*2 Corinthians*, 102).

[377] Furnish, *II Corinthians*, 231. See also Belleville, *Reflections of Glory*, 194–98; Hafemann, *Paul, Moses, and the History of Israel*, 338–39.

[378] Hafemann, *Paul, Moses, and the History of Israel*, 340. To be sure, proclaiming the gospel "requires boldness because it involves claiming that God has been uniquely revealed in the human form of Jesus Christ" (A. T. Hanson, "The Midrash in II Corinthians 3: A Reconsideration," *JSNT* 9 [1980], 15). But is Paul contrasting his courage with Moses' supposed lack of courage? I would argue that he is not. Philo appealed to Moses, who regularly communicated with God, as a prime example of bold, courageous speech (παρρησία). Not only did he speak and cry aloud to God, but Philo asserted (citing Exod 32:32; Num 11:12–13,22; Exod 5:22–23), Moses was so bold as "to make an outcry of reproach, wrung from him by real conviction, and expressing true emotion" (*Who Is the Heir of Divine Things?* 5.19). Philo viewed frank speech as a gift of God: "How vast is the boldness of the soul which is filled with the gracious gifts of God!" (*On Drunkenness*, 149). He also claimed that virtue fortified a man to speak freely and boldly (*Every Good Man Is Free*, 152) and that it was the fruit of wisdom (*Who Is the Heir of Divine Things?* 5.14).

[379] Acts 2:29; 4:13,29,31; 9:28; 13:46; 14:3; 18:26; 28:31; see also Eph 6:19–20; Phil 1:20. S. B. Marrow notes that in Acts boldness came as a gift of the Holy Spirit: "The apostles, no less than the Christian community itself, knew all too well that this *parrhēsia* is a divine gift to be prayed for, and not some moral virtue to be attained by dint of personal application, or acquired through repeated exercise: 'And now, Lord, look upon their threats and grant to your servants to speak your word with all boldness' (μετὰ παρρησίας πάσης, Acts 4:29). The immediate response to their prayer was that "they were all filled with the Holy Spirit and spoke the word of God with boldness" (μετὰ παρρησίας, 4:31) ("*Parrhēsia* in the New Testament," *CBQ* 44 [1982] 443).

finds *Wis* 4:20–5:1 to be the key conceptual parallel to 2 Cor 2:17 and 3:12.[380] But why would Paul need to defend himself to the Corinthians for proclaiming the gospel boldly and openly to the lawless who afflict him? The Corinthians would have no problem with such fearlessness. Nor is this assertion prompted by any criticism that he had been less than open with them about his intentions.[381] If they felt that he had been less than candid with them and had dishonorable motives, appealing to some contrast between himself and Moses would hardly convince them otherwise.

The word *parrēsia* is better understood in this context as referring to the right to speak freely and openly and to give frank criticism to cultivate moral improvement. Paul is talking about speech, not just his behavior. The word's usage had shifted from meaning freedom of speech in a political context to personal candor, speaking directly and bluntly.[382] Boldness related to freedom of speech and had to do with "speaking without restraint about the most painful things," "not mincing words."[383] It was, however, the characteristic of the true friend and not the flatterer (see 1 Thess 2:2; Phlm 8; Phil 1:20).[384] Plutarch connects it to a "father's frankness, foresight, and thoughtful concern for others."[385] The LXX version of Prov 10:10 provides a backdrop to understand Paul's meaning. It contrasts the one who "winks the eye with guile," perhaps a reference to sor-

---

[380] Hafemann, *Paul, Moses, and the History of Israel,* 341–42.

[381] So Thrall, *Second Epistle to the Corinthians,* 1:254–55.

[382] In 2:17 Paul says "we speak as persons of sincerity" who stand in God's presence, and in 4:2 he commends himself by open statement of the truth (see also 4:13 and 6:11).

[383] W. C. Van Unnik, "The Semitic Background of ΠΑΡΡΗΣΙΑ in The New Testament," in *Sparsa collecta: The Collected Essays, Part Two,* NovTSup 30 (Leiden: Brill, 1980) 290–306. P. Joüon, "Divers sens de παρρησία dans le Nouveau Testament," *RSR* 30 (1940) 239–42; H. Schlier, "Παρρησία, παρρησιάζομαι," *TDNT* 5 (1967) 871–76; and D. E. Fredrickson, "ΠΑΡΡΗΣΙΑ in the Pauline Epistles," 163–83. Schlier notes that within the political sphere the word had three shades of meaning: (a) the right to say everything; (b) openness to the truth that "resists the tendency of things to conceal themselves, and man's tendency to conceal them from himself"; and (c) candor. Marrow's inquiry into the word's usage reveals that the public exercise of *parrēsia* became "perilous as a result of the decline in democratic ideals," but "the freedom to speak openly and publicly clung to the basic meaning of the term even in its private manifestations" ("*Parrhēsia* in the New Testament," 434).

[384] Glad, in his analysis of the handbook of Philodemus, "On Frank Criticism," from Zeno's lectures, notes that "the frank speaker" "correctly guides his friends." Consequently, frankness is a key element in friendship ("Frank Speech, Flattery, and Friendship in Philodemus," 29, 32; see also C. E. Glad, *Paul and Philodemus: Adaptability in Epicurean and Early Christian Psychagogy,* NovTSup 81 [Leiden: Brill, 1995]). Plutarch says that frankness is "the most potent medicine in friendship" (*Adulator* 74 D). Philo concluded from Moses' outcry to God that "frankness of speech is akin to friendship" and that all of "the audacities of his bold discourse were uttered in friendship rather than in presumption" (*Who Is the Heir of Divine Things?* 5.19,21). The "audacity of courage" (θαρραλεότης; see θαρρέω in 2 Cor 7:16 and 10:1) belongs to a friend.

[385] Plutarch, *Precepts of Statecraft; Moralia* 802F–803A.

cery, which leads to sorrow, with the one who "reproves boldly," which leads to peace. Paul insists that he did not take them in by guile (12:16), certainly did not intend to bring them grief (2:2,4; 7:8–9), and wants them to make peace (13:11).

This statement in 3:12 means that Paul admonishes others with great confidence to bring about their moral reform. And this is the cause of resentment with some Corinthians. Philodemus observed that many are resentful of frank criticism, particularly those who are ambitious and desire prominence and reputation.[386] The Corinthian correspondence shows that some in the church suffer from these spiritual disorders, and there also is evidence that they have taken issue with the open and frank scoldings from one who seems socially inferior and so woebegone. Some thought Paul was too outspoken in his letters and that the insistent and forceful demands in his letters did not match his more bland and subdued presence (10:10). Philodemus identified obstinate students as "the strong," the disobedient who do not recognize their own sins. This teacher categorized the various dispositions of various students, and some of them fit what we know about the Corinthians to a tee: "recalcitrant," "obdurate," "puffed up," "disobedient," and "irascible," "difficult to cure." The "strong," according to Philodemus, are those "who cannot tolerate frank criticism on the part of others or who violently resist it."[387]

> When rebuked, they do not think that they have sinned or that their sins will be detected… . When rebuked they are irritated and their sinful disposition and pretentiousness are exposed… . Because they think they are perfect, they are more willing to engage in frank criticism of others than to receive it. They even resent being frankly criticized by those whom they recognize as more knowledgeable and as leaders. They thus claim to be wise and mature enough to correct others, since those who admonish others are called "more knowledgeable" and "wise"![388]

The test for the Corinthians (13:5–8) is not simply whether they will respond positively to Paul's defense of his ministry and take steps to heal their relationship but whether they will respond appropriately to his reproof of their behavior (see 12:19–21).

In his exposition of Exodus 34, Paul is therefore not countering opponents who may exalt Moses but explaining the source of his own bold-

---

[386] Glad, "Frank Speech, Flattery, and Friendship in Philodemus," 34–35. Philodemus (110–40/35 B.C.) was born in Gadara in Syria and was an Epicurean who wrote on a wide variety of topics. His influence touched the most learned and influential Romans of his time.

[387] D. Konstan, D. Clay, C. E. Glad, J. C. Thom, and J. Ware, *Philodemus on Frank Criticism: Introduction, Translation, and Notes,* SBLTT (Atlanta: Scholars Press, 1998) 11, 12.

[388] Ibid., 44.

ness.[389] His boldness derives from his conviction that God chose him to convey a life and death message (2:17), just as God chose Moses, and that God has made him sufficient for the task, just as God made Moses sufficient for his task. He therefore boldly seeks to persuade others (5:11) and to make an appeal for them to be reconciled to God (5:20). He does not vent his own petty grievances. He reproves others to evoke in them a godly sorrow that leads to salvation instead of death (7:9–10).

3:13 Paul begins his exposition of Exodus 34 by citing 34:33, "When Moses finished speaking to them, he put a veil over his face." When Moses left the presence of God on Sinai (Exod 34:27–29), his luminous appearance so terrified Aaron and the people that they were afraid to come near him (Exod 34:30).[390] Moses eventually coaxed them to return and presented them with the commandments of the Lord (Exod 34:31–32). After Moses finished speaking with them, he then placed a veil over his face.[391] The text in Exodus does not reveal explicitly why Moses donned the veil, and what follows in 3:13b–14 is Paul's explanation for this action.

Philo explains that "he [Moses] descended with a countenance far more beautiful than when he ascended, so that those who saw him were filled with awe and amazement; nor even could their eyes continue to stand the dazzling brightness that flashed from him like the rays of the sun."[392] Philo attributes the Israelites' inability to gaze at Moses' face to its "dazzling brightness." Later rabbinic traditions explained that Israel's sin with the golden calf was behind their inability to look at Moses' face.[393] Paul's interpretation of the reasons behind the veiling is notoriously obscure, and

---

[389] Against Belleville (*2 Corinthians,* 96) and many others who think that intruding missionaries appealed to Moses as a model of spirituality. Instead, Paul appeals to Moses to affirm that accessibility and openness are characteristic of the new covenant in contrast to the old covenant (Bultmann, *The Second Letter to the Corinthians,* 85).

[390] The LXX of Exod 34:30 reads that the outward appearance of his face "had been glorified" (ἦν δεδοξασμένη ἡ ὄψις τοῦ χρώματος τοῦ προσώπου αὐτοῦ). *Tg. Ps.-J.* gives an interpretive rendering of Exod 34:29: "And Moses did not know that the splendor of his features were made glorious, which happened to him from the splendor of the glory of the Shekinah of the Lord."

[391] Paul's citation agrees with the LXX (ἐπέθηκεν ἐπὶ τὸ πρόσωπον αὐτοῦ κάλυμμα) except that the verb ἐτίθει is in the imperfect tense. The imperfect implies that Moses did this habitually.

[392] Philo, *Moses* 2.70. In *On Flight and Finding* 165, Philo maintains that the one who wishes to "see the principal essence will be blinded by the exceeding brilliancy of his rays before he can see it." F. W. Danker cites the *Iliad* 18:203–6, which describes Achilles' head covered by the goddess Athena with a golden cloud and a brilliant flame encircling his head as a parallel text (*II Corinthians,* ACNT [Minneapolis: Augsburg, 1989] 5. This parallel shows that those coming from pagan background would have understood the divine significance of Moses' radiant face.

[393] See *Exod. Rab.* 41:1, cited above.

it has resulted in numerous competing explanations.[394]

The NIV translation "who would put a veil over his face to keep the Israelites from gazing at it while the radiance was fading away" camouflages most of the difficulties in the text. As in 3:7, the meaning of the verb *katargeō* (NIV "fading") is fundamental for unlocking Paul's meaning. In commenting on 3:7, I agreed with Hafemann that the verb means "to render inoperative," "to cut off." This means that Paul argues that the ministry of death came with such splendor "so that the sons of Israel were not able to gaze intently at the face of Moses because of the glory of his face which was being rendered inoperative *[katargeō]*." In 3:13 he gives added information. Moses placed a veil over his face "so that the sons of Israel not gaze intently on the end *(telos)* of that which was being rendered inoperative *(katargeō)*." Interpreters of this verse have attempted to solve three puzzles. What is the meaning of *telos?* What was it that was being rendered inoperative (or according to other interpretations "fading" or "being abolished")? And why did Moses veil his face?

Interpretations divide between two basic alternatives. Either Moses veiled himself because he wanted to hide something from the people, or Moses veiled himself because he wanted to protect something. One prominent view takes the participle in 3:13 *(tou katargoumenou)* to mean "to fade" and identifies what was fading as the glory on Moses' face. *Telos* has a temporal sense and refers to the termination of the glow from his face.[395] By veiling his face, Moses prevented the people from seeing the end of that waning glory. Bruce, for example, argues that Moses veiled his face when he left the presence of God so that the Israelites would not see that his was only a fading glory that needed constant recharging.[396] Thus the fading sheen on Moses' face contrasts with the unfading glory of God in the face of Christ (4:6).

Barrett concludes similarly that Moses veiled his face "that they might not see the glory come to an end and thus be led to disparage Moses as being of no more than temporary importance." The people might have asked how this human being could be God's agent, so Moses tried to conceal his human frailty. But Barrett tries to excuse any deception on Moses' part by claiming that he acted out of pastoral concern: "Moses acted as he did not with a view to concealing the truth but in order to persuade the children of Israel to accept it; they would be more likely to do

---

[394] Hanson goes so far as to say that chap. 3 is "the Mount Everest of Pauline texts as far as difficulty is concerned—or should we rather call it the sphinx among texts, since its difficulty lies in its enigmatic quality rather than its complexity?" ("The Midrash in II Corinthians 3," 19).

[395] Thrall, *Second Epistle to the Corinthians,* 1:256.

[396] F. F. Bruce, *Paul: Apostle of the Heart Set Free* (Grand Rapids: Eerdmans, 1977) 121; see also *I & II Corinthians,* 192.

so if they did not see the end of the glory."[397]
This interpretation falls to the ground because the noun "glory" *(doxa)* is feminine and the participle *(tou katargoumenou)* is either neuter or masculine. What was supposedly fading would not refer to the glory on Moses' face. Why would the Israelites have been disillusioned or even surprised that Moses' radiance began to fade the longer he was away from the source of the glory? They did not regard him as a divine figure. Besides these questions, this explanation attributes some measure of subterfuge on the part of Moses. If not guilty of outright chicanery, he was at least hiding something from the people. It is highly unlikely that Paul would have construed Moses' actions so negatively, even to make the point about his own openness and honesty.

An alternative to this view identifies what was fading as the old covenant. This view supposes that Moses sought to conceal the temporary character of the splendor of the old covenant that was destined to pass away.[398] Moses knew that the glory associated with the old covenant made on Mount Sinai was temporary and would come to an end with Christ. Martin, for example, interprets the fading glow on Moses' face as symbolic of "the temporary nature of nomistic religion."[399] He thinks Paul is saying that the Jews from the time of Moses "until the present day" show their blindness by viewing it as "the final embodiment of God's salvation."[400]

Others interpret the *telos* as referring to the aim of the law by appeal-

---

[397] Barrett, *The Second Epistle to the Corinthians,* 120. So also van Unnik, "'With Unveiled Face,'" 161.

[398] J. D. G. Dunn, "2 Corinthians III.17—'The Lord is the Spirit,'" *JTS* 21 (1970) 311.

[399] Martin, *2 Corinthians,* 68.

[400] Martin, *2 Corinthians,* 68. Both Martin and Collange (*Énigmes,* 96–97) argue that the key word for understanding how Paul interprets Moses' intentions is the verb τὸ ἀτενίσαι ("to gaze intently") that occurs only in vv. 7 and 13 in Paul's letters. It is usually translated "see" (RSV) or "look" (KJV). But if translated with its usual meaning, "to gaze intently," it can be interpreted to mean that Moses did not simply want to prevent them from seeing the glory that was radiating from his face dim. He wanted to keep them from fixing their attention on something that was only passing; namely, the covenant that Paul has described as written on tablets of stone (3:3,7), as something that kills (3:6), as a ministry of death and condemnation (3:7,9), and as something that is being annulled (3:11). The people could easily mistake what was to be annulled as something permanent and as their ultimate hope because of the glory that attended the giving of the law. Paul assumes in his interpretation that Moses recognized that his ministry of the letter would be annulled in spite of its great glory and attempted to prevent the people from focusing on what was only impermanent. Therefore, in Paul's view, Moses did not don the veil to fool the people but tried to prevent them from riveting their attention only on what was destined to be transcended. This may explain the "but" *(alla)* in 3:14: "but their minds were hardened" (cp. Deut 29:4; Isa 6:10; 29:10) which indicates that Moses' attempt failed. The people misconceived things, and they remain deluded as evidenced by the fact that they still keep their gaze focused only on the letter.

ing to Rom 10:4: "Christ is the end *[telos]* of the law." Hanson tries to make the case that Moses viewed the preexistent Christ in the tabernacle, so he put on the veil "to prevent the messianic glory from being seen by the Israelites." Moses resorted to such a device because he knew it was part of the divine plan that Israel would be blinded and not believe in the Messiah so that it would give opportunity for the Gentiles to believe.[401] This interpretation supposedly explains the contrast between Moses and Paul. Moses hid Christ; Paul proclaims Christ.[402] But how does putting a veil over his face hide the aim of the covenant? Such interpretations assume that Paul is using an allegorical method to interpret the text; the veil and what was fading or being annulled are mere ciphers representing something other than the description of a historical occurrence.[403]

The second basic alternative for understanding this verse proposes that Moses intended to protect something. Jones contends that it was the sacredness of the divine glory. "Moses had to hide his face because the people could not partake in his experience of the vision of God."[404] Hickling agrees that Moses acted on reverential grounds: "Moses, so Paul could well have thought, did not spare the Israelites the sight of the borrowed light's final extinction in order to allow them to think that it was still shining, but because the end—like the beginning—of the period of transfiguration was too sacred for human gaze."[405] The problem with this view is that Paul does not draw any special attention to its sacredness but to the fact that it was being rendered inoperative.

---

[401] Hanson, "The Midrash in II Corinthians 3," 13. In support of this view we might compare Gal 3:22–23: "But the Scripture declares that the whole world is a prisoner of sin, so that what was promised, being given through faith in Jesus Christ, might be given to those who believe. Before this faith came, we were held prisoners by the law, locked up until faith should be revealed." This interpretation, however, requires that Paul's reading of Exod 34 goes beyond the text, if not against the text, by importing this idea. Thrall believes that Moses "concealed the negative indication of the ultimate redundancy of the old covenant: the fact that by God's design its purpose was to perform only an interim function until its supercession by the Christ-event" (*Second Epistle to the Corinthians,* 1:258). She goes on to say that Paul may have attributed this intentional deception to Moses because he was charged with it himself by those who compared him unfavorably to Moses. Such an argument, however, shows how problematic it is to allow speculative hypotheses about the opponents' accusations against Paul to determine what Paul means.

[402] This interpretation fits well with Augustine's belief that the NT is concealed in the OT while the OT is revealed in the NT.

[403] Hafemann concludes: "These attempts all see symbols and metaphors where Paul is continuing to describe a historical occurrence" (*Paul, Moses, and the History of Israel,* 349, n. 45).

[404] P. Jones "L'Apôtre Paul: un second Moise pour la Communant de la nouvelle Alliance," *Foi et Vie* 75 (1976) 49.

[405] C. J. A. Hickling, "The Sequence of Thought on II Corinthians, Chapter Three," *NTS* 21 (1974) 391.

Hafemann's exhaustive study of these verses offers the best solution by helping us see how Paul's own interpretation of Exod 34:29–35 remained faithful to
the original context of Exodus 32–34.[406] Paul is not going beyond the text or
even against the text by imposing some theological motive, derived from Christian theology, on Moses' actions. He argues that Moses veiled himself to protect
the people of Israel. The Israelites were justifiably afraid, given their sin and
subsequent punishment. No hint appears in the text in Exodus or in contemporary Jewish tradition that the glory on Moses' face was fading.[407] The glory of
God was mediated on Moses' face, and the repeated veiling rendered inoperative (stopped, cut off) the effects of the glory on his face.[408] The veil hides the
glory of the Lord because, when the veil is removed, we see the glory of the
Lord (3:18).

The noun *telos* means "aim" but does not refer here to Christ as in Rom
10:4. When followed by the genitive of something, *telos* "is concerned with
'result, purpose, outcome, and fate, not termination.' Its connotations are
'teleological' rather than temporal when it occurs in biblical literature."[409]
Moses was protecting the people from a dire consequence if they gazed continually at the reflected glory of God radiating from his face. The *telos* of the
glory on Moses' face does not refer to some purpose or goal, or to Christ,

---

[406] Although offering different answers to various problems raised by the text, recent studies
reveal a consensus about Paul's treatment of Exod 34:29–35. It is assumed that Paul imposed his
Christian presuppositions on the text to find a typological/allegorical meaning that is not only arbi-
trary but contrary to the text's original meaning. See, e.g., D. Boyarin, *A Radical Jew: Paul and the
Politics of Identity* (Berkeley/Los Angeles/London: University of California Press, 1994) 100–101;
R. B. Hays, *Echoes of Scripture in the Letters of Paul* (New Haven: Yale University Press, 1989)
122–53; O. Hofius, "Gesetz und Evangelium nach 2. Korinther 3," in *Paulusstudien*, WUNT 51
(Tübingen: Mohr [Siebeck], 1989) 75– 120; M. Hooker, "Beyond the Things That Are Written? St.
Paul's Use of Scripture?" *NTS* 27 (1980) 295–309; P. von der Osten Sacken, "Die Decke des
Moses. Zur Exegese und Hermeneutic von Geist und Buchstabe in 2 Korinther 3," in *Die Heiligkeit
der Tora. Studien zum Gesetz bei Paulus* (München: Kaiser, 1989) 150–55; and C. K. Stockhausen,
Moses' Veil and the glory of the New Covenant. The Exegetical Substructure of II Cor 3,1–4,6, AB
116 (Rome: Pontifical Biblical Institute, 1989). Dumbrell identifies the serious implications of
such a view: "If Paul's argument here is simply a tour de force, then the Hellenistic congregations
to which he writes are being invited to regard Paul as the primary authority to which they must have
recourse and not the OT to which he himself seems to defer" ("Paul's Use of Exodus 34 in 2 Corinthians 3," 180).

[407] The rabbinic tradition has almost nothing to say about Moses' veil. There is one late comment that the divine glow continued even after Moses' death. If a hole was bored into Moses' grave,
the world would fill with light (*Pesiq. Rab.* 21). See also *Tg. Onq.* Deut 34:7.

[408] Hafemann, "Paul's Argument," 288–89. What was being rendered inoperative does not refer
to something that will happen only in the distant future but refers to something that occurs at the
time when Moses veiled his face (see Hafemann, *Paul, Moses, and the History of Israel*, 358).

[409] Thrall, *The Second Epistle to the Corinthians*, 1:257, citing R. Badenas, *Christ the End of
the Law: Romans 10:4 in Pauline Perspective*, JSNTSup 10 (Sheffield: JSOT, 1985) 79–80; see
also Hafemann, *Paul, Moses, and the History of Israel*, 357.

but to consequences. It concerns the death that divine glory inflicts upon "hardened hearts."

Israel's idolatry with the golden calf betrayed the hardened condition of the people.[410] It was not some minor lapse but something symptomatic of their incorrigible wickedness. The goal of the old covenant was the manifestation of the glory of God, but it had the effect of bringing death and condemnation to those with hardened hearts rather than transformation into glory (see 3:18).[411] If God's glory had continued in their midst during their hardened condition, the people would have been utterly destroyed (Exod 33:3,5).[412] Because of Israel's idolatry, Moses becomes the only link between the people and God (Num 12:7–8). He alone experiences God's glory and mediates it to the people (Exod 33:18).[413] Their hardened hearts made it necessary for Moses to wear a veil to compensate for the people's

---

[410] *Ps. Philo* 12:1–10 provides an interesting order in retelling the story of Moses' veil. It first reports that Moses came down from the mountain bathed in a light that surpassed the splendor of the sun and the moon, and then he made a veil for himself. Next, it recounts how the heart of the people was corrupted while he was on the mountain and provides an account of the golden calf incident. God intends to forsake the people but yields to Moses' plea to spare them. This account clearly connects the veil of Moses with the people's sin and God's holy wrath with God's long-suffering mercy.

[411] A secular and crude expression of this idea captured the popular imagination in the movie *Raiders of the Lost Ark*. When the Nazi villains opened up the recovered ark of the covenant, they were destroyed as they stared at the glorious power emerging from it. The hero and heroine are saved only by covering their eyes.

[412] Hafemann, *Paul, Moses, and the History of Israel*, 207. God's indescribable and potent glory required that the people abide by strict safeguards lest it destroy them. They had to be ceremonially washed and consecrated even though only priests could come near the holy mountain. They could not even touch the mountain's edge, and God warned Moses to prevent them from trying to break through the limits "to look," otherwise many of them would perish (Exod 19:21). A tradition in *Lev. Rab.* 20:10 maintains that the early deaths of Aaron's sons, Nadab and Abihu, resulted from a sentence of death received on Mount Sinai. They fed their eyes on the Shekinah, as Moses did, but were sinful. A parable that imagines the giving of the law as a symbol of Israel's betrothal to God is offered to explain why they did not die immediately (see Num 3:4; 26:61; 1 Chr 24:2). If a king celebrates the wedding of his daughter and finds something discreditable about the best man, he does not mar her joy by slaying him now but waits for another time. R. E. Otto cogently argues that this atmosphere of fear lies behind the reaction of Peter when he and two other disciples witnessed Jesus' transfiguration on the mountain. He translates his response as a question, "Is it good for us to be here?" (9:6). Gazing on the unveiling of Jesus' majestic glory without having been consecrated or ritually purified aroused his fear. Peter's offer to build the "tabernacles" (tents) was prompted by his terror and his desire to protect himself from being slain by this unapproachable glory. The tabernacles would veil the divine glory and prevent the three disciples, who knew themselves to be sinners, from being destroyed. For the disciples the unveiled glory was "graciously brief" ("The Fear Motivation in Peter's Offer to Build ΤΡΕΙΣ ΣΚΗΝΑΣ," *WJT* 59 [1997] 106–7, 110–12). The account of Jesus' transfiguration and the disciples' fear could provide another contrast for Paul's argument about the two covenants. The coming of the Spirit expels fear before the unveiled glory of God now revealed in the face of Jesus.

[413] Hafemann, 209, 215.

sinfulness. Wearing the veil was therefore Moses' way of *protecting* the stiff-necked people from "the death-dealing judgment of the glory of God" against sinners that is decreed in the old covenant. It prevented them from gazing dangerously long upon the glory mediated on Moses' face.[414]

Hafemann concludes that, like the fence around the bottom of Mount Sinai (Exod 19:12), "The veil of Moses makes it possible for the glory of God to be in the midst of the people, albeit now mediated through Moses, without destroying them."[415] The veil expresses God's judgment: God's reflected glory must be veiled because of their sinful state, otherwise it would have destroyed them.[416] The veil also expresses God's mercy. It makes possible for the glory of God to be brought into the midst of the people through Moses.[417] The veil embodies God's holy judgment while granting "the accompanying mercy of the renewed covenant." The people "could enjoy God's glory during the periods in which Moses spoke the words of the Lord to Israel, but they could no longer enjoy his uninterrupted presence in their midst."[418] Paul's interpretation of Exodus 32–34 stands at the end of a long line of canonical interpretations in which Moses' ministry was interpreted not only as an act of divine mercy and grace, but also as a ministry of judgment upon a rebellious people.[419]

Moses was helpless to do anything about the people's hardened condition. Consequently, they could not receive the full blessing of the old covenant.[420] The fault was not with the old covenant or with Moses but with the people who were sinful.[421] The people could not see the Lord's glory without being destroyed. Turning to the Lord, according to Paul, can only

---

[414] Ibid., 358. See also D. W. Oostendorp, *Another Jesus: A Gospel of Jewish-Christian Superiority in 2 Corinthians* (Kampen: Kok, 1967) 39–40 (open revelation of God's glory would have brought about their destruction, unable to stand in his holy presence); and D. A. Renwick, *Paul, the Temple, and the Presence of God,* BJS 224 (Atlanta: Scholars Press, 1991) 54, 138–44.

[415] Hafemann, *Paul, Moses, and the History of Israel,* 223.

[416] Had Moses not done so, "it would have destroyed Israel due to their 'stiff-necked' condition (cf. Exod 33:3,5). ... "[T]he veiling of Moses' face underscores the point of both Exod 32–34 and 2 Cor 3:7, that is, that due to Israel's hardened nature as manifested in her sin with the golden calf, Moses' mediation of the glory of God is now a ministry of death. The veil of Moses manifests YHWH's judgment against his rebellious people" (Hafemann, "Paul's Argument," 288–89).

[417] Hafemann, *Paul, Moses, and the History of Israel,* 224.

[418] Ibid., 354.

[419] See Num 14:26–35; Deut 1:34–46; 2:14–16; 9:6–8; 29:4; Pss 78:21–22; 95:10; 106:23,26; Jer 7:24–26; and Ezek 20:21–26.

[420] Paul understood Moses' veiling, which rendered inoperative God's glory and protected the people from the danger of God's immediate and abiding presence, as an indication that the ministry of condemnation "was, from the beginning, destined to be replaced by a 'new' covenant ministry" (Hafemann, "Paul's Argument," 294).

[421] H. A. Kent, Jr. "The Glory of Christian Ministry: An Analysis of 2 Corinthians 2:14–4:18," *GTJ* 2 (1981) 179.

be done in Christ through the Spirit.[422] The life-giving, transforming Spirit is now a present reality. Paul is bold compared with Moses because the Spirit has radically changed the people's disposition before God. Consequently, the glory of God no longer needs to "be veiled from those to whom he is sent, since its τέλος is life, not death."[423] Removing the veil is what happens when one turns to God. Christians can encounter the glory of God and live because the condemnation of the old covenant has now been permanently annulled for those who are in Christ.[424] Paul is not like Moses because the covenant of the Spirit is not like the old covenant, which the people of Israel broke (Jer 31:32).

VEILED ISRAEL (THEY, ISRAELITES) (3:14–17). **3:14–15** Paul continues his interpretation of the veil in Exodus 34 and reflects on its implications upon the sons of Israel "to this day."[425] It is possible to interpret the "but" in 3:14 as introducing the reaction of Israel which was the opposite of Moses' intent when he veiled himself.[426] Moses veiled himself, but their minds were hardened. We have argued, however, that the hardened nature of Israel, created by their idolatry, caused Moses to slip on the veil to cut off the dangerous effects of seeing the glory of God in their sinful state. The veiling, then, was not the cause of their obstinacy. The "but" must have its usual adversative meaning and *contrast* the statement in 3:13.[427] Paul is not like Moses in being very bold because Christians with the Spirit are not like Israel, whose minds were hardened.

---

[422] Philo stated that when Moses spoke for God he became "another man, changed both in outward appearance and mind and filled with the Spirit" (*Life of Moses* 2.271).

[423] Hafemann, *Paul, Moses, and the History of Israel*, 361.

[424] This reality does not mean that God no longer judges those who suppress the truth of the gospel because of their hardened hearts and blinded eyes (see Rom 1:18–32). The context of Israel's idolatry with the golden calf should serve as a stern warning to those Corinthians who feel no qualms about eating meat sacrificed to idols (1 Cor 8:1–13; 10:1–30; 2 Cor 6:14–7:1).

[425] The two verses are parallel 3:14b with the reference to "this day," "reading," "Moses" (= "the old covenant"), "veil," and "covers" (= "remains"). "Moses" in 3:15 refers to the old covenant (see Acts 15:21; Mark 10:3–4; 12:26; 2 Chr 25:4; Neh 13:1).

[426] So Belleville, *Reflections of Glory*, 219.

[427] On the οὐ ... ἀλλά construction, see Hafemann, *Paul, Moses, and the History of Israel*, 363–65. The ἀλλά in 3:14 introduces a positive contrast to the οὐ in 3:13a. He argues that the contrast is "not between Moses' intention and the 'hardened minds' of Israel, but between Paul's boldness and the fact that Israel's minds were hardened" (p. 365). Wright comments, "Moses had to use the veil because the hearts of the Israelites were hardened (unlike those of the new covenant people; this is the point of the ἀλλά, 'but,' at the start of v. 14)" ("Reflected Glory: 2 Corinthians 3," 180). The arguments against this sense (see Thrall, *Second Epistle to the Corinthians*, 1:262–63) are not persuasive.

The translation "hardened" better captures the meaning of *pōroō* than the NIV translation "made dull," a reading that implies that their problem was simply one of incomprehension from darkened perceptions. The people suffered from stone hard hearts, not simply dull minds.[428] A chorus of biblical witnesses ascribes the inability to see and hear to a sinful condition (see Isa 6:9–10; 29:10–12; Jer 5:21–24; Ezek 12:2; Mark 4:10–12; John 12:39–40; Acts 28:25–27).[429] Paul uses the noun form of the verb "to harden" in Rom 11:25 to explain why most of Israel has failed to respond to the gospel: "A hardening has come upon Israel" (see Rom 11:7–8).[430] In the context of his argument here, Paul implies that any who fail to see God's glory manifest in his own ministry of the Spirit are in the same hardened condition as Israel of old. For those who are hardened, Paul's ministry reeks with the odor of death.

The veil, then, is not simply a metaphor for Israel's failure to see and understand. As Paul sees it, Israel's fundamental problem is not a failure to comprehend the law but a failure to obey it (Rom 2:17–29; Gal 6:13). They do not suffer from an intellectual deficiency but from a moral one that prevents them from seeing and believing, hearing and understanding.[431] The veil comes to stand for this hardened condition that prevents those who may treasure, defend, and diligently study the law from apprehending God's true glory. From the very beginning, when the covenant was first read to them by Moses, they suffered from a spiritual hardening of the arteries. Paul insists that the people remain in that same condition

---

[428] In 2:11 Paul says we Christians know Satan's designs (τὰ νοήματα), the same word translated "minds" in 3:14. Paul may be warning that they must be careful for their own minds, which Satan will attempt to lead astray (11:3; Hafemann, *Paul, Moses, and the History of Israel*, 369).

[429] So also Provence, "Who Is Sufficient for These Things?" 80. It refers to the hardening of the will, not an obscuring of the perception. The veil represents a spiritual condition that explains the unbelief of the majority of Jews in his day (p. 77). Savage remarks that God has hardened Israel "by choosing to manifest his glory precisely where Israel, in its pride, would refuse to see it. In that way it could be ensured that when Israel did come to see the glory it would be on God's terms—when Israel had been humbled sufficiently to see the glory in the ignominy of the cross" (*Power through Weakness*, 143).

[430] Lambrecht notes that "the use of this terminology conveys a rather sad and pained attitude of Paul to the unconverted Jews ('they') which contrasts sharply with his boastful, self-confident and hopeful view of himself and the Christians ('we')" ("Structure," 270).

[431] This interpretation rules out views that Israel only misperceives the goal of the old covenant and the glory of God in the person of Christ by thinking that Moses is the final word, or failing to recognize that the glory of Moses is extinguished (Bultmann, *The Second Letter to the Corinthians*, 86), that the old covenant is obsolescent (Barrett, *Second Epistle to the Corinthians*, 120), or that it has been superseded by Christ (Bruce, *I & II Corinthians*, 192.

when the law is being read to them today.[432] Paul may be referring to the circumstances of his first preaching in Corinth, well known to his readers, when the local Jews opposed and reviled him and he was forced out of the synagogue (Acts 18:5–11).

The *epi* refers to the occasion when Moses read the commandments that God gave him on Mount Sinai (Exod 34:32–33).[433] Reading the old covenant does not refer to the Old Testament as opposed to the New, since the latter had not yet come into existence. Nor is "old" a negative assessment of the ministry of Moses as something antiquated, fusty, or passé.[434] It refers instead to the covenant made on Mount Sinai with Moses.[435] Provence comments, "Because the Holy Spirit was not shed abroad during the ministry of the Old Covenant, Paul can speak of a veil which lies upon the reading of the Old Covenant (v. 14) and, significantly, upon the hearts of the children of Israel (v. 15)."[436] The old covenant is not veiled, but Israel is.

Paul believes that Israel remains stiff-necked and refuses to turn to the Lord or submit to his will. The fault, however, is not in Moses or the law but in those who hear.[437] One of the foundations of Paul's faith was his conviction that in Christ, and only in Christ, the veil is abolished.[438] The subject of the verb *katargeitai* in 3:14 is not explicitly expressed. Paul gives no indication, however, that the subject has changed from "the same veil" in the first part of the verse, and the veil is the subject of the passive verb in 3:15. Israel's rejection of the only one who can remove the veil condemns them to

---

[432] Hafemann ("Paul's Argument," 293) contends that the focus is on the purpose and results of the old and new covenants: the old is being rendered inoperative while the new is abiding: "The Sinai covenant's mediation of the glory of God, which due to the hard hearts of Israel became an expression of God's condemnation (3:9) so that it had to be continually rendered inoperative by the veil (τὴν καταργουμένην) is now itself described as that which "was continually being rendered inoperative" (τὸ καταργούμενον, 3:11). In doing so, Paul creates a play on the use of καταργέω in which what happened to Moses' glory in Exod 34:29ff. becomes a metonymy for the old covenant of which it was a part." It is unlikely that Paul has in mind any reference to veiling the Torah scrolls in the synagogue (as a veil was on the lawgiver so it is on the law) or to veiling of the head in prayer. On the public reading of the law in the synagogue, see Acts 13:15 and 1 Tim 4:13.

[433] Hafemann, *Paul, Moses, and the History of Israel,* 370–71.

[434] See Matt 13:52: "Therefore every teacher of the law who has been instructed about the kingdom of heaven is like the owner of a house who brings out of his storeroom new treasures as well as old."

[435] Furnish, *II Corinthians,* 208. To say that they continue to be hardened in the present is an easy leap to make since the phrase πάντες οἱ ἄρχοντες τῆς συναγωγῆς ("all the rulers of the synagogue [congregation]") appears in Exod 34:31 in the LXX.

[436] Provence, "Who Is Sufficient for These Things?" 77.

[437] See Calvin, *The Second Epistle of Paul the Apostle to the Corinthians,* 47. Lambrecht points out that 3:14–17 emphasizes the guilt of the Jews for their unbelief lest one find Moses culpable in some way for their blindness ("Structure," 272).

[438] The NIV correctly reads ὅτι and translates it "because." The KJV reads it as a neuter singular relative pronoun ὅ τι: "which [veil] is done away in Christ."

continue in their hardened condition.[439]

Hafemann comments, "Only those whose hearts have been changed by the Spirit will accept the (new) covenant redemption (in Christ) and be enabled by the Spirit to keep its stipulations as revealed in the Law."[440] The seeming inglorious nature of the Messiah in whom Christians trust compounds the problem for Israel. Christ was not a figure of glory who vanquished the pagan oppressors and restored Israel's fortunes in the world but one who suffered and died on a cross. His fate "made a mockery of Jewish expectations" and "effectively nailed those expectations to a cross."[441] He became "a stone that causes men to stumble and a rock that makes them fall" (Rom 9:33; see Mark 12:10–11). Identification with this humble Messiah who endured the humiliation of death on the cross, however, abolishes one's former pride and fleshly boasts. But it also abolishes the veil that hides God's glory in Christ. Paul himself had suffered from the same blindness that now darkens Israel's vision. He looked at Christ from a fleshly perspective (5:16). When God caused the divine light to shine in his heart, he saw the crucified Jesus in a different way— as one who died for him because of his sin. This new perspective destroyed all his delusions of righteousness. He had to empty himself of his self-seeking desires and any wishful thinking about a Messiah who would exalt Israel to worldly prominence and who would celebrate his exemplary obedience to the law. To be crucified with Christ meant he had to discard as rubbish his noble heritage and laudable achievements, even his fervor for the law. In his own profound humiliation and shame, he saw God's compelling glory in Christ. He could no longer live for himself. Rather he must give himself to Christ to live and die for others.

3:16 Paul returns to the text of Exodus 34 and quotes freely from 34:34. When Moses went before the Lord in the tent of meeting, he would remove the veil, and then he would reveil his face when he returned to speak with the people. Several differences between Paul's quotation and the LXX ver-

---

[439] In Rom 11:11–32, Paul shows how God can use even willful disobedience to accomplish his purposes. Israel's blindness provided an opportunity for the Gentiles to believe and become members of God's people. We should remember, however, that not all Israel rejected the gospel. With perhaps the exception of Luke-Acts, our NT was penned by Jewish Christians. Acts records an enormous response to the gospel by the people, but it also records that every time it is preached to Jews it creates a divided response. It meets with neither wholesale repentance nor wholesale rejection (Acts 2:12; 4:4; 13:43–45,51; 18:4–8; 28:23–24). In fact, there was a divided response among Jesus' own disciples. Judas turned away to go to his own place (Acts 1:25). Peter declares, "Every soul that does not listen shall be destroyed from the people" (Acts 3:23; see Luke 1:16 and 2:34). Paul considers those Jews and Gentiles who believe in Jesus as "the Israel of God" (Gal 6:16; see Rom 9:6).

[440] Hafemann, *Paul, Moses, and the History of Israel,* 368.

[441] Savage, *Power through Weakness,* 140.

sion help elucidate what Paul means.[442]

First, "Moses" is omitted from the citation by Paul, and the verb "turn" has no explicit subject.[443] Second, the verb "enter" *(eiseporeueto)* in the imperfect tense in the LXX is changed to "turn" and is an aorist subjunctive.[444] Third, an element of condition is introduced by the "if."[445] Finally, the verb "remove" *(periaireitai)* is changed from an imperfect tense in the LXX to a present tense. In the Exodus passage the verb is clearly a middle voice so that Moses removes the veil when he comes into the presence of the Lord. In Paul's text the verb should be read as a passive voice so that the veil "is taken away."

The change from a spatial idea of "enter" to the verb "turn" is suggestive. In the Old and New Testaments the verb "turn" can refer to conversion (see Deut 4:30; 30:2,9–10; 2 Chr 30:9; Isa 6:9; Hos 6:1; see also *Tob* 13:6; Acts 9:35; 11:2; 15:19; 26:20). Paul interprets the experience of Moses in turning unveiled and beholding the glory of the Lord as an archetype for the experience of the Christian who turns to the Lord. This interpretation also holds Paul's hope for Israel (see Rom 11:23–24). Paul interprets the action of Moses as paradigmatic for unbelieving members of the nation of Israel in his own day.[446] *If* they turn to the Lord, they will have the veil of disobedience that sheathes their hearts and minds removed. The turning indicates "that there is a sense in which Israel must itself act to remove the veil."[447] On the

---

[442] The parallels in the two texts are underlined:
2 Cor 3:16 ἡνίκα δὲ ἐὰν ἐπιστρέψῃ πρὸς κύριον, περιαιρεῖται τὸ κάλυμμα.
Exod 34:34a ἡνίκα δὲ ἂν εἰσεπορεύετο Μωυσῆς ἔναντι κυρίου λαλεῖν αὐτῷ περιῃρεῖτο τὸ κάλυμμα.

[443] The "anyone" (τις) in the NIV is not in the text.

[444] It may have been suggested by the verb ἐπιστρέφω in Exod 34:31.

[445] Paul's text has ἐάν instead of ἄν (see E. Wong, "The Lord Is the Spirit," (2 Cor 3,17a)," *ETL* 61 [1985] 49–53).

[446] The ambiguity concerning the subject of the verb "turn" allows it to refer to the Exodus narrative, which describes Moses going back into the presence of the Lord and removing the veil and also to refer to those who follow Moses' pattern. In the latter context the verb has a moral-religious connotation (so Hughes, *Paul's Second Epistle to the Corinthians,* 114, n. 10). Sloan argues that Paul refers to Moses here, even though he does not specifically name him (see NEB). He contends that Paul is not concerned with how to remove the veil for others but with contrasting his ministry with that of Moses. Moses went before the Lord and removed the veil from his face ("New Covenant Hermeneutics," 141–42). But Paul is not simply contrasting himself with Moses. Moses is forced to wear the veil because of the people's hardheartedness. Paul draws a distinction between a ministry to people who are hardened, necessitating the veil to shield them from God's glory, and a ministry to a people whose hearts have been made pliant through the Spirit. The problem is stated in v. 15, "The veil covers their hearts." The solution is given in v. 16; the veil is removed by turning to the Lord, who is the Spirit. To argue, as W. J. Dalton does, that Paul only has in mind his Jewish adversaries in Corinth who need turn to Christ and that he does not refer to the conversion of Jews to Christ is a serious misreading of Paul ("Is the Old Covenant Abrogated (2 Cor 3:14)?" *AusBR* 35 [1987] 88–94). See Rom 11:11–21.

[447] Savage, *Power through Weakness,* 135. Some Jews in Corinth had done this (Acts 18:8).

other hand, turning to the Lord applies also to Gentile believers (see 1 Thess 1:9; Gal 4:9). In the new covenant every Christian can enter the presence of the Lord. But it is only by virtue of the Spirit who removes the heart of stone and writes God's law on our hearts that any can enter safely. Wright captures the thrust of Paul's argument, which is that "those who are in Christ, the new covenant people, are unveiled precisely because their hearts are unhardened (3.1–3,4–6)."[448]

This interpretation assumes that Exodus 34 continues to direct Paul's thought and that "Lord" refers to YHWH, not Christ.[449] In all of Paul's other quotations of the Old Testament the references to the Lord refer to God.[450] This reading fits the parallel reference in 1 Thess 1:9: "They tell how you turned to God from idols to serve the living and true God."[451]

The "if they turn" leads one to ask what prevents Israel from doing so. Paul's brief autobiographical sketches in Phil 3:2–9 and Gal 1:13–14 and his lament over Israel in Rom 9:30–10:12 may provide some clue.[452] As one who was zealous for the traditions of the fathers, Paul was imbued with pride and "an irresistible urge to exalt himself."[453] His confidence in his own merit derived from fleshly categories of life that gave him the basis for outboasting others as a rising religious star who outdid all his contemporaries (Gal 1:13–14). It provided him with his own righteousness (Phil 3:6,9), and that made him feel superior. He was self-absorbed—so self-absorbed that he could not see the glory of God in Christ and sought to destroy it. The law, when misinterpreted, seemed to encourage this do-it-yourself righteousness and engendered this national pride that looked down on others.[454]

---

[448] Wright, "Reflected Glory: 2 Corinthians 3," 183. This interpretation helps explain the basic differences between Moses, who had to veil himself to protect the people from God's glory, and Paul, who does not. The spiritual condition of the hearers is the crucial distinction.

[449] So Moule, "2 Cor 3:18b," 236; Dunn, "2 Cor III.17," 314–20; Furnish, *II Corinthians*, 211; and Hafemann, *Paul, Moses, and the History of Israel*, 392.

[450] Rom 4:8; 9:28,29; 10:16; 11:3,34; 15:11; 1 Cor 2:16; 3:20; 10:26; 14:21; and 2 Cor 6:17–18; 8:21 (see Dunn, "2 Cor III.17," 317; and Furnish, *II Corinthians*, 211).

[451] Others have argued from the reference to Christ in 3:14 that "the Lord" refers to Christ (I. Hermann, *Kyrios und Pneuma. Studien zur Christologie der paulinischen Hauptbriefe*, SANT 2 [Munich: Kösel, 1961], and still others that it refers to the Spirit from the statement that the Lord is the Spirit in 3:18 (see Belleville, *Reflections of Glory*, 256–63). Belleville notes the patristic tendency to use this verse in the service of Trinitarian controversy to argue that the Spirit is divine. She understands this to be an allegorization of the term "Lord." The term "Lord" refers to the Spirit (3:18). "Now the Lord to whom Moses turned was Yahweh; today the Lord to whom the Jew must turn is the Spirit" (Belleville, "Paul's Polemic," 301).

[452] What follows is adapted from Savage, *Power through Weakness*, 135–38.

[453] Ibid., 138.

[454] Israel's blind zeal for the law is not leavened with understanding (Rom 10:2) since they seek a righteousness based on works (Rom 9:32). It leads them to become arrogant "as though they were establishing 'their own righteousness'" (see Rom 10:3) (Savage, *Power through Weakness*, 137).

He reveled in his own achievements and failed to recognize that all that he had was a gift from God. When we exalt ourselves, even for such a praise-worthy virtue as our zeal for God, we blind ourselves to God's exaltation. Those who are consumed with their own glory, with pride and boasting, will miss the glory of God revealed in Christ; for it is a peculiar sort of glory, one that radiates from the humiliation of the cross.

3:17 Paul now explains the meaning of the verse from Exodus cited in v. 16. Belleville cogently makes the case that 3:17a, "Now the Lord is the Spirit," explains 3:16a, "But whenever anyone turns to the Lord"; and 3:17b, "and where the Spirit of the Lord is, there is freedom," explains 3:16b, "The veil is taken away."[455] If Paul is interpreting Exod 34:34, then the Lord would refer to YHWH, and the NEB translation best captures the meaning: "Now the Lord of whom this passage speaks is the Spirit."[456] The proximity of the divine presence caused Moses' transformation, and Paul would argue that every believer can experience the divine presence and the glorious transformation through the Spirit. Paul's ministry mediates the Spirit, whose function is to transform the lives of believers progressively into the image of Christ.[457]

But what kind of freedom does Paul have in mind? Freedom from what? The widespread idea that Paul has in mind freedom from the law should be

---

[455] Belleville, *Reflections of Glory,* 257–62. Others note that δέ is used in 1 Cor 10:4; 15:27,56; and Gal 4:25 to introduce an explanation of a scriptural text (Dunn, "2 Corinthians III.17," 312; Furnish, *II Corinthians,* 212; and Thrall, *Second Epistle to the Corinthians,* 1:274). The definite article with the Lord in 3:17a is anaphoric, pointing back to the previously mentioned "Lord" (without the article) in 3:16 and making clear that he is still under discussion. The phrase τὸ πνεῦμα κυρίου in 3:17b does not appear elsewhere in Paul's letters. Paul either includes the definite article with both nouns or omits it with both nouns.

[456] So Dunn, "2 Corinthians III.17," 313; Furnish, *II Corinthians;* and Thrall, *Second Epistle to the Corinthians,* 1:274. Paul takes up a term from the previous sentence citing a passage from the Scripture and elaborates on its meaning by repeating the term with its definite article and δέ in 1 Cor 10:4 and Gal 4:25. For other examples of this formula in Jewish literature, see Belleville, *Reflections of Glory,* 256–57. If, as we have argued, Paul has not interpreted Exodus 34 fancifully, it makes the proposal that "the Lord" refers to Christ quite unlikely (contra D. Greenwood, "The Lord Is the Spirit: Some Considerations of 2 Cor 3:17," *CBQ* 34 [1972] 467–72). Hafemann asserts that "Paul is not identifying Christ and the Spirit, but making it clear that Moses' experience of YHWH in the tent of meeting is equivalent to the current experience of the Spirit in Paul's ministry, even as Paul could refer in 3:3 to the Spirit unleashed in his ministry as the 'Spirit of the living God'" (*Paul, Moses, and the History of Israel,* 399). Even more unlikely is the conjecture that the text has somehow been corrupted. N. Turner suggested that οὗ ("where") was originally οὐ ("not"): "The Spirit is not freedom from the Lord" (*Grammatical Insights into the New Testament* [Edinburgh: T & T Clark, 1965] 128). Barrett (*Second Epistle to the Corinthians,* 124) counters that Paul expresses "freedom from" with the prepositions *apo* or *ek,* not with the use of the genitive (see Rom 6:18,22; 7:3; 8:2,21; 1 Cor 9:19).

[457] Bruce, *Paul,* 121.

dismissed.[458] The immediate context should guide the decision, not an importing of theological issues from Paul's other letters into 2 Corinthians.[459] In the context freedom has to do with freedom from the veil that only comes when one turns to the Lord (3:16,18). Because Israel did not have the Spirit to make their hearts receptive to God's law, they were kept from beholding God's glory. Using metonymy, Paul employs the term "the veil" to represent the people's hardheartedness that thwarted their ability to experience God's glory to its fullest extent.[460] If the veil represents the stiffnecked sinfulness of Israel, it follows as a corollary that when that veil is removed, freedom from the law of sin and death results.

In the age of the Spirit, there is no need for veils, which is what marks the contrast between Paul and Moses. Paul does not veil himself or his gospel but makes things evident and spreads the knowledge of God (2:14; 4:6) for all to see (3:2). The uncovered face of Paul that looks up to God also turns uncovered to others. "Freedom" parallels the boldness in 3:12.[461] Freedom is not freedom from some constraint. Paul has in mind "freedom of speech, boldness, openness, and honesty in proclaiming and defending the gospel (cp. 2:17; 4:1f.)."[462] Paul is free and can use boldness, not because he personally is different from Moses but because those who belong to the new covenant are different from those who belong to the old. He proclaims the gospel to the Corinthians boldly, without holding anything back. Malherbe notes how Paul's use of *parrēsia* is different from other moral philosophers of his day.

> While the moral philosopher was impelled by an awareness of his own moral freedom, acquired by reason and the application of his own will, to speak boldly to the human condition and demand its reformation, Paul regards his entire ministry, as to its origin, motivation, content and method, as being directed by God. God grants him the boldness to speak, and what he says is not philosophical or rational analysis of the human condition, but the gospel of God.[463]

---

[458] Barrett argues that "the Christian, in whose heart God's law is written by the Spirit, is not bound by legalistically conceived religion" (*The Second Epistle to the Corinthians,* 124). See Thrall, who believes that Paul has in mind freedom from the "the destiny of sin and death which goes with [the law]" (*The Second Epistle to the Corinthians,* 1:275). But in 1 Cor 7:19 Paul affirms that what matters is keeping the commandments of the law.

[459] See Rom 6:18,22; 8:2,21; 1 Cor 9:1,19; 10:29; Gal 2:4; 4:22–31; 5:1,13.

[460] See Hafemann, *Paul, Moses, and the History of Israel,* 371–74, on Paul's use of metonymy.

[461] Furnish maintains that it refers to "the freedom to speak and act without fear": "Apostolic boldness derives from the freedom which is granted under the new covenant, written on the heart by the action of the Spirit of the Lord" (*II Corinthians,* 237–38).

[462] Wright, "Reflected Glory: 2 Corinthians 3:18," 179.

[463] A. J. Malherbe, "Exhortation in 1 Thessalonians," in *Paul and the Popular Philosophers* (Minneapolis: Fortress, 1989) 59.

If this interpretation is correct, Paul salutes the Corinthians by comparing them favorably with the Israelites. Moses had to resort to a veil because of their hardened hearts. The greater glory of Paul's ministry does not require an even thicker veil to protect the people but no veil at all because the Spirit radically changes the disposition of the people's heart. Wright summarizes Paul's argument:

> "The reason we have boldness is this: you, unlike the Israelites before whom the glory (even of the old covenant) had to be veiled, possess the Spirit because you are within the new covenant, and you are therefore able to bear the bold, direct revelation of God's glory." The point Paul is making is that the open-faced style of ministry he employs is *appropriate* because of *the condition that he and his hearers share,* that is, unhardened hearts and the consequent Spirit-given ability to behold the glory of God.[464]

The foremost difference between Moses' ministry and Paul's is the work of the Spirit that enables all believers "to turn" and to enter into the Lord's presence.

UNVEILED CHRISTIANS (WE, CHRISTIANS) (3:18).   **3:18**   Paul concludes this section by combining the text of Exod 34:35 with a commentary. Moses wore the veil over his shining face until he went in to speak with the Lord; and Paul asserts that all Christians can, like Moses, approach the glory of the Lord with unveiled faces and experience the same transformation. The emphatic "we all" refers to the experience of all Christians, not just that of apostles or Christian ministers, because Paul is not simply contrasting himself with Moses.[465] It is "we" as opposed to the unbelieving Jews. In contrast to the Israelites who have a veil shrouding their hearts (3:15), Christians have the veil taken away (3:16).[466] Christians are "able to bear the bold, direct revelation of God's glory" because the state of their heart has been changed.[467]

---

[464] Wright, "Reflected Glory: 2 Corinthians 3:18," 184. Hafemann adds: "Paul can be bold, where Moses had to veil himself (3:12–13), precisely because Paul can expect that instead of destruction, those whose hearts have been changed will be transformed by their encounter with the glory of God on the face of Christ (3:18; 4:4–6)" ("The Glory and Veil of Moses in 2 Cor 3:7–14: An Example of Paul's Contextual Exegesis of the OT-A Proposal," *HBT* 14 [1992] 43).

[465] Sloan, following the text of p[46], argues for the omission of "all" so that Paul would only be referring to apostles. A scribe possibly added "all" to make the statement more inclusive ("New Covenant Hermeneutics," 149–50). See also Belleville, *Reflections of Glory,* 276. Fee argues more persuasively, however, that Paul concludes a similar defense of his apostolic integrity in 1:21–22 by referring to his readers as sharing in the benefits of the Spirit. He also includes the Corinthians in referring to the resurrection, "with you" in 4:14, and the judgment, "we all" in 5:10 (*God's Empowering Presence,* 314, n. 99).

[466] In 3:14 Paul uses the verb ἀνακαλύπτω ("uncover") to explain why Israel fails to see the glory of the Lord. In 3:16 he uses the perfect tense of the verb to state that Christians have had the veil taken away (in Christ) and that it stays removed.

[467] Wright, "Reflected Glory: 2 Corinthians 3:18," 144. He argues that Paul is not "dealing with his own ministry but with the state of heart of his hearers."

It is also "all" in contrast to the one, Moses. All Christians may approach the Lord as Moses did when he went up Mount Sinai into the presence of the Lord. The results are similar. Beholding with an unveiled face the glory of the Lord causes us to be transformed into the same image.

The NIV interprets the rare verb *katoptrizomenoi* to mean "reflecting as a mirror does."[468] This rendering implies that Paul continues to contrast himself with Moses. Unlike Moses, Paul's face is unveiled so that he reflects the Lord's glory to the people. But we have argued that Paul includes the Corinthians with the emphatic "we all," and lexical evidence tips the scale toward the translation "beholding in a mirror."[469] This meaning of the mirror image is found in 1 Cor 13:12: "Now we see but a poor reflection as in a mirror; then we shall see face to face. Now I know in part; then I shall know fully, even as I am fully known."[470] In 4:3–4 Paul repeats the three themes of the veil, glory, and image and writes that those who have been blinded by the god of this age "cannot see the light of the glory of the gospel of Christ" (4:4). Paul therefore is talking about the effects of the ministry of the Spirit: all who believe may now see, by means of a mirror, that glory.

To see by means of a mirror does not mean we see only "'indistinctly' or 'in a distorted way,' but indirectly as over against our eschatologically seeing him 'face to face.'"[471] In this mirror we see an image, a reflection of the glory of God, which is as close as human beings can ever get to this ultimate reality. As such it is provisional. Direct vision of God is "not for this world" but awaits the end of the age.[472] Christ, however, is the image of God (4:4;

---

[468] van Unnik, " 'With Unveiled Face,' " 167–68; Caird, "Everything to Everyone," 392; Plummer, *The Second Epistle of St. Paul to the Corinthians,* 105–6; see also Belleville, *Reflections of Glory,* 278–81.

[469] Paul uses other verbs of seeing in this section, ἀτενίζειν (3:7,13), αὐγάζειν (4:4), σκοποῦν (4:18), βλέπειν (4:18). Philo interprets Num 12:7–8 to mean that Moses received a clear vision of God's form as through a mirror (*Allegorical Interpretation* 3.100–101). See N. Hugedé, *La métaphore du miroir dans les épîtres de Saint Paul aux Corinthiens* (Neuchatel: Delachaux & Niestlé, 1957); R. Kittel, "κατοπτρίζομαι," *TDNT* 2:696; Bultmann, *The Second Letter to the Corinthians,* 93–97; F. W. Danker, "The Mirror Metaphor in 1 Cor 13:12 and 2 Cor 3:18," *CTM* 3 (1960) 428–29; Collange, *Énigmes,* 116–18; Furnish, *II Corinthians,* 214; Wolff, *Der zweite Brief des Paulus an die Korinther,* 77; and Lambrecht, "Transformation," 298–99. The alternative view that the verb κατοπτριζόμενοι means "reflecting" remains attractive, if not lexically established. Wright makes an interesting argument that the mirror in which Christians see the reflected glory of the Lord is other Christians. He argues that "God shines with the light of the gospel of Jesus Christ, into the hearts of his people, who then reflect his light, becoming mirrors in which others can see God's glory." In particular in 4:7–11 "the glory which is seen, as in a mirror, in Paul's ministry is the glory which shines through suffering" ("Reflected Glory: 2 Corinthians 3:18," 188, 189–90).

[470] Corinth's fame for producing excellent bronze mirrors is probably behind Paul's use of the imagery.

[471] Fee, *God's Empowering Presence,* 317.

[472] Barrett, *The Second Epistle to the Corinthians,* 125.

Rom 8:29; Col 1:15), and we have the privilege to see the glory of God in the face of Christ (4:6; cp. John 14:9). Therefore, Christ mirrors God for believers.[473] God is no longer isolated on a faraway mountaintop but may be met in the heart of the believer who turns to the Lord.[474] Lambrecht argues that "beholding" is "decidedly more than a visual or intellectual activity."

> It must be related with that existential confrontation which is contained in the preaching of the gospel. We are thus confronted with what God did in Christ. We see Christ as in a mirror, in the gospel and in that specific Christ way of life the gospel inspires. It is also an interior experience of God's active, "splendid" and forceful presence with us in Christ.[475]

We can never encounter God and remain unchanged. Beholding this glory effects our transformation as we are changed into a veritable likeness of him. In 1 Cor 11:7 Paul calls man "the image and glory of God" (see Gen 1:26–27; 5:1; Wis 2:23; Sir 17:3). The fall tarnished that image and glory, but not irreparably. Now it is being restored.[476] This transformation is brought about through Christ as the image into whom the believers are to grow (Eph 4:24). Kent writes, "No wonder the apostle exulted as he did at being involved in Christian ministry which could accomplish such a feat."[477]

We might have expected Paul to write "into the same glory" instead of "into the same image." Paul chose his words carefully because he knew that it is not our physical appearance that is being changed but our inner being! Outward appearances remain deceptive (5:12,16). God shines the divine light in hearts (4:6), and consequently it is only in our hearts where true glory can reside and only hearts that count with God. It is a moral axiom that we become like the gods we serve (see Rom 1:18–32). In beholding the true glory of the Lord reflected in Christ, our minds become transformed (Rom 12:2) so that we are not conformed to this world and its perceptions and values but conformed to Christ and the paradoxical pattern of his suffering and resurrection (Rom 8:29; Phil 3:10,21–22). The passive voice, "are being transformed," indicates that this transformation is something done by God, and Paul's exegesis makes clear that it happens through the Spirit.

---

[473] Paul uses this image because he "wants to suggest that Christ is the "mirror" of God. In that mirror we see the glory of the Lord; in Christ we see God reflected in all his glory!" (Lambrecht, "Transformation," 300–301).

[474] Moule, "2 Cor 3:18b," 236.

[475] Ibid., 302–3.

[476] The phrase "from glory to glory" can mean from the source of glory, the Spirit, to the glory possessed by believers (so Wright, "Reflected Glory: 2 Corinthians 3:18," 188), or it can mean from one degree of glory to another as the NIV renders it, "ever increasing glory." The latter seems the best option.

[477] Kent, "The Glory of Christian Ministry," 180–81.

Fitzmyer correctly emphasizes that the individual is "not transformed into Christ himself, as the pagan myths might suggest; rather, through that constant subjection to the reflected glory the person is gradually being transformed into a likeness of him."[478] Unlike the mystery religions, Christianity was primarily concerned with the moral reformation of persons (see Col 3:10). Hafemann remarks, "The dawning of the new covenant is thus the beginning of that obedience to God in response to his merciful redemption and restoration which characterizes the new creation (2 Cor 3:18; 5:17)."[479] The transformation is not instantaneous but must continually be made actual. Paul laments over the regression of the Galatians in this process: "My dear children, for whom I am again in the pains of childbirth until Christ is formed in you" (Gal 4:19). Clearly, this process will not be completed until the resurrection: "And just as we have borne the likeness of the earthly man, so shall we bear the likeness of the man from heaven" (1 Cor 15:49). But Paul's point is that through the Spirit we are able now to live a more Christ-like life, to join in Christ's saving enterprise (5:20), and to bring greater glory to God.

Many Christians have lost or never learned a sound doctrine of regeneration. They believe that the only thing that matters is their standing with God or with the church. They assume that a past decision for Christ or a decision to affiliate with a congregation determines their standing with God. Having

---

[478] J. A. Fitzmyer, "Glory Reflected on the Face of Christ (2 Cor 3:7–4:6) and a Palestinian Jewish Motif," *TS* (42 (1981) 644. The term μεταμορφόω ("transform") is used in mystery religions where the goal was transformation into the image of the god. J. Murphy-O'Connor argues that Paul draws on "the widespread Hellenistic belief that the vision of a god or a goddess had a transforming effect on the spectator" ("Pneumatikoi and Judaizers in 2 Cor 2:14–4:6," *AusBR* 34 [1986] 54). E.g., in Apuleius's novel, *The Golden Ass (Metamorphoses)* 11.23–24, the hero Lucius is transformed into the form of an ass after he dabbles with magic potions. He is transformed back into a man when he worships the goddess Isis. As an initiate of the goddess, he then begins to shine like her when he beheld her brilliant light. The verb also appears in apocalyptic literature to refer to the transformation of the elect in the new age (resurrection). According to *2 Apoc. Bar.* 50:3:

> As for the glory of those who proved to be righteous on account of my law, those who possessed intelligence in their life, and those who planted the root of wisdom in their heart— their splendor will then be glorified by transformations, and the shape of their face will be changed into the light of their beauty so that they may acquire and receive the undying world which is promised to them.

See also *2 Apoc. Bar.* 48:49; 51:4–10; *1 Enoch* 1:8; 5:7; 38:2,4; 45:4; 50:1; 58:3–6; 62:16; and 108:11–14. Jesus' transfiguration on the mountain gave the disciples a foretaste of this transforming glory when they caught a glimpse of a world invisible to them (Mark 9:1–8 / Matt 17:1–9 / Luke 9:28–36). "The scene functions like a hologram. For a brief moment, the disciples glimpse the truth as divine glory shines through the veil of suffering" (D. E. Garland, *Mark*, NIVAC [Grand Rapids: Zondervan, 1996] 343–44). See Matt 13:43, "Then the righteous will shine like the sun in the kingdom of their Father." Paul's vision of transformation differs from that of *2 Apoc Bar.* in that it is wrought by God's Spirit in those who have Christ planted in their hearts.

[479] Hafemann, "The Glory and Veil of Moses in 2 Cor 3:7–14," 43–44.

made that decision, they make no effort to allow the Spirit to renew them. The Spirit is not imposed upon us, and Christians must engage in spiritual disciplines that make the Spirit's work possible in changing our lives at the fundamental level. God's Spirit empowers us to do what we want to do and makes what we want to do to be what is right so that Christlikeness flows from us naturally.

Paul's concluding words in this verse read literally "as from the Lord of Spirit," which is rendered as a genitive of apposition by the NIV, "which comes from the Lord, who is the Spirit."[480] For Paul, human transformation can only be done by the Spirit. The Spirit's work is what distinguishes his ministry from that of Moses (3:6,8) and makes it so much more glorious.[481] God has made him sufficient by giving him a Spirit-endowed, Spirit-empowered ministry to those who are Spirit equipped. Fee summarizes well Paul's argument:

> Paul's ministry belongs to the time of the fulfilled promise, in which the Spirit is now available to all. The coming of the Spirit has brought the old to an end and has appropriated the work of Christ through whom the effects of the Fall have been radically reversed. Indeed, through Christ and by the Spirit we are being transformed so as to bear the likeness for which we were intended at the beginning. In the freedom that the Spirit provides, we have seen the glory of God himself—as it is made evident to us in the face of our Lord Jesus Christ— and we have come to experience that glory, and will do so in an ever-increasing way until we come to the final glory.[482]

(3) Christian Ministry: The Open Statement of the Truth (4:1–6)

¹Therefore, since through God's mercy we have this ministry, we do not lose heart. ²Rather, we have renounced secret and shameful ways; we do not use deception, nor do we distort the word of God. On the contrary, by setting forth the truth plainly we commend ourselves to every man's conscience in the sight of God.

³And even if our gospel is veiled, it is veiled to those who are perishing. ⁴The god of this age has blinded the minds of unbelievers, so that they cannot see the light of the gospel of the glory of Christ, who is the image of God.

⁵For we do not preach ourselves, but Jesus Christ as Lord, and ourselves as your servants for Jesus' sake. ⁶For God, who said, "Let light shine out of dark-

---

[480] Paul can refer to the Spirit of God in a variety of ways. See Rom 8:9, "Spirit", "Spirit of God," "Spirit of Christ"; Rom 8:13, "Spirit," "Spirit of God"; 1 Cor 12:3, "Spirit of God," "Holy Spirit," "Spirit"; 2 Cor 3:3 "Spirit of God"; 3:6, "Spirit."

[481] Fitzmyer notes the contrast with references from the Dead Sea Scroll that assert that the law illumines the face of the Teacher of Righteousness or the priests by which they illumine the Many ("Glory Reflected on the Face of Christ (2 Cor 3:7–4:6) and a Palestinian Jewish Motif," *TS* 42 [1981] 643).

[482] Fee, *God's Empowering Spirit,* 319.

ness," made his light shine in our hearts to give us the light of the knowledge of the glory of God in the face of Christ.

The chapter break at 4:1 is unfortunate since 4:1–6 is closely tied to what precedes. We have shown above how this passage fits in the structure of Paul's argument as the concluding section of an A B A′ structure.[483] It also continues the themes from 3:7–18.

1. "Having this ministry" (*diakonia;* 4:1) ties into the references to "ministry" *(diakonia)* in 3:7–9).

2. "Not losing heart," which is better translated "not being cowardly" or "not shrinking back" (4:1), refers back to Paul's apostolic frankness in 3:12.

3. The veiling of his gospel to those who are being destroyed (4:3) picks up the veil motif from 3:14–16.

4. The blinded minds (4:4) parallels the hardened minds of 3:14.

5. The inability to see (4:4; *augasai*) parallels the inability to gaze *(atenisai)* in 3:13.

6. The theme of glory so central to 3:7–18 reappears in 4:4,6.

This final unit of Paul's declarations about his ministry breaks into three segments. The first segment (4:1–2) reiterates how Paul commends himself to the conscience of others through the open statement of the truth (see 1 Thess 2:1–12). The second segment (4:3–4) characterizes the spiritual condition of those who do not see the glory of Christ in "our gospel." The third segment (4:5–6) summarizes the basic thrust of Paul's preaching.

COMMENDING HIMSELF THROUGH THE OPEN STATEMENT OF THE TRUTH (4:1–2). **4:1** Paul moves from the general experience of all Christians in 3:18 to his own particular experience as an apostle of the new covenant (see 3:6; 5:18).[484] The "we" is an authorial we.[485] God has made him sufficient for a ministry like that of Moses, who conveyed God's laws to human beings. Unlike Moses, his ministry writes these laws spiritually on people's hearts.[486] He understands this calling in terms of God's mercy (1 Cor 7:25; 1 Tim 1:13,16) as well as God's grace (1 Cor 15:9–10; Gal

---

[483] See above, p. 137f.

A   2:14–3:6

B   3:7–18

A′ 4:1–6

[484] Some argue that "therefore, since" (διὰ τοῦτο), refers forward to what is to come in the next clause, "having this ministry by God's mercy" (so Martin, *2 Corinthians,* 76; Thrall, *Second Epistle to the Corinthians,* 1:298). But the verse parallels 3:12, where the οὖν ("therefore") refers backward to the preceding section. "This ministry" Paul refers to is the ministry of the Spirit (3:8) and of justification (3:9) that allows him to be so bold with such glorious results (3:12,18).

[485] See the arguments in S. Kim, *The Origin of Paul's Gospel* (Grand Rapids: Eerdmans, 1981) 5–6.

[486] Harvey, *Renewal through Suffering,* 53.

1:15).[487] God took a blasphemer, persecutor, and insolent man (1 Tim 1:13) and turned him into a devoted apostle and humble servant of the church.

Paul refers to his calling when he says that "he has been mercied," and such language shows that he regards his ministry as a gift from God, not some personal achievement. With this gift comes the formidable responsibility to spread the gospel faithfully and to speak the truth forthrightly. The reference to mercy also reminds his readers how God has mercied him by delivering him from deadly persecution (1:10) and giving him the strength to carry on his ministry.

The verb translated in the NIV as "we do not lose heart" *(egkakoumen)* can have a variety of meanings.[488] It can mean "to become discouraged," and in the next section Paul lists plenty of reasons why he might lose heart in this sense of the word (see 4:8–9; 6:4–5). The constant threat of persecution, so fierce at times that it caused him to despair of his life (1:8), and the backstabbing by fellow Christians would have quickly demoralized many a lesser figure. But others contend that the verb means "to become weary" (see Gal 6:9; 2 Thess 3:13)[489] or "to be remiss," "to be lax," or "to be reluctant."[490] If we allow the context to help ascertain the meaning of the verb, the translation "to be cowardly or timid" fits best. The opening sentence of this unit would then parallel 3:12, [NIV "Since we have such a hope, we are very bold"] "Having such a hope we exercise much frank speech," and restates that thought in negative terms, [NIV "Since … we have this ministry … we do not lose heart"] "Having this ministry … we are not timid." In Eph 3:13 the verb follows a reference to boldness in 3:12. When the verb reappears in 2 Cor 4:16, its antonym is *tharreō,* "to be courageous, confident" (5:6). Paul therefore says that because he has this ministry "he does not draw in his horns."[491] He is not fainthearted. Plummer comments: "Such faintheartedness takes refuge in silence and inactivity, in order to escape criticism, and therefore is the opposite of παρρησια *[parrēsia]*."[492] The Spirit

---

[487] Before Moses received the vision of God's glory, God told him, "I will have mercy on whom I will have mercy" (Exod 33:19, cited in Rom 9:15).

[488] The reading ἐγκακοῦμεν (p[46], ℵ, A, B, D) is to be preferred over ἐκκακοῦμεν (C, Ψ, 0243 etc.).

[489] Harvey suggests it means "fatigue and lassitude, a natural consequence of a spell of physical weakness" (*Renewal through Suffering,* 53).

[490] Thrall, *Second Epistle to the Corinthians,* 1:298–99, following the extensive discussion in Baumert, *Täglich sterben und auferstehen,* 318–46.

[491] Bultmann, *The Second Letter to the Corinthians,* 99.

[492] Plummer, *The Second Epistle of St. Paul to the Corinthians,* 110. Furnish maintains that the verb ἐγκακοῦμεν "must be translated in such a way as to carry forward the thought of having much boldness (3:12), as well as in such a way to accord with what will be about apostles commending their actions to others, before God, without fear or trepidation (4:2)." He translates it "to shrink back" (*II Corinthians,* 217).

enables Paul to preach and minister an unveiled gospel.

4:2   In this verse Paul lists three ignoble practices he repudiates and then states what he does. First, he affirms that "we have renounced secret and shameful ways" (lit. "the hidden things of shame").[493] The NIV interprets this phrase as a qualitative genitive.[494] This alternative is the best option, but the phrase could also be interpreted as "things that lead to shame" or "things that are hidden because they are shameful" (see NEB, REB, "the deeds that men hide for their very shame"). This verse possibly alludes to the peddlers mentioned in 2:17 and has nothing whatsoever to do with Moses, as if Paul considered his practice of veiling his face as something deceptive. Moses does not come into view at all in this unit. When Paul says he renounces such shameful practices, he does not imply that he used to engage in them. He never did resort to them. The phrase contrasts his own boldness with those who attempt to cover up their true intentions. Those who act honorably, as Paul does, do not need to cloak their deeds in secrecy but are open to the view of the entire world, Christian and non-Christian.[495]

Second, he repudiates all deception. The noun "deception" translates a Greek word that literally means the readiness to do anything *(panourgia)*. When used in a bad sense, it applies to someone who is sly, crafty, deceitful, and tricky. Such persons will stoop to any ruse to accomplish their dishonorable purposes, and they usually resort to secret plots and intrigues. In 11:3 Paul connects such cunning to Satan, who beguiled Eve. The word also occurs in 1 Cor 3:19, where he cites Job 5:13, "He catches the wise in their craftiness," to denounce the foolish wisdom of this world that thinks that it can outfox God. Worldly shrewdness offers only fleeting success and will eventually ensnare the clever in their own tangled web of

---

[493] The middle voice of the verb ἀπειπάμεθα stresses "we for our part have renounced." It may imply that others have not done so (Murphy-O'Connor, "Pneumatikoi," 47).

[494] See Thrall, *Second Epistle to the Corinthians,* 1:1:300–303, "the secretive practices of disgraceful behavior."

[495] Philo wrote:

Let those who work mischief feel shame and seek holes and corners of the earth and profound darkness, there lie hid and keep the multitude of their iniquities veiled out of sight of all. But let those whose actions serve the common weal use freedom of speech (παρρησία) and walk in daylight through the market-place, ready to converse with crowded gathers, to let the clear sunlight shine (ἀνταυγάσοντες) upon their own life and through the two most royal senses, sight and hearing, to render good service to the assembled groups. (*Special Laws* 1:321).

But this reference to secrecy may also be related to a lack of candor. A fragment from Philodemus connects secrecy to unfriendly behavior and a failure to be forthright: "But to act in secret is necessarily most unfriendly, no doubt. For he who does not report [errors] is clearly covering up these things too from the most outstanding of his friends, and there will be no advantage for the one who hides [things]; for not one thing escaped notice" (Fr. 41 *Philodemus On Frank Criticism,* 55).

deceit.[496] The deceiver is the opposite of someone who is candid and forthright.[497]

Third, he repudiates any guileful misuse of the word of God. There is no indication that the Corinthians have accused Paul of distorting God's word.[498] Again he is picking up the statement in 2:17 in which he contrasts himself with the peddlers of the word of God. Paul plays off the ancient world's widespread suspicion and criticism of "fraudulent teachers of philosophy, out simply for their own gain."[499] He insists that unlike such con men he did not adjust, water down, or tamper with the gospel to stroke his listeners' egos or to avoid ruffling their feathers. He is not a flatterer using God's word only to delight the audience and bewitch them with enchanting interpretations that never question their conduct or character.

Finally, he lays out what he does do; he sets forth the truth plainly.[500] This last phrase again relates to his bold speech (see 6:6; 7:14); and in chaps. 10–13 he defends himself as one who has the truth of Christ (11:10), who speaks the truth even when it can be dismissed as foolish boasting (12:6), and who

---

[496] Paul uses both terms in 2 Cor 12:16: "Be that as it may, I have not been a burden to you. Yet, crafty fellow (πανοῦργος) that I am, I caught you by trickery (δόλος)!" It is possible that someone in Corinth raised questions about his handling of the collection.

[497] Seneca wrote: "A good man will do what he thinks it will be honourable for him to do, even if it involves toil, he will do it even if it involves harm to him, he will do it even if it involves peril; again, he will not do that which will be base, even if it brings him money, or pleasure, or power. Nothing will deter him from that which is honourable, and nothing will tempt him into baseness" (*Moral Epistles* 76.18).

[498] Martin's statement that "Paul's writing is polemically angled throughout as he continues his running debate with his detractors at Corinthians" is pure conjecture (*2 Corinthians,* 81). If they charged him with such unworthy motives, why would they bother to listen to him, let alone repent with godly sorrow from his moral admonishments? This interpretation is a classic case of mirror reading gone awry.

[499] Furnish, *II Corinthians,* 218. He cites Lucian, *Hermotimus* 59: "I certainly cannot say how in your view philosophy and wine are comparable, except perhaps at this one point, that philosophers sell their lessons as wine merchants their wines—most of them adulterating and cheating and giving false measure." Dio Chrysostom also criticizes the flatterer: "But he who in very truth is manly and high-minded would never submit to any such things, nor would he sacrifice his own liberty and his freedom of speech (παρρησία) for the sake of dishonourable payment of either power or riches, nor would he envy those who change their form and apparel for such rewards; on the contrary, he would think such persons to be comparable to those who change from human beings into snakes or other animals, not envying them nor carping at them because of their wantonness, but rather bewailing and pitying them" (*Orations* 77/78. 37).

[500] Philo's description of the sophists as "impostors, flatterers, inventors of cunning plausibilities, who know well how to cheat and mislead, but that only, and have no thought for honest truth" (*Who Is the Heir* 302) provides a possible backdrop for understanding with whom and with what Paul compares himself. Philo alludes to the sophists as absorbed in "the sophistries of deceitful word and thought" (ibid., 85) and interested only in argument for argument's sake, not with the truth (*The Worse Attacks the Better* 36). These references were called to my attention by B. W. Winter, *Paul and Philo among the Sophists,* SNTSMS 96 (Cambridge: University Press, 1997) 93.

does nothing against the truth but only for the truth (13:8; see 1 Cor 2:12–13). The letter written in tears and anguish of heart was such a statement of the truth. After he sent it, he momentarily had misgivings, fearing its effect. He had no intention of causing pain but wanted only to show his love and to bring about their penitence (2:4). The news that they did repent could only confirm for him that God called him always to speak the truth in love (Eph 4:25). He closes this letter by saying that he is doing the same thing again: "This is why I write these things when I am absent, that when I come I may not have to be harsh in my use of authority—the authority the Lord gave me for building you up, not for tearing you down" (13:10).

Paul never compromises the truth of the gospel even when the odds against him seem overwhelming. His fervent preaching of the truth of the gospel led to his having to defend it before the pillar apostles in Jerusalem. His account of this meeting in Gal 2:1–10 betrays some measure of ambivalence about their ratification of the gospel he preached to them. These reservations derive from his basic understanding of the implications of the truth of the gospel (2:5,14). He makes clear in the letter that he was dependent on no one for this gospel (1:17–18) and that the pillar apostles added nothing to him (2:6). The truth of the gospel does not depend on the certification of any human because it is not "according to man." Although he wants to set the record straight that the apostles before him did ratify his gospel and his mission, he knows that their seal of approval does not make the truth of the gospel any more true. His deep conviction is that the truth of the gospel does not depend on any human notarization, no matter how revered or holy an individual or group might be. Paul denounces all external criteria for the certification of divine truth or for the identification of God's people or God's apostles. The recognition of the truth of the gospel by the pillar apostles says more about their character and spiritual discernment than it says about Paul's gospel. Their authority depends entirely on whether they uphold the truth of the gospel. Consequently, he believes that his straightforward proclamation of the truth of the gospel is the only thing that can commend him as a preacher of the gospel.

"Commending ourselves" in the Greco-Roman context should not be understood as something negative. No one has accused Paul of recommending himself, as if this were something unprincipled.[501] The Corinthians would not have criticized him for commending himself to them since this was the normal means to establish relationships in the ancient world. Paul only emphasizes here how the way he has commended himself to the Corinthians and to others differs from the way some others have commended

---

[501] Against the views of Furnish, *II Corinthians,* 245, and many others. On the meaning of self-commendation, see above p. 154f.

themselves by means of letters (3:1). He commends himself by laying out the gospel plainly for everyone to judge for themselves.

How they assess this gospel will determine how they will be assessed by God. The expression "to every conscience of men" refers to people in general, not the Corinthians in particular. We have noted in the comment on 1:12 that "conscience" refers to the human faculty that recognizes right and wrong, the norms of moral conduct. Humans can examine what he says; and, if Satan has not blinded their minds, they can see its truth. Paul believes that the gospel is accessible to all; some, however, turn away or keep its messengers at arm's length. That is why Paul does not rely on human judgment because all too often humans rely on "fleshly" categories to make their judgments (1 Cor 4:3; 2 Cor 5:16).

THE SPIRITUAL CONDITION OF THOSE BLINDED TO THE GLORY OF CHRIST IN "OUR GOSPEL" (4:3–4). **4:3**   Paul returns to the theme that his gospel is an odor of death to those who are perishing (2:15–16). Bultmann correctly emphasizes that preaching the gospel presents people with the crisis of decision: "What is at stake in the question of faith is the either-or, God or Satan. There is not a third thing between."[502] If some should reject the gospel, that in no way discredits Paul's ministry.[503] His gospel is veiled only to those who are perishing (4:3). As Hodge puts it: "The reason or cause of this fact was not to be sought either in the nature of the gospel, or in the mode of its exhibition, but in the state and character of those who rejected it. The sun does not cease to be sun although the blind do not see it."[504] In the previous unit Paul uses the veil metaphorically as a symbol of the people's hard-heartedness. If the gospel is veiled to some, it is because their hearts have shriveled into a lifeless husk that will not or cannot respond.

What veils his gospel? That which Paul absolutely refuses to compromise—the scandal of the cross (1 Cor 1:23; 2:2). The veiling has nothing to do with the particular way Paul communicates the gospel—that it is too cryptic, too heavy, or too lackluster. It has to do instead with the fundamental nature of a gospel that strikes Greeks as foolishness and Jews as scandalous. This fundamental nature is that God defeats death and evil and reconciles the world through Christ's sacrifice, which puts an end to all human boasting. The Messiah whom God sent to save Israel was not a figure of glory who deposed Israel's pagan oppressors and restored her fortunes in the world. Instead, he suffered and died on a cross, and such a fate "made a mockery of Jewish expectations" and "effectively nailed those expectations to a cross."[505] He had become a "stone of stumbling and a rock of offense"

---

[502] Bultmann, *The Second Letter to the Corinthians,* 103.

[503] Paul may have in mind reference to the unbelieving Jews in Corinth (Acts 18:4–6).

[504] C. Hodge, *An Exposition of the Second Epistle to the Corinthians* (1859; reprint, Grand Rapids: Baker, 1980) 84–85.

[505] Ibid., 140.

(Rom 9:33, NASB; Mark 12:10–11). The Christian gospel offends those who want a more "tasteful" salvation plan.[506] Nietzsche was correct in his assessment that "the Crucified" who lies at the heart of the gospel "is the principle of death: anti-natural, symbolising consciousness of sin and foreboding authority of God, imposing a morbid principle on life."[507] He was wrong in his hope that a "Superman" could ever do what God has done.

Paul had suffered from the same blindness that darkens the vision of some in Israel. He looked at the promised Christ from a fleshly perspective (5:16)—from self-seeking desires and from wishful thinking about the glories of the Messiah who would exalt Israel to worldly prominence and himself as one who outshone all his contemporaries in zeal. His zealous campaign to be a good Jew kept him from being what God intended him to become, an apostle of Christ to the Gentiles. Only after Christ captured him (2:17; Phil 3:12) did he submit to God's righteousness and recognize God's glory in Christ. When the divine light was caused to shine in his heart, he saw the crucified Jesus as one who died for him because of his sin. All pride and boasting vanished. In his profound humiliation and shame, he could see God's compelling glory in Christ. By identifying with this humble Messiah who endured the humiliation of death on the cross, Paul's pride and boast was abolished and so was the veil of obduracy that hid God's glory in Christ. He had to empty himself to be crucified with Christ and put to death, discard as rubbish his self-centered desires and passions (even for the law). He could no longer live for himself but for Christ and others.

Those who look through the glass of a me-first culture can see no glory or power in giving one's life for others. The gospel Paul proclaims does promise glory, but not through the acquisition of worldly power. It comes instead through unconditional surrender of one's power to God. This divine paradigm so conflicts with human ways of thinking and acting that few ever recognize it for the truth that it is.

Paul's own sufferings also veiled his gospel because people do not want a suffering apostle who looks like a prisoner of war led in chains any more than they want a suffering Messiah who invites them to take up their cross and follow him. Most fancy worldly triumph, success, and preeminence that comes at minimal cost and exertion. They want something for nothing, and such an attitude makes them easy prey for the unscrupulous peddler who panders to their selfish aspirations.

Such desires only hasten their way along the road to perdition. But

---

[506] The imagery comes from F. Nietzsche's *Gay Science:* "What is now decisive against Christianity is our taste, no longer our reasons" (cited by S. N. Williams, "Dionysius against the Crucified: Nietzsche Contra Christianity, Part II," *TynBul* 49.1 [1998] 132).

[507] Williams, "Dionysius against the Crucified: Nietzsche Contra Christianity, Part II," 131.

Paul understands these persons to be perishing now. As Christians are now being transformed into the image of the glory of Christ, so those who reject Christ, the image of God, are now being malformed into the image of the god of this age, whom they serve. This god, however, wreaks only blindness, death, and destruction. The evidence of this false god's work in their lives is unmistakable in their moral deformity and spiritual collapse (see Rom 1:18–32). Paul does not have in view errant Christians. But if some in Corinth cannot see God's glory in Paul's ministry, they fall perilously close to the category of those who are being destroyed.

4:4 Paul blames another influence for the failure to believe: The god of this age has blinded the minds of unbelievers.[508] The phrase "god of this age" occurs only here in the New Testament, and most understand it as a reference to Satan.[509] Some, however, object that as a thoroughgoing monotheist Paul would not attribute divinity to an evil spirit. In 1 Cor 8:5 Paul dismisses them as "the so-called gods." Any suggestion that there was another god particularly troubled patristic interpreters since theological innovators seized on this verse to foist their errors on others. Marcion used this text to make his case for an inferior creator God and a supreme savior God. In confuting Marcion, Tertullian argued that Paul refers to God, who blinds the minds of unbelievers (*Against Marcion* 5.11; see also Hilary, Chrysostom, and Augustine). God is the only God of this age and the next. Plummer noted that "fear of the Manichean doctrine of two Gods, one good the other evil, no doubt produced this improbable interpretation."[510] The Arians appealed to this passage to argue that since Satan is called god of this world, Christ being called God is no proof of his true divinity. If Paul were actually referring to God here, it is strange that he does not characterize him as the God of all ages rather than simply

---

[508] The Greek text begins with the phrase "among whom," which is omitted in the NIV. This omission is justified in that it might suggest that unbelievers are not a subset of those who are perishing. Paul, however, sees the two as identical and substitutes "minds of unbelievers" for the simpler "their minds." By unbelievers Paul has in view non-Christians (1 Cor 6:6; 7:12–15; 10:27; 14:22–24) and not the intruders whom he calls servants of Satan (11:13–15)

[509] The term "Satan" appears in Rom 16:20; 1 Cor 5:5; 7:5; 2 Cor 2:11; 11:14; 12:7; 1 Thess 2:18; 2 Thess 2:9; and 1 Tim 1:20; 5:15. The term "devil" appears in Eph 4:27; 6:11; 1 Tim 3:6–7; 2 Tim 2:26; 3:3; Titus 2:3. He is called "Beliar" in 2 Cor 6:15 and "the serpent" in 2 Cor 11:3. Other terms appearing in Paul are "the tempter" (1 Thess 3:5), "the evil one" (2 Thess 3:3), and the "ruler of the realm [power] of the air, the spirit that is now at work among those who are disobedient" (Eph 2:2). In 1 Cor 2:6,8 Paul refers to the "rulers of this age," and the phrase "ruler of this world" appears in John 12:31; 14:30; and 16:11.

[510] A. Plummer, *The Second Epistle of Paul the Apostle to the Corinthians* (Cambridge: University Press, 1911) 39. See also id., *The Second Epistle of St. Paul to the Corinthians,* 115–16.

the God of this age.[511] Paul must be referring to Satan as the god of this age. He classifies Satan as a "god" because he has a dominion, however limited by the one true God, and has subjects whom Paul labels "unbelievers."[512]

Paul portrays the archenemy Satan as blinding unbelievers' minds.[513] This image derives from Jewish apocalypticism, which pictured the Prince of Light and the Angel of Darkness ruling different realms and engaged in a life-and-death struggle. It does not imply the inferiority or inherent evil of the created order.[514] But it does affirm that Satan's dominion, which consists of lawlessness, darkness, unbelief, the worship of idols, and moral defilement (6:14–7:1), is fundamentally incongruous with the kingdom of light ruled by God's beloved Son (Col 1:13). It also reminds the readers that Satan rules *only* this age, which in any case is judged and fallen and coming to nothing (see Gal 1:4; 1 Cor 2:6). Prayer can check his schemes (Luke 22:32), and the Spirit can neutralize his power. Paul is fully confident that "the God of peace will soon crush Satan under your feet" (Rom 16:20).

Satan has been defeated by the cross of Christ (Col 2:15). In his death throes, however, Satan still has the strength to besiege human minds and to incite them to embrace and exalt evil rather than God.[515] He continues to try

---

[511] Calvin insightfully observes how much the heat of controversy caused these interpreters to twist Scripture. They were "more anxious to refute" their theological opponents "than to expound Paul" (*The Second Epistle of Paul the Apostle to the Corinthians,* 54). Others have taken "the god of this world" as a genitive of apposition, "the god who is this world" (Collange, *Énigmes,* 133; Murphy-O'Connor, "Pneumatikoi," 44). They cite Phil 3:19 as a parallel: "Their god is their belly." Murphy-O'Connor infers that the spiritual ones in the congregation "have become slaves to the conventions of their world, and as such are equivalent to unbelievers." But Paul does not have Christians in view here, and we should not read the opponents' error into everything Paul says in 2 Corinthians.

[512] Calvin, *The Second Epistle of Paul the Apostle to the Corinthians,* 54.

[513] The reference to "their god is their stomach" in Phil 3:19 shows that Paul can use the term "god" for something other than God. "Satan" appears in 2:11; 11:14 and 12:7 and "Beliar" in 6:15. Paul therefore appeals to a common motif in lore about Satan where blindness and darkness symbolize Satan's reign: "Satan seeks to imprison humans in the darkness of the diabolical realm" (S. R. Garrett, "The God of This World and the Affliction of Paul: 2 Cor 4:1–12," in *Greeks, Romans, and Christians,* ed. D. L. Balch, E. Ferguson and W. A. Meeks [Minneapolis: Fortress, 1990] 109).

[514] Furnish, *II Corinthians,* 220, 247. He cites Philo, *Confusion of Tongues* 171–82, who asserted that there is one sovereign God, but he has commissioned many lesser powers and ministering angels to serve his purposes. The text from *T. Judah* 19:4, "The prince of deceit blinded me, and I sinned as a man and as flesh, being corrupted through sins . . ., is often cited as a parallel to Paul's idea. There is no reason to pursue some gnostic background for the term as Bultmann tries to do (*The Second Letter to the Corinthians,* 104–5). In Paul's Corinthians correspondence, God can use Satan to chastise an errant believer (1 Cor 5:5; and 1 Tim 1:20) and to send a message to a faithful apostle (2 Cor 12:7–9).

[515] In the interpretation of the parable of the sower, Satan snatches the seed sown along the path before it can take root (Mark 4:15).

to blind people to his defeat by leading them to disdain the scandal of the cross and to look for glory elsewhere (see 1 Cor 2:8). The "mind" *(noēma)* is the chief object of Satan's ploys (2:11). This counterspirit does all in his power to prevent humans from becoming the enlightened subjects of the one true God whose image can be seen in Christ.[516] Humans make themselves susceptible to his wiles with their preoccupation with the transient, unspiritual, earthly realm.[517] The mind blinded by Satan cannot think straight, and it rebels against God's truth (3:14).[518]

The word translated as "light" *(phōtismos)* occurs only here in the New Testament and may have a more active meaning, "an enlightenment that enlightens."[519] What the spiritually blinded are prevented from seeing is the glory of Christ, who is the image of God. In Paul's world an image was not considered something distinct from the object it represented, as if it were only a facsimile or reproduction.[520] As the image of God, Christ brings clarity to our hazy notions of the immortal, invisible God who lives in unapproachable light (1 Tim 1:17; 6:16).[521]

> In Christ we see who God is—Creator and Redeemer; what God is like—a
> God of mercy and love; and what God does—sending his Son to rescue people

---

[516] The verb αὐγάζω means "to see sharply" but can also mean "to shine." If the latter is its meaning, then the verb is intransitive, "so that the light may not shine forth [to them]" (REB "dawn upon"). In the context of being blinded, and the parallel with 3:13 and 3:18, however, the verb must mean "see" and is transitive, "so that [they] do not see the light" (RSV, JB). Philo uses the verb for "beholding as in a mirror" *(Life of Moses* 2.139).

[517] Barrett argues that this verse prevents any view that persons were "by nature incapable" of accepting the gospel *(The Second Epistle to the Corinthians,* 131). Furnish agrees but notes that Paul's purpose was to make certain that the cause of the unbelief was completely unrelated to Paul's gospel *(II Corinthians,* 247).

[518] Lambrecht comments, "If it had not been for the interference of Satan, the light of the gospel, which contains the glory of Christ, could have been contemplated simply and directly (and in fact is seen in that way by the Christians)" ("Transformation," 301).

[519] So Furnish, *II Corinthians,* 221. Philo asserts that God is light (Ps 27:1): "the archetype of every other light, nay, prior to and high above every archetype, holding the position of the model of the model" *(On Dreams* 1.75).

[520] H. Kleinknecht, *"eikon," TDNT* 2:389.

[521] Divine Wisdom was also regarded as the image of God: "For she is a reflection of eternal light, a spotless mirror of the working of God, and an image of his goodness" *(Wis* 7:26). In Paul's thinking, Christ has taken over all the functions of divine Wisdom. See H.-J. Klauck, "Erleuchtung und Verkündigung. Auslegungen zu 2 Kor 4,1–6," in *Paolo Ministro del Nuovo Testamento* (2 Co 2,14–4,6), ed. L. de Lorenzi, Monographic Series of "Benedictina": Biblical Ecumenical Section 10 (Rome: Benedictina, 1987) 286; and Thrall, *Second Epistle to the Corinthians,* 1:310. Philo regarded the Logos as the image of God and the firstborn of creation *(Allegorical Interpretation* 1.43; *On the Confusion of Tongues* 97; 146; *On Flight and Finding* 101; 146; *Special Laws* 1.81). Views positing some Eikon concept from Gnosticism (so G. W. MacRae, "Anti-Dualist Polemic in 2 Cor. 4:6," *SE* IV [TU 102: Berlin, 1968] 426–27) should be ignored as extraneous to the text.

from the dominion of darkness and bringing about the reconciliation of all creation through his death on a cross.[522]

Christ's death on the cross reveals most clearly God's love and power, but it befuddles or repels many as complete foolishness, since they see no glory radiating from such shame and dishonor. They cannot see how weakness and humiliation go with power and glory (see 2 Cor 13:4). It follows that they also cannot see this same glory reflected in the faces of those who serve the gospel and imitate Christ's humble service and suffering. Paul insists, however, that any who claim to know God and do not recognize God's image in Jesus Christ do not know the true God. Any who claim to hear God and do not hear God speaking in Jesus Christ are deaf to God's message. The implication is clear; those Christians who fail to see Christ's glory reflected in Paul's suffering as Christ's apostle are no less hardened than blind unbelievers.

THE BASIC THRUST OF PAUL'S PREACHING: CHRIST AS LORD; OURSELVES AS YOUR SLAVES (4:5–6). **4:5** Paul writes in 4:3 about "our gospel" being veiled, but such a statement shows how closely he identifies himself with the gospel that he was set apart to preach. But he knows full well that the gospel is not about him—"we do not preach ourselves." His ministry may be far more glorious than that of Moses, but it is not about his own personal glorification. What follows in 4:7–12 makes this reality clear. The gospel is not about Paul and his strength and virtue. It is about Christ, who imparts strength and virtue to frail, weak human beings and delivers them from Satan's bondage.

Some have claimed that Paul's assertion that he does not preach himself was intended to take a swipe at his rivals, whom he believed did preach themselves (see 10:12; 11:18). They had infiltrated the church with a self-promoting swagger and boastfulness and twisted the gospel to serve their own selfish ends. But it is not necessary to import a reference to rivals to understand this statement. Paul is neither insinuating that his opponents do this nor answering some charge against himself.[523] We must guard against

---

[522] Garland, *Colossians, Philemon,* 87. Calvin comments on Col 1:15 that in Christ, God shows us "his righteousness, goodness, wisdom, power, in short, his entire self" (*Commentaries on the Epistles of Paul the Apostle to the Philippians, Colossians and Thessalonians,* ed. J. Pringel [Grand Rapids: Eerdmans, 1948] 150).

[523] Possibly, he is contrasting himself with the generally negative picture of preachers and philosophers in the ancient world. E.g., Dio Chrysostom maintained that "the great majority [*hoi polloi,* see 2 Cor 2:17] of those styled philosophers proclaim themselves such, just as the Olympian heralds proclaim the victors " (*Orations* 13.11; cited by Furnish, *II Corinthians,* 223). In the context, Dio reflects on his exile and declares that it was not as grievous as some might imagine. In consulting the god Apollos in the temple, he felt bidden to keep on roaming, wearing humble attire so that people thought of him as a beggar or a philosopher. He did not proclaim himself to be such but gained that reputation from his listeners.

the tendency, so prevalent in commentaries, to view every statement in Paul's letters as a response to some external criticism or as a volley aimed at some imagined opponent. Here Paul simply makes a statement of fact (see 1:24; 10:8); he is not driven by selfish motives.

To preach oneself is to vaunt one's superior qualifications, to put on airs, and to turn the throne of Christ into a soap box from which to spout one's own pet themes and biases. No one is immune from the temptation to manipulate ministerial relationships to build a following rather than to build up a congregation or to exploit the gospel's "drama, pathos, solemnity, and majesty, for the display of one's own powers, one's ability, eloquence, humor, learning, gifts of popular exposition."[524] Some ministers may do this in blatant and crude ways; others may do it in more subtle and refined ways. Cranfield observes, "How often is that which is hailed as a successful ministry little more than success in winning a personal following!"[525] The temptation to preach ourselves is fed by congregations who are "prone to like to be entertained and to enjoy a minister's self-exhibition" and are prone "to indulge in a personality cult."[526] Clearly, Corinth was such a congregation, rallying around and exaggerating the importance of their ministerial heroes (1 Cor 1:12) and using their worship to show off their own individual gifts (1 Cor 14:26). They may have encouraged Paul's rivals in their boasting and berated him for his failure to display more dramatically his apostolic prowess.

Paul has used seeing imagery throughout this section (3:7,13; 4:4; see 4:18), but the truth of the gospel can only be appropriated through hearing the preached word. It is not blinded eyes that do not see, but blinded minds that do not hear and submit.[527] Paul saw the risen Christ on the road to Damascus, but it was God's message through Ananias that redirected his life and guided him along the path of loving service (Acts 9:10–19; see also his vision and Christ's command in 22:17–21). With the veil of blindness removed, he could see the glory of God in the face of Christ, and he recognized that the direction of Christianity is downward in the incarnation and outward in sacrificial labor for others. Consequently, he preaches two things: Jesus Christ as Lord and ourselves as your slaves for Jesus' sake.

---

[524] C. E. B. Cranfield, "Minister and Congregation in the Light of II Corinthians 4:5–7," *Int* 19 (1965) 163–64.

[525] Ibid., 164

[526] Ibid.

[527] By contrast, the ancient mystery religions stressed visual experiences. One official in the cult was called a hierophant, the one who shows sacred things; and the initiate into the mystery was called a "beholder." The adherents would stage initiation ceremonies at night so that "the contrast between light and darkness made the primal experience of enlightenment that much more vivid to the eyes and emotions" (M. Meyer, *The Ancient Mysteries: A Sourcebook* [San Francisco: Harper & Row, 1987] 5).

The first item is not surprising: Jesus Christ is Lord. Christless preaching quickly degenerates into vapid moralism. Hodge's comments provide an astute critique for any age:

> To make the end of preaching the inculcation of virtue, to render men honest, sober, benevolent and faithful, is part and parcel of that wisdom of the world that is foolishness with God. It is attempting to raise fruit without trees.[528]

Paul has already argued that no transformation can occur except through Christ (3:18). In 1 Cor 1:23 Paul says that he preached only Jesus Christ crucified. His statement that he preaches Christ as Lord indicates that the two ideas, Jesus Christ crucified and Jesus Christ as Lord, are identical. Humility goes together with his Lordship (see Rom 10:9; 1 Cor 12:31; Phil 2:10–11; 3:8). Although his glory is veiled to the many whose hearts are too ossified to comprehend it, the crucified Christ is the Lord of glory (1 Cor 2:8).

The second component of Paul's preaching *is* more surprising: ourselves as your slaves.[529] Only here does Paul speak of himself as the slave of his converts. His qualification "because of Christ" makes it clear, however, that he is not a slave of two masters. Being the slave of Christ who died for them (see 1 Cor 3:5; 4:1; Rom 1:1; and Phil 1:1) makes him their slave as well.[530] To be a slave of Christ means that all one's possessions, aspirations, time, and labor belong completely to him. It also means that if Christ is Lord, then those who proclaim his lordship cannot be lords themselves (see Luke 22:24–27; Mark 10:40–45). If Christ took the form of a slave, then those who follow him must be willing to give themselves over to serve others.[531] As Cranfield puts it, "One cannot sincerely or effectively preach Christ as Lord from the pulpit unless one is honestly trying to obey him as Lord in one's own life, day by day."[532]

Paul's depiction of himself as their slave for Jesus' sake reemphasizes his previous statement that he refuses to lord it over them (1:24) and prepares for the catalog of suffering that follows. The glory of God is manifested in the ministry of Paul in the same way it was manifested in the cross of Christ:

---

[528] Hodge, *An Exposition of the Second Epistle to the Corinthians,* 88.

[529] The word δοῦλος should be translated "slave," not "servant" as in the NIV. In our idiom "servant" tends to imply voluntary service, but a slave had no power over himself and was at the complete disposal of his master. Paul's exhortation to slaves not to work only to curry favor with the master when his eye is upon you "but with sincerity of heart and reverence for the Lord" applies also to himself (Col 3:22–24).

[530] We should note that in 11:20 he accuses the false apostles of turning the Corinthians into their slaves, preying upon them, acting presumptuously, and slapping them in the face as one would do with a slave.

[531] This is the very task of Israel: "He said to me, 'You are my servant, Israel, in whom I will display my splendor'" (Isa 49:3).

[532] Cranfield, "Minister and Congregation,"165.

"paradoxically, in self-emptying humility" and "in sacrificial service."[533] As Christ's abasement on the cross allows the light of God's power to shine more intensely, so the abasement of those who preach Christ's death allows the same light to shine more radiantly, pointing to God and not to the preacher.

The degradation he suffers as an apostle contrasts strikingly with the images of divine glory that pervade this section. The reason his critics cannot see the sufficiency of Paul's ministry is that their eyes have been blinded by the same veil that blinds Israel—the veil of pride and self-exaltation. This veil is woven from a culture that is given over to egocentrism and boasting. The boasting might differ in particulars from Paul's former strutting before God as a zealous Pharisee, but all boasting is rooted in the same foolish, human pride that led to man's fall in the beginning.

4:6 The "for" *(hoti)* introduces Paul's explanation of why he proclaims Christ as Lord and has become his obedient servant: God has shined a light in the darkest reaches of his heart. The God of light therefore acts quite differently from the god of this world, who blinds people, flings them into utter darkness, and hardens their hearts (4:4). Paul alludes here to the creation account in Gen 1:3–4: "God said, 'Let there be light.' "[534] The key terms, "God," "said," "light," and "darkness," occur in both contexts. Paul would attest that the same God who created light in the midst of chaos at the beginning of creation beamed that supernatural light into his own heart.[535]

The image of light shining reminds most interpreters of the account of Paul's own conversion experience recorded in Acts.[536] In Acts it is described as a light from heaven (Acts 9:3; 22:6,11; 26:13) and connected with glory (Acts 22:11; *doxa,* "brilliance"). Acts does not portray this event as some

---

[533] Savage, *Power through Weakness,* 152, 154.

[534] J. Jervell suggests that 3:18–4:6 is a midrash on Gen 1 (*Imago Dei,* 173–76; 194–97; 214–18).

[535] Strachan aptly comments: "So much of our religion is regarded as a quest in the dark, a venture of faith. God is regarded as waiting to be discovered. The Jewish and Christian conception is that God chooses his people, and reveals Himself to them (John 15:15)" (*The Second Epistle of Paul to the Corinthians,* 83). MacRae contends that Paul makes this statement lest those with a tendency toward a dualistic worldview (a problem in Corinth) might misinterpret 4:4 and the reference to the god of this world. The God who brings enlightenment is the God who created the world ("Anti-Dualist Polemic," 420–31).

[536] Furnish argues against this link because when Paul refers to his conversion in Gal 1:15–16 and 1 Cor 15:8 he uses the language of revelation rather than the language of illumination (*II Corinthians,* 251). But we need not limit Paul to the same language every time he refers to his conversion and call. These two passages also differ significantly from Phil 3:3–17, which addresses the experience of the total transformation of his life when he became a Christian.

internal awakening but as an external reality.[537] What Paul makes clear here is that the external reality became an internal reality—"who shone in our hearts." This glorious divine light illuminated the darkness that was in him but also revealed to him that he was not his sins, that is, he was not defined by the sins he may have committed. God offered new possibilities. Savage comments, "The one who is 'In Christ,' who shares the judgment pronounced on the crucified Messiah, is so humbled and divested of pride that he is able to see the exalted glory of the Lord."[538] Death with Christ therefore brings "clarity of vision." The Genesis backdrop explains how Paul understands conversion as an act of God's new creation (2 Cor 5:17).[539]

The parallel with Genesis is not precise, however; and it has led others to propose Isa 9:1 (LXX) as the background for Paul's assertion.[540] The use of the future tense in the Greek, "the God who said out of darkness light *will* shine," may suggest "that Paul understands his glory as a fulfillment of prophecy and thus as an eschatological light."[541] Savage concludes:

> The light which is shining in his heart ... is none other than the unapproachable splendour of God's own glory, a brilliance surpassing that of the sun and a brilliance not seen since creation. Indeed it is the long awaited light of the eschaton, heralding a new creation and commencing the day of salvation. As such it is a paradoxical glory, visible only to those whose pride has been shattered through judgement, a judgement precipitated by the re-creating energy of this very light.[542]

If Paul has Isaiah in mind, it would imply the divine light shining in him is "more brilliant than that of Moses and more powerful than that of creation"

---

[537] Thrall comments, "But he does not refer only to a purely interior experience of enlightenment even here, as though the illumination was not of any extraordinary kind but consisted simply of some religious truth" (*Second Epistle to the Corinthians*, 1:317). Kim argues that Paul has an "objective vision of the risen Lord. This affected Paul to the innermost part of his life, creating the conviction in the seat of his understanding, thought, feeling and will that what appeared to him was Christ, revealed in the glory of God" (*The Origin of Paul's Gospel*, 7).

[538] Savage, *Power through Weakness*, 146.

[539] Kim, *The Origin of Paul's Gospel*, 8–9.

[540] Paul uses the future tense φῶς λάμψει ("will shine," translated, "Let light shine"); it does not match the LXX phrasing in Gen 1:3, where an aorist subjunctive (γενηθήτω φῶς) is used. So Richard, "Polemics, Old Testament, and Theology," 360; Collange, *Énigmes*, 138–39; and Savage, *Power through Weakness*, 112–14, argue for the Isaiah passage. The phrase φῶς λάμψει is found only in 2 Cor 4:6 and Isa 9:1 (LXX; ὁ λαὸς ὁ πορευόμενος ἐν σκότει ἴδετε φῶς μέγα οἱ κατοικοῦντες ἐν χώρᾳ καὶ σκιᾷ θανάτου φῶς λάμψει ἐφ᾽ ὑμᾶς). Paul quotes heavily from Isaiah in his letters, which makes it a likely source. Elsewhere he cites Isaiah when he wishes to rebuke spiritual blindness (Rom 2; 3; 9–11 (eleven quotations); 1 Cor 1; 2 (two quotations); and 2 Cor 4–6 (three quotations). The words "light," "darkness," "shine," "blind," "reveal," "manifest" appear proportionately more in Isaiah than in all the rest of the prophets together.

[541] Savage, *Power through Weakness*, 112.

[542] Ibid., 126.

because it is "the great eschatological glory foretold in the prophets and destined to consummate history by reversing the proud ways of humankind." The glory of God can now be seen in the gospel as it is preached and lived out by the apostles. The Isaiah passage also brings up the theme of being a light to the nations (see Isa 42:6–7,16; 49:6; 60:12). Paul firmly believes that God called him to be a bearer of this light to the nations. God is not interested in bestowing private illumination and does not intend for the light to stay hidden in our hearts.[543] God caused the explosion of divine light in Paul's heart so that he might preach to the Gentiles (Gal 1:15).

Paul began this section by asking who is sufficient for the task. No one is; but God, who is the only source of light, wisdom, and stamina, made him sufficient and gave him a ministry more glorious than that of Moses, whose face was alight with the reflected glory of God. He concludes this section by affirming that his ministry reflects the light of the new age, the new creation, and the glory of Christ who is the image of God. Paul must next explain how this glorious ministry can be incarnated in weakness and suffering because some in Corinth see no glory about him at all. His voluntary acceptance of dishonor does not impair the glory of his ministry. The gospel "is carried and ministered by a broken body emblematic of the cross itself (see 4:7–12)."[544] Paul does not try to cover up his bodily frailty but insists that through it God is better able to convey the true comfort and glory of the gospel. Despite appearances, the wasting away of his outward body, tribulation, illness, and suffering, he, along with all Christians, is being transformed. What is visible to them now, therefore, is quite different from the anticipated glory of the future. As Christ's resurrection transformed his weak, perishable body into one of glory and power, no longer liable to decay and death (1 Cor 15:42–43; 2 Cor 13:4; Phil 3:20–21), so the same will happen to Paul in his resurrection.

(4) Self-Defense: Catalog of Afflictions: Always Being Given over to Death (4:7–15)

[7]But we have this treasure in jars of clay to show that this all-surpassing power is from God and not from us.

[8]We are hard pressed on every side, but not crushed; perplexed, but not in despair; [9]persecuted, but not abandoned; struck down, but not destroyed. [10]We always carry around in our body the death of Jesus, so that the life of Jesus may also be revealed in our body. [11]For we who are alive are always being given over

---

[543] Plummer translates the phrase πρὸς φωτισμὸν τῆς γνώσεως τῆς δόξης τοῦ θεοῦ to mean that God shone in Paul's heart "with a view to illumining men with the knowledge of the glory of God" (*The Second Epistle of St. Paul to the Corinthians*, 121). Kim avers: "God's shedding light in Paul's heart was not for its own sake, but it was for Paul to disseminate the light. ... Paul, who has experienced the light of the new creation at his conversion, is to convey it to others through his proclamation" (*The Origin of Paul's Gospel*, 7).

[544] Sloan, "New Covenant Hermeneutics," 144

to death for Jesus' sake, so that his life may be revealed in our mortal body. ¹²So then, death is at work in us, but life is at work in you.
¹³It is written: "I believed; therefore I have spoken." With that same spirit of faith we also believe and therefore speak, ¹⁴because we know that the one who raised the Lord Jesus from the dead will also raise us with Jesus and present us with you in his presence. ¹⁵All this is for your benefit, so that the grace that is reaching more and more people may cause thanksgiving to overflow to the glory of God.

Paul's acknowledgment that he always is given over to death gets at the core of the confusion and complaints about his apostolic ministry. How does the unsurpassed glory of the ministry of the Spirit harmonize with unrelenting death? How can such wonderful treasure be properly exhibited in such a lowly clay pot? Paul cannot cover up his tribulations and does not wish to do so. Instead, he exults in them and explains why the divine glory must be contained in the earthen vessel of his frail, pummeled body.⁵⁴⁵ It shows that his extraordinary apostolic power can only come from God and not himself. Rather than discrediting his apostolic ministry, Paul's hardships point to the all-transcending power of God working in and through him. This explanation gets at the heart of the gospel. The glory of the ministry must be seen in terms of both cross and resurrection (see 5:1–10). Paul reads the cross into all his experiences and interprets the ups and downs of his ministry theologically as carrying around in his body the death of Jesus to manifest the life (the resurrection) of Jesus. All his suffering is part of God's design to spread the gospel.⁵⁴⁶

The following structure shows the flow of Paul's thought:
4:7 But we have this treasure in jars of clay
    to (ἵνα, *hina*) show that this all-surpassing power
      is (ἤ, *ē*) from God and not from us.
4:8 In everything
    being hard pressed,   but not crushed;
    perplexed,   but not in despair;
4:9   persecuted,   but not abandoned;
    struck down,   but not destroyed.
4:10 We always
    carry around in our body the death of Jesus
      in order that *(hina)* the life of Jesus may also be revealed in our body.

---

[545] Hafemann, *Suffering and Ministry in the Spirit,* 63–64. He notes that while the catalog of sufferings in 2 Cor 4:7–12 is similar to that in 1 Cor 4:8–13 in arguing that God's power is made known through suffering, 1 Cor 4:8–13 is hortatory, focusing on the Corinthians to get them to imitate Paul's willingness to give up his rights to serve others, no matter what the cost in suffering. In 2 Cor 4:7–12 the thrust is apologetic, focusing on Paul and explaining how his suffering relates to the gospel message.
[546] Ibid., 67.

4:11 We always
>   are being given over to death for Jesus' sake
>   in order that *(hina)* his life may be revealed in our mortal body.
4:12 So then, death is at work in us,
>   but life is at work in you.

4:7   Paul begins this unit by announcing that we have this treasure in jars of clay. He writes in 5:1 that "we have a building from God, an eternal house in heaven, not built by human hands."[547] That building is for a time yet to come. Now is the time for earthen vessels (4:7), affliction (4:17), and being away from the Lord (5:6).[548] In this aeon treasure is stored and carried in earthen pots. Paul does not specify what he means by treasure. He could have in mind "the light of the knowledge of the glory of God in the face of Christ" (4:6), but that would also include the light of the gospel of the glory of Christ (4:3–4) that is so priceless and cherished by all Christians. It is more likely that means light revealed by the gospel than by his apostolic ministry (3:7–9; 4:1). But the treasure may also include his ministry since he describes it in terms of proclaiming the gospel of the glory of God (3:18; 4:4,6). He understands himself to be a vessel that contains and conveys a message.[549]

The term earthen vessels *(ostrakinoi skeuē)* implies something fragile, inferior, and expendable. Picturing himself as an ordinary, everyday utensil conveying an invaluable treasure is as striking an image as Paul's picture of himself as a defeated but joyous prisoner marching in God's triumphal procession (2:14).[550] Such an image underscores his weakness.

---

[547] See also the verb "to have" in 3:4,12; 4:1,13.

[548] J. Koenig, "The Knowing of Glory and Its Consequences (2 Corinthians 3–5)," in *The Conversation Continues: Studies in Paul and John,* ed. R. T. Fortna and B. R. Gaventa (Nashville: Abingdon, 1990) 166.

[549] Paul does not have in view that the body is the vessel for the soul or mind (see, e.g., Cicero, *Tusculan Disputations* I.xxii. 52; Philo, *On Dreams* 1.26; *Migration of Abraham* 193). The word "soul" (ψυχή) does not occur in 4:7–5:10 at all (and only appears in 1:23 and 12:15). Since the vessel suffers psychological distress, Paul does not consider it to be something solely corporeal (Thrall, *Second Epistle to the Corinthians,* 1:323).

[550] The image does not derive from some Gnostic metaphor for the contemptible nature of the human body (W. Schmithals, *Gnosticism in Corinth: An Investigation of the Letters to the Corinthians* [Nashville: Abingdon, 1971] 160–62). Nor does it derive from Cynic-Stoic imagery of humans as weak and perishable vessels (J. Dupont, *ΣΥΝ ΧΡΙΣΤΩΙ. L'union avec le Christ suivant St. Paul: Ière partie: 'avec le Christ' dans le vie future* [Bruges: Éditions de l'Abbaye de Saint André, 1952] 120–24.) E.g., Seneca wrote that our body is a "vessel that the slightest shaking, the slightest toss will break. ... A body weak and fragile, naked, in its natural state defenceless ... exposed to all the affronts of Fortune; ... doomed to decay" (*To Marcia* 11.3). But Furnish points out that Paul has no intention to contrast the mortal body to the immortal soul (*II Corinthians,* 278). It most likely is that the image derives from Paul's intimacy with the OT, which begins by avowing that God formed man from the dust of the ground (Gen 2:7; see 1 Cor 15:42–48) and typically views God as a potter (Job 10:9; 33:6; Isa 29:16; 41:25; 45:9; 64:8; Jer 18:1–10; Rom 9:21–23). The image of God as potter is even more prominent in the Dead Sea Scrolls (1QS 11:22; 1QH 1:21–23; 3:20–21; 4:29; 10:5; 11:3; 12:24–31; 13:15–16).

An earthen vessel is "quintessentially fragile," prone to breakage, easily chipped and cracked.[551] A breakable vessel offers no protection for the treasure (except from dust and water). The image therefore serves to emphasize the contrast between Paul's own pitiful weakness and the great power of God.

Second, the image highlights Paul's lowliness. He does not depict himself as an object d'art such as an exquisitely crafted Grecian urn, or bronze vessel, or delicate goblet with gold inlay. He has in mind earthenware jars or, perhaps, the small, cheap pottery lamps. Neither were things of beauty. They lacked any outward luster in contrast to the treasure, and their cheapness would disguise the fact that they contained anything valuable at all.[552] The contrast would emphasize the priceless value of the treasure compared to Paul's relative worthlessness. What the earthen vessel contains is the only thing that gives it importance.

Third, the image highlights Paul's expendability. Earthen vessels had no enduring value and were so cheap that when they were broken no one attempted to mend them. They simply discarded them. Broken glass was melted down to make new glass; an earthenware vessel, once hardened in a kiln, was nonrecyclable.[553] Easily broken, they were also easily replaced and not worth repairing. But the vessel is essential. A later rabbinic tradition makes this comparison:

---

[551] J. T. Fitzgerald, *Cracks in an Earthen Vessel: An Examination of the Catalogue of Hardships in the Corinthian Correspondence,* SBLDS 99 (Atlanta: Scholars Press, 1988) 167–68. The fragility of the clay vessel is the point of comparison in Job 4:18: "If God places no trust in his servants, / if he charges his angels with error, / how much more those who live in houses of clay, / whose foundations are in the dust, / who are crushed more readily than a moth!" See also Lam 4:2: "How the precious sons of Zion, / once worth their weight in gold, / are now considered as pots of clay, / the work of a potter's hands!" and Isa 30:14: "It will break in pieces like pottery, / shattered so mercilessly / that among its pieces not a fragment will be found / for taking coals from a hearth / or scooping water out of a cistern." Also Jer 19:1,10–11: "This is what the LORD says: 'Go and buy a clay jar from a potter. Take along some of the elders of the people and of the priests and go out to the Valley of Ben Hinnom, near the entrance of the Potsherd Gate. ... Then break the jar while those who go with you are watching, and say to them, "This is what the LORD Almighty says: 'I will smash this nation and this city just as this potter's jar is smashed and cannot be repaired.'"

[552] C. Maurer refers to a story in the Talmud (*b. Ta'can.* 7a) in which the Roman emperor's daughter mocks the outward ugliness of a rabbi by saying "glorious wisdom in a repulsive vessel" ("σκεῦος," *TDNT* 7:360). Plummer cites Epictetus (*Dissertations* III.9.18), who told a visiting rhetorician that his utensils (vessels, σκεύη) are made of gold but his discourse (word) is made of earthenware (ὀστράκινον τὸν λόγον; *The Second Epistle of St. Paul to the Corinthians,* 127).

[553] According to Jewish purity laws, it was impossible to render an earthen vessel ritually clean when it became defiled, so it was simply broken and discarded (Lev 6:28; 11:33–34; 15:12). A rabbinic tradition makes an argument about whether a heretic can be reformed from the premise that broken potsherds cannot be joined together again. Only vessels that have not yet been baked may be reformed (*Gen. Rab.* 14:7).

Just as wine cannot keep well in silver or gold vessels, but only in the lowliest of vessels—earthen ones—so words of Torah do not keep well in one who considers himself to be the same as silver or gold vessels, but only in one who considers himself the same as the lowliest of vessels—earthen ones.[554]

One therefore should not take Paul's image to mean that ministers are cheap and worthless, though they tend to be regarded or treated that way by the world and even by other Christians. Paul knows that as a minister of the new covenant he is a bearer of good tidings, a glorious divine treasure, even for those who despise him. In 2 Tim 2:20–21 he writes: "In a large house there are articles not only of gold and silver, but also of wood and clay; some are for noble purposes and some for ignoble. If a man cleanses himself from the latter, he will be an instrument for noble purposes, made holy, useful to the Master and prepared to do any good work." Solomon's drinking vessels were said to be made of gold (2 Chr 9:20). The vessels into which God pours his treasure are not gold but clay, made from the dust of the earth. They are not only sufficient for the job (see 2:16; 3:5); they are far more valuable than a golden receptacle because of the treasure they contain. But they are also vital because the medium is the message.

The image of clay jars expresses the wisdom of God, who "chose the foolish things of the world to shame the wise; God chose the weak things of the world to shame the strong, the lowly things of this world and the despised things—and the things that are not—to nullify the things that are (1 Cor 1:27–28). Why put treasure in an earthen pot, and divine treasure at that? To show that the treasure has nothing to do with the pot, "to show that this all-surpassing power is from God and not from us." The result is that no one, including apostles, may boast before God (1 Cor 1:29). Paul's image therefore captures "the paradox of his ministry: the glorious gospel borne about by those who are comparatively inferior, the powerful gospel by those who are weak."[555] He basically admits to being a cracked pot, one rejected, and afflicted, and subject to destruction. But "his weakness and vulnerability is necessary to the proper conveyance of the treasure of the gospel."[556] All can see that the power he imparts for the salvation of the world (Rom 1:16) does not derive from him but from God alone.

Paul continues his defense for exercising his apostolic right to criticize frankly the Corinthians by first pointing out that his all too conspicuous weakness that so annoys some of them is divinely intended to highlight God's strength. God houses this treasure in such lowly vessels so that others

---

[554] *Sipre Deut.* 48 to 11:22 (R. Hammer, *Sifre: A Tannaitic Commentary on the Book of Deuteronomy* [New Haven: Yale University Press, 1986 193].

[555] Savage, *Power through Weakness,* 166.

[556] Thrall, *Second Epistle to the Corinthians,* 1:324.

may see the true wellspring of the treasure and power and know that God can mightily use anyone. Paul has been talking of the sufficiency, glory, and boldness of his ministry, but the danger is that one (and particularly the Corinthians) might be tempted to reverence the conveyer of this spiritual power rather than the divine source. Putting this treasure in unremarkable household articles keeps "the pretensions and accomplishments" of the gospel's ministers from obscuring the fact that the power does not belong to them.[557] Paul confesses that no one looking at him would mistake him for something grand or be so taken by his grace and comeliness that they would then miss the source of power that was working in and through him to reconcile the world. In this way he undercuts his showy, bombastic, and pretentious rivals, whose manner was so different from his.

Second, Paul would affirm that God's power is only manifest in humans in their weakness and shame. Savage asks why Paul wrote "is" (*ē*, present subjunctive) in v. 7 rather than "might be manifest" or "might appear" or "might be found." He suggests that the answer is that Paul means to say that "it is only in weakness that the power may be of God." Paul's weakness "in some sense actually serves as the grounds for divine power."[558] If that is so, then 12:1–10 provides a helpful commentary on this verse: "The very existence of Christ's power in Paul was conditioned on the apostle's prior humility and weakness."[559] Human arrogance and pride make unwelcome divine power because "divine power does not manifest itself by making the believer powerful." Paul will make this clear in 12:9, where he claims that "power does not drive out weakness; on the contrary, it only comes to its full strength in and through weakness."[560] Paul therefore contends that he is most powerful when he is least reliant on his own resources and power.[561]

Third, v. 7 prepares readers for Paul's list of hardships that follows. If such a brittle vessel can survive intact the knocks and bangs that his ministry provokes, the credit does not belong to the durability of the pot but to the sustaining power of God. This, Paul would say, is the only explanation of why he has not been destroyed by all his afflictions. The afflictions have caused some stress fractures in the earthen vessel, but it remains whole

---

[557] Harvey, *Renewal through Suffering*, 56.
[558] Savage, *Power through Weakness*, 166.
[559] Ibid., 167.
[560] J. D. G. Dunn, *Jesus and the Spirit* (Philadelphia: Westminster, 1975) 329.
[561] B. Beck relates the circumstances surrounding the rebuilding of a bombed medieval church in London with just one wall and parts of two others left standing. One person in favor of rebuilding the church vociferously argued: "God must triumph in every situation. Never must he come off second best. That includes not letting terrorism triumph at St. Ethelburga." Beck thinks it would be a better witness to the gospel if the church were left a ruin. God does triumph: "But he does so precisely through the ruination of the cross, which stands forever in its starkness to witness what he has done" ("Reflections in 2 Cor 5:11–6:2," *Epworth Review* 21 [1994] 92).

because a divine glue holds it together.

Sadly for Paul, some in Corinth have failed to perceive any of this significance. Their response to him (see 1 Cor 4:8–13) is little different from the world's response to his message of Christ crucified, which is foolishness to the Greeks and a stumbling block to the Jews (1 Cor 1:23). Paul looks like a fool even though he is one for Christ's sake. He is weak, disreputable, hungry, poorly clothed, beaten, homeless, and easily dismissed as refuse and the dregs of all things (1 Cor 4:1–13). He hardly serves as an attractive endorsement for the advantages of becoming a Christian. They would, perhaps, more readily accept the counsel and censure of someone with a more regal bearing and a greater show of wisdom, strength, and honor. The Corinthians have therefore failed to see God's power at work in Paul's suffering, which suggests that they have failed to grasp the full meaning of the cross. They had differing views about how divine power should manifest itself in an apostle; and some apparently were asking, How can such a worthless vessel claim to be the agent for the glory of God? Plummer comments, "Those who get the treasure should not mock the shabby appearance of the vessel which brought it to them."[562] But more important, they should be able to see through the shabby appearance and behold God's glory in the one who suffers as Christ did.

When God entrusted apostles with the eternal treasure of the gospel, he did not endow them with immunity from illness, torment, or other human afflictions. The jar does not protect the treasure, nor the treasure the jar. But Paul's metaphor breaks down at this point. The treasure contained within can sustain them through every affliction, and his list of hardships makes this very point.

In contrast to the lists of hardships that appear later in the letter he speaks here in generalities. In 6:4–10 and 11:23–27 his lists become more specific: floggings, stonings, mobbings, imprisonments, labors, shipwrecks, muggings, sleeplessness, exposure, thirst, and hunger. These experiences of hardship in carrying out his ministry generated Paul's listing of his afflictions rather than some intent to follow a presumed literary pattern of hardship catalogs. The parallels with other Greco-Roman authors who recounted their hardships, however, reveals that Paul's readers would have been familiar with such catalogs. Horsley contends: "Because life was difficult for the vast majority of people in antiquity it is not surprising that the variety of adversities encountered was a common literary and philosophical preoccupation."[563] Therefore we should be cautious before accepting the claim that

---

[562] Plummer, *The Second Epistle of Paul the Apostle to the Corinthians,* 43.
[563] G. H. R. Horsley, "Review of Fitzgerald's, Cracks in an Earthen Vessel," *AusBR* 37 (1989) 83–84.

Paul is adopting a rhetorical convention in listing hardships to vouch for his legitimacy as an ideal sage.[564] The attitudes of other ancient moralists toward their hardships, however, help to throw in sharp relief Paul's distinctive attitude toward his afflictions. He differs significantly from the Cynic and Stoic philosophers of his day.

1. They appealed to their maltreatment or adversity to prove their superiority over circumstances. Epictetus believed that difficulties *(peristaseis)* "show what men are."[565] What they endured exhibited their true grit and moral constancy. For Paul hardships do not disclose what humans are made of but what God's power is like. They lay bare human weakness and reveal that the power, beyond all comparison, belongs entirely to God and not to any human however gallant he or she might be. While the sage claims to know his own strength and is full of self-confidence because of his self-sufficiency, Paul never boasts of his own stamina, self-discipline, or fortitude.[566] He can take no credit and knows that the gospel does not depend on human strength for its success. If he is stouthearted in the face of tribulation, it is only because of God's comfort and grace. Paul therefore knows only God's strength and is confident only in God (1:9–10).

---

[564] Horsley's review of Fitzgerald's *Cracks in an Earthen Vessel* sharply critiques it for identifying a literary catalog of hardships everywhere an allusion to suffering surfaces and for being undiscriminating ("an omnium gatherum approach") in the selection of passages (ibid., 82–87). For earlier research on tribulation lists, see A. Fridrichson, "Zum Stil des paulinischen Peristasenkatalogs. 2 Kor. 11,23ff.," SO 7 (1928–29) 25–29; and "Peristasenkatalog und res gestae: Nachtrag zu 2 Kor. 11,23ff.," SO 8 (1929) 78–82, who argued that the Greco-Roman descriptions of the wise sage is the primary background. For those who see the OT and Jewish apocalyptic as primary in determining the content, if not the form, of the catalog of trials, see Collange, *Énigmes*, 149; W. Schrage, "Leid, Kreuz und Eschaton: Die Peristasenkataloge als Merkmale paulinischer theologia crucis und Eschatologie," *EvT* 34 (1974) 141–75; and K. T. Kleinknecht, *Der leidende Gerechtfertigte. Die alttestamentlich-jüdische Tradition vom 'leidenden Gerechten' und ihre Rezeption bei Paulus*, WUNT 2/13 (Tübingen: Mohr [Siebeck], 1984) 208–304. R. Hodgson recognizes that Paul was not circumscribed by Stoic philosophy or by Jewish apocalyptic ("Paul the Apostle and First Century Tribulation Lists," *ZNW* 74 [1983] 59–80); and S. R. Garrett argues that Paul was influenced by both Stoic philosophy and the Jewish tradition as reflected in the *T. Job* ("The God of This World and the Affliction of Paul: 2 Cor 4:1–12," in *Greeks, Romans, and Christians: Essays in Honor of Abraham J. Malherbe* [ed. D. L. Balch, et al.; Minneapolis: Fortress, 1990] 99–117). Paul's direct quotation from Ps 115:1 (LXX) in 4:13 and Isa 49:8 in 6:2 would argue that the OT provides the primary framework for his understanding of his tribulations. On Paul's view of his suffering, see also E. Kamlah, "Wie beurteilt Paulus sein Leiden?" *ZNW* 54 (1963) 217–32; and C. G. Kruse, "The Price Paid for a Ministry Among Gentiles: Paul's Persecution at the Hands of the Jews," in *Worship, Theology, and Ministry in the Early Church: Essays in Honor of Ralph P. Martin*, ed. M. J. Wilkens and T. Paige (Sheffield: JSOT, 1992) 260–72.

[565] Epictetus, *Dissertations* I.24.1.

[566] Seneca wrote: "What element of evil is there in torture and in the other things which we call hardships? It seems to me that there is this evil,—that the mind sags, and bends, and collapses. But none of these things can happen to the sage; he stands erect under any load. Nothing can subdue him; nothing that must be endured annoys him" (*Moral Epistles* 71.26).

2. The Stoic and Cynic philosophers referred to their hardships to show how such troubles had no impact on their philosophic equilibrium or serenity. They assumed that an individual gained inner strength from holding philosophical convictions that enable one to endure hardships and be happy. For Epictetus, difficulties are overcome by reason and courage.[567] He wrote: "Show me a man who though sick is happy, though in danger is happy, though dying is happy, though condemned to exile is happy, though in disrepute is happy. Show him! … I fain would see a Stoic!"[568] By contrast, Paul does not think that some intellectual creed gives him the edge in overcoming suffering, and he never speaks of personal happiness.[569] Again, it is God's power as revealed in the death and resurrection of Jesus that energizes and reinforces him. Consequently, he thinks only in terms of service (4:5), faith (4:13), hope (4:14), thanksgiving (4:15), bringing glory to God (4:15), and the desire to make God happy (5:9). His abundant joy comes as a by-product from giving himself to his Lord, who loved him and died for him, and from giving himself to others.

3. In contrast to others, Paul does not downplay his suffering as trifling and make it a matter of indifference. Harvey comments: "The Stoic philosopher—and still more the Cynic—prided himself on his indifference to physical and mental suffering, and would often give a recital of what he had been through in order to demonstrate the power of the philosophy to make one able to rise above such purely external and short-term vicissitudes."[570] Paul regarded his suffering as inconsequential only when compared to the eternal glory that awaits him (4:17). In the meantime he freely confesses that he is not untouched by despair (1:8; 4:8), sleeplessness, or anxiety (11:27–28). He is not dispassionate about what has happened to him and has prayed fervently to God for things such as the thorn in the flesh to be removed (12:8). He does not believe that nothing is disastrous if only one has the right attitude toward it (such as apathy). The vocabulary in his list has affinity with the language of the suffering righteous one found in the Psalms (see 4:13) and the suffering servant in Isaiah (see 6:2).[571] In contrast to secular writers, Paul, like the psalmist,

---

[567] Epictetus, *Dissertations* IV.7.6–15.

[568] Epictetus, *Dissertations* II.19.24. Plutarch wrote that the wise sage "is not impeded when confined, and not under compulsion when flung down a precipice, and not in torture when on the rack, and not injured when mutilated, and is invincible when thrown down in a wrestling and is not blockaded under siege, and is uncaptured while his enemies are selling him into slavery ("Conspectus of the Essay," *Moralia* 1057D).

[569] Furnish, *II Corinthians*, 282.

[570] Harvey, *Renewal through Suffering*, 15–16.

[571] See C. M. Pate, *Adam Christology as the Exegetical and Theological Substructure of 2 Corinthians 4:7–5:21* (Lanham/New York: University Press of America, 1991) 92–96.

"speaks of deliverance, not of inward immunity."[572] What he goes through weighs him down with a crushing load of sorrow, but he is buoyed by the supreme assurance that God will deliver him through the suffering, if not from it. He also knows that, as an apostle, God may deliver him but only to suffer another day. Ultimate deliverance must await the moment when God will raise him with Christ.

This last point may be the most important for understanding Paul's purpose in listing his adversities. He is not simply trying to prove his legitimacy, to evoke empathy, or to show that he heroically risks "all for the gospel and for his congregations."[573] He wants those who see him only as "crushed, despairing, forsaken, or destroyed" to take a closer look. All his suffering has not destroyed him, not because he has made himself immune to it but because he rests secure in the hands of God, who upholds him. He faces rejection and dejection, but nothing will ever ultimately defeat him or destroy him because of God's love and power. To be sure, such an outlook on hardships accords with the view of Epictetus that God endows the individual with the internal strength "to enable us to bear all that happens without being degraded or crushed thereby."[574] But Paul's thought is primarily determined by Scripture and Christ's death and resurrection. The list therefore recalls the biblical motif of God helping the righteous. Daniel responds to the king, who asks:

> "Daniel, servant of the living God, has your God, whom you serve continually, been able to rescue you from the lions?" ... "My God sent his angel, and he shut the mouths of the lions. They have not hurt me, because I was found inno-

---

[572] Ibid., 329. The attitude found in *T. Jos.* 1:3b–7 is therefore closer to Paul's with its emphasis on God's saving acts.
These my brethren hated me, but the Lord loved me.
They wanted to kill me, but the God of my fathers preserved me.
Into a cistern they lowered me, the most High raised me up.
They sold me into slavery; the Lord of all set me free.
I was taken into captivity, the strength of his hand came to my aid.
I was overtaken by hunger, the Lord himself fed me generously.
I was alone, and God came to help me.
I was in weakness, and the Lord showed concern for me.
I was in prison, and the Savior acted graciously in my behalf.
I was in bonds, and he loosed me.
falsely accused, and he testified in my behalf.
Assaulted by bitter words of the Egyptians, and he rescued me.
A slave, and he exalted me.
[573] Against Witherington, *Conflict and Community in Corinth*, 388.
[574] *Epictetus, Dissertations* I.6.40. He also said that trials are necessary "because he [God] is training me, and making use of me as a witness to the rest of men" (*Dissertations* III.24.113). Paul understood his trials similarly but saw the witness of his sufferings as pointing away from himself to Christ and to God's redeeming power.

cent in his sight. Nor have I ever done any wrong before you, O king" (Dan 6:20,22).[575]

Paul responds to his detractors that his suffering does not discredit his ministry. Instead it attests to the power of God as he conforms his life to the cross of Christ. Roetzel's observations are helpful: "Ambiguous in their bare form, therefore, afflictions could be read either as signs of weakness, alienation, mortality, baseness, failure, and even divine rejection; or they could be viewed as symbolic participation in the death of Jesus (4:10)."[576] Paul interprets his suffering, "the dark side of human experience," as but the dark side of the cross that leads to resurrection. The catalog of experiences in 4:8–9 are presented in terms of dying and remaining alive and are directly connected to the death and resurrection of Jesus in 4:10–11. Even though Paul may look like death, his suffering is really the way to life and the way God has chosen to reveal and spread the gospel.[577]

4:8–9 The four pairs of participles set in antithesis in 4:8–9 illustrate what Paul means about being fragile and how power comes from God to save him. The NIV translates the phrase "in every way being afflicted" *(en panti thlibomeoni)* as applying only to the first contrast rather than all four; and since the exact phrase appears in 7:5, this rendering may be correct. But it may also apply to all four afflictions as outlined in our structure of the passage. The first term, "being afflicted," recalls Paul's opening reference to his recent affliction in Asia, which nearly dealt him a deathblow (1:8); and the theme of affliction dominates the letter. The noun "affliction" *(thlipsis)* appears nine times (1:4[2x],8; 2:4; 4:17; 6:4; 7:4; 8:2,13) and the verb *(thlibein)* three times (1:6; 4:8; 7:5). The fragile vessel is therefore "afflicted in every way," but the divine power goes to work, and he is "not crushed."[578] The noun form of the verb "crush" *(stenochōria)* is used as a synonym for affliction, but the verb here means "being confined or pressed." The REB aptly translates it "hard-pressed but never cornered." He is not crushed internally. His internal spirit is not gasping for breath.

The fragile vessel is "perplexed" (REB, "at wit's end"). Paul is not stoical about all of his troubles. He confesses to discouragement (see 1:8; Gal 4:20). Bauckham recognizes that such feelings can descend on any minister:

---

[575] "For the Lord does not abandon those who fear him, neither in darkness, or chains, or tribulation, or direst need" (*T. Jos.* 2:4).

[576] Roetzel, "As Dying, and Behold We Live," 9.

[577] In 4:10–11, the word "life" occurs three times.

[578] The negative οὐ appears with the participles when we would normally expect μή. The οὐ may be intended to make the antithesis more emphatic: "by no means" (so Fitzgerald, *Cracks in an Earthen Vessel,* 166; Savage, *Power through weakness,* 171; and Robertson, *Grammar,* 1137–38). Thrall, however, contends that it reflects the absolute use of the participle standing in the place of the indicative (see 5:12; 7:5; 8:19–20, 24; *The Second Epistle to the Corinthians,* 1:326).

Even without the physical dangers of Paul's career, anyone who throws himself
into the work of Christian ministry of any kind with half the dedication of Paul
will experience the weakness of which Paul speaks: the times when problems
seem insoluble, the times of weariness from sheer overwork, the times of
depression when there seem to be no results.[579]

But the divine power comes into play, and he is "not driven to despair." It is
difficult in English to capture Paul's play on words *aporoumenoi—exaporou-
menoi*. The *ek* is perfective: "perplexed to the final degree," and it may be
paraphrased "stressed, but not stressed out."[580]

The fragile vessel is "persecuted," but the divine power engages, and he is
not "forsaken" (NIV, "abandoned"), that is, by God. The same verb "forsaken" translates Jesus' cry on the cross (Mark 15:34; Matt 27:46, quoting
Ps 22:2). Paul knows from his experiences that God does not abandon his
own (Deut 4:31; 31:6,8).[581] That is why Paul is not crushed, despondent, or
destroyed, even when the Corinthians seemed to have abandoned him. God
sustains him through it all and enables him to continue to speak for God
(4:13). Paul also knows that in death God will not abandon him but will raise
him (4:14; 2 Tim 4:16–17).

The fragile vessel is "struck down." The verb *kataballein* can mean "laid
low by a blow or a weapon, abused or bullied, cast off or rejected, stricken
with an illness, or even slain."[582] In his persecutions Paul suffered physical
violence many times, but the divine power is always at work so that he is
knocked down but never knocked out (Phillips).

The assorted and sundry blows have caused some obvious stress fractures
in this earthen vessel, but it remains intact because it is held together by
God. Fitzgerald helps us to see the theological thrust of Paul's argument:

> Viewed as a whole, then, the hardships that Paul lists in his catalog have, as it
> were, caused cracks in him as an earthen vessel, but the vessel itself remains
> intact. The vessel is held together by the power of divine adhesive, and the light
> that shines (4:5–6) through these cracks is none other than the light of the life
> of Jesus (4:10–11).

God's use of a fragile, cracked vessel such as Paul is explicable only in light of
the divine folly displayed in the crucifixion. God's action vis-à-vis Paul's
weakness is consonant with God's action in Christ. Indeed, it is precisely
because his ministry exhibits the disparity between lowliness / weakness and

---

[579] R. Bauckham, "Weakness—Paul's and Ours," *Themelios* 4 (1982) 5–6.

[580] Furnish tries to capture the play on words with the translation "despairing, but not utterly
desperate" (*II Corinthians*, 254).

[581] See also Gen 28:15; Deut 31:6,8; Josh 1:5; 1 Chr 28:20; Pss 16:10 (LXX); 36:25,28 (LXX);
Jer 15:20; *Sir* 2:10; and Heb 13:5. See Hab 3:17–18.

[582] Furnish, *II Corinthians*, 255.

exaltation / power found in the cross that it is itself a part of the message about Christ that he proclaims.[583] Meeks points out that it is less precise to refer to this disparity as paradoxical.

That is, things ordinarily taken as signs of weakness are not simply redefined as powerful because they emulate the weakness of the crucified Jesus, although some of the statements by Paul may plausibly be taken that way. More often the pattern is dialectical or sequential: the Christ was first weak, then powerful; so too the Christians are weak and afflicted today but will be vindicated and glorious.[584]

It bears repeating that through the cracks the divine light shines to enlighten others. If Paul were a superman, faster than a speeding bullet and able to leap over tall buildings with a single bound, he could hardly proclaim the message of the cross. His weakness and God's power working in and through his weakness, however, is consonant with the folly of the cross. Christ crucified is not only his message, but it is also his model. He has become the suffering apostle of the suffering Messiah. We can learn from his example that ministers do not have to be wonderful, just faithful. Many labor under the enormous burden of trying to be wonderful in the eyes of others rather than simply trying to minister to them. Many a minister suffers burnout from trying to run a sparkling program, keeping up attendance while keeping down conflict, and preaching catchy sermons instead of preaching Christ. Paul knew suffering beyond the imagination of many but endured because he also knew the power of the resurrection (13:4). Most persons of average piety would be broken by such adversity. Yet piety does not rally him; it is the power of God at work within him. The task demands all he can give. And when he has given his all and finds it is not enough, God's power carries him through. This truth prevented Paul from thinking that he could do it all alone. But it also prevented him from avoiding doing anything except what was cautiously safe to avoid looking weak or like a failure. He knew that God works even through his limitations and failures. As one controlled by the love of Christ, he dared to reach beyond his limits because he trusted God's power to redeem all that he did.

4:10–11 Paul sums up his apostolic ministry with these words: "We always carry around in our body the death of Jesus." In 4:11 Paul comments on what he says in 4:10.[585] Paul's normal term for death is *thanatos* (see 1:9–10; 2:16; 3:7; 4:12; 7:10; 11:23). The term "death" *(nekrōsis)* is stark and may signify putrefying flesh that is stiff, swollen, and eaten away. It can

---

[583] Fitzgerald, *Cracks in an Earthen Vessel*, 176.

[584] W. A. Meeks, *The First Urban Christians: The Social World of the Apostle Paul* (New Haven: Yale University Press, 1983) 182.

[585] J. Lambrecht, "The *NEKRŌSIS* of Jesus: Ministry and Suffering in 2 Cor 4,7–15," in *Studies on 2 Corinthians*, BETL 112 (Leuven: University Press, 1994) 326.

refer to the process of either dying or decay or the final condition of death (see Rom 4:19). Perhaps Paul has both ideas in mind. He refers to the physical death and suffering of Jesus on the cross that is replicated in his own dying and being crucified with him (Gal 2:19). Paul's suffering continues to reveal God's saving activity as he carries around Christ's death and displays it for all to see. It is possible that he depicts himself here as the pallbearer of Christ.[586]

Duff offers the intriguing suggestion that Paul is using the imagery of Greco-Roman epiphany processions in which the devotees sought to attract attention and new converts to their cult with a parade. Such pageantry grew increasingly lavish, as devotees carried the symbols, sacred objects, and images associated with the rites and the saving action of the god or goddess. If Paul has such common religious spectacles in view, he employs another striking metaphor for evaluating his sufferings.[587] It parallels his other reference to a procession, the Roman triumph, in 2:14.

who always (time element)	always
leads [us] in triumph (procession)	carrying around the dying of Jesus
us in Christ (involvement of Paul)	in our body
and (conjunction)	so that
the scent of his knowledge	the life of Jesus
[he] manifests through us.	may be manifested in our bodies.

In contrast to the ostentatious golden vessels used in pagan processions, the gospel is unimposing and needs no swanky window dressing or pomp and circumstance.[588] The danger of such displays is that people will be so distracted by all the tinsel and glitter of the vessel that they will ignore what the vessel contains.

Paul is an earthen vessel, and his life and dying point to Christ. He does not strive to imitate Christ's sufferings as Ignatius did (see *Ign. Rom.* 6:3), but the sufferings of Christ are working themselves out in his life.[589] Harvey comments: "Physical debility and decay, instead of being in apparent contradiction to the promise of life proclaimed in the gospel, are now found to be a means by which the believer identifies with Jesus in his final hours of dying and so makes 'manifest' the new life which was the consequence of that death."[590] Paul preached Christ crucified (1 Cor 1:23), and his life and min-

---

[586] So Fitzgerald, drawing the parallel between a νεκρόφορος and the verb περιφέροντες (*Cracks in an Earthen Vessel*, 178).

[587] P. B. Duff, "Apostolic Suffering and the Language of Processions in 2 Corinthians 4:7–10," *BTB* (1991) 158–65.

[588] Duff cites Plutarch's complaint about gaudiness of processions so that the important elements of the rite are "buried under what is useless and superfluous." ("Apostolic Suffering," 161).

[589] Furnish, *II Corinthians*, 285.

[590] Harvey, *Renewal through Suffering*, 59.

istry are conformed to Jesus' humility and shame.[591] Consequently, his suffering "because of Jesus" should not be disparaged. For Paul, his "apostolic suffering and fragility are not just human pain caused by opposition and persecution. No, the dying of Jesus himself is present in it, visible in the body of the apostle."[592]

1. He endures it "unceasingly," "constantly." The "always" *(pantote)* in 4:10 is placed first in the Greek for emphasis (see 1 Cor 15:30–31), and the present tense of the participle "carrying about" reinforces this idea. He repeats the "always" *(aei)* in 4:11. He therefore does not consider his plight to be atypical of an apostle. It is not a matter of occasionally suffering for a period of time and then being delivered and set free from suffering.[593] Suffering is business as usual; but more than that, it is basic to his apostolic service. As Savage puts it:

> By faith Paul preaches the gospel, which in turn brings affliction, which then produces in him greater faith, which in turn creates greater boldness of speech, which then provokes additional affliction. For the minister of Christ, the pattern of believing—speaking—suffering is inescapable and perpetual.[594]

2. He is "handed over" as Jesus was.[595] The verb *paradidomai* is used for the handing over of Jesus to death (see 1 Cor 11:23; Rom 4:25; 8:32; Gal 2:20). The passive voice is a divine passive because Paul firmly believes that God's purposes lie behind his suffering. His suffering is on account of Jesus and forms part of God's paradoxical plan to sow the gospel in the world. God delivered him from the trials in Asia, but he is handed over again and again to death.

3. He endures it physically—in the flesh. Paul makes the extraordinary claim that in principle he shares the same weakness with Christ and suffers the same affliction. It becomes the basis for an even more extraordinary claim that through this weakness and affliction he manifests the life of Jesus in his mortal flesh (4:11). In 4:11 Paul switches from "body" *(sōma)* to "flesh" *(sarx)*. It is the body that is defenseless against the ravages of death,

---

[591] The verb παραδιδόμεθα ("handed over," "given over," NIV) is part of the tradition that Paul passed on to the Corinthians about Jesus' death with the phrase "the night he was handed over" (1 Cor 11:23; see Mark 9:31; 10:33). Paul's statement γὰρ ἡμεῖς οἱ ζῶντες εἰς θάνατον παραδιδόμεθα ("we who are alive are given over to death") closely parallels Isa 53:12: παρεδόθη εἰς θάνατον ἡ ψυχὴ αὐτοῦ ("his soul is given over to death").

[592] Lambrecht, "The *NEKRŌSIS* of Jesus," 325.

[593] Thrall, *Second Epistle to the Corinthians,* 1:330,

[594] Savage, *Power through Weakness,* 181.

[595] The verb could be middle: "We are always giving ourselves up to death for Jesus' sake." Fitzgerald argues for the middle voice so that Paul says he gives himself over as part of his imitation of Christ (*Cracks in an Earthen Vessel,* 180). But Paul does not present himself as heroic here, and it is more likely that it is passive.

and Jesus' death finds a new bodily expression in the brokenness of his apostles. Paul's statement in Gal 6:17 is comparable:[596]

death	stigmata
of Jesus	of Jesus
in the body	in the body
carrying around *(peripherontes)*	bearing *(bastazō)*

This suffering gives content to Paul's testimony in 1:5 that "the sufferings of Christ are ours in abundance."

4. His affliction bestows benefits for others by producing not only comfort (1:6–7) but life. Everyone could see Paul's physical frailty, which the persecution and suffering only magnified; but Paul was also aware of the stirrings of divine life in and through him. He carries about the death of Jesus for the purpose of disclosing his life, that is, his resurrection life, in order that others might be saved. Bauckham pinpoints the logic behind Paul's thinking, "If God's definitive salvific act occurred through the weakness of the crucified Jesus, then it should be no surprise that the saving gospel of the crucified Jesus should reach the Gentiles through the weakness of his apostle."[597]

Death and misery are therefore not boundless. Life prevails, but it is Jesus' life. Despite the overwhelming tribulations, Paul is not overwhelmed. The same divine power that raised Jesus from death is at work in him.[598] He is continually being renewed, although that renewal might be invisible to some (see 4:16). Savage concludes:

> The great irony is that it is precisely in submitting to the suffering meted out by the powers of the old age that Paul is able to repulse those very powers (vv. 8–9). Living as he does at the intersection of two ages he endures the "dyings" of the old order to receive the "life" of the new (vv. 10–11).

Hence, the "in order that" *(hina,* "so that," NIV) that appears in both v. 10 ("in order that the life of Jesus may also be revealed in our body") and v. 11 (in order that his life may be revealed in our mortal body"). The power of God becomes even more evident and effective through suffering, and this fact makes his suffering bearable. He does not mean that this power will be openly displayed at the end of time, but right now those with spiritual perception can see through the weakness and dying "much victory, power and glory."[599]

4:12 The "so that" *(hōste)* in 4:12 presents the startling conclusion

---

[596] Noted by R. C. Tannehill, *Dying and Rising with Christ,* BZNWKAK (Berlin: Töpelmann, 1966) 84.

[597] Bauckham, "Weakness—Paul's and Ours," 5.

[598] J. Lambrecht, "The Eschatological Outlook in 2 Corinthians 4:7–15," in *Studies on 2 Corinthians,* BETL 112 (Leuven: University Press, 1994) 340.

[599] Lambrecht, "The *NEKRŌSIS* of Jesus," 326.

from 4:10–11: death is at work in us and life in the Corinthians.[600] Paul understands his suffering as benefiting the Corinthians in some way (see 5:15, "for your sake" and Col 1:24), which matches his statement in 1:6, "If we are distressed [*thlibometha,* the same word in 4:8] it is for your comfort and salvation." We should not infer that Paul's suffering in itself has any salvific power. "It is because Paul shares in Christ's sufferings that his own are a benefit to others."[601] He lives out his new life in Christ and the paradox of gaining life by giving it for others. He is no longer self-concerned or self-indulgent but self-emptying like Christ. His missionary work will only result in more and more physical battering, but that physical affliction will result in more and more spiritual blessings for others. This pattern of suffering, mortality, and blessing confirms Paul's apostolic calling because they most fully exhibit God's power and Jesus' resurrection life as the source of his own life and ministry.

What also helps Paul bear up under his load of suffering is his conviction that it bears fruit in the life of others. "Life" refers to life received from God through Christ. It does not mean that they will escape tribulations themselves (1:6–7). They experience life when they accept this paradoxical message that losing one's life for Christ brings greater life.[602]

His suffering means that he joins the long line of God's righteous people who have always suffered (see Matt 5:11–12). Jesus' death on the cross, however, gives new meaning to the suffering of his followers. No longer is it simply the suffering of the righteous. It is becoming like Christ in his death (13:4)! Jesus' death and resurrection also "represents the overthrow of the old order."[603] Those who persecute Paul belong to this old order that is passing away. God's power that works through him far outstrips the third-rate forces opposing Paul. When they are through with their scorn, torture, and instruments of death, they are through; but God is not. They can only put people to death; God's power is able to raise the dead. This is why Paul is not completely crushed. He knows that when he is crushed, God will resurrect him.

4:13 In 4:13–15 Paul explains why he continues to speak. His suffering

---

[600] "Works" translates the verb ἐνεργεῖται as middle voice. Baumert argues for a passive meaning "is being worked," which would make it consistent with the other passive verbs in 4:10–11 (*Täglich sterben und auferstehen,* 72–73, 267–83). It would be a divine passive implying that God's power is working through the death.

[601] M. D. Hooker, "Interchange and Suffering," in *Suffering and Martyrdom in the New Testament,* ed. W. Horbury and B. McNeil (Cambridge: University Press, 1981) 78.

[602] Paul is not speaking ironically of life as a "happy life," as Calvin claims (*The Second Epistle of Paul the Apostle to the Corinthians,* 60). Calvin thinks that Paul is chiding them for living happily and freely and taking their ease in security "at the very time Paul was struggling with infinite hardships."

[603] Savage, *Power through Weakness,* 176.

and preaching (both are interconnected) are for the sake of the Corinthians and for the purpose of reaching more and more people, whose response will lead to the greater glory of God. It will increase thanksgiving to the glory of God (see 1:11).

Paul completes this first discussion of his hardships in the letter by citing Ps 115:1 (LXX = Ps 116:10 MT): "According to what is written, 'I believed; therefore I have spoken.'" The "same spirit of faith" may refer to (1) the same spirit of robust, enduring faith that motivated the psalmist. This interpretation influences the rendering in the NIV, which understands it to be a disposition. The psalmist was also beset by travail and trusted in God, who delivered him. Therefore he spoke words that made evident his salvation.[604] (2) The phrase may also refer to the Holy Spirit, who engenders faith (1 Cor 12:9; Rom 8:14–16; Gal 3:2,5,14; 5:5; see also 1 Cor 2:4–5; 1 Thess 1:5–7). The same Spirit that generated the psalmist's faith and imbued his speech (see Acts 1:16) also works through Paul.

The first option seems the best since Paul repeats the psalm in the second half of the verse but changes it into the present tense and the first person plural, adding *kai* ("also") twice for emphasis: "We also believe, wherefore we also speak." He compares his own situation in which his faith inspires his bold speech despite his suffering at the hands of the unrighteous to that of the psalmist. Both are righteous sufferers whose manifold afflictions will not silence them. The content of Paul's faith, however, is different from the psalmist's because it is founded on the good news of the death and resurrection of Jesus Christ. It is this gospel that he preaches (4:2, "open statement of the truth"; 4:4, "the gospel"; 4:5, "preaching Jesus Christ"). For Paul the gospel is not some abstract theory that can be accepted and hidden away in the heart. It requires proclamation, and proclaiming it to a hostile world is perilous. Paul does not shrink from speaking this gospel boldly to unbelievers and to any believers who get out of line, whatever the consequences, because this is his calling in Christ.

4:14 Paul speaks boldly because his faith reveals to him that beyond earthly tribulation lies the assurance that God will resurrect him. Those who belong to Christ and experience his living power in this life will also belong to him on the other side of death and will therefore be raised with him. Those conformed to his death in this life will also experience the same vindication in resurrection (Phil 3:10–11). As Christ's death brought us life, so Christ's resurrection makes possible the life to come. All of Paul's apostolic ministry of proclamation "is grounded in his faith certainty of a final out-

---

[604] The phrase "the spirit of faith" could also be interpreted as a genitive of content, "the spirit which is faith" (so J. Murphy-O'Connor, "Faith and Resurrection in 2 Cor 4:13–14," *RB* 95 [1988] 548).

come: his resurrection after death—firmly based on Christ's past resurrection—and what can be called a gathering for ever of all Christians with Jesus in the presence of God."[605] Death is chiseling away and breaking him down, but it has no final power over him. For this reason he is willing to speak boldly, to put himself in danger every hour, to die daily, to fight with both literal and metaphorical beasts (1 Cor 15:30–32). If this hope were not true, they would have every reason to jeer him as a pitiful fool (1 Cor 15:17–19). It would also justify their failure to follow his example and to invest all their energy in trying to get and preserve the so-called good life in the here and now. This hope is true, however, and any contempt for Paul's afflictions betrays a grievous misunderstanding of the gospel established by Christ's death and resurrection.

The verb in the phrase "to present us with you in his presence" *(paristanai)* is used (1) for presenting something in the open, to make manifest; (2) for presenting a cultic offering (Rom 12:1); (3) for placing something at the disposal of someone or something else (Luke 1:19; Rom 6:13,16); (4) for presenting someone before a king in a court ceremony; or (5) for presenting someone to stand before a judge (Acts 22:33; 27:24). The last option is the most likely in the context. Paul declares that all persons will come before the judgment throne of Christ (5:10; see also Rom 14:10–11; Col 1:22). This verse would then provide an introduction to 4:16–5:10, in which Paul moves from discussion of the certainty of the resurrection (4:16–5:8) to appearing before the judgment seat of Christ (5:9–10).

We should not overlook the phrase "with you." Paul understands himself to be intimately joined to other Christians. He does not believe that he stands on a higher spiritual plateau because of his apostolic calling or his manifold sufferings for Christ. He understands himself to be the one who presents them as a bride before Christ (11:2), and he wants to be able to present them as a pure virgin (see Col 1:28). But he also sees himself as standing with them.[606] His goal in his Corinthian correspondence is to create this sense of bonding and community. They are prone to see themselves as individuals, economically and religiously self-sufficient, and only minimally interdependent with other believers. Paul seeks to build up community. He reminds them that they share the same suffering and comfort (1:5–7), that they are each other's boast before the Lord Jesus (1:14), that they have been established together in Christ (1:21), that they are the source of each other's joy (2:3–5), and that they will stand

---

[605] Lambrecht, "The Eschatological Outlook," 348.

[606] This sense of solidarity with his converts is beautifully expressed in his references to the Macedonians as his joy and his crown (Phil 2:14–18; 1 Thess 2:19–20). It would be shameful for him to stand before Christ alone and to realize that his work among his churches had all been in vain.

together before the Lord. Those who name Christ as Lord may differ with one another and from one another, but they will not be separated from one another before God.

4:15 Paul's last sentence in this unit avows that his ultimate goal as Christ's apostle is to bring glory to God.[607] The "all things" refers to Paul's suffering and his speaking. All the suffering he has endured has been caused by his faithful preaching of the gospel to the Gentiles. It is therefore for them. Had he played it safe or retreated at the first signs of danger, they may never have heard the gospel. His speech, including his harsh censure of their ethical lapses, is also for them. His frank speech does not come from his lack of love for them (6:11–12), nor is it intended to belittle them (7:8). He wants only to reconcile them to God. He is their slave (4:5) as Christ took the form of slave to give his life for others (Phil 2:7), and therefore all his work and affliction "is for your benefit."

Some Corinthians fail to appreciate fully the benefits they have received through Paul's ministry. Normally Paul would not mind the neglect and the derision if it were not for the reasons behind it: their failure to understand the full implications of the gospel they have received.

In Rom 5:20 Paul uses the verb *pleonazein* to describe sin that increases, but here he affirms that grace also expands.[608] "Grace" in this verse does not simply refer to God's forgiveness of sin but to the "gra-

---

[607] The syntax of the second half of this verse is problematic. Literally it reads "so that the grace having been made more through the more might abound thanksgiving to the glory of God." The prepositional phrase διὰ τῶν πλειόνων ("through the more") could go with the participle πλεονάσασα ("made more") or περισσεύσῃ ("might abound"). The two verbs πλεονάσασα ("made more") or περισσεύσῃ ("might abound") could be transitive or intransitive. Thrall lists four options (*The Second Epistle to the Corinthians*, 1:345–46):
1. "So that grace, having increased, may cause thanksgiving through the agency of more and more people to abound to the glory of God."
2. "So that grace, having increased, may, on account of the thanksgiving of the more and more people, abound to the glory of God."
3. "So that grace, having increased the thanksgiving through the agency of more and more people, may abound to the glory of God."
4. "So that grace, having increased though the agency of more and more people, may cause thanksgiving to abound to the glory of God."
Barnett cuts through the thicket of the syntax with the following structure (*The Second Epistle to the Corinthians*, 244):
For all things
are for you
    in order that the increasing grace may overflow   PURPOSE
    through the thanksgiving of more [people]   MEANS
    to the glory of God.   GOAL
[608] There is a play on words between πλεονάσασα ("having increased") and πλειόνων ("the many"), which is lost in the NIV's paraphrase "reaching more and more people." Paul does not refer to "all" people because all do not respond.

cious divine power at work in the hearts and lives of the readers."[609] Paul understands that God's grace should always lead to human gratitude. His goal is to bring as many as possible to faith (1 Cor 9:19–23) with the result that the more who receive this grace (see Rom 4:20), the more will be the thanksgiving redounding to God's glory. Paul does not gauge his success as an apostle by the numbers of converts, but that does not mean that a growing number of converts is not important to him. His suffering is part and parcel of his missionary task to draw more and more people to Christ. His preaching, which brings about his apostolic suffering, gives more and more people the chance to hear and to respond to the gospel. Their thankful response to his speaking brings more and more glory to God.

Paul expresses his confidence knowing that his suffering is for the glory of God, that it is temporary, that it effects the renewal of the inner person, and that God is preparing an eternal abundance of glory beyond all measure for him (and other Christians). He has set his sights on eternal, invisible realities.

(5) The Resurrection Hope (4:16–5:10)

[16]Therefore we do not lose heart. Though outwardly we are wasting away, yet inwardly we are being renewed day by day. [17]For our light and momentary troubles are achieving for us an eternal glory that far outweighs them all. [18]So we fix our eyes not on what is seen, but on what is unseen. For what is seen is temporary, but what is unseen is eternal.

[1]Now we know that if the earthly tent we live in is destroyed, we have a building from God, an eternal house in heaven, not built by human hands. [2]Meanwhile we groan, longing to be clothed with our heavenly dwelling, [3]because when we are clothed, we will not be found naked. [4]For while we are in this tent, we groan and are burdened, because we do not wish to be unclothed but to be clothed with our heavenly dwelling, so that what is mortal may be swallowed up by life. [5]Now it is God who has made us for this very purpose and has given us the Spirit as a deposit, guaranteeing what is to come.

[6]Therefore we are always confident and know that as long as we are at home in the body we are away from the Lord. [7]We live by faith, not by sight. [8]We are confident, I say, and would prefer to be away from the body and at home with the Lord. [9]So we make it our goal to please him, whether we are at home in the body or away from it. [10]For we must all appear before the judgment seat of Christ, that each one may receive what is due him for the things done while in the body, whether good or bad.

---

[609] Thrall, *Second Epistle to the Corinthians,* 1:344

4:16 The "therefore" (*dio*) emphatically draws the self-evident inference from Paul's preceding remarks in 4:7–15. Paul repeats the statement in 4:1 (*ouk egkakoumen;* NIV "we do not lose heart") and launches a new development in his argument that justifies why he ministers as he does and preaches as boldly as he does. Rather than connecting the meaning of the word *egkakein* in 4:1 to discouragement, losing heart, or giving up, it is argued that it is related to Paul's apostolic boldness. Paul does not need to give grounds for his "indomitable spirit" to the Corinthians.[610] Instead, he needs to explain why, in spite of his shameful condition as one who is afflicted, persecuted, and always being given up to death (4:8–11), he does not "draw in his horns," "is not timid," but is bold in preaching an *unveiled* gospel. Furnish comments, "The context here (see especially 4:2–6,7,10–12,13,15) makes it certain that Paul is not referring to boldness in facing death, but to boldness in preaching the gospel despite all manner of afflictions and despite the way some have falsely interpreted those."[611]

The initial *alla* ("but," omitted in the NIV) regards the preceding as settled and introduces the next stage of his argument that has to do with the dissolution of the earthen vessel and the sure promise of a resurrection body for the faithful: "But even if our outward man is being destroyed, but our inner man is being renewed day by day." The double adversatives add emphasis and begin a series of contrasts between the present affliction and the eternal glory that follows.

outward man / inner man (4:16)
wasting away / being renewed (4:16)
slight / beyond measure (4:17)
momentary / eternal (4:17, 18)
affliction / glory (4:17)
what can be seen / what cannot be seen (4:18)
tentlike house / building from God (5:1,2)
earthly / heavenly (5:1)
destroyed / eternal (5:1)
stripped naked / clothed (5:2–4)
mortality / life (5:4)
preparation, the guarantee of the Holy Spirit / not yet (5:5)
sight / faith (5:7)
at home in the body / away from the Lord (5:7–9)

The image of the outer and inner man is at home in Hellenistic philosophy, and it is possible that Paul adopts here the "popular philosophical ter-

---

[610] As Martin, e.g., contends (*II Corinthians,* 91).
[611] Furnish, *II Corinthians,* 288.

minology from the marketplace."[612] But Paul does not understand this contrast as referring to some inner part of a person as opposed to the outer flesh. Thrall describes the outer as the whole person "as seen by others from without" and the inner person as "one's unseen personality, visible only to God and (in part) to oneself."[613] Furnish defines the "outer person" as "that aspect of one's humanity which is subject to the various assaults and hardships of historical existence (4:8–9) and which, because of its vulnerability to these, may be likened to *earthen pots* (4:7)."[614] Paul's mortal existence is constantly wasting away and rushing headlong toward death. Paul's inner existence, united with Christ, is always being renewed and proceeding toward ever increasing glory (3:18; 4:11). He is not opposing body and soul, but the inner human being from the outer human being, existence determined by worldly circumstances and possibilities from existence determined by the power of the One who raised Christ from the dead. The outer person is what belongs to this world that is temporary and crumbling and what those who only evaluate things from a fleshly perspective can see. By contrast, the inner person belongs to what has ultimate significance and is being transformed and prepared for resurrection life through God's matchless power.

The battering Paul has taken in the service of Christ has left him the worse for wear and makes him a shamed figure in the eyes of the world. His deteriorating physical condition and shameful plight caused some in Corinth, who took account of such things, to wonder out loud about his power as an apostle. They may have assumed that God would do a better job of safeguarding and bringing honor to an authorized messenger of the gospel. Some in the ancient world interpreted affliction as a sign of god's judgment and as something dishonorable. After surviving the shipwreck on the journey to Rome and landing safely on the island of Malta, the islanders

---

[612] Harvey, *Renewal through Suffering*, 62. See Windisch, who cites references from Plato, *Republic* 589a; *Symposium* 216d–e; Plotinus, *Ennead* V.1.10; VI.4.14; I.4.4.; II.3.9; and the *Corpus Hermeticum* I.18; XII.7–8 (Der zweite Korintherbrief, 152–53). Furnish adds references from *Marcus Aurelius* III.3; X.38; and Philo, *Every Good Man Is Free* 111; *On Husbandry* 9; *On Noah's Work as a Planter* 42; and *The Worse Attacks the Better* 22–23 (*II Corinthians,* 261). H. P. Rüger demonstrates that the concept of the inner and outer person matches the rabbinic distinction between the impulse of good and impulse of evil and that Paul chose the Hellenistic terms to accommodate his audience ("Hieronymous, die Rabbinen und Paulus. Zur Vorgeschichte des Begriffspaars 'innerer und äusserer Mensch,'" *ZNW* 68 [1977] 132–37).

[613] Thrall, *Second Epistle to the Corinthians,* 1:349–50. This view is supported by Paul's contrast between the inner person and the (outward) members in Rom 7:22–23 to describe a person's inner struggle, not visible on the surface, to try to obey the law. This parallel would argue against the view that the outer person is one who belongs to this age while the inner person belongs to the age to come.

[614] Furnish, *II Corinthians,* 289.

were sure when they saw a viper hanging from Paul's hand that he must have been guilty of some great crime for which the gods were now belatedly punishing him. "Though he escaped from the sea, justice has not allowed him to live" (Acts 28:5). They expected him "to swell up or suddenly fall dead, but after waiting a long time and seeing nothing unusual happen to him, they changed their minds and said he was a god" (Acts 28:6). Like the Maltese islanders, some Corinthians were judging Paul only from outward appearances and from a wrongheaded view about how God works in this world and what God has in store for those who faithfully serve. Paul will confess in 5:16 that he too once judged Christ from the same outward, worldly criteria and, as a result, entirely misjudged him. Only after his conversion could he see beyond the damning judgment of the law, that everyone hanged on a tree is accursed of God (Deut 21:22–23; Gal 3:13), and recognize that the crucified Jesus was "the Son of God who loved me and gave himself for me" (Gal 2:20). He now no longer looks at persons from this superficial, worldly perspective; and the Corinthians should not either—particularly God's apostles, who pattern their lives after the sacrificial suffering and death of Christ.

The Corinthians need to understand that the Christian's inner life is constantly being transformed into glory even as its earthly embodiment decays and dies. The present tense, "being renewed" *(anakainoutai),* points to a continuing process (see Col 3:10). The phrase "day by day" suggests that it is "not progressively accomplished but is repeated all over again each day."[615] Paul has said that this renewal comes through continual fellowship with the risen Christ and the power of the Spirit so that the believer "is being transformed into his likeness with ever-increasing glory" (3:18). His image is the exact reverse of the plot in Oscar Wilde's novel, *The Picture of Dorian Gray.* In that story the vain Dorian Gray has his portrait painted; and when it is finished, he laments: "How sad! I shall grow old and horrible, but this picture never will be older. If it were I who was to be always young, and the picture that was to grow old! I would give my soul for that!" He got his wish. The portrait became a mirror of his soul, which showed every sign of evil and aging. He locked it away to prevent the world from seeing the truth about himself and deceived others with an outward appearance of one who was young, pure, and handsome. The contrast between the loathsome, evil, and wrinkled visage on the canvas fed by mad, ravenous passions, and his exquisite outward appearance grew more stark every day. In Paul's case others may only see a withered, crushed apostle, pounded by overwhelming hardships. If they do not look at him with the eyes of faith, they will not see the real Paul on a portrait locked away in heaven that is ever being transformed into the likeness of Christ. As his outward life conforms ever more

---

[615] Furnish, *II Corinthians,* 262.

closely to the crucified Christ, his inward life conforms ever more closely to the glorified Christ.

Harvey comments:

> It was one thing for a philosopher to say that the inner man is impervious to outer vicissitudes, or that the immortal soul cannot be harmed by the dissolution of the mortal body; or indeed for the pious Jew to say that adversaries may constitute an inner 'testing' by which the character is chastened and purified. It was quite another thing for Paul to say that such experiences actually had a positive value, that they were a "source of renewal."[616]

That is precisely what Paul emphasizes. He understands that through his suffering he shared Christ's death and received new life (see Phil 3:10–11). Savage captures Paul's thought:

> It is precisely because his outer man is decaying that his inner man is being renewed day by day (v. 16). His outer afflictions serve to multiply the glory of his inner man (v. 17). His critics fail to see this increasing weight of glory because it is accumulating in his heart (v. 6), a place hidden to their externally minded outlook."[617]

Most cannot see this transformation because they only look at the outer surface of humans. From this vantage point, it looks like Paul is falling apart instead of being gloriously renewed. Caird explains this process well and why God designed it so:

> But it is a secret process, invisible both to the outsider and to the believer himself, known only to faith. To protect that faith from the encroachments of pride, which would turn spiritual renewal into a human achievement instead of accepting it as a gift of grace, God has provided that the process be concealed within an 'earthenware vessel,' a perishable body subject to pain and decay (4:7; cp. 12:7–9). Those whose eyes are not on the seen and transient, but on the unseen and eternal, can detect beneath the decay of the outer nature an inner life which is being daily renewed (4:16–18).[618]

The Christian's life is "hid with Christ in God" (Col 3:3). That some Corinthians do not recognize this fact troubles Paul, since only the eyes of faith can see that what God has done through the death and resurrection of Christ and what God promises to do for believers. Their blindness suggests that they have failed to understand the full significance of Christ's shameful death or to understand that the discernible presence of the Holy Spirit in their lives serves as a guarantee of this future glory. In the eternal realm,

---

[616] Harvey, *Renewal through Suffering,* 63.

[617] Savage, *Power through Weakness,* 183.

[618] G. B. Caird, *Paul's Letters from Prison,* New Clarendon Bible (Oxford: Clarendon, 1976) 202.

there is no suffering; in the temporal realm, suffering indicates more surely than anything else that one is a follower of Christ.

The next five sentences begin with the connecting particle "for" *(gar)* and explain further Paul's stance toward his afflictions:

4:17 For our light and momentary troubles are achieving for us an eternal glory that far outweighs them all.

4:18b For what is seen is temporary, but what is unseen is eternal.

5:1 Now [for] we know that if the earthly tent we live in is destroyed, we have a building from God, an eternal house in heaven, not built by human hands.

5:2 Meanwhile [for indeed] we groan, longing to be clothed with our heavenly dwelling,

5:4 For while we are in this tent, we groan and are burdened, because we do not wish to be unclothed but to be clothed with our heavenly dwelling, so that what is mortal may be swallowed up by life.

4:17   Paul characterizes the present, which is marked by tribulation, as brief in duration and trifling in comparison to what God has in store for believers. He uses the same terms to describe this glory *(hyperbolē,* "beyond all measure"; *baros,* "weight") that he used to describe his sufferings in Asia when he says that he was unbearably crushed (1:8; *hyperbolē,* "beyond all measure"; *ebarēthēmen,* "we were weighed down").[619] He now evaluates that affliction and all his afflictions differently. The incredible, eternal weight of glory beyond all comparison outweighs any earthly afflictions and makes them look like a tiny storm in a teacup (see also Rom 8:18; 2 Thess 1:5). Since the persecution affects only the outer nature that is wasting away, it is destined to pass and to be replaced by something far more glorious. On earth, our afflictions seem never ending while the more sublime moments seem to pass by in a flash. Looking at things from the vantage point of God's new aeon puts everything, including affliction, in its true perspective.

Furnish contrasts Seneca's praise for the man who treats his affliction as of small account because of his ability to reason things out with Paul's argument. Paul regards his suffering in this way because of his faith and hope in God who will deliver him.[620] He does not commend his personal discipline

---

[619] Lit. the phrase καθ᾽ ὑπερβολὴν εἰς ὑπερβολὴν would read "according to surpassing unto surpassing." Furnish suggests it means "to the nth degree" *(II Corinthians,* 262) and translates it "absolutely incomparable." For other uses of the noun see 1:8; 4:7; 12:7; and the adverb 11:23.

[620] Furnish, *II Corinthians,* 290 (citing Seneca, *Moral Epistles* 41.4–5). Paul's view accords with an eschatological perspective that present suffering is tied to divine necessity that will ultimately lead to the redemption and vindication of the faithful. See, e.g., *2 Apoc. Bar.* 48:49: "For assuredly as in a little time in this transitory world in which ye live, ye have endured much labour, / So in that world to which there is no end, ye shall receive great light" (see also 15:7–7; 21:22–23; 51:14).

or equanimity in the face of adversity that would overwhelm the normal person. He acclaims the God whose Spirit works in him and through his sufferings to bring about his inner transformation. Implicit in this statement is Paul's belief that God is working through this trouble, not in spite of it, to bring about the eternal abundance of glory in us.[621]

4:18 The NIV correctly renders the genitive absolute, "not fixing our eyes," as a conclusion from what precedes. Paul focuses his attention on what is really real and ultimately significant (see Phil 3:14). The statement implies that those Corinthians who disparage Paul's suffering have fixed their eyes on all the wrong things because they can see nothing of God's glory in Paul's ministry as a suffering apostle. Rather than openly berating them for their spiritual myopia, he tries to unfold the paradox for them. Their culture had conditioned them to see and appreciate only a counterfeit glory and honor. Those with honor in this culture were the elite who ruthlessly beat down all others around them to preserve their pride of place. If the Corinthians allow themselves to continue to be seduced by such a twisted value system, they will miss the authentic glory and honor that reside less conspicuously in the hearts of those who have been beaten down by a malevolent world but who will be raised up by God. Suffering is so visible and inner transformation so invisible, except to the eyes of faith.[622]

Spiritual transformation cannot be documented in a laboratory with empirical experiments any more than the truth of the resurrection can be proven scientifically. To believe that God raised Christ from the dead after such a shameful death requires extraordinary faith. To believe that God will do the same for Christ's followers who are conformed to Christ's death requires just as much faith, since all the outward evidence suggests otherwise. Paul's supreme confidence in God's promise and God's power rips away the veil of suffering and tears that otherwise would blind him to the glorious heavenly existence that comes after death (see Phil 3:19). The contrast between the seen and unseen, the temporary and the eternal, is carried over to 5:1 where what is visible and temporary is the earthly tent-house; what is not seen and is eternal is the heavenly building from God.

---

[621] The passive voice, κατεργάζεται ἡμῖν ("are achieving for us, NIV"), points to God as the agent (see Phil 2:12–13). The thought would parallel Rom 8:28, "We know that all things work together for good for those who love God, who are called according to his purpose" (NRSV). The "all things" refer to the sufferings of those who love God (Rom 8:18,35–39; and 5:3–4). The "good" refers to their ultimate salvation, not simply good things happening in their lives. Paul affirms in Romans that nothing can really harm those who give their lives to God, but even grievous things serve to help them on their way to salvation, confirming their faith and drawing them closer to God.

[622] Cp. 1 Sam 16:7: "But the LORD said to Samuel, 'Do not consider his appearance or his height, for I have rejected him. The LORD does not look at the things man looks at. Man looks at the outward appearance, but the LORD looks at the heart.'"

The unfortunate chapter division at 5:1 has misled many to isolate Paul's discussion of the resurrection in 5:1–10 from its context which begins in 4:16. This artificial partition prevents readers from seeing how these verses function in Paul's total argument. In these verses, Paul is not engaged in an isolated polemical excursus against a gnostic view that believed that the human spirit shed the earthly body and ascended "naked" heavenward to join the divine fullness, as some have argued.[623] Nor is he pursuing the theme of our future heavenly existence for its own sake. Instead, he cites his confidence in the Christian's certain resurrection as a justification for his present conduct.[624] The "for" in 5:1 connects what follows to what precedes so that 5:1–10 is not an isolated unit but a continuation of Paul's defense of his apostolic boldness (2:14–7:4). It is therefore to be interpreted in the context of Paul's discussion of his apostolic suffering as one who is hard pressed, hunted down, and struck down.[625] Now he turns to his ultimate consolation—the resurrection that puts his suffering in the proper perspective.[626]

Before examining these verses we should note the parallels with his earlier exchange about the bodily resurrection in 1 Cor 15:42–58. Both passages use clothing imagery: "For the perishable must clothe itself with the imperishable, and the mortal with immortality. When the perishable has been clothed with the imperishable, and the mortal with immortality" (1 Cor 15:53–54a; see 2 Cor 5:2–4). The term "perishable" *(phthora)* in 1 Cor 15:50,53 implies the body's destruction (2 Cor 5:1). Both passages cite or allude to the same Scripture, "he will swallow up death forever" (Isa 25:8):

1 Cor 15:54b	"Then the saying that is written will come true: 'Death has been swallowed up in victory.'"
2 Cor 5:4c	"So that what is mortal may be swallowed up by life."

Both passages acclaim God for preparing us for this victory announced in Scripture (2 Cor 5:5) or for accomplishing that victory (1 Cor 15:57).

---

[623] So Bultmann, *The Second Letter to the Corinthians,* 135–37.

[624] F. Lang, *2 Korinther 5,1–10 in der neueren Forschung* (Tübingen: Mohr [Siebeck], 1973) 194. Lang's study examines the views of 108 different scholars on this passage.

[625] J. Gillman, "A Thematic Comparison: 1 Cor 15:50–57 and 2 Cor. 5:1–5," *JBL* 107 (1988) 445. Furnish comments that the function of 5:1 "is not to introduce a new topic but to help undergird the renewed statement of apostolic confidence in 4:16a" (*II Corinthians,* 291). Thrall also argues that in this section "Paul elaborates on the theme of 4:16–18"—the "contrast between earthly existence with its decay and anxieties and the invisible and eternal sphere" (*Second Epistle to the Corinthians,* 1:357).

[626] A. C. Perriman correctly recognizes that "these verses are neither dogmatic nor polemical but intensely personal, emerging from the deeply felt contradiction between the experience of bodily affliction and the future hope" ("Paul and the Parousia: 1 Corinthians 15:50–7 and 2 Corinthians 5:1–5," *NTS* 35 [1989] 519).

But the two discussions of the resurrection also differ from one another. First, in 1 Cor 15:1 Paul begins by saying that "I want you to know that" and in 15:50 "I say that." He is making a case *about* the resurrection of the dead—how the dead are raised. In 2 Cor 5:1 he begins by saying "we know that" and is arguing from the resurrection—how the resurrection makes our troubles seem slight and short-lived. The torrent of suffering that seems to engulf his ministry in shame will be nullified by the resurrection. He argues from what he believes to be a shared belief about the resurrection hope.

Second, the antithetic imagery in 1 Corinthians 15 is "flesh and blood" versus "the kingdom of God" and "what is perishable" versus "what is imperishable." In 2 Corinthians 5 he contrasts the "earthly tent-house" with "a building from God not made with hands, in the heavens." The emphasis in 1 Corinthians 15 is on the incompatibility of the two opposites; in 2 Corinthians 5 it is on replacement after destruction.

Third, in 1 Corinthians 15 Paul uses end time language referring to the Parousia of Christ (1 Cor 15:52). That language is absent from 2 Corinthians 5, nor is there any reference to the mystery of transformation (see 1 Cor 15:51). Although the passages deal with a similar topic, resurrection, the issues being addressed are different.

Paul's statements in 5:1–10 must be read in the context of his continuing defense of his ministry and frank speech. Paul is less concerned about describing the hows and wherefores of our future heavenly existence than in describing how his confidence in this future existence affects his current existence.[627] His purpose is not to answer speculative questions about the life to come and when we receive the spiritual body but to show how the assurance of the life to come changes everything for the Christian in the present. It gives meaning to his suffering in this mortal life and galvanizes his conduct and ministry. The declaration at the end of this unit (5:9–10) that he aims to please God because we all will be judged before Christ's tribunal according to what we have done in the body reveals what keeps him doing what he is doing.

If Paul is arguing against anyone it would be those who have misread how life in the Spirit affects human experience in this world. Paul's commentary on the life to come clarifies that "following Jesus on this side of the divide

---

[627] Lang, *2 Korinther 5,1–10*, 194. Lang believes that Paul devalues his competitors' glorification of the earthly house by calling it a tent and by removing it from earth to heaven, and he postpones occupation of the heavenly house to the future. C. J. Roetzel concurs: "In response to critics who claimed to be so alive with the glory of the risen Lord that they had overcome the gulf imposed between life in the divine and human worlds, Paul reaffirms the reality of that present separation" ("As Dying, and Behold We Live," *Int* 46 [1992] 15). We would not want to import the hypothetical view of Paul's competitors into this text. Paul does not specifically mention opponents here and is not trying to correct any particular error about the resurrection. If some in Corinth held such views, which is not unlikely, Paul's statements only indirectly challenge them.

provides no immediate escape from death's burden in all of its multiform expressions—human frailty, physical handicaps, declining strength in age, or lack of prowess or success—and living death in this world as an epiphany of the resurrected one is no way synonymous with absolute alienation."[628]

Against those in Corinth who may claim that they have already bridged the gap between the human and the divine—something Paul's frailty and suffering betray that he has not done—he argues that the gap still remains. The harsh realities of life still press against us. Against those who may offer assurances that we can be above it all in the here and now, Paul offers only the promise of a future resurrection. Meanwhile, one must suffer with Christ. Against those who saw themselves as having risen above human limits, Paul argues that those limits still exist until we receive an eternal building from God. Against those who judged him already and gave him failing grades as an apostle because of his shameful condition, Paul argues that the ultimate judgment is yet to come and all will have to stand before the judgment seat. He is fully confident of his vindication, but he does not take that acquittal for granted and serves the Lord as if everything were in doubt. Against those who may claim to possess God's glory here and now, Paul claims that any allotment of glory in this life pales beside the glory which is to come in the future. Against those who think that they can have glory apart from the cross, Paul argues that glory comes only to those who faithfully bear the cross (Phil 3:10).

Therefore this section continues his case that his affliction does not discredit the gospel or its proclaimer but is a means of renewing the inner man. Not only is the inner man renewed, but the all-surpassing power of God will clothe him with an eternal, heavenly dwelling when his frail, mortal body of clay finally succumbs.

Paul began this letter by telling the Corinthians about his deliverance from the brink of death by God's grace. Harvey asks, "But suppose it resulted in death: would that invalidate the argument?"[629] Obviously, the answer is no. Many times God delivers the faithful; but many times they are not delivered. Surviving near death experiences and earthly afflictions is not the only way Christians experience divine vindication. They will experience it also in death. We, that is, all Christians, know that when we die we have a building from God, not made with hands, eternal in the heavens" (5:1). Paul therefore expresses supreme confidence that the present mortification of his outer person will culminate in glorious transformation and a heavenly body which earthly words and images strain to describe but can never fully capture.

5:1 The formula, "now we know" *(oidamen gar),* appears elsewhere in Paul's letters (Rom 7:14; 8:22).[630] It suggests that the Corinthians know and

---

[628] Roetzel, "As Dying, and Behold We Live," 16–17.

[629] Harvey, *Renewal through Suffering,* 66.

[630] A variation, "knowing that" (εἰδότες ὅτι), occurs in 4:14 and 5:6; see also "for you know" (γινώσκετε γάρ) in 8:9 and "you know that" (γινώσκετε ὅτι) in 13:6.

believe this and that he is rehearsing a doctrine that he had already taught them.[631] It is highly unlikely that Paul is unveiling for them some new development in his thought. His faith in the resurrection is expressed in 1:9 and 4:14. He assumes that their faith informs them that when our earthly tent-house is destroyed we will have a building from God.

It is easy to get lost in Paul's shifting metaphors that describe death and resurrection: tearing down a tent, a house not made with hands, taking off and putting on clothing, nakedness, and being away from home and being at home.[632] He begins by referring to "our earthly tentlike house."[633] The "earthly" contrasts with the "heavenly" (1 Cor 15:40; Phil 2:10; 3:19) and refers to something that belongs to this temporal world. Here "earthly tent" refers to the physical body and connotes something sufficient for its purpose, yet transitory and subject to wear and tear.[634] The earthly tent is syn-

---

[631] Windisch, *Der zweite Korintherbrief,* 158; and Barnett, *The Second Epistle to the Corinthians,* 259. Some commentators believe that it conveys that they may know it (Furnish, *II Corinthians,* 446) or that they ought to know it. Paul appeals to a basic article of belief that most, if not all, Christians accept. But if the Corinthians do not accept this belief, then it undermines his point. It is best therefore to assume that Paul argues from an accepted article of faith.

[632] The images Paul uses suggest (1) replacement: one kind of house is exchanged for another (5:1); (2) addition: clothing is put on; and (3) elimination: the mortal is swallowed up. Replacement and elimination imply some kind of discontinuity; addition implies some kind of continuity (Gillman, "A Thematic Comparison," 453).

[633] Lit. "our earthly house of the tent (or tabernacle)" (ἡ ἐπίγειος ἡμῶν οἰκία τοῦ σκήνους) = "our earthly tentlike house."

[634] W. Michaelis cites a saying attributed to Democrates: "The world is a tent, life a passage; you come, you see, you depart" ("σκηνή," *TDNT* 7:369). The most apt parallel is found in *Wis* 9:13–18:

For who can learn the counsel of God?
   Or who can discern what the Lord wills?
For the reasoning of mortals is worthless,
   and our designs are likely to fail;
for *a perishable body* weighs down the soul,
   and *this earthy tent* burdens the thoughtful mind.
We can hardly guess at what is on earth,
   and what is at hand we find with labor;
   but who has traced out what is in the heavens?
Who has learned your counsel,
   unless you have given wisdom
   and sent your holy spirit from on high?
And thus the paths of those on earth were set right,
   and people were taught what pleases you,
   and were saved by wisdom.

Other suggestions that it refers more generally to earthly existence (see Isa 38:12; Job 4:19) or is an allusion to the tabernacle (see 1 Chr 9:23, LXX, and T. W. Manson, "Hilasterion," *JTS* 46 [1945] 1–10) are less probable. Thrall entertains the possibility that "just as the tabernacle was the temporary abode of God during the desert wanderings of the Israelites, so man in his earthly life is only a temporary, transient temple. Or the point may be that the believer's earthly existence is a life of pilgrimage and separation from the Lord." But she rejects this option except as playing a minor part in Paul's argument (*Second Epistle to the Corinthians,* 1:361).

onymous with our body (4:10), our mortal flesh (4:11), and "our outer person" (4:16), as well as the earthen pot (4:17). Tent life is a ready metaphor for humankind's brief sojourn in this world, and it depicts "the instability, and thus the vulnerability, of one's mortal existence."[635]

The verb translated "is destroyed" also means "to tear down," and is particularly appropriate for the image of striking a tent.[636] The reference is to physical death. The aorist passive verb highlights death's finality compared with continuously carrying around the dying of Jesus while Paul is alive and serving the Lord (4:10–11).[637] The human mortality rate remains steady at 100 percent, and Paul squarely addresses this reality.[638] Death remains our most feared enemy, and the fear of death could present the most stultifying threat to the boldness Paul exercises in his ministry. He explains why he is not tempted to recoil in the face of daily danger.

The subject of death, however, has universal relevance; and Paul frequently speaks of it. Minear observes, "Touch the epistles at any point, examine the dynamics of his mission, overhear the line of argument in any debate, and you encounter a reference to some form of dying."[639] But whenever Paul talked of death he also spoke of life. We should not interpret this passage as showing that Paul had recently come to terms with his own mortality after his recent scrape with death in Asia. Paul must have done that long ago. It does reveal that he did not embrace death as good, though he might regard it as preferable. Death was something related to sin (Rom 6:23; 7:9,11) which destroys life, and death ensnares all in its web since all have sinned (Rom 5:12). Death therefore reigns invisibly as

---

[635] Furnish, *II Corinthians*, 293.

[636] Many point out the interesting parallels between 2 Cor 5:1 and Jesus' saying in Mark 14:58, "I will destroy" (καταλύσω) = "is destroyed" (καταλύθη); "I will build" (οἰκοδομήσω) = "building" (οἰκοδομή); and "made without hands" (ἀχειροποίητον). But how they may relate is difficult to unravel.

[637] A. Lincoln claims that the verb is only applicable "to the death of a believer before the Parousia and not to what happens to those who survive and are alive at Christ's return" (*Paradise Now and Not Yet: Studies in the Role of the Heavenly Dimension in Paul's Thought with Special Reference to His Theology*, SNTSMS 43 [Cambridge: University Press, 1981] 62). Those who are still alive at Christ's return will not be "destroyed."

[638] Gillman contends that "the destruction ... of the tentlike house designates primarily the physical death of believers, but also encompasses the termination of the earthly life of those who are still living at the Parousia" ("A Thematic Comparison," 446). M. J. Harris insists that ἐάν does not bear its normal conditional sense here because the statement "if I die" would need to be qualified with "before the Parousia" ("2 Corinthians 5:1–10: Watershed in Paul's Eschatology?" *TynBul* 22 [1971] 34–35). But this interpretation begs the question and projects the idea of the Parousia onto the text when it is not specifically mentioned. Every other use of ἐάν in 2 Corinthians bears its regular conditional sense (3:16; 8:12; 9:4; 10:8; 12:6; 13:2).

[639] P. S. Minear, "Some Pauline Thoughts on Dying: A Study of 2 Corinthians," in *From Faith to Faith*, ed. D. Y. Hadidian (Pittsburgh: Pickwick, 1979) 91.

a power, a last enemy. The only death that is good is dying with Christ, dying to oneself (Rom 6:6), dying to sin (Rom 6:2,10), dying to the law and its tyranny (Gal 2:19–20), dying to the world (Gal 6:14), and dying to the elemental spirits of the world (Col 2:20). Paul did not ultimately fear physical death because he knew that its power had been exhausted in Christ's death and resurrection.

But what happens when we die? Paul does not give us a "blueprint of the next life but only hints about its nature."[640] Gillman is correct in his analysis of Paul's statements in 1 Corinthians 15 and 2 Corinthians 5: "It would be going too far ... to press, as many do, both passages for systematic answers to such questions as *when* the resurrection body is received (death or Parousia?), *what* the nature of the intermediates state is, or *how* the transformation of the earthly body takes place."[641] Paul did not write this passage to answer questions we might have about the when, what, or how; he only intends to affirm his confidence in the Christian's transformation in the life after death.

The phrase "a building from God ... an eternal house in heaven, not built by human hands" has quickened the imaginations of interpreters. Thrall lists no less than nine proposals for the meaning of "building."[642] But the context indicates that Paul has in mind the individual resurrection body. If an earthly tent-house refers to the earthly body, then the building from God would most likely refer to its opposite, the spiritual body.[643] The parallel with 1 Corinthians 15 also lends support to the view that Paul has in mind the

---

[640] Best, *2 Corinthians,* 46.

[641] Gillman, "A Thematic Comparison," 441.

[642] Thrall, *Second Epistle to the Corinthians,* 1:363–68. In addition to our interpretation that it refers to the resurrection body, some contend that (1) the "building" echoes Jesus' words to his disciples, "In my Father's house are many rooms; ... I am going there to prepare a place for you" (John 14:2). It refers to this heavenly habitation that is already a reality (Hodge, *An Exposition of the Second Epistle to the Corinthians,* 485–88). The problem with this view is that "house" (οἰκία) would then have two different senses in one verse (earthly house = body; and house made without hands = abode). (2) Others have argued that the "building" has an ecclesiological dimension rather than anthropological (see Rom 14:19; 15:12; 1 Cor 14:3,5,12,26; 2 Cor 10:8; 12:19; 13:10) and refers to the body of Christ, the church (J. A. T. Robinson, *The Body,* SBT 1 [A. R. Allenson, 1952] 76; E. E. Ellis, "II Corinthians v.1–10 in Pauline Eschatology," *NTS* 6 [1960] 217–18). The problem is that the contexts where the image of a building for the church appears are totally different from 2 Cor 5:1–10, and we cannot restrict Paul's use of an image to only one meaning. (3) Another view interprets the building to be the heavenly temple. In Israel's history a tent becoming a building might refer to the tabernacle and temple. The temple that Christians look forward to is one not made with hands or subject to the ravages of assaulting armies and refers to his dwelling in the temple of the Lord's Presence (Mark 14:58; 1 Cor 3:16; Eph 3:10; Heb 9:11; so K. Hanhart, *The Intermediate State* [Groningen: V. R. B. Kleine, 1966] 160–61). Others interpret it to represent (4) the interim heavenly body; (5) the inner man; (6) the resurrection body of Christ; (7) a metaphor for the glory of the eschatological age (the new Jerusalem); or the heavenly dimension of present existence (Furnish, *II Corinthians,* 294–95).

[643] Harris, "2 Corinthians 5:1–10," 39.

spiritual, resurrection body in 2 Cor 5:1. He refers to the resurrection body as a body from God (1 Cor 15:38), spiritual (1 Cor 15:44,46), imperishable (15:42,52–54), and heavenly (15:40,48–49).

The assertion "we have" *(echomen)* brings up the question, When do we have it and what do we have? Do we receive an interim building at death and must await the coming of Christ and the general resurrection before we receive the resurrection body? Or do we receive it at death? Those who argue that Paul believes that we have this resurrection body at the Parousia maintain that Paul's use of the present tense ("we have") expresses his conviction that this future possession is so certain that it can be regarded as already a reality.[644]

But it is more probable that Paul understands the Christian to receive the resurrection body immediately at death. It would be small consolation to know that this heavenly dwelling is only another partial fulfillment of what is to come and that one must wait in limbo until the consummation.[645] Interpreters who take this text to refer to some form of intermediate state argue that Paul finds this state of limbo undesirable and consequently prefers to remain alive until the Parousia of Christ so that he will avoid it. Barrett writes that Paul dreads death "because it would be a much happier thing to survive till the *parusia,* that is, not to die, be buried, pass some time *naked,* and then be raised up, but to be transformed immediately (I Cor. xv.51) by the substitution of a spiritual body for the natural body (I Cor. xv. 44), to put on the new dwelling over the old."[646] Such an interpretation seems to contradict Paul's statements in Phil 1:23–24. With the prospect of death looming over him, he confesses that his personal preference is for death (something far better) because he will be with Christ. We can surmise that it is also better because it will bring an end to his earthly "conflict" (Phil 1:29), "sorrow upon sorrow" (Phil 2:27), and "affliction" (Phil 4:14). But he concludes that his personal desires will be overruled in God's providence by the necessity that

---

[644] So Windisch, *Der zweite Korintherbrief,* 160; Barrett, *The Second Epistle to the Corinthians,* 134; H. Hanse, "ἔχω," *TDNT* 2:825; Martin, *2 Corinthians,* 104; and A. T. Robertson, who comments, "The condition is future in conception, but the conclusion is a present reality, so confident is Paul of the bliss of heaven" (*A Grammar of the Greek New Testament in the Light of Historical Research* [Nashville: Broadman, 1934] 1019). Furnish observes that the sentence is conditional, and other Pauline examples of "*ean* with the aorist subjunctive and the present indicative makes what follows dependent on the fulfillment of the condition, and in these cases the present tense seems to be the sign of an axiomatic formulation (Rom 7:2–3; 1 Cor 7:39; 8:8; 14:23; 15:36)" (*II Corinthians,* 265).

[645] To argue that he longs for this spiritual body to be given to him while he is still alive on earth so that he might avoid this imperfect condition is to make Paul say something different from what he actually says.

[646] Barrett, *The Second Epistle to the Corinthians,* 156.

he return to the Philippians to strengthen their faith (Phil 1:24–26). This conclusion derives from his prior conviction that God always acts for the best interest of His people as a whole. As a slave of Christ (Phil 1:1), he serves as his Master wills, not as he wills. Therefore he believed that God will deliver him from his imprisonment because of his pastoral responsibilities. The attitude reflected in Philippians is not that of one who wants to continue living to escape the limbo into which death would plunge him.

The present tense of "we have" means that there is no homeless interlude between the destruction of the earthly tent house and receiving the building from God. Harris argues against the view that the heavenly body will be received at the Parousia of Christ: "The moment when the consolation is needed must be the moment when the consolation is given; and the consolation received at death cannot simply be identical with that assurance of the future acquisition of the resurrection body which is already possessed during life."[647] The "we have" points "to an immediate succession between two forms of embodiment without implying a long-standing or even momentary coexistence of two bodies."[648] Harris paraphrases this verse, "'As soon as our earthly tent-dwelling is taken down, we are the recipients of a building from God.'"[649] Christians therefore will never be "homeless."

The description of the building as something "not made with hands, eternal in the heavens" and not the word "building" is the key for interpreting its meaning. "Not made with hands" contrasts something that is temporary, impure, and incomplete (made with hands) with something enduring, incorruptible, and finished—something made by God.[650] Its description as "eternal in the heavens" hardly describes an interim dwelling, which implies some lesser form of existence. These adjectives express Paul's confidence that at death believers receive a permanent (eternal), spiritual (not made with hands), heavenly form of existence.[651] Quite simply, Paul says here that

---

[647] Harris, "2 Corinthians 5:1–10," 41. J. Osei-Bonsu counters that Paul seeks to console those worried about who have died before the Parousia with exactly the same idea in 1 Thess 4:13–18 ("Does 2 Cor 5.1–10 Teach the Reception of the Resurrection Body at the Moment of Death?" *JSNT* [1986] 87).

[648] Harris, "2 Corinthians 5:1–10," 43.

[649] Ibid.

[650] In Scripture something "made with hands" is connected to idolatry and implies impurity (Lev 26:1,30; Isa 2:18; 10:11; 16:12; 19:1; Dan 5:4,23; 6:26; Acts 7:48; 17:24; Col 2:11).

[651] Thrall, *Second Epistle to the Corinthians,* 1:369–70.

when Christians die they have resurrection bodies.[652] If eternal life is already present and discernible in the lives of those who bear the Spirit (5:5), then it follows that they will have a heavenly body at death and do not need to sleep or wait for resurrection.[653] The thrust of his argument matches Paul's reasoning in Rom 8:11, "And if the Spirit of him who raised Jesus from the dead is living in you, he who raised Christ from the dead will also give life to your mortal bodies through his Spirit, who lives in you" (see 2 Cor 4:14).

This interpretation raises another question that has occupied Paul's interpreters; did Paul's view of the resurrection of the dead evolve since he wrote 1 Thess 4:13–18 and 1 Corinthians 15? The classical view assumes that Paul's recent brush with death caused him to reflect more on death and, specifically, more about his own death. They assume that his recent peril made him suddenly aware that his death before the return of Christ was more likely. He subsequently changed his view from a general resurrection that will occur at the Parousia as evidenced in 1 Thessalonians 4 and 1 Corinthians 15 to a belief in resurrection at death in 2 Corinthians 5.[654] C. H. Dodd's famous reconstruction of this supposed maturation in Paul's thinking contended that he also underwent a second conversion between his writing

---

[652] C. H. Talbert, *Reading Corinthians: A Literary and Theological Commentary on 1 and 2 Corinthians* (New York: Crossroad, 1987) 160. The question of "when" has perhaps too much engaged the attention of scholars who interpret this passage. Paul is not addressing this issue. Our difficulties with this issue are compounded by the enormous difficulty in trying to grasp what happens in conditions of time and space so different from our own (see W. Lillie, "An Approach to II Corinthians 5:1–10," *SJT* 30 [1977] 59–70). R. Cassidy notes that "Time is simply a human device, a way of relating events which we experience in our physical existence" ("Paul's Attitude to Death in II Corinthians 5:1–10," *EvQ* 43 [1971] 216–17). Confined by our perceptions of time and matter, we cannot comprehend God's time sequence. *4 Ezra* 5:41–42 tries to answer the question about what those who die before us will do and those who die after us. It explains that death is like a circle in which the beginning and end are identical. Every death is equidistant from eternity. It concludes, "For those who are last there is not slowness; for those who are first there is no haste." Bruce points out that earth bound time is meaningless to those who have died and for the believer who dies there would be no consciousness of any interval of time between death and resurrection (Paul: Apostle of the Heart Set Free, 312, n. 40). Whatever God's timetable for the resurrection, Paul believes that resurrection is the next thing the dead in Christ experience, not waiting.

[653] Hanse, "ἔχω," 825.

[654] B. F. Meyer traces the development of this view to O. Pfleiderer, *Paulinism: A Contribution to the History of Primitive Christian Theology*, 2 vols. (London: Williams & Norgate, 1877; German 1873) and E. Teichmann, Die paulinische Vorstellungen von Auferstehung und Gericht und ihre Beziehungen zur jüdischen Apokalyptik (Freiburg-Leipzig: Mohr, 1896). As they understood it, Paul developed "from supernatural Jewish fancies to a reasonable Hellenistic wisdom" ("Did Paul's View of the Resurrection of the Dead Undergo Development?" *TS* 47 [1986] 384). Most recently, G. Luedemann has revived this older view (*Paul the Apostle to the Gentiles: Studies in Christology* [Philadelphia: Fortress, 1987] 212).

1 and 2 Corinthians, "from harsh and fanatic dualism to maturity of experience."[655] This so-called conversion manifested itself particularly with his break from what Dodd regarded as his crude Jewish apocalypticism found particularly in 1 Thessalonians 4.[656]

Others contend that Paul did not change his view on the end time resurrection but changed his view of the intermediate state of those who have died before the resurrection. He shifted from a more Sheol like existence of Christians resting asleep in the grave until the Parousia to a more blessed and conscious state of union with Christ.[657]

A stronger case can be made that Paul's views on what happened to the believer at death did not change. Paul was not a beginning seminarian trying to hammer out what he believed and adjusting his beliefs with each new experience or each new idea that he came across. The agenda prompting Paul's discussion of the topic in 1 Thessalonians, 1 Corinthians, and 2 Corinthians are completely different. Such limited evidence does not allow us access to the state of Paul's mind.[658] Meyer challenges the emphasis on "development" as a solution to problems, citing H. A. A. Kennedy: "But in an age when the notion of development is regarded as the key to all problems, it is perhaps natural that scholars should use it in explaining certain phenomena which look like antinomies in the Pauline Epistles."[659] Meyer chides scholars for pretending to be objective in developing an imagined trajectory of Paul's development of his beliefs regarding the resurrection when at the basis of their theories lies "a common repugnance toward apocalypticism as intrinsically perverse and illusory."[660] We should also question whether Paul's recent experience in Asia would have so unnerved him that he lost confidence that he would survive until the Parousia and then began to rethink his view about those who died in Christ. The danger of death was hardly something new for Paul. In 11:25 he reports that once he was stoned (in Acts 14:19, it says he was stoned and left for dead) and that three times he was shipwrecked. In 1 Cor 15:30–32 he declares that he faces perils every hour and death every day. Are we to believe that only now after the misadventure in Asia

---

[655] C. H. Dodd, "The Mind of Paul: I," NTS (Manchester: University Press, 1953) 81.

[656] Ibid., 126.

[657] P. Hoffmann gives a summary of authors holding this view (*Die Toten in Christus: Eine Religionsgeschichtliche und exegetische Untersuchung zur paulinischen Eschatologie*, NTAbh n.s. 2 [Münster: Aschendorff, 1978] 4–20). So F. F. Bruce, *1 and 2 Corinthians*, 200–206; and *Paul: Apostle of the Free Spirit*, 309–13.

[658] Furnish, *II Corinthians*, 292.

[659] H. A. A. Kennedy, *St. Paul's Conception of the Last Things* (London: Hodder & Stoughton, 1904) 24; cited by Meyer, "Did Paul's View of the Resurrection of the Dead Undergo Development?" 368.

[660] Meyer, "Did Paul's View of the Resurrection of the Dead Undergo Development?" 384.

does he hear death's knell and begin to worry that he might not survive until the Lord's return? Only now does he contemplate the state of the dead between burial and resurrection? Berry asks appropriately, "Are we to suppose that he was the sort of man who would hold one view when the death of others was under consideration, only to adopt another, more congenial, view when his own death seemed imminent?"[661] If so, then Paul is guilty of adjusting his theology to suit his own personal dreams. According to Paul's brief account of his affliction in Asia in 1:8–11, it served to deepen his confidence in God rather than to shake it. Finally, we have already noted that the opening statement in this verse, "for we know," does not suggest "that Paul is making here a fresh departure in doctrine."[662]

We conclude from the parallels that in 2 Corinthians 5 Paul expands on his assertions in 1 Corinthians 15 rather than altering them.[663] The focus of the two passages, however, is quite different. In 1 Corinthians 15 Paul presses the necessity of a bodily transformation; in 2 Cor 4:16–5:10, he is working out the ultimate resolution of his apostolic suffering.[664]

Before moving on, we should say a word about what influence Paul's Jewish background may have had on his beliefs about the resurrection and immortality. We should not simply assume that they are an outgrowth of that background. Jewish views on the resurrection and immortality were remark-

---

[661] R. Berry, "Death and Life in Christ: The Meaning of 2 Corinthians 5:1–10," *SJT* 14 (1961) 61.

[662] Ibid., 62. If Paul were supplementing or changing his views expressed in 1 Cor 15:35–58, then it is strange that the key terms used in that passage, resurrection (15:42), transformation (15:52), and references to the Parousia (15:52), do not occur in 2 Cor 5:1–10 (see Furnish, *II Corinthians,* 292). But C. Brown provides evidence that Paul did not change his eschatological language and ideas by noting the parallels between 1 Thess 5:1–11 (an example of Paul's earliest writing) and Rom 13:11–13 (an example of Paul's later writing). In both passages Paul regards the end as imminent (1 Thess 5:2; Rom 13:11) and uses the same contrasts between night and day (1 Thess 5:4; Rom 13:11), sleeping and waking (1 Thess 5:6; Rom 13:11), and drunkenness and sobriety (1 Thess 5:7; Rom 13:13). The verb "put on" also occurs (1 Thess 5:8; Rom 13:12) ("Present," *NIDNTT* 2:925).

[663] J. Dupont contends that 2 Corinthians 5 is an explication of what Paul said in 1 Corinthians 15 (*SYN CHRISTŌ L'union avec le Christ suivant saint Paul* [Paris / Bruges: Abbaye de Saint-André, 1952] 139).

[664] Gillman, "A Thematic Comparison," 441. Gillman argues that the two passages can be viewed in terms of "two sides of a coin." At one moment Paul seems to be looking at one side of the coin (e.g., destruction of the earthly body at death in v. 1) and in the next moment at the reverse side of the coin (e.g., reception of the resurrection body, which in terms of 1 Thess 4:13–18; 1 Cor 15; and Phil 3:20–21 occurs at the Parousia) without concentrating on the interval in between. That aside, the main point to be argued is that bodily transformation, explicit in 1 Cor 15:50–57, is implicit in 2 Cor 5:1–5 (p. 442). He concludes that there is no shift in view but only in the use of "more literal, abstract, and anthropological terminology in 1 Cor 15:50–55 to a rather intricate development of metaphorical language in 2 Cor 5:1–4" (p. 454).

ably diverse.[665] Paul's pre-Christian conception of the afterlife may have been that the dead were dead or perhaps kept in some intermediate state until the power of God brought them back to life at the resurrection. His encounter with the resurrected Christ which so redirected his life, however, must also have determined his views on the resurrection. The power of God had already raised Christ as the first fruits of those who died (1 Cor 15:20). Bruce comments:

> What had been for Paul previously the resurrection *hope* was now, so far as Jesus was concerned, more than a hope; it was a *fait accompli*. Since God raised Jesus from the dead, he would assuredly raise those of them who passed through death before the Parousia of Jesus—his advent in glory when their resurrection would take place—whether they belonged to the patriarchs and prophets of the old age or to believers of the new age.[666]

Paul's understanding of Christ's resurrection and his conviction that God's power will also transform our humble bodies to be conformed to his glorious body (Phil 3:21) makes passages from Second Temple Judaism less useful as a backdrop for understanding 2 Cor 5:1–10.

This leads us to three conclusions that will guide the interpretation of the following verses. (1) The burning conviction that radiates from Paul's discussion of Jesus' death and resurrection is that those who are conformed to his death and suffer with him will assuredly be glorified with him (Rom 8:17). (2) Death will not shatter the Christian's intimate union with Christ in this life, even for a moment. On the contrary, death will perfect that union. (3) Paul's declaration that we have a building from God clearly implies that "Man is not immortal because he possesses or is a soul. He becomes immortal because God transforms him by raising him from the dead."[667]

5:2 Paul's next statement expresses his yearning for this heavenly house. The phrase *kai gar,* translated "meanwhile," is one of four clauses in this section that begins with "for" (*gar;* see 4:17; 5:1,4). The translation in the NIV, "meanwhile we groan," omits *en toutō* ("in this"), which refers to this earthly body (NRSV, "For in this tent we groan"). The sentence does not fully explain why we groan, but we can easily infer the reason. Our earthly condition is marked by suffering and affliction (see 1:8; 4:7–15; 6:4–10; 11:23–27), and we know that we have a heavenly dwelling with God. The

[665] G. W. E. Nickelsburg documents the wide range of views about the time, mode, and place of resurrection in Second Temple Judaism (*Resurrection, Immortality, and Eternal Life in Intertestamental Judaism, HTS* 26 [Cambridge: Harvard University Press, 1972]). H. C. C. Cavallin found eight references to the intermediate state: *4 Ezra* 7:78, 100; 4:35–42; *2 Apoc. Bar.* 30:1–5; 50:1–51:16; Josephus *J. W.* 2.8.14 §163; 3.8.5 §§374–75; *Ant.* 18.1.3 §14 (*Life after Death: Paul's Arguments for the Resurrection of the Dead in 1 Cor 15* [ConBNT 7/1: Lund: Gleerup, 1974]).
[666] F. F. Bruce, "Paul on Immortality," *SJT* 24 (1971) 461.
[667] M. J. Harris, "Resurrection and Immortality: Eight Theses," *Themelios* 1 (1976) 53.

translation "groan" for *stenazō* (see also 5:4) does not imply here despair, agony, or mournful dejection but is related to his hopeful longing. Paul does not groan from hopeless futility but from an earnest desire to receive the culmination of our salvation that awaits us. One has said that sighs are the natural language of the heart. For Paul, sighing is the natural language of one whose heart has turned toward God and hungers for God's final redemption.

Romans 8:17–27, which was penned when Paul was in Corinth, is an important parallel for understanding his meaning here. In both passages suffering is interpreted as preliminary to eternal glory (Rom 8:17–18; 2 Cor 4:17). Hope for something not seen also appears in both passages (Rom 8:24–25; 2 Cor 4:18; 5:7). Both contexts refer to the assurance provided by God's Spirit (Rom 8:23; 2 Cor 5:5). The verb *stenazō* appears in Rom 8:23, where Paul speaks of Christians who have the firstfruits of the Spirit groaning *(stenazomen)* "inwardly as we wait eagerly for our adoption as sons, the redemption of our bodies" (Rom 8:23).[668] In Rom 8:26 the Spirit intercedes with groanings too deep for words *(stenagmois alalētois)*. The parallel shows how the verb expresses "the tension between suffering and hope."[669] Barnett correctly states: "This is not the 'groaning' of doubt or fear, or even of mortality, but of hopeful 'longing,' as of a woman in prospect of childbirth (cf. Rom 8:23–25)."[670] "It is not that such groaning is a merely existential, creaturely anxiety or a sense of hopelessness. Quite to the contrary, it is eschatological and full of sure hope (so 4:16)."[671]

The sighing grows out of what Paul says in 4:18, "We fix our attention on what is unseen and eternal." Windisch cites Epictetus, who said, "The person who learns how to deal with outward circumstances 'will not groan' any longer under 'this paltry body' made of clay."[672] By contrast, Paul, a brittle earthen pot, copes bravely with his arduous outward circumstances, which would break him. Nevertheless, he groans because he knows that we have an immortal heavenly dwelling prepared for us, and he longs to possess it. Now, in this life, he feels the pain of separation from what he regards as his true home.

---

[668] The parallels are noted by Furnish, *II Corinthians,* 295–96.

[669] Thrall, *Second Epistle to the Corinthians,* 1:371.

[670] Barnett, *The Second Epistle to the Corinthians,* 261.

[671] Ibid., 264. Harvey contends that his groaning is not caused by any sense of vulnerability to his afflictions "but is part of our very existence as Christians" (*Renewal through Suffering,* 67). "For a Christian, the justification for 'groaning' was the consciousness that, though baptized, one had not yet fully 'put on' all that the new life in Christ demanded and made possible, and the constant yearning to put on, as it were, further layers of this covering " (p. 68). It is not that the human condition causes his groaning, but that being in this earthly body means that we "are not yet in the state of perfect redemption" (J. Schneider, "στενάζω ...," *TDNT* 7:601).

[672] Windisch, *Der zweite Korintherbrief,* 163; Furnish, *II Corinthians,* 296. They cite Epictetus, *Dissertations* I.1.9–12.

Therefore he yearns "to be clothed with our heavenly dwelling." The verb translated "to be clothed" *(ependysasthai)* means "to put on" or "put on over," "to be further clothed."[673] Some claim that this doubly compounded verb *(epi + en + dyomai)*, which only occurs here and in 5:4 in the New Testament, connotes something different from 1 Cor 15:53–54, where the verb *endyein* ("to put on") appears. They argue that in 1 Corinthians 15 Paul uses the verb *endyein* to refer to the resurrection from the dead when "the perishable must clothe itself with the imperishable, and the mortal with immortality" (1 Cor 15:53). By contrast, the verb *ependyomai* in 2 Cor 5:2,4 is said to apply to the experience of believers at the Parousia of Christ who are "overclothed." But such an interpretation places more weight on the preposition than it can bear.[674] Harris suggests that Paul uses the double compound verb to stress a continuity in the process of moving from the earthly tent dwelling to the heavenly building. One does not first have to slip off the earthly body before being garbed in the heavenly one. Paul therefore does not picture himself being denuded before being clothed.[675] The doubly compounded verb reinforces the effect of "we have" "by emphasizing that the moment of death is also the moment of investiture."[676] This interpretation helps explain Paul's emphasis in the next verse.

5:3 The Greek conditional particle *ei* plus the intensive particle *ge* and the conjunction *kai* that begin v. 3 may be translated, "If indeed then we have been clothed, [then] we will not be found naked."[677] The NRSV, however, opts for the textual variant "having put off" *(ekdysamenoi)* probably because "having put on" *(endysamenoi)* would seem to leave us with a seemingly banal tautology: "being clothed, we will not be found

---

[673] On clothing see Matt 17:2; Rev 3:4; 6:11; 7:9; Isa 7:22; 8:14,26; and 9:2,9,17,24–26. "The bright embroidered robe" "made ready in its home on high" in the *Hymn of the Pearl* 82 ff. shows that these kinds of ideas were common.

[674] J. H. Moulton argues that the simple compound verb ἐνδύω is no different in meaning from the doubly compounded verb ἐπενδύομαι (*A Grammar of the New Testament Greek, Vol. I, Prolegomena* [Edinburgh: T & T Clark, 1908] 115). Harris also points out that in 1 Cor 15:53–54 the verb "put on" does not refer exclusively to the resurrection of the dead but to what is experienced by all mortal human beings, whether dead or alive, when they are transformed ("2 Corinthians 5:1–10," 44). See also Bultmann, *The Second Letter to the Corinthians,* 134.

[675] As Harris says: "It was to be a case of addition without prior subtraction, a case not of investiture succeeding divestiture but of 'superinvestiture' without any disvestiture" ("2 Corinthians 5:1–10," 44).

[676] Ibid., 44–45.

[677] Robertson observes that "the feelings are sharply involved when γέ is present" (*A Grammar of the Greek New Testament,* 1147). No English equivalent for the word exists. Some important texts (p[46] B D F G 33 1175) read εἴπερ ("if indeed," "if after all," "since") that is behind the translation in the NIV, "because." It emphasizes all the more the soundness of the basic premise.

naked."[678] But "having put on" is not only the best attested reading, it is the hardest.[679] Why, if Paul had originally written "put off," would a later scribe change it to "put on"? The supposed tautology was probably intentional on Paul's part to emphasize that we will not be disembodied ghosts but will experience this complete salvation at death.[680] He might have thought that this point needed underscoring for those at Corinth who still harbored ideas that a disembodied state was preferable.[681] Paul does not believe in nor value an immaterial existence.[682]

What does Paul intend to connote by the image of nakedness? Some interpreters take it in an ethical sense to refer to our guilty moral state so that being clothed or being naked have to do with God's favorable or unfavorable judgment.[683] Although Paul was not nonchalant about the prospect of the judgment (see Phil 3:8–11), as one who was in Christ he had no fear of being found guilty before God. Standing before God's tri-

---

[678] The NRSV follows the 26th edition of the Nestle-Aland text, which accords unusual weight to only but a handful of manuscripts (D*c a fc Marcion Tertullian), which read ἐκδυσάμενοι ("having put off"). The basis for this choice is internal evidence. B. M. Metzger argues that "put off" is the better reading because of this banal tautology created by "having put on" and because it would be more in tune with Paul's vivid and paradoxical thought: "inasmuch as we, though unclothed, shall not be found naked" (*A Textual Commentary on the Greek New Testament* [London/ New York: UBS, 1971] 579–80). The other reading ἐκλυσάμενοι can be dismissed as a scribal misreading of ΕΚΛ for ΕΚΔ.

[679] Most MSS have the reading ἐνδυσάμενοι ("having put on," NIV, REB, NJB). See also M. E. Thrall, "'Putting on' or 'Stripping off' in 2 Corinthians 5:3," in *New Testament Textual Criticism: Its Significance for Exegesis: Essays in Honour of Bruce M. Metzger,* ed. E. J. Epp and G. D. Fee (Oxford: Clarendon, 1981) 221–37.

[680] Thrall, *Second Epistle to the Corinthians,* 1:377. Furnish's argument that "having been clothed" refers to baptism (see Gal 3:27, putting on Christ) and "to clothe over" refers to its final fulfillment is not convincing (*II Corinthians,* 298).

[681] Bultmann insists that Paul is countering those who long for this very thing—to be disembodied at death (*The Second Letter to the Corinthians,* 135; see also T. F. Glasson, "2 Corinthians v.1–10 versus Platonism," *SJT* 43 [1990] 145–55). But this issue should not be taken as the main concern of Paul's argument. He is not engaged here in a polemic against Gnostic views of the afterlife nor arguing about the details of the resurrection; rather he is arguing from the certainty of the resurrection.

[682] J. N. Sevenster, "Some Remarks on the *GYMNOS* in II Cor. V. 3," in *Studia Paulina in honorem Johannis de Zwaan septuagenarii,* ed. J. N. Sevenster and W. C. van Unnik (Haarlem: Bohn, 1953) 202–14.

[683] This view is shared by many church fathers; see K. Staab, *Pauluskommentare aus der griechischen Kirche* (Münster: Aschendorff, 1933) 27. See also Murphy-O'Connor, *Theology,* 52; W. Mundle, "Das Problem des Zwischenstandes in dem Abschnitt 2 Kor. 5, 1–10," in *Festgabe für A. Jülicher* (Tübingen: Mohr, 1927) 101; R. F. Hettlinger, "2 Corinthians 5:1–10," *SJT* 10 (1957) 190; and E. E. Ellis, "2 Corinthians 5:1–10," 219–21, who think nakedness should be interpreted in a Hebraic sense. As the nakedness of Adam and Eve in Gen 3 represented their guilt, so it does here (see also Ezek 16:37,39; 23:26,29). The contrast is between being in Adam and naked or being in Christ and clothed.

bunal is not in the purview of this verse, and "being naked" does not refer to spiritual alienation from Christ.[684] Paul is not referring to the plight of the godless who do not receive a glorious body because, unlike believers, they are not clothed with Christ or robed with his righteousness.[685] The immediate context suggests that being naked refers to a disembodied state, a soul stripped of its body.[686] "To be clothed," means the opposite, to have a bodily existence.[687] To be naked means to lack a bodily existence. In this verse Paul essentially repeats what he says in 5:1–2 to emphasize that the believer will never be found in a bodiless state.[688] Redemption was not redemption from the body, but redemption of the body (Rom 8:23). Nakedness, some incorporeal existence, is an absurd idea to him because of the resurrection of Christ; and his assertion that we will not be found naked links with his earlier insistence in 1 Cor 15:35–44 that "the future life is a bodily one."[689] If we prune away the metaphorical language in this verse, Paul simply says that the dead rise with a body. If this is correct, we should not read into his imagery an interim period or an interim state. Nor should we read into this verse any dread of some naked state. Instead, this assertion should be understood as expressing the solace that Paul's resurrection hope gives him: "we shall not be found naked."

5:4 Paul repeats his personal longing for transformation expressed in 5:2 and expands on it. "For while we are in this tent, we groan and are burdened" recalls the burden of afflictions that nearly crushed him in Asia

---

[684] *Against Collange,* 215–18, 225; Furnish, *II Corinthians,* 298; Harvey, *Renewal through Suffering,* 68. Their logic is that "being clothed" elsewhere in Paul means putting on Christ. Being naked must be its opposite. But the clothing metaphor need not have the same connotations everywhere it is used. Context must decide. He is not thinking of judgment here or of putting on Christ as a defense. Though Paul states that he is determined to remain faithful to Christ because of his fear of coming before the judgment seat of Christ (5:9–10), in this verse he is clearly referring to bodies, first with the image of tents and buildings and next with the image of clothing.

[685] Calvin, *The Second Epistle of Paul the Apostle to the Corinthians,* 67.

[686] Such an image would have been readily understood in a Hellenistic context (see Plato, *Cratylus* 403B; *Gorgias* 523E–524D). Philo describes the death of Moses in this way: "He began to pass over from mortal existence to life immortal and gradually became conscious of the disuniting of the elements of which he was composed. The body, the shell-like growth which encased him, was being stripped away and the soul laid bare (ἀπογυμνουμένης) and yearning for its natural removal hence" (*On the Virtues* 76). He also describes his death as ἀποικία, "settlement away from home" (*On the Virtues* 77). Some interpret 1 Cor 15:37–38 as referring to the soul stripped of its physical body at death to receive a new spiritual body.

[687] We find the image of the body as a garment which clothes humans and death and resurrection as putting off mortal clothing and putting on immortal in *4 Ezra* 2:45; *2 Enoch* 22:8; *2 Apoc. Bar.* 49:3; *Apoc. Abr.* 13:15; and *T. Abr.* 15:7.

[688] Thrall, *Second Epistle to the Corinthians,* 1:379.

[689] E. Schweizer, "σῶμα," *TDNT* 7:1060. This is not to say that Jews could not conceive of a bodiless existence in the afterlife, see *1 Enoch* 102–4.

(1:8) and the catalog of apostolic suffering in 4:8–12. In a world of sin and death, we are beset with frustration and adversity. Seneca complained of "this clogging burden of a body to which nature has fettered me" (*Moral Epistles* 24.18), and he believed that the burden would only be relieved when the body was obliterated. Paul thinks of a quite different burden and does not groan to be rid of this body. Instead, he groans to receive his heavenly body and to be with his Lord.

The statement "because we do not wish to be unclothed but clothed over" does not mean that he recoils at the prospect of being disembodied or consigned to some incomplete, interim state where he must wait for the Second Coming before receiving his resurrection body—his further clothing.[690] He affirms in 5:8 that being away from the body, that is, physical death, means that he will be present with the Lord. Why would he have any aversion to this state? It is more likely that he expresses a natural, human aversion to death itself. The metaphor of "putting off" simply refers to death, which fits well the aspect of the verb's aorist (past) tense. Paul understands death as a punishment for sin (Rom 6:23; 1 Cor 11:29–30). Death is therefore a fearful experience for humans, and Paul knows that death is the last enemy to be destroyed (1 Cor 15:26). Death is not a liberation from earthly toil and trouble; it is itself the problem. Resurrection is the answer.[691] Paul also knows that it is unlikely, as Christ's apostle, that he will die in his sleep. Just as one may fear an operation that promises to lead to new physical health, one may have a healthy fear of death though it promises to lead to a new, glorified life. Jesus' intense distress before the prospect of a terrible death was overcome by intense prayer (Mark 14:32–42; Heb 5:7).

Nevertheless, Paul wants to be "clothed" so that all that is mortal in him might be devoured by life. Again, this is not a reference to being alive at the Parousia and having a spiritual body somehow drawn over an earthly one so that it does not have to decompose in a grave. "Mortality" refers to the death of Jesus at the beginning of the listing of hardships in 4:11: "For we who are alive are always being given over to death for Jesus' sake, so that his life may be revealed in our mortal body" (see also Rom 6:12; 8:11; 1 Cor 15:53–54). Paul is saying that in this earthly body he suffers; and though he has no death wish, he earnestly wants to receive

---

[690] Not all Jews found such a disembodied state repugnant. *Jub.* 23:31 says, "And their bones will rest in the earth, and their spirits will increase joy."

[691] See O. Cullmann, "Immortality of the Soul or Resurrection of the Dead," in *Immortality and Resurrection,* ed. K. Stendahl (New York: Macmillan, 1965) 12–20.

the heavenly body—being over-clothed with a glorious body, and life.[692]

"Swallowed up by life" alludes to Isa 25:8, which is also cited in 1 Cor 15:54: "When the perishable has been clothed with the imperishable, and the mortal with immortality, then the saying that is written will come true: 'Death has been swallowed up in victory.'" Gillman notes three variations from the citation of Isa 25:8 in 1 Cor 15:54. First, Paul omits an introductory fulfillment formula and has a *hina* clause expressing result: "so that what is mortal may be swallowed up by life." Second, Paul substitutes "mortality," what directly permeates human life, in place of "death," which is personified as a cosmic power (1 Cor 15:26,54–55). Third, he replaces the phrase "in victory" with an agent, life.[693] Life, then, is personified as the agent that swallows up mortality. Paul has mentioned the "life of Jesus" in 4:10–11. Recalling this previous reference reminds us that this is not simply a discourse on the topic of the resurrection. The allusion reinforces what Paul says about the main issue in this section—his defense of his apostolic style. His suffering for Christ in this mortal life, carrying around the death of Jesus, will be rewarded. The life of Jesus manifested now in an apostle's unbecoming and tattered mortal flesh will be the power that transforms this same mortal flesh into a glorious body conformed to his image. The resurrection perfects our salvation, which can only be partial in this body in which we receive only a pledge, not the full reality. This body weighed down and wasting away will be transformed.

5:5 Paul now affirms that God, who accomplishes all that is promised in Scripture, made (*katergazetai,* "prepared," "equipped") us "for this pur-

---

[692] The verb "overclothed" reflects a "rejection of the alternative view of the soul's entry into heaven by shedding the body" (P. Perkins, *Resurrection: New Testament: Witness and Contemporary Reflection* [Garden City: Doubleday, 1984] 309). This perspective argues against the traditional interpretation of 2 Cor 5:1–10 that assumes that Paul is contemplating the possibility of his pre-Parousia death and that he envisaged and dreaded an interval of disembodied existence for the soul ("nakedness") between death and the Parousia, when he would receive the individual, heavenly body. This view is proposed by G. Vos, "Alleged Development in Paul's Teaching on the Resurrection," *PTR* 27 (1929) 206–21, and more recently by Osei-Bonsu, "Does 2 Cor 5.1–10 Teach the Reception of the Resurrection Body at the Moment of Death?" 81–101. In my opinion Paul does not find himself in a "Catch 22" position between the very best state of being at home in the Lord in a glorified body and the dreaded state of being at home with the Lord but away from the body (nakedness), as W. L. Craig contends ("Paul's Dilemma in 2 Cor 5:1–10: A 'Catch 22'?" *NTS* 24 [1988] 145–47). In Rom 8:11 Paul writes, "If the Spirit of him who raised Jesus from the dead is living in you, he who raised Christ from the dead will also give life to your mortal bodies through his Spirit, who lives in you." The mortal body will have a share in the resurrection, but it will be clothed over with a glorious bodily existence (Schweizer, "σῶμα," 1061).

[693] Gillman, "A Thematic Comparison," 450; also G. Dautzenburg, "'Glaube' oder 'Hoffnung' in 2 Kor 4,13–5,10," in *The Diakonia of the Spirit* (2 Co 4:7–7:4), ed. L. de Lorenzi, Monographic Series of "Benedictina": Biblical Ecumenical Section 10 (Rome: Benedictina, 1989) 91–92.

pose" (lit., "for this very thing").[694] This thing is the clothing event mentioned in 5:4—the complete transformation of what is perishable to what is imperishable. It also refers to 4:17, where the same verb *katergazetai* appears: "For this slight momentary affliction is preparing for us an eternal weight of glory beyond all comparison." The life given by God overwhelms mortality.[695] Some Corinthians fail to see this abiding invisible force working in Christians, forming them for heaven by conforming them to Christ. They see only the wasting away of Paul's outer nature and do not see that he is daily being transformed inwardly (4:7–15). The transient, surface reality of our lives that so many in this world prize and spend billions trying to preserve will eventually be destroyed. The only thing that matters then is what has been happening to a person internally. Those who are in Christ will have their decrepit, decaying outer frames replaced with an eternal glory beyond imagining.

God has poured the Spirit into the lives of believers as surety for this promise. Paul's remarks in 1 Corinthians reveal his vexation with some Corinthians for misconstruing their experience of the Spirit. They viewed the Spirit only as an inrush of heavenly power into their lives. Their boastful self-importance as "spiritual ones" vitiated the gospel's goal to set us all as equals before God. This passage does not clarify what the experience of the Spirit means. It appeals to the Spirit's undeniable presence in the lives of believers as the capstone of his argument about the inner person and the coming age. Christians are united by faith to Christ and have received the Spirit of Christ, which gives them a foretaste of the life to come.[696] The inward renewal produced by the Spirit culminates in the Christian's complete transformation at the end. But the Spirit received in this life is only a guarantee of this future transformation, not the actual transformation (2 Cor 1:22, 5:5; see also Eph 1:14; Rom 8:23, "first fruits of the Spirit").[697] In this life Christians must live with suffering and live by faith. Their treasure is in clay pots, or, to switch metaphors with Paul, in a makeshift, perishable tent.

---

[694] Some texts (D F G 81) have the present κατεργαζόμενος ("is preparing") rather than the aorist κατεργασάμενος ("has prepared). Perriman argues that the δέ that begins the statement "points to the paradox of God being the author of a very human and unrealizable desire," the premature longing for the new life to come ("Paul and the Parousia," 520).

[695] Romans 8:11 is similar, "If the Spirit of him who raised Jesus from the dead is living in you, he who raised Christ from the dead will also give life to your mortal bodies through his Spirit, who lives in you."

[696] See S. Cox, "The Earnest of the Spirit," *Exp* 24 (1884) 416–26; Kennedy, "St. Paul's Conception of the Spirit as Pledge," *Exp* 4 (1901) 274–80; C. L. Mitton, "Paul's Certainties 5: The Gift of the Spirit and Life beyond Death—2 Corinthians v. 1–5," *ExpTim* 69 (1957–58) 360–63; and K. von Erlemann, "Der Geist als ἀρραβών (2 Kor 5,5) im Kontext der paulinischen Eschatologie," *ZNW* 83 (1992) 202–23.

[697] Paul argues in 1 Corinthians that the true mark of the spiritual person is willingness to bear bodily suffering for Christ.

This mortal life is marked by being burdened down, groaning, and longing because our humanity cordons us off from full fellowship with the Lord. But in all this outward suffering, an unseen power and an unseen reality sustain Paul. Paul's whole life is suffused with confidence because of the assurance of the resurrection (1 Cor 15:12–34,49). This does not mean that he lives in an other-worldly haze, dreaming of heaven.[698] He finds great joy and comfort in this life, despite its sufferings, because of the Spirit. The Spirit's presence in the lives of believers betokens that some of the splendor of the world to come has already broken into this present evil age. The writer of Hebrews recognizes this truth when he speaks of those "who have tasted the heavenly gift, who have shared in the Holy Spirit, who have tasted the goodness of the word of God and the powers of the coming age" (Heb 6:4b–5).

How do Christians know that the promise of a heavenly existence is real? Paul's answer is that the experience of the transforming and uplifting power of the Holy Spirit now in their lives is the one piece of empirical evidence that shows that God promises are real. Paul had no need to convince the Corinthians of the Spirit's transforming power, and he appeals to it to make his case for the amazing transformation that awaits Christians at death. If they accept his point, they will no longer judge him or anyone else according to twisted worldly values and hopes. They will look beyond corporeal existence that hides this inner transformation to see how God is preparing them for something far greater.

5:6–8 Paul's whole life is suffused with confidence because of the hope of the resurrection (1 Cor 15:12–34,49). It steels him to face the hardships which come his way and to proclaim the gospel boldly. It also explains why he speaks freely to the Corinthians and does not cloak his thoughts behind insincere flattery or artful guile. He can abandon himself entirely to his mission because he knows that God will not abandon him in death, for he knows the Lord has determined a glorious destiny for him. He knows that Christ dwells in heaven, and the believer cannot be present with him in the same way "he hopes to be after death."[699] This does not imply that the believer is not "with Christ" now (see Gal 2:20) or is alienated from him in some way, only that the believer is not with Christ fully. Nor does it imply some alienation from Christ. The next statement, "we walk by faith, not by sight" (5:7), makes this clear. The term "faith" used here almost as a synonym for "hope" recalls 4:18, where Paul talks about fixing the eyes on what is unseen and eternal.[700] He expresses the longing of those who know themselves to be

---

[698] See further, Garland, *Colossians, Philemon*, 214–15.

[699] Thrall, *Second Epistle to the Corinthians*, 1:386.

[700] Rom 8:24–25 provides a parallel: "For in this hope we were saved. But hope that is seen is no hope at all. Who hopes for what he already has? But if we hope for what we do not yet have, we wait for it patiently."

exiled from their true home in this present evil age.[701] The separation is spatial and qualitative. He longs to move from incomplete fellowship to full fellowship, from indirect, partial, and enigmatic vision to seeing face to face, from unfulfilled hope to fulfillment.

Living by faith and not by sight means that as we walk with God we have no literal pillar of cloud or fire to guide us as Israel of old had.[702] Paul believes that our life in Christ is hidden (see Col 3:1–4), so he cannot prove it from outward appearances (see 4:18). And those who judge things only by outward appearances (physical weaknesses, suffering, near death experiences) cannot see the whole truth about him or any other Christian (see 1 John 3:2). Only faith can take measure of the unseen eternal realities of the next aeon, where all this present weakness and mortality will be transformed into something sublime.

Paul repeats his confidence yet is not ashamed to express his preference to be away from the body (a metaphor for death) and at home with the Lord (a metaphor for resurrection).[703] The picture he paints shows that as soon as we are away from the physical body we are present with the Lord in a new dimension that is qualitatively different from our experience of the Lord's presence in this body.[704] He does not have a death wish, however. In 1:10 he rejoices over God's past deliverance, and he fully expects God to deliver him again. Such an earnest hope reveals his orientation in life and insures that this hope will be fulfilled.

5:9–10 Paul now switches themes, moving from assurance to warning, as he discusses the implications of this confidence.[705] These verses contain an implicit forewarning: we must all appear before the judgment seat of God.[706] It is this divine judgment seat (bēma), not Pilate's (Matt 27:19; John 19:13), not Gallio's (Acts 18:12,16–17), not the court of public of opinion, that ultimately counts. No one, including Christians, can escape it.

---

[701] J. Murphy-O'Connor's contention that Paul quotes in 5:6b a slogan from his opponents, the *pneumatikoi*, is not persuasive ("'Being at home in the body we are in exile from the Lord' (2 Cor 5:6b)," *RevBib* 93 (1986) 214–21.

[702] Plummer, *The Second Epistle of Paul the Apostle to the Corinthians*, 49.

[703] The μᾶλλον may mean "we are content rather to depart" or "the more do we think it well."

[704] Harris argues that the image of dwelling in the company of the Lord "must be referring to some heightened form of inter-personal communion, particularly since the Christian's eternal destiny would scarcely be depicted as qualitatively inferior to his experience of fellowship with Christ upon earth while walking διὰ πίστεως." The verb "suggests a settled permanent mutual fellowship" ("2 Corinthians 5:1–10," 46–47).

[705] διο καί means "it follows also."

[706] The *bēma* from which public proclamations and judicial pronouncements were made was prominently located in the center of Corinth's lower agora (see E. Dinkler, "Das Bema zu Korinth," in *Signum Crucis* [Tübingen: Mohr (Siebeck) 118–23]. Paul's reminder that the Corinthians will stand before a far more imposing, divine judgment seat would have struck a chord.

We cannot melt into the crowd. We will be held accountable for our individual actions and commitments. The chances that anyone might fool the God who knows even our subconscious thoughts are nil. Paul's remarks drive home four points that are particularly important for the Corinthians.

1. Paul reminds them that "immortality" is not something humans innately possess; our future life rests entirely in the hands of God who graciously bestows it on Christians after they have been judged for what they have done in this mortal body.

2. What humans do in the body has moral significance and eternal consequences.[707] Everyone who is mindful of their mortality must therefore be mindful of their morality. Schweizer comments that the body, "far from being a burdensome envelope for the divine soul, is the very place where man is tested and in terms of which he will be questioned in the judgment."[708] Our moral responsibility before God means that Christians can never be indifferent to such things as sexual immorality (1 Cor 5:1–13), trying to gain advantage over others in the courts of the unrighteous (1 Cor 6:1–8), consorting with prostitutes (1 Cor 6:12–20), dining at the tables of idols / demons (1 Cor 10:14–22), or humiliating other brothers and sisters in Christ (1 Cor 11:7–22). Paul sums it up in his warning in 1 Cor 6:9–10:

> Do you not know that the wicked will not inherit the kingdom of God? Do not be deceived: Neither the sexually immoral nor idolaters nor adulterers nor male prostitutes nor homosexual offenders nor thieves nor the greedy nor drunkards nor slanderers nor swindlers will inherit the kingdom of God.

He expresses his worry in 2 Corinthians that some still "have not repented of the impurity, sexual sin and debauchery in which they have indulged" (12:21). Therefore it behooves them to test themselves (13:5) before they undergo the final testing by God when they are remanded before the judgment seat of Christ (see also 1 Cor 3:10–15; 4:5; Rom 2:4–6; 14:10–12).[709]

If we hope to be conformed to Christ's glorious body in the next life, we must be conformed to his character in this life. Barnett summarizes the point well:

> The teaching about the judgment seat before which all believers must come reminds us that we have been saved, not for a life of aimlessness or indifference, but to live as to the Lord (5:15). This doctrine of the universality of the

---

[707] Paul may have pointedly placed emphasis on what is done in "the body" because some in Corinth had denigrated the moral significance of the body (E. Synofzik, *Die Gerichts-und Vergeltungsaussagen bei Paulus. Eine traditionsgeschichtliche Untersuchung* (Göttingen: Vandenhoeck & Ruprecht, 1977) 75–76.

[708] Schweizer, "σῶμα," 1062.

[709] This theme of judgment occurs throughout the Bible; see Eccl 12:14; Matt 16:27; and Rev 20:11–15.

judgment of believers preserves the moral seriousness of God. ... The sure prospect of the judgment seat reminds the Corinthians—and all believers—that while they are righteous in Christ by faith alone, the faith that justifies is to be expressed by love and obedience (Gal 5:6; Rom 1:5), and by pleasing the Lord (v. 9).[710]

3. The reference to what we have done in the body refers back to 4:10, where the verb *phaneroō* also appears. "The suffering of the apostles 'in the body' is the means by which the power of God and the life of Jesus are manifested."[711]

4. We must hold assurance and warning in tension. On the one hand, we might be tempted to succumb to despair when we are lashed by one affliction after another. The promise of God's transcendent purpose to deliver us from death as Christ was raised from the dead and the earnest of the Spirit sustains us. On the other hand, we might be tempted to become "puffed up" and repose in false assurance. The certainty of God's judgment (see 1 Cor 3:1–17; 4:1–5; 5:1–5; 6:9–11; 9:24–27; 10:1–12; 11:27–34) should call forth our obedience.

Paul takes to heart his warnings to others and says that his ambition is to have Christ's approval whether in the body or out of the body. He does not state precisely how we are to please the Lord, but we can infer from the context that it comprises speaking boldly the gospel (3:12; 4:1,13; 5:20; 6:7,11), taking with good courage the suffering that ensues (4:7–12,16–17; 6:4–5,8–10), living by faith, fully confident of the resurrection (4:13–14,17–18; 5:7), avoiding the taint of idolatry (6:14–7:1), and bringing glory to God (4:15) by living out the message of Christ's reconciling death (5:19–21). Paul does not shrink from his manifold sufferings in the service of the gospel, nor does he have any craven fear of his various persecutors. He will not back down before influential members of the Corinthian congregation or inflated, superfine apostles because he fears only the judgment of God. The reference to the seat of judgment prepares for his sharp admonition in 6:14–7:1.

(6) Persuading Others to Be Reconciled (5:11–21)

[11]Since, then, we know what it is to fear the Lord, we try to persuade men. What we are is plain to God, and I hope it is also plain to your conscience. [12]We are not trying to commend ourselves to you again, but are giving you an opportunity to take pride in us, so that you can answer those who take pride in what is seen rather than in what is in the heart. [13]If we are out of our mind, it is for the

---

[710] Barnett, *The Second Epistle to the Corinthians,* 277. Thomas À Kempis: "You can be certain of this: when the Day of Judgment comes, we shall not be asked what we have read, but what we have done; not how well we have spoken, but how well we have lived."

[711] Perriman, "Paul and the Parousia," 516.

sake of God; if we are in our right mind, it is for you. [14]For Christ's love compels us, because we are convinced that one died for all, and therefore all died. [15]And he died for all, that those who live should no longer live for themselves but for him who died for them and was raised again.

[16]So from now on we regard no one from a worldly point of view. Though we once regarded Christ in this way, we do so no longer. [17]Therefore, if anyone is in Christ, he is a new creation; the old has gone, the new has come! [18]All this is from God, who reconciled us to himself through Christ and gave us the ministry of reconciliation: [19]that God was reconciling the world to himself in Christ, not counting men's sins against them. And he has committed to us the message of reconciliation. [20]We are therefore Christ's ambassadors, as though God were making his appeal through us. We implore you on Christ's behalf: Be reconciled to God. [21]God made him who had no sin to be sin for us, so that in him we might become the righteousness of God.

Lambrecht charts an A B A′ structure for Paul's arguments from 5:11–6:10:

A 5:11–13 Self–Defense
B 5:14–21 Emissary of Christ
A′ 6:1–10 Self–Defense[712]

SELF-DEFENSE: REITERATION OF THE LETTER'S THEME STATEMENT (5:11–13). While Paul may not have consciously structured the passage in this way, this outline does help us see more clearly the development of his thought. In 5:11–13 he reiterates the letter's theme stated in 1:12–14. Paul's tone is hopeful, almost pleading. He knows that he is accountable to God and stands in reverential awe of God's final judgment. It is said that whatever it is that one fears the most that is what one will serve the most. Paul is steeped in the Old Testament tradition that understands fear of the Lord as the beginning of wisdom (Prov 1:7), but he understands it be the basis of faithful service as well. Paul's supreme awe of God motivates him to act as he does and prevents him from vainly trying to rely on his own meager resources. He does not fear that God will condemn him since he longs to be with the Lord (5:8).[713] His life is an open book to God and to the Corinthians as well. He is confident before God because he knows that God judges the heart. He is vexed before the Corinthians because they judge by appearances. God knows him and upholds his ministry; the Corinthians should also know him and do better to uphold the ministry of their apostle.

In 5:14–21 Paul "situates his apostolic way of life within the whole of

---

[712] J. Lambrecht, "'Reconcile Yourselves ...' A Reading of 2 Corinthians 5,11–21," in *Studies on 2 Corinthians,* ed. R. Bieringer and J. Lambrecht, BETL 112 (Leuven: University Press, 1994) 364–65.

[713] Only those who disobey God should feel terror about standing before God's throne (Rom 2:1–11).

God's salvific plan and in connection with the Christ event."[714] In the first part of this unit, 5:14–17, the focus is Christocentric. He draws out the implications of Christ's death, which brings about a new creation and necessitates a dramatic change in the way Christians must now regard others. In the second part, 5:18–21, the focus is theocentric. He illustrates what God has done in Christ with the image of reconciliation. The argument falls into the another A B A pattern. The unit is introduced by the phrase in 5:18a, "All this is from God."

A God's Act of Reconciliation (5:18b–19b)
    who reconciled us to himself through Christ
    and gave us the ministry of reconciliation
    that God was reconciling the world to himself in Christ,
    not counting men's sins against them.
    B The Ministry of Reconciliation (5:19c–20)
        And he has committed to us the message of reconciliation.
        We are therefore Christ's ambassadors,
        as though God were making his appeal through us.
        We implore you on Christ's behalf:
        Be reconciled to God.
A God's Act of Reconciliation (5:21)
    God made him who had no sin
    to be sin for us,
    so that in him we might become the righteousness of God.

God's act of reconciliation in Christ did not end with Christ's death and resurrection. It continues in the ministry of apostles like Paul who have been given the task of proclaiming it to the world.

5:11 The fear of the Lord relates to Paul's conviction that everyone, apostles included, will stand before God and give account for what he or she has done (5:10). In 1 Cor 3:10–15 Paul pictures himself as an expert builder who laid a solid foundation for building up this church by preaching Christ crucified. He was careful in how he built because he knows that God's judgment will reveal whether he erected his building with gold, silver, and costly stones that will survive the fiery test or with wood, hay or straw that will be laid waste by the fire.[715] Fear refers to a religious consciousness, a reverential awe of God,

---

[714] Lambrecht, "Reconcile Yourselves," 366.

[715] *Sir* 1:30 refers to the fear of the Lord (cited by Furnish, *II Corinthians*, 322):
    Do not exalt yourself, or you may fall
      and bring dishonor upon yourself.
    The Lord will reveal your secrets
      and overthrow you before the whole congregation,
    because you did not come in the fear of the Lord,
      and your heart was full of deceit.
The context in *Sirach* ties this discussion of "fear of the Lord" to the divided mind and hypocrisy.

that directs the way one lives. Paul does not live in unhealthy dread of God's judgment because he knows the love of Christ who gave himself for him. But his extraordinary experience of God's love and forgiveness does not deaden his consciousness that God remains a holy and righteous God. The "fear of the Lord" reappears in 7:1 (see 7:11). Many live like the rich fool of Jesus' parable and forget to factor God into their business spread sheets. God calls them fools (Luke 12:20). The epithet recalls the words of the psalmist who says, "A fool says in his heart that there is no God" (Ps 14:1; see Ps 36:1 cited in Rom 3:18). Persons may never say anything like this out loud, but they live their lives as if there were no God, fooling themselves into believing that earthly realities such as money and power will somehow protect them from their tottering finitude as they plan how to make their futures more happy and secure. Others may try to anesthetize themselves from any perturbing fear of God. They contrive a sugary theology with an indulgent and permissive God who winks at all that we do or have become. By contrast, Paul works knowing that God will scrutinize all that he says and does. As Christ's ambassador (5:20), he must be particularly circumspect. In the ancient world "envoys were responsible for their mission and although this responsibility was not always well defined, envoys were sometimes tried and punished both in the Greek polis and in Rome when they failed in their mission or agreed to conditions unacceptable to the ratifying body."[716]

Fear of God determines Paul's apostolic existence as he strives to persuade others about the seriousness of their plight without God and the abundance of God's mercy in Christ. The NIV renders the verb *peithō* as having a conative force, "we try to persuade men," which implies an attempt that is not necessarily successful (see Acts 26:28). But Paul has been effective in persuading people, and the nuance of "trying" is inherent in the idea of "persuading."[717] What he wants to make clear is that he persuades others by God's means and according to God's standards, not with the trappings of a gilded rhetoric or with seductive trickery. Nor does he dictate to others what they are to believe by lording over their faith. He trusts in the merits of the gospel, paradoxical and scandalous as it is, to pass any honest scrutiny and allows his hearers to decide for themselves its truth.

Paul uses the verb *peithō* with a negative connotation of "pleasing" in a polemical context in Gal 1:10: "Am I now trying to win the approval of men, or of God? Or am I trying to please [*peithō*] men? If I were still trying to please [*peithō*] men, I would not be a servant of Christ." Some interpreters argue that Gal 1:10 is a parallel to 2 Cor 5:11 and that Paul must be responding to critics who have charged him with winning his converts by unscrupu-

---

[716] S. Perlman, "Interstate Relations," in *Civilization of the Ancient Mediterranean: Greece and Rome,* ed. M. Grand and R. Kitzinger (New York: Scribner's, 1988) 1:672.

[717] Lambrecht, "Reconcile Yourselves," 367–68.

lous means.[718] In this view the idea of persuading would be connected to "adulterating the gospel so that he might please his hearers."[719] But there is no compelling reason to assume that his use of the verb "to persuade" in 2 Corinthians connotes some kind of shady rhetorical style. It is more likely from the immediate context that Paul has in mind his evangelistic task (Rom 15:17–19).[720] The statement ties in to his previous assertion that by setting forth "the truth plainly we commend ourselves to every man's conscience in the sight of God" (4:2; see 4:13). To argue that he is responding to some criticism about his method of swaying others is unjustified mirror reading.[721] This entire section, 2:14–7:3, is more profitably read as a defense of his letter of tears that persuaded the Corinthians of their error and not as an answer to some criticism that he used "questionable methods of ministry when he was present with them."[722] Paul's assertion at the conclusion of this unit, that God makes his appeal through us and his call for them to be reconciled to God (5:20), puts this statement in 5:11 in its proper context. Persuading others is part of what God has called him to do as one charged with a message of reconciliation. It is not "persuasion of a special kind," minus the deceitful practices.[723] Persuasion is necessary to convince others of the truth of this paradoxical gospel and to win them to God.[724] It is also imperative when dealing with a fractious and rebellious congregation. Persuasion would also include convicting others of their sin to lead them to godly sorrow. One consumed by the fear of the Lord generates true persuasion. Paul's statement should therefore be taken at face value: he persuades others in the fear of the Lord who knows him, which implies that he does so in a straightforward and honorable way as one answerable to God.

Paul knows that one can delude others with a show of piety and even

---

[718] Bultmann believes that the word is an opponent's barb (*Exegetische Probleme des zweiten Korintherbriefs* [Darmstadt: Wissenschaftliche Buchgesellschaft, 1963] 13). Furnish contends that Paul's critics "have accused him of trying to 'persuade people' in devious ways." He suggests that the word should be put in quotation marks (*II Corinthians*, 322). Thrall thinks that the criticism came initially from Jewish opponents in Corinth who, in turn, influenced Jewish Christian members (*Second Epistle to the Corinthians*, 1:402–3).

[719] So Kruse, *2 Corinthians*, 119.

[720] So Windisch, *Der Zweite Korintherbrief*, 176.

[721] Given the Corinthians' interest in showy rhetorical displays, it is unlikely that they would have viewed such "persuasion" in a negative sense. Why would they have criticized Paul for this?

[722] As Barnett contends (*The Second Epistle to the Corinthians*, 281).

[723] As Furnish would read it (*II Corinthians*, 323).

[724] Bultmann argues that it most naturally means "to seek to win men" ("πείθω ...," *TDNT* 6:2). In Acts the verb πείθειν ("to persuade) most frequently appears with a positive connotation of persuading persons to believe (see 13:43; 17:4; 18:4; 19:8,26; 23:23; 26:28; 28:23–24). It has a negative sense in Acts 14:19; 19:26; and 23:21. Lambrecht concludes, "Paul tries to win over people by preaching the message, to persuade them by means of the proclamation of the gospel" ("Reconcile Yourselves," 166).

deceive oneself, but one can never hoodwink God, who examines our souls with a jeweler's eye. He therefore has no interest in appearing to be holy, only in seeking real holiness. He exudes confidence that God knows his true self and that his ministry and his motivation are completely in accord with God's will. Paul wishes that what he knows to be plain to God were just as plain to the Corinthians (see 1:14), but their actions betray that not all appreciate his ministry.[725] This statement in 5:11 picks up the theme of the letter expressed in 1:12–14:

> Now this is our boast: Our conscience testifies that we have conducted ourselves in the world, and especially in our relations with you, in the holiness and sincerity that are from God. We have done so not according to worldly wisdom but according to God's grace. For we do not write you anything you cannot read or understand. And I hope that, as you have understood us in part, you will come to understand fully that you can boast of us just as we will boast of you in the day of the Lord Jesus.

Paul assumes that mature Christians have the gift of discernment and can judge matters for themselves. He can only leave it to their conscience to evaluate the evidence. But he insists that if they knew him the way God, who examines every recess of his heart, knows him, they would change their unkind opinions of him and would not be so taken with the outward displays and charms that their heathen culture finds so enchanting and persuasive. Paul's hope in writing this letter is that they will finally recognize that he serves them, not himself, that he wishes to exalt them before God, not himself, and that his bold admonishments are all part of his ministry to get them to accept God's reconciliation so that they may stand with him acquitted before God.[726] They need to examine their own consciences and question whether their own lives are governed by the fear of God.

5:12 Paul's statement that he is "not trying to commend ourselves to you again" does not mean that he worries that they might misconstrue his defense as reverting again to boastful ways. I have already argued that there was nothing inherently wrong with commending oneself in Paul's culture. It refers to self-introduction.[727] The key word is *again*.[728] Boastfulness does not seem to be a Corinthian complaint against Paul; if any-

---

[725] The verb "to be plain" appears in 2:14; 3:3; 4:10,11; 5:10,11(2x); 7:12; and 11:6. Here it refers back to 5:10 "appear." The perfect tense of the two verbs (πεφανερώμεθα, πεφανερῶσθαι) refers to the abiding situation that his past ministry among them established.

[726] Barnett claims that "to you" suggests that Paul is defending himself to the Corinthians against outside opponents (*The Second Epistle to the Corinthians*, 278). He refers to them as "shadowy opponents." In this passage they are so shadowy that they may simply be shadows of the interpreters' imaginations.

[727] See the discussion of the idea of self-commendation in 3:1.

[728] So also Thrall, *Second Epistle to the Corinthians*, 1:403.

thing, they may feel that he is not boastful enough, at least, according to their cultural conventions. It is unlikely, then, that Paul alludes to a cocky and inflated view of himself which the Corinthians found distasteful. Instead, he is insisting that he is not reintroducing himself to them as an apostle. He only wants them to take pride in him (literally, "to have a boast in behalf of us").[729] Boasting here has a positive connotation. He wants to give them an incentive to boast about him [us] as he has boasted about them to the Macedonians (9:2).

The context would suggest that he wishes them to value "his total generous and genuine self-involvement" described in 4:8–12; 6:4–10.[730] He writes as he does to give them something to say to those whose boasts derive only from worldly pretensions. His goal is to open up for them a new way to interpret the evidence so they can reevaluate his ministry from God's point of view and defend him against any detractors. Paul does not specify who these detractors might be. He may intend the reference to "those who take pride in what is seen" (lit., "those who boast in the face") indefinitely so that it would apply to anyone who might fall into that category and might cast scorn on the apostle. The implied critics may be mutinous members of the Corinthian congregation, recent intruders who have overstepped their bounds, or external antagonists, such as his earlier Jewish adversaries who opposed him and reviled him (Acts 18:6,12–13). We find no need to pinpoint specific opponents behind this criticism. The tendency to take pride in appearances is a widespread problem among humans and can infect rival Jews, rival missionaries, or disaffected Corinthian Christians. What Paul says about the glory of the gospel and his ministry, having treasure in clay jars, and living by faith in God's promise that a glory beyond all measure awaits those who die in Christ, can be used to counter anyone whose judgments are addled by spurious worldly values, whether they are members of the congregation, meddling guests, or malicious outsiders.

Whoever they are, they boast in appearances—what is external, superficial, and transitory—instead of the heart—what is internal, essential, and eternal.[731] Paul knows that what he is has been made plain to God. First Samuel 16:7 could provide a theological basis for his confidence. There the Lord warns Samuel that Eliab, Jesse's firstborn son, was not the one who was to be anointed by the prophet: "But the LORD said to Samuel, "Do not consider his appearance or his height, for I have rejected him. The LORD does not look at the things man looks at. Man looks at the outward appearance, but the LORD looks at the heart." God chose the least expected, the youngest of the sons. When humans make judgments on the basis of appearances and normal expectations, they are likely to

---

[729] A textual variant has ὑμῶν (p[46] B ℵ 33). This reading would mean they could boast about themselves because they know him to be a trustworthy, valorous apostle (so Collange, Énigmes, 248–49). The reading ἡμῶν, however, best supports the sense of Paul's argument in this section.

[730] Lambrecht, "Reconcile Yourselves," 169.

make false judgments. The visible realm is incomplete, illusive, and subject to the ravages of decay. Worldly primacy and power, even ecclesiastical power, does not always equate with success in God's eyes. The eternal realm provides the only definitive and lasting values from which to make sound spiritual judgments. The Corinthians therefore should be making their judgments from the Spirit's vantage point rather than looking at such things as earthly status, worldly honor, and physical appearance.

5:13 Paul affirms that all he does is for God, or for them, and not for himself. The NIV translates the verb *existēmi* to refer to being out of one's mind, and this rendering would parallel its usage in Mark 3:21—people were saying that Jesus "had gone out of his mind." The verb can also refer to "ecstasy" (Acts 10:10; 11:5; and 22:17) and is used in Acts 22:17 to describe a vision Paul had in Jerusalem.[732] Some therefore understand Paul to be alluding to religious ecstasy expressed in mystical experiences and speaking in tongues.[733] This view assumes that Paul distinguishes the rare moments of spiritual rapture when he is in special communion with God from his normal, rational state when he communicates to his fellow humans. Paul makes such a distinction in 1 Cor 14:2–4:

---

[731] The word translated in the NIV by the phrase "what is seen" is lit. "face" (πρόσωπον). The word occurs in 1:11; 2:10; 3:7,13,18; 4:6; 5:12; 8:24; 10:1,7; 11:20. Furnish correctly notes that boasting in the face "may also be called boasting *kata sarka*" (see 11:18; *2 Corinthians*, 308). Thrall conjectures from the reference to Moses' face in 3:7–18 that the criticism comes "from non-Christian Jews, who compare Paul to his disadvantage with the glorious figure of Moses, with his transfigured face." They appeal to the glorious figure of Moses as attesting the glorious splendor of the old covenant and do not recognize the glory of the new covenant written on the heart. "They perceive Paul's lack of outward 'Mosaic' glory and fail to recognise his credentials in the form of the community he has founded. It is to give his converts a means of reply to these people that he has written chaps. 3–4" (*Second Epistle to the Corinthians*, 1:404–5). This view assumes that Paul's mention of Moses was prompted by opponents who appealed to him. If this is not the case, as we have argued, then this argument falls to the ground. It also assumes that Paul is trying to help the Corinthians, who already support Paul, in their debates with Jewish opponents. But the tone of these chapters suggests instead that Paul is having to defend himself against internal opposition. Criticism directed at him by outsiders may well feed the disaffection that some in Corinth feel toward him, but Paul's primary target in his defense is the Corinthians themselves, not outsiders.

[732] Thrall notes that Philo uses the nouns μανία and ἐκστάσις as virtual synonyms for "madness" (*Who Is the Heir* 264) and thinks that "it is not unreasonable to suppose that Paul could use the intransitive form of ἐξίστημι as the equivalent of μαίνομαι" (*Second Epistle to the Corinthians*, 1:406). M. Hubbard offers counterevidence that seriously challenges the view that these two verbs are roughly synonymous ("Was Paul Out of His Mind? Re-Reading 2 Corinthians 5.13," *JSNT* 70 [1998] 39–64). The verb ἐξίστημι is used more frequently in the NT to describe the terrified or amazed reaction to a miracle (Matt 12:23; Mark 2:12; 5:42; 6:51; Luke 8:56; 24:22; Acts 2:7,12; 8:9,11,13; 9:21; 10:45; 12:16) or some divine revelation (Luke 2:47). The noun ἔκστασις is used to describe the reaction to a miracle (Mark 5:42; 16:8; Luke 5:26; and Acts 3:10) and three times to describe a trance in which one receives a revelation (Acts 10:10; 11:5; and 22:17).

[733] The verb ἐξέστημεν would then be regarded as a gnomic aorist. Its aspect would be timeless, simply stressing the general fact of such ecstasy.

For anyone who speaks in a tongue does not speak to men but to God. Indeed, no one understands him; he utters mysteries with his spirit. But everyone who prophesies speaks to men for their strengthening, encouragement and comfort. He who speaks in a tongue edifies himself, but he who prophesies edifies the church.

If that distinction applies here, then Paul's point could be that neither his ecstatic experiences nor his rational experiences are "undertaken for my own benefit or glory."[734]

On the other hand, Paul may be downplaying the value of ecstatic visions in contrast to his more flamboyant opponents who put great stock in them as part of their apostolic credentials. He talks of his ecstatic visions in 12:1–7 only reluctantly, while his opponents apparently publicly prided themselves on their celestial revelations. Paul knows, however, that apostles who are forever in a state of frenzied ecstasy will not be much use to a community in need of sober-minded direction.[735] Paul may be saying, "If we do experience ecstasy, then that is something between us and God [not something to be displayed before others as proof of the spiritual character of our ministry], but if we are in our right mind [and, use reasonable, intelligible speech], that is for your benefit."[736] The Corinthians' fixation on such things, however, suggests that they would be prone only to criticize Paul for his shortage of thrilling visions. Thrall suggests, "They might have wished to have seen him in an ecstatic condition, to which they could bear testimony."[737] They could then vaunt his spiritual bona fides to external critics. Paul responds to such criticism that they can only depend on his sober and rational arguments, not any dazzling religious ecstasy.

These interpretations perhaps read too much into what Paul actually says.[738] The question of his apostolic credentials is not in view here. In this context Paul is not reacting to any criticism about his paucity of ecstatic

---

[734] Barrett, *The Second Epistle to the Corinthians,* 166–67.

[735] Furnish contends: "Paul is mindful of the criticism that the authenticity of his apostolate has been supported by no 'religious' evidence in the form of public displays of ecstasy. In response he disallows the pertinence of ecstatic experiences for the question of apostleship (v. 13a) and emphasizes instead the commitment of his apostolate to the preaching of the gospel (v. 11a) and to the care of those who have received it" (v. 13b). The phrase "to God" means that these ecstatic experiences "are a matter between himself and God" (Furnish, *2 Corinthians,* 321, 324). Barnett concurs that Paul is arguing that such ecstatic experiences do not legitimate his ministry: "The evaluation of ministry is to be sought in the public realm, not the private" (*The Second Epistle to the Corinthians,* 278–79).

[736] Kruse, *2 Corinthians,* 121.

[737] Thrall, *Second Epistle to the Corinthians,* 1:407.

[738] J. W. Fraser observes, "There is no real ground for taking Paul's own use of ἐξέστημεν, applying it to them and ascribing ecstatic experiences to them" ("Paul's Knowledge of Jesus: II Corinthians V.16 Once More," *NTS* 17 [1971] 308).

experiences. It is more likely that the NIV translation connecting it to some kind of madness is correct. Ecstasy is the opposite of self-control and can refer to all kinds of behavior that may seem irrational.[739] Someone, such as his Jewish opponents, may be accusing him of some kind of mental instability—he has gone mad.[740] Or those in Corinth "who thought highly and confidently of themselves and their outward status and show could have regarded Paul as abnormal."[741] He was perhaps too eccentric for their tastes.

If the aorist (past) tense of the verb is interpreted historically ("if we were once beside ourselves") and not timelessly, referring to a present condition, then Paul may allude to some past action. Since he uses the present tense for being in his right mind, he may be deliberately contrasting what he is now in writing to them with something that happened previously that may be interpreted as being mad.[742] The REB reads, "If these are mad words, take them as addressed to God; if sound sense, as addressed to you." We have argued, however, that this large section contains Paul's defense of his impassioned letter of tears in which he boldly confronted them with their sin, and the use of the aorist may refer to that previous letter of tears (2:4). He was beside himself with grief and says that he regretted writing what he did in such strong language the minute he sent off the letter (7:8). But between himself and God, this vigorous rebuke was a well-intentioned attempt to reconcile them not only to himself but also to God. In 11:2 he admits to feeling a "divine jealousy" for them as a father who has promised his daughter in marriage to one husband Christ and intends to present her "as a chaste vir-

---

[739] Hubbard argues from Aristotle's use of the verb ἐξίστημι to refer to something in the orator's style that is detrimental (*Rhetoric* 1408b, 1418a) that Paul alludes to a criticism of his speech as unpolished and excessive ("Was Paul Out of His Mind?" 57–64).

[740] In Acts 26:24–25 the Roman governor Festus accuses Paul of madness (μαίνη), and Paul responds that he is in right mind (σωφροσύνης = σωφρονοῦμεν in 2 Cor 5:13).

[741] Fraser, "Paul's Knowledge of Jesus," 308. Belleville comments that it might seem madness to exult in suffering for others (4:8–9), and Paul counters that what the world regards as madness is for God (*2 Corinthians,* 148). Kruse offers another option: "Even if we are mad [as some say], that is but the result of our faithfulness to God in preaching a pure gospel, but if we are in our right mind [as we are], then that is for your sake [who benefit from the sober truth]" (*2 Corinthians,* 121).

[742] Lambrecht contends that it refers to his past exaggerated behavior in commending himself and translates it, "If we have been immoderate ..." It may parallel Paul's description of his boasting in 11:23, "I am out of my mind to talk like this" (παραφρονῶν λαλῶ). He thinks that the verb "to be open" should be supplied in 5:13: "For if we acted somewhat beyond measure, our intentions were known to God, we were open to God; if now we are acting in a rational, controlled way, we are completely honest and open to you." Paul would be defending himself that God knows his past exaggerations were well intended and "the Corinthians should recognize that his sober-minded apostolic life is transparent to them" ("Reconcile Yourselves," 172–73). Marshall thinks that it might be a reference to his "uncontrolled enthusiasm" (*Enmity in Corinth,* 333). He claims that his opponents complained that "his speech is unrestrained and impulsive and betrays his lack of education in the accompanying social graces" (pp. 339–40). Similarly, Danker suggests that Paul's emotionalism appeared to tip in the direction of imbalance and fanaticism (*II Corinthians,* 78).

gin" (11:2). Such deep attachment to the Corinthians accounts for the anguish and reproaches that burst forth in the letter of tears. In 7:9b he explains that they "became sorrowful as God intended and so were not harmed in any way by us." He is more restrained in this letter, and he assures them that it too is also for their benefit.

"If we are in our right mind, it is for you." "Right mind" refers to "mental sobriety." They should know him well enough to realize that whatever he does is for God or for them and not for himself. His previous letter was not written from personal pique at the one who offended him or to cause them grief. It was to bring them back to God (2:9–11; 7:9,12). What he writes now to them is more sober and restrained but has the same purpose.

AN EMISSARY OF CHRIST FOR RECONCILLIATION (5:14–21). **5:14–15** What drives Paul to dedicate himself to God and to others? Paul expands on his motives with a doctrinal exposition of what Christ's death means for his own life and ministry.[743]

In both Greek and English the phrase "the love of Christ" can imply (a) Christ's love for Paul (subjective genitive); (b) Paul's love for Christ (objective genitive); or (c) both Christ's love and Paul's love. While Christ's love came first in giving his life for others, Paul responds to this divine compassion with his own love, feeble and unstable as it is. Since Paul describes what God has done in Christ as an expression of love and means of reconciliation, Christ's love for him (Gal 2:20; Eph 5:21; 2 Thess 2:16) is the primary reference; but he could not ignore his own response of love for Christ (Eph 6:24).[744]

The verb "compels" *(synechein)* only appears elsewhere in the New Testament in Phil 1:23. It can mean "to hold together," "to enclose," "to hold fast," or "to constrain." Many interpret it in a positive sense: Christ's love impels him to action. But the negative sense would fit the captive metaphor in 2:14. Christ's love, expressed in his death, holds him fast as the controlling factor in his life.[745] The NEB translates it Christ's love "leaves us no choice." Thrall understands it to mean "Christ's self-sacrificing love restrains Paul from self-seeking."[746] What seemed to the casual observer to have been an ignominious and powerless death on a cross actually exerts enormous power for good on those who submit to it. In R. Bolt's *A Man for All Seasons,* Sir Thomas More's daughter Margaret pleads with him not to persist in his resistance to the king and beseeches

---

[743] The γάρ in 5:14 gives the reasons for what he says in 5:11–13.

[744] So C. Spicq, "L'étriente de la charité," *ST* 8 (1954) 124; M. Zerwick, *Biblical Greek* (Rome: Pontifical Biblical Institute, 1963) 13; and D. B. Wallace, *Biblical Greek Beyond the Basics* (Grand Rapids: Zondervan, 1996) 120, who classifies it as a "plenary genitive."

[745] The image appears in a love poem of Ovid (*Art of Love* 1.2.27–30), who identifies himself as a "recent spoil" bearing his "new bonds with unresisting heart."

[746] Thrall, *Second Epistle to the Corinthians,* 1:408.

him: "But in reason! Haven't you done as much as God can reasonably want?" More responds, "Well, ... finally ... it isn't a matter of reason; finally it's a matter of love."[747] The love of Christ keeps Paul from living for himself and instead causes him to pour out his life for others. Barnett comments that for Paul "egocentricity has given way to Christocentricity."[748]

"We are convinced" is related to his present judgment *(krinantas)* that differs markedly from his past judgment (see Acts 26:9).[749] He now understands that one died for *(hyper)* all. The preposition *anti* would express more undeniably that Christ died "instead" of all, but the preposition *hyper* was used more prevalently during this era to express this idea.[750] The context suggests that it has a substitutionary meaning.

All humans were under sin and merited the just punishment of death (Rom 3:9–18,23; 5:12). We can say that one died as a representative of all and brought benefits to all because that one died instead of all.[751] It follows that "If 'one died for all,' then such a 'one' must be uniquely significant."[752] While belief in God today is almost universal, much of the world stumbles over ascribing anything universally significant about Jesus of Nazareth. They may admire his pithy sayings and lament his tragic martyrdom. The lifeblood of the gospel, however, courses from the central truth that in Christ God became one with the human race, that he died for all, and that his resurrection breaks the stranglehold of death.

How many people are covered by the "all"? Texts such as Col 1:20, which speaks of God reconciling "to himself all things, whether things on earth or things in heaven, by making peace through his blood, shed on the

---

[747] R. Bolt, *A Man for All Seasons* (New York: Vintage, 1960) 81; cited by W. H. Gloer, "2 Corinthians 5:14–21," *RevExp* 86 (1989) 397.

[748] P. Barnett, *The Message of 2 Corinthians,* The Bible Speaks Today (Leicester/Downers Grove: IVP, 1988) 111.

[749] The NIV translates the participle causally. Furnish contends that it is modal, "our decision having been this" (*II Corinthians,* 310).

[750] See A. T. Robertson, *The Minister and His Greek New Testament* (Nashville: Broadman, 1977) 35–42; and Wallace, *Biblical Greek Beyond the Basics,* 383–89.

[751] J. D. G. Dunn argues for the representative view of Jesus' death ("Paul's Understanding of the Death of Jesus as Sacrifice," in *Sacrifice and Redemption: Durham Essays in Theology* [Cambridge: University Press, 1991] 35–56). He contends that "substitution" tells only half the story: "There is, of course, an important element of Jesus taking the place of others—that, after all, is at the heart of the sacrificial metaphor. But Paul's teaching is not that Christ dies "in the place of" others so that they escape death (as the logic of substitution implies). It is rather that Christ's sharing their death makes it possible for them to share his death." He clarifies that the terms "representation," "participation" are also inadequate, but they have the advantage of conveying "the sense of a continuing identification with Christ in, through, and beyond his death" (*The Theology of Paul the Apostle* [Grand Rapids: Eerdmans, 1998] 223).

[752] Barnett, *The Second Epistle to the Corinthians,* 289.

cross," and Rom 8:32 which affirms, "He who did not spare his own Son, but gave him up for us all," suggest that God intended that the benefits of Christ's death reach everyone (see also Heb 2:9; 1 John 2:2). The "all" would encompass all humanity. The benefits of Christ's death are not limited to his fellow Jews but extend beyond accepted boundaries to include male and female, slave and free, Jew and Gentile.[753] But those who stubbornly refuse to submit to Christ and rebuff God's reconciliation choose to remain in condemnation. Consequently, only believers profit from Christ's death.

From this assertion Paul draws the inference that "all die."[754] What is the reasoning behind this conclusion? How is it that "all" die? We might expect Paul to have written instead, "One died; therefore all were saved from death."[755] Paul's statement is written in a kind of theological shorthand. Its full meaning is expressed well by Tasker: "Christ's death was the death of all in the sense that they should have died; the penalty of their sins was borne by him (1 Cor 15:3; 2 Cor 5:20); He died in their place."[756] Paul's purpose in this section is not to expound on the death of Christ but to argue from it. Consequently, he leaves out some basic premises about the theological reasons for Christ's death which the Corinthians already knew, namely, that all were liable to death because of their sin and that God sent his own Son in the likeness of sinful flesh to deal with sin and to restore sinners (Rom 8:3). The syllogism consists of these omitted premises:

[All humanity was condemned to death because of sin]
[Christ identified with all sinful humanity and died.]
Therefore all died.

The conclusion "Christ died, therefore all died" only makes sense if Christ died as the proxy or substitute for all humanity. But humans did not select Christ to die for us; God did. Christ's submission to God's will was a supreme act of self-giving love.

The next verse (5:15) further explains and qualifies what this atoning death entails: "And he died for all, that those who live should no longer live for themselves but for him who died for them and was raised again."[757] This

---

[753] In his letter to the Romans, written from Corinth, Paul expresses his wonder that Christ died not for the righteous or even for the good person but for all unrighteous humankind. While we were yet enemies—God took a calculated risk of seeking to transform enemies into those who are at peace with God.

[754] He uses an inferential particle ἄρα meaning "therefore," "consequently," "as a result."

[755] Windisch, *Die zweite Korintherbrief,* 182.

[756] R. V. G. Tasker, *The Second Epistle to the Corinthians,* TNTC (Grand Rapids: Eerdmans, 1958) 86.

[757] Paul's assertions do not contain novel ideas for the Corinthians. He has shared this theology with them before and apparently does not feel any need to elaborate more fully what he means. We, however, need to fill in the gaps in his argument.

restatement of 5:14 suggests that Paul refers to all *believers* who die to themselves with Christ. The "all" applies to all who no longer live for themselves (see "all who believe," Rom 4:11; and "all who call upon him," Rom 10:12). The death he envisions is death to the self, so that one can have life with Christ.[758] Tannehill insists that this statement "is merely a different formulation of the motif of dying with Christ."[759] All who join themselves to Christ must die with him. Paul therefore understands death here to be more than the medical definition "when the brain waves stop sparking and the heart stops pushing the blood through our system."[760] It is death to Sin, the Flesh, and the Old.[761] We appropriate the benefits of Christ's death for all when we accept by faith the message of reconciliation that his death proclaims and when we are baptized into his death. As the sin of Adam is the story of all humanity, the passion of Jesus is the story of all humanity in that it reflects God's judgment and punishment for sin. When we die with Christ, we escape the law's judgment and the clutches of death.

The reference to Jesus' sacrificial death allows Paul to apply subtle pressure on any Corinthians who are still slaves to self-love. This clause implies that "you should no longer live for yourself" and thereby "shifts the debate from its turbulent you-versus-me to a Christ-versus-us axis."[762] In doing so, Paul makes clear that more ultimate matters are involved in this dispute between them. Christ's death must change the way we live here and now on earth, not simply insure our entrance into God's eternal presence. Anyone who expects to live in the resurrection must respond properly to Christ's death. This response requires more than intellectual assent to the proposition that Christ's death atones for sins; it must mold how one lives. This response provides the essential criterion for discerning who truly belongs to Christ and who does not. Those who belong to Christ do not live for themselves. In societies given to self-promotion, self-fulfillment, and self-indulgence, Christians will stand out as distinctively differ-

---

[758] This option makes more sense in the context than to assume that Paul has in mind all persons who die in sin as Lambrecht, e.g., contends: "Just as in Rom 5,15 through Adam's sin, 'the many' died (in sin), so in 2 Cor 5, 14 in the redemptive death of the new Adam, Christ, all died because of their [sins and died to sin, i.e they live (cf. 15b)" ("Reconcile Yourselves," 378, n. 31). It also makes more sense to assume that all die potentially and their actual death awaits their response by faith (Barrett, *The Second Epistle to the Corinthians,* 168–69), or that the old has come to an end (interpreting it from an eschatological perspective; Furnish, *II Corinthians,* 327–28).

[759] R. C. Tannehill, *Dying and Rising with Christ,* BZNWKAK 32 (Berlin: Töplemann, 1966) 66.

[760] Minear, "Some Thoughts on Dying," 100.

[761] In Rom 5:1–11 Paul refers to Christ's death bringing reconciliation, and in the next paragraphs he talks about baptism into Christ's death (6:3–7), death to the law (Rom 7:4–5), Christ's resurrection (Rom 6:4–5,9–10), walking in newness of life (Rom 6:4), and being brought from death to life (Rom 6:13).

[762] Minear, "Some Thoughts on Dying," 101–2.

ent. They live only for Christ and give up their own rights for the good of others and do not insist on having their own way.

The self-denial of first-century Christians like Paul would have caught the attention of his contemporaries, if only to mystify them. Judge observes:

> A feature of St. Paul's thought is his fascination with the self-abasement of Christ, and the meaning of that in terms of the atonement. He could see, contrary to all human expectations, a marvelous outcome from the apparent disaster. So in his own career of setbacks and humiliations he was led by the analogy with Christ's suffering to see a quite opposite kind of ideal to that of the ethical philosophers, the ideal of the man who could give himself up for others. Self-protection was the first aspect of Greek thought which I think that Paul fundamentally rejected.[763]

The gift of redemption that comes through Christ's death and resurrection requires that we change the way we live. We are no longer to allow our selfish desires to twist the way we regard or treat others. To accept death with Christ so that our own longings, purposes, and securities are also put to death requires the risky venture of faith. But Paul insists that Christ controls the reins of his life so that he no longer is driven to kick against the goads. He instead lives to serve others, particularly, the Corinthians (4:12,15; 5:13). What Paul finds crucially important in this section is what Christ's death means for how he must evaluate others and how they should evaluate him. As others now misread Paul, so he once misread Christ.

5:16 What does it mean to live for Christ? The "so" *(hōste)* draws the conclusions from 5:14–15. From now on, we regard no one "according to the flesh" *(kata sarka,* "from a worldly point of view," NIV).[764] The emphasis is on "no longer" *(mēketi),* "from now on" *(apo tou nun),* and "no longer" *(nun ouketi).* The phrase "from now on," however, has eschatological overtones and therefore refers to something beyond the point of Paul's conversion when he surrendered all his evaluations and decisions to the wisdom of the cross.[765] Christ's death is the turning of the ages. It reveals that this world is passing away and shows that all attachments to it are unimportant and vain. Tannehill writes:

> If Paul were only able to assert that "for me" or "in my view" the old world has passed away, he would not be able to argue as he does that others may no longer judge him according to the flesh, for they would be entitled to their

---

[763] E. Judge, "St. Paul as a Radical Critic of Society," *Interchange* 16 (1974) 195.

[764] The verbs translated "regard" in the NIV are οἴδαμεν, ἐγνώκαμεν, and γινώσκομεν, which mean "to know." For one schooled in the Hebrew Scriptures "to know" has a direct effect on how one behaves (Lambrecht, "Reconcile Yourselves," 383).

[765] The phrase also has an eschatological thrust in Luke 22:69, but not in the other NT occurrences (Luke 1:48; 5:10; 12:52; 22:18; John 8:11; Acts 18:6).

viewpoint as he to his. Paul's whole argument in these verses depends upon the reality of the presence of the new aeon.[766]

For Paul truth is not relative or simply a matter of personal taste; it rests in the objective reality of what God has done in Christ.

Paul affirms that "we regard no one from a worldly point of view (*kata sarka*, "according to the flesh")—though we once regarded Christ in this way, we do so no longer." The latter half, "though we once regarded Christ in this way," has generated a number of different interpretations.[767] One prominent view takes the phrase "according to the flesh" as modifying the pronoun "no one" and the noun "Christ." The statement then becomes a reference to the historical Jesus. It is then inferred that Paul had no interest in the Jesus of history, only the exalted Christ of heaven. Bultmann provides the classic statement of this view:

For Paul, Christ has lost his identity as an individual human person. He knows him no longer "after the flesh" (2 Cor 5:16). Instead, Jesus has become a cosmic figure, a body to which all belong who have been joined to him through faith and baptism.[768]

Several considerations make this view untenable. Paul has cited the tradition about what Jesus said about divorce in his advice on marriage and divorce (1 Cor 7:12). He also cited the tradition of Jesus' last supper, which he had delivered to the Corinthians, to correct the abuses at their Lord's Supper (1 Cor 11:23–25). That tradition of what the earthly Jesus said and did was clearly important and authoritative and not an insignificant part of Paul's preaching.[769] But the key argument against this view is the pattern established by Paul's use of the phrase *kata sarka* elsewhere. When Paul construes the phrase *kata sarka* with a noun or proper name, the phrase *follows* the noun (Rom 1:3; 4:1; 9:3,5; 1 Cor 1:26; 10:18).[770]

---

[766] Tannehill, *Dying and Rising with Christ,* 69.

[767] The differing translations of the phrase κατὰ σάρκα ("according to the flesh") reveal the problem: NRSV "from a human point of view"; NAB "in terms of human judgment"; GNB "according to human standards"; JB "in the flesh"; Moffatt "what is external"; Phillips "as a man." We can dismiss the view that κατὰ σάρκα is a Gnostic gloss that interrupts the flow of thought from 5:11–15 to 5:17 (so, e.g., W. Schmithals, *Gnosticism in Corinth: An Investigation of the Letters to the Corinthians* [Nashville: Abingdon, 1971] 302–15).

[768] R. Bultmann, *Primitive Christianity in its Contemporary Setting* (New York: Word, 1956) 197. In his commentary Bultmann writes: "The Christos *kata sarka* is Christ as he can be encountered in the world, before his death and resurrection. He should no longer be viewed as such" (*The Second Letter to the Corinthians,* 155). See also J. Weiss, *Paul and Jesus* (London: Harper, 1909) 41–53; and W. Bouset, *Kyrios Christos* (Nashville: Abingdon, 1970) 169.

[769] See Dunn, *The Theology of Paul the Apostle,* 182–206.

[770] Fraser, "Paul's Knowledge of Jesus," 298; Furnish, *II Corinthians,* 313; and F. W. Danker, "Exegesis of 2 Corinthians 5:14–21," in *Interpreting 2 Corinthians 5:14–21,* ed. J. P. Lewis (New York: Mellen, 1989) 114–15. When the phrase modifies the verb, it may precede or follow the verb (Rom 8:4,12; 2 Cor 1:17; 10:2–3; 11:18; Gal 4:23).

In this sentence the pronoun "no one" and the noun "Christ" *precede* the phrase, and it should therefore be read adverbially. In addition to this pattern, Fraser notes that the references to Jesus and to Christ throughout 2 Corinthians reveal that Paul uses both names to refer to the whole gamut of Christ's work, to Christ before the passion, to Christ in the passion and resurrection, and to what happened to Christ after these events. He concludes that "'Christ cannot be considered apart from the historical Jesus.'"[771] Finally, Paul says that he knows no one *kata sarka*. To be consistent, this interpretation would require him to mean that he never met anyone in the flesh, which makes nonsense. This statement that he no longer knows Christ *kata sarka* therefore has nothing to do with any presumed disinterest in the earthly Jesus. Paul refers instead to the measuring scale by which he knows or judges others, namely, unspiritual, worldly standards. Paul does not reject knowledge of "Christ after the flesh," just an "according to the flesh" view of Christ.

To judge others according to worldly standards, or from a sinful point of view, only furthers division and discord rather than fostering reconciliation. Paul does not specify what these standards are, but from the context they must be related to outward appearances (5:12). The primary reason for raising this issue is the Corinthians' misjudgment of his ministry, which they have assessed according to the worldly paradigms with which they are more familiar. Paul confesses that he (using an authorial "we") viewed reality and persons from a fleshly perspective which used only human yardsticks to measure others. False, superficial criteria led him to esteem those who appeared to be wise, influential, of noble birth, and strong, and to disdain those who were none of these things. Before he was captured by Christ, such worldly norms warped his judgments as they do all who live under the thralldom of sin and whose veiled, benighted minds screen out God's truth.

Paul's opening salvo in 1 Corinthians, "But God chose the foolish things of the world to shame the wise; God chose the weak things of the world to shame the strong" (1 Cor 1:26–27), sounds the same theme. The same ones who find the servile shame of Christ's crucifixion to be folly or a scandal

---

[771] Fraser, "Paul's Knowledge of Jesus," 299. F. F. Bruce writes: "For Paul there was a personal continuity and indeed identity between the crucified Jesus and the exalted Lord: in so far as the words and deeds of the earthly Jesus were relevant for the knowledge of the exalted Lord, an interest in them was not tantamount to an endeavor to 'know Christ after the flesh.' To know Christ after the flesh was to cherish that unregenerate estimate which had marked Paul's earlier days. Henceforth for Paul the Christ was identical with the crucified and exalted Jesus, and to view all men in relation to him was to have done with knowing them 'after the flesh'—i.e., from an unregenerate point of view" ("Further thoughts on Paul's Autobiography," in *Jesus und Paulus,* ed. E. E. Ellis and E. Grässer [Göttingen: Vandenhoeck & Ruprecht, 1978] 25).

will also be repulsed by Paul's lowly condition. In comparison to the wise, strong, and honored of this world, Paul looks like a fool who is weak and dishonored. As someone hungry and thirsty, ragged, brutally treated, homeless, cursed, and a laborer who works with his hands, he is deemed "the scum of the earth, the refuse of the world" (1 Cor 4:8–13). Others see only death in Paul. He responds, "Behold we live!" He also insists that those who recognize that we are now living at the end of the ages must change their epistemology accordingly. As one puts it, we now are to know according to the cross.[772] But this yardstick should be expanded to include the resurrection and the Spirit. We know according to the cross, according to resurrection (see 4:14; 5:1–10), and according to the Spirit (3:16–18; 4:13). Understanding the full meaning of the cross and resurrection and fully experiencing the Spirit brings an enlightenment that causes Christians to see things and other persons in new ways.

Consequently, Paul now sees others according to their standing with Christ (see Rom 14:8–12) and concedes that all his previous judgments of others were wrong. God's verdict on our sin condemns us all and destroys any illusions of superiority or inferiority. Jew and Greek, slave and free, male and female are all on the same level before God. All share a kinship with one another because of sin but also share kinship with one another because Christ died for all to redeem all. When we see that we are all sinners dead in our sins and needing reconciliation from God, and when we accept Christ's shameful death on the cross as our death, then all previous canons we used to appraise others must be scrapped.[773]

The *ei kai* ("even if," "though" NIV) in the second half of the verse is interpreted by some as a hypothetical condition, and the "we" is understood as not applying only to Paul. Even if we—whoever that might be—regarded Christ according to the flesh, we do so no longer. While the first class condition assumes the reality of the case, it does not require that it actually was the case. One can "if" anything. But Paul's confession of his zeal in persecuting the church (1 Cor 15:9; Gal 1:13–15; Phil 3:6) and his citation of Deut 21:23 that pronounces anyone hanged on a tree as accursed (Gal 3:13) suggest that Paul's sinful disposition controlled how he had first reacted to Christ. He confesses in Phil 3:4–6 that before being captured by Christ his whole life was oriented around flesh categories.

---

[772] J. L. Martyn, "Epistemology at the Turn of the Ages: 2 Corinthians 5:16," in *Christian History and Interpretation: Studies Presented to John Knox,* ed. W. R. Farmer, C. F. D. Moule, and R. R. Niebuhr (Cambridge: University Press, 1967) 285.

[773] Paul came to understand that all humanity stood under the curse of the law and was on death row, but through Christ's death God provided the means for each one to receive a reprieve. The only catch is that we must be willing to accept this judgment on our sin and God's unmerited mercy and must also accept others as our brothers and sisters for whom Christ also died.

Therefore it is more likely that Paul refers to his own pre-Christian evaluation of Jesus as Messiah in this verse.[774] As Fraser argues, "Paul is not likely simply to be giving a detached academic account of Christian epistemology or Christology without bringing his own extraordinary experience into play."[775] It takes no stretch of the imagination to assume that a zealous, law-observant Pharisee would have pegged Jesus as a charlatan and blasphemer whose crucifixion revealed him to be accursed by God.[776] He must have raged at anyone who proclaimed the crucified Jesus as the promised Messiah. The rumors about his resurrection only perpetuated and magnified the original mischief. Paul's self-centered devotion to the law had blinded him to the glory of God in the person of Christ. Only when the Lord encountered him on the Damascus road was he constrained to recognize the truth. This compelling encounter caused him to change his mind about everything he had previously held dear, but it also changed his mind from one corrupted and veiled by sin to one that could now see the very heart of God. Jesus had been raised by the power of God; he was the Son of God, and the exalted Lord. Paul learned that Jesus' crucifixion was not God's retribution against some imagined blasphemy committed by a counterfeit prophet but a vicarious sacrifice for the sins of humanity. God revealed to him that the object of his spiteful hatred, Jesus, whom the Nazarenes called Christ, had died for him making him the beneficiary of staggering sacrificial love. He also learned that his righteousness according to the law (Phil 3:6) was nothing more than filthy rags. The crucifixion exposed the deep seated evil hidden in his own heart.

Judging Christ according to human standards continues in various forms. Few today regard Christ as negatively as so many did in the first century. Many view him as a good and wise man who died a tragic death. Modern scholars, dressed in the garb of academic expertise,

---

[774] It is not impossible that Paul may have known about Jesus or met him in Jerusalem, but we cannot argue it from this verse. It makes more sense to argue that Paul has some prior acquaintance with Jesus from the Damascus road encounter. The Jewish scholar, J. Klausner, contended that the vision would not have been possible if Paul "had not seen Jesus one or more times during [his] lifetime," most likely when he was disputing with the Pharisees and perhaps when he was crucified (*From Jesus to Paul* [New York: Macmillan, 1943] 312–16). If Paul were intending to refer to any acquaintance with the historical Jesus here, however, it is more likely that he would have written "in the flesh" rather than "according to the flesh" (Fraser, "Paul's Knowledge of Jesus," 298). In this context he refers to his former outlook on all persons including his attitude toward Christ. He is not talking about his personal acquaintance with all persons, and consequently we should not project that interpretation on to his statement about knowing Christ.

[775] Fraser, "Paul's Knowledge of Jesus," 310.

[776] Fraser catalogs various views of the meaning of the phrase and dismisses many as conforming to the "theological fashion" of the day (ibid., 301–7).

tend to make Jesus over into their own image, and, in the process, eliminate any eternal claim he might exert on their lives. Some present him as a revolutionary who gathered a band of desperadoes to bring about a social liberation of the oppressed peasants. Others present him as an itinerant, nonviolent teacher spouting pithy maxims; still others as a charismatic healer trying to reform Judaism.[777]

All of these evaluations miss the mark and are no closer to the truth than the uneducated guesses of Jesus' contemporaries, who imagined him to be some recycled prophet, John the Baptist, Elijah, or some other prophet (Mark 8:28). Those who judge him according to the Spirit, however, draw a different conclusion. He is the Son of God sent by God to redeem humankind and to reconcile them.

5:17   In this next verse Paul makes four crisp antithetical statements. They are launched by a condition, "If anyone is in Christ." This phrase, "in Christ," can mean several things that are not mutually exclusive: that one belongs to Christ, that one lives in the sphere of Christ's power, that one is united with Christ, or that one is part of the body of Christ, the believing community. Paul's assumption is that being in Christ should bring about a radical change in a person's life.

The next statement is very terse and reads literally "new creation." The subject and the verb must be supplied. Translations usually choose between two options: "he is" (NIV), implying that the person is a new being, or "there is" (NRSV), implying that a new situation has come into being. The pronoun "anyone" seems to imply that Paul has individuals in mind. In the context, he is talking about changing one's way of looking at things; and this change, which occurs at conversion, is a subjective experience. Later rabbinic texts refer to proselytes becoming new creatures, and a similar idea may have been part of Paul's thinking.[778]

On the other hand, Paul also conceives that Christ's death and resurrection marks a radical eschatological break between the old age and the new.[779] Christ is the divider of history."[780] Paul also never uses the noun "creation" *(ktisis)* to refer to an individual person (see Rom 1:2,25; 8:19–22,39), and the concept of a new creation appears prominently in Jewish apocalyptic texts that picture the new age as inaugurating something far more sweeping than individual transformation—a new heaven and a new

---

[777] D. E. Garland, *Mark,* NIVAC (Grand Rapids: Zondervan, 1996) 336.

[778] In the tale of Joseph and Asenath, when Asenath converts to Judaism, she is told, "You will be renewed and formed anew and made alive again" *(Jos. As.* 15:4). Later rabbis claimed that bringing a heathen near to God is as though someone had "created him" *(Gen. Rab.* 39:4).

[779] If we are to read τὰ πάντα ("all things") before "new," it would embrace the whole cosmos (see Rom 11:36; 1 Cor 8:6; 15:27–28; Eph 1:10–11; Col 1:15–20).

[780] Barnett, *The Second Epistle to the Corinthians,* 287.

earth.[781] The translation "there is a new creation" would mean that the new creation does not merely involve the personal transformation of individuals but encompasses the eschatological act of recreating humans and nature in Christ. It would also include the new community, which has done away with the artificial barriers of circumcision and uncircumcision (Gal 6:15–16; see Eph 2:14–16) as part of this new creation.

Christians see the world in a new way and become new when they are joined to Christ. Beasley-Murray comments: "United to the risen Lord, the believer participates in the new creation of which Christ is the fount and the life."[782] Translating the words literally, "new creation," without inserting a pronoun would allow for both options since the eschatological reality of the new creation effected by Christ's advent makes possible that subjective change in individuals who become new creations in Christ. Paul's declaration is the corollary to his earlier affirmations that we are being transformed (3:16,18; 4:16–17)—so much so that the believer becomes a new creation. The new heaven and new earth and the complete transformation of believers remain a future hope, but for Christians they are so certain to be fulfilled that their lives are controlled by this new reality that still awaits consummation. For individuals to become a part of this new creation, they must choose to be in Christ.

"The old has gone!" Again, this phrase can be interpreted to refer to the "old order" or to everything that controlled the individual's pre-Christian existence. Both are true. The old order is passing off the stage (1 Cor 7:31). The individual's whole being, value system, and behavior are also changed through conversion. We are dead to sin but alive to God in Christ (Rom 6:11). Denney writes of Paul: "The past was dead to him, as dead as Christ on his cross, all its ideas, all its hopes, all its ambitions were dead in Christ, he was another man in another universe."[783]

"The new has come!" Paul believes that the "new thing" that Isaiah foretold God would do has come to pass in Christ.[784] It is greater than the exodus from Egypt (Exod 14–15) and greater than the deliverance from Babylon (Isa 48:18–19). God has now delivered us from the bondage of sin and led us back from the exile of our estrangement from God to a new reconciled relationship. The NIV omits the particle "behold" *(idou)* that prefaces this statement, probably because it sounds archaic, and inserts an

---

[781] See Isa 65:17; 66:22; and postbiblical expectation of a new creation in *1 Enoch* 45:4–5; 72:1; 91:15–16; *2 Apoc. Bar.* 32:6; 44:12; 57:2; 73–74; *4 Ezra* 7:75; *Jub.* 1:29; 4:26; *Ps.-Philo* 3:10; 16:3; 32:17; 1QH 3:19–23b; 11:9–14; 13:1,11–12; 15:13–17a; 1QS 4:23–26; 11QTemple 29:7b–10.

[782] Beasley-Murray, "2 Corinthians," 42.

[783] J. Denney, *The Second Epistle to the Corinthians,* The Expositor's Bible (London: Hodder & Stoughton, 1908) 206.

[784] Isa 42:9; 43:16–21; 48:6; 65:17; 66:22.

exclamation mark at the end of the sentence instead. This word, however, "is ordinarily used by biblical writers to mark an unusual moment or deed" (cp. Rev 21:5, "Behold, I make all things new").[785] "Behold" also prefaces Paul's interpretation of Isa 49:8 in 6:2: "Behold, now is the time of God's favor, behold now is the day of salvation."[786] The important new thing is God's reconciliation that enables us to become the righteousness of God (5:21) and brings us salvation (6:2). This new thing not only begets new values, it also begets new behavior (1 Cor 6:9–11).

5:18 In 5:18–21 Paul shifts from a focus on Christ to what God has done and reflects on the role his apostleship plays in God's redemptive plan of reconciling the world.[787] The Corinthians can only appreciate Paul's apostolic work when they understand it as part of God's work to reconcile the world. If they want to see God's glory, they can see it most clearly in Paul's reconciling ministry to the world that requires self-sacrifice and inevitably results in suffering. This explains why this passage about God's reconciling work appears in Paul's defense. In this section Paul is not primarily concerned to set forth his doctrine of atonement but to establish the basis of his ministry of reconciliation. Everything begins with God's initiative: "All this from God." He then amplifies what he means with two parallel statements:

5:18   God reconciled us to himself through Christ
        gave us a ministry of reconciliation
5:19   reconciling the world to himself in Christ, not counting men's
        sins against them.
        And he has committed to us the message of reconciliation.
He concludes by listing the results of God's initiative:
5:20   We are therefore Christ's ambassadors, as though God were
        making his appeal through us. We implore you on Christ's behalf:
        Be reconciled to God.
5:21   God made him who had no sin to be sin for us, so that in him we
        might become the righteousness of God.

This unit contains three key assertions. (1) God is the driving force behind the redemption of humankind. Reconciliation comes solely at God's initiative. (2) God acted through Christ's death, and Christ alone is the means of reconciliation. (3) God continues to act through those who have

---

[785] Furnish comments, "Here the expression not only calls attention to what follows but lends an almost triumphal note to the affirmation" (II Corinthians, 315–16).

[786] The NIV substitutes "I tell you" for the word "behold" and omits an exclamation point.

[787] Lambrecht, "Reconcile Yourselves," 376. Thrall comments, "It is natural that the one theme [apostolic ministry] should evoke the other, since the apostolic message of the cross (1 Cor 1:18) is the message of God's love for sinners (Rom 5:8)" ("Salvation Proclaimed V. 2 Corinthians 5:18–21: Reconciliation with God," *ExpTim* 93 [1982] 227).

been reconciled. They have the privilege and responsibility to share in this great divine enterprise and are to call others to be reconciled to God.

Christians undermine this great calling whenever they are riven with their own irreconciliation. Paul understands that he cannot fulfill his vision of going to Spain to preach a gospel of reconciliation while leaving behind an unreconciled church where Jew does not accept Gentile (see Rom 15:24). This concern to bring Jewish Christians and Gentile Christians together is the primary motive behind the collection for Jerusalem, the topic taken up in chaps. 8–9.[788]

When Paul says "all this" (lit. "all these things) is from God, he makes clear that the new creation (5:17) is exclusively God's work. He continues in this mode by asserting that humans have done nothing to reconcile God; God has instead acted to reconcile them. Reconciliation therefore begins with God, who acts unilaterally. It is effected through Christ, whose death removed the barrier (see Isa 59:2) to reconciliation. Christ's death, however, requires our response as we accept reconciliation with God and work to reconcile ourselves with our fellow humans.[789]

Paul is the only author in the New Testament to use the noun "reconciliation" *(katallagē)* and the verb "to reconcile" *(katallassein).*[790] When the verb is used in the active voice, Christ or God is always the subject; when it is used in the passive voice, humans are the subject. In other words, "God reconciles; man is reconciled."[791] Reconciliation assumes ruptured relationships, alienation, and disaffection. The problem, however, is not with God, as if God were some cruel taskmaster from whom humans rebelled. Human

---

[788] F. Stagg, "Exegesis of 2 Corinthians 5:14–21," in *Interpreting 2 Corinthians 5:14–21: An Exercise in Hermeneutics,* ed. J. P. Lewis, SBEC 17 (Lewiston/Queenston/Lampeter: Mellen, 1989) 165.

[789] The phrase "through Christ" parallels Rom 5:10, "We were reconciled to him through the death of his Son." "Through Christ" therefore implies "through the death of his Son" and refers to the crucifixion (see 2 Cor 5:14).

[790] The noun appears four times (Rom 5:11; 11:15; 2 Cor 5:18,19) and the verb six times (Rom 5:11[2x]; 1 Cor 7:11; 2 Cor 5:18,19,20). The verb ἀποκαταλλάσσω appears in Eph 2:16 and Col 1:20,22.

[791] Thrall, "Salvation Proclaimed," 227–28. By contrast the verb appears in *2 Macc* 1:5; 5:20; 7:33; 8:29 for something humans do to prod God to be reconciled to them. It was not an essential part of Hellenistic religion since pagan deities were not viewed as having any personal relationship to humanity (F. Büchsel, ἀλλάσσω …," *TDNT* 1:254). I. H. Marshall ("The Meaning of 'Reconciliation,'" in *Unity and Diversity in New Testament Theology,* ed. R. A. Guelich [Grand Rapids: Eerdmans, 1978] 120–21) shows that the word ἀλλάσσω was used in four different ways that differ significantly from Paul's usage:
   a. active sense: someone who mediates between two groups
   b. passive / deponent: someone who persuades someone to relinquish hostility towards himself
   c. passive: an offended person who is persuaded to give up his hostility
   d. with a direct object to refer to offenses that made reconciliation necessary.

sinfulness created the problem, and this sinful condition had to be dealt with before there could be any reconciliation. Sin incurs God's holy wrath, so it could not be treated lightly or swept under the rug. God can never be reconciled to sin, but God does not turn away from sinners in disgust and leave them to their just desserts. Instead, while humans were still in open revolt, God acted in love (Rom 5:8) to bring the hostility to an end and to bring about peace (see Rom 5:1; see Isa 32:17). This peace is not simply a cessation of hostilities or an uneasy truce. It refers to the mending of the broken relationship that results from God justifying us (making us right) through faith and changing us from enemies to friends (GNB).

Cranfield perceptively comments on Paul's switch from the metaphor of justification in Rom 5:1–9 to the metaphor of reconciliation in Rom 5:10–11:

> Justification is a judicial term used in the law courts. A judge may acquit an accused person without ever entering into any personal relationship with the him or her. He just announces the verdict, not guilty. The accused hardly expects to be invited over for dinner by the judge, and probably hopes that he will never see him again.[792]

The shift to the reconciliation metaphor takes what God has done through Christ a step further. The judge enters into a personal relationship with the accused. This is necessary because the judge is the one who has been sinned against and is the focus of the personal hostility. God does not simply make a bookkeeping alteration by dropping the charges against us. God gives himself to us in friendship. Because of our extreme hostility toward God, this investment is accomplished at unspeakable cost.

Paul offers us insight into his theology of ministry when he asserts that God gave to us the ministry of reconciliation. Paul uses the noun "ministry" *(diakonia)* for his apostolic service.[793] The image may derive from the humble servant who waits at table. Roloff argues that the use of the term in early Christian tradition to denote ministry derives from what Jesus did at the last supper (John 13:1–17; see also Mark 10:45).[794] If that is the case, Paul's

---

[792] C. E. B. Cranfield, *A Critical and Exegetical Commentary on the Epistle to the Romans,* ICC (Edinburgh: T & T Clark, 1975) 1:259.

[793] The verb "to minister" (διακονεῖν) and the nouns "ministry" (διακονία) and "minister" (διάκονος) appear in Paul's letters thirty-five times out of the one hundred occurrences in the NT. Twenty of these thirty-five occurrences are in 2 Corinthians. See R. Bieringer, "Paul's Understanding of Diakonia in 2 Corinthians 5,18," in *Studies on 2 Corinthians,* ed. R. Bieringer and J. Lambrecht, BETL 112 (Leuven: University Press, 1994) 413–28; S. Aalen, "Versuch einer Analyse des Diakonia-Begriffes im Neuen Testament," in *The New Testament Age,* ed. W. C. Weinrich (Macon: Mercer, 1984) 1:1–13. See also J. N. Collins, *Diakonia: Re-interpreting the Ancient Sources* (New York/Oxford: Oxford University Press, 1990).

[794] J. Roloff, "Anfänge der soteriologischen Deutung des Todes Jesu," *NTS* 19 (1972–73) 38–64.

conception of apostleship is modeled on Christ's death on the cross, and the apostolic office is a representation of Christ's service. Others argue that it arose from the servant role of Israel in Isa 51:16 and 59:21. The way Paul uses the term in this context does not highlight the menial nature of the work or imply some humble status. Instead, it refers to activity "done on behalf of another." He regards himself to be an authoritative spokesman for God, authorized in his missionary work to be a mediator of God's revelation.[795] This assertion captures Paul's understanding of what an apostle is: someone "acting in God's service," but this role "does not raise him above the community or give him privileges." Quite the contrary, it is the source of his great suffering.[796] The hardships Paul lists in 6:4–10 "explain what makes Paul's *diakonia* to be *diakonia*."[797] In 11:23 his list of hardships show that he is a better "servant of Christ" than his rivals.

The phrase "ministry of reconciliation" can mean that his ministry has its origin and is made possible by the grace of reconciliation (genitive of origin). It can also mean that his ministry is characterized by reconciliation, a reconciling ministry (qualitative genitive); or his ministry proclaims, offers, or brings about reconciliation (objective genitive). It can also mean that reconciliation is the content of his ministry (genitive of content). It is hard to decide among the various options since all have a measure of truth.[798] The last seems to be the best alternative given the context in which Paul refers to the "word of reconciliation" (5:19) and how he expands theologically on what God has done to bring about reconciliation. But Paul does not simply proclaim something, namely, that the cross was an event in the past which took away the sins of the world; he lives the message himself (see 4:10).[799] The ministry of reconciliation therefore involves more than simply explaining to others what God has done in Christ. It requires that one become an active reconciler oneself. Like Christ, a minister of reconciliation plunges

---

[795] Paul refers here only to his own apostolic ministry because that is what he is defending and therefore is not referring to the general task of all Christians. In 3:8–9 he uses the term *diakonia* to refer to his apostolic ministry and preaching of the gospel. Apostles are the first to proclaim to people what God has done through Christ's death and resurrection. That does not mean that this task is left only to apostles. M. A. Getty writes: "Justification is not an event that happened in past history but a dynamic of faith challenging all believers to participate in the work of reconciling the world to God" ("The Primacy of Christ," *TBT* 23 [1985] 23). All Christians are called to ministry, and all are therefore called to a ministry of reconciliation. Georgi believes that this concept of being God's envoy derives from a Cynic background and that the unusual concentration of the term in 2 Corinthians is because the opponents used it (Georgi, *Opponents,* 28). Against this view see the cogent arguments of J. N. Collins, "Georgi's 'Envoys' in 2 Cor 11:23," *JBL* 93 (1974) 88–96.

[796] Bieringer, "Paul's Understanding of *Diakonia*," 425–26.

[797] Ibid., 427.

[798] In 3:9 he refers to "the ministry of righteousness."

[799] Bieringer, "Paul's Understanding of *Diakonia*," 427–28.

into the midst of human tumult to bring harmony out of chaos, reconciliation out of estrangement, and love in the place of hate.

Paul's strained relationship with the Corinthians makes the reconciliation metaphor apt. His role as reconciler is clear in both of Paul's letters to the Corinthians. In 1 Corinthians Paul tries to remedy the "I" disease that inspires the party spirit and squabbling: "I belong to Cephas, Apollos, Paul, Christ" (1 Cor 1:12). He intervenes to restrain wealthier members from trying to gain advantage over others by bringing legal action against poorer members in pagan courts (1 Cor 6:1–11). He arbitrates conflicts concerning marriage, reminding them that God has called them to peace (1 Cor 7:15). He cautions the ones with knowledge to be considerate of scruples of the weak regarding anything associated with idols (1 Cor 8:1–13). He rebukes the entire congregation for celebrating a Lord's Supper that leaves poor members humiliated and hungry (1 Cor 11:17–34). In 2 Corinthians he insists that they forgive the offender who has repented (2:5–11), and the entire letter seeks to bring reconciliation between himself and the church. Clearly, reconciliation does not entail glossing over sin or ignoring it for the sake of maintaining harmony. Paul confronts it directly and forcefully, so forcefully in the letter of tears that it temporarily deepened the breach in his relationship with the Corinthians and prompted this letter to mend any hurt feelings. But Paul knows that there can be no real reconciliation without an acknowledgment of sinful behavior and repentance for it.

5:19 The phrase *hōs hoti,* which the NIV renders "that," has suggested to some that Paul draws on a traditional formulation used in the church's worship.[800] The *hōs* ("as") makes a transition and the *hoti* introduces a quotation: "As it is said." It is strange, however, that Paul would quote a supposed tradition that does not surface elsewhere in the New Testament, since the image of reconciliation is uniquely Pauline. Marshall draws the more reasonable conclusion that Paul is using language that he has previously formulated as part of his preaching.[801] If this is correct, the phrase could be

---

[800] E. Käsemann argues that it introduces a pre-Pauline hymnic fragment that Paul quotes here ("Some Thoughts on the Theme 'The Doctrine of Reconciliation' in the New Testament," in *The Future of Our Religious Past,* ed. J. M. Robinson [New York: Harper & Row, 1971] 52–57). He bases this conclusion on (1) the introductory formula; (2) the imperfect periphrastic, which is rare in Paul; (3) the plural of the noun "trespasses" rather than Paul's more frequent singular; (4) the third person pronouns "their" and "them" as opposed to the first person "us" in 5:18–19; and (5) the present participle, "not charging," as opposed to the aorist (has reconciled, has given). Furnish translates it "as it is said" (*II Corinthians,* 317). Martin takes it in a recitative sense, introducing a quotation (*2 Corinthians,* 153). Trying to guess the wording of the hypothetical original and how Paul may have altered it (as Martin does, 140–45) is, in my opinion, a less than productive exercise. Thrall thoroughly critiques these views and rejects the theory that Paul cites a tradition (*Second Epistle to the Corinthians,* 1:445–49).

[801] Marshall, "The Meaning of 'Reconciliation,'" 129–30.

translated "as you should know" or "it is a well known," for what follows is not new to the Corinthians.[802] On the other hand, what follows reiterates and clarifies what Paul has just written in 5:18. Therefore it may be better to translate *hōs hoti,* "that is."[803] It explains that "God is bringing the world back into forgiven relationship with himself, and he is doing this by means of a 'word' entrusted to the apostles."[804]

The NIV translation also alters the literal word order in the Greek that reads, "God was in Christ the world reconciling to himself." This phrase can be construed so that it emphasizes the incarnation: "God was in Christ, reconciling the world to himself" (KJV, REB). But Paul's theological agenda here does not center on affirming the incarnation. The same may be said of translating the phrase as a predicate nominative: "It was God who in Christ was reconciling the world to himself." The option chosen by the NIV to render the phrase as an imperfect periphrastic is the most likely: "In Christ God was reconciling the world to himself." The "in Christ" has an instrumental force—through Christ. Paul explains what God intended to accomplish by Christ's death and resurrection. The imperfect tenses convey the idea of incomplete action, but it is incomplete only in the sense that God's act of reconciliation requires a human response.[805] As Beck rightly comments, "There is no reconciliation when one side is willing to put the past behind them and the other side merely takes advantage of it."[806] He notes that reconciliation requires both sides to acknowledge the wrong, and for the injured party to let go of the pain. God has confronted us with our transgressions but has taken the initiative in Christ to resolve the problem they have created. God has let go of the pain of our wilful rebellion and does not count our trespasses against us. But it remains for us to accept that we have done wrong, to repent of it, and to accept God's offer of friendship. Not all will do so; some will defiantly continue to snub God.

It is more likely that "the world" refers to humankind in this context rather than to the whole created order (see Col 1:20,22).[807] It picks up the "all" from 5:14–15 and points to the references "to their trespasses" and "against them."[808] Since the object of God's reconciliation is not limited to "us" but also includes "the world," we who have responded to God's work

---

[802] Lambrecht, "'Reconcile Yourselves,'" 184.

[803] Another option is to take the phrase ὡς ὅτι to mean "because," and what follows provides the explanation for what is said in 5:18.

[804] Barnett, *The Second Epistle to the Corinthians,* 306.

[805] Why the switch to the imperfect from the aorist in 5:18? The imperfect implies that the action has not been completed. Thrall calls it "a 'disguised aorist,' employed for reasons of style and rhythm" (*Second Epistle to the Corinthians,* 1:434).

[806] Beck, "Reflections on 2 Corinthians 5:11–6:2," 88.

[807] In Rom 11:15, "For if their rejection is the reconciliation of the world, what will their acceptance be but life from the dead?" Here the world means "the Gentiles" (11:12).

may not look down on "the world." At one time we too were very much part of that world and needed reconciliation to God no less (see 1 Cor 6:9–11).

God's act of reconciliation is summed up in his canceling the debt of sin (see Col 2:13–14). The word translated "sins" by the NIV is "transgressions" *(paraptomata)*. Transgressions are not simply sins that one commits in ignorance. Transgression is deliberate sin, doing what we know to be disobedience to God. This defiant mutiny is far more serious and created what seemed to be an unbridgeable gulf between us and God. But God wiped clean the register of transgressions through Christ's death. The files containing the records of our shortcomings and offenses have been deleted. Thrall comments that "disregard of human sinfulness would be an expression not of love but of transcendent indifference. What has changed, then, is not God's fundamental disposition toward mankind, but rather his means of dealing with sinfulness which has caused the state of estrangement."[809]

Paul's assertion, "and he has committed *[themenos]* to us the message of reconciliation," may echo Ps 104:27 (LXX = Ps 105:27), which claims God placed in Moses and Aaron the words and the signs they performed.[810] This scriptural echo seems likely since Paul has already compared himself to Moses in chap. 3. But Hofius claims that Paul refers instead to God directly accomplishing his word rather than instructing his apostles what to say. He cites Ps 77:5 (LXX = 78:5 MT) as a better parallel that emphasizes (1) the accomplishment of the word by God himself; (2) the covenant instruction that the word be published in Israel; and (3) obedience by the proclamation of the word.[811] This pattern matches the context in 5:18–20: (1) the accomplishment of the word of reconciliation (5:19); (2) entrusting the apostle with the ministry of preaching reconciliation (5:18); and (3) the working out of this ministry in proclamation (5:20).[812] This latter half of the verse is a crucial part of Paul's defense. The apostles' proclamation is all part of God's reconciling activity. The apostles proclaim this reconciliation in both word and behavior. They go where alienation is most evident, resentments most inflamed, and wounds most festering, which inevitably leads to suffering.

God did not deputize Paul to make people feel good about themselves and their relationship to God but to effect a real peace. This task means that

---

[808] Barnett, *The Second Epistle to the Corinthians,* 307. Barrett, however, claims that the lack of a definite article preceding the noun κόσμος ("world") emphasizes "the nature rather than the particularity of the object of the verb—it is a whole world he reconciled—including perhaps the rebellious heavenly powers of Col i 19f." (*The Second Epistle to the Corinthians,* 177).

[809] Thrall, *Second Epistle to the Corinthians,* 1: 431.

[810] Ps 104:27: ἔθετο ἐν αὐτοῖς τοὺς λόγους τῶν σημείων καὶ τῶν τεράτων ἐν γῇ Χαμ.

[811] Ps 77:5: καὶ ἀνέστησεν μαρτύριον ἐν Ιακωβ καὶ νόμον ἔθετο ἐν Ισραηλ ὅσα ἐνετείλατο τοῖς πατράσιν ἡμῶν τοῦ γνωρίσαι αὐτὰ τοῖς υἱοῖς αὐτῶν.

[812] O. Hofius, "Gott has unter uns aufgericht das Wort von der Versöhnung" (2 Kor 5:19)," *ZNW* 71 (1980) 11–13.

he must always point to something beyond himself, not to himself, to what God has done in Christ, not what he is doing for Christ.

5:20 Paul identifies himself as an ambassador of Christ. Our modern perception of an ambassador as an official of the highest rank chosen and certified by a government to represent it before another helps us appreciate the magnitude of Paul's claim. He is Christ's spokesman. He does not act on his own authority but under the commission of a greater power and authority who sent him. Paul therefore understands himself to be divinely authorized to announce to the world God's terms for peace.[813]

Comparing the way ambassadors normally functioned in the ancient world points up some rather noteworthy differences about Paul's commission. First, in ancient times ambassadors were considered to be inviolate and were never to be imprisoned. There were cases where ambassadors were scorned, mistreated, or assaulted; but this kind of mistreatment was condemned as a breach of a universally accepted custom, which Livy refers to as the "law of the nations regarding envoys."[814] Such abuse met with swift retribution if the ambassadors represented a greater power. By contrast, being Christ's ambassador has not given Paul a sacrosanct status in the eyes of this world nor any diplomatic immunity. He is an ambassador in chains (Eph 6:20), incarcerated, beaten, and dishonored (2 Cor 6:4–10). While other ambassadors might wear gold chains and pendants as tokens of the wealth and power of those they represented, the insignia of Paul's embassy is his chains. The chains are not something to be ashamed of (2 Tim 1:16) but the appropriate credentials for an envoy of Jesus Christ who was himself put to death by worldly powers.[815] God will not be trifled with, however, nor will God allow Christ's ambassadors to be abused without penalty.

Second, the surviving documents and inscriptions that provide us with some record of ancient diplomacy make it quite clear that envoys were

---

[813] This reference to being Christ's ambassador implies Paul's independence from the Corinthians. C. Forbes points out that an ambassador's position "is guaranteed by his sender, not those to whom he is sent" ("Comparison, Self-Praise and Irony: Paul's Boasting and the Conventions of Hellenistic Rhetoric," *NTS* 32 [1986] 14).

[814] Livy, *Histories* XXX.25; see also Caesar, *Gallic Wars* III.9. Perlman observes: "In every case envoys were protected and given safe exit even in times of war; however, the inviolability of envoys was less observed in Greece (although heralds were sacrosanct) than in Hellenistic world and in Rome, where failure to observe it was regarded to be transgression of the law of nations. Refusal to receive Roman envoys was regarded by the senate as *casus belli* and a similar refusal by the Roman Senate was an indication of hostile intentions" ("Interstate Relations," 672).

[815] Jesus instructed his disciples, "A student is not above his teacher, nor a servant above his master. It is enough for the student to be like his teacher, and the servant like his master. If the head of the house has been called Beelzebub, how much more the members of his household!" (Matt 10:24–25).

usually sent to others as a sign of friendship and good will, to establish a relationship, to renew friendly relations, or to make an alliance. Their purpose was to renew or establish "goodwill," "friendship," and "alliances."[816] God's purpose in sending Christ and his envoys has the same end—to put an end to hostilities and to bring about a reconciliation. God sends out envoys to continue to announce that now is the day of salvation and reconciliation.

Third, in the era when Paul writes, various cities and provinces usually sent their ambassadors to Rome to plead their cases before the emperor or to offer tribute to gain some imperial favor. Philo describes participating in such a delegation to the emperor Gaius (Caligula) to make an appeal on behalf of Alexandrian Jews who were suffering brutal persecution at the hands of their fellow citizens.[817] The Roman emperor, who sent out decrees effecting everyone in the world (Luke 2:1), did not send ambassadors to a city or province to negotiate (as in *2 Macc* 11:34–38). Instead, he sent governors to rule those who were already subjected or armies to crush any resistance. Consequently, ambassadors from these conquered realms streamed to Rome.[818] Augustus boasts of all the ambassadors who came to him from the remote fringes of the empire and beyond:

Royal embassies from India, never previously seen before any Roman general, were often sent to me. Our friendship was sought through ambassadors by the Bastarnians and Scythians and by the kings of the Sarmatians, who live on both sides of the Don river, and by the kings of the Albanians and of the Iberians and of the Medes.[819]

From this boast, we can see a notable contrast between God and the emperor Augustus. An all-powerful God does not wait for humanity to make their appeals to him but sends out ambassadors to make appeals to humanity.

A fourth point has to do with those who were chosen as ambassadors in the ancient world. Our picture of ambassadors as career diplomats residing in foreign embassies does not fit the situation in the first century. Those selected to go on embassies were drawn from the ranks of the distinguished families in their homeland. For some, the opportunity to go as an envoy had the honor of community recognition attached to it, and

---

[816] See R. K. Sherk, *Rome and the Greek East to the Death of Augustus* (Cambridge: University Press, 1984).

[817] Philo, *Embassy to Gaius.*

[818] Plutarch indirectly testifies to the great number of embassies that descended on Rome in explaining why these ambassadors proceeded first to the temple of Saturn to register with the prefect of the treasury there. He noted that in the past the officials of this temple used to care for foreign ambassadors if they got sick and would bury them if they died. He goes on to say that the large volume of embassies had now made it too expensive to continue the practice, but the ambassadors continued the tradition of visiting that temple (*The Roman Questions* 43).

[819] *The Accomplishments of Augustus, Res Gestae Divi Augusti* 31.

many received commendations.[820] For others, going on an embassy was considered to be one of the burdens of being part of the ruling elite. Many did not welcome the prospect of having to leave one's home for a prolonged period of time or having to undergo the long and strenuous journey to wherever they might have to go, usually to Rome. When one finally arrived, one had to wait for an undetermined period for the emperor to grant the embassy an audience when an envoy would deliver an oration in hopes of gaining a favorable opinion. The fright that was attached to this appearance before the emperor and his officials is expressed in the following account from the time of Constantine:

> Nor is it any small matter to make a request on one's own behalf to the emperor of the whole world, to put on a brave face before the eyes of such majesty, to compose one's expression, to summon up one's courage, to choose the right words, to speak without fear, to stop at the right moment and to await the reply.[821]

Many times social pressure was brought to bear on the ambassadors to undertake the journey at their own expense. This is why Plutarch says that an exile should choose for himself the best spot that he can in which to live. Choose a native land "that does not distract you, is not importunate, does not command: 'pay a special levy,' 'go on an embassy to Rome,' 'entertain the governor,' 'undertake a public service at your own expense.'"[822] By contrast Paul does not consider being an ambassador of Christ an onerous task but an enormous privilege to become part of God's saving enterprise in the world. He does not worry that he must pay his own way. He does not complain because he had been imprisoned so many times, suffered countless beatings, and had endured stonings, shipwrecks, and deadly dangers from his countless journeys. He did not travel first class but frequently wound up hungry, thirsty, and exposed to the cold (2 Cor 11:23–28). He did not endure these things for personal glory or reward but because God shone in his heart and gave him the light of the knowledge of the glory of God in the face of Christ (2 Cor 4:6). He simply could not stay home and keep silent (1 Cor 9:16). He committed himself to this ministry for the sake of the gospel (1 Cor 9:23)

---

[820] A stele from Lete in Macedonia (119 B.C.) honors M. Annius for putting the duty to his city above everything else in serving as an envoy (Sherk, *Rome and the Greek East,* # 48).

[821] *Panegyrici Latini* VIII (5) 9, 3, cited by F. Millar, *The Emperor in the Roman World (31 BC–AD 337)* (Ithaca: Cornell University Press, 1977) 385. Rivals were known to attempt to take advantage of the ambassador's absence from home and to initiate legal proceedings against him. See Cicero, *Against Verres,* II.xliv.109. Traveling expenses were usually allocated for the embassy, but sometimes they were not. Cicero presents the case of ambassadors from Rhodes to Athens who were not given money for their traveling expenses and who refused to set out (*De Inventione* II.xxix.87).

[822] Plutarch, *On Exile,* 602 C.

and for sake of the one who loved him and gave himself for him (Gal 2:20). What is awesome for Paul is not that he is granted an audience before the majesty of any earthly kings but that he speaks the word of God.

An ambassador makes the case for the one who sent him. He proclaims, appeals, entreats (5:20), and urges (6:1). Paul, however, implies that he does not simply speak as God's representative but that the living Lord speaks directly through him. This statement might be misinterpreted to mean that the word of God is whatever the apostles may preach and opens the door to false apostles who will unscrupulously manipulate the gullible for their own ends. True apostles have been instructed by God, and Paul will address the issue of true and false apostles and how to tell the difference in chaps. 10–13. Here he wants to make the point that God's word dictates the apostle's word, not vice versa. The implication is barbed. If the Corinthians fail to heed Paul's remonstrations with them, they turn their backs not just on their apostle but on God. This insinuation is the key issue in this section. Paul was not just venting his spleen in his painful and frank letter to them; God was making an appeal to them through Paul to be reconciled. Paul's statement that God makes his appeal through us still holds true two millennia after he penned these words to the Corinthians, and his words remain forceful and convincing and can be ignored only at great peril.

Paul climaxes his theological discussion by suddenly imploring the Corinthians to be reconciled to God. Gloer reads the implication of this appeal correctly; Paul is summoning the Corinthians, not unbelievers. "While this is, indeed, the 'universal missionary entreaty' of the church to the world, in this context it is addressed to the Corinthian Christians who are alienated from Paul and highlights the continual claim of the new way of living in Christ."[823] Why does Paul implore those who are already Christians to be reconciled to God? They had already accepted the gospel message. Calvin explains it that we sin every day, therefore we must be reconciled every day. But the aorist tense would not be suited to refer to something that must be repeated every day.[824] Barrett's comments are more apt:

> Reconciliation is an act of God's grace, carried out on the cross and offered freely to men. It is for them to receive it, but it may be received more or less effectively [just as] Paul claimed that he had labored more abundantly than oth-

---

[823] Gloer, "2 Corinthians 5:14–21," 403. Kruse comments that it may well "reflect language of his evangelistic preaching, but here the appeal is directed to members of the Corinthian church" (*2 Corinthians,* 128). S. E. Porter argues that it makes better sense of the grammar and discourse structure as an appeal to the "unreconciled." God has rendered the hearers reconciled and Paul calls upon them "to become ministers with a message of reconciliation" ("Reconciliation and 2 Cor 5,18–21," in *The Corinthian Correspondence,* ed. R. Bieringer, BETL 125 (Leuven: University Press, 1996] 702–4).

[824] Calvin, *The Second Epistle of Paul the Apostle to the Corinthians,* 80.

ers. The Corinthians had indeed been reconciled to God, but it was for them to receive the reconciliation more effectively.[825]

The fundamental problem behind the Corinthians' misunderstanding of Paul and their discord is that they are not fully reconciled to God.[826] It explains why the values of the pagan society encircling them continue to make inroads and interfere with their obedience to God and why they are so easily beguiled by false apostles. Paul tells them to be reconciled to God because they have fallen short because of their bickering, sinful lifestyles, and participation with idols, all of which necessitate his frank reproof.[827] Paul has made known his eagerness to be reconciled with the Corinthians and the provocateur who abused him (2:5–11), and later in the letter he rejoices at their repentance (7:12). But he will not retract his bold criticism that caused some of the hard feelings just to win them back and settle for an uncertain peace. The breach was caused by serious transgressions, and it is not enough for each of them to let bygones be bygones. He wants to purge them of all animosity and misgivings toward him so that he can then build on the reconciliation and strengthen the bonds between them. Hence the renewed plea to be reconciled to God.

The verb "be reconciled" *(katallagēte)* is in the passive voice and may reflect a divine passive: "Be reconciled to God by God." The reconciliation is something they receive from God.[828] But some active response is required. The passive form of the verb occurs in 1 Cor 7:11, where Paul expects the estranged marriage partner to effect a reconciliation, not simply receive it (see Matt 5:24). The imperative mood also expects those commanded to make some kind of active response. God's action to bring about reconciliation therefore requires our response before reconciliation can become a reality. That response requires the following elements.

1. Reconciliation obliges us to come to terms with the alienation and our responsibility for it. We must recognize our culpability for the ruptured relationship.

2. The key phrase in the call to be reconciled is "to God." Humans may attempt to reconcile with one another, but if they are not also reconciled to God there will be no real reconciliation. Reconciliation obliges us to reorder our lives around God. Our changed orientation, when we no longer live to ourselves, will spill over into all our relationships with others. Continuing to harbor enmity toward others belies any claim to be reconciled to God.

---

[825] Quoted from the discussion of Lambrecht's paper, "Reconcile Yourselves," 411.

[826] Ibid., 391.

[827] Martin comments, "The plea is a renewed call to them to leave their hostile dispositions and suspicions of both his message and his ministry and accept his proffered reconciliation, already given to the ringleader (2:5–11; 7:12)" (*2 Corinthians,* 137).

[828] Barnett, *2 Corinthians,* 311.

3. Reconciliation requires that we jettison all worldly criteria for evaluating others. We must look at others from God's vantage point.

4. Those who are reconciled to God are reconciling.[829] Mead protests the history of the Western church from A.D. 400–1900:

> The faith of the church was regarded as a deposit of doctrines expressing historical, objective acts of God. The doctrines could be, and were stated in a creed. The business of the church toward men was to bring them into a believing connection with the doctrines. Thus, there were three separable things: what God has done, doctrines expressing it, and the church's function as an instrument to apply "it" to men."[830]

Paul is not interested in the *abstract doctrine* of reconciliation but in the *concrete task* of reconciliation. The church not only is to preserve sound doctrine but is called by God to be, as apostles were, a reconciling force. That means it must adopt the status of a servant and must be active in a ministry of helping and healing.

5:21 This verse explains how God did not count the trespasses against us (5:19) and made possible our reconciliation. From the time of Ambrosiaster and Augustine, interpreters have argued that Paul means that Christ became a "sin offering."[831] This view fits nicely with Isa 53:10, which expresses the Lord's will "to crush him and cause him to suffer," and to make "his life a guilt offering." The word "sin" *(hamartia)* is sometimes used for sin-offering *(hatta°t)* in the LXX.[832] And Paul depicts Christ's death as a kind of cultic sacrifice in Rom 3:25 and 1 Cor 5:7 (see Rom 8:3). There are problems with this view, however. The word *hamartia* does not have the meaning "sin offering" elsewhere in the New Testament, and if Paul intends that meaning here, then he uses the word with two quite different meanings in the same sentence. In the first instance he states that Christ did not know sin, and there is no indication that he intended a quite different meaning for the word *sin* in the second instance. If Paul had intended to use the noun in the quite different sense of "sin offering," it would have been more fitting to use the verb "presented" or "offered" rather than "made." "Sin" also contrasts with "righteousness," and interpreting the word as "sin offering" destroys the parallel structure of the sentence:

Christ who knew no sin
God made him sin

[829] C. B. Cousar, "II Corinthians 5:17–21," *Int* 35 (1981) 183.

[830] R. T. Mead, "Exegesis of 2 Corinthians 5:14–21," in *Interpreting 2 Corinthians 5:14–21: An Exercise in Hermeneutics,* ed. J. P. Lewis, SBEC 17 (Lewiston/Queenston/Lampeter: Mellen, 1989) 161.

[831] For a history of the interpretation of this verse see S. Lyonnet and L. Sabourin, *Sin, Redemption, and Sacrifice: A Biblical and Patristic Study,* AB 48 (Rome: Biblical Institute, 1971) 185–296.

[832] See Lev 4:8,20,21,24,25,29,32; 5:9,12; 6:17,25; 8:2,14; Hos 4:8; Num 6:14.

We [who are sinners]
Become the righteousness of God

Paul therefore intends to say that Christ is made a sinner. The New Testament, however, proclaims that Christ was without sin (John 8:46; 14:30; Heb 4:15; 1 Pet 2:22; 1 John 3:5). By metonymy, using an abstract term in place of a more concrete term and by saying it was "for us," he protects Christ's sinlessness.[833] Galatians 3:13 offers an important parallel. Paul asserts that Christ became a curse in order that blessing might come to others. This statement matches what he says here: Christ became sin in order that others might become the righteousness of God. Paul is not focusing on Jesus' human life but on his inglorious death. Christ experienced the consequences for human sin. The one who lived a sinless life died a sinner's death, estranged from God and the object of wrath. He was treated as a sinner in his death.[834]

The next question is whether Paul's sees this death as representative ("in behalf of us," "for our benefit") or substitutionary ("in our place"). Hooker argues for the representative position: "It is as man's *representative, rather than as his substitute, that Christ suffers, and it is only as one who is fully human that he is able to do anything effective for mankind, by lifting man, as it were, into an obedient relationship with God."[835] But there is widespread evidence for the use of the preposition *hyper* in a substitutionary sense to mean "instead of another" or "in the place of another."[836] McLean argues that "Christ does not become human in order to stand in solidarity with humanity but to stand in its place and to participate in a twofold imputation: he receives the burden of humanity's sin while humanity receives God's righteousness."[837] He makes the case that the substitutionary idea fits widespread apotropaeic rituals in the Mediterranean in which the victim functions in a substitutionary role by taking the place of the threatened community and assuming this burden. McLean concludes:

> Christ becomes a transgressor through an act of substitution. Paul is not satisfied with noetic processes: it is not enough for God to reckon humanity to be righteous, nor is a new self-understanding among Christians sufficient. A real

---

[833] Lambrecht, "Reconcile Yourselves," 388.

[834] Windisch sees an allusion to the scapegoat (Lev 16:21) on the Day of Atonement (*Der zweite Korintherbrief,* 198).

[835] M. D. Hooker, "Interchange in Christ," *JTS* 22 (1971) 358.

[836] See Isa 43:3–4 LXX ("in exchange for you"); John 11:50; *1 Clem* 5:1, "his flesh in the place of our flesh"; and *Diogn.* 9.2, 5, where the preposition ὑπέρ with the genitive occurs six times and concludes with "oh what a sweet exchange" (ἀνταλλαγή).

[837] B. H. McLean, *The Cursed Christ: Mediterranean Expulsion Rituals and Pauline Soteriology,* JSNTSup 126 (Sheffield: Academic Press, 1996) 112.

transfer of sin and curse to Christ was essential. Christ must truly become polluted.

... A real death was necessary to put real distance between saved Christians and the power of sin.[838]

God provided Jesus to stand in for sinful humanity. Even though Jesus was sinless, God deals with him as though he were a sinner by letting him die an accursed death. In the Jewish cult the animal offered up to atone for sins "had to be holy, without defect, precisely so that both priest and offerer could be confident that the death it died was *not its own.*"[839] The result of this transaction is that "we might become the righteousness of God." We do not simply have righteousness from God, we are the righteousness of God as a result of being in Christ (see 1 Cor 1:30; 6:11). We are given his righteousness only as we are in him, and will be raised like him only if we live in him.[840]

(7) Paul's Commendation as a Minister of God (6:1–10)

[1]As God's fellow workers we urge you not to receive God's grace in vain. [2]For he says,

"In the time of my favor I heard you,
    and in the day of salvation I helped you."

I tell you, now is the time of God's favor, now is the day of salvation.

[3]We put no stumbling block in anyone's path, so that our ministry will not be discredited. [4]Rather, as servants of God we commend ourselves in every way: in great endurance; in troubles, hardships and distresses; [5]in beatings, imprisonments and riots; in hard work, sleepless nights and hunger; [6]in purity, understanding, patience and kindness; in the Holy Spirit and in sincere love; [7]in truthful speech and in the power of God; with weapons of righteousness in the right hand and in the left; [8]through glory and dishonor, bad report and good report; genuine, yet regarded as impostors; [9]known, yet regarded as unknown; dying, and yet we live on; beaten, and yet not killed; [10]sorrowful, yet always rejoicing; poor, yet making many rich; having nothing, and yet possessing everything.

The NIV puts the paragraph break with a new heading at 6:3 instead of 6:1 (so also REB, NRSV). The participles in 6:3–4 (*didontes* and *syni-*

---

[838] Ibid., 144. Thrall concurs with this view: "Christ became identified with sinful humanity, exchanging the situation proper to his own sinlessness for the condition consequent upon human sin. In this second half the second element is described. Through their relationship with Christ, men and women may exchange their sinful condition for the state designated 'God's righteousness'" (*Second Epistle to the Corinthians*, 1:442).

[839] Dunn, *The Theology of Paul the Apostle*, 221.

[840] In Rom 5:1–11 Paul starts with justification and ends with reconciliation. Here he begins with reconciliation and ends with justification.

stantes) could be independent of the main verb in 6:1 and used instead of a
finite verb (see Rom 5:11), and the NIV chooses to render them as finite
verbs, "we put" and "we commend." The verb *(parakaloumen)* in 6:1, translated "urge," is the same verb in 5:20 *(parakalountos)* and translated
"implore." Using the same verb ties 5:20 and 6:1 together, and the quotation
from Isaiah in 6:2 explains the urgency behind Paul's appeal. The chapter
break therefore may be inappropriate here, but 6:1–2 does form a bridge to
what follows in 6:3–10. These verses take up what precedes by summarizing
it and prepare for what follows.[841] In the commentary we will treat 6:1–2
with 6:3–10.

In 6:3–10 Paul presents the case why the Corinthians should honor both
him and his appeals, and it fits the following structure:[842]

6:3a Declaration: "We put no stumbling block in anyone's path"
6:3b Reason: "so that our ministry will not be discredited"
6:4a Declaration: "as servants of God we commend ourselves in every
way"
6:4b–10 a compendium of what is commendable about his ministry
The resumé of his ministry (6:4b–10) falls into the following pattern:
6:4c–5 nine hardships prefaced by the preposition *en* and introduced by
"in great endurance" (the only noun in the list modified by an
adjective)[843]
6:6–7b eight qualities of his ministry prefaced by the preposition *en*
("in")[844]
6:7c–8b three combinations introduced by *dia* (translated as "with," and
"through")
6:8c–10 seven pairs of antitheses introduced by *hōs* ("as")

6:1 "As God's fellow workers" is a bold statement that translates one
word in Greek "working together" *(synergountes)*. The verb has no object,
but most translations assume that it refers to working together with God.
Paul could be referring to his human coworkers; but since this phrase follows 5:20, where he asserts that God gave him a ministry of reconciliation
and that God makes his appeal through him, he surely has in mind working
with God.[845] This statement reminds them of his divine commission and

---

[841] Lambrecht, "'Reconcile Yourselves,'" 403.
[842] Obviously, the traditional verse divisions are less than helpful here.
[843] One word, "troubles," is common to the first list of hardships in 4:8–12; five words, "beatings," "imprisonments," "hard work," "sleepless nights," "hunger," are common to the third list in
11:23–28.
[844] Furnish notes the last term, "in the power of God," provides an apt conclusion and summary
(*II Corinthians,* 355).
[845] Paul identifies Timothy as God's coworker in 1 Thess 3:2. Paul also refers to Apollos and
himself as God's coworkers (NIV, "God's fellow workers") in 1 Cor 3:9, although Furnish understands the term to mean "coworkers for God" (*II Corinthians,* 341).

authority while also asserting that what he does is God's work, not his. Working together with God means that he sets out to accomplish God's objectives, not his own. In the context that objective concerns reconciliation. God sent Christ as his agent to make reconciliation possible. God uses ambassadors like Paul to continue that agenda—to call people to be reconciled to God, to make known that God does not count their sins against them and that God loves them and yearns for them to repent.

Yet Paul directs his call for reconciliation specifically to the Corinthians (5:20), and he implores them not to receive God's grace in vain *(eis kenon)*.[846] The grace refers to God's reconciling work in Christ. Paul apparently took this warning to heart himself. He wrote to the Corinthians about his call to be an apostle: "But by the grace of God I am what I am, and his grace to me was not without effect *[kenē]*. No, I worked harder than all of them—yet not I, but the grace of God that was with me" (1 Cor 15:10). He assumes that they have received God's grace, but what would make it all for nothing? Lapide cites Anselm: "He receives grace into a vacuum … who does not work with it, who does not give it his heart, and who, through sloth, makes that grace ineffectual, by not doing all that he can to express it in good works."[847] This interpretation makes this statement an applicable warning to all Christians, but Paul has something more specific in view for the Corinthians than allowing God's grace to produce fruit in their Christian life. The admonition that follows in 6:14–7:1 suggests that their continuing association with idols would cause their faith to founder on the rocks.[848]

6:2 Paul explains the gravity of the situation with a verbatim quotation from Isa 49:8 (quoting the LXX, not the Hebrew text). The acceptable time ("the time of my favor") is when God mercifully answered prayer and acted for Israel's salvation. Paul then provides a commentary on what this passage means now. It refers to something even greater than the return from exile in Babylon. The "now" refers to the eschatological change of the ages inaugurated by Christ's death (see Rom 3:21,26; 5:9,11; 6:22; 7:6; 8:1). The day of salvation applies to the deliverance from sin's captivity through Jesus' cross and resurrection. The acceptable time ("the time of God's favor," NIV) refers to God's timetable that completely ignores what is acceptable or timely to humans. The implication would be clear to those in Paul's age who were familiar with the ancient cliché "to seize the day." To become acceptable to God, one must accept God's offer of reconciliation. Yet hearing the promise is no guarantee that the promise will be received. They must obey as long as it is still called "Today" (Heb 3:13).

---

[846] This is the only finite verb in this section (vv. 1–10, aside from the parenthesis in v. 2).

[847] Lapide, *The Great Commentary of Cornelius à Lapide,* 84.

[848] See further J. Gundry-Volf, *Paul and Perseverance: Staying in and Falling Away,* WUNT 2/37 (Tübingen: Mohr [Siebeck]) 277–80.

Plummer suggests that Paul may have turned to this passage in Isaiah because Isaiah's case resembled his own. In the Isaian context (Isa 49:1–6), the prophet presents his credentials. The Lord formed him from his mother's womb to be his servant, to reconcile Israel to be a light to the nations, so that God's salvation may reach to the end of the earth (see Gal 1:15). But when the prophet delivered his message, he met with a less than enthusiastic response from the people. He expresses his bitter disappointment, "I have labored in vain" (49:4), while also expressing his confidence that his cause is with the Lord: "For I am honored in the eyes of the LORD and my God has been my strength" (Isa 49:5). Plummer writes, "Although men despise him, God will honour him by confirming his message; and the God who has had compassion on Israel in spite of their sins, will have compassion on all the nations. ... Word for word this is true of the Apostle."[849] Danker thinks that Paul understands himself to be like the servant in Isaiah who invites "Israel to share in the benefits of the new age and at the same time proclaims the grace of God to the Gentiles."[850] As God raised up Isaiah to speak through him and call the people out of Babylon, so God has raised up Paul as a mouthpiece to comfort and admonish the Corinthians.[851]

6:3 Paul now moves on to present what is commendable about his ministry. He commends himself by his purity of motives and the evident power of God that has sustained him through all his trials and afflictions. His deeds match his words.[852] He is quite different from the Cynics who gathered crowds on street corners, alley ways, and temple gates. Their contemporaries generally regarded them as "foul-smelling frauds."[853] Dio Chrysostom

---

[849] Plummer, *The Second Epistle of St. Paul to the Corinthians,* 190–91; see also J. Lambrecht, "The Favorable Time: A Study of 2 Corinthians 6,2a in its Context," in *Studies on 2 Corinthians,* ed J. Lambrecht and R. Bieringer, BETL 112 (Leuven: University Press, 1994) 524.

[850] Danker, *II Corinthians,* 85.

[851] A. T. Hanson argues that Paul applies the citation to Christians as well. He wishes to assure "the Corinthians that as they share in the sufferings of Christ so they are also to share in his vindication" (*The Paradox of the Cross in the Thought of St. Paul,* JSNTSup 17 [Sheffield: JSOT, 1987] 56). But the purpose of the passage seems more defense of Paul than assurance for the Corinthians.

[852] Danker argues that in what follows Paul translates the Jewish servant figure from Isaiah into terms that a Greco-Roman audience would understand and appreciate (*II Corinthians,* 91). He provides a convenient summary of principle Roman virtues celebrated by philosophers: "ability to endure suffering *(patientia);* justice *(iustitia);* fidelity to a trust *(fides);* steadfastness of purpose *(constantia);* wisdom and deliberation in action *(concilium);* simplicity of living *(frugalitas);* unflinching performance in the face of difficulties and hazards *(fortitudo);* reverence for deity and authority figures *(pietas);* morality *(castitas)* especially honoring marriage. The Greeks emphasized uprightness *(dikaiosyne);* self-control *(sōphrosynē);* endurance *(hypomonē);* and courage *(andreia)* (89).

[853] S. K. Stowers, "Social Status, Public Speaking and Private Teaching: The Circumstances of Paul's Preaching Activity," *NovT* 26 (1984) 62, citing Seneca, *Epistles* 5.1; 29:1; Martial 4.5.3; and Dio Chrysostom, *Orations* 34.2; 32.9.

complained about their hit and run tactics:

> But to find a man who in plain terms and without guile speaks his mind with frankness *(parrēsiazomenon),* and neither for the sake of reputation *(doxēs)* nor for gain makes false pretensions, but out of good will and concern for his fellow-men stands ready, if need be, to submit to ridicule and to the disorder and the uproar of the mob—to find such a man as that is not easy, but rather the good fortune of a very lucky city, so great is the dearth of noble, independent souls and such the abundance of toadies [flatterers, *kolakōn*], mountebanks, and sophists.[854]

Paul lets the Corinthians know that he is just such a man whom God has enabled to hold up under every pressure. In listing his qualities he is trying indirectly to encourage them to emulate his cruciform life. His life and work are "a model and example of his message."[855]

Paul asserts that he has "put no stumbling block in anyone's path." This means that he does not do anything that would discredit his witness and turn others away from the gospel.[856] He implies that if they have accepted God's grace in vain, it is not because of anything he has done.

Paul expresses the purpose of his upright behavior: "so that our ministry will not be discredited."[857] The apostle is not concerned about his own personal reputation but the reputation of the ministry and its effectiveness (see Phil 1:15–18). The censure he dreads does not come from humans but from God (see 1 Cor 4:2–5). To be discredited before humans is one thing; to be discredited before God is quite another. People inevitably find fault with human ministers, and trying to avoid this by ministering "defensively," skirting around anything that might evoke possible criticism, will still meet with criticism. Worse, a ministry directed by what others might think is so neutralized that it is ultimately worthless to God.

6:4–5   We commend ourselves as ministers *(diakonoi,* "servants," NIV) of God should.[858] Paul's different statements about commending himself may be confusing, but he does not say here that we commend ourselves *to you* as he does in 5:12. He is talking about commending himself in general (see 4:2, "commending ourselves to every conscience"). He is saying to the Corinthians, this is the way I commend myself to others in the world; this is

---

[854] Dio Chrysostom, *Orations* 32.11.

[855] Ibid., 80.

[856] This "stumbling block" (προσκοπή) differs from the "scandal" (σκάνδαλον), which the gospel evokes because the gospel is inherently offensive. The stumbling block refers to some moral failure on the part of the preacher that would cause others to spurn the gospel. See also 1 Cor 8:13.

[857] The "our" is not present in some Greek texts, and Furnish argues for translating it "this ministry" (*II Corinthians,* 343).

[858] Furnish, *II Corinthians,* 343. "Ministers of God" is in the nominative, and so he cannot mean that we commend ourselves as ministers of God.

the way you should commend me to others (12:11). He may also be saying that this is what you as Christians should emulate to make sure that you do not receive God's grace in vain. God did not call them to be bystanders applauding the dedicated sacrificial service of God's servants. They are called to serve as well.

Paul's service for God brings much hardship. He has not landed a soft assignment as Christ's ambassador. A ministry of reconciliation requires that one must go to those who are unreconciled and impenitent, to claim those claimed by Satan, to march boldly into the dens of vice, ignorance, and deviltry. It is dangerous work, as Christ's crucifixion reveals. The demonic powers do not lie down weakly in submission when the gospel is preached. But they rise up and lash out viciously in a desperate attempt to prevent it from taking hold.

If the phrase "by much endurance" in 6:4 goes with the opening clause "we commend ourselves as servants of God with much endurance," then what follows illustrates what Paul endured.[859] Endurance is not one of the afflictions but a positive quality by which he commends himself. Afflictions in themselves do not commend anyone, but his great endurance of afflictions does (see Rom 5:3–4; 15:4; Col 1:11).[860] Some may regard his suffering as a disqualifying feature. From Paul's perspective, however, he would be disqualified if he attempted to evade suffering that comes from his apostolic service. Enduring it confirms that he is a servant of God and that God sustains him through it all. He therefore does not view his suffering as an apostle as a tedious detour; it is rather the main highway. It is not punishment for wrongdoing, but the suffering of one who is righteous.

A list of nine hardships follow that may be grouped into three sets of three under the categories of general suffering, suffering endured at the hands of others, and suffering endured by way of self-discipline.[861] The first group falls into the broad category of "troubles," a prevalent word in the letter (1:4,8; 2:4; 4:17; 7:4; 8:2,13); hardships ("calamities," see 1 Cor 7:26), and "distresses ("anguish," see 4:8; 12:10; Rom 8:35). The next set of three is more specific in which he is the object of mistreatment: beatings (see 11:23); imprisonments (11:23); and riots (mobbed in tumults; see Acts 13:50; 14:19; 16:19–20; 17:5–8,13; 19:23–20:1). The final set of three stems from his devotion to his missionary labor. The word translated "hard work" can suggest the toil that brings on exhaustion. In 1 Thess 2:9 he speaks of working night and day to support himself, which may explain his "sleepless

---

[859] The REB renders it: "As God's ministers, we try to recommend ourselves in all circumstances by our steadfast endurance: in affliction ..."

[860] Hafemann, *Suffering and Ministry in the Spirit,* 73–74.

[861] Bruce, *I and II Corinthians,* 212; Harris, "2 Corinthians," 357; and Barnett, *The Second Epistle to the Corinthians,* 326–27.

nights" (11:27). He used the night hours to work at his trade, or perhaps to preach and teach "because others, too, would be work-bound from dawn to dusk" (see Acts 20:7–12).[862] The word translated "hunger" is used elsewhere in the New Testament for fasting. It may refer to the times "he neglected to eat to give more time to his evangelistic task.[863] Or, it may mean that he went hungry (see 1 Cor 4:11 and 11:27) because he refused to accept support from others. The hardships reveal that he has received crushing blows that have not crushed him.

6:6–7b The list now changes from hardships to ethical qualities that characterize his ministry. "Purity" refers to his guiltless conduct (see 1 Thess 2:3). "Understanding" best translates the word for knowledge *(gnōsis)*. Moral integrity without knowledge can create almost as much havoc as a lack of integrity. Paul does not refer simply to intellectual knowledge but to the kind of knowledge that counts with God (11:6). It refers to the ability "to size up a situation and adopt appropriate measures."[864]

"Patience and kindness" refer to how he responds to all the abuse. Barnett, however, notes that "patience is reactive, kindness is proactive."[865] Paul does not strike back in anger when attacked (see 1 Cor 4:13, "when we are slandered, we answer kindly"; and his response to the offender in 2 Cor 2:5–10). Lapide tells an ancient story of missionaries to Japan who had made no progress until a man spat in the face of one of them and he simply wiped his face and continued preaching as if he had suffered nothing. They so admired this fortitude that they honored them as "men descended from heaven" and began to embrace the faith these men not only preached but lived.[866] But "patience and kindness" also apply to the way Paul deals with his congregations and to his frank criticism of them. One of Dio's complaints against the Cynics was that they were "sometimes brutally harsh rather than seeking to benefit their hearers."[867] Paul's kindness softens the rebuke that might momentarily sting so that they know it is for their own good.

---

[862] Furnish, *II Corinthians*, 355.

[863] Plummer, *The Second Epistle of St. Paul to the Corinthians*, 195. Hanson points out that to interpret it as voluntary fasting would make Paul out to be more like the Pharisee in Jesus' parable about the Pharisee and the tax collector who boasts of his fasting to God (*The Paradox of the Cross*, 64).

[864] Danker, *II Corinthians*, 91. Barrett points to the use of the word "knowledge" in 1 Pet 3:7 and thinks that it might mean "Christian insight and tact" (*The Second Epistle to the Corinthians*, 186).

[865] Barnett, *The Second Epistle to the Corinthians*, 328.

[866] Lapide, *The Great Commentary of Cornelius à Lapide*, 87.

[867] A. J. Malherbe, "'Gentle as a Nurse': The Cynic Background to 1 Thessalonians 2," in *Paul and the Popular Philosophers* (Minneapolis: Fortress, 1989) 45. Stowers reports that Epictetus worried that philosophers became impatient with novices and turned them away with harsh language ("Social Status, Public Speaking and Private Teaching," 69).

The presence of the phrase "in the Holy Spirit" is perhaps surprising in a list of ethical attributes. Consequently, some have thought that Paul means "with a holy spirit." Barrett comments: "Now it is certainly unlikely that Paul simply should throw in a reference to the Third Person of the Trinity in the midst of a series of human ethical qualities ('knowledge, patience, kindness, the Holy Spirit, love …'); and the evidence adduced from his usage elsewhere seems to give adequate support to the view that in this verse *spirit (pneuma)* means the human spirit, and that *holy* is a description of its ethical quality." Barrett appeals to 1 Cor 7:34, where Paul says "the unmarried woman is anxious about the things of the Lord "in order that she might be holy *(hagia)* both in body and spirit" (see also 7:1; 12:18).[868] The actual term "holy spirit" does not occur in this text, however, and "holy" normally refers to the Spirit (see Rom 5:5; 9:1; 14:17; 15:13,16; 1 Cor 12:3; 1 Thess 1:5–6; Titus 3:5). "Holy Spirit" is joined to the ethical qualities of peace and joy (Rom 14:17; 15:13). Knowledge (1 Cor 12:8), forbearance, kindness, love (Gal 5:22) are associated with the Spirit, and therefore it may not be as odd to include the Holy Spirit in this list as Barrett assumes. Paul is, after all, engaged in a ministry of the Spirit (3:6,8,17–18).

The following reference to the "power of God" reveals that he is thinking in terms of some divine force working in his life and ministry. The Spirit fosters these virtues, and "they are evidence of his indwelling presence."[869] Walking in the Spirit is the foremost requirement for effective ministry that will not be discredited before God and is a mandatory credential of ministerial character. It insures that ministry will be carried out in purity. The qualifications for apostleship are not to be sought in grand, external displays. If manifestations of the Spirit are genuine, there will be a visible effect on the internal character of the apostle.

"In sincere love" (see Rom 12:9) implies that others may feign love. Paul's frank but gentle criticism is one of the surest signs of his genuine love for them. "In truthful speech" may refer back to 1:17–20 and would be contrasted with flattery. He brings up his truthfulness again in 7:14.[870] In the context of 2 Corinthians, "truthful speech" refers to Paul's not mincing words when he needs to correct people for their sins. He does not flatter and

---

[868] Barrett, *The Second Epistle to the Corinthians,* 187. So also Plummer, who finds it "scarcely credible that St. Paul would place the Holy Spirit in a list of human virtues in a subordinate place, neither first to lead, nor last to sum up all the rest" (*The Second Epistle of St. Paul to the Corinthians,* 196).

[869] Bruce, *I and II Corinthians,* 212.

[870] The phrase "word of truth" may also be interpreted as a genitive of content, "by the word, which is truth," or as an objective genitive, "by the declaration of the truth" (REB; see 4:2; Gal 5:7; Eph 1:13; Col 1:5; 2 Tim 2:15). The latter would mean that he refers to God's truth rather than to his own truthfulness.

cajole but speaks the truth. Paul's freedom in Christ allows him to speak truthfully even if such speech may cause grief.

The final quality in the list is "in the power of God" (see 4:7, "the all-surpassing power is from God"; and Rom 1:16; 15:19; 1 Cor 1:18; 2:4–5; 1 Thess 1:5). Paul does not operate in his own strength but in the power of God, which brings salvation. He explains this more fully in 1 Cor 2:4–5: "My message and my preaching were not with wise and persuasive words, but with a demonstration of the Spirit's power, so that your faith might not rest on men's wisdom, but on God's power."

In summary, Paul assumes that the gospel is discredited by those ministers who are lustful, impure, ignorant, overbearing, indignant, rude, unkind, and hypocritical in their love, cultivating those whom they think can benefit them in some way. Such ministers have neither the Holy Spirit nor the power of God.

6:7c–6:8b Paul next switches to three combinations of terms introduced by the preposition "with" *(dia)*. The ambiguity of the genitive case allows the first phrase, "weapons of righteousness," to be understood in several ways.

1. It can be a genitive of content and mean "weapons consisting of righteousness." That would convey the idea that our righteousness becomes our weapon. The parallel term in Rom 6:13, where Paul urges them to present their members to God as "instruments of righteousness" as contrasted with "instruments of unrighteousness" suggests that Paul may have in mind human righteousness here.[871]

2. "Weapons of righteousness" could also be a qualitative genitive and mean "righteous weapons." But the term righteousness more likely refers to either God's righteousness or human righteousness rather than simply having an adjectival force.

3. Finally, "weapons of righteousness" could be a subjective genitive and mean "weapons provided by righteousness." This last option understands the righteousness to be God's and is the best interpretation. Paul has just referred to the power of God, and the righteousness of God is far more potent as a weapon than human moral qualities (see Rom 1:16–17; see Rom 13:12, "armor of light"). Later in the letter he will remind them that his weapons of warfare are not "fleshly" *(sarkika)* but have divine power (10:4).

The military image (see also 10:4; Rom 13:12; Eph 6:11–17; 1 Thess 5:8) means that Paul does not go out into the world unprotected and dodging Satan's shafts as best he can. He is armed by God. Why does he say weapons for the left and right? It may be a way of saying that he is fully outfitted or that he has weapons "applicable to every situation."[872] Interpreters have

---

[871] So Thrall, *Second Epistle to the Corinthians,* 1:462.

often noted that in combat, the right hand is used for offense (sword, spear, lance) and the left hand for defense (shield). The GNB paraphrases it, "We have righteousness for our weapon, both to attack and to defend ourselves. Barclay translates it, "Goodness has been our armour both to commend and to defend the faith." But some have interpreted left and right allegorically to represent adversity and prosperity. If so, then Paul would be saying that with righteousness in his arsenal adversity does not fell him and make him despondent, nor does prosperity overly elate him.

This latter interpretation fits best the following pairs, "glory and dishonor," "bad report and good report." These terms fit a chiastic a b b′ a′ pattern:

glory   dishonor
bad report   good report

Paul suffered insults and also basked in praise for the benefits he brought to others through the gospel. The Lycaonians, for example, worshiped Barnabas and Paul as gods in one moment and stoned them and left them for dead in the next (Acts 14:8–19). Paul was indifferent to fame and abuse because he had a divine, internal gyroscope to help maintain his equilibrium when the swings in the responses to him, from respect to shame, were so dramatic. Insults did not devastate him; praise did not puff him up. His desire to please only God kept him on an even keel.

6:8c–10 The list next shifts to seven pairs of antitheses all introduced by "as" *(hōs)*. These can be taken in several ways.[873] The first item may refer to the outward appearance, while the second refers to the essential, inward reality of Paul's life.[874] Or, the first item may refer to the false estimate formed by those who judge him according to worldly standards, while the second reflects "the true judgment of those who are in Christ."[875] In other words, the first item refers to the worldly assessment of apostles, the second to God's judgment of them.[876] The problem with this view is that the first detail in the antithesis is not entirely false; Paul admits that he is indeed "dying," "beaten," and "poor."

Perhaps, then, the first item in the antithesis refers to Paul's reputation, true or false, the second to the reality, or that both items are complementary, albeit paradoxical, truths about Paul's existence.[877] The latter seems to be the best option for understanding these antitheses. With the exception of the first antithesis, Paul does not merely appear to be unknown, dying, beaten,

[872] Danker, *II Corinthians*, 93.
[873] See Thrall, *Second Epistle to the Corinthians*, 1:463.
[874] Talbert, *Reading Corinthians*, 170–71.
[875] Furnish, *II Corinthians*, 357.
[876] Bruce, *I and II Corinthians*, 212.
[877] Thrall, *Second Epistle to the Corinthians*, 1:464.

sorrowful, poor and having nothing. He is. But that is not the whole story. The first element is connected to the brief and shadowy realities affecting a clay vessel. The second element is related to the presence of the all-surpassing power from God (4:7) in his life. The first is temporary, destined to pass away; the second is eternal (4:18).

The NIV, for some reason, reverses the order of the pair in the first two antitheses. The Greek has "impostors" ("deceivers" who lead others astray, see 2 John 7) first followed by "genuine" ("true," "righteous," "honest"). The Corinthians do not regard him as an impostor. Paul has in mind the opinions of outsiders. Most commentators, however, think that Paul has his rival apostles in the back of his mind who "refused to recognize his apostleship."[878] Paul is not commending himself to the Corinthians, but outlining how he commends himself to the conscience of others. The Corinthians do not deny that he is a genuine apostle; they simply choose to differ with him on certain issues and to follow their own spiritual insights. Churches who have difficulty with pastors whose style of ministry they do not like, for whatever reason, do not deny that such pastors were ever called to ministry. They only wish that they were called to serve somewhere else. If the Corinthians thought that Paul was some kind of imposter, they would never bother to read his letters or heed his emissaries. This passage is not part of a "long apologia for the apostolic office (2:14–7:4)," as some declare, but a defense of his frank criticism of the Corinthians.[879] Paul is talking about how most of the world evaluates him. From the hostile world's point of view, he is no minister from God, only a fraud who preaches foolishness and leads his followers down the garden path to destruction.[880]

The next antithesis extends this confusion about Paul's identity. He is unknown by most. He does not refer to his obscurity. He is certainly known at least by reputation among Christians in many places (see Gal 2:14). But do they *really* know him? Certainly, no one knew him as Saint Paul; but, more important, few knew him as he insists God knows him (see 5:11).

"Dying, and yet we live on" and "beaten (*paideuomai,* which also can mean "disciplined") and yet not killed" recalls Paul's interpretation of his hardships in 4:16 (see 4:10,12). It also echoes Ps 118:17–18 (LXX 117:17–18):

---

[878] Barrett, *The Second Epistle to the Corinthians,* 189.

[879] Contra Barnett, *The Second Epistle to the Corinthians,* 317.

[880] We can compare Lucian's fictional tale, *The Passing of Peregrinus,* about a Cynic philosopher who became a Christian for a brief period early in his life and is portrayed as an unscrupulous impostor. He advanced by learning Christian lore, becoming a "Prophet, cult-leader, head of the synagogue and everything, all by himself," interpreting their books, and even composing some. Lucian presents him as a charlatan and notoriety seeker who profited from the support of simple-minded Christians. He considers them to be "poor wretches" because they have convinced themselves that they will be immortal and therefore willingly give themselves over to custody. Preyed upon by clever liars, they are easily taken in and believe doctrines "without any definite evidence."

I will not die but live,
and will proclaim what the LORD has done.
The LORD has chastened me severely,
but he has not given me over to death.

The scriptural reverberation reminds us that the source of Paul's endurance and equilibrium is not his philosophy, as the popular philosophers of his day proclaimed, but his God.[881]

The account of Paul's mission adventures in Acts offers vivid pictures of times when Paul was "beaten, and yet not killed." In 11:24–25 Paul names five times when he was lashed, three times when he was beaten with rods, and once when he was stoned and left for dead. Such a battering would destroy a lesser man serving a lesser god.

Paul admits to being sorrowful. The painful visit and the mutinous disobedience of the Corinthians caused him immeasurable sorrow (2:1–3). He was grief stricken that his own kinsmen, the Jews, who were the heirs of God's promises turned their backs on their Messiah (Rom 9:2). He was heartsick when illness and calamity struck his coworkers, particularly when they risked their lives, as Epaphroditus did, to offer him assistance (Phil 2:27). But most who read Philippians do not remember this passage where Paul said that he would have had "sorrow upon sorrow" had Epaphroditus not been spared. Most remember only the joy that radiates throughout this epistle, though Paul wrote it from prison with his life hanging in the balance (see also Acts 16:19–26). The joy that Paul exudes through all the persecutions is reminiscent of the Beatitudes (see also 1 Pet 1:6–7).[882]

6:4–5 in troubles, hardships and distresses; in beatings, imprisonments and riots	Blessed are those persecuted for righteousness sake (Matt 5:10)
6:6 in purity	Blessed are the pure in heart (Matt 5:8)
6:8 through glory and dishonor, bad report and good report; genuine, yet regarded as impostors	Blessed are you when people insult you, persecute you and falsely say all kinds of evil against you because of me (Matt 5:11 / Luke 6:22)
6:10 sorrowful, yet always rejoicing	Blessed are those who mourn (Matt 5:4)
6:10 poor, yet making many rich; having nothing, and yet possessing everything	Blessed are the poor (Luke 6:20 / Matt 5:3)

Fixing his eyes on the unseen, eternal glory that awaits him buoys his spirit so that he is always rejoicing.

---

[881] Harvey, *Renewal through Suffering,* 75.
[882] Hanson, *The Paradox of the Cross,* 69.

His ministry keeps him poor, yet he makes many rich. Paul models himself after Christ (8:9). No one could accuse him of getting rich off the gospel (Acts 20:33). He chose his poverty so that he would not compromise the gospel with even the appearance that he was in it for money (6:3). He wanted to avoid becoming ensnared in the anxieties of this world (1 Cor 7:31) and to avoid becoming a burden to others (11:9; 12:16). Yet he is confident that he makes others rich through his preaching. Reminding the Corinthians that they share in the riches of God's gifts (see 1 Cor 3:22, "all things are yours") prepares for his appeal in chaps. 8–9 (see 8:9; 9:11) that they should share with others from their material bounty.

Paul concludes that in spite of "having nothing" he "possesses everything." This was a current adage applied to popular philosophers, but Paul understands it from a religious point of view. Philo's application of the adage to Moses fits Paul's conviction:

> For if, as the proverb says, what belongs to friends is common, and the prophet is called the friend of God, it would follow that he shares also God's possessions, so far as it is serviceable. For God possesses all things, but needs nothing; while the good man, though possessing nothing in the proper sense, not even himself, partakes of the precious things of God so far as he is capable.[883]

In this unit Paul lays out for the Corinthians his commendation as God's minister. It paves the way for his climactic ethical appeal in 6:11–7:3.

(8) Who Christians Are and Who They Are Not (6:11–7:3)

[11]We have spoken freely to you, Corinthians, and opened wide our hearts to you. [12]We are not withholding our affection from you, but you are withholding yours from us. [13]As a fair exchange—I speak as to my children—open wide your hearts also.

[14]Do not be yoked together with unbelievers. For what do righteousness and wickedness have in common? Or what fellowship can light have with darkness? [15]What harmony is there between Christ and Belial? What does a believer have in common with an unbeliever? [16]What agreement is there between the temple of God and idols? For we are the temple of the living God. As God has said: "I will live with them and walk among them, and I will be their God, and they will be my people."

[17]"Therefore come out from them
  and be separate,
  says the Lord.
  Touch no unclean thing,
  and I will receive you."
[18]"I will be a Father to you,

---

[883] Philo, *Life of Moses,* 1.156–57

and you will be my sons and daughters, says the Lord Almighty."
¹Since we have these promises, dear friends, let us purify ourselves from
everything that contaminates body and spirit, perfecting holiness out of reverence
for God.
²Make room for us in your hearts. We have wronged no one, we have corrupted no one, we have exploited no one. ³I do not say this to condemn you; I
have said before that you have such a place in our hearts that we would live or
die with you.

Furnish calls 6:14–7:1 an "enigma," "neither its origin nor its place in the
context being entirely clear." It leaves off the warm, emotional affirmation of
Paul's love for the Corinthians and his earnest appeal for them to open their
hearts to him (6:11–13) and launches an unexpected, flinty exhortation to
separate themselves from unbelievers and to purify themselves. In 7:2–3
Paul harks back to his pledge of love for them and his appeal for them to
show him the same affection. The transition in 6:14 is so abrupt that some
argue that 7:2–3 follows naturally from 6:11–13:

> We have spoken freely to you, Corinthians, and opened wide our hearts to you.
> We are not withholding our affection from you, but you are withholding yours
> from us. As a fair exchange—I speak as to my children—open wide your
> hearts also (6:11–13). … Make room for us in your hearts. We have wronged
> no one, we have corrupted no one, we have exploited no one. I do not say this
> to condemn you; I have said before that you have such a place in our hearts that
> we would live or die with you (7:2–3).

The exhortation in 6:14–7:1 with its collage of Old Testament citations clearly
digresses from this poignant entreaty, and some consider it a foreign body
somehow inserted into the text, though no extant text of 2 Corinthians omits it.
The text also contains a high percentage of unique vocabulary.[884] The introduction to the chain of quotations from the Old Testament is unusual since
Paul does not introduce quotations with "as God said" elsewhere and normally
distinguishes the quotations from one another (compare Rom 9:25–29; 10:18–
20; 15:9–12).[885] The text also shares similarities with writings from the Dead

---

[884] Six words occur only here in the NT: ἑτεροζυγέω ("yoke together"), μετοξή ("have in
common"), συμφώνησις ("harmony"), Βελιάρ ("Belial"), συγκατάθεσις ("agreement"),
μολύσμος ("contaminates"). Three words that occur only here in Paul's letters derive from the OT
quotes: ἐμπεριπατέω ("walk among"), εἰσδέχομαι ("receive"), and παντοκράτωρ ("Lord
Almighty"). Four words do not appear in the Greek OT: ἑτεροζυγέω (except as an adjective, Lev
19:19), συμφώνησις, συγκατάθεσις, and Βελιάρ. The word θυγάηρ ("daughter") occurs only
here in Paul's letters.
[885] Paul does not cite Lev 20:12; Isa 52:11; or 2 Sam 7:14 elsewhere in his letters.

Sea Scrolls.[886] Benoit colorfully described this passage as "a meteor fallen from the heaven of Qumran into Paul's epistle."[887] Others find the sectarianism in the text to be foreign, if not completely incompatible, with Paul's thought. These problems have led scholars in the last century to the conclusion that the passage is extraneous to 2 Corinthians, and they have postulated many theories concerning its origin.[888] Though no consensus exists regarding the source of this supposed interpolation, the result of these studies is that the burden of proof rests upon those who would argue that it comes from Paul's hand and that it is integral to his argument. Consequently, before we can begin the interpretation of this unit, we first need to resolve these critical issues regarding its origin and how it fits in Paul's argument.[889]

Those interpreters who argue that 6:14–7:1 did not belong originally in its location in 2 Corinthians propose various theories as to its source. Some propose that it does not come from Paul's hand but was composed by an unknown Christian who reworked an Essene paragraph or composed it himself and introduced it when he was editing the letter. Betz goes so far as to identify it as an "anti-Pauline" fragment written by someone in the Jewish Christian party opposed to Paul.[890] Some argue that Paul himself inserted a text from another source, perhaps Essene, to address a particular issue.

Others claim more reasonably that the passage does come from Paul but that it did not originally belong to 2 Corinthians. They suggest that it was a fragment from a previous letter to the Corinthians, perhaps the letter of tears, or the first letter Paul wrote to them, both of which are now lost. Paul

---

[886] The parallels are noted by J. A. Fitzmyer, "Qumran and the Interpolated Paragraph in 2 Cor vi 14–vii 1," *CBQ* 23 (1961) 271–80; and J. Gnilka, "2 Kor, 6.14–7.1 in Lichte der Qumranschriften und der Zwölf-Patriarchen-Testamente," in *Neutestamentliche Aufsätze. Festschrift für Prof. Josef Schmid zum 70. Geburtstag* (Regensburg: Pustet, 1963) 86–99 = "2 Cor 6:14–7:1 in the Light of the Qumran Texts and the Testaments of the Twelve Patriarchs," in *Paul and Qumran. Studies in New Testament Exegesis;* ed. J. Murphy-O'Connor (Chicago: Priory, 1968) 48–68. They note such things as the dualism, opposition to idols, a similar use of OT texts, cleansing the flesh, Belial, and insistence on separation. N. Dahl comments, "Even persons like myself who are reluctant to assume much direct influence of the Qumran sectarians upon the New Testament will have to admit that 2 Cor. 6:14–7:1 is a slightly Christianized piece of Qumran theology" ("A Fragment and Its Context: 2 Corinthians 6:14–7:1," in *Studies in Paul* [Minneapolis: Augsburg, 1977] 63).

[887] P. Benoit, "Qumran and the New Testament," in *Paul and Qumran. Studies in New Testament Exegesis,* ed. J. Murphy-O'Connor (Chicago: Priory, 1968) 5.

[888] For a brief history of the interpretation of this passage from the reformation to the twentieth century, see W. J. Webb, *Returning Home: New Covenant and Second Exodus as the Context for 2 Corinthians 6.14–7.1,* JSNTSup 85 (Sheffield: JSOT, 1993) 16–30.

[889] It is telling of the state of scholarship on this passage that Lambrecht entitled an article on it, "The Fragment 2 Corinthians 6,14–7,1, A Plea for Its Authenticity," *NovT* 48 (1978) 143–61; reprinted in Studies on 2 Corinthians, ed. R. Bieringer and J. Lambrecht, BETL 112 (Leuven: University Press, 1994) 531–49.

[890] H. D. Betz, "2 Cor. 6:14–7:1: An Anti-Pauline Fragment?" *JBL* 92 (1973) 88–108.

alludes to this first letter in 1 Cor 5:9–10.

> I have written you in my letter not to associate with sexually immoral people—not at all meaning the people of this world who are immoral, or the greedy and swindlers, or idolaters. In that case you would have to leave this world.[891]

This description of the contents of this first letter seems, to some, to match 2 Cor 6:14–7:1. They read sections in 1 Corinthians as taking up and clarifying the statements in this passage that the Corinthians misconstrued. "Do not be yoked together with unbelievers" is explained further by Paul's instructions on marriage to an unbeliever (1 Cor 7:12–15). "What agreement is there between the temple of God and idols" is dealt with in more detail in the discussion of eating idol food at a pagan temple and in someone's home (1 Cor 8–10). "Come out from them and be separate" is clarified as referring to immoral Christians and not the immoral of this world (1 Cor 5:9–11).[892] These correlations do not prove that 6:14–7:1 was originally part of the first letter Paul sent to the Corinthians. They show instead that such problems were endemic in Corinth and that Paul continually needed to address them.

Others imagine that this fragment was originally part of 1 Corinthians and somehow was inserted here, or that it was dislocated from its original context in 2 Corinthians. All these theories present more problems than they pretend to solve, and most interpreters who adopt them generally skip the basic task of explaining the mechanics of how such an interpolation would have been carried out or why it would have been undertaken.[893] What were the motives behind such a peculiar interpolation, that, according to these interpreters, fits so badly with its context? Danker contends that "the early editors of what is now 2 Corinthians did a skillful job of mending the seams, for vv. 11–13 constitute an appropriate transition."[894] Apparently, it was not skillful enough to fool the expert detection of modern scholars; and Danker does not even offer a guess as to the purpose of such editing. On the other hand, if this is an "appropriate transition," why could it not stem from Paul? Webb points out that other recognized interpolations in the New Testament have clear textual critical evidence omitting the passage and "good reasons can be shown as to *why* a later scribe inserted the text." The proponents of a later interpolation theory offer no clues about why

---

[891] The world is filled with immoral persons, and one cannot but help come in contact with them. By "immoral men" Paul meant those who bear the name Christian who are guilty of immorality, greed, idolatry, reviling, drunkenness, and robbery. The church is not in the business of judging outsiders, but they are to exercise internal discipline.

[892] The problem with this view is that sexual immorality is not explicitly addressed in 2 Cor 6:14–7:1, and the "unbelievers" would have to be immoral Christians rather than what seems the more likely meaning, "unbelieving heathens."

[893] See Introduction, p. 38f.

[894] Danker, *II Corinthians*, 96.

this so-called fragment was inserted here with such a supposedly jarring effect.[895]

It will not do to argue that the digression in Paul's argument was caused by a pause in dictation or to imagine that he suddenly felt a burst of concern prompting an excursus unrelated to his primary argument. If there were such a pause, it leaves unexplained why 7:2 so nicely picks up the thought from 6:13. Nor is it satisfactory to argue that Paul inserted a pre-Christian Essene tradition that was recast by a Christian. The parallels between 6:14–7:1 and the Dead Sea Scrolls do not require that this passage originated with the Essenes. Ideas, particularly those rooted in Old Testament texts, do not flow in pipelines.[896] The theories connecting this text to the Dead Sea Scrolls appeared during the first flush of interest in the discovery and publication of the Scrolls when their influence in the New Testament was seen to be pervasive. Years of reflection on the significance of the Scrolls allows for a more prudent assessment of their impact on the New Testament writings. Murphy-O'Connor reminds us:

> Qumran was a closed community. Dissemination of its teachings was forbidden (1QS 9:16–17), and secrecy was reinforced by writing certain documents in code (e.g. 4Q186). Specifically Qumran ideas, therefore, are extremely unlikely to have penetrated Jewish life in Palestine, and still less in the Diaspora. [897]

---

[895] Webb, *Returning Home*, 163. He cites John 5:3b–4; 7:52–8:11; Acts 8:37; and 1 John 5:7–8. See also Mark 16:9–20. Webb notes that they dismiss the problem by saying it is "difficult to answer" (G. Bornkamm, "Die Vorgeschichte des sogenannten Zweiten Korintherbriefes," in *Gesammelte Aufsätze*, BEvT 53 [Munich: Evangelischer Verlag, 1971] 193, n. 3); "not clear" (Gnilka, "2 Cor 6:14–7:1," 67); "remains unsolved" (Fitzmyer, "Qumran and the Interpolated Paragraph," 217); "for reasons unknown" (Betz, "2 Cor. 6:14–7:1: An Anti-Pauline Fragment?" 108); or "impossible to say how it came to Corinth" (Georgi, T*he Opponents of Paul in Second Corinthians,* 12). Those who do attempt some explanation require such an imaginative stretch that it makes Paul's authorship of the passage seem far more probable. F. Lang contends that Paul's summons for them to open wide their hearts might have caused someone concern among those who believed that Christians' hearts could be too open to their heathen world and so they composed these words of constraint (*Die Brief an die Korinther,* NTD [1936; revised, Göttingen: Vandenhoeck & Ruprecht, 1986] 310–11). R. P. C. Hanson claims that the Corinthians had three letters of Paul, one complete (2 Cor 1–9), a fragment of 111 words (2 Cor 6:14–7:1), and an incomplete letter (2 Cor 10–13). He conjectures that the leaders of the Corinthian church did not want to admit they had allowed the letters of the great apostle Paul to be lost and did not want to circulate their letters mutilated and unedited. Consequently they published all three together (*II Corinthians,* TBC [London: SPCK, 1954] 21–22).

[896] S. Sandmel coined the phrase "parallelomania" to caution against falling into these kinds of traps ("Parallelomania," *JBL* 81 [1962] 1–13; noted by Martin, *2 Corinthians,* 193).

[897] J. Murphy-O'Connor, "Philo and 2 Cor 6:14–7:1," *RevBib* 95 (1988) 59. He thinks that there may have been "elements of the wider Essene movement in Asia Minor, but their teaching is known only from documents that antedate the foundation of Qumran." He finds the parallels in the *Testaments of the Twelve Patriarchs* and Philo to be far more significant. G. Sass points out that the similar passages in the DSS occur in a schema of blessings and curses that is not present in this passage ("Noch Einmal: 2 Kor 6,14–7,1 Literarkritische Waffen gegen einen 'unpaulinischen' Paulus," *ZNW* 84 [1993] 42–44).

He concludes from parallels in *Testament of the Twelve Patriarchs* and Philo that the language and ideas of 6:14–7:1 are perfectly at home in Hellenistic Judaism.[898] The tide may be turning regarding the authenticity of 6:14–7:1 as a growing list of scholars now argue from a variety of perspectives that Paul wrote this passage and that it fits into the logical flow of Paul's argument.[899] The objections to Pauline authorship do not withstand close scrutiny. Other passages in Paul have rare vocabulary; and, as Fee comments, "the presence of hapax legomena can never be the sole factor in determining authorship."[900] It can only be decisive when there is an extremely high percentage of unique vocabulary, and that only holds true when one can rule out the subject matter as a factor in generating the number of unique words and when these words differ significantly from the author's ordinary vocabulary to express similar ideas or when they are completely foreign to the author's time. In this case none of these criteria apply. The quantity of hapax legomena is not extraordinary. The passage

---

[898] See *T. Levi* 19:1: "And now, my children, you have learned everything. Choose for yourselves light or darkness, the law of the Lord or the works of Beliar." *T. Dan* 6:10, "Forsake all unrighteousness and cling to the righteousness of God." *T. Naph.* 2:6 refers to the law of Beliar, and in 2:10 it says, "You are unable to perform the works of light while you are in darkness." *T. Jos.* 20:2, "The Lord will be with you in the light, while Beliar will be with the Egyptians in the dark." Sass also draws attention to *Jub.* 1:15–26 as a more significant parallel concerning the restoration of the people ("Noch Einmal: 2 Kor 6,14–7,1," 45–47).

[899] For specialized studies on this passage, see G. D. Fee, "II Corinthians vi. 14 – vii. 1 and Food offered to Idols," *NTS* 23 (1977) 140–61; M. E. Thrall, "The Problem of II Cor, VI.14–VII.1 in Some Recent Discussion," *NTS* 24 (1977) 133–38; J. D. M. Derrett, "2 Cor 6,14ff. a Midrash on Dt 22,10," Bib 59 (1978) 231–50; J. Lambrecht, "The Fragment 2 Corinthians 6,14–7,1, *A Plea for Its Authenticity,*" 531–49; J. Murphy-O'Connor, "Relating 2 Corinthians 6.14–7.1 to its Context," *NTS* 33 (1987) 272–75; and "Philo and 2 Cor 6:14–7:1," 55–69; G. K. Beale, "The Old Testament Background of Reconciliation in 2 Corinthians 5–7 and Its Bearing on the Literary Problem of 2 Corinthians 6.14–7:1," *NTS* 5 (1989) 550–81; D. A. DeSilva, "Recasting the Moment of Decision: 2 Corinthians 6:14–7:1 in Its Literary Context," Andrews University Seminary Studies 31 (1993) 3–16; Webb, *Returning Home;* F. Zeilinger, "Die Echtheit von 2 Cor 6:14–7:1, *JBL* 112 (1993) 71–80; Sass, "Noch Einmal: 2 Kor 6,14–7,1," 36–64; R. Bieringer, "2 Korinther 6,14–7,1 im Kontext des 2. Korintherbriefs: Forschungsüberblick und Versuch eines eigenen Zugangs," in *Studies on 2 Corinthians,* ed. R. Bieringer and J. Lambrecht, BETL 112 (Leuven: University Press, 1994) 551–70; M. Goulder, "2 Cor. 6:14–7:1 As An Integral Part of 2 Corinthians," *NovT* 36 (1994) 47–57; and J. M. Scott, "The Use of Scripture in 2 Corinthians 6:16c–18 and Paul's Restoration Theology," *JSNT* 56 (1994) 73–99.

[900] Fee, "II Corinthians vi. 14 – vii. 1 and Food offered to Idols," 8.

in 1 Cor 4:7–13 has almost the same number (eight).[901]

A chain of Old Testament quotations also appears in Rom 3:10–18 where Paul does not distinguish the biblical authors cited, and he uses a phrase similar to "as the Lord said" (6:16) in 2 Cor 4:6, "For it is God who said," and has "says the Lord" in Rom 12:19. The apparent care in which the Old Testament quotations are altered to fit the context points against the use of a previously compiled testimony or a preexisting fragment.[902] The quotations also fit closely with the outer shell, 6:14–15 and 7:1 which indicates that the passages were chosen and redacted to fit the outer shell rather than being a preexisting catena thrown together haphazardly.[903] Olley traces the logic of the series of quotations and confirms this view. He concludes that the texts chosen focus on the "incompatibility of being God's temple/people/children and participating in worship of other gods."[904] Olley's contribution helps explain how the Old Testament passages in 6:17d–18 relate to the issue of idolatry, something we will argue is the primary issue in this exhortation.[905]

The presumed shift in the argument also can be dismissed as imaginary. Paul uses digressions regularly, and 6:11–13 and 7:2–4 bracket 6:14–7:1 to form an A B A′ structure common in Paul's letters. We would disagree with

---

[901] Three of the words derive from the OT quotations: ἐμπεριπατέω ("walk among"), εἰσδέχομαι, ("receive"), and παντοκράτωρ ("Lord Almighty"). The other expressions are not outside Paul's lexical orbit. (1) Phil 4:3 has σύζυγος ("yoke-fellow" as a parallel to coworker, συνεργός (see 6:1 συνεργοῦντες). The possibility of its converse, being "other yoked" (ἑτεροζυγοῦντες, 6:14) with a non-Christian, would not be a totally foreign idea. (2) The noun μετοχή (6:14, "sharing," "participation," "in common" NIV) appears in the verb form μετέχω ("share") in 1 Cor 9:10, 12; 10:17, 21; 30. The noun κοινωνία ("partnership") and the verb μετέχω appear together in 1 Cor 10:16–17. See also συμμέτοχος ("sharers together") in Eph 3:6; 5:7. (3). σύμφωνησις ("harmony," "agreement," 6:15) appears as an adjective σύμφωνος ("harmonious") in 1 Cor 7:5. (4) μολύσμος ("defilement," "everything that contaminates," NIV, 7:1) appears in the verb form μολύνομαι ("defile") in 1 Cor 8:7. (5) The antonym of the verb καθαρίζω ("to cleanse," "purify," 7:1) appears as an adjective in 1 Cor 7:14: the spouse married to the believer is consecrated, "otherwise your children would be unclean (ἀκάθαρτα), but as it is, they are holy." Here cleansing belongs closely to holiness, and holiness is listed as the opposite of impurity in Pauline parenesis (Rom 6:19; 1 Thess 4:7; see 1 Cor 6:11). (6) Belial is a common name in Jewish apocalyptic tradition. (7) συνκατάθεσις is a synonym for συμφώνησις and may reflect Exod 23:32: "You shall make no covenant with them or their gods." Grammatically the construction "partnership" plus the dative and πρός has no parallel in Paul, but Lambrecht lists several Pauline grammatical traits in the passage ("The Fragment 2 Corinthians 6,14–7,1: A Plea for Its Authenticity," 545). μὴ γίνεσθε ("do not be," Rom 12:16; 1 Cor 7:24); "for we [you] are … " (6:14; Phil 3:3; Gal 5:5); "therefore having these" (2 Cor 3:12; 4:1, 13); and ἐπιτελέω ("complete," 7:1; Rom 15:28; 2 Cor 8:6,11[2x]; Gal 3:3; Phil 1:6).

[902] Lambrecht, "The Fragment 2 Corinthians 6,14–7,1, A Plea for Its Authenticity," 544.

[903] Webb, Returning Home, 66–70.

[904] J. W. Olley, "A Precursor of the NRSV? 'Sons and Daughters in 2 Cor 6:18," NTS 44 (1998) 204–12.

[905] Olley's contribution therefore advances Fee's argument since he did not recognize how all the quotations related to the matter of idolatry and suggested that a preexisting catena was "merely carried over."

Barrett who maintains "Paul not infrequently allows himself to wander from his point, and then brings himself back to it with something of a jerk."[906] We are not convinced that this is a major digression from Paul's point in this section. In the immediate context Paul appeals to the Corinthians to repent: "We implore you on Christ's behalf: Be reconciled to God" (5:20). "As God's fellow workers we urge you not to receive God's grace in vain. For he says, "In the time of my favor I heard you, and in the day of salvation I helped you." I tell you, now is the time of God's favor, now is the day of salvation" (6:1–2).[907] Paul bids them to open wide their hearts to him (6:13) and continues with another second person plural imperative in 6:14 ("do not be").[908] Opening wide their hearts to Paul (6:13) requires that they do what he instructs them to do. In 7:2 he resumes the thought from 6:13, but its phrasing suggests that there always was a disjuncture after 6:13."[909] The statement "I have said before" in 7:3, which repeats the statement in 6:11, would be strange if it followed immediately. It makes more sense as a deliberate reference back to 6:11–13 after the interruption.[910]

The placement of this passage here in 2 Corinthians also fits a pattern of argument found elsewhere in Paul. Scott notes that Paul's citation of a combination of Scriptures in Rom 3:10–18 marks the end of a major section of Paul's argument in that letter (Rom 1:18–3:20), and in the same way the citation of a combination of Scripture marks the end of his argument in 2:14–7:4.[911] Goulder displays how the sequence of argument in 1 Corinthians 4–6 parallels the sequence of argument in 2 Corinthians 5–7.[912] According to Goulder, the argument in 1 Corinthians 4–6 runs as follows:

A   Paul reminds those who are misjudging him (4:3) that he is to be regarded as a servant of Christ and a steward of the mysteries of God (1 Cor 4:1–5). When the Lord comes, he will disclose the purposes of the heart and then each will receive commendation from God (4:5).

B   In contrast to the Corinthians who think that they already reign, Paul lists his deprivations and persecutions as an apostle. This ironic weakness is the true token of his apostleship (1 Cor 4:6–13).

C   He asserts his authority over them as a father over his children (1 Cor 4:14–21). He does not want to make them ashamed (4:1) or to discipline the

---

[906] Barrett, *The Second Epistle to the Corinthians,* 194.

[907] Sass argues that the form fits the exhortation to those who are already converted (see Rom 6:17–19; 1 Cor 9–11; 1 Thess 4:3–12; "Noch einmal: 2 Kor 6,14–7,1," 48).

[908] We should note that 6:14–7:1 continues the use of stark contrasts that are found throughout 4:16–5:10.

[909] Lambrecht, "The Fragment 2 Corinthians 6,14–7,1, A Plea for Its Authenticity," 540.

[910] Tasker, *The Second Epistle to the Corinthians,* 101–2.

[911] Scott, "The Use of Scripture in 2 Corinthians 6:16c–18 and Paul's Restoration Theology," 96.

[912] Goulder, "2 Cor. 6:14–7:1 As An Integral Part of 2 Corinthians," 48–49.

arrogant with a rod (4:21). He prefers to come "with love in a spirit of gentleness" (4:21).

D He asserts his authority because of the blatant sins in the community—the man living with his father's wife and the law suits against one another (5:1–13; 6:1–11)—which they seem to condone by their silence. He is appalled that they would tolerate such behavior and warns of its corrupting effects. They are to be new and unleavened (5:6–8), and therefore he urges them not to have anything to do with such persons: "Drive out the wicked person from among you" (5:13).

The argument in 2 Corinthians 5–7 is similar in reacting to those who are boastful (5:12) and runs as follows:

A Paul affirms that his ministry is greater than that of Moses as a servant of Jesus Christ (and of them; 2:14–4:6), and a servant of God (6:4), and that God has given him a ministry of reconciliation (5:18) and appointed him as an ambassador for Christ (5:20). He also affirms that God knows what he is and, he hopes, the Corinthians will know also (5:11). Consequently, he should not have to commend himself to them again (5:12). He no longer evaluates others according to human standards and implies that they should not use these standards either (5:16).

B He then recounts more fully his deprivations and sufferings (4:8–12; 6:4–10; cp. 1 Cor 4:11–12).

C He makes his appeal to the Corinthians' affection as his children (6:11–13; cp. 1 Cor 4:14–15).

D He stresses the Corinthians' holiness in contrast to others who are unclean (6:14–18; cp. 1 Cor 5:7–8; 6:9–11).

E Finally, he demands that they separate themselves from the sources of corruption (2 Cor 6:17, cp. 1 Cor 5:7, 5:13).[913]

These similarities in the argumentation strongly suggest that 6:14–7:1 always belonged where it is placed in this letter.

The major question that must be answered is how does this passage fit in the flow of Paul's discussion. If 2:14–7:3 is an integral unit, as we have argued, it would be strange for Paul to digress at the end of it and more likely that the end marks the capstone of his argument. All the imperatives in this section occur at the end ("be reconciled" 5:20; "we beg you not to

---

[913] Goulder discovers the same pattern of argument in 2 Cor 10–13 ("2 Cor 6:14–7:1," 52):

A Let the opponents reckon that he is also of Christ (10:7), that he is not inferior to the super apostles (11:5) and that he is a better "servant of Christ" than they are (11:23).

B He expands at even greater length on his deprivations and weaknesses (11:23–33)

C He makes a fatherly appeal in 12:14–18.

D He then challenges them to a pure spiritual life in 12:19–21.

E He then brings up the issue of discipline, warning them that he will return and expressing hopes that he will not have to exercise authority severely (13:10).

receive the grace of God in vain" 6:1; "open wide your hearts," 6:13; "do not be yoked," 6:14, "come out," "be separate," "do not touch" 6:17; "make room for us in your hearts," 7:2). Paul is not flying off on some tangent in 6:14–7:1; instead this passage marks the climax of his argument.[914] Its main topic is the problem of associations with idolatry which, we propose, was one of the roots of the dissension in Corinth and the focus of the previous severe letter. We have contended that 2:14–7:3 is a defense of Paul's frank criticism of the Corinthians in this letter and now argue that Paul recapitulates his exhortation in that letter in 6:14–7:1 to reinforce the seriousness of the problem. Paul employs rhetorical skill and pastoral tact in placing this strongly worded warning at the end of his long defense of his frank criticism and before his joyous affirmation of them for responding to his letter and to his emissary Titus. After boldly reiterating the same ultimatum he issued in his severe letter, he will next move on to praise them for their godly sorrow and repentance (7:4–16). He brackets this climactic warning with professions of his love for them perhaps to make the harsh medicine easier to swallow.[915] But he also insists that they must reciprocate his love and care for them by opening their hearts again to him. This entails heeding his warnings and calling a halt to their defiance and muttering in the ranks.

If this proposal is correct, then this passage is not "a piece of 'common' parenesis meant for Christians who live in the midst of manifold dangers in a Gentile world."[916] The Corinthians did live in a world filled with various trade guilds and associations in a city dotted with pagan temples and pervasive idolatry. But I would argue that 6:14–7:1 is specifically composed for the Corinthian situation to address the problem of forming appropriate boundaries for the Christian community to ward off the deleterious effects of idolatry. Goulder is on target in pointing out the strong overlap of language between 6:14–7:1 and 1 Corinthians 8 and 10, making it likely "that the particular question Paul has in mind is that of idol meat."[917] We find the same contrast between God and idols (6:14 and 1 Cor 8:4–6) and between Christ/Lord and Beliar/demons (6:14; 1 Cor 10:21). The words *koinōnia*

---

[914] Witherington cites Quintilian (*Training in Oratory*, 4.3.12; 4.3.9) that digressions may occur at any point and may be characterized by greater vehemence and freedom of speech than the surrounding argument (*Conflict and Community*, 402–4). But this rhetorical permission to digress does not prove that Paul is doing so here. Using quite different methodology (structuralism), D. Patte argues that this passage functions as the conclusion of the discourse ("A Structural Exegesis of 2 Corinthians 2:14–7:4 with Special Attention on 2:14–3:6 and 6:11–7:4," *SBLSP* (1988) 23–49).

[915] R. E. Brown suggests parenthetically, "In the present sequence the passage serves as an indicator that all has not been healed at Corinth and prepares for the corrective chaps. 10–13" (*Introduction to the New Testament* [New York: Doubleday, 1997] 546).

[916] Lambrecht, "The Fragment 2 Corinthians 6,14–7,1 A Plea for Its Authenticity," 548.

[917] Goulder, "2 Cor 6:14–7:1," 50–51.

("fellowship") and *metochē* in 6:14 also appear together in 1 Cor 10:16–17 (using the verb form of the noun, *metechein,* "partake") in comparing the Lord's Supper with idol feasts. Even the extremely rare word *molysmos* ("defilement," "everything that contaminates," NIV) in 7:2 appears in the verb form in 1 Cor 8:7 with reference to the weak person whose conscience "is defiled." The admonitions in 1 Corinthians, "do not become idolaters" (10:7), "flee from idolatry" (10:14), and "do not eat it" (10:28) match the tenor of commands in 6:14–7:1 to "come out from them," to "be separate," to "touch no unclean thing," to "purify themselves from everything that contaminates." The most reasonable conclusion to draw from this overlapping vocabulary is that the idol-meat question had not gone away. Paul may allude to it again in 12:21 where he expresses his fear that when he returns to Corinth he will discover that "many who have sinned earlier and have not repented of the impurity, sexual sin and debauchery in which they have indulged." He has in mind the impurity caused by joining in celebrations in idols' temples and not being discriminating in eating idol meat, as well as the sexual sins listed in 1 Corinthians 5–6 and the arrogance that insists, "Everything is permissible" (10:23).

Since many new converts came from a background of idol worship, they may not have readily understood or accepted the need for strict boundaries regarding other gods. In their religious background "no deity demanded exclusive worship from his or her devotees."[918] Syncretism was habitual. Individuals could choose from a cafeteria line of deities to worship, and they usually chose those gods whom they hoped would offer the greatest assistance in helping them to lead successful lives. The more gods the merrier— as long as the gods served the needs of the worshiper. The exclusive claim placed on Gentile converts entering into covenant with the God of Israel would have been a new concept and would have caused some difficult adjustments.

Paul links idol food to idolatry in 1 Cor 10:19–20. He does not permit idol food at all if one knows it to be idol food. He never says, "Eat idol food if the weak are not caused to stumble." He permits one to eat any food bought in the meat market or served in another's home without inquiring about its origins or history. But if one knows that the food is sacrificed food, Paul then insists that one must abstain.[919] Paul may have rejected Jewish

---

[918] Best, *Second Corinthians,* 65.

[919] If Paul condoned eating idol food, he would not only have been the first but the only early Christian to do so (P. J. Tomson, *Paul and the Jewish Law: Halaka in the Letters of the Apostle to the Gentiles,* Compendia Rerum Iudaicarum ad Novum Testamentum [Assen/ Maastricht: Van Gorcum / Minneapolis: Fortress, 1990] 185). For a thorough investigation of this issue that corrects the common errors made by Western interpreters, see A. Cheung, *Idol Food in Corinth: Jewish Background and Pauline Legacy,* JSNTSup 176 (Sheffield: Academic Press, 1999).

food laws that built up barriers between Jewish and Gentile Christians, but he never condoned eating what was known to be idol food. He did not reject the restrictions that separated Christians, who are exclusively tied to the one true God, from pagans who relate to many gods and lords.[920] Social meals in temples could never be purely secular or only nominally connected to idolatry since idolatrous rites were frequently performed over food.[921]

Paul's discussion of this issue in 1 Corinthians 8–10 could not have been the first time he ever raised this subject. Denunciation of idol worship and avoidance of any associations with idols was part of his missionary preaching. We can see his uncompromising attitude toward idolatry in the vice list in Gal 5:20, his condemnation of idolaters (among others) in 1 Cor 6:9, and his commendation of the Thessalonians for turning from idols to God (1 Thess 1:9). According to Acts 19:11–40, Paul stirred up troubles in Ephesus preaching against idolatry. In a world permeated with idolatry, this issue would have had to be addressed immediately for newly converted Christians. Cheung notes that idol food is the earliest and most important issue confronting new converts anywhere many gods and many lords are worshiped.[922] Consequently, the issues discussed in 1 Corinthians 8–10 would not have suddenly dawned on them months later when the weak supposedly objected to the strong's exercise of their freedom by participating in idol feasts. Paul would have had to address such issues during his eighteen-month stay in Corinth.[923]

This scenario suggests that the dispute over idol food was not one raging among the strong and weak Corinthians but was a dispute between Paul and the Corinthians. There is no hint that the weak ever challenged the right of the strong to eat idol food. What Paul fears is not factionalism in the church over this issue but the so-called strong destroying the weak. The ones with knowledge are the shapers of opinion in the Corinthian church. Apparently, they have taken issue with Paul's previous prohibitions concerning idol food

---

[920] In his discussion in Rom 14:1–15:13 about not passing judgment on other Christians over food, Paul assumes that the food has been blessed: "they give thanks to God" (Rom 14:6). In 1 Cor 10 the question is whether or not the food can be blessed. For Jews, forbidding anything associated with idolatry required no explanation in contrast to the rules covering pure and impure food, which did. It was self-evident from their exclusive allegiance to God.

[921] See P. D. Gooch, *Dangerous Food: 1 Corinthians 8–10 in Its Context,* Studies in Christianity and Judaism 5 (Waterloo: Wilfrid Laurier University Press, 1993) 15–45.

[922] Cheung, *Idol Food in Corinth,* 141, n. 82.

[923] B. W. Winter constructs an alternative scenario. He argues that the issue has to do with the civic right some Corinthian Roman citizens possessed to participate in feasts held in the temple of Poseidon in Isthmia celebrating the quadrennial Caesarian Games and Imperial Contests that were held in 55. The Corinthian Christians who possessed these rights were understandably reluctant to forego their social privileges or to fail to show civic loyalty ("The Achaean Federal Imperial Cult II: The Corinthian Church," *TynBul* 46 [1995] 169–78).

and have countered with clever arguments and slogans. They were not asking, "Can we eat idol food?" but "Why can't we eat idol food? Hurd reconstructs the Corinthians' challenge:

> We find nothing wrong with eating idol meat. After all, we have knowledge. We know that an idol has no real existence. We know that there is no God but one. For those in Christ all things are lawful, and as far as food is concerned everyone knows that "food is meant for the stomach and the stomach for food." We fail to see what is to be gained by the avoidance of idol meat. You know yourself that when you were with us you never questioned what you ate and drank. Moreover, what of the markets? Are we to be required to inquire as to the history of each piece of meat we buy? And what of our friends? Are we to decline their invitations to banquets because of possible contamination by idol meat?[924]

We can only surmise what happened. When Paul was present, he denounced anything associated with idols. After he left, the more prominent members of the congregation would be strongly tempted to eat idol food because of social pressure; and they buckled under this pressure and justified it with an "enlightened" view of Christian freedom. Carter points out "It is evident that those who had contact with the outside world through their attendance at idol feasts, or their use of the law courts and prostitutes, neither shared the apostle's concern about the boundaries of the community, nor his rejection of city life outside those boundaries."[925] They were seeking their own social good and then justifying it theologically, unconcerned about what effect it might have on others.[926] Like stubborn teenagers who may challenge the limits placed on them by their parents, the Corinthians refuted Paul's prohibitions. In 1 Corinthians 8–10 Paul responds to their rebuttal and tries to persuade them by other means.[927] Often he may seem to agree with them in principle but points out to them the error of their application of the principles. He is primarily interested in strengthening their Christian identity and social unity, which requires maintaining the boundaries that set the community apart from the surrounding society. That requires avoiding anything that plainly smacks of idolatry no matter how unreasonable, inconvenient, or unsociable such withdrawal might seem to the Corinthians.

This letter and 6:14–7:1 suggest that this controversy, like most controversies, was not settled overnight. It continued to simmer and perhaps was behind the confrontation that prompted Paul's retreat and the tearful, severe letter. Paul repeated his strong objections to associations with anything idol-

---

[924] J. C. Hurd, Jr., The Origin of 1 Corinthians (New York: Seabury, 1965) 146.
[925] T. L. Carter, " 'Big Men' in Corinth," *JSNT* 66 (1997) 50.
[926] See Cheung, *Idol Food in Corinth,* 118–24.
[927] Ibid., 108–17.

atrous; but, as the next section (7:5–16) reveals, in greater confidence that they have taken seriously and will take seriously his warnings.

The Structure of 6:11–7:3

John Chrysostom understood well Paul's rhetorical strategy. He notes that Paul shifts from commending his ministry to his profession of love for them to a frank reproach: "for if even from his own good deeds, he that rebuketh be entitled to reverence; yet still, when he also displayeth the love, which he bears toward those who are censured, he maketh his speech less offensive."[928] Hughes also notes that Paul has "graciously cushioned" his direct and unequivocal warning in 6:14–7:1 between two passages expressing his affection for them (6:11–13; 7:2–3). The admonition "is direct and to the point," but "it is still administered in the spirit of love, not censoriousness." He takes it as a model for other pastors to emulate. Paul is "plainspoken" without being "crushing and harsh" in correcting those who "are placing themselves in a position of the gravest spiritual peril."[929]

The charge that follows 6:11–13 begins with an introduction containing the main admonition: "Do not be yoked together with unbelievers" (6:14a). The basis for this directive is given in the form of five rhetorical questions (6:14b–16a), followed by a series of Scriptural prooftexts (6:16b–18). The five rhetorical questions begin with *tis,* "what?" asking what two mutually exclusive domains have to do with each other, expecting negative answers. No reasonable person could conceive of these radically different domains having any "partnership" (*metochē,* "in common" NIV), "fellowship" *(koinōnia),* "harmony" *(symphōnēsis),* "portion" *(meris;* "in common" NIV) and "agreement" *(synkatathesis)*—all synonyms. Each question serves to remind the Corinthians of who they are as Christians and who they are not:

Who Christians Are	Who Christians Are Not
"righteousness" (see 5:21; 1 Cor 1:30)	"wickedness"
"light" (see 4:6)	"darkness" (4:6)
"[members of] Christ" (see 1 Cor 6:15)	"Belial" (4:4)
"believers" (see 2 Cor 5:7)	"unbelievers" (4:4)
"temple of God" (see 1 Cor 6:19)	"idols" (see 1 Cor 5:10–11; 6:9–10; 10:14; 12:2)

The reference to the temple of God (6:16a) leads to the assertion that "we are the temple of the living God" and God's covenant promise to be present among the people.

---

[928] John Chrysostom, *Saint Chrysostom: Homilies on the Epistles of Epistles of Paul to the Corinthians,* NPNF 1st ser. XII [Grand Rapids: Eerdmans, 1969; the Oxford translation revised by T. W. Chambers] XIII.1 (162).

[929] Hughes, *The Second Epistle to the Corinthians,* 244.

The medley of Old Testament quotes explain *(gar)* why righteousness and lawlessness, et cetera, are mutually exclusive. They are bracketed by the formula "as God has said" and "says the Lord Almighty" (6:16b–18).

The conclusion in 7:1 contains an exhortation based on these promises: "Because we have these promises, be holy." The Corinthians are to separate themselves from unclean things that are morally polluting and idolatrous. Participation in the promises hinges on their moral uprightness and avoiding the contamination of idols.

Paul is dealing with a controversial subject and a contentious opposition, and his use of questions allows his readers to supply the answers themselves. The Scriptural proofs then buttress those answers. This approach to the problem reveals that Paul wants them to think through the issues themselves and does not wish to force his opinions down their throats. Reconciliation requires that they be convinced in their own minds that Paul is right on these matters.

6:11–12   Paul uses a Hebraic idiom for speaking, "Our mouth stands opened (perfect tense) to you," which means here that he has spoken freely or frankly to them and continues to do so (REB, "we have spoken very frankly").[930] He cannot stay silent when they stand on a dangerous precipice where one false step will lead to their spiritual ruin. John Chrysostom interprets this statement to mean "that 'we discourse unto you on all points with freedom, as unto persons beloved, and suppressing nothing, reserving nothing.'"[931]

This is the only place in Paul's correspondence with the Corinthians that he directly addresses them as Corinthians.[932] Thrall suggests that this address makes what he says refer "to everything he has written since the opening greeting 'to the church of God which is in Corinth.'"[933] Comparing it to the other instances when Paul directly addresses his readers, Harris claims that Paul only does so "when his emotions were deeply stirred."[934] John Chrysostom assumes that the addition of the name "is a mark of great love, and warmth, and affection; for we are accustomed to be repeating continually the bare names of those we love."[935] These last two options should be combined to explain why Paul addresses the Corinthians directly.

---

[930] Furnish regards the idiom as describing "the free and candid expression of one's thoughts and feelings" (*II Corinthians,* 360). See Judg 11:35–36 (LXX); Job 3:1 (LXX); *Sir* 51:2; and Matt 5:1. This interpretation is more accurate than Barrett's negative rendering, "I have let my tongue run away with me" (Barrett, *The Second Epistle to the Corinthians,* 191).

[931] Chrysostom, *Homilies on Second Corinthians,* XIII.1 (162). Philodemus says, "There is nothing so grand as having one to whom one will say what is in one's heart and who will listen when one speaks" (Fr. 28; Philodemus, *On Frank Criticism,* 45).

[932] See Gal 3:1, "O foolish Galatians"; and Phil 4:15, "Philippians."

[933] Thrall, *Second Epistle to the Corinthians,* 1:468.

[934] Harris, "2 Corinthians," 358.

[935] John Chrysostom, *Homilies on Second Corinthians* XIII.1 (p. 342).

The perfect tense ("we have opened wide our hearts to you") implies that as he had loved them before he continues to love them now. It is as if to say that the breach in their relationship was not caused by him. He may have disapproved of their conduct and sternly rebuked them so that they would change, but such frank criticism does not mean that he abandoned his affection for them. There is plenty of room for them in Paul's heart. Jesus' teaching, "For out of the overflow of the heart the mouth speaks" (Matt 12:34; Luke 6:45), provides a commentary to what Paul means. What he has said to them flows from his love for them. If they are his letter of recommendation written on our hearts (3:2), he wants them to be a good letter of recommendation—which explains his chastisement. He is not interested in restoring good relations with those who lives are not right with God simply for the sake of peace and harmony. He will not back down in proclaiming God's absolute demand for ethical purity (see 12:20–21).

There is no restraint on Paul's affection for them, but he frankly accuses them of closing their hearts to him. Literally it reads: "You are not constricted by us, but you are constricted in your bowels"—the seat of emotion and compassion (see 1 John 3:17). The verb *(stenochōrein)* means "to narrow," "to cramp," "to constrict." We have the expression "narrow-minded" but not the expression "narrow-hearted," and therefore we need to adopt another figure of speech to express affection and loss of affection. Their love has grown cold, while he professes that he still loves them with heated passion. He has opened his heart to them; they have closed theirs and, in effect, squeezed him out of their hearts by treating him with distrust and suspicion.

If they do love him, that love is best shown by their obedience. If they refuse to accept his teaching and reproof, they have closed their hearts not only to him, but also to the Spirit.

6:13   "As a fair exchange" interprets the phrase that literally reads "the same recompense" *(tēn autēn antimisthian),* and it can also be rendered "in return," "in fair understanding," "as a fair return," or "in recompense in kind." Paul is asking them to show some reciprocity, the key element of friendship in the ancient world. Seneca writes that it is a disgrace to have received something that is greatly prized and not acknowledge it so that one does not accept the debt incurred.[936] It is possible that the Corinthians have trouble accepting that they have "received" everything and that it came through the ministrations of one so lowly (1 Cor 4:7). The cannot deny, however, that they owe their new spiritual life to Paul's ministry of reconciliation (5:17–20). Seneca also expounds that asking for a return on benefits given "is a very sensitive social act."[937] He says, "It is not easy to say whether it is

---

[936] Seneca, *On Benefits* 4.6.2–3.
[937] Ibid., 2.11.1; 2.17.7; 5.25.1; 6.27.2.

more shameful to repudiate a benefit or to ask the repayment of it."[938]

Paul's appeal for them to reciprocate in kind would normally be a delicate issue, but he escapes any social embarrassment by reminding them (1 Cor 4:14–15) that he is their father: "I speak as to my children."[939] This does not mean that he speaks "as he would to children."[940] They *are* his children, and he brings up this filial relationship because it permits him to speak as he does—demanding a return for parental affection from children. As their spiritual parent, Paul has loved and nurtured them; and they owe love to him in return. Sirach highlights this universally accepted duty of children:

> Remember that it was of your parents you were born;
> how can you repay what they have given to you? (7:28 NRSV)

Philo writes that "none can be more truly called benefactors than parents in relation to their children."[941] Paul therefore has every right to expect and to demand love from his children in return for his love.

He calls for them to be reconciled to God (5:20) and to open their hearts to him. For Paul the two are intertwined. This interconnection makes sense if the issue at the bottom of the dispute concerns their associations with idolatry. They cannot be reconciled to God and reconciled to Paul if they continue in heathen practices. Some have noted the connection of enlarged hearts to the Old Testament warning against worshiping other gods in Deut 11:16, "Be careful, or you will be enticed to turn away and worship other gods and bow down to them."[942] The LXX has "do not broaden your hearts."[943] In Deuteronomy the enlarged heart has a negative connotation and is related to pride swelling up in the people because of the bounty of the land whereas Paul uses the idiom in a positive sense to refer to open and joyous affection.[944] It is remotely possible, however, that Paul intends that they enlarge their hearts for him rather than for idols.[945]

6:14 Paul couches the main admonition in vivid imagery: "Do not be

---

[938] Ibid., 1.1.3.
[939] The "my" is not in the Greek text.
[940] Barrett, *The Second Epistle to the Corinthians,* 192.
[941] Philo, *Special Laws* 2.229. See also Philo, *On the Decalogue* 112; Aristotle, *Nichomachean Ethics* 8.11.1–4; and Seneca, *On Benefits* 5.5.2.
[942] Thrall, "The Problem of 2 Corinthians VI.14–VII.1, 147; and Murphy-O'Connor, "Relating 2 Corinthians 6.14–7.1 to Its Context," 272–75.
[943] Deut 11:16 LXX: πρόσεχε σεαυτῷ μὴ πλατυνθῇ ἡ καρδία σου καὶ παραβῆτε καὶ λατρεύσητε θεοῖς ἑτέροις καὶ προσκυνήσητε αὐτοῖς.
[944] Webb, *Returning Home,* 170–71.
[945] Alternatively, Beale suggests that the image derives from Isa 60:5, which matches the wording of Ps 119:32 (LXX 118:32). It would recall the motif of the exilic return and restoration of the people ("The Old Testament Background of Reconciliation in 2 Corinthians 5–7," 569, 576–77; see also Webb, *Returning Home,* 151–54).

yoked together with unbelievers." The verb *heterozygountes* is difficult to render. It literally means "other yoked" and is perhaps best translated "unequally yoked." In Lev 19:19 (LXX) the adjectival form occurs in the prohibition of mating different species of cattle, which explains the translation choice "mismated" in the RSV. It could be related to the prohibition of entering into "the partnership of marriage with a member of a foreign nation."[946] But in the context here, the image cannot be limited to marriage (see 1 Cor 7:39) and must include broader associations.[947] Plutarch uses the word to mean something akin to "ally" which would fit well in this context.[948]

Barrett paraphrases it well, "You must not get into double harness with unbelievers" ("harness yourselves in an uneven team," NJB). Paul has in mind an alliance with spiritual opposites, and the image of harnessing oneself to someone who is spiritually incompatible evokes images of spiritual disaster. Those who bear Christ's yoke (Matt 11:30) cannot share it with others who deny Christ. Those who harness themselves together with unbelievers will soon find themselves plowing Satan's fields. One can only be a true yokefellow (Phil 4:3) with a fellow Christian.

But does "unbelievers" *(apistoi)* mean those who do not believe in Christ? Several other candidates have been proposed.[949]

1. Some argue that they are immoral or faithless Christians.[950] They read this verse in light of 1 Cor 5:9–10 and assume that Paul is not telling them to shun pagans. Otherwise, they would have to withdraw from the world, but telling them to shun those who bear the name Christians who are guilty of the same sins: immorality, greed, idolatry, reviling, drunkenness, robbery. They are not to eat (the Lord's Supper) with such persons and to drive these wicked persons from their midst.

2. Another view claims that "unbelievers" represent "untrustworthy persons" in general as opposed to trustworthy persons like Paul.[951] Paul would then be commending himself to the Corinthians, but the word "unbeliever" never has this meaning in Paul.

3. Based on his interpolation theory that 6:14–7:1 was composed by Paul's Jewish Christian opponents, Betz claims that "unbelievers" refer to Gentile Christians who do not keep the Torah.[952] But this view is untenable,

---

[946] Philo, *Special Laws* 3.29.

[947] Deuteronomy 22:10 prohibits plowing with an ox and donkey together, but the verb ἑτεροζυγέω does not appear.

[948] Plutarch, *Cimon* 16.10; noted by Scott, "The Use of Scripture in 2 Corinthians 6:16c–18 and Paul's Restoration Theology," 75, n. 7.

[949] For a summary and critique of the various views, see Webb, *Returning Home,* 184–99.

[950] Goulder identifies them as "immoral/non-Pauline Christians" ("2 Cor 6:14–7:1," 53–55).

[951] J. D. M. Derrett, "2 Cor 6,14ff. a Midrash on Dt 22,10," *Bib* 59 (1978) 231–50.

[952] Betz, "2 Cor. 6:14–7:1: An Anti-Pauline Fragment?"

and no evidence exists that the word ever had this meaning.

4. Still others claim that Paul refers to the intruding false apostles.[953] Being "other yoked" would mean to follow their teaching. But this view requires that the reference to idols in 6:16 be taken in a metaphorical sense. Setting "idols" over against "the living God" suggests, however, that Paul has literal idols in view. One also wonders how "idols" could possibly be connected in any way to Judaizing false apostles? The quotation from Isa 52:11 in 6:17 would also make no sense since it visualizes Israel coming out from the midst of unclean heathens. The command to purify yourself and to touch no unclean thing is more applicable to dissociating themselves from pagan gods than Christian apostles.[954]

5. The option which makes the most sense in the context understands the *apistoi* to be non-Christians. Paul uses the word consistently in the Corinthian correspondence to refer to outsiders (see 1 Cor 6:6; 7:12,13,14(2x),15; 10:27; 14:22(2x),23,24; 2 Cor 4:4). The references to idols, the terms associated with separation from foreign gods, and the sharp antitheses that permit no compromise all indicate that "unbelievers" do not refer to false brothers who claim allegiance to Christ, however misguided, but to non-Christians who espouse values, beliefs, and practices that are antithetical to the Christian faith. The "unbelievers" are therefore the "unconverted Gentiles who inhabit the dark world of idolatry and immorality in such a city as Corinth."[955]

For Paul it is an either/or situation. Fellowship with God excludes all other fellowships—particularly those associated with idolatry. The Corinthian Christians were surrounded by pagan values and practices. Just because they have been sealed by the Spirit does not mean that they can be careless about their relationships and associations with the world.

Paul's clarification in 1 Cor 5:9–10 makes it clear, however, that he is not asking them to shun pagans altogether. He assumes that they will shop in the market (1 Cor 10:25) and encourages them to go to dinner at a pagan's home if they are invited and disposed to go (1 Cor 10:26). But he does want to form their spiritual identity so that they are distinguished from the pagan society surrounding them and will realign their values accordingly. Christians hold values dear that others reject. They must not allow themselves to be hitched to the same yoke as those whose beliefs are hostile to Christian faith. Therefore, Paul pleads with them to withdraw from these unholy alliances.

---

[953] So Collange, *Énigmes,* 305–6; D. Rensberger, "2 Corinthians 6:14–7:1—A Fresh Examination," *Studia Biblica et Theologica* 8 (1978) 25–49; Goulder, "2 Cor. 6:14–7:1 As An Integral Part of 2 Corinthians," 53–57; and Beale, "The Old Testament Background of Reconciliation in 2 Corinthians 5–7," 573.

[954] See further Webb for nine major problems with this view (*Returning Home,* 193–96).

[955] Barnett, *The Second Epistle to the Corinthians,* 345.

Does Paul have something specific in mind? Furnish does not believe the admonition "warrants particularizing" and views it only as a general counsel akin to what we find in Jas 1:27, "to keep oneself from being polluted by the world."[956] But the context suggests that Paul directs his admonition to something definite, and several proposals have been made. He could refer to taking grievances before pagan courts (1 Cor 6:1–11), visiting temple prostitutes (1 Cor 6:12–20), entering mixed marriages (1 Cor 7:39) with their dangerous association with idolatry (see Deut 7:3–4; Exod 34:16; Josh 23:6–13)—though Paul is clearly against ending such marriages unnecessarily (1 Cor 7:12–15). The most likely reference, however, is to eating meat offered to idols at pagan temples and in the homes of pagan associates. Paul associates this practice with idolatry even if the Christian eating this food has no intention of bowing down to serve idols. Webb allows that the admonition might cover "a number of cases not explicitly mentioned within the Corinthian correspondence: maintaining membership in a pagan cult, attending ceremonies in pagan temples (related to trade guilds, or to birth, death, and marriage, or the Isthmian games), employment by pagan temples, pagan worship in the home, etc."[957] He thinks the most probable options are visiting temple prostitutes and joining in pagan temple feasts.

The basic admonition is justified by a series of rhetorical questions beginning with the polarity between righteousness and lawlessness *(anomia)*.[958] The noun translated "in common" *(metochē)* refers to "a relationship involving shared purposes and activities."[959] Righteousness refers back to 5:21: "We have become the righteousness of God."[960] Lawlessness must then refer to those who willingly violate God's laws. The contrast between "righteousness" and *anomia* appears in Rom 6:19, "Just as you used to offer the parts of your

---

[956] Furnish, *II Corinthians,* 372.

[957] Webb, *Returning Home,* 214.

[958] A series of rhetorical contrasts is found in *Sir* 13:15–20:
Every creature loves its like,
   and every person the neighbor.
All living beings associate with their own kind,
   and people stick close to those like themselves.
What does a wolf have in common with a lamb?
   No more has a sinner with the devout.
What peace is there between a hyena and a dog?
   And what peace between the rich and the poor?
Wild asses in the wilderness are the prey of lions;
   likewise the poor are feeding grounds for the rich.
Humility is an abomination to the proud;
   likewise the poor are an abomination to the rich.

[959] J. P. Louw and E. A. Nida, *Greek-English Lexicon of the New Testament Based on Semantic Domains,* 2d. ed. (New York: UBS, 1989) 1:447.

[960] Paul uses righteousness in an ethical sense in Rom 6:19.

body in slavery to impurity and to ever-increasing wickedness *[anomia]*, so now offer them in slavery to righteousness leading to holiness." This statement would parallel what Paul says in 7:1: "make holiness perfect."

"What fellowship can light have with darkness?"[961] Paul characterizes the life of Gentiles before becoming Christians as an ethical and theological darkness (Eph 5:8; 1 Thess 5:4–5; see also 1 Pet 2:9; 1 John 1:5–7).[962] Immorality, anger, strife, vengeance, violence, and oppression thrive in such murk. Before their conversion, Gentiles were in bondage to the prince of darkness (the pretender to light, 2 Cor 11:14) and his evil dominion (see Eph 6:12). He even describes his own life as a devout Jew as one of darkness (4:6). But God has redeemed Christians from the dominion of darkness and transferred them to the kingdom of light (Col 1:12–13). Consequently, the "deeds of darkness" must be put away (Rom 13:12; see 1 Thess 5:5).

God has also called Christians into fellowship with his Son, Jesus Christ (1 Cor 1:9), and therefore they can only have true fellowship with him and with other Christians. The early church was marked by a keen sense of fellowship with one another (see Acts 2:42; Gal 2:9). "Shared faith in Christ has a bonding character and welds us to others who share the same experience of faith."[963] But in this context the word "fellowship" *(koinōnia)* refers to some kind of partnership. Christian partnership is best illustrated by Paul's relationship to the Philippians and to Philemon. Paul is especially attached to the Philippians because they joined him in a partnership to spread the gospel (Phil 1:5; 4:15). Paul also calls Philemon his partner (Phlm 17). He could not make such an unheard of request for Philemon to accept Onesimus back as a brother and not as a slave (Phlm 16) unless he was confident in this partnership and in Philemon's Christian convictions. A pagan associate would have laughed in his face, or worse, at such an inconceivable request.

6:15 "What harmony is there between Christ and Belial?" "Harmony" *(symphōnēsis)* suggests some kind of mutual agreement (see Matt 20:2,13) or an alliance (Gen 14:3; Isa 7:2 LXX). Danker paraphrases it: "Does anyone think that God would sign a contract with idols?"[964] The inference is then "how can a Christian engage in any activity that compromises God's interests?"[965]

---

[961] This word appears in *4 Kgdms* 17:11 (LXX) for entering into fellowship with the gods of high places (see 2 Kgs 17:11–12).

[962] In the OT darkness represents death (Job 10:22; Ps 143:3), Sheol (Ps 88:12), and God's judgment (Ps 105:28; Jer 23:12; Ezek 32:8; Amos 5:18, 20; Zeph 1:15).

[963] Garland, *Colossians Philemon*, 320.

[964] Danker, *II Corinthians*, 99.

[965] From the Greek word translated "harmony" we get the English word "symphony." This evokes another image: Can anyone imagine playing in a symphony composed of violins and pneumatic drills?

The contrasts in this verse between light and darkness, Christ and Belial, are rooted in Paul's conviction, stated in 4:4, that "The God of this age has blinded the minds of unbelievers, so that they cannot see the light of the gospel of the glory of Christ, who is the image of God." The God of this world (Belial) only spreads darkness by blinding people. Consequently, there can be no harmony between Christ, who is light, and dark Belial. Belial is a Hebrew word *(beliyya'al)* that may mean "worthlessness" (see 1 Sam 25:25), "ruin," or "wickedness."[966] In the intertestamental period it was used as a name for Satan, much as Lucifer was once a popular name for Satan in English. In the Dead Sea Scrolls, Belial appears as the arch enemy of God (1QM 13:11 the "angel of enmity; his domain is darkness, his counsel is for evil and wickedness").[967] Paul possibly chose the term Belial because he wanted a personal name as the antithesis of Christ.[968] In 1 Cor 10:20 he warns them that participating in pagan feasts is to share in the worship of demons. Christ and demons do not belong at the same table.

If we ask, "What does a believer have in common with an unbeliever?" as the NIV renders it, the answer is, "Much in every way."[969] Both are sinners loved by God, and both experience the same kinds of troubles and anxieties. The word translated "in common" *(meris),* however, means "lot," "share," or "portion"; and this meaning presents a quite different picture.[970] Christians give thanks to the Father because he has qualified them "to share in the inheritance of the saints in the kingdom of light" (Col 1:12). Unbelievers have no share in the community or in the promises.

---

[966] The Greek has *Beliar.* When the Hb. בְּלִיַּעַל *(bly'l)* was transliterated into Gk., the *l* and *r* were frequently interchanged.

[967] See also 1QM 1:1,5,13,15; 1QS 1:18,24; 2:19; CD 4:13; 5:18; 12:2; 4QFlor 8–9; and *Jub.* 1:20; *T. Reuben* 4:11, 6:3; *T. Sim.* 5:3; *T. Levi* 18:12; 19:1; *T. Judah* 25:3; *T. Dan* 1:7; 5:10–11; *T. Naph.* 2:6; *T. Jos.* 20:2; *T. Benj.* 6:1; and *Mart. Isa.* 1:8; 2:4; 3:11. *Sib. Or.* 3:63; 73 refers to the law of Beliar, and in 2:10 it reads, "You are unable to perform the works of light while you are in darkness."

[968] Murphy-O'Connor suggests that Paul does not use the term "Satan" because Satan can be associated with believers ("Philo and 2 Cor 6:14–7:1," 62). See Rom 16:20; 1 Cor 5:5; 7:5; 2 Cor 2:11; 11:14; 12:7; 1 Thess 2:18; 2 Thess 2:9). Less likely is the suggestion that Belial might be a pun found in rabbinic literature, where the word *beli Jol,* "having no yoke," appears (see *Sipre Deut.* 117; *b. Sanh.* 111b; so Barrett, *The Second Epistle to the Corinthians,* 198; Martin, *2 Corinthians,* 200; and Barnett, *The Second Epistle to the Corinthians,* 348).

[969] *Pistos* as a reference to one who believes does not appear elsewhere in Paul. Murphy-O'Connor contends that it refers to commitment to the transitory, visible and material realm and paraphrases the text: "Do not blend belief with unbelief" ("Philo and 2 Cor 6:14–7:1," 64–65). But Paul does use *apistos* to refer to an unbeliever, and the contrasting pairs demands "believer" (Talbert, *Reading Corinthians,* 172).

[970] Webb points out that "the lot of those who serve idols is often contrast with the lot of those who serve Yahweh (e.g., LXX Isa 17:14; 57:6; Jer 10:16; 13:25; and 28 [51]:18–19)" (*Returning Home,* 61, n. 1).

6:16 "What agreement is there between the temple of God and idols?" (see 2 Kgs 21:7; 23:6). The word "agreement" *(sygkatathesis)* refers to some kind of consensual affiliation, such as a pact joining persons together in common cause. The verb form is found in Exod 23:33 (LXX) in the prohibition of joining with the inhabitants of the land in some kind of agreement because of their idolatry. This is not a general appeal but directly relates to a major issue at Corinth. Paul clarifies the metaphor by identifying the community as the temple of the living God (1 Cor 3:16–17; 6:19–20).[971]

He next provides a series of proofs from Scripture to reinforce the main admonition in 6:14 and sets them off by citing them as the word of God: "as God has said" (6:16b) and "says the Lord Almighty" (6:18b).

Why did he choose to cite these particular texts? The answer will help reveal his purpose in this passage. Webb argues that the texts follow a chiastic pattern and fit a new covenant and second exodus/return theology.[972]

A Promise	of presence 6:16
	of relationship—covenant formula
	B Imperative of separation (6:17ab)
	B′ Imperative of separation (6:17c)
A′ Promise	of presence (6:17d)
	of relationship—covenant formula (6:18)[973]

Olley shows more convincingly that each text has been chosen "from contexts of worship of God, whether linked with the temple or in opposition to worship of other gods."[974] The link between the texts is this protest against pagan worship. The first citation 6:16b comes from Lev 26:11–12. The context deals with setting the people apart from worshiping idols so that they may properly revere God's holy place:

> Do not make idols or set up an image or a sacred stone for yourselves, and do not place a carved stone in your land to bow down before it. I am the LORD your God. Observe my Sabbaths and have reverence for my sanctuary. I am the LORD (Lev 26:1–2).

---

[971] J. Coppens, "The Spiritual Temple in Pauline Letters and its Background," *SE VI* (TU 112, Berlin: Töpelmann, 1973) 63, shows that "the idea of a spiritual sanctuary to be realised in mankind had pervaded Jewish circles." The reading "we are" is to be preferred over "you are," which is assimilated to the second person in 6:14, 17 and 1 Cor 3:16.

[972] Webb, *Returning Home,* 32–33.

[973] Webb contends: "The promises of regathering, a new heart, and a covenant bond (your God-my people) are all associated with forsaking idolatry. Egypt and Babylon become paradigms for idol worship, so that those who journey back to Jerusalem must leave their idols behind. Ultimately, the journey back to Jerusalem was to worship Yahweh in the new eschatological temple" *(Returning Home,* 59–60).

[974] Olley, "A Precursor of the NRSV? 'Sons and Daughters' in 2 Cor 6:18," 212.

The citation in 6:17 combines Isa 52:11 with Ezek 20:34 (LXX). Isaiah 52:11 is cited in 6:17ab, and its context refers to carrying the Lord's vessels out of Babylon. This sacred cultic task (see Num 1:50–51) necessarily precludes any contamination with idols. Ezekiel 20:34 (LXX) is cited in 6:17d, and it refers to gathering the people for purging the rebels (Ezek 20:38). The context again alludes to the persistent worship of other gods (Ezek 20:39). This quotation therefore contains "a note of warning" and reinforces "the need to be separated from the worship of idols if the hearers are to be 'God's people'" (see Ezek 20:41).[975]

Second Samuel 7:14 and Deut 32:18–19 are joined together in 6:18.[976] The Deuteronomy text is not as obvious, and the reasons for identifying it as a source will be dealt with below. If this identification is correct, however, the context in Deuteronomy indicts "the people of Israel for abandoning God (v. 15), serving 'strange gods' (v. 16), and sacrificing to demons and other deities (v.18). Further, v. 18 refers specifically to God as parent (father-mother [who fathered and gave birth to you])."[977] Deuteronomy 32:20–21 chides rebellious children who worship other gods and yet then promises that they will be cleansed.

Olley's analysis of the Scripture citations and their contexts confirm that they were not chosen haphazardly. He concludes: "Each in its own way reinforces both in warning and promise the call to give sole undivided allegiance to God as his 'people,' his 'sons and daughters.'"[978] The passages bear every sign of having been chosen to address the specific dangers of idolatry that, we have claimed on other grounds, lie at the heart of Paul's aggravation with the Corinthians and the cause of much of their conflict.

The first citation comes from Lev 26:11–12, "I will put my dwelling place among you, and I will not abhor you. I will walk among you and be your God, and you will be my people." Ezekiel 37:27 has also been proposed as the source: "My dwelling place will be with them; I will be their God, and they will be my people.[979] Resolving the matter is difficult, but the consistent opposition to worshiping other gods in the other passages and the warnings against idolatry emphasized in the shell surrounding the catena of quotations gives the edge to Leviticus.

---

[975] Ibid., 208.

[976] I am indebted to Olley for this reference ("A Precursor of the NRSV? 'Sons and Daughters in 2 Cor 6:18," 210–11).

[977] Ibid., 210–11.

[978] Ibid., 212.

[979] Webb argues that Ezek 37:27 is the primary citation since it fits an eschatological restoration theme he finds in this passage (*Returning Home*, 33–37). Scott claims that the conflation of Lev 26:11–12 with Ezek 37:27 "presents the promise of the New Covenant in conscious continuity with the Sinai Covenant" ("Scripture," 81–82). This seems to read far too much into Paul's intention.

The passage as cited from Lev 26:11–12 has been slightly altered. The second person is changed to the third person—"you" to "they" (possibly influenced by Ezek 37:27). "I will live among them" is added in place of "put my dwelling (or tent, tabernacle) among you" (Lev 26:11) to help interpret the phrase "I will walk among them." This passage serves to confirm that they are the temple of God where God dwells. It also attests that the covenant promise is now a reality for believers in Christ without any physical temple or tabernacle. But the emphasis is on God residing among the whole community and not just in "the temple" of the individual's body (1 Cor 6:19). The temple was assumed to be the home of God, and "I will live with them" means that God dwells in their midst. Everyone in the ancient world knew that defiling a temple in any way was a serious offense that courted disaster. The context of Lev 26:11–12 emphasizes the absolute necessity for the people of God to separate themselves from the worship of idols so that they can duly reverence God's holy place.

6:17 The second quotation cites Isa 52:11:

> Depart, depart, go out from there!
> Touch no unclean thing!
> Come out from it and be pure,
> you who carry the vessels of the LORD.

Again slight changes appear. The conjunction "therefore" ("wherefore," *dio*) has been added so that the citation gives the constraints required by their relationship to God: one must become holy. The text is abbreviated so that the reference to "those who bear the vessels of the Lord" is absent. The order is also inverted to make it fit better the new context. The third and fourth lines are placed before the second.[980] Finally, the reference to Babylon is omitted. The pronoun is changed from her *(autēs)*, "come out of her midst," referring to Babylon, to "their" *(autōn)*, "come out of their midst." The text is no longer read as applying to a real departure from Babylon but to a metaphorical departure. "Says the Lord" is also added to the text.

"I will receive you" is not appended as a short explanation; rather, it is a quote from Ezek 20:34 (LXX). The verb *eisdechomai* means more than simply "receive," "welcome," or "accept." In the context in Ezekiel, "God is

---

[980] Cp. the transposition of 1 Kgs 19:10 in Rom 11:3.

gathering people for purging, removing rebels who are worshiping idols."[981] This citation from Ezekiel interprets the one from Isaiah: God rescues with a mighty hand and then purges (Ezek 20:38). The phrase translated "I will receive you" therefore contains a note of warning rather than welcome. "It is reinforcing the need to be separated from the worship of idols if the hearers are to be 'God's people.'"[982]

This mixed quotation emphasizes that God's people are to be separate from the nations and their idolatry. "Touch no unclean thing" reflects a fear of impurity from physical contact with something contaminated and prepares for the command to "purify yourselves" in 7:1.[983]

6:18 The last citation comes primarily from 2 Sam 7:14: "I will be his father, and he will be my son. When he does wrong, I will punish him with the rod of men, with floggings inflicted by men." In the citation, the third person singular "he," referring to the son of David, becomes a second person plural "you," referring to the church.[984] "Son" is put into the plural and "daughters" is added.

"Daughters" occurs only here in Paul's writings which prompts the question, Why has it been added?[985] Some have argued that the addition

---

[981] Olley, "A Precursor of the NRSV? 'Sons and Daughters in 2 Cor 6:18," 207–08. The entire context of Ezek 20:34–41 is relevant in which the phrase καὶ εἰσδέξομαι ὑμᾶς, "and I will receive you" occurs twice: "I will bring you from the nations and [LXX καὶ εἰσδέξομαι ὑμᾶς, "and I will receive you"] gather you from the countries where you have been scattered—with a mighty hand and an outstretched arm and with outpoured wrath. I will bring you into the desert of the nations and there, face to face, I will execute judgment upon you. As I judged your fathers in the desert of the land of Egypt, so I will judge you, declares the Sovereign LORD. I will take note of you as you pass under my rod, and I will bring you into the bond of the covenant. I will purge you of those who revolt and rebel against me. Although I will bring them out of the land where they are living, yet they will not enter the land of Israel. Then you will know that I am the LORD. As for you, O house of Israel, this is what the Sovereign LORD says: 'Go and serve your idols, every one of you! But afterward you will surely listen to me and no longer profane my holy name with your gifts and idols. For on my holy mountain, the high mountain of Israel, declares the Sovereign LORD, there in the land the entire house of Israel will serve me, and there I will accept them. There I will require your offerings and your choice gifts, along with all your holy sacrifices. I will accept you as fragrant incense when I bring you out from the nations and [LXX καὶ εἰσδέξομαι ὑμᾶς, "and I will receive you"] gather you from the countries where you have been scattered, and I will show myself holy among you in the sight of the nations.'"

[982] Ibid., 208. Other proposals are Ezek 11:17; Zeph 3:20; Isa 52:12b; and an interpretation of 2 Sam 7:14; see Webb, *Returning Home*, 44–47.

[983] See Lev 5:2–3; 7:19,21; 11:8; 24–28; and Num 19:11–13. The context of Isaiah pictures the people in a holy procession traveling back to Jerusalem and carrying the Lord's vessels. With such a sacred task they cannot be tainted by association with any other gods (Num 1:50–51).

[984] D. Juel calls it a "'democratization' of messianic promises" (*Messianic Exegesis: Christological Interpretation of the Old Testament in Early Christianity* [Philadelphia: Fortress, 1988] 108, n. 34). Webb calls it a rereading of the Davidic covenant in light of the community-oriented new covenant" (*Returning Home*, 54).

[985] Betz argues that the phrase is un-Pauline "and would not have been used by anyone who, like the apostle, believed that the distinction between male and female had been abolished in Christ" ("2 Cor 6:14–7:1, An Anti-Pauline Fragment?" 106).

expresses a Pauline concern to assert the equality of male and female in Christ and to raise women to a place of equality with men. The promise, originally addressed to the male king, is now applied to males and females, who in Christ the king have equal status before God.[986] The problem with this view is that when Paul uses the word "sons" he always understands it generically. He would not have thought that the word "sons," in this context, excluded women and that "daughters" needed to be added to insure their inclusion. Furnish points out that Paul uses the phrase "sons of God" in Gal 3:26 in the context of mentioning the equality of the male and female (see also Gal 4:5–7), and he apparently felt no need to add "daughters" in an attempt to be less discriminatory.[987] Another reason must be found to explain the phrase "sons and daughters."

Since Paul is citing the Old Testament and fusing different passages, a more obvious source for the phrase would be the Old Testament. Beale claims that the word "daughters" was "occasioned by the OT promises of the restoration of Israel in which 'daughters' are often mentioned with 'sons' (Isa 43:6; 49:22; 60:4)."[988] This line of reasoning is helpful, but not as persuasive as Olley's proposal that Deut 32:19 lies behind the phraseology. Again the context is important:

> They made him jealous with their foreign gods
>   and angered him with their detestable idols.
> They sacrificed to demons, which are not God—
>   gods they had not known,
>   gods that recently appeared,
>   gods your fathers did not fear.
> You deserted the Rock, who fathered you;
>   you forgot the God who gave you birth.
>
> The LORD saw this and rejected them
>   because he was angered by his *sons and daughters.*
> "I will hide my face from them," he said,
>   "and see what their end will be;
> for they are a perverse generation,
>   children who are unfaithful.
> They made me jealous by what is no god
>   and angered me with their worthless idols.
> I will make them envious by those who are not a people;

---

[986] Plummer, *The Second Epistle of St. Paul to the Corinthians,* 210; Barrett, *The Second Epistle to the Corinthians,* 201; Héring, *The Second Epistle of Saint Paul to the Corinthians,* 51; Martin, *2 Corinthians,* 207; and Witherington, *Conflict and Community,* 406.

[987] Furnish, *II Corinthians,* 375.

[988] Beale, "The Old Testament Background of Reconciliation in 2 Corinthians 5–7," 572.

I will make them angry by a nation that has no understanding.
For a fire has been kindled by my wrath." (Deut 32:16–22)

Paul referred to Deuteronomy 32 in his warning against participating in
idol worship in 1 Cor 10:20 (Deut 32:27) and 10:22 (Deut 32:17), as well as
in his reference to Christ as the rock (1 Cor 10:4; Deut 32:18).[989] Deuteronomy 32 is therefore clearly associated in Paul's mind as a source for combat-
ing the problems of idolatry. Again, the quotation from the Old Testament
derives from a context that attacks any connection with idols.

The conclusion of the catena of Old Testament quotations is marked by
"says the Lord Almighty." This is the only place in Paul's letters where the
name "Lord Almighty" *(kyrios pantokratōr)* occurs.[990] It refers to God as
all powerful and ruler of everything. Olley concludes:

> If *all* the OT passages cited or alluded to in 2 Cor 6:14–18 thus contain an
> undercurrent of warning against treating God lightly by combining the worship
> and service of him with that given to other gods, it is appropriate that the more
> awesome title for God is then used, κύριος παντοκράτωρ.[991]

7:1   The phrase "since we have these promises" identifies these Old Testament passages as promises from God that relate to the restoration of the
people of God. It also calls to mind Paul's opening words in this letter: "For
no matter how many promises God has made, they are "Yes" in Christ. And
so through him the "Amen" is spoken by us to the glory of God" (2 Cor
1:20). But the promises are also set in a context of warning. They are not
unconditional, for they bring with them a solemn responsibility that can be
disregarded or disdained only at great peril. Christians possess the promise,
but they do not yet have its fulfillment.[992] The people will be restored *and
then* scrutinized by God. The phrase translated "out of reverence for God" is
literally "in the fear of God," the very thing that Paul has said motivates his
ministry (5:11; see 1 Cor 2:3; 2 Cor 7:11). Consequently, Paul gives a second admonition that is related to the first in 6:14: they must purify themselves from everything that contaminates.[993] We can compare this command

---

[989] Olley, "A Precursor of the NRSV? 'Sons and Daughters in 2 Cor 6:18,'" 211. He writes, "It
is above all in Deut 32 that 'Rock' is a description of God (and of idols as 'rocks; that provide no
protection)."
[990] The shorter phrase, κύριος παντοκράτωρ, translates צְבָאוֹת יהוה (Yahweh Sabaoth;
"Lord of Hosts"; see 2 Sam 5:10; 7:8 and elsewhere). Revelation has the fuller phrase κύριος ὁ
θεὸ ὁ παντοκράτωρ (Rev 1:8; 4:8; 11:17; 15:3; 16:7,14; 19:6,15; and 21:22).
[991] Olley, "A Precursor of the NRSV? 'Sons and Daughters in 2 Cor 6:18,'" 210.
[992] Thrall, *Second Epistle to the Corinthians,* 1:480.
[993] Concern for ritual purity was not solely an issue for Jews. Everyone in the ancient world
knew that temples must be entered in purity and that sacral rites must be done properly in purity.
These laws were also understood in a moral sense (see examples cited by Danker, *II Corinthians,*
99–100).

with 1 Cor 6:10–11. God has cleansed them, but this cleansing is for naught if they persist in defiling associations.

The word translated "contaminates" in the NIV is the noun *molysmos*, and it appears only here in the New Testament and three times in the LXX. It refers to religious defilement from worshiping other gods. In *1 Esdr* 8:80, it is used to denote the pollution created by the inhabitants of the land with their idolatry. In *2 Macc* 5:27, Judas Maccabee retreats to the desert to escape the idolatry and pollution of the temple imposed by Antiochus Epiphanes. The word also appears in a judgment oracle against the false prophets for the defilement they have brought to Jerusalem that was worse than that of Sodom and Gomorrah (Jer 23:15 [LXX]). The verb form appears in 1 Cor 8:7 to refer to cultic defilement (see also Isa 65:4; Jer 23:11; *2 Macc* 14:3).

Defilement "of body and spirit" means that the entire person, externally and internally, is corrupted by idolatrous practices in much the same way that sexual relations with a prostitute corrupts both body and spirit (1 Cor 6:15–18). Paul still must convince some in Corinth that participation in anything publicly associated with idols endangers their spiritual lives.

Therefore Paul calls them to perfect their "holiness." The verb "to perfect" *(epitelein)* means "to bring to completion," "to bring to its intended goal" and does not mean that they are to become perfect.[994] In the greetings of both letters to the Corinthians, Paul emphasizes that they have been set apart (1 Cor 1:2) and called to be "holy ones" ("saints," "those who are set apart," 1 Cor 1:2; 2 Cor 1:1). Barnett comments, "The holiness that is to be perfected is covenantal rather than developmental or progressive in character."[995] Holiness is "something that God gives to Christians (1 Cor 1:30; 2 Thess 2:13) but also something Christians strive to complete (1 Cor 7:34; 1 Thess 4:1–8; Rom 6:19), as well as something that God will ultimately complete (1 Thess 3:13)."[996]

In Galatians Paul combines the indicative "we live by the Spirit" with the imperative "let us keep in step with the Spirit" to address their problems (Gal 5:25). In the same way, he combines the indicative "you were washed, you were sanctified [*ēgiasthēte* = "made holy"], you were justified in the

---

[994] See G. Delling, "τέλος ...," *TDNT* 8:61–62.

[995] Barnett, *The Second Epistle to the Corinthians,* 357.

[996] Talbert, *Reading Corinthians,* 172–73. Watson, who does not believe this passage comes from Paul, finds addressing believers as "the agents of their own cleaning and as capable of completing or perfecting their consecration or holiness" to be "an extraordinary statement from Paul's pen." He concludes "It is difficult to imagine the author of Galatians and Romans conceiving of anyone but God as the agent of cleansing or the perfecter of holiness" (*The Second Epistle to the Corinthians,* 76). But it is not unimaginable for the author of Philippians, who wrote "work out your salvation with fear and trembling for it is God who works in you to will and to act according to his good purpose" (Phil 2:12–13).

name of the Lord Jesus Christ and by the Spirit of our God" (1 Cor 6:11)
with the imperative "perfect holiness" (2 Cor 7:1) to address the Corinthians' problems. Purifying themselves and perfecting their holiness would
mean, in this context, withdrawing from any unholy alliances and association with idolatry.

7:2 Paul repeats and therefore reinforces his appeal from 6:13, "Make
room for us in your hearts." The Corinthians need to broaden the boundaries
of their hearts to include Paul while establishing tighter the boundaries to
shut out any possible connection to idolatry. Paul also includes in this appeal
a reproach as he did in 6:12 ("We are not withholding our affection from
you, but you are withholding yours from us"): "We have wronged no one,
we have corrupted no one, we have exploited no one." Many interpreters
assume that the accusation relates to the Corinthians' suspicions about his
handling of money (see 12:16–18). But he may also be accused of causing
someone a business loss from his uncompromising insistence that they cut
off all partnerships with idolaters. From Paul's perspective profits derived
from something unchristian can bring no profit to the Christian. Perhaps it
refers to the stern discipline he urged in 1 Corinthians 5 or his insistence that
they not take other Christians to court but rather accept being wronged or
defrauded (1 Cor 6:7). Harvey submits that Paul may not be responding to
specific charges at all but only giving a conventional defense.[997]

7:3 Paul's reproach of the Corinthians for holding him in suspicion is
softened by saying that he has no intention of condemning them and by
repeating that they occupy an important place in Paul's heart (6:11).
Throughout this section he implies that unjust charges have been raised
against him and tolerated, if not believed, by the Corinthians. The problem
is, as Harvey notes, that "a successful defense might become an effective
prosecution: by proving one's innocence one would be directing the judge's
attention to the offence of the plaintiffs in bringing the accusation in the first
place."[998] Danker is aware that "the basic social concern about shame" lurks
behind his statements. Paul wants to make sure they understand his motives.
He does nothing to cause them shame. Like a good parent who loves a child
with all his heart, he has no desire to destroy his children's ego when correcting them (see Col 3:21). These words confirm his gentle disposition and

---

[997] Harvey, *Renewal through Suffering,* 77. He adds: "These words could be drawn from the
standard repertory of phrases used by a righteous man to protest his innocence in the face of those
who drew damaging evidence from his afflictions—similar expressions can be found in the psalms
and in Wisdom literature (which were demonstrably at the back of Paul's mind), and if indeed Paul
had recently survived a particularly life-threatening experience they would be an appropriate way
of reiterating his innocence and the 'assurance' (παρρησία) with which 'the just man ... confronts
those who oppressed him' (*Wisdom* 5.1)."

[998] Ibid.

good will in frankly confronting them. Because he has such affection for them, he has no interest in condemning them. He wants instead to boast about them. In fact, we cannot disparage those who are truly in our hearts. These Corinthian children cause him enormous pride and incomparable joy; but, because he truly loves them, he will frankly challenge them when they are in the wrong. His goal is not simply to negotiate a truce, but to correct their error.

Paul vividly expresses his immeasurable love for them and their unbreakable union: "that we would live or die with you" (lit. "so that to die together and to live together"). Most translations ignore the purpose nuance in this clause, expressed by *eis to* plus the infinitive, and turn it into a simple statement.[999] The NIV does this with its translation "that." It correctly interprets the unexpressed subject of the infinitives, however, as "we." Lambrecht understands the "we" to include the apostles and the Corinthians and takes it to mean "in order that we die together and live together."[1000]

This phrase may simply express Paul's deep affection and abiding friendship for the Corinthians. It could reflect a military image of a soldier's allegiance to his commander that makes him willing to die for him in battle and live out the difficult life of a warrior with him. Ittai, for example, swears to David, "As surely as the LORD lives, and as my lord the king lives, wherever my lord the king may be, whether it means life or death, there will your servant be" (2 Sam 15:21). If this is the backdrop, Paul would be expressing his loyal devotion to the Corinthians whatever the sacrifice.

On the other hand, the order "to die ... to live" in the Greek text seems strange, but it should not be reversed as it is in the NIV translation. The order is intentional and may have a Christological nuance referring to dying with Christ to live with Christ.[1001] Paul may therefore be alluding to their Christian destiny together. Lambrecht argues that while the phrase may have its roots in the everyday use of language that expresses absolute fidelity, it no longer has that meaning here. Paul is not simply expressing comradeship with the Corinthians. He has altered the secular expression from "to live and to die" to "to die and to live" to reflect "the christological destiny which awaits both himself and the Corinthians."[1002] His phrasing refers to "future death in Christ and future life in Christ after death." The bond between them

[999] J. Lambrecht, "To Die Together and to Live Together: A Study of 2 Corinthians 7,3," in *Studies on 2 Corinthians,* ed. R. Bieringer and J. Lambrecht, BETL 112 (Leuven: University Press, 1994) 572.

[1000] Ibid., 573.

[1001] G. Stählin, "'Um mitzusterben und mitzuleben,' Bemerkungen zu 2 Kor 7,3," in *Neues Testament und christliche Existenz,* ed. O. Betz and L. Schottroff (Tübingen: Mohr [Siebeck], 1973) 503–21.

[1002] Lambrecht, "To Die Together and To Live Together," 579, 586.

will therefore remain "in future death and future life."[1003]

But Paul has been dying for them already (4:12), which has resulted in his death-like condition that so repels some in Corinth. Rather than evoking their love for him, his sacrifices have caused them to heap scorn on him. When they come to understand and appreciate his cruciform life and ministry, they will also understand their mutual destiny in Christ.

How might this passage apply today? In a seminal article Barclay observed a stark contrast between the issues dealt with in 1 Thessalonians and those in 1 Corinthians. Although these two churches were founded by Paul within months of one another, "these sibling communities developed remarkably different interpretations of the Christian faith."[1004] He isolates one neglected factor that may explain this phenomenon—their respective social relations with outsiders.

One finds clear evidence in 1 Thessalonians that the church is experiencing conflict with outsiders (1 Thess 1:6; 2:2,14–16; 3:3) and feeling the sting of their alienation from society and society's hostility toward them (1 Thess 4:5,13; 5:7). No reference to conflict in the relations of Christians with outsiders, however, appears in 1 or 2 Corinthians. On the contrary, Paul contrasts his own situation of affliction and dishonor with their relative tranquility (1 Cor 4:9–13; 15:30–32; 16:9). The Corinthians appear to be getting on quite well in their community. Leaders participate in feasts in the dining rooms of pagan temples (1 Cor 8:10), and some are invited to share meals in the homes of unbelievers (1 Cor 10:27). Unbelievers drop into the house church to observe their worship (1 Cor 14:24–25). Some members of the Corinthian church therefore appear *too* well integrated into pagan society and have no religious scruples about their associations with unbelievers. In Corinth little countercultural impact, so central to the preaching of the cross, is evident (1 Cor 1:18–25). Their faith apparently did not create any significant social and moral realignment of their lives. For some, it was more important to maintain friendly relations with pagan acquaintances and family members and to keep their good opinion than it was to show absolute loyalty to the one God or to respect the feelings of weaker Christian brothers and sisters. As a result the Corinthians experience little of the social ostracism faced by the Thessalonians.

Paul does not expect them to withdraw from the world (1 Cor 5:10), nor does he reject contact with unbelievers in everyday life, particularly to witness to the gospel (1 Cor 9:19–23; 10:32–33). But Paul viewed the world with dark apocalyptic spectacles and makes it clear that "bad company ruins

[1003] Ibid., 580.
[1004] J. M. G. Barclay, "Thessalonica and Corinth: Social Contrasts in Pauline Christianity," *JSNT* 47 (1992) 50.

good morals" (1 Cor 15:33). Here in 6:14–7:1 he makes it more specific: they must not allow themselves to be harnessed together with pagans but must purify themselves and perfect their holiness as part of their exclusive covenant commitment to God. Barclay writes, however, that the Corinthian church

> ... is not a cohesive community but a club, whose meetings provide important moments of spiritual insight and exaltation, but do not have global implications of moral and social change. The Corinthians could gladly participate in this church as one segment of their lives. But the segment, however important, is not the whole and the centre. Their perception of their church and of the significance of their faith could correlate well with a life-style which remained fully integrated in Corinthian society.[1005]

The church in every age must walk a narrow tightrope as it tries to be in the world but not of it. To do this, Christians need a proper sense of their own identity and of appropriate boundaries. Christians must always be on guard against the pulls of the surrounding paganism and must resist religious entanglements that will compromise their loyalty and commitment to Christ and jeopardize their witness and their ultimate destiny.

Such sectarianism displayed in this passage may not be familiar to modern readers who know Paul primarily as the one who so vigorously defended eating with Gentiles in Antioch (Gal 2:11–21). Nor is it very palatable in an age of relativism and tolerance. The exclusivism reflected in this passage may trouble some as being little different from fussy narrow-mindedness that afflicted the Pharisees who consistently grumbled against Jesus for eating with and receiving sinners. The difference is that Jesus was reaching out to sinners to proclaim the gospel and to reform them. Paul himself does the very same thing (1 Cor 9:20–23), but never does he permit Christians to join any activities that bring discredit to the name of Christ or to form any alliances with those who openly deny Christ.

3. The Report from Titus (7:4–16)

Paul now returns to the subject he left off in 2:13, his anxious wait for news from Titus. This unit may be structured as follows:

7:4 Paul's boldness toward the Corinthians brings joy
　7:5–7 Titus's arrival comforts Paul in his affliction
　　7:8–13a The purpose and effect of the tearful letter
　7:13b–15 Titus's report proved Paul's boast
7:16 Paul's boldness toward the Corinthians brings joy

[1005] Ibid., 71

Paul's joyous declaration of his confidence in the Corinthians surrounds the account of successfully meeting up with Titus and his encouraging word about the Corinthians' response.

(1) Paul's Boldness toward the Corinthians Brings Joy (7:4)

⁴I have great confidence in you; I take great pride in you. I am greatly encouraged; in all our troubles my joy knows no bounds.

7:4 Many consider 7:4 to be the concluding sentence of the section beginning in 2:14, but it functions more as a hinge-joint, ending the previous passage and beginning the next.[1006] The repetition of its vocabulary in the succeeding verses shows that it prepares for what follows:

"confidence" *(parrēsia)*	7:16 *(tharreō)* (see 3:12)
"pride" ("boast"; *kauchēsis*)	7:14 (see 1:12; 8:24; 11:10,17)
encouraged ("comfort"; *paraklēsis*)	7:6 (verb form, *parakaleō*) 7 (noun and verb form) 7:13 (see 1:3,4,5,6; 8:4,17)
"joy" *(chara)*	7:7 (verb form, *chairō*); 7:9 (verb form); 7:13,16 (verb form; see 1:15, 24; 2:3)
"in all our troubles" *(thlipsis)*	7:5 (verb form, *thlibomai*)
"my joy knows no bounds" *(hyperperisseuomai tē chara)*	8:2 "their overflowing joy *(hē perisseia tēs charas)*

In the opening of the letter Paul expressed worry that he had grieved them (2:2; see 7:8–9). If he caused them grief, he wonders aloud, who will bring joy to him? As his children, they ought to make him rejoice (2:3), and now we learn five chapters later that indeed they have (7:4,13). His confidence in them (2:3) has proven to be well founded (7:4,14). Paul treads carefully around the touchy subject of his severe letter in which, he confesses, he may have been too blunt. He gently assures them that he never intended to cause them grief (7:4) but is glad that the grief that the letter generated turned out to be a godly grief (7:8–9). While many try to hide their emotions, Paul expressed his freely. The Corinthians deeply pained him when they withdrew their affection from him, and he was just as deeply overjoyed by signs that they had rekindled their love for him.

[1006] Barnett, *The Second Epistle to the Corinthians,* 362–64. He points out that 7:5–16 does not merely resume 2:12–13 but "serves to lead into the remainder of the letter" (p. 365). Talbert believes that 7:4 marks out an inclusio with 7:16 (*Reading Corinthians,* 138). Furnish comments that the connections with what follows are not to be attributed to the contrivance of a clever redactor (*II Corinthians,* 393; so also Bultmann, *The Second Letter to the Corinthians,* 181; Martin, *2 Corinthians,* 216).

According to the NIV translation, Paul expresses "great confidence" in the Corinthians. Olson contends that "the epistolary expression of confidence is best interpreted as a persuasive technique rather than as a sincere reflection of the way the writer thinks the addressees will respond to his proposals or to himself."[1007] From this perspective, Paul resorts to this convention only to soften them up before making his request about renewing their zeal for collection for the poor of the saints in Jerusalem since such effusive praise would create a sense of obligation. But Paul is not resorting to such manipulative tactics. His response is fervent; his joy, genuine and profound. But the word translated "confidence" *(parrēsia)* by the NIV is better translated as "boldness of speech."

Paul therefore returns explicitly to the topic of his frank letter by referring again to his plainspokenness that the Corinthians could mistake as a sign of unwarranted audacity which would inflame their enmity: "Great is my boldness of speech toward you" (see 6:11, "We have spoken freely to you, Corinthians, and opened wide our hearts to you").[1008] He can speak boldly to them because of his confidence in them.

An ancient Arabian proverb has it that a frank talk is good soap for the heart, but it can also border on impudent presumption. Boldness of speech and speaking the truth can create animosity—particularly in a hierarchical society if the one giving the frank criticism is perceived to be located on the lower end of the social spectrum. Paul is sensitive to this ticklish situation. He knows that the candor necessary for correcting another's error does not always go down easily, especially when it comes from a letter and not in person. In his hot letter to the Galatians in which he calls them foolish and bewitched (Gal 3:1), Paul laments, "Have I now become your enemy by telling you the truth?" (Gal 4:16). Marshall observes, "Many thought that *parrhēsia* [boldness] was evidence of an enemy rather than a friend and doubted friendship's capacity to withstand reproach from that quarter. Censure was never far from insult in Greek society."[1009] Consequently, in

---

[1007] S. N. Olson, "Pauline Expressions of Confidence in his Addressees," *CBQ* 47 (1985) 282–95

[1008] S. B. Marrow argues, "It is not a question of his having 'much confidence' in them, as the RSV translates it, but of his having that frankness to address them openly, to speak to them candidly, and to exhort them boldly" ("Parrhesia and the New Testament," *CBQ* 44 (1982) 445). See also W. C. Van Unnik, "The Christian's Freedom of Speech," *BJRL* 44 (1961–62) 466–88, particularly pp. 473–74. Furnish translates it, "I feel I can speak quite candidly to you" (*II Corinthians,* 385). Windisch cited Philo (*Who Is the Heir* 6): the servant speaks frankly to his master when he knows that he had done no wrong and that his words and deeds are for his master's benefit (*Der zweite Korintherbrief,* 223). See also D. E. Fredrickson, "*PARRHSIA* in the Pauline Epistles," in *Friendship, Flattery and Frankness of Speech: Studies on Friendship in the New Testament World,* NovTSup 82 (Leiden: Brill, 1996) 163–64.

[1009] Marshall, *Enmity,* 152–53; see also Malherbe, "Gentle as a Nurse," 208–14.

1 Corinthians, Paul tried to put his forthright indictment of their internecine spats in a softer light so that they would not misunderstand his intent: "I am not writing this to shame you, but to warn you, as my dear children" (1 Cor 4:14).[1010]

In returning to the subject of the accusatory letter in 7:4, Paul restates the main thrust of the previous chapters that he has spoken to them with all candor—the candor appropriate to Christ's apostle and one who truly loves them. From 2:14 to this point Paul has justified his license to be so frank with them, and he now explains that his frankness is a compliment to them. One has freedom of speech when one addresses those whom one trusts (6:11). He takes pride in them (lit., "great is my boast in behalf of you"), and he has been "greatly encouraged" by them (literally "I have been filled [perfect tense] with comfort"). The theme of mutual encouragement (comfort) is important in the letter (1:3–7). He overabounds with joy (the same phrase used in 1:4) in the midst of affliction because they have responded so well to his candor.

The reference to affliction leads into his recollection of troubles continuing in Macedonia when he went there to look for Titus. After Titus arrived with good news from Corinth, the joy that welled up in his heart alleviated all the pain (cf. 1 Thess 3:6–10). His boasting about their faithfulness sets the theme for 7:4–16. In 7:14 he concludes that his boast about them to Titus was not shown to be empty bluster but was proven true.[1011] Their positive response shows how well founded his boasting was to Titus. He will tell them that he has shared his great confidence in them with the Macedonians (9:2). The Corinthians' initial zeal for the collection spurred the enthusiasm of the Macedonians for the project. He trusts that such boasting will also prove to be well founded (9:3–5).

(2) Titus's Arrival Comforts Paul in His Affliction (7:5–7)

[5]For when we came into Macedonia, this body of ours had no rest, but we were harassed at every turn—conflicts on the outside, fears within. [6]But God, who comforts the downcast, comforted us by the coming of Titus, [7]and not only by his coming but also by the comfort you had given him. He told us about your longing for me, your deep sorrow, your ardent concern for me, so that my joy was greater than ever.

[1010] See further B. Fiori, "'Covert Allusion' in 1 Corinthians 1–4," *CBQ* 47 (1985) 85–102; and D. R. Hall, "A Disguise for the Wise: ΜΕΤΑΣΧΗΜΑΤΙΣΜΟΣ in 1 Corinthians 4:6," *NTS* 40 (1994) 143–49.

[1011] Philodemus offers the advice in his handbook, *On Frank Criticism,* that the wise man "mixes praises and blame; the pupil 'will be regained in that manner, namely, when the sting of censure is followed by praise'" (cited by C. E. Glad, "Frank Speech, Flattery, and Friendship in Philodemus," in *Friendship, Flattery and Frankness of Speech: Studies on Friendship in the New Testament World,* ed. J. T. Fitzgerald, NovTSup 82 [Leiden: Brill, 1996] 38).

7:5   Paul resumes the account where he left off in 2:12–13 about his travail and his quest for news from Titus. The abrupt transition from 7:3 matches the abrupt transition between 2:13 and 2:14, but it does not mean that a fragment of material—perhaps from the letter of tears—has been interpolated into the letter. The supposed seams do raise questions, however. Why did Paul leave off the story about not finding Titus only to pick it up so much later in the letter?[1012] This section is not simply a resumption of 2:12–13. It gives the foundation for his many appeals to this point—his joy over their repentance that confirmed his supreme confidence in them.[1013] But it also prepares for the following appeal for them to complete the collection that they had begun so hopefully. Titus is to play a major role in helping the Corinthians get ready for the collection, and his enthusiastic report to Paul about their reception of him primes them for his return. Paul intends to build them up as obedient stewards of God's grace.

He first discloses that his woes continued *even* when he came to Macedonia: "This body of ours [literally "our flesh"] had no rest." The flesh grows weary and is subject to all manner of woe. The use of the perfect tense communicates that this affliction was lasting. The term "flesh" has a neutral meaning here and connotes our creatureliness that is frail and vulnerable (see 4:11 [NIV "our mortal body"]; 12:7 "thorn in the flesh"; and Mark 14:38). Instead of getting a breather after facing deadly peril in Asia (1:8–11), his afflictions continued in Macedonia. "In every way" recalls the catalogue of calamities in 4:8–9: "We are hard pressed on every side, but not crushed; perplexed, but not in despair; persecuted, but not abandoned; struck down, but not destroyed." We do not know exactly where he was in Macedonia or what precisely his afflictions were, but Paul has taken pains to explain that, as an apostle in a world where the god of this age rules, he can expect hostility and little or no rest from troubles.

"Fightings without and fears within" suggests that the affliction was both external and internal. Paul had suffered serious persecution before in Macedonia (see Acts 16–17; Phil 1:30; 1 Thess 2:2), and we learn that the church in Thessalonica continued to face intense oppression (1 Thess 1:6–8; 2:2,14; 3:1–5; 2 Thess 1:4). The "fights" need not refer to physical threats but may refer to quarrels (see Jas 4:1–2), perhaps with the same

---

[1012] We may wish that Paul had included more details about what happened during Titus's visit, but the Corinthians already know that, and he did not need to give them this information. What is important to them is what Titus reported to Paul and how Paul responded. Paul therefore focuses on this response in this section.

[1013] Furnish, *II Corinthians*, 392.

opposition that caused him earlier grief.[1014] But it may also relate to spiritual warfare, to doing battle with Satan.

The "fears within" suggest that the external pressure was aggravated by worry. Paul hints at his apprehension about how his letter would be received, and he may have worried that his work in Corinth, the capital of Achaia, might turn out to have been in vain (6:1). Obviously, Paul never believed that his work was "finished" with any church after he left the scene. He never thought to himself, "I did my part, now it is someone else's turn to worry about them." Harris is on target: "It probably seemed to Paul that from the human point of view his whole future as apostle to the Gentiles was related to the Corinthians' reaction to his assertion of authority in the letter delivered by Titus. And now the nonarrival of Titus tended to confirm his worst fears."[1015] He may also have been worried about the safety of Titus— particularly when the traveler faced danger from rivers, bandits, false brothers, and danger in the city, in the country, and at sea (11:26). Just as his spirit had no relief in Troas (2:13), his body had no rest in Macedonia—until Titus showed up with good news.

7:6 Paul confesses to being plagued by "fightings without and fears within," but the answer to the struggle comes in the opening exclamation of 7:6: "But God"! In Rom 8:31 Paul exults, "If God is for us who can be against us?" The answer is "plenty," but the enemy can never ultimately defeat us. Here Paul returns to the opening words of this letter, where he praises the God of all comfort (see 1:3–4). We learn from this passage more precisely what that comfort entailed: the safe arrival of Titus, the good news from Corinth with their warm reception of Titus, their longing for Paul and sorrow over what had happened, and their zeal to make things right.

Paul says that God comforts the "downcast" (*tapeinos,* "humble," "low"), and again alludes to the prophet Isaiah and the promise that God comforts the unfortunate sufferers:

Shout for joy, O heavens;
rejoice, O earth;

[1014] Furnish translates the word μάχαι as "disputes" (*II Corinthians,* 386), and Kruse also argues that the use of the word in 2 Tim 2:23; Titus 3:9; Jas 4:1 suggests that it refers to quarrels and disputes with unbelievers or Christians (*II Corinthians,* 144). Acts states that Paul's antagonistic Jewish brethren chased him from city to city, and they may have continued to plague him and the churches (see 1 Thess 2:14–16; Phil 3:2–3).

[1015] Harris, "2 Corinthians," 362. Marshall points out that people of quality in the ancient world feared the loss of friendship and the transfer of loyalty to someone else more deeply than they feared the loss of wealth because it meant that they would lose, perhaps permanently, services, benefits, status, and reputation (*Enmity in Corinth,* 280–81). For Paul the loss of status and reputation was not as serious as losing the Corinthian church to false apostles with their false gospel and losing its support as a strategic cog in the worldwide mission of taking the gospel to the Gentiles.

burst into song, O mountains!
For the LORD comforts his people
and will have compassion on his afflicted ones. (Isa 49:13)[1016]

But the whole crisis with Corinth had brought Paul low and was a humiliating experience for him. Paul therefore may also be alluding to a criticism leveled at him. In 10:1 the word *tapeinos* appears: "I appeal to you—I, Paul, who am 'timid' *[tapeinos]* when face to face with you, but "bold" when away!" In 10:1 the word has a derogatory sense and connotes someone who is "'servile,' 'abject,' 'ineffectual,' 'inferior.'"[1017] Indeed, someone bedeviled by fightings without and fears within is the personification of one who is demeaned and wretched. God, however, does not regard those who suffer affliction, poverty, and defeat, or those who are unpretentious and self-effacing in the same way that the world regards them. God looks upon the lowly with favor and brings them comfort: "The LORD is close to the brokenhearted / and saves those who are crushed in spirit" (Ps 34:18). Paul knew what it was like to be abased and what it was like to abound (Phil 4:12). In any and all circumstances he trusted that God's comfort would strengthen him. He was "downcast" (NRSV), but not for long.

7:7 Paul rejoices no less when his coworkers also experience God's comfort. Titus received comfort from his time with the Corinthians, and he passed that comfort along to Paul with the report of their remorse. The image of "comfort" in this letter is something like a baton that one passes to another Christian as we compete in a challenging and exhausting contest. The hurt, repentance, and renewal of friendship have deepened the relationship among all three parties: Paul, Titus and the Corinthians.

The Corinthians were longing to see Paul (*epipothēsis,* cf. 1 Thess 3:6), apparently regretting his departure and failure to return. The word may connote a tender affection, an attachment to Paul that is mixed with a nuance of anxiety or pain (see 9:14; Phil 1:8).[1018] If they long to see Paul again, it means that they are prepared for his return, something that he will bring up repeatedly in what follows (9:4; 10:2,6; 12:14,20,21; 13:1,2,10). Their yearning therefore bodes well that his next visit will not be another painful one.

Their deep sorrow (*odyrmos;* "lamentation," "mourning") may be contrition over their past behavior or a sense of loss from Paul's decision to continue to stay clear of Corinth.[1019] Their former indifference has been transformed into "ardent concern" (*zēlos,* see 7:11) for him. This zeal is manifest in their discipline of the offender, which Paul seeks to rein in

[1016] τοὺς ταπεινοὺς τοῦ λαοῦ αὐτοῦ ("the humble of his people").
[1017] W. Grundmann, "ταπεινός ...," *TDNT* 8:19.
[1018] C. Spicq, *Theological Lexicon of the New Testament,* trans. and ed. J. D. Ernest (Peabody, Mass.: Hendrickson, 1994) 2:60.
[1019] Thrall, *Second Epistle to the Corinthians,* 1:489.

before it becomes harmful (2:6), and their desire to remedy the situation and repair the damage. Paul hopes that they will apply this zeal in carrying out his instructions for the collection and in defending him more vigorously against those who would badger him and hold him up to ridicule.

Paul repeats his expression of exultation in 7:4: Titus brought good news that multiplied the joy Paul felt when he finally arrived.[1020] Five things evoked Paul's joy: (1) Titus's safe arrival; (2) the comforting news about their longing for Paul, their mourning over the unpleasant incident, and their zeal to reform; (3) the Corinthians' repentance caused by their godly sorrow; (4) Titus's joy over the situation; and (5) the confirmation of his boast about them. His expression of joy confirms that the bond between them has not been irretrievably broken as he had feared.

(3) The Purpose and Effect of the Tearful Letter (7:8–13a)

[8]Even if I caused you sorrow by my letter, I do not regret it. Though I did regret it—I see that my letter hurt you, but only for a little while—[9]yet now I am happy, not because you were made sorry, but because your sorrow led you to repentance. For you became sorrowful as God intended and so were not harmed in any way by us. [10]Godly sorrow brings repentance that leads to salvation and leaves no regret, but worldly sorrow brings death. [11]See what this godly sorrow has produced in you: what earnestness, what eagerness to clear yourselves, what indignation, what alarm, what longing, what concern, what readiness to see justice done. At every point you have proved yourselves to be innocent in this matter. [12]So even though I wrote to you, it was not on account of the one who did the wrong or of the injured party, but rather that before God you could see for yourselves how devoted to us you are. [13]By all this we are encouraged.

7:8 Paul partially apologizes for any pain his letter may have caused them but delights over its ultimate results.[1021] The letter is the same letter of tears, now lost, that Paul refers to in 2:4. He says that it distresses him to

---

[1020] The μᾶλλον could mean "rather," "on the contrary." His grief turned to joy. Or it could mean "all the more" as the NIV renders it.

[1021] The definite article in Greek, τῇ ἐπιστολῇ, indicates a specific letter and not just "a letter" as in the KJV. Furnish notes that Paul uses the first person singular so as not to implicate his associates (*II Corinthians*, 397). The NIV translation, "I see that," assumes that the textual variant γάρ was absent from the original text (βλέπω γάρ). But the γάρ has wide ranging support among different textual traditions and best explains the other readings that attempt to clarify the construction by omitting it or turning it into a participle βλέπων. Metzger notes that the UBS Greek New Testament committee was split on their decision, but the explanation that "copyists rightly sensed that a new portion of the discourse begins with εἰ καὶ μετεμελόμην (whence B inserts δέ after εἰ) as an adversative conjunction), and therefore the main clause was taken to begin at βλέπω, with the consequent omission of γάρ, or at νῦν χαίρω, with the substitution of the participial form βλέπων as a gloss for βλέπω γάρ" is the most convincing (*A Textual Commentary on the Greek New Testament*, 581). See also Barrett, *The Second Epistle to the Corinthians*, 210; and Thrall, *Second Epistle to the Corinthians*, 1:490–91.

have distressed them which reveals his underlying fear that his boldness in this earlier confrontational letter might have driven them further away from him. Paul knows that no one can minister effectively while running roughshod over the feelings of others, and he takes no pleasure in wounding anyone. His "weighty and strong" (10:10) words are not intended to wreck relationships. But he is glad that the sharp letter hit the mark.

Danker cites as an apt parallel the advice of Libanius for repairing a relationship:

> I did not give a second thought to words that I had said to you, for I never suspected that they could have caused you pain. But if you were offended by them, please know, most excellent of all men, that I shall never repeat one of them, for I am interested only in being of service to my friends and not to cause them pain (*Epistles* 15).[1022]

But we should note several contrasts between Paul's remarks and this piece of ancient advice. (1) Paul is not fawning over them with a feigned apology. (2) He fully knew that his letter might cause a severe reaction. (3) He would do it again if necessary. He disciplined them for their own good. (4) He is an apostle responsible for preaching the gospel and effecting moral reform in others. That may sometimes cause pain, but he is not in the business of making everyone feel good.

Paul had no intention of venting his wrath on the disobedient in Corinth. His advice to fathers in Col 3:21 not to embitter their children so that they become discouraged shows that he knows that disciplining others means that one always walks a fine line. Heartless chastisement can reap harmful results as much as laxity and indifference. He confesses that he had misgivings that perhaps he did the wrong thing. But he has already told them his purpose in writing: so that his next visit would bring joy instead of pain (2:3), to show his love (2:4), and to test their obedience (2:9). Now he makes clear that he also wrote so boldly out of great confidence. Their obedience would reveal to them their real earnestness for Paul (7:11–12).

The reason that he is not really sorry for the anguish that his candidness caused them is that their grief only lasted a little while (compared to his, we might add), that it evoked godly sorrow, and that it resulted in their repentance and made them want to redress the wrong. Consequently, they were not harmed in any way ("suffered no loss," 7:9).

7:9 He rejoices over their repentance that implies regret over their previous course of action and their sorrow "according to God," that is, sorrow in accordance with God's will.[1023] That may mean God-intended sorrow that caused them to suffer no loss from us (NIV "were not harmed in any

---

[1022] Danker, *II Corinthians,* 107.
[1023] Martin, *2 Corinthians,* 230.

way by us"). Héring claims that "the loss" Paul refers to is his failure to return to Corinth, but it is far more significant than that. It relates to forfeiting the rewards of the next life and their salvation (7:10). Paul uses the verb "to lose" or "to forfeit" in cautioning the Corinthians about how they build on the foundation he laid by the grace God gave to him (1 Cor 3:10–15). In the last judgment, those who build on this foundation will have their work shown for what it is when it is tested by fire. "If what he has built survives, he will receive his reward. If it is burned up, he will suffer loss; he himself will be saved, but only as one escaping through the flames" (1 Cor 3:14–15). Kruse contends that "Paul may have felt that the Corinthians' positive response to his 'severe' letter had saved them from such a loss."[1024] If so, the letter saved them from harm rather than harmed them.

7:10 Although Paul and his associates may be a fragrance of life for some but death for others (2:15), as a minister of reconciliation he proclaims a message in this world that opens the way for life, not death. What he regretted is not regrettable because godly grief was its positive result.

Godly grief differs from a worldly grief in several ways. The first difference is what causes the grief. Worldly grief is caused by the loss or denial of something we want for ourselves. It is self-centered. It laments such worldly things as failing to receive the recognition one thinks one deserves, not having as much money as one wants, not getting something one covets. The kings of the earth weeping and mourning over the destruction of "Babylon," terrified at her torment that will soon befall them, and the merchants of the earth weeping and mourning "over her because no one buys their cargoes any more" (Rev 18:9–11) are examples of worldly grief. The inventory of their cargo follows (Rev 18:12–13), and last of all on the list are "bodies," a normal word for slaves. Because of his Christian conviction, John goes on to identify them as the "souls of men," as human beings, not "living tools," as Aristotle classified slaves.[1025] These merchants are slave traders who are grief stricken because they have nowhere to sell their cargo and make their heartless profits. By contrast, a wonderful example of godly grief was penned by the converted slave trader, John Newton, who came to recognize and confess his wretchedness and blindness in the hymn "Amazing Grace."

A second difference involves its results. The selfishness of worldly grief gives rise only to despair, bitterness, and paralysis. It causes our souls to drown in self pity or turns the sorrow into a cankerous sore. Many lead lives filled with regrets like Esau's when he sold his birthright (see Heb 12:17). Judas was overcome with grief by his betrayal of his master, but it led to

---

[1024] Kruse, *2 Corinthians,* 145; see also Hughes, *The Second Epistle to the Corinthians,* 269–70. Cp. Phil 3:7–11.

[1025] Aristotle, *Politics* 1.2.4.

despair and the desperate act of taking his own life, not to repentance. Godly grief, on the other hand, leads to repentance.[1026]

God can use this kind of sorrow because it moves one to action. The classic example is the prodigal son who "came to himself" and went home to confess his unworthiness to his father. Godly grief is therefore not to be regretted. It cracks the whip that motivates us to go to God, and our salvation takes root in it. John Chrysostom argued that sorrow is good for nothing but sin. It fails to mend most ailments. For example, sorrow over the loss of money does not restore the money. Sorrow over the loss of a child does not bring the child back to life. Sorrow over sickness does not cure the sickness. Sorrow over sin, however, can be positive when that sorrow kindles repentance.[1027] It incites us to seek to do something about the problem by taking the past tense and allowing God to turn it into his future tense. John Newton knew himself as the greatest of sinners, but after coming to God, he composed these words:

How sweet the name of Jesus sounds
  In a believer's ear!
It soothes his sorrows,
  heals his wounds,
And drives away his fear!

Surprisingly, in speaking to Christians, Paul says that their repentance leads to salvation. Repentance in the New Testament usually describes sinners or unbelievers turning to God (Rom 2:4; 2 Pet 3:9). We would think that those who were Christians would already have the assurance of salvation.[1028] But Paul's worries about the Corinthians (see 5:20; 6:1,14–7:1) are evident. Later in the letter, he will express his fear that not all will have repented of the "impurity, sexual sin and debauchery in which they have indulged" (12:21). Repentance implies remorse for sins that wound and anger God and the desire to make amends and to desist from sinning again. Paul fears that any refusal to own up to their sins will lead to a hardening that will calcify their hearts and make true repentance all the more difficult.[1029]

[1026] Cp. a similar thought in *Sir* 4:20–22:
Watch for the opportune time, and beware of evil,
  and do not be ashamed to be yourself.
For there is a shame that leads to sin,
  and there is a shame that is glory and favor.
Do not show partiality, to your own harm,
  or deference, to your downfall.

[1027] John Chrysostom, *Homilies on Second Corinthians,* XV.2.

[1028] *T. Gad* 5:7 is apropos: "For according to God's truth, repentance destroys disobedience, puts darkness to flight, illumines the vision, furnishes knowledge of the soul, and guides the deliberative power to salvation."

[1029] Possibly the word "salvation" does not refer to their ultimate redemption but only to the spiritual health of the community (see 1:6; and Phil 2:12). Repentance brings about reconciliation. "Death" would refer to their spiritual death, not ultimate death. But the word "salvation" has the meaning "redemption" in 6:2.

7:11   Paul's bold letter woke the Corinthians up to the gravity of the matter. In 2:9 he says that he wrote the letter to see their character *(dokimē)*, and now he asserts that they have demonstrated it. Whether we like it or not, "Human existence stands under the divine testing in which it must prove itself."[1030] The Corinthians are under their apostle's searching eye and also God's.

Paul gives a second catalogue (see 7:7) of the results of his letter and Titus's visit. The visit has shown their "earnestness" *(spoudē,* "diligence," "zeal"). The NIV interprets the next word *apologia* ("defense") to refer to their eagerness to clear themselves.[1031] The visit also evoked "indignation" *(aganaktēsis),* presumably at the person who wronged Paul, and "alarm" *(phobos,* "fear"). The fear may refer to a fearful respect for Paul and some apostolic punishment (see 1 Cor 4:21),[1032] a reverential awe of divine reprisals for rebuffing one who claims to be acting for God (5:20),[1033] or simply being caught off guard and having the seriousness of the matter driven home to them.[1034]

Paul again mentions their longing *(epipothēsis),* presumably for Paul's return, which signals that they want the relationship to be fully restored. The translation "what concern" *(zēlos)* is a weak translation and should at least be "ardent concern." They are displaying zeal, but Paul does not specify zeal for what. Zeal in itself is not always good, because it can be misdirected (Rom 10:2). It may be zeal for God, or a renewed zeal for Paul after their rather listless defense of him. Or it may mark a reversal of their former apathy and their lackadaisical approach to the disciplinary matter. The latter is the more likely option, since he felt the need to allay the severity of their punishment of the offender and encourage them to restore him (2:5–11). This interpretation also fits the next word.

They are now ready to see justice done *(ekdikēsis),* and this must refer to punishment of the offender (2:6). But the last phrase is puzzling: "At every point you have proved yourselves to be innocent in this matter." Paul delicately refers to it only as "this matter," leaving modern readers to puzzle over what matter this might be. Barrett argues that the offender was an outsider, not a Corinthian. He interprets the dative case "in this matter" as a dative of respect: "as far as this affair was concerned, the persons in question were ἁγνοί [*hagnoi,* pure, innocent]." He then contends that the Corinthians

---

[1030] W. Grundmann, "δόκιμος ... ," *TDNT* 2:257.

[1031] Ironically, the Corinthians have forced Paul to defend himself in this letter by their accusations (see 12:19).

[1032] Barrett, *The Second Epistle to the Corinthians,* 211; and Hughes, *Paul's Second Epistle to the Corinthians,* 274.

[1033] Plummer, *The Second Epistle of St. Paul to the Corinthians,* 223; Héring, *The Second Epistle to the Corinthians,* 55; and Martin, *2 Corinthians,* 235.

[1034] Belleville, *2 Corinthians,* 197.

had always been guiltless in the matter and now proved their innocence to Titus.[1035] But the reference to their "deep sorrow" in 7:7 suggests some measure of guilt on their part, and they took steps to make amends. Whatever the involvement of the majority of Corinthians in the case—perhaps they only failed to take Paul's side in the dispute—Paul is interested only in praising them for having now repented.

7:12 Paul again specifically mentions the severe letter. His statement that "it was not on account of the one who did the wrong or of the injured party, but rather that before God you could see for yourselves how devoted to us you are" does not mean that he *did not* write to make sure that they discipline the one who did wrong and champion the one who was wronged. He is using a form of comparison that communicates that his greater purpose was the ultimate good of the church. Plummer points out that this idiom serves to highlight the last part of the phrase. He compares it with Hos 6:6, "I desire mercy and not sacrifice."[1036] It is not that God does not want sacrifice but that God particularly wants mercy. Paul did want them to discipline the wrongdoer, but he insists that he wrote primarily to show them that they were indeed devoted to him. He wishes to make clear that healing their strained relationship and restoring their friendship was utmost in his mind. Their inaction in the face of the offender's defiance may have concealed temporarily their true loyalty to Paul. Paul's reprimand therefore was not aimed only at an individual but at the whole church.

The reprimand, painful as it was, worked by stirring them to action. Their zeal to punish the offender showed their devotion to Paul and to the gospel. Paul's explanation for the letter shows that a minister of reconciliation is not intent on making sure that punishment is meted out to those who may deserve it (to strike back) or to protect the honor of his person or his office. He is interested only in resolving the wrong and insuring that reconciliation occurs.

Again, Paul's delicate phrasing of things leaves us in the dark. Who is the injured party? It could have been a member of the congregation, whose identity we can only guess, who had been injured in some way. It could also have been Timothy, who was mistreated in some way during his last visit, which may explain why Paul dispatched Titus to visit them next instead of Timothy. Or he may be referring to himself with a tactful circumlocution. Paul insisted earlier that he had forgiven the offender—"if there was anything to forgive" (2:10). This absolution would also apply to Timothy as the cosender of the letter. It may seem, then, that the injured party was someone other than Paul and Timothy, but we cannot be sure. Without any clear evi-

---

[1035] C. K. Barrett, "Ο ΑΔΙΚΗΣΑΣ (2 Cor 7:12)," in *Essays on Paul* (Philadelphia: Westminster, 1982) 112.

[1036] Plummer, *The Second Epistle of St. Paul to the Corinthians*, 224.

dence, we can only speculate who this person might be. We may also be thrown off by Paul's extremely delicate phrasing to avoid any direct reference to his mistreatment at the hands of the Corinthians. It is more likely that Paul is alluding to himself in a roundabout way as he tiptoes around the original dispute so as not to rouse old feelings of hurt. Paul's main point, however, is to reassert that the whole church was wronged by what happened (see 2:5). The whole incident has been made known before God, and God is the proper judge of it.

In 2:4 Paul says that he wrote the letter to let them know how much he cared for them. He makes clear that the personal issues are not as important as preserving community and the enduring relationship between them. He cares for them and wants them to acknowledge how much they care for him and are indebted to him.

(4) Titus's Report Proved Paul's Boast (7:13b–15)

In addition to our own encouragement, we were especially delighted to see how happy Titus was, because his spirit has been refreshed by all of you. [14]I had boasted to him about you, and you have not embarrassed me. But just as everything we said to you was true, so our boasting about you to Titus has proved to be true as well. [15]And his affection for you is all the greater when he remembers that you were all obedient, receiving him with fear and trembling.

7:13b Paul "rejoiced in the joy of Titus" and received encouragement. The verb for encouragement occurs in the perfect tense *(parakeklēmetha)* and is related to the theme of comfort (7:6). If 2 Corinthians 10–13 is a later letter, then Titus was overly optimistic and misread the depth of their repentance. Paul's confidence in the Corinthians was also misplaced; and, indeed, his statements in 12:20–21 seem to contradict this confidence. But not all the news that Titus brought from Corinth was cheering. Paul learned that some were still upset by his canceled visit (1:15–2:2). And there are clear hints throughout chaps. 1–7 that residual problems still exist in the church. Paul is a skillful pastor, however, and does not focus only on the negative. He does not wish to bring the Corinthians to heel by destroying their egos. Although we get the impression that all is not completely well, Paul can honestly share his joy over their favorable response.

7:14 Their positive response confirms Paul's veracity; what he said to them and to Titus was true. From these remarks we can infer two significant points about the situation. First, they "certainly preclude the notion that Titus had been sent to deal with a church in open rebellion against its apostle."[1037] The picture of an extremely bitter dispute between the

---

[1037] Furnish, *II Corinthians,* 397.

Corinthians and Paul that some interpreters have painted may be too negative and alarmist. Second, Titus may not have been to Corinth before this trip. Titus seems to know the Corinthians only from Paul's enthusiastic reports about them. This possibility would rule out the hypothesis that chaps. 10–13 were written before chaps. 1–9, since Paul asks in 12:18: "I urged Titus to go to you and I sent our brother with him. Titus did not exploit you, did he? Did we not act in the same spirit and follow the same course?"

His boasting about them to Titus did not prove empty as he trusts that his boasting about them to the Macedonians will also not prove empty (9:2; see 8:24). This verse serves to prepare them for his specific appeal for renewing their zeal for the collection. Titus, whom they refreshed (perfect tense, indicating continuing results), will be sent back to them to complete the collection (8:16–24).

7:15 Titus reported that the church had been obedient in disciplining the wrongdoer. He was not sent to the community in a thundering rage to bring the Corinthians in line, but he reports that they responded to his authority "with fear and trembling." This same attitude characterized Paul's first preaching of the gospel to them (1 Cor 2:3). Beasley-Murray explains it this way:

> At that time Paul had been anxious that the word of God should not be frustrated by his inadequacy, and he cast himself on the mercy and grace of God, knowing that without them he could achieve nothing. Titus perceived in the way the Corinthians received him as the messenger of the Lord a like attitude, for they submitted to the word of God, they too cast themselves on the mercy of God in respect to their sins and they sought his grace for fuller obedience.[1038]

"Fear and trembling" refer to "the anxiety of a man who knows his limitations to do the will of God, but equally his faith that the Lord is not only Judge but Redeemer and that the grace is able to make even him adequate for his task, provided that he rests in faith on that grace."[1039]

(5) Paul's Boldness toward the Corinthians Brings Joy (7:16)

[16]I am glad I can have complete confidence in you.

7:16 The NIV translation "I am glad I can have complete confidence in you" is widely accepted. If it is correct, it must be qualified. Paul's confidence is based on the Lord working in and through them, not solely in them. But the verb *tharreō* parallels the noun *parrēsia* ("frank criti-

---

[1038] Beasley-Murray, "2 Corinthians," 56.
[1039] Ibid.

cism," "boldness") in 7:4, and its meaning here is "to be bold" (negatively "to show audacity") rather than "to have confidence."[1040] Spicq contends that this Stoic meaning of the verb applies both here and in 10:1–2. He interprets it to mean that Paul rejoices at "'being able in all things to be bold with' the Corinthians, to speak to them undiplomatically, with evangelical liberty and authority, and thus to communicate to them painful truths."[1041] Paul told them what he thought, and his thoughts are an open book—not camouflaged by insincere flattery or artful guile (see 6:11). We take this statement, "I am bold with you," to mark the conclusion of Paul's defense of his boldness (3:12; 7:4). After the discussion of the collection in chaps. 8–9, he will take up the theme again in 10:1 from another angle. In 7:16 he writes, "I am bold with you" *(tharrō en humin);* in 10:1 he writes, "I am bold with you" *(tharrō en humin).*[1042] But now, having praised the Corinthians for their renewed obedience, he seeks more proof of their zeal by their enthusiastic response to his project for the saints in Jerusalem. Paul therefore turns his attention to reviving their lagging preparations for the collection.

[1040] See W. Grundmann, "Θαρρέω, (θαρσέω)," *TDNT* 3:25.

[1041] Spicq, *Theological Lexicon of the New Testament,* 2:192.

[1042] The NIV translation of 7:16, "I can have complete confidence [θαρρῶ] in you," and of 10:1–2, "I, Paul, who am 'timid' when face to face with you, but 'bold' [θαρρῶ] when away! I beg you that when I come I may not have to be as bold [θαρρῆσαι] as I expect to be toward some people who think that we live by the standards of this world," fails to let the reader see the connections between the verses.

III. INSTRUCTIONS FOR THE COLLECTION FOR THE SAINTS (8:1–9:15)

1. Renewing the Corinthians' Commitment to the Collection (8:1–15)

The subject abruptly shifts in chaps. 8–9 to raising funds for the churches in Judea. This sudden turn in the argument, which seems to have nothing to do with what precedes, has caused many scholars to think that someone has inserted an independent letter or letters at this point. But the mention of Titus in 7:6–7,13–15 provides an appropriate connection to Paul's instructions for a project in which Titus is to play a major role (8:6,16–24). Switching his style to that of a commendatory and administrative letter to deal with the new subject of the collection is appropriate.[1] Paul mentions that his afflictions continued when he arrived in Macedonia (7:5) and that the Macedonians were going through a severe trial as well (8:2). The description of this affliction in 8:1–2 matches Paul's references to his afflictions in Asia in 1:8. One of the themes in this letter is his concern to explain how his afflictions could issue in "life" for others (4:12).[2] The Macedonians' afflictions and extreme poverty that result in overflowing joy and an extraordinary desire to help others fits this *leitmotif*.[3]

Cranfield comments, "The Church's need of money is a matter which it is difficult to handle with graciousness, sensitiveness and dignity."[4] Paul handles the issue deftly, and his lengthy discussion shows how important planning and administration are to the success of any ministry. Paul engages in evangelism as a front line missionary working in the trenches. He is a sensitive pastor and wise theologian. He is a visionary who has planned a worldwide project with enormous theological ramifications. He is also an administrator who does not shy away from handling the essential details, delivering theological pep talks to those who have grown indifferent to the task, delegating responsibilities, and soothing ruffled feathers.

The Jerusalem project offers the Corinthians the chance to participate in something greater than themselves. Generosity is not something innate to human beings. Seneca recognized that people needed to be taught how to give, receive, and return willingly.[5] This is no less true of Christians, and in these two chapters Paul shows why and how the Corinthian Christians should contribute to this fund. His discussion can be outlined as follows:[6]

---

[1] A. E. Harvey writes: "Paul certainly had an urgent request to make of the Corinthians, but of the kind which he always preferred to speak of somewhat indirectly. He also evidently needed to express his personal confidence in Titus, who would be assisting in the transaction. What [is] more natural than that he should adopt a more official tone and use some well-tried techniques of persuasion" (*Renewal through Suffering: A Study of 2 Corinthians*, Studies of the New Testament and Its World [Edinburgh: T & T Clark, 1996] 81). V. D. Verbrugge discusses fund-raising in the Greco-Roman society and letters requesting such gifts (*Paul's Style of Church Leadership Illustrated by His Instructions to the Corinthians on the Collection* [San Francisco: Mellen Research University Press, 1992] 145–243). He comments that we have grown accustomed to receiving appeals for donations from a wide variety of sources using a wide variety of methods, but this practice was "virtually unknown in antiquity" (p. 244). Paul's request to solicit funds for a group of people is unique.

[2] Paul mentions "affliction" in 1:4–6,8; 2:4; 4:8,17; and 6:4, but not in chaps. 10–13.

[3] Harvey, *Renewal through Suffering*, 82.

[4] C. E. B. Cranfield, "The Grace of Our Lord Jesus Christ: 2 Corinthians 8,1–9," *Communio viatorum* 32 (1989) 105.

[5] Seneca, *On Benefits* 1.4.3.

[6] See also C. H. Talbert, "Money Management in Early Mediterranean Christianity: 2 Corinthians 8–9," *RevExp* 86 (1989) 361.

A 8:1–15 The Corinthians' need to complete their collection
    8:1–5 Example: God's grace given to the Macedonians
    8:6–8 Direction: Bring to completion this act of grace (excel in this grace of
        giving)
    8:9 Example: God's grace in the sacrifice of Jesus Christ
    8:10–12 Direction: Finish the work (willingness sanctifies the gift)
    8:13–15 Divine principle: Equity (Scripture citation)
    **B 8:16–9:5 The administration of the funds by Titus and the acclaimed
        brothers**
        8:16–24 Commendation of Titus and the brothers
        9:1–5 Explanation for sending the brothers: Avoiding shame
**A′ 9:6–15 Divine principles of giving: Why the Corinthians need to give
    generously**
    9:6–7 Divine principle: (Scripture citation)
    9:8–10 Divine principle: (Scripture citation and interpretation)
    9:11–15 Concluding summary of what this service will achieve

(1) Example: God's Grace Given to the Macedonians (8:1–5)

**¹And now, brothers, we want you to know about the grace that God has given
the Macedonian churches. ²Out of the most severe trial, their overflowing joy and
their extreme poverty welled up in rich generosity. ³For I testify that they gave as
much as they were able, and even beyond their ability. Entirely on their own,
⁴they urgently pleaded with us for the privilege of sharing in this service to the
saints. ⁵And they did not do as we expected, but they gave themselves first to the
Lord and then to us in keeping with God's will.**

8:1   Paul begins his appeal by informing the Corinthians how the grace
of God has been given to the churches in Macedonia, presumably, Philippi,
Thessalonica, and Berea.[7] "Grace" is a key word that appears ten times
throughout these two chapters with differing nuances.[8] Here it refers to
human generosity, which Paul understands to be something given by God.
Grace is God's unconditional benevolence toward us. When people are
spontaneously generous toward others, Paul takes it as clear evidence that
God's grace is working in and through them.[9] Dahl calls the gift of money to
others "a visible sign of an invisible grace."[10] Attributing their generosity to

---

[7] The phrase "we want you to know" is not infrequently used as a transition marker in Paul's
letters (see Gal 1:11; 2 Cor 1:8; Phil 1:12). See D. De Silva, "Measuring Penultimate against Ultimate Reality: An Investigation of the Integrity and Argumentation of 2 Corinthians," *JSNT* 52
(1993) 42–43.

[8] It occurs ten times in these chapters out of the eighteen times it appears in the letter (8:1,4,6,
7,9,16,19; 9:8,14,15). The NIV renders it as "grace" (8:1,9; 9:8,14); "act of grace (8:6); "grace of
giving" (8:7); "offering (8:19); "privilege" (8:4); and "thanks" (8:16; 9:15).

[9] In Rom 12:8 Paul lists contributing to the needs of others as a gift given by grace.

[10] N. A. Dahl, "Paul and Possessions," in *Studies in Paul* (Minneapolis: Augsburg, 1977) 31.

God's grace may reflect Paul's marveling over how this project was "unfolding without his personal intervention; everything is happening as if it were a gesture of grace performed by God for the sake of the Macedonians (8:1)."[11] It is interesting that Paul understands that God's grace does not lighten the Macedonians' afflictions nor remove their deep poverty. Instead, it opens their hearts and their purse strings to others.

Paul hopes that the Corinthians will take heart from the example of the Macedonians. It may seem that he is playing one church off the other: impoverished churches over against affluent churches, churches from the north versus churches from the south. But Paul is not stooping to any gimmicks in fund raising. He is not trying to raise a larger amount by inciting competition between churches to see who can raise the most. The amount does not matter; the spirit behind the giving does. If the Corinthians want to compete with the Macedonians, they should compete for the most joyful and willing attitude, not over the amount of money contributed. Attitudes of the heart, however, are far more difficult to measure and to compare, so humans tend to resort to flesh categories (5:16) to evaluate giving and spirituality. By contrast, Paul commends the Macedonians for their overflowing joy and willingness to sacrifice for others in the midst of their own suffering.

Paul asserts, however, that the Macedonians can take no credit for this joyful, willing attitude. It all comes from God's grace *given* to them. Paul therefore bases his appeal to the Corinthians on the grace of God that continues to be richly poured out in the lives of Christians. Paul's approach to fund-raising is grounded in solid theological principles, and it should lead the Corinthians to ask themselves, Where is the evidence of the grace of God that has been given to us?

8:2 The Macedonians experienced an up welling of generosity during a severe test of affliction. The New Testament evidence suggests that they were no strangers to persecution (see Acts 16:20; 17:50; Phil 1:29–30; 1 Thess 1:6; 2:14; 3:3–4). The word translated "test" *(dokimē)* has a different nuance than the word for testing *(peirasmos)* that is related to temptation.[12] It "points more to the positive outcome of such a test than to the test itself."[13] The test proved their Christian character.

The Macedonians also suffered from extreme poverty that Paul vividly

---

[11] D. Georgi, *Remembering the Poor: The History of Paul's Collection for Jerusalem* (Nashville: Abingdon, 1992) 72.

[12] The word ἡ δοκιμή ("test," "ordeal") appears in 2:9; 9:13; 13:3. The cognate τὸ δοκιμίον ("testing," "proven genuine by testing") appears in Jas 1:3, where James says that the testing of their faith produces perseverance, and in 1 Pet 1:7, where the testing of their faith, tested by fire, results in praise, glory, and honor.

[13] H. D. Betz, *2 Corinthians 8 and 9: A Commentary on Two Administrative Letters of the Apostle Paul*, Her (Philadelphia: Fortress, 1985) 43.

expresses as "down to depths of poverty." Persecution and social ostracism probably caused this rock bottom poverty. Their poverty matches that of the saints in Jerusalem that was also caused by persecution and may have generated their empathy with them.[14]

In spite of persecution and poverty, they experienced an abundance of joy, which resulted in a wealth of generosity (the Greek uses cognates, "the abundance of their joy abounded ...").[15] In the New Testament the Christian's experience of joy has no correlation to his or her outward circumstances. Paradoxically, Christians can experience joy in the midst of great persecution and personal suffering.[16] Poverty overflowing into wealth also may seem paradoxical, but it fits the crazy-quilt logic of the gospel: joy + severe affliction + poverty = wealth. Here, wealth relates to a wealth of generosity and joy multiplied.[17] Material wealth, on the other hand, may cloak spiritual poverty, as Christ's condemnation of the wealthy but tepid church at Laodicea reveals (Rev 3:14–22). That church considered itself rich and prospering, but the Lord considered it "wretched, pitiful, poor, blind and naked." By contrast, Christ praises the poverty stricken church at Smyrna, also beset by affliction, as rich (Rev 2:8–11). The Macedonian churches were, like Smyrna, members of a specially blessed category in the eyes of the Lord: rich poor churches. Murphy–O'Connor reflects on the Macedonians' benevolence:

> Despite all their own difficulties they did not turn inwards; their concern was for others, the one proof of "authentic love" (2 Cor 8:2–8). It was this that released the divine power into the world. What a contrast to the church at Corinth, whose internal divisions risked putting a stumbling-block in the way of the conversion of both Jews and Greeks, and even endangered other Christians (1 Cor. 10:32–33)![18]

In this passage Paul is too tactful to put things quite so bluntly; but he holds up the supreme sacrifice of the Macedonian's in the face of extreme poverty as an example for the Corinthians. The Macedonians' giving to help

---

[14] See R. Jewett, *The Thessalonian Correspondence: Pauline Rhetoric and Millenarian Piety* (Philadelphia: Fortress, 1986) 165–66. See 1 Thess 2:14.

[15] The verb translated "welled up" (περισσεύω) also appears in 8:7 (2x, "excel"), 9:8 (2x, "abound"), and in 9:12 ("overflow"); see also 1:5; 3:9; and 4:15.

[16] Matt 5:10–12; Acts 5:41; Phil 1:12–18; Jas 1:2; and 1 Pet 1:6–7.

[17] Furnish interprets the phrase "the wealth of their generosity" as epexegetical, "the wealth, which is their generosity" (*II Corinthians*, 400). The word translated "generosity" (ἁπλότης) appears only in Paul's letters in the NT and means "simplicity," "singleness," "sincerity," "willingness," or "sincere concern" or "kindness." It comes to mean generosity as those with a singleness of concern for another's need stand ready to help.

[18] J. Murphy-O'Connor, "Paul and Macedonia: The Connection Between 2 Corinthians 2.13 and 2.14," *JSNT* 25 (1985) 102.

others who were also beleaguered by persecution and poverty follows the pattern of Jesus Christ mentioned in 8:9 who willingly accepted poverty and turned it into wealth for others.

8:3–4 Paul says that they gave as much as they were able and beyond what they were able.[19] He did not ask for any specified amount or percentage. The Macedonians had not prospered and given from their surplus. Instead, they gave out of their poverty more than could be expected or even thought wise. Paul emphasizes that they did this of their own accord.[20] This word could go with what precedes (KJV, JB, NRSV) or, as the NIV punctuates it, with the next sentence in 8:4. If it is part of v. 3, their giving was spontaneous and voluntary. If it goes with v. 4, they urgently pleaded to participate entirely on their own (see also REB). This reading would imply that Paul originally was not going to ask them to participate, which is strange, since he had been in partnership with the Philippian congregation who helped him in his mission enterprise in other cities (Phil 4:15–16). But in 1 Cor 16:1–4 Paul only mentions giving directions for the collection to the Corinthians and the churches of Galatia.

Paul's primary reason for emphasizing that the Macedonians responded voluntarily is to make clear to the Corinthians that he did not constrain them in any way. They volunteered, either to give sacrificially, or to participate. Since Paul encourages the Corinthians to give willingly, he may be referring to how the Macedonians gave. The Macedonians considered it a privilege to contribute. The word translated "privilege" is the same word "grace" *(charis)* that rings throughout these two chapters. They did not plea poverty to evade any obligation; they pled with Paul instead to allow them to join in this service. By contrast, Paul has to plead with the more affluent Corinthians to follow through on their first pledge.

Paul gives the impression that he was taken aback by the Macedonians' eagerness and generosity. They gave beyond their means and did so without Paul's encouragement, let alone his insistence. If it comes from "grace," then it cannot come from coercion. They gave beyond anything he anticipated because they gave of themselves.

The quantity of what they gave does not matter to Paul, but the spirit in which they gave does. With God, a couple of "mites" can far outweigh a ton of gold bullion. In keeping with this divine outlook, Paul never mentions the word money when talking about this project. He cloaks the whole enterprise in language that has both a formal administrative character and a theological character. It is a "ministry." The word "ministry" *(diakonia)* had a technical

---

[19] The word δύναμις, "power," "ability," can refer to one's financial capacity.

[20] αὐθαίρετοι (αὐτός + αἱρέομαι) means "to choose for oneself, of one's accord." The adjective appears in 8:17 to refer to the response of Titus at the prospect returning to Corinth.

meaning in Judaism for supporting the needs of the poor.[21] For Paul, however, this ministry is far more than simply delivering aid to poor people. It had major theological consequences and was something he was prepared to risk his life to carry out. Business language is therefore hardly adequate to describe it, and so Paul resorts to theological language.

"grace," "privilege" (*charis*, 8:4,6,7,19)
"partnership," "sharing" (*koinōnia*, 8:4)
"service," "ministry" (*diakonia*, 8:4; 9:1,12,13)
"earnestness" (*spoudē*, 8:8)
"love" (*agapē*, 8:7,8,24)
"willingness" (*prothymia*, 8:11,12,19; 9:2)
"generosity" (*haplotēs*, 8:2; 9:11,13)
"abundance" (*perisseuma*, 8:14)
"liberal gift" (*hadrotēs*, 8:20)
"undertaking" (*hypostasis*, 9:4)
"blessing" "generous gift" (*eulogia*, 9:5)
"good work" (*ergon agathon*, 9:8)
"the yield of your righteousness" (*ta gennēmata tēs dikaiosynēs hymōn*, 9:10)
"service" (*leitourgia*, 9:12).[22]

In the process Paul creates a new meaning for the word, *koinōnia* ("partnership," "fellowship").[23] This is the first use of the word for monetary collections.[24] As the Philippians had formed a partnership with Paul in his mission work beyond Philippi (Phil 1:5; 4:15), all the Macedonian churches want to form a partnership with other Christians in Judea. They beg to participate.[25] Murphy-O'Connor remarks:

---

[21] See Acts 6:1; 11:29; 12:25; Rom 15:25,31; and its usage here in 2 Cor 8:4; 9:12–13. Furnish also cites *T. Job* 11:1–3; 12:2; 15:1,4,8 (*II Corinthians*, 401).

[22] In Rom 15:28 Paul also refers to it as "fruit" (*karpos*).

[23] The NIV correctly renders the Greek phrase "grace and sharing" as a hendiadys, "the grace of sharing."

[24] M. McDermott, "The Biblical Doctrine of KOINΩNIA, II. Part," *BZ* 19 (1973) 222. "Here for the first time the spiritual union among Christians is seen as the basis of the demanded sharing of material goods." McDermott notes that Paul was so influenced by "the religious context of the collection" that he chose "a word with positive religious connotations instead of the secular λογία" ("The Biblical Doctrine of KOINΩNIA," *BZ* 19 [1973] 72–73).

[25] A parallel can be found in *T. Job* 11:1–3, which cites the response of others to Job's care for the poor: "There were also certain strangers who saw my eagerness, and they too desired to assist in this service. And there were still others, at that time without resources and unable to invest a thing, who came and entreated me, saying: 'We beg you, may we also engage in this service. But we own nothing, however. Show mercy on us and lend us money so we may leave for distant cities on business and be able to do the poor a service. And afterward we shall repay you what is yours.'"

This spontaneous recognition of charity as the essence of Christianity won them a place in his affections to which no other community could aspire, and which merited them the accolade of 'partners in the gospel.' (Phil 1:5,7). They made the good news something real and vital by demonstrating the power of grace."[26]

Paul does not specifically identify the "saints" who are the recipients of the "ministry" (see Rom 15:26).[27] Expressing love for the saints in material ways, whoever they may be (see Col 1:4; Phlm 5), is one measure that Paul uses to gauge the maturity of a church's or individual's faith. Christians, like young children, need to grow out of their natural self-centeredness and learn to share with others. When they show evidence of this, Paul praises them profusely.

8:5 The literal rendering of the Greek that they gave "not as we had hoped" suggests to English ears some disappointment on Paul's part when, in truth, what they did was beyond his hopes. They gave beyond any reasonable hope. "First" (in an emphatic position), they gave themselves to the Lord. The "first" refers to the priority of importance, not to time. They also gave of themselves "to us," which means that they dedicated themselves to Paul's project. This phrase betrays that Paul recognizes how important the churches' relationship to him is to the success of the project. If they are not prepared to give themselves to him, they are not likely to give to the relief fund. The past enmity between Paul and the Corinthians has threatened to suspend their participation. The Macedonians' eagerness to participate allows Paul to use them as a model for the Corinthians. In doing so he makes clear that this surprising turn of events stemmed entirely from their dedication to the Lord. Paul puts their generosity in the context of their Christian commitment but also brings out their loyalty to him in a subtle way. Again, Paul leaves the Corinthians to draw the proper inferences for themselves. Generosity stems from devotion to Christ. Have the Corinthians surrendered themselves first to the Lord? Paul implies that devotion to Christ will also issue in support for Christ's apostle.

With the phrase "by the will of God" Paul makes more specific that the impetus for generosity comes from God and is related to God's grace. Furnish comments that Paul "attributes it neither to his own successful ministry ... nor to their own selfless action. It is God working in them,

[26] J. Murphy-O'Connor, *The Theology of the Second Letter to the Corinthians* (Cambridge: University Press, 1991) 80.

[27] On the basis of Rom 15:31, where Paul mentions *"my* ministry for Jerusalem," P. Barnett believes that Paul's various references to "ministry" in these chapters refer to Paul's ministry to Jerusalem to which his churches contribute (*The Second Epistle to the Corinthians*, NICNT [Grand Rapids: Eerdmans, 1997] 397; see also Furnish, *II Corinthians*, 401).

just as it will be when the Corinthians have completed their contribution to the fund (9:4)."[28]

(2) Direction: Bring to Completion This Act of Grace (8:6–8)

[6]So we urged Titus, since he had earlier made a beginning, to bring also to completion this act of grace on your part. [7]But just as you excel in everything—in faith, in speech, in knowledge, in complete earnestness and in your love for us— see that you also excel in this grace of giving.
[8]I am not commanding you, but I want to test the sincerity of your love by comparing it with the earnestness of others.

8:6 Paul now turns from the example of the Macedonians to the Corinthians' responsibility in this ministry. Their initial zeal for the venture has evidently flagged, and they need more coaxing to insure that they will do what they promised. Their waning commitment to this ministry is attributable to the deteriorating relations between them and Paul that culminated in the painful visit and the painful letter. Perhaps the shadowy opponents downplay the offering's necessity in hopes of undermining Paul's influence.[29] Charges of some kind of fraud may also be lurking in the background. Paul's refusal to accept support from the Corinthians may have fed vicious rumors that he schemed to siphon off some of the money from the fund. He would then receive support from them surreptitiously while avoiding any obligation to them as their client. We do not know what was the cause behind their procrastination, but Paul capitalizes on the renewed good will of the community toward him to raise the issue again.

Paul has urged Titus to return to Corinth to help them fulfill their earlier promise.[30] The verb *epitelein* means to "complete successfully something

---

[28] Furnish, *II Corinthians*, 413. Barnett, however, argues that "through the will of God" is generally restricted to Paul's apostleship (1 Cor 1:1; Eph 1:1; Col 1:1; and 2 Tim 1:1) and that Paul is referring to the Macedonians' recognition of Paul's apostleship and authority. In giving themselves to the Lord they also recognized Paul as an apostle (*The Second Epistle to the Corinthians*, 399). But Barnett himself points to Rom 15:32 as an exception to the use of the phrase "through the will of God," and Paul's apostleship or authority is not at issue in these chapters. The phrase is best understood as connected to the Macedonians' giving.

[29] If external opponents are indeed behind the alienation between Paul and the Corinthians, we learn that they are not shy about taking advantage of them (11:20); and scuttling the collection would have left that money available for themselves.

[30] Betz claims that the verb παρακαλέω ("urge," NIV) has the technical meaning "summon" or "appoint" found in administrative writings and does not mean "entreat," as it means elsewhere in Paul (*2 Corinthians 8 and 9*, 54). But this interpretation of the verb as an "official" term seems to read too much into an earnest request. It is unlikely that Titus actually began the collection as Barnett would have it (*The Second Epistle to the Corinthians*, 401, n. 53). The collection had clearly already started in Corinth when Paul wrote 1 Cor 16:1–4, and Paul's account of Titus's recent visit to the church implies that it was his first visit (7:14). During this visit Titus must have made some attempt to revive their interest in the project.

already begun" or "to bring something to conclusion." Paul sent Titus to resume the collection, to finish what he and they started. We cannot be sure, but it is most likely that Paul refers to the recent past when Titus delivered the severe letter and remained in Corinth to revive their commitment to Paul.

This verse becomes a delicate admonition for the Corinthians to follow through on their initial commitments. Rather than scold the Corinthians for not having finished, Paul instead praises them for their initial enthusiasm. They remain in the beginning stages, however; and he delegates the responsibility for helping them finish it to Titus. His warm reception by the Corinthians makes him the ideal candidate to fulfill the task.

8:7 Paul continues his affirmation by praising them for excelling in almost everything: faith, speech, knowledge, earnestness, and love. Some interpret this as barbed tribute. Murphy-O'Connor, for example, contends, "When he is being totally sincere he compliments a community on its faith, hope and charity (1 Thess 1:3; 2 Thess 1:3; Col 1:4–5) or its partnership in the gospel (Phil 1:5)."[31] Nevertheless, Paul would not risk alienating the Corinthians again with some cutting remark that they could take the wrong way. Hugo Grotius observed in the seventeenth century: "Paul was not ignorant of the art of rhetoric, to move people by praising them."[32] People are moved to anger if they detect that they are the butt of ironic jabs. This is not irony. He genuinely gives thanks for the Corinthians that they have in "every way been enriched in every way—in all your speaking and in all your knowledge" (1 Cor 1:5).[33] They are "not lacking in any spiritual gift" (1 Cor 1:7). Here he attests to their abundance of gifts and wants them to match it "with an equal abundance of generosity."[34] The verb translated "excel" *(perisseuein)* is used in 8:2 to describe how the Macedonians' depths of poverty "welled up" into a wealth of generosity. It is better translated "overflow." The Macedonians "overflowed" with generosity, and the Corinthians "overflow" with gifts. Paul hopes that these riches in gifts will lead to the same kind of overflowing generosity, literally, "in this grace."

Paul lists the gifts in two triads each beginning with "all" *(pas):*

all faith, speech, knowledge;

all earnestness, love, grace.

The Corinthians may have matured in faith, in the sense of trusting God, so

---

[31] Murphy-O'Connor, *The Theology of the Second Letter to the Corinthians*, 81.

[32] Cited by Betz, *2 Corinthians 8 and 9*, 8.

[33] The verb πλουτέω ("to become rich") appears in 1 Cor 4:8; 8:9; the adjectives πλοῦτος and πλούσιος ("rich") in 8:2,9; and the verb πλουτίζω ("make rich") in 1 Cor 1:5; and 2 Cor 6:10; 9:11.

[34] Cranfield, "The Grace of Our Lord Jesus Christ," 106. Georgi argues that Paul wants "to make the Corinthians see that participation in the collection was the consequence of all the gifts of grace *(charismata)* they had previously been granted" (*Remembering the Poor*, 82).

that he could mention it as something in which they now abound (see 2 Cor 1:24).[35] On the other hand, it seems more likely that "faith" corresponds to the list of spiritual gifts in 1 Cor 12:8–10 and refers to a wonder working faith (see 1 Cor 13:2) rather than the faith that saves.[36] "Speech" may refer to their eloquence (NJB); but again, it is more likely to refer to the spiritual speech such as tongues and prophesy that so captivates them (see 1 Cor 12:10,28; 13:1–2). "Knowledge" refers to their spiritual insight—the knowledge to understand all mysteries (1 Cor 13:2). Interpreting these riches in light of Paul's discussion of them in 1 Corinthians helps us recognize that while Paul values such things, they do not top the list of what he thinks is most important for the upbuilding of the community (1 Cor 8:1–3). Paul interprets these gifts as tending to build up the individual rather than the community. Consequently he would prefer that they cultivate those gifts which cause them to focus more outwardly on others. The second triad does this.

He can confirm their "eagerness" or "zeal." Paul may be referring to their earnestness in their response to Titus (7:11–12). He rejoices that they wanted to do what was right concerning the offending brother, and he hopes that they will show the same zeal in doing what is right regarding the collection.

The next gift presents a knotty textual problem. The evidence is divided. Some texts read, "your love in (among) us" (literally, "the from you in us love"); others read "our love in (among) you."[37] The two variants would have been pronounced exactly the same: *hymōn* (your) / *hēmōn* (our), *hēmin* (in us) / *hymin* (in you).[38] Scribes making copies of the text at the same time may have heard different words as someone read from an exemplar and caused the variants. Which is the best reading?

Some argue for the reading "our love for you" because Paul previously reproached them for having squeezed him out of their hearts (6:12) and implored them to make room in their hearts for him (7:2). This internal evidence suggests that he could hardly presume that they overflowed in love for him. On the other hand, Paul does proclaim his deep love for them (6:11; 7:3). But Paul is speaking about the "graces of the Corinthians" and to mention his own love for them as something they excel in

---

[35] So Betz, who claims that "the goals of 1 Cor 1:4–7; 15:58 have been reached" (*2 Corinthians 8 and 9*, 56–57).

[36] So Furnish, *II Corinthians*, 415.

[37] The reading ἡμῶν ἐν ὑμῖν is found in p[46] B 1746 it[r] cop[sa bo] Origen. The reading ὑμῶν ἐν ἡμῖν is more widely attested geographically in ℵ C D G K P Ψ.

[38] On Greek pronunciation see C. C. Caragounis, "The Error of Erasmus and Un-Greek Pronunciation of Greek," *Filologia Neotestamentaria* 8 (1995) 151–85. The same variant between ὑμῶν and ἡμῶν occurs in 8:9: Christ became poor "for our sake" or "for your sake."

would disturb the sense.[39] According to Paul's explanation in 7:12, Paul wrote the severe letter so that they might make their zeal for him known. This statement assumes that this zeal was momentarily obscured, not completely lost. Their positive reaction to Paul's letter and to Titus's visit permits him now to say that they love him.[40] In 8:8 Paul says that he is testing the genuineness of their love, so he must be speaking here about the love they possess for him, rather than the love he has for them.

The phrase "see that you also excel in this grace of giving" is hyphenated by the NIV to suggest that a break occurs in the syntactical sequence of the listing of the gifts. It reads literally, "in order that *(hina)* you abound in this grace also." The *hina* may express expected consequence: "I am pointing this out so that you may excel in this gracious work too"; a wish or exhortation: "I wish or exhort that you excel in this gracious work also"; or an alternative form of the imperative as the NIV translates it, "see that you also excel." This last option is the best.[41] Verbrugge argues that Paul uses this construction as "one of the least direct ways that Paul could use to express the imperatival idea." It "expressed more of a wish than a command, and people who were not in a superior or authoritative position to the recipient of the letter tended to use it."[42] It forms a marked contrast with the simple imperative in 1 Cor 16:1–2:

> Now about the collection for God's people: Do what I told the Galatian churches to do. On the first day of every week, each one of you should set aside [literally, let each one set aside, third person imperative] a sum of money in keeping with his income, saving it up, so that when I come no collections will have to be made.

Paul apparently no longer feels free to make such direct commands as he did earlier. But he always prefers to lay out principles rather than lay down rules (compare his lengthy discussion about idolatry in 1 Cor 8–10). In these two chapters on the collection, Paul spends most of his time explaining the princi-

---

[39] J. H. Bernard, "The Second Epistle to the Corinthians," in *The Expositor's Greek Testament* (Grand Rapids: Eerdmans, 1979) 3:86. Precisely for this reason some argue that a scribe may have changed the text from the harder reading. But those who argue for this reading assume that Paul would have been unlikely, given what he says in 6:12 and 7:2, to list the Corinthians' love for him as one of the things they excelled in. But this argument makes "your love for us" the harder reading.

[40] This is not to say that their love equals that of the Philippians, for example, or that their love is perfected. Betz comments, "There is ample evidence in the Corinthian correspondence to suggest that the apostle had considerable difficulty in making them understand the notion of love. . ." (*2 Corinthians 8 and 9*, 58). See 1 Cor 4:21; 8:1; 13:1–13; 14:1; 16:14,24; 2 Cor 2:4,8; 8:8,24; 9:7; 11:11; 12:15; and 13:11,18.

[41] See C. J. Cadoux, "The Imperatival Use of ἵνα in the New Testament," *JTS* 42 (1941) 165–73; A. R. George, "The Imperatival Use of ἵνα in the New Testament," *JTS* 42 (1944) 56–60; and W. G. Morrice, "The Imperatival ἵνα," *BT* 23 (1972) 326–30.

[42] Verbrugge, *Paul's Style of Church Leadership*, 47–51.

ples that should motivate generosity rather than ordering the Corinthians to do what he wants.

Yet Paul is not shy about telling them that they need to abound in graciousness or charity. It is abundance in the second triad of gifts (earnestness, love, and grace) that determines whether the abundance in the first triad (faith, speech, and knowledge) has any spiritual validity. A deficiency in the second calls into question whether their faith, speech, and knowledge are in any way meaningful to God. Paul has talked about the participation of the Macedonian churches in the collection as a sure sign that God's grace had been given to them (8:1). The Corinthians' participation would reveal that God's grace is just as active among them.

8:8 Paul is moving cautiously and does not want to leave the impression that he is giving them orders (1 Cor 7:6,25; contrast 1 Cor 16:1–2). He is sensitive to any charges that he domineers over their faith (1:24). He also does not want them giving because of some external compulsion. In his letter to Philemon, he deals with his fellow Christian in the same way and does not command him what to do (Phlm 8,14).[43] Paul takes the freedom of Christians seriously. They may choose to take part or not. Their participation is purely voluntary (2 Cor 9:5,7), and voluntary collections depend on the goodwill of the donors. Consequently, Paul does not command but instead invites, encourages, and lays out divine principles gleaned from Scripture. He hopes that they will respond out of hearts that have been freed by the gospel and fired by God's grace. This does not mean that he sits by passively in wishful anticipation that they will choose the right thing. He is their spiritual director, and he spends two chapters outlining the reasons why they should participate. He does not want them giving for the wrong reasons. On the other hand, we should not ignore today that the discipline of giving, even for the wrong reasons, may eventually lead to a person giving for the right reasons. But Paul has the highest expectations that the Corinthians will give for the right reasons, and he offers a theological rationale for why they should give.

The life of faith always brings its tests, and Paul equates the collection with a test. He says in 2:9 that he wrote the letter of tears to see if they

---

[43] As I read Paul's request of Philemon, he "wants to win obedience, not force compliance that is only a superficial conformity to expectations ('eye-service,' Col. 3:22). Paul trusts Philemon's Christian faith and believes that his faith will guide his decisions. He refuses to bulldoze his moral responsibility by dictating to him what he must do. Developing morally wise Christians is like helping a child learn to ride a bicycle. The child needs encouragement, steadying, and pointing in the right direction; but the parent must finally let go if the child will ever learn to pedal, steer, and balance alone. If Christians are ever to grow in Christ, leaders need to point them in the right directions, but they must let go and let them decide for themselves the obedience Christ requires of them" (D. E. Garland, *Colossians Philemon*, NIVAC [Grand Rapids: Zondervan, 1996] 368).

would stand the test (that he might know their character, *dokimē*). They passed that test, submitting to Paul's authority. Now he moves to another test. The Macedonians came through in a severe "test" of affliction and gave generously (8:2). For the Corinthians it is a test to see if their love—something that Paul thought needed more work (1 Cor 12:31–13:13)—is genuine, authentic. Paul leaves them with the implied question, What will they do when faced with their test?[44]

"Love" in this sentence does not have an object and can refer to their love for Paul (8:7) or their love for Christ. Paul speaks earlier of the love of Christ constraining him in all that he does (5:14). It is possible that he intends for them to show their love for Christ and Christ's love for them by showing their love for their fellow Christians. Paul knows that words expressing love come cheaply and can be faked; genuine love will show up in the checkbook.

(3) Example: God's Grace in the Sacrifice of Jesus Christ (8:9)

[9]For you know the grace of our Lord Jesus Christ, that though he was rich, yet for your sakes he became poor, so that you through his poverty might become rich.

8:9   Paul increases the potency of his entreaty by appealing now to the example of our Lord Jesus Christ. The sacrifice of the Macedonians for others is one thing; the sacrifice of Christ for others is quite another. As Cranfield puts it, "The grace of our Lord Jesus Christ" "denotes the utterly undeserved, royally free, effective, unwearying, inexhaustible goodwill of God, active in and through Jesus Christ, God's effective, overflowing mercy."[45] It sums up God's merciful action toward humanity. When we have been the beneficiaries of such undeserved grace, how can true Christians shut their hearts or purses to brothers and sisters in need or begrudge every penny they may share with others (see 1 John 3:16–20)? God's lavishness in the gift of grace and the depths of Christ's sacrifice requires that Christians be liberal in their giving to others. A halfhearted response ill befits the total sacrifice that Christ made for us.

Paul employs a brief christological confession in the service of his ethical exhortation (see Phil 2:5–11). "Though he was rich" means that Christ did not exploit his status for his own advantage. Instead, he relinquished that

---

[44] Barnett notes that the verb δοκιμάζειν is commonly used by Paul in his letters to express "the outworking principles of Christian belief" (see Rom 2:18; 12:2; 14:22; 1 Cor 11:28; 2 Cor 13:5; Gal 6:4; and Eph 5:10). He also notes: "Δοκιμάζειν should be contrasted with πειράζειν, which generally means testing intended to produce failure" (*The Second Epistle to the Corinthians,* 406, n. 7).

[45] Cranfield, "The Grace of Our Lord Jesus Christ," 106.

status to serve others (Phil 2:6).[46] His riches "describe that estate of the pre-existent Christ which elsewhere in the New Testament is presented as 'the glory which I had with thee before the world was made'" (John 17:5), or as "being in the form of God" and having "equality with God" (Phil 2:6).[47]

The affirmation that Christ became poor for our sakes has been taken in an economic sense to mean Christ's literal poverty during his earthly life. We do not know that Jesus was literally impoverished, however, and he was probably no worse off economically than any other Palestinian subjugated under Roman rule and their puppets, client kings and the priestly aristocracy. To be consistent, an economic interpretation would imply that through Christ's material poverty others were made materially rich. This hardly applies for the Macedonians. The riches therefore can only be spiritual riches which make one's material possessions irrelevant. Christ's "poverty" must refer to something other than having no place to lay his head (Matt 8:20).

It is far more likely that "he became poor" is an ingressive aorist that refers to the incarnation, the state Christ assumed in taking on this mortal life. Becoming poor refers to his "emptying himself" (Phil 2:6; see also Rom 15:3; Heb 12:2) and suggests that this is something he did voluntarily. Schelkle comments: "Christ renounced the divine fullness of power in which he dwelt with the Father, abandoned the heavenly glory which was his as the Son of God. He chose the poverty of human existence so that through his poverty he could impart the eternal riches of redemption to the poverty of all for whose sake he became poor."[48] But how does this make us rich? Paul must also be thinking of Christ's death on the cross: "Christ became 'poor' by accepting the radical impoverishment of a degrading and humiliating death in which everything was taken from him."[49] Christ's incarnation climaxed in his death, and the principle of interchange—he became poor; we

---

[46] Paul did the same (6:10: "poor, yet making many rich; having nothing, and yet possessing everything"). He makes no provision for his personal comfort and cares only that Christ is preached (see Phil 1:18).

[47] F. B. Craddock, *The Pre-existence of Christ in the New Testament* (Nashville / New York: Abingdon, 1968) 166.

[48] K. Schelkle, *The Second Epistle to the Corinthians*, New Testament for Spiritual Reading (New York: Herder & Herder, 1969) 123–24. Craddock comments: "Although free and sovereign over all created powers of the universe, he himself came under these powers, tasting the full measure of their thrust, even to the cross. This he did for our sake" (*The Pre-existence of Christ in the New Testament*, 168).

[49] Murphy-O'Connor, *The Theology of the Second Letter to the Corinthians*, 83. J. Denney noted: "The New Testament knows nothing of an incarnation which can be defined apart from its relation to atonement. Not Bethlehem but Calvary is the focus of revelation" (*The Death of Christ* [London: Tyndale, 1960] 179; cited by P. Barnett, *The Message of 2 Corinthians*, The New Testament Speaks Today [Leicester / Downers Grove: IVP, 1988] 144).

became rich—is the same as in 5:21: "Jesus gave up his righteousness
(becoming 'sin') in order that believers might become the 'righteousness of
God.'"[50] Lapide cites the summary of benefits we received from Christ's
impoverishment so beautifully expressed by Gregory of Nazianus:

> Christ was made poor that we through His poverty might be rich. He took the
> form of a servant that we might regain liberty. He descended that we might be
> exalted. He was tempted that we might overcome. He was despised that He
> might fill us with glory. He died that we might be saved. He ascended, to draw
> to Himself those lying prostrate on the ground through sin's stumblingblock.[51]

The riches of salvation are not something that only await us in glory but
are spiritual blessings that we can experience right now (see 1 Cor 1:4-5;
3:22). The test for the Corinthians will be whether this spiritual enrichment
will have any tangible effect on the way they share their economic riches
with others.[52] Paul drives home the point in the next chapter that God makes
us rich so that we can be generous with others (9:11).

Christ's sacrifice becomes the real motive for giving, not trying to copy or
to outdo some sibling community. Paul asks them to respond to what Christ
has done for them: "And he died for all, that those who live should no longer
live for themselves but for him who died for them and was raised again"
(5:15). Furnish, however, argues that Paul does not present Christ as an
example to follow. He claims that Paul does not mean "Do what Christ did,"
or even "Do for others what Christ has done for you." It is rather, "Do what
is appropriate for your status as those who have been enriched by the grace
of Christ."[53]

But it is hard to see how Christ's self-giving cannot be a model for the
self-giving of all Christians—including how they should give their
money.[54] The self-emptying of Christ for Christians should lead them to
empty their pocketbooks for others, if only in proportion to what they
have. Paul followed Christ's example in his own way of life as one who
emptied himself for others, becoming poor, and bearing great hardships to
reach others with the gospel. Yet Paul is not asking the Corinthians to give
as Christ has given to them, or even to give of their lives to others in the

---

[50] Furnish, *II Corinthians*, 417.

[51] C. Lapide, *The Great Commentary of Cornelius à Lapide: II Corinthians and Galatians*,
trans. and ed. W. F. Cobb (London: John Hodges, 1897) 114, citing *Orat, 1 in Pascha*.

[52] Cranfield expounds, "True riches differ from the transitory riches of this world." Humans
seek after these earthly riches with "such fierce and relentless competitiveness" and "without any
sense of shame." They "can only be possessed at the price of making others poorer (as the rich get
richer, the poor get poorer ...)" ("The Grace of Our Lord Jesus Christ," 108).

[53] Furnish, *II Corinthians*, 418.

[54] D. Horrell, "Paul's Collection: Resources for a Materialist Theology," *Epworth Review* 22
(1995) 77.

same way he has as their apostle, nor even to give out of their impoverishment as the Macedonians have. Paul asks them only to give a fair share, a proportion of what they have, and promises that they will receive blessings in return. But he reminds them that Christ did not give his fair share! His gift was way out of proportion, and there was no guarantee that there would be a flood of gratitude to God for this inexpressible gift. Such unmerited grace from their Lord should inspire the Corinthians to be gracious to others who are in need. Craddock comments: "The drama of redemption took place where we live, in history, in Jesus of Nazareth. Therefore let us express it where we live, says Paul, in the circumstances of each day's life, for example, in the sharing of one's purse with those in need."[55]

From the examples of the Macedonians and Christ the Corinthians can learn the following:

1. True giving requires giving of oneself, not just giving money. The gospel is not about what we can get from God but what God has given to us so that we can give of ourselves to others.

2. One can give out of extreme poverty, and one can give out of measureless riches. Those who are disinclined to be generous when they are poor are not likely to become suddenly generous when they are rich.

3. Giving is related to the grace of God experienced in Christ. The recipients are not required to have done anything to merit the gift except to be in need. The givers are made generous because of God's grace working on them, in them, and through them.

(4) Direction: Finish the Work (8:10–12)

[10]And here is my advice about what is best for you in this matter: Last year you were the first not only to give but also to have the desire to do so. [11]Now finish the work, so that your eager willingness to do it may be matched by your completion of it, according to your means. [12]For if the willingness is there, the gift is acceptable according to what one has, not according to what he does not have.

8:10 Paul does not command them on this matter but does give them authoritative counsel (see 1 Cor 7:25,40). He wants to motivate them through reasoning since genuine benevolence for others is not something that created by dint of a command. He also does not want to seem to criticize them, but he does want to tell him what he thinks is best. Their original intention was good, but if they do not carry it out, it would make them look

[55] F. B. Craddock, "The Poverty of Christ," *Int* 22 (1968) 168.

bad.[56] Paul shows his affirming leadership style by praising what can be praised, namely, their willingness to commit to the ministry in the first place, and by permitting "the Corinthians' self-respect to function as an internal incentive."[57] But he clearly, if subtly, communicates that talk is cheap; now is the time to produce. Boswell's old adage that the road to hell is paved with good intentions applies. Therefore Paul thinks it is in their best interest to complete what they were so willing to start because: (1) they have already begun and they should not leave something undone (8:11); (2) nothing is accomplished if what is started is not finished; (3) they get no credit for initial enthusiasm that disintegrates before the task is finished.[58]

8:11–12 The only imperative in the chapter appears in 8:11 and strikes the heart of Paul's concern that they finish what they started.[59] Paul is not trying to recruit them at the last minute; they were the first to get involved. Now, he is trying to get them to reverse their last minute foot dragging. Putting off something not only results in dwindling motivation to complete the task, their delay calls into question their initial willingness. Seneca remarks that "A benefit ... should not be given tardily, since, seeing that in every service the willingness of the giver counts for much, he who acts tardily has for a long time been unwilling."[60]

The phrase translated "according to your means" (lit., "out of what you have") parallels the phrase in 8:3, "according to their ability." Paul does not ask them to do as the Macedonians did and go beyond their means but only to give according to their means. They are not to go into debt, to become

---

[56] The phrase translated "last year" (ἀπὸ πέρυσι) does not necessarily mean a year ago as it tends to do in English idiom but refers instead to the previous calendar year. That could be a month to twenty-three months ago; no definite span of time is indicated (Furnish, *II Corinthians*, 405). Since there was no universally accepted calendar, the Jewish new year began in autumn, the Roman in January, the Athenian in midsummer, dating matters become further complicated. The only thing we can be sure of is that the Corinthians had started on the collection before the Macedonians and that some time has passed. When Paul wrote 1 Corinthians, the collection had already been launched (1 Cor 16:1–4). In the meantime there had been the intervening painful visit, the severe letter, and Titus's visit and return to Paul. Paul had since moved from Ephesus to Troas to Macedonia. Certainly many months have passed.

[57] Murphy-O'Connor, *The Theology of the Second Letter to the Corinthians*, 84.

[58] Betz, *2 Corinthians 8 and 9*, 64. The verb συμφέρειν, translated "what is best for you," means "to be advantageous, profitable, or expedient." In 12:1 he tells them that the boasting he has been forced to engage in is unprofitable and confers no benefit on anyone. In 1 Corinthians, Paul has warned them that though they may believe everything is permissible, not everything is beneficial (1 Cor 6:12; 10:23). He thinks that he knows what is best for building up the community. In 1 Cor 12:7 he says that the spiritual gifts have been given "for the common good." In the same way, their following through on the collection will confer benefits on the needy saints and will also be advantageous for their common good.

[59] It reads literally: "But now complete also the doing [task], in order that just as [there was] readiness to will thus also to complete from what you have."

[60] Seneca, *On Benefits* 1.1.8.

disadvantaged or overburdened. Paul's goal is not unreasonable; he is not trying to raise record amounts. His instructions in 1 Cor 16:2 to set aside a sum of money each week reveals that he knows he is dealing with many who have limited resources, and a significant amount will only be accumulated over time. Whatever they give generously, he assures them, is acceptable to God. God does not expect the widow's mites, "all that she had to live on" (Mark 12:44), but God does expect generosity and giving gifts without a begrudging spirit. What matters to God is only what is in the giver's heart. In the Corinthians' case the smallest gift is greater than the grandest intention that goes unfulfilled.

In the New Testament the principle "in proportion to what you have" (see also 1 Cor 16:2) replaces the principle of the tithe found in the Old Testament. The tithe only puts the focus on how much one is required to give and allows one to ignore how much is kept for oneself. Some can give far more than the tithe and have more than enough to provide all the necessities of life. Others barely have two mites for their daily needs. We can find the idea of giving in proportion to what one has in the book of *Tobit*. Concerning almsgiving it says:

> For those who act in accordance with truth will prosper in all their activities. To all those who practice righteousness give alms from your possessions to all who live uprightly, and do not let your eye begrudge the gift when you make it. Do not turn your face away from anyone who is poor, and the face of God will not be turned away from you. If you have many possessions, make your gift from them in proportion; if few, do not be afraid to give according to the little you have. So you will be laying up a good treasure for yourself against the day of necessity. For almsgiving delivers from death and keeps you from going into the Darkness; Indeed, almsgiving, for all who practice it, is an excellent offering in the presence of the Most High (*Tob* 4:6–11, NRSV).[61]

As the thriving capital of Achaia, Corinth was far more wealthy than the Macedonian cities, and the congregation had some members who were relatively well off. Paul does not mention anything about their poverty, so we can assume that they were not in the same financial straits as the Macedonians. One wonders, then, if Paul does not share this piece of wisdom about giving according to your means for the poor in the congregation who were so easily slighted and humiliated by the others (see 1 Cor 11:20–22). If the slaves in the Corinthian church were also contributing to the fund, it

---

[61] Josephus explains the rights of the poor to share in the harvest: "For one must not account as expenditure that which out of liberality one lets men take, since God bestows this abundance of good things not for our enjoyment alone, but that we may also share them generously with others; and He is desirous that by these means the special favor that He bears to the people Israel and the bounty of his gifts may be manifested to others also, when out of all that superabundance of ours they too receive a share from us" (*Ant.* 4.8.21 §237).

could only be a token amount, if anything. Barclay notes that the only money they could donate "would be taken from their savings with which they might hope one day to purchase their freedom! The greater their generosity, the less their chance of manumission."[62] Paul is not asking for such bold sacrifices, but he is asking for proportionate giving.

(5) Divine Principle: Equity (8:13–15)

[13]Our desire is not that others might be relieved while you are hard pressed, but that there might be equality. [14]At the present time your plenty will supply what they need, so that in turn their plenty will supply what you need. Then there will be equality, [15]as it is written: "He who gathered much did not have too much, and he who gathered little did not have too little."

8:13–15 Stinginess has a way of expressing itself through suspicion of others and rationalizing its tightfisted ways. Paul is aware that some miserly members of the congregation might gripe, "Others will be profiting from our hard earned money." "We have to bear the brunt of the burden while the poor get rich off us." "We have enough financial troubles of our own, why should we have to help others we do not even know?" Paul is realistic; unless one has the spirit of Christ, one does not want to bear a greater burden so that others might be relieved. He therefore tries to deflect any possible complaint by assuring them that the Jerusalem church is not going to live the high life from these gifts.

Paul does not ask the Corinthians to give more than others because they are better off. He asks them only to give what they can. The example of the Macedonians shows that Paul is not placing an unequal burden upon them. He does not want them to become hard pressed in offering relief to others. The word translated "hard pressed" *(thlipsis)* in the NIV is the same word in 8:2 that refers to the Macedonian's "test of affliction" ("out of the most severe trial," NIV). The Corinthians' giving to this fund, even sacrificially, will hardly compare with the severe affliction which the Macedonians endured. In spite of their dire circumstances, these Christians did not believe they were too hard pressed to give what they could and beyond what they could. But Paul is not asking the Corinthians to put themselves into debt by contributing. The principle undergirding the whole project is one of equity *(isotēs, "equality," NIV). It relates to "justice" and "fairness."

Paul does not write "so that there might be equality," as the NIV renders it, but instead he writes unexpectedly "but out of equity" *(all' ex isotētos).*[63] Paul is not talking about the purpose for their giving—to create equality—

---

[62] J. M. G. Barclay, "Paul, Philemon and the Dilemma of Christian Slave Ownership," *NTS* 37 (1991) 179–80.

[63] Georgi, *Remembering the Poor,* 87.

but the ground of their giving—from equality.[64] Sharing from their surplus
to give to this fund accords with a divine principle about equity and material
goods. Calvin comments

> that riches which are heaped up at the expense of our brethren are accursed and
> will soon perish and their owner will be ruined with them, so that we are not to
> imagine that the way to grow rich is to make provision for our own distant
> future and defraud our poor brethren of the help that is their due. I acknowl-
> edge indeed that we are not bound to such equality as would make it wrong for
> the rich to live more elegantly than the poor; but there must be such an equality
> that nobody starves and nobody hordes his abundance at another's expense.[65]

Two principles emerge from Paul's discussion: giving in proportion to what
one has, and giving on the basis of equity so that each has enough. The Corinthians' current abundance will supply their current lack.

Instead of finishing the sentence in 8:13, Paul leaves it incomplete and
starts another in 8:14. Georgi paraphrases 8:14–15, "At this point in time
your abundance is added to their shortage, so that their might be equity;
as it is written: 'Who had much, did not have more, and who had little,
did not have less.'"[66] Most do not believe that the expression "at the
present time" *(en tōi nyn kairōi)* carries any particular eschatological significance but only refers to the present time of need suffered by the saints
in Jerusalem. But Paul's use of the phrase in Rom 3:26; 8:18; 11:5 and
2 Cor 6:2 suggests that it might indeed have eschatological overtones.
Barnett interprets it to mean:

> As God imposed "equality" within Israel during the wilderness pilgrimage, so
> at "the present time" under the "new covenant" (3:2–6; cf. 6:16), when there is,
> by fulfillment, an "Israel of God" (Gal 6:16), there is also to be "equality." In

---

[64] Philo apparently understood ἰσότης ("equity") to be a divine force that was instilled with a
cosmic nature and closely associated with δικαιοσύνη ("justice"). It had a mystical component
and a charismatic component as grace granted from above. Thus it lost its connection to community. The key passage is Philo's use of the word in *Who Is the Heir* 141–206 (particularly 145).
Georgi argues that Paul has the same understanding of the word (Georgi, *Remembering the Poor,*
88–89). Against this view C. K. Barrett argues that Paul was not the same kind of thinker as Philo,
who had a tendency to take a fundamentally moral concept and "personify it in cosmic and mystical
directions" (*The Second Epistle to the Corinthians,* HNTC [New York: Harper & Row, 1973] 227).
Equity "remains a fundamentally moral concept." Dio Chrysostom's quotes Euripides, "Equality
… knitteth friends to friends, / Cities to cities, allies to allies (*Orations* 17.9–10, cited by Furnish,
II Corinthians, 407). But Paul connects equity to something that God ordained and controlled during the wilderness wanderings through manna.

[65] J. Calvin, *The Second Epistle of Paul the Apostle to the Corinthians and the Epistles to Timothy, Titus and Philemon,* CNTC [Grand Rapids: Eerdmans, 1964] 114.

[66] Ibid., 89.

this time of God's eschatological fulfillment (v. 14) that "equality" is to be voluntary (vv. 3, 8–9), joyous, and generous (v. 2).[67]

In Rom 15:25–31 Paul makes it clear that the gospel is a gift that creates an obligation of gratitude that should be shown by the return of material gifts. Paul specifically refers to the Macedonians and Achaians as spiritual debtors to those in Jerusalem (Rom 15:26–27; cp. Phlm 17–19). He explains, "For if the Gentiles have shared in the Jews' spiritual blessings, they owe it to the Jews to share with them their material blessings" (Rom 15:27b; cp. John 4:22, "Salvation is of the Jews"). Peterman shows that in the ancient world, "When a person receives a benefit it is considered a social obligation to show gratitude. This gratitude is primarily displayed in a counter gift or favour."[68] The collection becomes a way of paying off a spiritual debt to those in Jerusalem.

Given the Corinthians' sensitivities to the intricacies of such social relations, however, Paul does not come right out and say in so many words that they are debtors to the mother church in Jerusalem. He also shows sensitivity to the social rules of the time by emphasizing future reciprocity. The protocol of gift giving in this culture took for granted that whenever there was disparity in the exchange of gifts, the one who outgave the other gained status as the superior while the other moved down a rung in the status ladder. That explains why Paul stresses that the Corinthians' plenty now will supply the needs of the saints "so that in turn their plenty will supply what you need." No one will outgive the other and attain a higher status over the other. Hanson expresses it this way: "The Corinthians give now, not as the richer members condescending to give to their poorer brethren, but as brothers who know that, in Christ, their present supplying of the needs of the Christians in Jerusalem will be answered by the people of Jerusalem in some way and at some time supplying their need."[69]

Paul's statement leaves open the possibility that they will repay in kind with material gifts if the Corinthians ever have need. But in chap. 9 Paul will give a Christian twist to the convention of gift giving. He stresses that God rewards those who are generous with the poor. This theological affirmation changes entirely the dynamics behind gift exchange with its expectation of reciprocity and brings it more in line with the gospel. The implication is that

---

[67] Barnett, *The Second Epistle to the Corinthians*, 416. R. R. Melick, Jr. makes a similar point: "If God were supervising the distribution of resources, as he was in the desert when he supernaturally supplied their needs, there would be adequate supply for all and equitable distribution. The Corinthians had the responsibility of acting God-like in their stewardship of resources" ("The Collection for the Saints: 2 Corinthians 8–9," *CTR* 4 [1989] 110).

[68] G. W. Peterman, *Paul's Gift from Philippi: Conventions of Gift Exchange and Christian Giving*, SNTSMS 92 (Cambridge: University Press, 1997) 177.

[69] R. P. C. Hanson, *II Corinthians*, TBC (London: SPCK, 1954) 69.

the bond between them is triangular because God repays those who are generous to the poor (9:6–11). He also spiritualizes their reciprocity. If the unlikely possibility ever comes to pass that their fortunes should be reversed, the Jerusalem Christians will share material gifts with the Corinthians. But immediately they will offer up prayers of thanksgiving and intercession for them (9:12–14).

Paul steers carefully through the intricate maze of cultural expectations regarding gift exchange and social reciprocity yet clearly implies that Christians cannot sit idly by and let the Christians starve who sent the gospel their way. God intends that there be fairness in the distribution of what people need to live. They will lose nothing in sharing with their needy brothers and sisters in Christ. But they will face God's judgment if they keep for themselves a surplus that could have been used to help others on the edge of survival.

The quotation from Exod 16:18 from the miracle of the manna caps this stage of Paul's argument:

> And when they measured it by the omer, he who gathered much did not have too much, and he who gathered little did not have too little. Each one gathered as much as he needed. Then Moses said to them, "No one is to keep any of it until morning." However, some of them paid no attention to Moses; they kept part of it until morning, but it was full of maggots and began to smell. So Moses was angry with them (Exod 16:18–20).

The manna was distributed "each according to his need," and Paul takes this as a divine pattern for the distribution of material possessions. Strachan, among many others, fails to see how the quotation is relevant since, he claims, it does not illustrate the principle of give and take, except that in God's scheme of things it does not pay to be selfish.[70] But the principle of give and take is not the point. God's justice demands equality, and Paul interprets this to apply to the equality of sharing. Trying to amass more than one's fair share, hoarding it, or clutching it desperately is a futile waste of energy. One ends up with a pile of rot. Paul interprets the account from Exodus as teaching that one can share with others and still have enough.

The "enough" has to do with what is necessary. Unfortunately, the contin-

---

[70] R. H. Strachan, *The Second Epistle of Paul to the Corinthians*, MNTC (London: Hodder and Stoughton, 1935) 138. R. B. Hays notes that one could twist this Scripture to mean exactly the opposite of what Paul intends. Someone could argue. "Why worry about sharing goods if God will provide miraculously for those in need? Thus, a literalistic objector could protest that Paul's appeal to the story is unpersuasive and illogical: how can Paul turn an account of supernatural divine grace into an authorization for mutual sharing in the church?" (*Echoes of Scriptures in the Letters of Paul* [New Haven / London: Yale University Press, 1989] 88–89). Some therefore play down the connection of the quotation to the narrative and reduce it to mean that God intends equality among his people (as does A. Plummer, *A Critical and Exegetical Commentary on the Second Epistle of St. Paul to the Corinthians*, ICC [New York: Scribner's, 1915] 245).

uation of the story of the manna in the wilderness illustrates how humans never seem to feel that enough is enough. Sinful humans are not satisfied with their omer apiece and invariably want to squirrel away more for themselves and have something saved for a rainy day. They also grow dissatisfied with plain old manna from heaven and crave luxuries (see Num 11:5–6). Anxiety over possessing and keeping such things throttles any generosity as we worry that we may not have enough for ourselves. But our selfishness and covetousness is in turn stifled by the divine principle of equality that turns our excess spoils into spoilage reeking to heaven.

This divine principle—no one has a surplus; no one has a shortage—was enforced by God in the time of the wilderness. Now it is voluntary, dependent on the working of God's grace in the hearts of Christians. The principle governs Paul's advice on handling money. He told the Corinthians earlier that they should not depend on their money but live independently of it (1 Cor 7:29–31). He warns others to beware of greed (Rom 1:29; 1 Cor 6:10; 2 Cor 3:5; Eph 4:19; 5:3,5; and 1 Tim 6:10) and to provide for those in need (Rom 12:13; 2 Cor 9:8; Gal 6:6–10; Eph 4:28; and 2 Thess 3:13). The most remarkable statement appears in Eph 4:28, that one should work so that one may "have something to share with those in need" (cp. 1 Thess 4:12). On the other side, he warns others from trying to take advantage of others' generosity (see 2 Thess 3:8–12).

Paul applies the divine principle of equity to sharing material gifts with the poor in Jerusalem. Hays concludes that Paul uses the story about the manna "to good effect in depicting the Corinthians' material 'abundance' (2 Cor 8:14) as a superfluous store that could and should be made available to supply the 'wants of the saints.'"[71] But the sharing of material gifts is a sign of a spiritual equity. Paul sees this project as the outworking of an even greater divine principle that is creating a worldwide fellowship of people in Christ. They are interconnected to one another through Christ and have equal access to God's grace. They trust in God's daily provision, and no one needs to hoard their material blessings since God provides abundantly. If they lack anything, they need not fret. God has provided other Christians an abundance so they can help. God has also poured out grace to make Christians generous.

The Significance of the Collection

Why does Paul invest so much energy in this collection for the saints in Jerusalem? Several reasons may have made it so important to him. (1) First, it was an act of almsgiving to relieve the poverty of Christians in Jerusalem.[72] Although

---

[71] Hays, *Echoes of Scriptures in the Letters of Paul*, 90.

[72] In Acts 24:17 Paul refers to it as "alms for my nation." Acts is primarily interested in showing Paul's loyalty to the nation and the hope of Israel in this section, however, and does not go into any detail about the significance of the reception of the offerings.

Paul hardly touches on the need of the saints in Jerusalem, he does refer specifically to the "poor of the saints who are in Jerusalem" in Rom 15:26. "Of the saints" is a partitive genitive referring to poor people who belong to the saints. Paul mentions their need (lack) in 8:14 and 9:12. We know that famine was not unfamiliar to this area, for it prompted an earlier relief effort (see Acts 11:28). Some had voluntarily given up their property to help others in the community (Acts 4:32–37). We can guess that the church also faced persecution (Gal 1:22–23; 1 Thess 2:14–15) which compounded their poverty since they were unlikely to receive aid from the unbelieving Jewish community.

Almsgiving was very much a part of the religious piety of Judaism, and Paul would have been deeply influenced by it (Rom 12:13; Eph 4:28). The Old Testament injunctions to care for the poor as well as the practice of the early Jerusalem church to accept financial responsibility for one another (Acts 2:43–47; 4:32–37; 6:1) would have been a sufficient motivation for him to respond to their needs. While Paul considers this offering to be an act of charity for those who were suffering in Jerusalem, it had a greater significance for him than that. If the need in Jerusalem was so urgent, the arrangements for the collection were taking a long time (8:10). Other reasons besides a critical relief effort must have inspired Paul's efforts.

Second, some have argued that Paul carried out the collection because he was discharging an obligation. While Paul's Jewish sensitivity to the needs of the poor and needy (Ps 112:9) undergirds his concern that they receive help, his specific concern for *the poor of Jerusalem* needs explanation. Galatians 2:6–10 records a concordat between the "pillar" apostles of the Jerusalem church, James, Peter, and John, and Paul. Paul says that they did not add anything to his gospel but recognized and affirmed his ministry and extended to him the right hand of fellowship. They ask only that he remember the poor (Gal 2:10).[73] Paul's expres-

---

[73] Against K. Holl, who claimed that "the saints" and "the poor" were technical terms for members of the Jerusalem church and not poor people, that the offering was a test of Paul's loyalty to the Jerusalem church or of his subservience to its authority, and that it was a version of the temple tax gathered among the synagogues of the Diaspora as a sign of Jewish unity ("Der Kirchenbegriff des Paulus in seinem Verhältnis zu dem der Urgemeinde," in *Gesammelte Aufsätze zur Kirchengeschichte* [Tübingen: Mohr (Siebeck), 1928] 2:44–67). The money is a kind of tax that is due them. So also K. F. Nickle, *The Collection: A Study of Paul's Strategy*, SBT 48 (Naperville: Alec R. Allenson, 1966) 74–99; Bruce, "Paul and Jerusalem," *TynBul* 19 (1968) 10; and B. Holmberg, *Paul and Power: The Structure of Authority in the Primitive Church as Reflected in the Pauline Epistles* (Philadelphia: Fortress, 1978) 39–41. L. E. Keck has convincingly challenged this view ("The Poor among the Saints in the New Testament," *ZNW* 56 [1965] 100–129). He shows that it is questionable to assume that the poor in Gal 2:10 and in Rom 15:26 meant anything other than simply the poor people. The collection was definitely not a tax like the half-shekel tax that was collected from Jews throughout the world to support the temple. The collection of funds for the temple does offer a precedent, but it is not related to what Paul is doing. The temple tax was regressive; rich and poor owed exactly the same amount. What Paul asks from the Corinthians is a willing gift in proportion to what one has. K. Berger identifies the collection as almsgiving and contends that the Gentile churches would have viewed it as some kind of substitute in lieu of becoming circumcised and offering sacrifices. The gifts would have recognized Israel's priority in salvation history and demonstrated their allegiance to Israel ("Almosen für Israel: Zum Historischen Kontext der Paulinischen Kollekte," *NTS* 23 [1976–77] 180–204).

sion of eagerness to help the poor indicates that he would have done so at his own initiative.[74] Also his eagerness for the success of the collection reflected in his other letters would be inexplicable if it were an obligation that the pillar apostles laid on him. He says that the Gentiles are in debt to the church in Jerusalem (Rom 15:27), but he understands it to be a spiritual debt. Paul's terms for the offering stress its theological significance as an occasion for the grace of God, and he emphasizes its purely voluntary nature. His fear, expressed in Rom 15:31, that the saints might not accept the offering rules out the possibility that this was some kind of tax. If this were some tax that Gentiles were obligated to pay to Jerusalem, Paul would not need to fret that it would not be accepted. How could they reject something that they had required?

The word "grace" *(charis)* is Paul's favored word in describing the project (1 Cor 16:3; 2 Cor 8:6,7,19). Verbrugge notes that "grace" refers to "something freely given, whether it be what God gives us in Christ, or what we give to God or others." It comes undeserved and does not require others to have done something to be worthy of it before it is given to them.[75] The generosity of the Gentile churches with those whom they knew only by reputation was a sign of God's grace working itself out in their lives. They had indeed been blessed by them since they shared with them the gospel, but the gospel brings with it an obligation to become a blessing to others. While Paul does see this gift as repaying a spiritual debt (Rom 15:27), it is not the primary motive behind his efforts.

Paul may have felt some sense of debt to the mother church for quite different reasons. He had violently persecuted it and tried to destroy it (Gal 1:13). But his relations with the pillar apostles as he reports it in Galatians 2 betrays no sense of any need to atone for past sins. The collection, then, is something more than simply a repayment of some kind of debt.

Third, Paul's worry, expressed in Rom 15:31, that his service might not be accepted by the saints is a crucial piece of evidence. He asks the Romans: "Pray that I may be rescued from the unbelievers in Judea and that my service in Jerusalem may be acceptable to the saints there, so that by God's will I may come to you with joy and together with you be refreshed" (Rom 15:31–32). If this were simply an emergency relief effort for people who were starving, why does Paul need to ask the Romans to pray that poor people will find it "acceptable"? The answer is to be found in the long history of conflict over the acceptance of uncircumcised Gentile Christians by the more traditional, law observant Jewish Christians. The problem was that this was Gentile money. If the Jewish Christians accept this tangible sign of love and indebtedness from Gentile Christians, then they have, in effect, accepted them as their brothers in Christ and fellow heirs of the promises. The collection shows that Christian faith overcomes the deepest racial barriers that formerly separated Jews from Gentiles.

This concern to show the solidarity between Jew and Greek in Christ is the primary motivation behind the collection. Horrell notes that Paul did not organize

[74] Georgi claims Paul made two collections. one at the instigation of the pillar apostles and this one at his own initiative (*Remembering the Poor*, 43–49).
[75] Verbrugge, *Paul's Style of Church Leadership*, 328.

collections for other churches who also suffered persecution and poverty, and therefore he apparently saw special spiritual significance in the offering for Jerusalem.[76] Paul wants to do more than send them relief; he wants to establish unity between the Jewish Christian Jerusalem church and the Gentile churches he founded. He yearns for all Christians to understand that since we all belong to Christ, we all belong together. The collection is part of his ministry of reconciliation to bring an end to the hostility between Jew and Gentile and to break down the dividing walls of hostility. The church will then know the unity of the Spirit in the bond of peace: "There is one body and one Spirit—just as you were called to one hope when you were called—one Lord, one faith, one baptism; one God and Father of all, who is over all and through all and in all" (Eph 4:4–6). If Paul were just sending relief aid to Jerusalem, he could have sent it on with the messengers from the churches. He decided to deliver the gift in person. Paul was fully aware of all the risks involved, but he must have felt that it was crucial that the gift be properly interpreted as evidence of the bond between Jews and Gentiles in Christ.[77]

A fourth possible motivation behind the collection may be Paul's desire to demonstrate the success of the Gentile mission to non believing Jews. It would reveal that God was indeed working among the Gentiles and that God was not the tribal deity of the Jews but the God of all people who justifies all the ungodly who submit in faith (Rom 3:29–30). It therefore may have had some eschatological significance for Paul.[78] Paul did not think that this project would usher in the end of the age, but he may have believed that it would show what God had been doing among the Gentiles was a fulfillment of ancient prophecies as they sent gifts to Zion (Isa 2:2–4; 60:1–9; Mic 4:1–3; Hag 2:7; and Zech 14:14). Paul shares his pain over Israel's unbelief with the Romans: He would be willing to lose his salvation, if it were possible, if only his people would believe (Rom 9:2–3). He did hope that non-believing Jews would be provoked to jealousy as they witness the Gentiles receiving blessings intended for Israel, that they would recognize that this offering was a fulfillment of ancient prophecies, and that it might spark their conversion (Rom 10:19; 11:11–14). There is no explicit mention of the collection in Romans 11, but it may provide a backdrop for better understanding why Paul turns from his mission in Gentile territory to return to Jerusalem. He explains why he cannot come to Rome as he had always hoped and planned but must backtrack. He tells them that though he is the apostle to the Gentiles, until God gives up on the people of Israel, he cannot. Perhaps this offering might crack the hardening that has come upon Israel. If their obduracy has brought blessing to the Gentiles by the proclamation of the gospel outside the land, how much more blessing will come if the people who had priority in God's plan of salvation

[76] Horrell, "Paul's Collection," 77.

[77] Dahl, "Paul and Possessions," 32.

[78] So J. Munck, *Paul and the Salvation of Mankind* (Atlanta: John Knox, 1959) 299–308; Nickle, *The Collection*, 129–42; F. F. Bruce, "Paul and Jerusalem," 22–25; and Barrett, *The Second Epistle to the Corinthians*, 27–28.

believe and give their wholehearted support for proclaiming the gospel to all the world?

We read in Rom 15:25–26 that Achaia and Macedonia did make contributions to the collection. Galatia, however, is omitted, though, according to 1 Cor 16:1, they were originally part of the undertaking. It is possible that Paul's letter to the Galatians failed to achieve its aim, and the churches withdrew from the project. It is more likely that they are not mentioned because, unlike Achaia and Macedonia, the persons in that province had no connections to the church in Rome. The goal of unity has always been elusive because the church keeps fragmenting. Achtemeier suggests that Acts is silent on the collection project because it failed.[79] Perhaps so, but not ultimately. Paul was arrested in Jerusalem, a martyr for Christian unity. He did not regard his imprisonment as a setback for the gospel. Instead he saw it as serving the advancement of the gospel, for he introduced each of his captors to the gospel (Phil 1:12; see Acts). He also did not give up on his grand vision of the unity of Christ's body. The relations with the Jerusalem church would become a moot point as the city and its temple would soon lie in smoldering ruins. The need to show the unity of Christ's body by acts of concrete love, however, remains relevant.

2. The Administration of the Funds by Titus and the Acclaimed Brothers (8:16–9:5)

Paul explains the careful arrangements he is making for the collection. Many ministers come up with grand plans that fail for lack of realistic planning, detailed supervision, clear-cut guidelines, and determined execution.

(1) Commendation of Titus and the Brothers (8:16–24)

[16]I thank God, who put into the heart of Titus the same concern I have for you. [17]For Titus not only welcomdor appeal, but he is coming to you with much enthusiasm and on his own initiative. [18]And we are sending along with him the brother who is praised by all the churches for his service to the gospel. [19]What is more, he was chosen by the churches to accompany us as we carry the offering, which we administer in order to honor the Lord himself and to show our eagerness to help. [20]We want to avoid any criticism of the way we administer this liberal gift. [21]For we are taking pains to do what is right, not only in the eyes of the Lord but also in the eyes of men.

[22]In addition, we are sending with them our brother who has often proved to us in many ways that he is zealous, and now even more so because of his great confidence in you. [23]As for Titus, he is my partner and fellow worker among you; as for our brothers, they are representatives of the churches and an honor to Christ. [24]Therefore show these men the proof of your love and the reason for our pride in you, so that the churches can see it.

---

[79]P. Achtemeier, "An Elusive Unity: Paul, Acts, and the Early Church," *CBQ* 48 (1986) 1–26.

8:16–17   Paul now informs the Corinthians about the envoys he has sent to them to help with the final arrangements: Titus, whom they know, the brother famous among the churches for his ministry in the gospel, and another whom he has found earnest. They will also reinforce his exhortations on the collection, but Paul delicately tiptoes around the issue so that the Corinthians might not perceive their coming as putting undue pressure on them.

The Corinthians might be surprised to see Titus again so soon, so Paul writes a commendatory explanation.[80] His main intention is to dispel any hint of coercion on his part. He also makes clear that he is not coercing an underling to return to the Corinthians. He sends his equal partner, Titus, who wanted to return to them of his own accord. Murphy-O'Connor notes that this "little vignette is illustrative of Paul's dealings with his assistants: he does not order a subordinate, but asks a 'partner' (8:23)."[81] Paul is not a taskmaster that demands that his junior assistants go hither and yon. He urges Titus to go and interprets his readiness to accept this responsibility as another grace from God, and so he gives thanks to God.[82]

Titus loves the Corinthians as Paul loves them. His zeal for the project is the same as Paul's. Note that the "zeal" (weakly translated by the NIV as "concern") he feels for them has been given to him by God. Paul has mentioned the earnestness of the Corinthians (8:7; 7:11,12) and the Macedonians (8:8). He now mentions Titus's zeal, which becomes an example for them. (1) Titus on his own initiative accepted Paul's appeal to return; they should, on their own initiative, accept Paul's appeal to give. (2) Titus is more than eager; they should be more than eager.[83]

8:18   The renowned brother who is being sent with Titus is praised by all the churches for his service to the gospel. Paul does not identify who these churches might be. Conceivably, he is known everywhere in Paul's mission field and beyond, but it is more likely that Paul means all the churches in Macedonia and Achaia. The churches sing his praises for what he does for the gospel (lit., "in the gospel"). The NIV interprets the phrase to mean "service to the gospel" (also REB), but the NRSV takes it to refer to his proclaiming the gospel (also GNB, NAB).[84] It may have a more general

---

[80] The verb ἐξῆλθεν is an epistolary aorist and is correctly translated by the NIV as "is coming to you" (see also συνεπέμψαμεν ["sending along with"] 8:18, 22; and ἔπεμψα ["I am sending"] 9:3; and cp. Acts 23:30; Phil 2:28; Phlm 12).

[81] Murphy-O'Connor, *The Theology of the Second Letter to the Corinthians,* 85. Betz claims that παράκλησις ("appeal") in 8:17 is a technical term for a legal mandate (*2 Corinthians 8 and 9,* 70–71). But it is more likely that it simply refers to Paul's urgent appeal or encouragement.

[82] "Paul means that he made the request and found it unnecessary—Titus was already anxious to go" (Barrett, *The Second Epistle to the Corinthians,* 228).

[83] K. Quast, *Reading the Corinthian Correspondence* (New York / Mahwah: Paulist, 1994) 144.

[84] If this interpretation is correct, brothers famous for preaching must also engage in administration!

meaning that could include a wide variety of activities for the gospel, since Paul refers to Euodia and Syntyche as contending with him side by side "in the gospel" (Phil 4:3). On the other hand, one of the most important tasks "in the gospel" is proclaiming it. The phrase clearly is associated with preaching in Rom 1:9; 1 Cor 9:18; 2 Cor 10:14; and 1 Thess 3:2, where Timothy is identified as "God's fellow worker in spreading the gospel of Christ" (NRSV "in proclaiming the gospel"). Paul's usage of this term indicates that this brother is celebrated for his preaching.

It is odd to recommend persons without giving their names, and this omission has raised speculation about why Paul does not name the brothers accompanying Titus. Paul omits the names of his adversaries, not his supporters.[85] Several explanations have been proposed. (1) Some have argued that the names were removed by later scribes because they were judged unsuitable for some reason, such as falling into a heresy.[86] This alternative seems far-fetched. (2) Since Paul did not appoint them but they were elected by the churches, it is possible that he sought to lower their profiles in the delegation. He did not want to give them any more status than necessary and did not want to diminish the authority of Titus, who was the key figure chosen by Paul. By omitting their names, Paul implies that there are "two levels of authorization within the delegation. Titus alone was authorized in the full sense, while the brothers derived their authority from him." Had they arrived without Titus or taken an independent course of action they would have had no letter of recommendation.[87] (3) Betz claimed that Paul's method of appointing was by apostolic decree; the Greek churches operated through the democratic process.[88] Therefore Paul did not name those whom he did not appoint. (4) Another possibility is that this first envoy was a Corinthian Christian who had gone to Macedonia to work there in the gospel (see the contacts between Corinth and Macedonia in 2 Cor 11:9; 1 Thess 1:7–8). Paul's eulogy would have flattered and relieved the Corinthians: the emissary was one of their own, not "a critical Macedonian," and was widely recognized for his contributions to the mission of the gospel.[89] This choice may have been a diplomatic gesture.[90]

---

[85] For the adversaries in Corinthian correspondence, see 1 Cor 3:10; 5:1,5; 2 Cor 2:5–10; 7:12; 10:10; and 11:5. For naming his supporters, see 1 Cor 16:10–15; Rom 16:1; Phil 2:20–25; Col 4:7–10; Titus 3:12–14; Acts 15:22,25,27.

[86] H. Windisch, *Der zweite Korintherbrief*, MeyerK (Göttingen: Vandenhoeck & Ruprecht, 1924) 262. Heretics' names were omitted to avoid giving them any notoriety (see *Ign. Smyrn.* 5:3). Georgi also believes that names were deleted in a later edition of the letter but does not know why (*Remembering the Poor*, 73).

[87] Betz, *2 Corinthians 8 and 9*, 73–74.

[88] Ibid., 75.

[89] Murphy-O'Connor, *The Theology of the Second Letter to the Corinthians*, 86.

[90] A. T. Robertson tries to explain the absence of the name with the unlikely suggestion that the article before "brother" functions as a possessive pronoun so that Titus came with his own brother (*A Grammar of the Greek New Testament in the Light of Historical Research* [Nashville: Broadman, 1934] 770).

Perhaps (5) the emissary is someone already known to the Corinthians; and since he arrived with the letter, it would have been unnecessary to name him. But Paul identifies both the men who accompanied Titus as the messengers (apostles) of the churches (8:22). This implies that they were not chosen to go to Corinth to help them complete their donations but to represent the churches of Macedonia in Jerusalem (8:19; see 1 Cor 16:3). They accompany Titus now to assure anyone who might question the integrity of the project that it is being carried out in a virtuous and unimpeachable way. If someone suspects foul play or that a conspiracy is afoot, they will have to implicate the Macedonian churches as well. Paul does not commend these escorts by name because they are not sent to work with the Corinthians.[91] What is only important to Paul are the qualifications of these men who insure with Titus the probity of this undertaking. The first emissary stands out for his work in the gospel, the recognition of that work by all the churches, and his appointment by the churches (8:19).[92]

8:19–20 Money is a sensitive issue and frequently sparks controversy, and Paul reminds them that this fund is a "grace" that is "being ministered" by us for the purpose of bringing glory to the Lord and to show our good will (8:19). Then he explains that he is taking every precaution to be above reproach.[93] By having these well-known representatives from Macedonia

---

[91] Guesses at the identity of the brother include almost everyone associated Paul. It cannot be Timothy since he is a cosender of the letter (1:1). Ancient tradition has long identified him as Luke (see Phlm 24; Col 4:4; 2 Tim 4:11) from the following inference. The first long "we passage" in Acts begins in 16:11, when Paul establishes his work in Macedonia. If the we passages refer to Luke as Paul's travel companion, he would have been familiar to the Macedonians. In Acts 20:4 no representative of Philippi is named, and it could be Luke. Barnett opines, "One who was capable of writing the gospel, as Luke was, may well have been famous for his preaching of the gospel" (*The Message of 2 Corinthians,* 149). Other plausible candidates come from the entourage listed in Acts 20:4 who traveled with Paul to Jerusalem: Macedonians: Sopater of Beroea; Aristarchus and Secundus of Thessalonica; Asians: Tychicus and Trophimus; and Galatians: Gaius of Derbe. Another suggestion is that it was someone from Judea such as Judas Barsabbas (Acts 15:22; Nickle, *The Collection,* 18–22). We will never know for sure, but the most likely choices would seem to come from this list of emissaries in Acts 20:4. Tychicus stands out as one who is not only mentioned in Acts 20:4 but also in Eph 5:21; Col 4:7; 2 Tim 4:12; and Titus 3:12; and he qualifies as a close companion of Paul.

[92] The word χειροτονηθείς originally meant to elect by show of hands and then generally to elect. In discussing the logistics of transporting the temple half-shekel tax (incumbent on every Jewish male, Exod 30:11–16) to Jerusalem, Philo reports that men of the highest repute were chosen from every city to deliver the funds (*Special Laws* 1.78).

[93] Recent events had made collecting money for Jerusalem an even more sensitive issue. Josephus reports that a Palestinian Jew and three cohorts were instructing people in Rome on the law. They induced one of the notable converts, Fulvia, to send valuables for the temple in Jerusalem. Rather than conveying the goods to Jerusalem, they absconded with them. When their dishonesty was discovered, it created such an uproar that the emperor Tiberius ordered all Jews to be banished from Rome (*Ant.* 18.3.5 § 81).

accompany Titus, Paul makes it clear that he does not intend for this project to line his own pockets.[94] With someone appointed by other churches and not by Paul, there can be no doubts about his own honesty regarding what will happen to the funds. Paul recognizes that the power of one's witness corresponds directly to one's reputation for integrity. He cannot allow the project to become shrouded in malicious rumors that all is not above board.[95] He therefore takes steps to ensure that there be not the slightest hint of any impropriety.

8:21 Paul cites Prov 3:4 (LXX) in 8:21: "For we take forethought for the good not only before the Lord but also before men" (cited again in Rom 12:17) to underscore his honorable intentions. His motives and actions are an open book to God, who scrutinizes him. Still, he also wants to be completely open to people. This recalls his statement in 4:2 that he commends himself to every man's conscience in the sight of God. Though he can accept being held in ill-repute (6:8; 1 Cor 4:10), he does not welcome dishonor and will do nothing to warrant it (see 1 Pet 2:20; 3:13–17). The gospel may be scandalous, but his behavior and sincerity must be exemplary to both believers and unbelievers. Too often Christians have brought discredit to themselves and to the Christian faith in the eyes of the world by mishandling donations through fraud or by receiving disproportionately high salaries for their "service" in the gospel. Paul is sensitive to any charges that he might be guilty of corruption (see 2:17; 4:2; 7:2; 11:7–12; 12:14–18). He therefore bends over backwards to keep everything open and public and to avoid the slightest impression of any self-seeking in all of his ministry (6:3), especially with regard to a collection of a substantial sum of money.

8:22 This concern for propriety leads to the mention of another person who will accompany Titus. He is identified as "our brother," which distinguishes him from the first one mentioned who is identified as "the brother." This may mean that he is a well-known and longtime companion of Paul. No mention is made of his election by the churches but it may be assumed. Paul

---

[94] The verb στέλλεσθαι appears only here and in 2 Thess 3:6 in the NT. In 2 Thess 3:6 it means "to avoid," "to keep away from," and this is how the NIV renders it here. Barnett thinks it may have the meaning "send" as a cognate of ἀπόστολοι (8:23) and as parallel to verb συμπέμπειν in 8:18,22. He notes that Philo uses it in this sense (*Embassy to Gaius* 216). K. H. Rengstorf claims it expresses the thought "inasmuch as I see to it, or take steps" ("στέλλω ..." *TDNT* 7:588–90). J. Héring also understands it to mean "to set out on a task, to undertake" (*The Second Epistle of Saint Paul to the Corinthians* [London: Epworth, 1967] 63). Furnish translates it "we are taking this action" (*II Corinthians,* 423). The advantage of interpreting the verb in this way is that it connects more clearly to what follows: "We are dispatching [Titus and the brother] lest anyone blame us."

[95] Pagans and Christians recognize the significance of integrity. Furnish (*II Corinthians,* 434) cites Cicero: "But the chief thing in all public administration and public service is to avoid even the slightest suspicion of self-seeking" (*On Moral Obligation* II. xxi. 75).

highlights that he is fully acquainted with him and that he has proven himself zealous in many things, many times. Now he is all the more zealous because of his confidence in you. This last remark removes any potential competition or rivalry between the two regions. The one who represents the Macedonian churches has every confidence that the Corinthians will come through with shining colors.

8:23 Paul rounds out this paragraph on the administration of the program with a final reference to Titus and the brothers and their qualifications. The abrupt way the Greek reads, "whether Titus .... whether our brothers," requires adding a verb to make sense of it. Barnett suggests the translation, "Whether [anyone asks about] Titus or the brothers."[96] If anyone questions Titus, he is Paul's partner and a coworker "for you" *(eis hymas),* not "among you" (NIV). Titus is therefore Paul's partner "because he works with him for the Corinthians."[97] The brothers are "apostles" (sent ones) of the churches, which means that they are their messengers, agents, or representatives (see Phil 2:25). They are not Paul's coworkers in Corinth but mostly bystanders to endorse that everything that Paul and his emissary undertakes is honorable.

More important, these brothers are identified as *doxa Christou.*[98] The NIV renders this phrase as an objective genitive "an honor to Christ"—they bring glory to Christ by the quality of their lives. They are dedicated to the gospel of the glory of Christ (4:4). This phrase could also mean that they reflect the glory of Christ as Paul is "the aroma of Christ" (2:15) or the Corinthians are "a letter of Christ" (3:3). Paul probably has more in mind than the prosaic idea that they are a credit to Christ. "Glory" is connected to revelation. Watson comments, "The glory of God is that which makes the invisible God visible, that which makes God known." Distinguishing them as "the glory of Christ" implies that Christ is made known through these delegates.[99] Rather than blinding others to the glory of Christ as the god of this age does (4:4), they proclaim the gospel.

The three who come to Corinth are more than envoys. They become a standard of Christian living which the Corinthians would do well to emulate. In 8:24 Paul entreats the Corinthians to live up to his boasts about them.[100]

[96] Barnett, *The Second Epistle to the Corinthians,* 425–26.

[97] J. Y. Campbell, ΚΟΙΝΩΝΙΑ and Its Cognates in the New Testament," *JBL* 51 (1932) 362.

[98] The phrase could apply instead to the Macedonian churches (NRSV). Barnett argues on theological grounds that the church comprises the source of brightness (Phil 2:15) or the glory of Christ (*The Second Epistle to the Corinthians,* 427). Since Paul is talking about the envoys here and not the churches, the phrase most likely describes these men as being of the highest repute.

[99] N. Watson, *The Second Epistle to the Corinthians,* Epworth Commentaries (London: Epworth, 1993) 95.

[100] The participle ἐνδεικνύμενοι ("show") is used with an imperative sense and fits Paul's indirect approach in asking the Corinthians to give.

8:24 Paul reemphasizes the appeal in 8:7–15 to fulfill their commitment. They are to show the proof of their love to these men and to the churches. This exhortation intimates that the proof of their love is not shown by simply receiving these emissaries with open arms but by contributing liberally to help the saints.

The notion of showing proof of faith or love can be theologically dangerous. God does not say, "If you love me, then prove it by doing this or giving this." Paul understands, however, that the Corinthians' generosity is proof that God's grace is at work in them. Genuine beneficence is not something that one can fake or produce on demand, because it will always be begrudged. It ensues naturally from experiencing God's grace.

Paul's appeal to their pride to show others their generosity is also theologically dangerous. But Christians and churches do not always make the right ethical decisions when left to themselves. Accountability to others keeps us from always doing what we want and serving our own selfish desires. Paul assumes that Christians live and act out of a communal context and that they are answerable to each other. The decisions made by the Corinthians regarding this matter will have immediate repercussions for the whole church. Knowing that our fellow Christians are watching what we do may help us to be more responsible in allowing God's grace to work in our lives.

Is Chapter 9 a Separate Letter?

From our outline of Paul's discussion about the collection, we obviously do not regard chap. 9 to be a separate letter that has been joined to chap. 8 by a later editor. Some interpreters have vigorously argued that this was indeed the case, that chap. 9 comprises a different circular letter that was sent to the churches of Achaia, while chap. 8 was sent specifically to Corinth.[101] We need to settle this matter before continuing our discussion.

The proposed solution that imagines that this is a second letter with its greeting, customary note of thanksgiving, and concluding benediction deleted presents far more complicated difficulties than the minor problem in 9:1. In 9:1 Paul says he does not need to write them about the ministry to the saints after he has just done so in chap. 8 and then he proceeds to discuss it for another fourteen verses in 9:2–15. Why did Paul need to write a second letter saying basically the same things? Betz's argument that this second letter (chap. 9) was sent to other churches in Achaia does not withstand careful scrutiny. What Achaian cities would be candidates for receiving such a letter? Cenchrea (see Rom 16:1) is part of Corinth. Others object that Achaia could hardly refer "to the cities from the province *apart from* Corinth, any more than the word 'France' today would be

---

[101] Notably Betz, who has written an entire commentary on these two chapters and argues throughout that they are two separate letters with two different addressees and distinctive purposes (*2 Corinthians 8 and 9*, 94; see also Windisch, *Der zweite Korintherbrief*, 286–88; Georgi, *Remembering the Poor*, 75–79; and R. P. Martin, *2 Corinthians*, WBC (Waco: Word, 1986) 249–50, 281.

understood as referring to that country *apart from* Paris."[102] Achaia is mentioned in the address in 1:1, and so it is not surprising for Achaia to be mentioned again in the letter. In fact, this regional reference to Achaia in 9:2 serves to balance the regional reference to Macedonia in 8:1.

Betz bases his argument primarily on his supposition that chaps. 8 and 9 contain two separate parts of a rhetorical speech. Even if his rhetorical analysis is correct, that does not prove that these two chapters were originally separate documents. The entire letter is composed of a variety of arguments and rhetorical styles.[103] It is better strategy to try to make sense of the text as it stands rather than to pile hypothesis upon hypothesis.

Many other commentators have argued that chap. 9 makes good sense following chap. 8, so there is no need to resort to complicated theories about two different letters. While it may surprise us that Paul says it is superfluous to write to them at all about the ministry for the saints and then to repeat his appeal, Furnish comments: "There is no serious difficulty ... in reading the verses as a continuation of the preceding discussion. Paul acknowledges that because he has been *boasting* to the Macedonians about the commitment of the Achaian churches (including Corinth) to the fund for Jerusalem (v. 2a) it is *superfluous* for him to *be writing* them about contributing" (v. 1).[104]

The last time Paul specifically mentioned "the ministry for the saints" was in 8:4 when he was talking about the Macedonians' unanticipated generosity. Paul now adds that they were inspired to give to the fund when they heard of the Achaians' dedication to the cause. He emphasizes that he does not want his boast about them to be empty, and therefore warns them that other Macedonians may be coming with him. It will be highly embarrassing to him and to them if the Macedonians show up and find the Corinthians unready to make their contribution to the project.[105]

Stowers delivers the death blow to the hypothesis that chaps. 8 and 9 are fragments of two separate letters. He shows conclusively that the meaning of the expression *peri men gar* in 9:1, the only argument for the partition of chaps. 8 and 9 that "is susceptible to anything resembling 'objective' verification or falsification," demands that it interlocks with what precedes.[106] Betz had claimed that the phrase does not connect to what precedes but instead introduces the body of a new letter that the hypothetical editor of 2 Corinthians had attached after

---

[102] Harvey, *Renewal through Suffering*, 88.

[103] B. Witherington III, *Conflict and Community in Corinth: A Socio-Rhetorical Commentary on 1 and 2 Corinthians* (Grand Rapids: Eerdmans, 1994) 413, n. 7.

[104] Furnish, *II Corinthians*, 438.

[105] M. J. Harris points out: "Without the discussion of chapter 8 immediately preceding, the allusive reference to 'the brothers' in vv. 3,5 would be scarcely explicable; this argues for the unity of these two chapters" ("2 Corinthians," EBC [Grand Rapids: Zondervan, 1976] 10:374).

[106] S. K. Stowers, "*Peri Men Gar* and the Integrity of 2 Cor. 8 and 9," *NovT* 32 (1990) 340–48. J. Lambrecht adds further arguments to establish beyond reasonable doubt that 9:1–5 was originally connected to 8:24 and that chaps. 8 and 9 belonged together from the beginning ("Paul's Boasting about the Corinthians: A Study of 2 Cor. 8:24–9:5," *NovT* 40 [1998] 352–68).

removing its salutation.[107] Stowers' analysis of ninety instances of the phrase in other texts reveals that it was used in four ways: (1) to "introduce a reason, warrant, or explanation for what was just said" (see Acts 28:22); (2) to provide a specific instance after a general statement or claim which could be translated, "now back to the case of ..."; (3) "to introduce the main or most important topic or subtopic among several which have been or could be discussed"; and (4) "to introduce quotations or references to what others have said" providing a "reason, explanation, or example for what was said previously."[108] His conclusion is that the phrase "expresses a close relationship—a reason, warrant, explanation, subtopic—to what precedes."[109]

The central exhortation appears in 8:24, "Therefore show these men the proof of your love and the reason for our pride in you, so that the churches can see it." What follows in 9:1–4 "provides a warrant and explanation" for why Paul is pressing them to be ready. They both could be embarrassed if the delegation from Macedonia arrives and they are not ready.[110] Stowers concludes: "The results of this study make it most implausible to think of chaps. 8 and 9 as fragments of two letters. Indeed the only argument for that case that might be subject to verification has been shown wrong."[111]

Paul's continuation of his discussion in 9:6–15 to remotivate the Corinthians to give generously may also be related to the Corinthians' cultural conventions about giving and receiving. These conventions were at odds with Paul's biblical understanding of the spiritual significance of giving. He needs to reeducate them on what it means to give to others. Paul approaches giving from a Jewish perspective found in the Old Testament: "There will always be poor people in the land. Therefore I command you to be openhanded toward your brothers and toward the poor and needy in your land" (Deut 15:11; see Exod 23:10–11; Deut 14:28–29; 24:19–22). This view differs significantly from the perspective in the Greco-Roman world. Peterman points out: "Generally speaking ... in Greco-Roman society generosity toward the poor out of compassion for them in their state was not considered a virtuous act and therefore could expect no reward from God. It was more blessed to give than to receive among the Greeks and Romans, not because of the display of compassion seen therein, but because giving displayed one's personal virtue and social power."[112]

He goes on to cite Saller's study: "The most basic premise from which the Romans started was that honour and prestige derived from the power to give to others what they needed or wanted."[113] Good works, therefore, were normally

---

[107] Betz, *2 Corinthians 8 and 9*, 26–27; 90–91. His views reflect those of A. Halmel, *Der zweite Korintherbrief des Apostels Paulus: geschichtliche und literarkritische Untersuchungen* (Halle: Niemeyer, 1904) 11–18; and Windisch, *Der zweite Korintherbrief*, 268– 69.

[108] Stowers, "*Peri Men Gar* and the Integrity of 2 Cor. 8 and 9," 341–43.

[109] Ibid., 345.

[110] Ibid., 346–47.

[111] Ibid., 347.

[112] Peterman, *Paul's Gift*, 156. He cites H. Bolkestein, "Almosen," *RAC* 1 (1950) 302.

[113] R. P. Saller, *Personal Patronage under the Early Empire* (Cambridge: University Press, 1982) 126.

done to bring praise to oneself. In this mindset it is more blessed to receive honor and that is why one gives. Peterman notes, "In the Greco-Roman world the only nonmaterial return that givers could expect would be the honour the receiver(s) pay to the giver."[114] For example, Seneca insists that the only return one can expect from gifts is from the receiver, not from God.[115] Those who are poor and socially inferior and cannot repay benefits in some material way can only repay in giving honor. In this cultural context people gave to others who were capable of giving them something in return, either through repayment in kind or through the bestowal of honor by lauding them publicly.

By contrast, Paul expects the Corinthians to do good works to poor people whom they have never met to bring praise to God and not to themselves. Paul's request also goes beyond what is envisioned in Deut 15:11. The land is not the promised land, and the brothers are not fellow Jews. Christians are not bound to any one land, and their brothers are not circumscribed by any one tribe or nation. Brothers in Christ extend across national boundaries and racial barriers. Gentile Christians and Jewish Christians in lands far from Jerusalem are obligated to the poor Jewish Christians suffering there. The recipients of this gift will then direct their thanksgiving and praise to God, not to the Corinthians, because they know that God is the true source of all giving. What is new for those who are immersed in a pagan culture and suffused with pagan values is that God requires charity for the poor, that God rewards charity with eternal recompense, and that our charity brings ultimate glory to God and not to ourselves.

If some Corinthians are influenced by a Roman perspective about giving, this lengthy and seemingly repetitive discussion presenting a biblical perspective is necessary to bridge the cultural gap. It is a new concept for most Corinthian Christians that sharing with others in need is a service to God, that opening their hearts to the poor in Jerusalem and giving generously will enhance their spiritual welfare, and that God richly rewards such generosity.[116] Many in Corinth may have found it difficult to absorb.[117] This new way of looking at giving and receiving requires more than a perfunctory letter on how the Corinthians should fulfill their pledges and how their giving will be administered. It requires in depth theological instruction. This is what Paul provides in chap. 9 as he continues his bid to reignite the Corinthians' enthusiasm for the ministry for the saints.

---

[114] Peterman, *Paul's Gift*, 149. He points to Aristotle who said "Honor (τιμή) is the due reward for virtue and beneficence" (*Nicomachean Ethics* 8.14.2) and Plutarch who said "rulers should show philanthropy to their friends and the friends should shower them with love and honor" (*Moralia* 808D).

[115] See Peterman, *Paul's Gift*, 68, 89.

[116] See Matt 6:4; 19:21; Luke 6:38; 7:4–5; 12:33; 14:12–14; 18:22; and Acts 10:4.

[117] When Christians showed compassion on the poor and gave sacrificially, they stood out from their contemporaries, who viewed things so differently. C. H. Talbert cites Justin Martyr (*Reading Corinthians: A Literary and Theological Commentary on 1 and 2 Corinthians* [New York: Crossroad, 1987] 155): "And they who are well to do, and willing, give what each thinks fit; and what is collected is deposited with the president, who succors the orphans and the widows, and those who, through sickness or any other cause, are in want, and those who are in bonds, and the strangers sojourning among us, and in a word, takes care of all who are in need" (*Apology* I, 67).

Finally, we should note that the beginning of chap. 8 and the end of chap. 9 form a kind of inclusio as the same words which occur in the introduction to the topic reappear in the conclusion.

hē charis tou theou ("the grace of God")	8:1; 9:14
diakonia ("ministry," "service")	8:1; 9:12,13
dokimē ("test")	8:2; 9:13
haplotē ("generosity")	8:2; 9:13 (9:11)
perisseuō ("abound")	8:2; 9:12 (8:7[2x]; 9:8[2x])

The conclusion is that the two chapters were sent as part of the same letter to the Corinthians.

(2) Explanation for Sending the Brothers: Avoiding Shame (9:1–5)

¹There is no need for me to write to you about this service to the saints. ²For I know your eagerness to help, and I have been boasting about it to the Macedonians, telling them that since last year you in Achaia were ready to give; and your enthusiasm has stirred most of them to action. ³But I am sending the brothers in order that our boasting about you in this matter should not prove hollow, but that you may be ready, as I said you would be. ⁴For if any Macedonians come with me and find you unprepared, we—not to say anything about you—would be ashamed of having been so confident. ⁵So I thought it necessary to urge the brothers to visit you in advance and finish the arrangements for the generous gift you had promised. Then it will be ready as a generous gift, not as one grudgingly given.

9:1–3 The NIV translation "There is no need ..." ignores the phrase that begins the sentence with *peri men gar*, "for to begin with."[118] The "for"

---

[118] The περὶ μὲν γάρ is different from περὶ δέ ("now concerning") that introduces a new topic (1 Cor 7:1,25; 8:1; 12:1; 16:1,12; 1 Thess 4:9; 5:1). Betz contends that the phrase refers to "that which follows without connection to what has gone before" (citing Acts 28:22; 2 Corinthians 8 and 9, 90; see also Windisch, *Der zweite Korintherbrief,* 268–69). The περὶ μὲν γάρ in Acts 28:22 actually points back to what precedes. Stowers points out that it "hardly serves an introductory function" but instead comes at the conclusion of the Jewish leaders' response to Paul's speech. It is closely related to what precedes in providing the reason why they want to hear more about what he has to say ("*Peri Men Gar* and the Integrity of 2 Cor. 8 and 9," 341). F. F. Bruce calls it "resumptive" rather than introducing some new topic (*I and II Corinthians,* NCB [Grand Rapids: Eerdmans, 1971] 225). But what does it resume? Plummer believes it refers back to the sending of the brothers (*The Second Epistle of St. Paul to the Corinthians,* 253). C. K. Barrett believes it refers back to the issue of boasting in 8:24 (*The Second Epistle to the Corinthians,* HNTC [New York: Harper & Row, 1973] 232). Dahl believes that it refers back to the previous topic before the recommendation of the brothers in 8:16–24 ("Paul and Possessions," 39). Furnish suggests that μὲν could anticipate the δέ in 9:3: "While on the one hand there is no need to write to you ... on the other hand, I am sending the brothers ..." (*II Corinthians,* 426). Stowers shows that the phrase "signals" that Paul is treating the main point expressed in 8:24, "the Corinthian reception of and preparation for the delegation," in light of his boasting about them to the Macedonians ("*Peri Men Gar* and the Integrity of 2 Cor. 8 and 9," 347). He concludes: "The expression introduces the subtopic of the potentially embarrassing situation caused by Paul's boasting. At the same time 9:1–4 provides a warrant and explanation for Paul's exhortation in 8:24" (347–48).

(gar) resumes what has preceded and explains why he has been so confidently boasting about their love to others (8:24). Not translating this explanatory conjunction, or translating it "now" (NRSV), obscures the connection of this sentence to what precedes.

Paul begins tactfully by saying that he does not need to say anything more about their giving to this project. Harvey compares it with our convention, "I am sure I do not need to remind you, but ..."[119] Most people subconsciously employ a kind of mental air defense system to deflect any appeals for money that their radar screen picks up as approaching their way. Paul may be anticipating this resistance and trying to put them off their guard.[120] But he may truly believe that it is superfluous to say any more to them for a number of reasons. First, the collection is not some new scheme that Paul has just dreamed up. He had already discussed, some time ago, the purpose of this ministry for the saints and had outlined the steps they needed to take to get ready (1 Cor 16:1–4). They were enthusiastically involved from its inception and know what their duty is. Second, Titus will take care of any further questions or details when he arrives, since that is the purpose of his mission. Third, Paul may also consider it unnecessary to write about it because he is now confident after their reconciliation that their response will be abundant. It shows his faith in the Corinthians; they really do not need his exhortation (cp. 1 Thess 4:9; 5:1). In fact, he tells them that he has already boasted of their eagerness to the Macedonians. He does need to tell them about the mission of Titus and the arrival of the envoys from Macedonia. He also needs to warn them that he has been boasting to others that Achaia has been ready for some time. That boasting could come back to haunt them both and bring shame if it should prove hollow.

His exhortation to complete what they started, expressed in 8:11, may reveal that Paul was perhaps overly enthusiastic in representing the progress of their preparations to the Macedonians.[121] It does show the Corinthians that, while they might not have been completely loyal to him during the recent dispute, Paul remained completely loyal to them and continued to put them in the best light to other churches.[122] Paul may have thought that they were ready because of their auspicious start and has since found out that their efforts have floundered because of their deteriorating relationship with him.

The verb "stirred" *(erethizein)* like the English word, "provoke," can have a negative meaning "to irritate" or "to provoke" (Col 3:21) or a positive

---

[119] Harvey, *Renewal Through Suffering*, 87.

[120] See Betz, *2 Corinthians 8 and 9*, 91.

[121] Betz notes that the verb παρασκευάζειν ("ready to give") is a military term that describes preparation for military action, but not its completion (*2 Corinthians 8 and 9*, 92).

[122] Murphy-O'Connor, *The Theology of the Second Letter to the Corinthians*, 89.

connotation "to stimulate through competition" (in sports and education). Here it means that their enthusiasm has stirred up the Macedonians. He uses the Macedonians in 8:1–5 as an example to urge the Corinthians to give. Now he says that he used the Corinthians as an example to urge the Macedonians to give. But Paul has not met with universal success. He was only able to spur on "most of them." The reason is that charity for strangers was something foreign to the prevailing cultural mores in Paul's day. Money was to be earned for oneself and to be enjoyed by oneself and one's household. Something so unprecedented as collecting money to send to people they did not know and who were not of the same race could not expect to receive everyone's ardent support.

Paul now relays his concern that his boast about the Corinthians that provoked others to give might prove to be hollow. Keeping up the initial enthusiasm for a project over a sustained period has proven difficult. It will cause him great chagrin and humiliate them if they come up empty. He adds another reason for sending the brothers (whom he does not introduce again). Their presence is likely to encourage them to get their gift ready. By completing their contribution before Paul arrived with other Macedonians, both Paul and the Corinthians will avoid being shamed. Paul does not want some hasty collection put together at the last minute. He takes care in his administration of the project so that it will be done right, and he delegates others to attend to the task.

9:4 Paul refers to an impending visit in 2:3; 12:14; and 13:1; and he assumes that some from Macedonia will be coming with him. If the Corinthians have nothing to add to the funds for the saints, Paul will be humiliated by his empty boasting about them, not to mention the embarrassment they would feel. By tying his honor to the Corinthians, Paul forges another link that joins them together. They will both lose honor if the Corinthians fail to follow through. But Paul's greatest concern is unspoken; their default might endanger the whole project.[123] As their zeal impelled others to contribute, their apathy might have the opposite effect. Paul may worry that the Corinthian's failure to participate would undermine his entire mission to Jerusalem.

The NIV, along with most English translations, renders the last word in the verse *(hypostasis)* as "confidence" or "assurance." But no other examples of the usage of the word with this meaning exist.[124] The word means "project" or "plan."[125] The end of this verse is therefore better translated,

---

[123] Furnish, *II Corinthians*, 427–28.

[124] BAGD, 847; Barrett, *The Second Epistle to the Corinthians*, 234; see R. E. Witt, "Hypostasis," in *Amiticiae Corolla*, ed. H. G. Wood (London: University Press, 1933), but Furnish contends that there is no evidence for that meaning (*II Corinthians*, 427).

[125] H. Koester, "ὑπόστασις," *TDNT* 8:584–85. He is followed by Betz, who translates it "project" (*2 Corinthians 8 and 9*, 95), and Furnish, who translates it "undertaking" (*II Corinthians*, 427). Martin's claim that it means "eventuality" is less defensible (*2 Corinthians*, 284).

"we would be put to shame—not to say anything about you—in this project (undertaking)." Paul is not solely concerned with the prospect of embarrassment if his faith in them is shown to have been misplaced. If they back out on their original commitment, the whole project could falter. The theological importance that he attached to this undertaking would make its failure a bitter pill for him to swallow.

9:5 Paul mentions that they had already pledged to make a generous gift. If they renege on their promises, they would be pledge dodgers. Betz notes that the names of pledge dodgers were published in the Athenian Agora.[126] The Corinthians would be familiar with such public dishonor, and Paul may be asking them, "Do you want to be known as pledge-dodgers?"[127]

They should not be motivated to give simply to avoid shame, however. Paul therefore encourages them to be ready so it is indeed a gift of blessing and not greediness. This new term, "gift of blessing," is related to a thank offering given in response to benefits received.[128] In 1 Cor 4:7 Paul reminds them: "For who makes you different from anyone else? What do you have that you did not receive? And if you did receive it, why do you boast as though you did not?" Covetousness and greed seem to have been a problem with some in the community (see 1 Cor 5:10,11; 6:10). The collection project was supposed to attest to the partnership of the Gentile churches with the Judean churches. If Paul has to beg or coerce them to contribute, it would not be a testament of their love, but instead a testament of their unwillingness. The phrase translated "not as one grudgingly given" *(mē hōs pleonexian)* does not quite capture Paul's uneasiness. The word *pleonexia* means "greediness," or "covetousness"; and Paul may be suggesting that avarice may cause them to give less than they should. In 2:11 and 7:2, however, the verb form of the word appears with the meaning "outwit" and "exploit"; and the noun may carry this meaning here. It would fit the potential quandary that Paul is so eager to avoid. If they raise the sum they contribute only after Paul and the others arrive, it will seem as if he is exploiting them in some way. The NRSV translates it "extortion" (see also REB).[129] Moffatt perhaps translates it best, "not as money wrung out of you." If it

---

[126] Betz, *2 Corinthians 8 and 9*, 96.

[127] The most infamous pledge dodgers are Ananias and Sapphira (Acts 5:1–11). This story, probably unknown to the Corinthians, reveals that such attempts to cheat or to perform less than one promised was not unknown in the church.

[128] Betz, *2 Corinthians 8 and 9*, 97. Furnish suggests there might be a wordplay between λογεία, the term for the collection he used in 1 Cor 16:1, and εὐλογία (*II Corinthians*, 428).

[129] Plummer objects: "'Not of extortion' makes πλεονεξία apply to the Apostle and his three envoys; 'that this might be ready, because you are so willing to give, and not because we force you to do so.' The meaning rather is 'that this may be ready as a generous gift and not as a grudging contribution'" (*The Second Epistle of St. Paul to the Corinthians*, 256).

appears that Paul has twisted their arms to get them to give, they will come off as ungrateful, stingy givers. If the money donated to the saints comes as a levy squeezed out of them, it may provide some needed assistance for the poor, but it will undermine the whole intent of the project. This gift is not a tax, nor is it to be a burden that weighs them down with guilt. All too often people give out of a sense of guilt rather than from a glad heart, and Paul does not want the Corinthians to feel that this offering was somehow imposed upon them. Generous giving only comes when it is voluntary and not coerced.

Paul uses a new term for the offering in this verse, "blessing" *(eulogia)*. The NIV is not incorrect to render it as "a generous gift" because it refers to the rich bounty that comes from giving a blessing. The idea of blessing, however, should not be obscured. In the Bible an act of blessing calls down the grace of God on others. By sharing their material substance with the saints, they are blessing them spiritually and materially.

3. Divine Principles of Giving: Why the Corinthians Need to Give Generously (9:6–15)

⁶Remember this: Whoever sows sparingly will also reap sparingly, and whoever sows generously will also reap generously. ⁷Each man should give what he has decided in his heart to give, not reluctantly or under compulsion, for God loves a cheerful giver. ⁸And God is able to make all grace abound to you, so that in all things at all times, having all that you need, you will abound in every good work. ⁹As it is written:

"He has scattered abroad his gifts to the poor;

his righteousness endures forever."

¹⁰Now he who supplies seed to the sower and bread for food will also supply and increase your store of seed and will enlarge the harvest of your righteousness. ¹¹You will be made rich in every way so that you can be generous on every occasion, and through us your generosity will result in thanksgiving to God.

¹²This service that you perform is not only supplying the needs of God's people but is also overflowing in many expressions of thanks to God. ¹³Because of the service by which you have proved yourselves, men will praise God for the obedience that accompanies your confession of the gospel of Christ, and for your generosity in sharing with them and with everyone else. ¹⁴And in their prayers for you their hearts will go out to you, because of the surpassing grace God has given you. ¹⁵Thanks be to God for his indescribable gift!

It is one thing to chide a church for being dilatory in their giving. It is something else to motivate individuals in the church to be free and unselfish in their giving. How does one develop in individuals such a happy spirit about giving? Church leaders throughout the ages have faced the same challenge that confronted Paul. In the next verses Paul presents four principles that are not directed to the Corinthian church as a whole but to individuals whose contributions will make up the church's gift. First, he appeals to a proverb to make the point that bountiful giving leads to bountiful rewards; stingy giving leads to stingy rewards (9:6). Second, he cites Scripture to encourage giving generously and freely because God loves a cheerful giver (9:7). Third, he refers to God's readiness to provide all that is necessary for generosity (9:8–10). Paul reassures those who might worry that they do not have enough seed to sow to attain a rich harvest. God will provide all that they need. Fourth, he maintains that their generosity will bring a great harvest of thanksgiving to God (9:11).

The benefits for giving that Paul sketches out in this unit can be summed up as follows:

1. It will make them spiritually rich (9:8–10).
2. It will bring thanksgiving to God (9:11–13).
3. The recipients will respond with prayers for them (9:14).
4. It will advance the well being and solidarity of the worldwide Christian community (9:13–14).

9:6 Paul's first point draws on a well-known analogy from farming: those who sow sparingly will get a spare harvest, those who so generously will get a generous harvest.[130] "Generously" in the NIV renders "upon blessings" *(ep' eulogiais)* and may be explained as "upon the principle of blessings." What does this mean? No farmer considers sowing as a loss of seed because the harvest will provide the seed for the next season. Consequently, no sower begrudges the seed he casts upon the ground or tries to scrimp by with sowing as little as possible. He willingly sows all that he can and trusts that God will bless the sowing with a bountiful harvest. If the farmer, for some reason, stints on the sowing, he will cheat himself of that harvest. The more he sows, the greater the harvest he will reap and the more he will have for sowing for the next harvest. Applying this analogy to giving means that plentiful giving will result in a plentiful harvest. But what kind of harvest is reaped by generosity?

The idea that generosity to the poor would meet with overflowing blessing in return was common in Jewish thinking (cp. Prov 11:24–25; Mal 3:10; *Sir* 35:10–11). In recent times this idea has been perverted by unscrupulous ministers to entice people to believe that the more they give the more they we will get in return. They appeal to greed to encourage others to open their pocketbooks, and they give ultimately to get more for themselves.[131] But this verse must be interpreted in terms of what follows. Paul does not pass

---

[130] Proverbs 11:24 provides a biblical parallel: "One man gives freely, yet gains even more; / another withholds unduly, but comes to poverty."

[131] An old English proverb warns, "He who serves God for money will serve the devil for better wages."

this principle off as a shrewd investment strategy on how to reap greater material blessings by giving a portion of it to others. If one gives in hopes of attaining greater material prosperity, then one will harvest only spiritual poverty. Paul makes clear in what follows that God rewards generosity with material abundance to make it possible for people to be even more generous.

9:7 Paul's second reason is directed specifically to individuals: "Each man should give what he has decided in his heart to give." The verb "should give" is not in the text and must be supplied. Plummer claims that the absence of a verb makes the request more forcible, but Verbrugge argues just the opposite.[132] Paul omits the imperative and thereby softens the force of what he wants them to do.[133] Throughout these two chapters, Paul goes out of his way to avoid giving the impression that he is trying to force this project upon them. What the Corinthians are to do is clear, but Paul does not come right out and tell them to do it.[134] This approach means that if they comply, they will do so out of obedience to their Lord who gave himself for them, not out of obedience to Paul.

Paul echoes Scripture to bolster the need to give generously: those who give spontaneously from the heart are especially prized by God. In the Old Testament, giving reluctantly or under compulsion is portrayed as cancelling out any benefit that could be received from the gift while giving with a glad heart promises reward from God: "Give generously to him and do so without a grudging heart; then because of this the LORD your God will bless you in all your work and in everything you put your hand to" (Deut 15:10). Scripture assumes that what is crucial is the attitude of the one who gives, not the amount. God, who knows and appraises our hearts, values only those gifts that come as a free expression of the deepest part of our souls. Gifts given under some sense of external compulsion will always be halfhearted at best. That is why the amount makes no difference if it is given with a glad heart (8:12).[135] But if it is given resentfully with a gloomy countenance, that atti-

---

[132] Plummer, *The Second Epistle of St. Paul to the Corinthians*, 231.

[133] Verbrugge, *Paul's Style of Church Leadership*, 259.

[134] Paul uses a similar strategy in his request to Philemon about Onesimus.

[135] Seneca writes: "Let us give in the manner that would have been acceptable if we were receiving. Above all let us give willingly, promptly, and without hesitation. ... No gratitude is felt for a benefit when it has lingered long in the hands of him who gives it, when the giver has seemed sorry to let it go, and has given it with the air of one who is robbing himself. Even though some delay should intervene, let us avoid in every way the appearance of having deliberately delayed; hesitation is the next thing to refusing, and gains no gratitude. For, since in the case of a benefit the chief pleasure of it comes from the intention of the bestower, he who by his very hesitation has shown that he made his bestowal unwillingly has not "given," but has failed to withstand the effort to extract it" (*On Benefits* 2.1.1–2). A rabbinic tradition list four types of almsgivers: "he that is minded to give but not that others should give — he begrudges what belongs to others; he that is minded that others should give but not that he should give — he begrudges what belongs to himself; he that is minded to give and also that others should give — he is a saintly man; he that is minded not to give himself and that others should not give — he is a wicked man" (*m. 'Abot* 5:13).

tude cancels any merit the gift might have no matter its amount.

Paul underscores this point with a line from Prov 22:8 (LXX) that is absent from the Hebrew text, "for God loves a cheerful giver."[136] The LXX has God "blesses" a cheerful giver. The Hebrew text reflects the idea of blessing in Prov 22:9, "A generous man will himself be blessed, for he shares his food with the poor." It is not that God does not love the one who gives grudgingly or not at all but that God loves, in the sense of "approves," the one who is delighted to give to others. God loves a cheerful giver because that is precisely what God is, a cheerful giver.

Horrell reflects on how this verse can be twisted to mean something other than Paul intended:

> The comfortable rich who wish to remain so may interpret this to mean that if they can only give a little cheerfully, and would resent giving more, then God would rather they give only a little. Paul, it is clear, puts things rather differently: where the grace of God abounds, there people of their own free-will abound in good deeds (9:8), like the righteous one whom the scripture describes as scattering gifts freely to the poor (9:9).[137]

9:8   The third reason for giving is that God is lavishly generous and abundantly supplies us with everything necessary to have enough for our own needs and to be generous with others. The phrase "all grace" is quite broad in scope, covering the material blessings and the spiritual motivation to share them. Most people become miserly in their giving because they worry that they will not have enough for themselves. Paul assures them that God will supply them with plenty for their needs at all times and uses alliterative repetition to carry his point: "All grace … so that in all things at all times, having all that you need, you will abound in every [all] good work."

Reluctance to sow generously, then, reflects a refusal to trust that God is all sufficient and all gracious. It also assumes that we can only give when we are prospering and have something extra that we will not need for ourselves. Paul says that at all times God provides us with all that we need so there is

---

[136] A wide variety of Jewish traditions place an emphasis on cheerfulness in giving (see particularly Deut 15:7–11). A later rabbinic tradition interprets the teaching "receive all men with a cheerful countenance" to mean that "if one gives his fellow all the good gifts in the world with a downcast face, Scripture accounts it to him as though he had given him naught. But if he receives his fellow with a cheerful countenance, even though he gives him naught, Scripture accounts it to him as though he had given him all the good gifts in the world" (ʾAbot R. Nat. 13). Philo argues that in no other action does one resemble God as in showing kindness in redressing the misfortunes of neighbors: So then let not the rich man collect great store of gold and silver and hoard it at his house, but bring it out for general use that he may soften the hard lot of the needy with the unction of his cheerfully given liberality" (Special Laws IV.74). In T. Job 12:1 Job says, "On occasion a man cheerful of heart would come to me saying, 'I am not wealthy enough to help the destitute. Yet I wish to serve the poor today at your table.'"

[137] Horrell, "Paul's Collection," 79.

never any time when we cannot be generous.

In 9:8 the word "having all you need" translates *autarkeia,* a word that Greek authors used to mean "self-sufficiency" or "contentment." The Cynics and Stoics of Paul's day understood self sufficiency to be related "to freedom from external circumstances and other people."[138] In this tradition one developed this self-sufficiency by disengaging oneself from human needs and from other humans. Paul does not use this term in a philosophical sense but in an economic sense. Having enough does not simply mean reducing one's craving for material goods and becoming independent from everyone. It means reducing what one wants for oneself so that one has enough to share with others and create an interdependence with them.[139] Having what is sufficient helps Christians "to relate more effectively to other people, not to withdraw from them."[140]

For Paul, having all you need means having enough for every good work. Paul's point is that "God will provide the means to be generous, that one can sow *liberally* (which also means freely and cheerfully, v. 7a) in the confidence that God will bestow a liberal harvest."[141] The more we give, the more we will be given by God to share with others. We may not have all the money that we want, but we will have all the money we need to be abundant in our giving to others.

When God gives us our resources, God gives us more than we need, not so that we can have more, but so that we can give more to others. God does not bestow material blessings so that one can hoard them for oneself or withdraw from others but so that they might be shared with others. The whole purpose of the collection, therefore, is not to establish the independence of the Gentile Christians from the Jewish Christians in Jerusalem but to deepen their interdependence.[142]

Paul also differs from the Cynics and Stoics in the use of *autarkeia* in his assumption that self-sufficiency does come from one's own earnest self-discipline. It is a gift of God. Therefore "self-sufficiency" is a misnomer, since it is sufficiency that comes from God not from the self (see

---

[138] Furnish, *II Corinthians*, 442.

[139] Ibid., 447.

[140] Ibid., 448.

[141] Ibid., 447.

[142] This concept comports well with a similar understanding about almsgiving that is found in the Babylonian Talmud: "Tinnius Rufus asked: Why does your God, being the lover of the needy, not Himself provide for their support? R. Akiba replied: By charity wealth is to be made a means of salvation; God the Father of both the rich and the poor, wants the one to help the other, and thus to make the world a household of love" (*b. B. Bat.* 10a).

Phil 4:11–13).[143] Paul believes that God bestows both the generosity and the resources for generosity which explains why he lists "liberality" as a spiritual gift (Rom 12:8).

Paul assumes in this verse that the most valuable thing about money is that we can use it for every good work. He avoids the plural "works," which he tends to connect with "works of law" and the ritual acts of piety, such as circumcision, and observing food laws. "Every good work" here refers to acts of charity (see 1 Cor 15:58) and is little different from what James says about supplying the needs of the brother or sister who is naked and lacks daily food (Jas 2:14–17).[144] Abounding in every good work comes from abounding in God's grace. Every good work does not earn grace; grace, already received, generates the good work.

Paul is trying to teach the Corinthians about the value of money that differs significantly from the value attached to it in their culture (and almost every other culture, ancient and modern). Peterman shows a correspondence between what Paul writes here in 9:8–13 and what he writes to the Philippians. He draws important conclusions from these texts that are particularly relevant in any culture awash in crass materialism.[145]

1. Christians should know contentment (*autarkeia,* "having enough") in every state.

2. Money is a commodity that should be used in the service of others *(leitourgia),* not something to display one's virtue publicly, to gain honor, or to bring others into one's orbit of power.

3. Reward can only be expected from God, not from others, an Old Testament view that runs counter to Greco-Roman social expectations. Giving to others in need reaps spiritual dividends from God.

4. God bestows the material wealth that we share with others, and consequently God, not the giver, is the one who is to be blessed and thanked.

---

[143] In Horace's *Satires,* Davus the slave is allowed to speak freely and says: "Who then is free? The wise man, who is lord over himself, whom neither poverty nor death, nor bonds afright, who bravely defies his passions, and scorns ambition, who in himself is a whole, smoothed and rounded, so that nothing from outside can rest on the polished surface, and against whom Fortune in her onset is ever maimed" (2.7.83–87).

[144] Cp. 1 Tim 6:18–19: "Command them to do good, to be rich in good deeds, and to be generous and willing to share. In this way they will lay up treasure for themselves as a firm foundation for the coming age, so that they may take hold of the life that is truly life."

[145] He spots the following parallels:

9:8	αὐτάρκεια	Phil 4:11 αὐτάρκης (adjective)
9:10–11	God's reward	Phil 4:19
9:12	λειτουργία	Phil 2:25,30
9:12	thanks to God	Phil 1:3
9:13	κοινωνία	Phil 1:5; 4:15
9:13	εὐαγγέλλιον	Phil 1:5; 4:15

5. Sharing with other Christians is identified as *koinōnia*—joining in partnership with them. In no way should the benefactors assume that the recipients of their gifts become their social inferiors or are obligated to return the favor with material benefits.

6. Giving to others proves that one's confession of Christ as Lord is true.

9:9 Paul again resorts to Scripture to make his point, citing Ps 111:9 (LXX, Hb. text 112:9): "He has scattered abroad his gifts to the poor; his righteousness endures forever." The word "poor" *(penēs),* meaning "one who is destitute," appears only here in the New Testament. The Greco-Roman culture assumed that it was pointless to give anything to a pauper. The only repayment he could make was with his praise, which was worthless. The biblical concern for those in abject poverty differs markedly from this view. Showing benevolence to the poor and needy is a sign of righteousness in the Old Testament.

"His righteousness" may therefore refer to the moral uprightness of the pious man, as in the psalm. Giving to the poor is a sign of a right relation with God (see Dan 4:27). As God's righteousness is demonstrated by mighty deeds, so human righteousness is demonstrated by actions—particularly in giving to the poor. The word "righteousness" takes on a meaning that is closer to what one finds in Matthew. Righteousness is something one does; and here, as in Matt 6:1–4, it involves giving alms to the poor and showing mercy to the oppressed. But how does the righteousness of a humane and compassionate person abide forever? It may simply mean that the righteous "will be remembered forever" by God (Ps 112:6).

In Ps 111:3, however, it refers to God's righteousness enduring forever. It is more likely that Paul understands "his righteousness" in the citation to refer to divine righteousness. God is the subject of the previous verse, "God is able to make all grace abound to you" (9:8), and Paul's interpretation of the psalm in the next verse (9:10) assumes that the subject of the psalm is God, "Now he who supplies the seed ..." If "his righteousness" refers to God's righteousness, then the meaning would accord with what Paul has maintained throughout this section; charity comes from God. The Lord is gracious and merciful to provide all that we need and shows his righteousness in scattering gifts to the poor. The charitable acts of Christians, then, are all "part of that larger righteousness of God by which they themselves live and in which they will remain forever (v. 9)."[146] Their righteous acts are "taken as the acts of God."[147]

---

[146] Furnish, *II Corinthians,* 449.

[147] Murphy-O'Connor, *The Theology of the Second Letter to the Corinthians,* 92. He argues that it fits the unity of Psalms 110–111 (LXX).

9:10   God is the one who provides, scatters, and multiplies.[148] God is the source of the seed (Isa 55:10–11), which is likened to righteousness (Hos 10:12), and God produces the crop. Paul's interpretation of the psalm is drawn from his observation of the farming process. The seed planted provides a harvest and enough seed to plant next year's harvest. But this statement also reflects the basic confession of Judaism that God graciously provides all of the bounty of nature. The Hebrew would have understood the opening phrase of Jesus' parable of the rich fool, "the ground of a certain rich man produced a good crop" (Luke 12:16), to mean that God produced the crop. This idea also emerges in the parable of the seed that grows of itself *(automatē)* and the farmer does not know how (Mark 4:26–29). Paul's statement that he planted, Apollos watered, but God gave the growth (1 Cor 3:6) shows that he shares this basic presupposition that all harvests come from God, not from the farmers. The one who is generous acts on the assured faith that God bountifully supplies bread for the sower and multiplies the seed corn for future harvests.

The phrase "the harvest of your righteousness" now applies "righteousness" to humans, "your righteousness." The harvest of righteous deeds, like the harvest of the field, does not come from us, but from God. The righteousness that we become through Christ's sacrificial death (5:21) works itself out in our sacrificial generosity to others. A lack of generosity calls into question whether or not we have truly received the righteousness of God. Paul's point is that God makes us righteous through Christ and gives us seed money for a harvest of generosity. The more we sow, the greater the harvest; and the greater the harvest now, the greater the harvest will be in the future.[149]

The principle Paul lays out is similar to the crass economic principle that the rich get richer and the poor get poorer. The generous get richer; the miserly grow poorer—a truth memorably captured in secular literature by the characters of Ebenezer Scrooge and Silas Marner. But growing richer may not mean wealth the way the world measures wealth. They are spiritually richer and regard whatever material resources they may possess as providing enough for themselves (see 1 Tim 6:8) and enough to give to others who have nothing. The problem with being tight-fisted is that the closed fist prevents us from receiving anything more from God. When we are open handed with others, our hands are also open to receive more from God. MacGregor writes:

---

[148] Betz, *2 Corinthians 8 and 9*, 114.

[149] Furnish comments, "Because liberal sowing leads to a liberal harvest (cf. v. 6), one may expect progressively larger harvests as there is ever more seed available for sowing in the next season. If the Corinthians will contribute generously to the collection, they will see how God can multiply their resources for yet more generous giving" (*II Corinthians*, 449).

A selfish man is never rich. His day is as long as his neighbour's, yet he has no leisure except for his own amusements, no sympathy or concern beyond his own perplexities, no strength but to fight his own battles, and no money except for his own need; what haunts his mind at every turn is the dread of having too little for himself.[150]

Martin Luther said: I have had many things in my hands that I lost; the things that I placed in the hands of God I still possess.

9:11 The first half of the verse summarizes Paul's point in the previous verses: God will provide the means for them to be generous. They will not be enriched so that they can become like the rich fool who sits back in comfort and says to himself, "You have plenty of good things laid up for many years. Take life easy; eat, drink and be merry" (Luke 12:19). They are enriched solely to give them every opportunity to be generous with others. God is generous in giving people wealth so that they may be generous with others. What we do with our money, then, becomes a litmus test for our relationship to God. If we try to hoard it or to spend it all on ourselves, that should set off alarm bells that our relationship with God is out of balance or worse, nonexistent. The rich fool with his bulging barns and bumper crop wondered where he could store all his good things to preserve them all for himself. It apparently never crossed his mind that he had plenty of storage in the mouths of the needy. Those who are decisive and resourceful in trying to find ways to use God's bounty to help others, as the rich fool was decisive and resourceful in finding ways to feather his own luxuriant nest, are those who are righteous in God's eyes (see 8:2) and who live out God's righteousness.

In the middle of outlining the principles explaining why the Corinthians should be generous, Paul reminds them that he is not talking about generosity in general. He wants them to be generous for this particular project that is "being worked through us." Paul is the agent who initiated the undertaking that will allow their generosity not only to issue in a harvest of righteousness but also to produce a worldwide impact on Christ's church. The project that he is administering brings a focus to their giving which amplifies its significance. It therefore requires that they emulate the Macedonians (8:5) in giving themselves first to the Lord and then to Paul in giving to the ministry for the saints.

The second half of the verse introduces the theme of thanksgiving by those who receive their gifts, and this idea is developed in the next verse (see 1:11; 4:15). Giving to others becomes a kind of thank-offering to God that multiplies itself. We thank God for what we have received; others thank God

---

[150] W. M. MacGregor, *Jesus Christ Son of God*, 215, as cited by Strachan, *The Second Epistle to the Corinthians*, 143–44.

for what they have received from us.

9:12   Paul now explains why "generosity will result in thanksgiving to God." "This service that you perform" translates the Greek phrase "the ministry of this service" *(hē diakonia tēs leitourgias tautēs)*. The ministry is the same word used in the "service for the saints" (8:4; 9:1), but here it refers to the rendering or execution of something. The word translated "service" *(leitourgia)* was used in Paul's day for public service, such as the contributions of money or services for a specific cause by the wealthier residents of the city-state.[151] The rich were expected to spend a portion of their wealth to promote the common good. They received honors in return, such as public praise and honorific inscriptions lauding their service and preserving their honor after death.[152] The word would recall for the Corinthians the benefactions that the wealthy made as patrons of their city or social group. Participating in the "service" Paul administers is not something that only the very rich can do, even the poorest can be, so to speak, public patrons.

But the word *leitourgia* was also used for priestly ceremonies (see Num 8:22). Paul used the word in the sense of public service (Phil 2:30) and in the sense of religious sacrifice (Phil 2:17; 4:18). Paul combines the two meanings in this verse. The rendering of their service is an act of benevolence for the common good and a spiritual offering to God.

The purpose of the collection that Paul gives here is twofold, material and spiritual. It supplies the needs of the saints and abounds in thanksgivings offered to God. Their gift is not just a service for the poor, it is a service to God because of the thanksgiving that will redound to God's glory. The recipients of their gifts cannot help but lift their voices in thanksgiving to God.

9:13   "The proof of this ministry" ("this service by which you have proved yourselves," NIV) recalls Paul's description of the Macedonians in 8:2. They proved themselves in severe affliction.[153] God does not always test us through affliction. Some of the most difficult tests come when we must prove ourselves obedient to God in times of relative prosperity. If the Corinthians follow through generously on their commitment to this ministry, they will have passed this test. Their obedience will also bring glory to God from the recipients as they praise God for it.

Their sharing with fellow Christians means that the dividing lines of race

---

[151] Verbrugge, *Paul's Style of Church Leadership*, 147–48.

[152] An example would be the inscription naming Erastus (perhaps the same Erastus Paul mentions in Rom 16:23) who paved the plaza in the theater area with Acrocorinthian limestone. With the abbreviations spelled out, the inscription reads: *[——] Erastus pro aedilitate sua pecunia stravit.* J. H. Kent translates it: "——] Erastus in return for his aedileship laid (the pavement) at his own expense" (*The Inscriptions 1926–1950, Vol 8 Part 3 of Corinth* [Princeton: ASCSA, 1966] no. 232).

[153] διὰ τῆς δοκιμῆς τῆς διακονίας ταύτης parallels ἐν πολλῇ δοκιμῇ θλίψεως (8:2).

and national heritage have indeed been broken down in Christ. It also accomplishes what Paul believes is God's will in this matter: a concrete gesture of love that signifies the unity of the churches. The gift is also part of their confession of the gospel of Christ. The "obedience of your confession" could be a subjective genitive, "obedience created by your confession"; an objective genitive, "obedience to your confession"; or a genitive of apposition, "the obedience which is one's confession." The first option seems best. Confession is to be more than the mouthing of pious clichés; it should lead to actions that speak louder than words. The confession "Jesus Christ is Lord" kindles their generosity for the saints of Jerusalem and proclaims that Jesus is Lord of both Jews and Gentiles who are full partners together in the gospel. The Jewish Christian recipients should interpret this expression of authentic love from Gentiles as a sign of God's miraculous grace on all. The one gospel of Christ brings reconciliation to those who were formerly strangers and bitter antagonists.

9:14 Bestowing gifts on others was expected to win thanks, but Paul assumes that the recipients of their aid will respond with thanks to God and intercessory prayers for them. They will recognize that the grace manifested in their giving comes from the surpassing grace of God working in their lives. Either Paul does not want to confide his feelings of trepidation, which are freely expressed in Rom 15:31, that the saints in Jerusalem may not be so effusive in their thanks to God as he hopes, or something occurred between the time he wrote this line and when he wrote Romans that caused his trust in the saints' spiritual discernment to fade. On the eve of his departure for Jerusalem with the offering for the saints, he asks the Romans to pray that it will be accepted by them in the spirit that it was given.

If the Corinthians' love is genuine, however, it is the need of the saints in Jerusalem, not the expectation of their grateful response, that motivates their generosity. Paul, however, envisages that they will receive this sacrificial gift gratefully with an outpouring of thanks to God. Paul is not trying to build castles in the air. He knows that some Jewish Christians in Jerusalem still harbor prejudice against uncircumcized Gentiles. Yet he hopes that this gift will help break down that bias as they recognize that God's grace is being poured out "even on the Gentiles" (see Acts 11:45). Gift giving was the primary way friendship was established in the ancient world, and Paul anticipates that the gift will create a bond between Jewish and Gentile Christians. Their hearts will go out to you (lit., "longing for you"), and they will offer up intercessory prayers in your behalf.[154]

---

[154] Talbert believes that Paul assumes that "the prayers of the poor were especially efficacious," citing *Herm. Sim.* 2:5–6 ("Money Management in Early Mediterranean Christianity," 367).

9:15 Paul concludes this section on a note of confidence that the Corinthians will indeed comply, and so he offers thanks to God with the word that runs throughout this section, "grace" (*charis,* "thanks"). The thanks is not offered to the Corinthians for being well-disposed to Paul's grand scheme and opening their purses to others. It is instead directed to God, who is the author of all perfect gifts. Paul gives thanks here specifically for the "indescribable" (inexpressible) gift.[155] This may refer to a number of things that are all connected together: the gift of salvation, the gift of God's Son, the gift of God's grace (8:1,4,6,7,16,19; 9:8). Most likely it refers to 8:9, "the primary gift of God which has established the whole framework of Christian life and fellowship within which Paul's preaching and collection alike stand."[156]

These words of thanksgiving conclude Paul's appeal to the Corinthians to renew their ardor for the undertaking and to fulfill their promise. They eveal that "all Christian giving is carried out in the light of God's inexpressible gift."[157] Remembering thankfully Christ's sacrifice (8:9) and God's grace, which human words fail to capture fully, should cause them to finish the preparations for their gifts diligently, unselfishly, and cheerfully. Their gift models the kind of *inexpressible gift* that God has given to them.

If Rom 15:26–27 is any indication, Paul's appeals in these chapters were successful. He reports that both Macedonia and Achaia have been pleased to share in the spiritual blessings of the Jews and in return to share their material blessings with them.

---

[155] The word ἀνεκδιήγητος ("indescribable," "inexpressible") appears only here in the NT and does not appear in the LXX.

[156] Barrett, *The Second Epistle to the Corinthians,* 241.

[157] C. Kruse, *2 Corinthians,* TNTC (Grand Rapids: Eerdmans, 1987) 169.

IV. WARNINGS IN PREPARATION FOR PAUL'S NEXT VISIT
   (10:1–13:10)
   1. Preparations for Paul's Coming Visit (10:1–11)
   2. Proper Commendation (10:12–18)
   3. Paul's Defense (11:1–21a)
      (1) Appeal to Bear with Foolishness (11:1)
      (2) Justification for Foolishness: His Zeal for the Church (11:2–3)
      (3) Justification for Foolishness: The Church's Readiness to Bear
          with Fools (11:4)
      (4) Justification for Foolishness: He Is Not Inferior to the Super-
          apostles (11:5–6)
      (5) Contrast between Paul and the Superapostles (11:7–15)
      (6) Justification for Foolishness: The Church's Readiness to Bear
          with Fools (11:16–21a)
   4. Paul's Foolish Boasts (11:21b–12:13)
      (1) Topic of Boasting: Jewish Lineage (11:21b–22)
      (2) Topic of Boasting: Greater Hardships (11:23–29)
      (3) Topic of Boasting: Things That Show His Weakness and God's
          Power: Escape from Damascus (11:30–33)
      (4) Topic of Boasting: Things That Show His Weakness and God's
          Power: Paul's Stake in the Flesh (12:1–10)
      (5) Foolish Boasting and the Signs of a True Apostle (12:11–13)
   5. Paul's Return to Corinth (12:14–21)
   6. Warning: Paul May Have to Be Severe in Using His Authority
      When Present (13:1–10)
   7. Benediction (13:11–14)

IV. WARNINGS IN PREPARATION FOR PAUL'S NEXT VISIT (10:1–13:10)

The Relationship of Chapters 10–13 to the Rest of 2 Corinthians

To this point in the letter, Paul has defended his frank criticism in his severe letter to the Corinthians (2:14–7:3) and exulted over their demonstration of loyalty to him during Titus's visit (7:4–16). His report of their desire to make amends encouraged Paul to press them to complete their collection and to give generously (8:1–9:15). But in chaps. 10–13 Paul unexpectedly switches from a conciliatory posture to a combatant one. He indicts the

Corinthians for an assortment of vices that he fears they still engage in (12:20–21) and warns that he may have to be severe with them when he next visits them (13:10). He chastises them for being hoodwinked by a different gospel and a different Jesus and being led astray from a pure devotion to Christ (11:2–4). He chides them for thinking that they are wise while putting up with fools (11:19). Paul devotes most of his attention, however, to defending himself against unnamed detractors; and he attacks boastful interferers as fools and worse, as false apostles, deceitful workers, and ministers of Satan masquerading as ministers of God (11:13–15). Since Paul accuses his opponents of "illegitimacy and ignorant pretentiousness" (10:2,7,12,15; 11:5,13–15; 12:11), many assume that these same charges have been leveled against him. In these chapters he launches a counterattack that turns the charges back on his accusers.[1] He pulls out all stops in trying to rally the Corinthians to his point of view and to reject these false teachers who have beguiled and badgered them.

Many interpreters have wondered how the scorching blast in these chapters could follow an appeal for money. This sudden change in tone and the passionate intensity of Paul's self-defense have led more than a few interpreters to regard these chapters as a fragment of a separate letter to the Corinthians that someone, for unknown reasons, edited and appended to another letter (or other letters).[2] Some consider the evidence so convincing that the burden of proof is placed on those who hold to the integrity of the epistle, and we have tried to make the case for letter's unity throughout the commentary. But if one can make sense of the canonical text as it stands, it seems more reasonable to place the burden of proof on those who argue for partition theories. They must explain how and why one would have edited

---

[1] J. T. Fitzgerald, "Paul, The Ancient Epistolary Theorists, and 2 Corinthians 10–13: The Purpose and Literary Genre of a Pauline Letter," in *Greeks, Romans, and Christians: Essays in Honor of Abraham J. Malherbe*, ed. D. L. Balch, E. Ferguson, and W. A. Meeks (Minneapolis: Fortress, 1990) 198.

[2] Many have noted logical inconsistencies between statements found in chaps. 1–7 and chaps. 10–13. (1) Paul's opening statement in 1:24, "You stand firm in the faith" (NRSV) seems to contradict his closing warning in 13:5, "Examine yourselves to see whether you are in the faith." The NIV translation of 1:24, "it is by faith you stand firm," however, eliminates any possible contradiction by translating it as a theological statement rather than an affirmation of the Corinthians' faith. (2) Paul's expression of joy and comfort over signs of their repentance (7:4,11) seems to be negated by his stern warning that he fears that he will need to exercise strict discipline against those who still resist or make light of his authority (10:2) and those who continue in immorality (12:20–21). A. Plummer contends that it makes more sense for expressions of fears and warnings to precede joyous commendation and suggests that this incongruity argues for chaps. 10–13 being an earlier, harsh letter (*A Critical and Exegetical Commentary on the Second Epistle of St. Paul to the Corinthians*, ICC [New York: Scribner's, 1915] xxxi). But Paul's commendation and joy in chap. 7 has to do with their godly sorrow over a particular matter (7:11), and the stern warning in 6:14–7:1 shows that Paul does not regard every issue in the church to have been resolved.

the epistle in such a supposedly unsatisfactory way. Nevertheless, it is necessary to rehearse some of the arguments for this section's original unity with the rest of the letter.[3] Several key themes that appeared in the earlier parts of the letter reappear in these chapters.

First, Paul appeals *(deomai)* to the Corinthians to be reconciled to God in 5:20, and now he begins a more extensive appeal in 10:1–2 *(deomai)* for them to repent so that he will not have to exercise the same boldness in person that he exhibited in his earlier letter. That boldness is based on the confidence *(pepoithēsis)* he has claimed throughout the letter (1:15; 3:4; 10:2). He states in 2:3 that he wrote the severe letter so that he might avoid another painful face to face confrontation. That remains his concern. He earnestly wants to spare them (1:23), but he needs to warn them that he stands ready to avenge all disobedience (10:6) and will not give them another reprieve (13:2). The same purpose that inspired his severe letter motivates this letter: "This is why I write these things when I am absent, that when I come I may not have to be harsh in my use of authority—the authority the Lord gave me for building you up, not for tearing you down" (13:11).[4]

Second, he continues to make a rebuttal of any foolish triumphalism (2:14–16). God works through human weakness. Barnett suggests that the emphasis on divine grace in chaps. 8–9 "forms a fitting prelude to his exposition of power in weakness as opposed to triumphalism in 10:12–12:13."[5]

Third, Paul continues to rebut any suggestion that he is somehow insufficient as an apostle (2:16; 3:5–6). He is the equal of the so-called superlative apostles. In fact, he shows through his "foolish boasting" that he is by far their superior. The establishment of the church in Corinth constitutes all the proof he needs that he has done the signs of an apostle.

Fourth, the issue of commendation resurfaces (see 3:1; 4:2; 5:12; 6:4; 10:12; 10:18; and 12:11). Paul asserted that he did not need to commend

---

[3] Hypothetical psychological explanations for the change in tone will not suffice to resolve the issue. There is no justification for believing that Paul's dictation of the letter was interrupted by a sleepless night that resulted in a sour mood or that bad news suddenly arrived alerting him to the danger that Corinth was not as securely in his camp as Titus had led him to believe.

[4] Plummer cites the parallels between Paul's explanation for his failure to visit them as expected and writing the severe letter instead because he wanted to spare them (1:23; 2:3) and the statements in 13:2,10 that this was also the purpose of this letter as a remarkable coincidence. It confirms for him that chaps. 10–13 originally comprised the severe letter (*The Second Epistle of St. Paul to the Corinthians,* xxxi). But it is no less likely that Paul continues to have misgivings about his upcoming visit to Corinthians and continues to take every precaution to avert another painful experience. He takes no pleasure at the prospect of having to exercise his authority to discipline them and hopes to preclude its necessity through positive reinforcement in commending them for matters in which they are obedient and issuing stiff warnings if any continue in their disobedience.

[5] P. Barnett, *The Second Epistle to the Corinthians,* NICNT (Grand Rapids: Eerdmans, 1997) 451, n. 6.

himself to the Corinthians again because he was not responsible for the breach in the relationship. The rivals, however, have falsely commended themselves, boasting beyond measure, and working their way into the community's life. When they challenged Paul, the Corinthians should have defended and commended him (12:11).

Fifth, we have argued that 2:14–7:3 is primarily a defense of his boldness and frank criticism of them in the severe letter. After a brief interlude with the appeal for them to renew their commitment to the collection, Paul now returns to the topic of his boldness to make sure that they understand that he will be no less bold when he meets them face to face than he was in his earlier letter. The same apostle who wrote weighty, reproachful letters will also take action when he arrives in person.[6] Chapters 2:14–7:3 therefore defend the past while chaps. 10–13 prepare for the future—his next visit to them (10:2,6; 11:9; 12:14,20,21; 13:1,2,10; see 9:4). Now he writes severely again, another bold letter, with frank criticism to build them up, not to destroy them (10:8; 13:10), to insure that his anticipated visit will not be painful. He does not want to be severe in his use of authority when he arrives.

While such vehemence might seem strange after an expression of confidence, it may be part of Paul's pastoral method. We have cited earlier Dio Chrysostom's picture of the ideal Cynic who tries to lead all men to virtue and sobriety "partly by persuading and exhorting, partly by abusing and reproaching, in the hope that he may thereby rescue somebody from folly." He then cites Homer (*Iliad* 12.267): "With gentle words at times, at others harsh."[7] Paul's harsher tone in these chapters may be tied to his rhetorical strategy as he gathers up previous topics in a final emotional appeal. Barnett suggests that "Paul may be observing the existing rhetorical convention in (written) speeches from the Hellenistic era that conclude with a powerful peroration calculated to stir the hearers to appropriate attitudinal and behavioral change."[8] He notes that this section is deliberately "emotional in tone, geared to arouse anger at the injustice of the case."[9] While he does not propose to solve the question of the letter's integrity, DiCicco makes the case that Paul employs rhetorical strategies of appealing to his good character *(ethos)*, arousing emotions *(pathos)*, and pointing to the logic of his argument *(logos)*—what Aristotle and other classical rhetoricians claimed were absolute requisites for persuading others—to prove to the Corinthians his

---

[6] The phrase "before God in Christ we speak" (κατέναντι θεοῦ ἐν Χριστῷ λαλοῦμεν) in 2:17 and 12:19 appears nowhere else in Paul's letters. It addresses the issue of his boldness as one who reproaches them with divine authority.

[7] Dio Chrysostom, *Orations* 77/78.38; noted by C. E. Glad, *Paul and Philodemus: Adaptability in Epicurean and Early Christian Psychagogy*, NovTSup 81 (Leiden: Brill, 1995) 72.

[8] Barnett, *The Second Epistle to the Corinthians*, 452.

[9] Ibid., 18.

legitimacy as their apostle and to show the illegitimacy of his detractors.[10] The rift between Paul and the Corinthians has been wrenching for both parties; and in these last chapters Paul uses a wide range of rhetorical devices, irony, sarcasm, mock humility, and contrast to bring the Corinthians in line with the gospel.[11] He therefore pushes emotional buttons and gives logical arguments in a final climactic appeal before he makes his next visit to them.[12] Having established some basis for his confidence in their spiritual competency, he can now appeal to their good judgment to make the right decision about him.

Sixth, the use of irony that pervades these chapters, particularly 11:1–12:10, provides an interesting piece of evidence. Holland defines irony as "the pretense that what is said 'hides' from the reader the true state of affairs while in fact revealing it."[13] Irony allows him " 'to speak like a fool' in his own defense, saying things that must be said 'but which he could not say *in proper persona.*' "[14] Paul specifically calls the listener's attention to the fact that he is employing this rhetorical strategy by speaking as a fool, and it allows him to invite them "to look past the surface meaning of the text in

---

[10] M. M. DiCicco, *Paul's Use of Ethos, Pathos, and Logos in 2 Corinthians 10–13,* Mellen Biblical Press Series 31 (Lewiston/Queenston /Lampeter: Mellen Biblical Press, 1995).

[11] J. Lambrecht: "The style is vivid and emotional: pleading and paranesis, biting irony. Bitter sarcasm, threat and condemnation go hand-in hand. The tone is both apologetic (self defense vis-à-vis the faithful of Corinth) and, indirectly, polemical (attack against the opponents, the intruders)" ("Dangerous Boasting: Paul's Self-Commendation in 2 Corinthians 10–13," in *The Corinthian Correspondence,* ed. R. Bieringer, BETL 125 [Leuven: University Press, 1996] 328.

[12] E. A. Judge notes a parallel to Paul's concern about his status with the Corinthians in Dio Chrysostom's *Oration to the Corinthians,* thought to be composed by his pupil Favorinus: "Like Paul, he had been treated with contempt by the Corinthians, after initially being lionised, and his speech is an elegantly self-centered reprimand to them after he was restored to favour" ("Paul's Boasting in Relation to Contemporary Professional Practice," *AusBR* 16 [1968] 46).

[13] G. Holland, "Speaking Like a Fool: Irony in 2 Corinthians 10–13," in *Rhetoric and the New Testament: Essays from the Heidelberg Conference,* ed. S. E. Porter and T. H. Olbricht, JSNTSup 90 (Sheffield: Academic Press, 1993) 250. Holland points out elsewhere that irony does not necessarily mean "saying one thing and intending its opposite"; "the intended meaning of what is said is only different than its apparent meaning." It is "often associated with litotes and exaggeration, that is, with either saying less or more than what is actually meant." The boaster (ἀλαζών) "simulates, pretending to be what he is not, while the εἴρων dissimulates, pretending not to be what he is" (Holland, "Paul's Use of Irony as a Rhetorical Technique," in *The Rhetorical Analysis of Scripture: Essays from the 1995 London Conference,* ed. S. E. Porter and T. H. Olbricht, JSNTSup 146 [Sheffield: Academic Press, 1997] 235). In Ps. Aristotle, *Rhetoric to Alexander,* we find irony defined as "saying something while pretending not to say it, or calling things by the opposite names: 'It appears that whereas these honourable gentlemen have done our allies a great deal of harm, we base creatures have caused them many benefits.' … In vituperations also you should employ irony, and ridicule your opponent for the things on which he prides himself" (1434a; 1141b 23; cited by C. Forbes, "Comparison, Self-Praise and Irony: Paul's Boasting and the Conventions of Hellenistic Rhetoric," *NTS* 32 [1986] 10).

[14] Holland, "Speaking Like a Fool: Irony in 2 Corinthians 10–13," 251.

order to find its deeper, 'true' meaning." Holland continues: "The intention of the Foolish discourse, and 2 Corinthians 10–13 as a whole, is to induce the reader to see things the correct way, that is, with the spiritual insight proper to the Christian believer rather than 'according to the flesh.' "[15] But this is a risky and difficult form of argumentation because the audience may easily misunderstand it.[16] The reason is that irony

> takes its point only indirectly, by a dissimulation that is meant to be transparent to the rhetor's political supporters, its proper interpretation involves a much more complicated mental transaction on the part of the audience than do most other forms of rhetoric. There is always the chance that the rhetor's irony will be misunderstood, and that he will fail to communicate the message he intends.[17]

Holland cites the argument of Booth "that the mental process involved in detecting and decoding irony is itself conducive to a sympathetic view of the rhetor, since it is based on the belief that the rhetor is 'our kind of person.' The task of interpreting irony forms a little communication conspiracy between the rhetor and the members of his audience."[18] The audience knows that the author knows that they would catch the irony and that it would not go over their heads. The conspiracy creates a bond between author and audience. In poking fun at the norms, the writer provokes shame that will lead either to anger or to repentance, as well as a rejection of the norms.

In my opinion Paul risks this rhetorical strategy here because he has reason to believe that it will not provoke more anger but will lead instead to more repentance and the rejection of these false norms. The word from Titus declaring their zealous desire to make things right between them is the basis for this confidence.[19]

Structure of 10–13

The outline of these chapters falls into a chiastic structure.

A 10:1–11 Warning that he can be as bold to punish disobedience when

---

[15] Ibid.

[16] Holland, "Paul's Use of Irony as a Rhetorical Technique," 234.

[17] Ibid.

[18] Ibid., 238, citing W. C. Booth, "The Pleasures and Pitfalls of Irony: or, Why Don't You Say What You Mean?" in *Rhetoric, Philosophy, and Literature: An Exploration,* ed. D. M. Burks (West Lafayette, Ind.: Purdue University Press, 1978) 11.

[19] I would argue that the primary object of his reproof is the Corinthians, members of the Corinthian congregation who have mistaken Paul's meekness and gentleness for weakness (10:2,10) and have been charmed by the false norms of the rivals and members of the congregation guilty of sin (12:21; 13:2; see 6:14–7:1). The rivals who have slithered into the congregation's good graces are basically written off by Paul and only indirectly addressed.

present as he is in his letters [set off by inclusion with the idea "when present," "when absent," and the verb *logizomai* (10:2,11), and the inconsistency between his letters and his presence (10:1b; and 10:10)][20]

B 10:12–18 Self-Commendation and God's Commendation [set off by inclusion with the verb commend, *synistemi* (10:12,18)]

C 11:1–21a Bearing with Foolishness [set off by inclusion with the verb "bearing," *anechomai* (11:1,419,20)]

C′ 11:21b–12:13 Paul's Foolish Boasts [set off by inclusion by his declaration that he is speaking as a fool (11:21; 12:11)][21]

B′ 12:14–21 Paul's Return to Corinth [set off by inclusion with his reference to coming to them again (12:14,21)]

A′ 13:1–10 Warning that he may have to be severe in his use of authority [marking an inclusion with 10:1–11 with the reference to being absent and present (10:1–2; 13:10) and the authority the Lord gave to him for building up and not tearing down (10:8; 13:10)].[22]

1. Preparations for Paul's Coming Visit (10:1–11)

[1]By the meekness and gentleness of Christ, I appeal to you—I, Paul, who am "timid" when face to face with you, but "bold" when away! [2]I beg you that when I come I may not have to be as bold as I expect to be toward some people who think that we live by the standards of this world. [3]For though we live in the world, we do not wage war as the world does. [4]The weapons we fight with are not the weapons of the world. On the contrary, they have divine power to demolish strongholds. [5]We demolish arguments and every pretension that sets itself up against the knowledge of God, and we take captive every thought to make it obedient to Christ. [6]And we will be ready to punish every act of disobedience, once your obedience is complete.

[7]You are looking only on the surface of things. If anyone is confident that he belongs to Christ, he should consider again that we belong to Christ just as much as he. [8]For even if I boast somewhat freely about the authority the Lord gave us for building you up rather than pulling you down, I will not be ashamed of it. [9]I do not want to seem to be trying to frighten you with my letters. [10]For some say,

---

[20] B. K. Peterson's rhetorical analysis identifies 10:1–11 as the *propositio* in which he lays out three main topics to be discussed in the *probatio*: (1) Paul too belongs to Christ (10:7), developed in 11:1–15. (2) Paul is able to boast in his authority without shame (10:8–10), developed in 11:16–12:13. (3) Paul will act with consistency (10:11), developed in 12:14–18 (*Eloquence and the Proclamation of the Gospel in Corinth*, SBLDS 163 [Atlanta: Scholars Press, 1998] 93).

[21] The necessity of boasting or boasting of weakness is repeated at the beginning of each of the three subsections: 11:30–33; 12:1–5; 12:6–10.

[22] Cp. M.-A. Chevallier who divides the text differently ("L'argumentation de Paul dans II Corinthiens 10 à 13," *RHPR* 70 [1990] 3–15).

"His letters are weighty and forceful, but in person he is unimpressive and his speaking amounts to nothing." [11]Such people should realize that what we are in our letters when we are absent, we will be in our actions when we are present.

The Corinthians' regard for Paul had been steadily undermined both by actions on his part that they have misconstrued and by the encroachment of rivals who made inroads by disdainfully comparing Paul to themselves. Because these mischief makers have met with an embarrassing measure of success, Paul has found himself in the uncomfortable position of having to defend himself against their annoying smear campaign and to explain his deportment as an apostle. Paul is compelled to answer criticism that he is weak and cowardly (10:1,10; 11:7; 13:3–4), that he somehow lacks apostolic power (12:12), and that his refusal to accept support from the Corinthians and to work at a trade instead denigrates his apostleship and reflects badly on them (11:7–9; 12:13–18; see 1 Cor 9:3–18). He in turn reproves the Corinthians for allowing bogus apostles to drive a wedge between them and for failing to defend him against their defamation of his character (12:11). While reaffirming his love for them (11:11; 12:15), he expresses distress over their error and issues stern warnings about their wrongheaded disregard of the truth (10:5–6,11; 13:1–4,10). His hope is that their obedience will be complete (10:6), that their faith will increase (10:15), that they will be made perfect (13:9), and that they will hold to the faith (13:5)—the faith originally preached to them by Paul. His attitude toward the rivals, however, is quite a different story. Paul insinuates that they are guilty of comparing themselves with themselves and commending themselves unduly (10:12); poaching on Paul's mission field (10:14); being ignorant of the true source of authority, the Lord (10:12b,17–18); seducing the Corinthians as Satan did Eve (11:2–3); preaching another Jesus, Spirit, and gospel (11:4); and boasting unduly (10:15; 11:12; see 5:12). He explicitly brands them false apostles, deceitful workers, and emissaries of Satan who have only disguised themselves as apostles of Christ (11:13,15).

Paul never names or addresses these rivals directly, which has prompted many hypotheses about their identity. But they must remain nameless "certain ones." What we can know about these opponents can only be inferred from the text. They apparently are proud of their Jewish heritage (11:22), skillful in the rhetorical arts (11:6, and therefore strongly influenced by the Hellenistic environment), and boastful of various accomplishments, visions, and revelations that they claimed proved that Christ speaks in them (13:3). From Paul's point of view, however, they are aligned with the forces of evil, are thoroughly evil themselves, and should be blocked from having any influence over the community.

The heart of the quarrel concerns Paul's authority over the Corinthian church; but, as Paul himself insists, he is not simply engaged in a personal defense (12:19). Barrett has his finger on the pulse of Paul's argument when he writes: "It is the nature of the apostolic Gospel, and the apostolic authority behind it, that are at stake."[23] Paul defends his reputation, but it is more to save the community from fools and a false gospel than to save his reputation.

10:1 After pleading for the Corinthians to renew their zeal for the collection for the saints of Jerusalem, Paul takes up again his own cause and the issue of his supposed lack of boldness when he is at close quarters with the Corinthians. He makes clear that he is not spoiling for a fight. He does not want to have to be hard on them when he next returns to Corinth, but he does want to remove all doubts about his supposed shortage of courage in face-to-face confrontations. He is fully prepared to confront them in person. Paul launches this appeal to cut off any possible support for the meddling false apostles so that his upcoming visit will not be another painful one.[24] His entreaty in vv. 1–2 introduces two key ideas that he will address: (1) the mistaken opinion of some that he wavers between boldness in his letters and timidity in person, and (2) his own conviction that his style of ministry is modeled after Christ.

Paul begins this section authoritatively with an emphatic, "Now I Paul myself" *(autos egō Paulos).*[25] This is the language of presence which teasingly brings up the complaint that some have against him: "I who am timid [humble] when face to face with you but bold when I am away—I beg of you that when I am present." This statement is not Paul's own evaluation of his deportment. Rather it picks up the criticism of someone in Corinth who "says" this (10:10). He intends to debunk any illusion that some might have that he is only bold when he fires off hot letters from a safe distance to be delivered by his associates. He stresses that he is present to them through this letter. Nevertheless, he is acutely aware of the difference between being present in person and being present through written correspondence and therefore underscores that the acknowledged forcefulness of his letters is not some false front. A continuity exists between the apostle who writes these letters and the apostle who will soon come to them in person.

Peterson contends, "The emphatic self-reference in our passage, then, is intended to introduce the weight of Paul's apostolic authority, remind the Corinthians just who is addressing them, and, Paul hopes, get them to lis-

---

[23] C. K. Barrett, *The Second Epistle to the Corinthians,* HNTC (New York: Harper, 1973), 245.

[24] παρακαλῶ periods in Paul's letters are regularly preceded by thanksgivings or doxologies to God. This appeal is preceded by a thanksgiving in 9:12–15 and therefore follows the same pattern found in Rom 12:1, preceded by a doxology in 11:33–36, and 1 Thess 4:1, preceded by doxological prayer in 3:11–13 (B. Witherington, III, *Conflict and Community in Corinth: A Socio-Rhetorical Commentary on 1 and 2 Corinthians* [Grand Rapids: Eerdmans, 1994] 432). This pattern provides another argument for the integrity of the letter.

[25] Paul uses the emphatic "I Paul" in Gal 5:2; Eph 3:1; and Col 1:23 (cp. Phlm 9).

ten."[26] Paul may be dissociating what he says in these chapters from his coauthor Timothy, who is named in the salutation (1:1).[27] But after talking about the visit of Titus and the brothers to Corinth (8:6,16–19,22,24; 9:3–5), it is more likely that he now addresses the prospect of his own visit to Corinth (10:2) and he uses this expression to distinguish it from that of the brothers.[28] He is defending *his* authority, explaining the theological significance of *his* weakness, and warning of *his* power and willingness to discipline the disobedient vigorously when *he* comes.[29]

Paul again does not seek to lord it over them; he exercises his authority first by beseeching them (see 2:8; 5:20; 6:1).[30] He still brandishes only the power of persuasion based on the truth in Christ, and he trusts that the Corinthians will make the correct judgment from what he has written. If any in Corinth might be misled into thinking that Paul is not as strong as the more imperious interlopers, he wants to set them straight. He packs high-powered, divine weapons, but "the meekness and gentleness of Christ" always govern their use. Paul therefore begins his appeal by highlighting the virtues of Christ, whom he represents as his ambassador and after whom he patterns his ministry (4:10; 13:3–4). He appeals to the extraordinary power that Jesus employed with an even more extraordinary meekness and kindness.

Meekness (*praytēs,* "moderation," mildness") was used in classical literature for "a calm and soothing disposition" that contrasted with "rage and savagery." "It implies moderation … which permits reconciliation."[31] It was a virtue hailed in leaders who should be slow to anger, willing to accommodate, and capable of showing pity. In keeping with this usage, Josephus uses it to refer to rulers who were courteous or of a gentle disposition, benevolent to all.[32] Ancient writers esteemed this virtue because it "'mellows' all rela-

---

[26] Peterson, *Eloquence and the Proclamation of the Gospel in Corinth,* 76.

[27] D. A. Black, *Paul, Apostle of Weakness: Astheneia and its Cognates in the Pauline Literature,* American University Studies (New York/Berne/Frankfurt on the Main/Nancy: Peter Lang, 1984) 133.

[28] C. Wolf, *Der zweite Brief des Paulus an die Korinther,* THKNT (Berlin: Evangelische Verlaganstalt, 1987) 195.

[29] Lambrecht points out a number of motifs appearing in chaps. 10 and 13 ("Dangerous Boasting: Paul's Self-Commendation in 2 Corinthians 10–13," 330, n. 10). Paul speaks of his absence/presence (10:1–2,11; 13:2,10), his anticipated arrival (10:2,4–6,11; 13:1,2,10), his threat not to spare them (10:2,11; 13:2,10), their disobedience (10:6; 13:1–2,5,9–10), his letters (10:9–11; 13:10), his divine authority to build up and not to tear down (10:8; 13:10), being tested and approved (10:18; 13:3,5–7), and being of Christ (10:7; 13:3,5).

[30] See 1 Cor 1:10; 4:16; 16:15.

[31] C. Spicq, *Theological Lexicon of the New Testament,* trans. and ed. J. D. Ernest (Peabody: Hendrickson, 1994) 3:161, citing Plato *Symposium* 197d; Aristotle *Nicomachean Ethics* 1125b; and Chilon in *Stobaeus* 4.7.24.

[32] Josephus, *Ant.* 14.3.3 § 46; 19.7.3 §330.

tions ... between citizens ... even while it remains implacable toward enemies."[33] It was viewed as a key virtue in those who had power over others. It kept them from the excesses of severity and tyranny and encouraged leniency, thus helping them to win over their adversaries.[34] The "mild look" and "soft voice" of the one who is meek presupposes a self-mastery that controls any intemperate feelings from boiling over. This virtue was particularly crucial for a teacher who must be patient and not irascible with the errors of his pupils and the challenges from any detractors.[35]

The Greek Old Testament adds a distinct nuance to the word in applying it to those who are submissive to the divine will (Ps 132:11). In the New Testament, Jesus presents himself as "gentle [meek] and humble in heart" (Matt 11:29) to explain why his "yoke" is easy for those who are weary, burdened, harassed, and helpless (Matt 9:36). Jesus' yoke is easy because he "treats his disciples as yokefellows rather than as camels and donkeys to be loaded down (23:4)."[36]

Paul has mentioned his meekness before in his dealings with the Corinthians. He told them that they may have ten thousand guardians in Christ but not many fathers (4:15). The guardian *(paidagōgos)* was a slave childminder who, in Greek plays, became a comic type caricatured as harsh and stupid and recognizable by his rod.[37] Paul asks the Corinthians if they wanted him to come with a rod (NIV "whip") as a *paidagōgos* to administer harsh discipline or to come with love and a spirit of meekness as a father (1 Cor 4:21).[38] He makes it clear that he would much rather come as a gentle and serene father (1 Cor 4:15). His lengthy correspondence with them reveals that he prefers trying to persuade rather than to rail against them and to coax them into submission with reasoned arguments rather than to beat them into submission. This earlier passage reveals Paul's basic stance toward discipline: he always wants to be in a position

---

[33] Ibid., 162 citing Isocrates *Panegyricus* 116; Xenophon *Cynegeticus* 2.1.29; Plato *Republic* 2.375; *Timaeus* 18a.

[34] It is applied to Moses (see Num 12:3; *Sir* 45:4; Philo *Life of Moses* 1.26; 2.279; and Josephus *Ant.* 3.5.7 § 97).

[35] Spicq, *Theological Lexicon of the New Testament,* 164.

[36] D. E. Garland, *Reading Matthew: A Literary and Theological Commentary on the First Gospel* (New York: Crossroads, 1993) 133. If Paul refers to characteristics of Jesus' earthly life, it assumes that the Corinthians must have known something of the tradition that depicted Jesus as meek and gentle.

[37] H. D. Betz, *Galatians,* Her (Philadelphia: Fortress, 1977) 177.

[38] "Meekness" is a fruit of the Spirit (Gal 5:23), and Paul encourages the Galatians to deal with those caught in transgression in a spirit of meekness (Gal 6:1; see also Eph 4:12; Col 3:12; 2 Tim 2:25; Titus 3:2). Timothy, as a man of God, is to pursue "righteousness, godliness, faith, love, endurance and gentleness [meekness]" (1 Tim 6:11).

in which he can be mild toward those he regards as his children.[39] He knows that punishment, harsh or otherwise, can inflict shame and inflame bitterness and has the potential to drive the offender from the faith (2:5–11; see also Eph 6:4; Col 3:21). As their spiritual father, Paul expects obedience from his churches, but he believes that a father's discipline should be tempered by love, compassion, kindness, and patience (Col 3:12) and that Christ's apostle, in particular, should emulate the model of Christ's meekness and gentleness.

The noun "gentleness" (*epieikeia*, "kindness," "reasonableness, "fairness," "clemency," "moderation") reinforces the idea of indulgence. It was regarded as an essential quality in judges since justice must go hand-in-hand with mercy.[40] Spicq writes, "For those in positions of superiority, *epieikeia* is an easy-going quality that moderates the inflexible severity of wrath, a fairness that corrects anything that might be odious or unjust in the strict application of the law."[41] Josephus records an Essene elder predicting when Herod was still a child that he would become "King of the Jews" and admonishing him "to love justice and piety toward God and mildness toward your citizens."[42] The noun, adjective, and adverb are

---

[39] R. Leivestad argues that "the meekness and gentleness of Christ" is a hendiadys that refers to the manner of Christ's coming into the world, not his leniency or indulgence ("'The Meekness and Gentleness of Christ' II Cor X.1," *NTS* 12 [1966] 156–64). In Christian texts the two terms describe a "gentle, humble and modest attitude as a general Christian ideal, not the magnanimity and generosity to be exercised by authorities" (p. 160). Leivestad appeals to the presence of the phrase "in gentleness and meekness" in *Diogn.* 7:4–5 and interprets it to mean: "The real paradox is not that God sent a mild and merciful ruler instead of a tyrant, but that he sent his Son without any royal glory at all, in the shape of an ordinary, simple man. The point is the humble state more than the humble behaviour" (p. 161). He concludes about its usage in 2 Cor 10:1: "Paul is not referring to the lenience and indulgence of the heavenly judge, nor even to his mild and gracious attitude during his earthly life; he is alluding to the fact of the kenosis, the literal weakness and lowliness of the Lord" (p. 163). Paul wants the Corinthians to recognize that his appearance as one who is humble is "an imitation and a continuation of the kenosis of Christ, of the paradoxical demonstration of divine δύναμις working through human ἀσθένεια" (p. 164). While this interpretation of the two terms fits well with the overall thrust of Paul's argument in chaps 10–13, the parallel with 1 Cor 4:21 points instead to the way Paul treats the Corinthians, particularly in matters of discipline. Leivestad asserts that the context defines the terms' function, and in this context Paul's attitude and his use of authority are at issue. The Corinthians are put off by what they regard as an inconsistency between his threatening letters and his mild and timid presence. His rivals seize upon his meekness and gentleness in his face to face encounters with the Corinthians to suggest that he has no real authority: He is all bluster with no follow through. Paul explains that his demeanor emulates Christ's meekness and gentleness.

[40] Spicq, *Theological Lexicon of the New Testament,* 2:34–35.

[41] Ibid., 35.

[42] Josephus, *Ant.* 15.10.5 § 375.

applied to God in the LXX to describe God's mildness and forbearance.[43] "Gentleness" appears as an essential quality in a church leader (1 Tim 3:3). The bishop is not to be prone to violence or vindictiveness but should be moderate, gentle, and serene. According to James, those who have the wisdom from above show gentleness as well as being pure, peaceable, willing to yield, and full of mercy (Jas 3:17).

Appealing to Christ's virtues of meekness and gentleness does two things. First, it shows that Paul takes for granted his status of authority over them as their spiritual director since these are the virtues "of those who voluntarily do not make full use of the power that their superior position justly allows."[44] Christ who reigns over Christians as their Lord and judge is known by them as meek and gentle. Rejecting an arrogant and domineering attitude over his charges does not mean that Paul lacks authority, as some infer, but instead it means that Paul is like Christ.[45] His gentle demeanor and lack of aggressiveness in person are not to be taken as signs that he lacks confidence or fortitude but as evidence of his conformity to Christ's example. Second, the reference to these virtues shows his basic goodwill toward them. He is open and conciliatory and hopes that his moderation and leniency will make a more drastic show of his authority quite unnecessary.[46] But if this approach fails, he promises not to be lenient again when he comes (13:2).

The opponents concede that Paul could be bold and severe in his letters, and he tries to help them understand that his goal was to make it unnecessary for him to take disciplinary action when he arrived. He will warn them that they should not mistake his lowly demeanor for cowardice or impotency. Instead, it conforms to the paradigm of the meekness and gentleness of Christ.

Although gentleness and meekness were primarily viewed in secular literature as virtues for those in power, "humility" (*tapeinos,* NIV "timid") was not. It was not highly regarded in the ancient world and did not have the positive, moral sense of being modest and void of wrongful pride. Paul uses

---

[43] *1 Kgdms* 12:22; Ps 85:5; *Wis* 12:18; *Bar* 2:27; Dan 3:42; 4:27; *2 Macc* 9:27; and *3 Macc* 3:15; 7:6. In *Pr Azar* 19 (=Dan 3.42 LXX), Azariah prays for God to deal with them "according to your kindness" (ἐπιείκεια) and abundant mercy.

[44] Fitzgerald, "Paul, The Ancient Epistolary Theorists, and 2 Corinthians 10–13," 194, n. 26, noting J. de Romilly, "Fairness and Kindness in Thucydides," *Phoenix* 28 (1974) 95–100.

[45] Barnett comments that Paul "presents himself to them in ministry as the model of 'Christ' himself." He "exemplifies in a concrete and visible way a lifestyle that was both heard from and seen in Christ himself, and by it he now appeals to the Corinthians" (*The Second Epistle to the Corinthians,* 459–60).

[46] An example of this virtue is found in 2 Cor 2:6–11, where he insists that the community be considerate, kind, and forgiving to the offender. Compare Paul's gentleness in 1 Thessalonians 2. He says that he came gently as a nurse and was not abusive (see A. J. Malherbe, "'Gentle as a Nurse': The Cynic Background to I Thess ii," *NovT* 12 [1970] 203–17).

the word "humble" in 7:6 in the sense of one who is "lowly" and "down-cast." When his opponents describe Paul as being "humble," they understand it to be a reproach. Humility was an attitude suitable to one who was "base, ignoble or despised," not the attitude of any self-respecting person.[47] Lucian wrote: "The humble-witted [are] ... neither sought by their friends nor feared by their enemies ... [but are] ever cringing to the man above."[48] Here was the problem. The Corinthians have mistaken Paul's gentleness for timidity, something they regarded as more fitting for one who was servile, demeaned, and abased than an apostle of the exalted Christ.[49] Dio Chrysostom comments: "Certainly foolish persons universally scorn men of no reputation and pay no heed to them, even though they may chance to be giving most excellent advice; but, on the other hand, when they see men being honoured by the multitude or by persons of greatest power, they do not disdain to be guided by them."[50]

Paul has admitted that the world viewed him as one who was dishonored and of no reputation (6:8). The world's scorn of Christ's apostle has unfortunately permeated this church, imbued as it is with the world's values.

Some person or persons in Corinth therefore must have belittled Paul as too lowly to suit their ideal of towering apostolic leadership.[51] He will derisively ask them in 11:20–21 if they would prefer him to be more ruthless. The Corinthian culture embraced "those who projected themselves with vigor and force."[52] They gladly put up with Paul's haughty rivals who enslave them, prey upon them, take advantage of them, lord it over them, and strike them in the face (11:20). Some apparently found this manner of wielding authority—speaking loudly and whacking with a big stick—far more impressive than Paul's more humble and timorous approach. His response drips with sarcasm, "To my shame I admit that we were too weak for that!" (11:21). But his point in these chapters is that he only appears to be weak and that he is really powerful in Christ who works in his weakness. They have misread his weakness and have failed to see how God's power uses and overcomes weakness. He will therefore turn the tables on them by

---

[47] Spicq, *Theological Lexicon of the New Testament*, 3:369.

[48] Lucian, *The Dream* 9; cited by T. B. Savage, *Power through weakness: Paul's Understanding of the Christian Ministry in 2 Corinthians*, SNTSMS 86 (Cambridge: University Press, 1996) 24, n 39.

[49] An example of Paul's forbearing gentleness can be found in 2:6–11, where he requests that the community be kind to the one he had demanded be disciplined.

[50] Dio Chrysostom, *Orations* 57.3.

[51] J. L. Sumney argues that the conflict swirls around the Corinthians' assumption "that true apostles should be impressive individuals. They should be dynamic and persuasive speakers and have a commanding demeanor" (*Identifying Paul's Opponents: The Question of Method in 2 Corinthians*, JSNTSup 40 [Sheffield: Academic Press, 1990] 162).

[52] Savage, *Power through Weakness*, 69.

arguing, "If he were not weak, the power of God could not become perfect in him."[53] His weakness then becomes something in which he can boast (11:30; 12:9–10).

Paul's opening sentence in this section, "By the meekness and gentleness of Christ, I appeal to you," is incomplete. What follows in 10:2–6 clarifies the nature of his appeal. He can be as bold and able to destroy arguments in person as he can in letters. Those who oppose him or treat his admonitions lightly are therefore forewarned. He is ready to wage war but pleads that he not have to do so. The meekness of Christ that they have witnessed in him does not compel him to continue to turn the other cheek when challenged by those in the congregation who are headstrong and flout his authority or to sit idly by as overbold interlopers, ministers of Satan, engage in a hostile takeover to wrest this church from his orbit of influence. Like Christ, who boldly confronted Pharisees and chief priests when they challenged his authority in the temple, Paul is prepared to come to Corinth with guns blazing. But he first begs the Corinthians not to force a showdown. He does not seek vengeance against the trespassers who have infringed on his ministry, but he will defend himself. His defense is for the good of the community in danger of being seduced by a different gospel and another Jesus (11:4) as much as it is to salvage his slandered reputation (Rom 12:19).

10:2 Whether Paul will be meek and gentle when he next visits them depends on how they respond to this letter. He prefers meekness but will show his boldness if necessary. He now begs them to obey, but his entreaty contains a thinly veiled threat that sets the stage for this anticipated visit.[54] They need to prepare themselves for his arrival by completing their collection so that they will not be embarrassed before the Macedonians who will come with him. More importantly, they need to prepare themselves with a thorough moral reformation so that Paul can spare the rod when he comes; and then both of them can be spared another painful visit.

In these opening verses Paul alludes to charges that have been raised by those who wish to impugn his reputation and undermine his influence. First, the reference to the discrepancy between his mighty letters and his weak presence points back to the painful visit alluded to in 2:1 when he was publicly humiliated in a nasty confrontation and quietly withdrew

---

[53] Leivestad, "The Meekness and Gentleness of Christ," 162.

[54] J. Calvin comments: "All Christian teachers should make this their invariable method, first to strive with gentleness to bring their hearers to obedience and to appeal to them kindly, before they go on to visit punishment on rebelliousness" (*The Second Epistle of Paul the Apostle to the Corinthians and the Epistles to Timothy, Titus and Philemon,* CNTC [Grand Rapids: Eerdmans, 1964] 131).

rather than stay to battle it out. He responded with the severe letter and did not return as expected. His threat in an earlier letter to discipline them (1 Cor 4:18–21) and his apparent failure to follow through, coupled with his abrupt departure after the quarrel, may have given credence to the suspicion that he was not a spiritually authoritative apostle but a man of the flesh who was cowardly and ineffectual.[55] He was, as it were, only a "paper" apostle. By contrast, the intruders appeared to embody the very apostolic ideals that Paul's detractors claimed he lacked. They displayed a more commanding spiritual presence, spoke with greater eloquence, and flashed more conspicuous evidence of divine authority (11:20). To use an image from a popular film, some in Corinth had been inclined to regard Paul as if he were like the Wizard of Oz when he was finally exposed as a fraud. The wizard frightened people when he hid behind his curtain pulling levers and projecting a menacing image on a large screen with noisy sound effects. But he turned out to be bumbling and timorous when met face-to-face without his elaborate props to shield him. To their mind, Paul cuts a sorry figure when he is present with them and only dares to browbeat them in letters when he is safely out of reach (10:1,10).

A second accusation may be related to the first, that Paul "walks according to the flesh" (NIV "we live by the standards of this world"). This phrase is open to a variety of interpretations. It may refer to their opinion that he acts from worldly motives and may be tied to accusations that he is inconsistent and unreliable (see 1:12,17).[56] He says one thing and does another as his fancy strikes him.

A third problem relates to his unimposing physical presence and ineffective speech. His bodily presence *(parousia)* is weak (10:10); his speech is of no account (10:10; 11:6). He is less than awe-inspiring. Paul's oratory leaves much to be desired according to the rhetorical standards they prize. His physical appearance and perhaps his mannerisms and speech make him ineffective and seemingly incompetent. He does not project

---

[55] Plummer claims that they see him as "at once a coward and a bully" (*The Second Epistle of St. Paul to the Corinthians*, 275).

[56] G. Theissen notes the various theories proposed by German scholars (*The Social Setting of Pauline Christianity: Essays on Corinth* [Philadelphia: Fortress, 1982] 64, n. 44): (1) Paul reproached those in Corinth who caused strife as behaving in a fleshly manner (1 Cor 3:1–3). Since Paul has also caused strife, they have countered with the same charge. (2) An angel of Satan has caused his illness, revealing that he behaves in a fleshly manner. (3) Paul is regarded as some kind of sorcerer. (4) Paul was not a pneumatic person but was still caught in the fleshly realm of existence.

success as the world would recognize it.[57]

We can only guess at the other possible charges by reading between the lines. Does someone accuse him of not belonging to Christ in some way (10:7)? Is this related to their general opinion of his rhetorical clumsiness that is then presumed to reflect some spiritual inadequacy? Do they think that he somehow lacks charismatic power appropriate for an apostle (12:12; 13:3–4)? Certainly, they are less than pleased with his continuing to work at a trade. They regard such work as serving only to lower him (11:7–9; see 1 Cor 9:3–18). Do some accuse him of conniving avarice by refusing to accept overtly anything from them because he plans to skim money off the top from their collection (11:7–9; 12:14–18)? He probably also compared badly with the interlopers when it came to airing his divine visions and ecstatic experiences, and this vision deficit may have also served to lower their esteem of his spiritual prowess.

Paul's purpose is not to get into a shouting match with his detractors but to recapture the goodwill of his listening audience so that they might make a favorable judgment about him themselves. He will do so by establishing his character as a genuine apostle, pushing emotional buttons, drawing on irony to show the foolishness of his opponents, and presenting sound arguments with which no reasonable judge could disagree.

10:3–6 The opponents think that Paul is "humble," but he will not cower and grovel before his detractors. He employs a series of martial metaphors in 10:3–6 to reinforce this point. He wages war (10:3); he has weapons of warfare to destroy strongholds (10:4); he tears down raised obstacles (10:5); he takes captives (10:6); and he stands on military alert, ready to punish the rebels (10:6).[58] Many today have an impression that Paul was

---

[57] Black shows that Paul uses the term "weakness" (ἀσθένεια) anthropologically to refer to humanity's general powerlessness in relation to God, Christologically to refer to weakness as the place where God exhibits his power, and ethically to refer to weakness as a characteristic of immature believers who must not be condemned (*Paul, Apostle of Weakness*, 84–168; 228–46). But weakness also has class and status associations. "'Weakness' is shameful and frequently has connections to the lower classes. On the other hand, the description 'strong' connotes those who are important and influential, usually nobles or well-to-do" (H. Stansbury, "Corinthians Honor, Corinthian Conflict: A Social History of Early Roman Corinth and Its Pauline Community" [Ph.D. diss., University of Michigan, Ann Arbor, 1990] 428). Stansbury argues: "The language ... connotes superiority in influence and honor in relation to other members of the community, but the basis for defining these unequal status positions varies according to context. The marks of a strong person can encompass a mix of variables, including wisdom, liberty, wealth, social status, and lifestyle. A person would not have to possess all of these variables to reckon himself "strong," for the community's system of honor was yet in flux, and an individual might rate any particular variable above another" (p. 430). Paul intends to upset the whole value system that ranks people socially as strong and weak and allows people to assert superiority over others (see 2 Cor 12:10).

[58] Malherbe notes that being "ready" was a phrase used of military preparedness ("Antisthenes and Odysseus and Paul at War," in *Paul and the Popular Philosophers* [Philadelphia: Westminster, 1989], 93, citing Polybius, *The Histories* 2.34.2; Philo, *On the Embassy to Gaius* 259; and Dionysius of Halicarnassus, *The Roman Antiquities* 8.17.1; 9.35.6; 9.12.14). See also *1 Macc* 7:29; 12:50.

pugnacious and uncompromising, hard to get along with, and always on the warpath against this or that opponent.[59] It is interesting to discover that the Corinthians' perspective of their apostle was quite the opposite and that Paul feels compelled to convince the Corinthians that he is not timid but bold. The picture that some have of a combative, cantankerous Paul needs to be reevaluated.[60]

Paul begins his defense against the negative appraisals of his ministry style with irony. "For though we walk according to the flesh" (NIV, "for though we live in the world") repeats the same phrase from the previous verse which broaches one of the charges leveled against him, "walking according to the flesh" (NIV, "we live by the standards of this world"). By repeating this phrase, Paul would seem to grant the criticism directed against him about being "fleshly," but he tweaks the meaning of word "flesh" to give it a quite different connotation.[61] It does not apply to living according to misguided humans standards but to live a human existence that is subject to all the limitations that our corporeality places upon us. "To live in the flesh" means that he possesses no supernatural powers but is a frail clay vessel that is wasting away and given over to death (4:7–10,16; 6:4–5). Paul concedes he walks in the flesh, which means that he is subject to bodily weakness and thorns in the flesh. He then returns to the negative meaning of "flesh" from the previous verse to insist that he does not wage war according to the flesh by using misguided humans standards.[62] "To wage war according to the flesh" (NIV, "to wage war as the world does") means that one relies on flimsy human resources that are void of any divine power and that one is likely to resort to shameful, underhanded means to gain the desired victory. Paul's methods are not fleshly methods. He does not rely on cunning or deception to insure that he will win. His power is God's power, which means that he fights according to God's rules of engagement. He has an arsenal of powerful, divine weapons at his disposal. In what follows, Paul appeals to the three stages of the campaign in ancient siege warfare (*strateuometha*

---

[59] One example among many that could be cited is the comment of E. Best, "Paul, I am sure, was not an easy person to get on with. He dominated others; his language was over-vehement" ("Paul's Apostolic Authority—?" *JSNT* 27 [1986] 21).

[60] N. R. Peterson contends: "Some in Corinth have apparently been persuaded by other apostles that Paul's exercise of his authority in Corinth is overbearing and not matched by his personal qualifications" (*Rediscovering Paul: Philemon and the Sociology of Paul's Narrative World* (Philadelphia: Fortress, 1985). On the contrary, just the opposite is true.

[61] Other examples where he appears to concede their criticism only to turn it against them occur in 10:10; 11:6,7–8,16.

[62] For Paul, life in the sphere of the flesh requires a fight with spiritual weapons against spiritual foes (Rom 13:12,13; 1 Cor 9:7; 2 Cor 6:7; Eph 6:11–17; 1 Thess 5:8; and 1 Tim 1:18; 2 Tim 2:3–4). The enemy consists of arguments, obstacles to the knowledge of God, thoughts, and disobedience.

with three dependent participles): destroying defensive fortifications, taking captives, and punishing resistance when the city is finally brought to submission.[63] He may *walk weakly,* but he *fights strongly.*[64]

Divinely powerful spiritual weapons enable him to lay siege to his opponents, but he does not specify what spiritual siege craft he has in mind. He has referred previously to the power of God working through him with weapons of righteousness for the right hand and for the left (6:7). From references elsewhere in the Corinthian correspondence, we can assume that he has in view the truth of the gospel, epitomized in the word of the cross (1 Cor 1:18,23–24; 2:5; 2 Cor 6:7; see Rom 1:16), and the knowledge of God (2:14; 4:6).[65] Other spiritual weapons referred to in the New Testament such as prayer, divine wisdom, and holy conduct may also be assumed to be part of his arsenal. As Paul develops his argument in these chapters, however, he reveals that in God's hands even his weakness becomes a mighty weapon through which God works powerfully—perhaps because it is so disarming.

While Paul does not elaborate on the weapons at his disposal, he does emphasize their effect and likens his opponents to mutinous resisters holed up in the city of Corinth and miscalculating that their ramparts and battlements will protect them. Everyone in the ancient world knew, however, that the advantage was always on the side of the attacker with his siege engines and not with the fortified city. No matter how well defended cities might be,

---

[63] The imagery derives from well-known realities of siege warfare in the ancient world. In the account of the Maccabean struggles, Judas and his brothers struck "Hebron and its villages and tore down its strongholds and burned its towers on all sides" (*1 Macc* 5:65). The description of the Romans mentions them attacking the Greeks: "Many of them were wounded and fell, and the Romans took captive their wives and children; they plundered them, conquered the land, tore down their strongholds, and enslaved them to this day" (*1 Macc* 8:10, presumably referring to the time when the Achaean League of Greece was defeated and Corinth destroyed in 146 B.C.). Paul may understand himself in light of the OT as a wise man assaulting ungodliness: "A wise man attacks the city of the mighty / and pulls down the stronghold in which they trust" (Prov 21:22; the LXX has "in which the ungodly [οἱ ἀσεβεῖς] trust"). In the story of the tower of Babel, they said, "Come, let us build ourselves a city, with a tower that reaches to the heavens, so that we may make a name for ourselves and not be scattered over the face of the whole earth" (Gen 11:4). Witherington draws attention to Eccl 9:14–16: "There was once a small city with only a few people in it. And a powerful king came against it, surrounded it and built huge siegeworks against it. Now there lived in that city a man poor but wise, and he saved the city by his wisdom. But nobody remembered that poor man. So I said, 'Wisdom is better than strength.' But the poor man's wisdom is despised, and his words are no longer heeded." He concludes that Paul portrays himself as "the poor sage who must deliver his besieged converts from the lofty walls the opponents built against them, and yet his wisdom is being despised" (*Conflict and Community in Corinth,* 438). Malherbe points out that the imagery was current in philosophical debate and argues that Paul "describes his own weapons in terms approximating the self-description of the rigoristic Cynics and his opponents' fortification in terms strongly reminiscent of the Stoic sage" ("Antisthenes and Odysseus and Paul at War," 112).

[64] Savage, *Power through Weakness,* 66.
[65] Furnish, *II Corinthians,* 462.

they would eventually fall to the resourceful and determined general.[66] How much more is this the case on the spiritual level when "the city" is up against God's weaponry. Human bulwarks and parapets, no matter how high and lifted up, can never withstand God's power.

Paul assures them that he has the capacity to destroy strongholds. He does not identify what these high bulwarks represent, except to say that they are related to arguments that oppose the knowledge of God. These bulwarks may therefore refer to the assortment of intellectual arguments that humans construct in an attempt to stave off the truth of the gospel. More specific to the Corinthian resistance, they may refer to conceptual barriers they erected to rationalize their defiance of Paul's moral and theological correction. When he says that we demolish "arguments" *(logismoi)* or, if we choose a more derogatory translation, "sophistries," he refers back to 10:2, where he proposes *(logizomai)* to show boldness against those who reckon *(logizomenous)* that he operates by the world's standards. These specious arguments that he intends to destroy therefore appear to be specifically about him and not just defenses against the gospel. Goulder raises the right question and gives the obvious answer to it: "Why does Paul want to assert his authority? Because people are not behaving properly, and he needs to stop it."[67]

"Every pretension that sets itself up" (NIV) translates the Greek phrase that reads literally "every high thing lifted up." It refers to another defensive fortification, "a raised rampart."[68] This tower has been lifted up against the knowledge of God. Paul has said earlier that he is led in God's triumph so that the knowledge of God spreads like a fragrance in every place through him (2:14). He understands himself to be a conduit for knowing God because God commanded the light to shine out of the darkness and shone in his heart to give him "the light of the knowledge of the glory of God in the face of Christ" (4:6). He has commended himself to others as God's servant because of his knowledge of God and his purity, patience, kindness, genuine love and truthful speech (6:6). Consequently he will concede only that his speech might not measure up to the rhetorical standards of certain ones but will insist that they cannot call his knowledge of God into question (11:6). When it comes to the only kind

---

[66] The extraordinary example of the siege and fall of the seemingly impregnable fortress of Masada is a case in point.

[67] M. Goulder, "2 Cor. 6:14–7:1 as an Integral part of 2 Corinthians," *NovT* 36 (1994) 48.

[68] Malherbe cites the use of the word *hypsos* in Aeneas Tacticus (*On the Defense of Fortified Positions* 32.2) to "throw up in opposition wooden towers or other high structures." He explains that "Paul's use of the less usual *hypsoma* may have been suggested by *ochryōma and noēma,* and is in any case an example of his play on nouns that end in *-ma,* which, according to BDF 488.3, belongs "to the dainties of the Hell. artists of style" ("Antisthenes and Odysseus and Paul at War," 92–93). Paul plays with words. He will throw down (καθαίρεω) what has been lifted up (ἐπαίρω).

of knowledge that matters, he is no untrained apprentice. Again the reference to knowledge of God is personally connected to Paul's apostleship. Those who have set up barricades against the knowledge of God have set up obstacles to block Paul's influence in the community and have tried to refute his insights into the meaning of the gospel.

Paul therefore has every intention of taking captive every thought for Christ. The word translated "thought" *(noēma)* is rendered elsewhere as "mind" and "design." It is connected in this letter to the activities of Satan, either as part of Satan's designs to outwit us (2:11), or as the object of Satan's assault. In 3:14 the minds of the Israelites were hardened, necessitating Moses' veil. In 4:4 Paul says that the minds of unbelievers have been blinded by the God of this world to keep them from seeing the light of gospel of the glory of Christ. In 11:3 he candidly says that Satan has ensnared the Corinthians "thoughts" in the same way he deceived Eve. Satan holds their minds hostage, and Paul is prepared to fight a pitched battle to liberate them.

Since Paul pictured himself earlier as Christ's captive being led in his triumph (2:14), it is ironic that he now portrays himself as a military general who must breach the stronghold that in this case obstructs them from seeing the truth. Christ's prisoners who have been snatched from Satan's clutches can take the offensive and capture others for the gospel. Paul intends to take them prisoner, which, paradoxically, is the only way to be set free from Satan. Their thoughts need to come under the Lordship of Christ and to be liberated from the captivity of Satan.

Paul also stands ready to punish every disobedience.[69] Whose disobedience does he have in view? Many interpreters assume that he is thinking of the outsiders. When he comes to Corinth, he will have to confront boldly the outsiders who are undermining his ministry and preaching another gospel (11:4). That might explain why he promises to punish them "once your obedience is complete" (10:6). As Furnish reads it, "When Paul is certain enough of the basic Christian commitments of the congregation, then his own hand will have been strengthened to deal with *every disobedience* of the interlopers."[70]

---

[69] The Moffatt translation captures the military metaphor by translating it "to court-martial anyone who remains insubordinate."

[70] Furnish, *II Corinthians,* 461, 464; so also C. K. Barrett, *The Second Epistle to the Corinthians,* HNTC (New York: Harper & Row, 1973) 253–54; and R. P. Martin, *2 Corinthians,* WBC (Waco: Word, 1986) 306–7. Peterson goes so far as to say, "The anticipated obedience of the Corinthians is distinguished from the hopeless and doomed disobedience of the intruders" (*Eloquence and the Proclamation of the Gospel in Corinth,* 86). Whether Paul's protest related to the violation of the agreement in Gal 2:6–10, as F. F. Bruce (*I and II Corinthians,* NCB [Grand Rapids: Eerdmans, 1971] 34; and Martin (*2 Corinthians,* WBC [Waco: Word, 1986] 316), contend, is impossible to prove until the identity of the opponents can be firmly established. C. Kruse notes that "Paul may have regarded Achaia off limits for the Jewish Christian intruders who aggravated the situation in Corinth." But he goes on to say that the crime of tampering with the truth of the gospel (11:4), being false apostles, deceitful workers, who disguise themselves as apostles of Christ (11:13) is far more serious (*2 Corinthians,* TNTC [Grand Rapids: Eerdmans, 1987] 175).

But how will Paul punish these intruders except to evict them? Paul is primarily interested in correcting the disobedience of the Corinthians themselves. The disobedient include those who think that Paul walks according to the flesh, are guilty of sexual immorality, continue in their associations with idolatry (12:21; 13:2), and promote false apostles. It is not that Paul needs to rally the Corinthians to his side so that in concert with them he can give the intruders the boot. Paul does not want to take over their own responsibility to examine themselves and to discipline wrongdoers (see 1 Cor 5:1–5; 6:1–11). When their obedience is complete, they need to take action as they did when the majority disciplined a previous offender (2:6).

From these opening verses of Paul's defense, we can glean several insights about Paul's views on how to exercise spiritual leadership. First, we see that his aim is not to destroy people who oppose him but to destroy their specious arguments (10:4)! All too often, people, rather than their wrongheaded opinions, become the object of any attack. The opponents do a hatchet job on the reputations of others and build themselves up to secure their own position of power. Paul knows that "if anyone destroys God's temple, God will destroy him" (1 Cor 3:17). He does not name names because he is not out to triumph over individuals so that he can rule the roost. He wants only to rescue the Corinthians from the grips of foolishness that will only lead to infidelity to Christ.

Second, Paul, by letter and by personal visit, wants them to acknowledge the truth of his gospel and the basis of his authority so that they will be obedient. But he has no desire to fashion them into his worshipful disciples. His goal is to make them obedient to God (see 2:9; 7:15; 12:21; and 13:2). As Furnish puts it so well: "Paul does not wish to use his authority to strengthen his hold over the Corinthians, but only to strengthen their grip on the gospel, their faith."[71]

Third, Paul promises in 10:5 that he will punish those who are disobedient when the obedience of the Corinthians is complete, that is, when they get in line again with the gospel. This means that Paul does not wish to exercise his authority independently of the Corinthians but intends to act only in concert with them.

R. May identifies five kinds of power that leaders can exert.[72] (1) Exploitative power uses physical force or the threat of violence and leaves the other with no choice but to comply. (2) Manipulative power uses the covert cunning of the con man rather than the gunman. (3) Competitive power employs an I win / you lose strategy. Only one can win, and it results in shrinkage of

---

[71] Furnish, *II Corinthians*, 477.

[72] R. May, *Power and Innocence: A Search for the Sources of Violence* (New York: Norton, 1972) 105–113.

community. (4) Nutrient power is likened to the parents' care for their children; they exercise their power to do them good. Problems arise when "care" becomes smothering and when it insists on doing children good the parents' way. Such methods create dependency.

> Developing morally wise Christians is like helping a child learn to ride a bicycle. The child needs encouragement, steadying, and pointing in the right direction; but the parent must finally let go if the child will ever learn to pedal, steer, and balance alone. If Christians are ever to grow in Christ, leaders need to point them in the right directions, but they must let go and let them decide for themselves the obedience Christ requires of them.[73]

(5) Integrative power works with the other person to enable them to grow both mentally and spiritually. As Paul portrays matters in these chapters, we get the picture that his rivals have been exploitative, manipulative, and competitive in their use of power. He insinuates that they enslave, devour, seek to gain control, put on airs, and strike the Corinthians in the face, either metaphorically with insults or literally with blows (11:20). Some Corinthians readily submitted to their domination, mistaking this brazen behavior for the apostolic ideal. They then interpreted Paul's gentle restraint as weakness (10:1). By contrast, Paul uses integrative power: "we work with you for your joy" (1:24; see 13:10). These chapters illustrate that Paul asserts his authority for building up the Christian community, not himself (12:19; 13:9–10); and his manner becomes a model for how to exercise authority in the church. Wall insightfully comments: "When we continue to position ourselves to gain power over others rather than to empower them as agents of God's grace, our congregations and families will simply fail to bear witness to God in our world."[74]

10:7 The NIV takes the verb *blepete* in the phrase *ta kata prosōpon blepete* as an indicative and interprets it to mean, "You are looking only on the surface of things" (so also ASV, GNB).[75] It would reflect a key problem in the Corinthians' spirituality. *Ta kata prosōpon* (lit. "the things according to the face") would refer to outward appearances. They see only things that are superficial and ultimately meaningless (see also 2 Cor 5:12).[76] They fail to recognize that as God's foolishness is wisdom (1 Cor 1:18–25), so weakness in Christ is strength (12:9; 13:3–4). Because externals easily impress them, they are taken in by ostentation and swagger. The false apostles who serve the master of disguise, Satan (11:13–15),

---

[73] D. E. Garland, *Colossians Philemon,* NIVAC (Grand Rapids: Zondervan, 1998) 368.

[74] R. W. Wall, *Colossians and Philemon,* IVPNTC (Downers Grove: IVP, 1993) 188.

[75] The KJV translates it as an interrogative in the indicative: "Do ye look on things after the outward appearance?"

[76] This assumes that τὰ κατὰ πρόσωπον is equivalent to τὰ κατὰ σάρκα, "mere externals" (so R. Bultmann, *The Second Letter to the Corinthians,* ed. E. Dinkler, trans. R. A. Harrisville [Minneapolis: Augsburg, 1976] 187).

have consequently dazzled and bamboozled them.

The NRSV, however, renders the verb *blepete* as an imperative and interprets the object *ta kata prosōpon* to be what is staring them in the face: "Look at what is before your eyes" (so also REB, JB). In every other occurrence of the verb *blepete* in Paul's letters it is an imperative.[77] Kruse takes Paul to mean "Look at what is patently obvious!"[78] Holland renders it, "Look at the things that are in front of you."[79] The phrase *kata prosōpon* recalls their evaluation of him in 10:1, where they say that "according to the face," "in person," he is lowly. The problem is that they have looked at Paul when he was present with him and came to the wrong conclusion that he was "weak" (10:10b). Paul accepts that judgment on one level, but they do not understand the spiritual significance of his weakness, nor do they understand that this apparent weakness does not mean that he is not Christ's or that he is without divine authority. He therefore demands that the Corinthians reconsider the evidence that will require them to admit his status as a man in Christ (10:7b).[80] They need to see their very existence as a church as ample proof of the power of God working through Paul in spite of his weakness. It is difficult to decide between these two interpretations; but the preponderance of Paul's usage of the verb *blepete* as an imperative, "Look!" argues for this second alternative, "Look at what is before your eyes."

"If anyone is confident that he belongs to Christ, he should consider again" implies that they have neglected a key piece of evidence. He should go on to consider this fact for himself: If you are Christ's, so are we.[81]

What does "to be of Christ" mean? It could refer simply to being a Christian, but it is unlikely that the Corinthians doubt that Paul is a Christian and that Paul needs to reestablish that fact. He also puts it hypothetically and not as a simple fact, almost as if it were a matter of conceit, "if any has confidence in himself."[82] It could refer to being a disciple of Jesus during his earthly ministry, but Paul could not make this claim. A

---

[77] 1 Cor 1:26; 8:9; 10:12,18; 16:10; Gal 5:15; Phil 3:2; and Col 2:8.

[78] Kruse, *2 Corinthians*, 176.

[79] Holland, "Speaking Like a Fool: Irony in 2 Corinthians 10–13," 253.

[80] Peterson comments, "Since Paul himself is at the moment absent, they must look at the signs of his presence among them still" (*Eloquence and the Proclamation of the Gospel in Corinth*, 89).

[81] Barrett suggests that Paul means "let him have another look at himself" (*The Second Epistle to the Corinthians*, 256). If this is correct, then Paul will challenge them later to examine themselves to see if they meet the test whether Jesus Christ is truly in them (13:5).

[82] Elsewhere in the NT the verb form πείθω ("persuade," "have confidence") followed by the reflexive pronoun has a negative connotation. See Luke 18:9, "To some who were confident of their own righteousness and looked down on everybody else, Jesus told this parable"; and Rom 2:19–20, "If you are convinced that you are a guide for the blind, a light for those who are in the dark, an instructor of the foolish, a teacher of infants, because you have in the law the embodiment of knowledge and truth."

more likely option is that it has something to do with a special relationship to Christ that bestows some kind of distinctive authority as Christ's
servant or apostle. The reference to his boasting in his authority in the
next verse would confirm this view. It would then be parallel to the phrase
"apostles of Christ" and "servants of Christ" in 11:13,23.[83] In the same
vein it could also refer to having the power of Christ working in or speaking through the individual and would parallel the statement in 13:3,
"proof that Christ is speaking in me." They apparently want more proof
that Christ speaks through him (13:4) since he is so rhetorically subpar
and since most assume that one cannot be wise without being eloquent.[84]
The rivals may also have cast doubt on Paul's spiritual power because of
a perceived shortage of the signs of the true apostle, "signs and wonders
and mighty works" (12:12). Barnett comments, "They doubted that he
was a Spirit-empowered minister."[85] Paul, however, points to the only
logical conclusion from the evidence: if they are Christ's, then the one
who betrothed them to Christ must be as much Christ's as they are. Paul
may appear to be demeaned in the flesh, but spiritual perception will penetrate beneath the surface to see his true nature as a man in Christ. Paul is
saying: "Look at the evidence before your very eyes but look at it with
spiritual perception so that you can see beneath the surface to the divine
reality. If anyone doubts that I am Christ's, then how did it happen that
this church was founded through my preaching? Your existence as
Christ's church is the primary evidence that I am Christ's servant and that
the Spirit of Christ works powerfully through me."

10:8 The issue of boasting that is so prominent in these chapters (see
10:8,13,15–17; 11:10,12,16–18,30; and 12:1,5,6,9) first surfaces in this
verse. Paul seems to be defending himself against the charge that he inappropriately boasted of his authority. Presumably, someone took issue with
his authoritative demands in the previous letter of frank criticism. Paul's tendency to take their accusations and to subvert them with sarcasm and irony
throughout this section should caution us from accepting this statement as
Paul's own perception of what he did.[86] This charge of boasting too much in

[83] So Martin, *2 Corinthians,* 309; and Kruse, *2 Corinthians,* 176.

[84] See D. Litfin, *St. Paul's Theology of Proclamation: 1 Corinthians 1–4 and Greco- Roman rhetoric,* SNTSMS 79 (Cambridge: University Press, 1994) 245.

[85] Barnett, *The Second Epistle to the Corinthians,* 470.

[86] See "His letters are weighty and forceful, but in person he is unimpressive and his speaking amounts to nothing" (10:10); "We do not dare to classify or compare ourselves with some who commend themselves" (10:12); "I may not be a trained speaker, but I do have knowledge" (11:6); "I repeat: Let no one take me for a fool. But if you do, then receive me just as you would a fool, so that I may do a little boasting" (11:16); "In fact, you even put up with anyone who enslaves you or exploits you or takes advantage of you or pushes himself forward or slaps you in the face. To my shame I admit that we were too weak for that!" (11:20–21).

his authority reflects the perspective of his opponents, *not* his own view.[87] They call it immoderate boasting because Paul's powerless position in the status hierarchy of a place like Corinth, plus the poor impression he makes in person with his less than stellar oral performance, would seem to disqualify any claims he would make to having authority over them.[88]

The rivals are trying to dislodge Paul from his rightful role of spiritual leader of the church by challenging his authority and belittling his adequacy as a rhetor. As Winter imagines it, his opponents "could have argued convincingly that if the secular *ekklēsia* [assembly] of Corinth demanded of speakers a facility in oratory, then the *ekklēsia tou theou* [assembly of God] in the same city should flourish with teachers of no less ability. Paul lacked the necessary prowess."[89] Judge first observed about these chapters that the struggle was "with rhetorically trained opponents for the support of his rhetorically fastidious converts."[90] Paul's deficiency in this regard caused them to disparage any claim he made to authority over them as vain boasting that he could not justify.[91]

Paul does not believe that he boasted excessively or too freely because his boasting was not beyond limits but according to the field assigned him by God (10:13).[92] He did not boast in the labors of others but in his own

---

[87] See E. Käsemann, "Die Legitimität des Apostels. Eine Untersuchung zu II Korinther 10–13," *ZNW* 41 (1942) 36.

[88] A. J. Dewey defines boasting as representing "the action of a person who, in the eyes of those he has challenged socially and in view of the larger public audience, has gone beyond the limits of perceived status" ("A Matter of Honor: A Social-Historical Analysis of 2 Corinthians 10," *HTR* 78 [1985] 210). I would argue that Paul's perceived status as determined by the criteria of the culture were behind the criticism and not doubts about his commissioning by Jesus in comparison to the Jerusalem apostles.

[89] B. W. Winter, *Philo and Paul among the Sophists,* SNTSMS 96 (Cambridge: University Press, 1997) 221.

[90] E. A. Judge, "The Reaction against Classical Education in the New Testament," *Journal of Christian Education* 77 (1983) 13.

[91] The question does not have to do with the legitimacy of his calling as an apostle but with their dissatisfaction with his manner of carrying out his apostolic authority. If they did not believe that he was a legitimate apostle, his rivals would not boast about being his equal (11:12). They have compared themselves to him and argued that they are better apostles because of their more magnetic and electrifying style.

[92] Lambrecht shows that 10:8 serves an annunciatory function to 10:12–18 by introducing three themes which will specifically be dealt with in these verses, authority, boasting and commendation ("Dangerous Boasting: Paul's Self-Commendation in 2 Corinthians 10–13," 329–30). He shows the following parallelism of vocabulary and motif:

v. 8	vv. 12–18
somewhat too much	not beyond limits (10:13,15)
I boast	we will boast (10:13)
authority	the measure of the *kanōn* (10:13; see 10:15)
God gave	God has assigned (10:13)
building up	proclaiming the good news (10:14–16)
shall not be put to shame	whom the Lord commends (10:18)

Lambrecht (p. 331) suggests that 10:7–12:13 might be regarded as a "sort of digression" inserted between 10:6 and 12:14 in much the same way that 2:14–7:4 interrupts 2:13 and 7:5.

(10:15), and his boasting was therefore in the Lord (10:17). Consequently, he defends his authority as something given to him by God; and he will not be put to shame for speaking of it or for wielding it.[93] The passive voice *(aischynthēsomai)* implies being put to shame rather than simply being ashamed (cp. Phil 1:20). Shame comes when one exceeds one's social boundaries; and he certainly has not exceeded his, as he will argue in 10:12–18. But Paul has in view Christ's judgment seat (5:10): "It is the Lord who judges me" (1 Cor 4:4). He will not be condemned or dishonored by Christ for exercising the authority God gave to him.[94]

Paul talks about his right *(exousia)* not to work but to be supported by them in 1 Cor 9:4–6,12,18, although he foregoes that right. Here the authority *(exousia)* refers to the right to discipline and to bind and to loose (e.g., see 1 Cor 5:1–5; 7:15). He will insist that the power of Christ rests upon him despite his apparent weaknesses. In fact, it works through his weaknesses (12:9), which conforms to the divine pattern revealed in the crucifixion: "For to be sure, he was crucified in weakness, yet he lives by God's power. Likewise, we are weak in him, yet by God's power we will live with him to serve you" (2 Cor 13:4). At the conclusion of his argument in chap. 13, Paul reveals that he has not backed down an inch as he reasserts his authority over them: "This is why I write these things when I am absent, that when I come I may not have to be harsh in my use of authority—the authority the Lord gave me for building you up, not for tearing you down" (13:10).[95] His letters are weighty (10:10) because of the authority the Lord has given to him.[96]

Paul insists, however, that this authority, expressed in his frank criticism, is not for destroying them (see 1 Cor 5:5, "the destruction of the flesh") but for building them up. The image of besieging is therefore not altogether apt for what Paul does. His divine task is not to attack and to tear down others. God called him to found and build up congregations.[97] He was not chosen to be a divine disciplinarian or inquisitor, smelling out heresy and dishing out punishment. He will watch over them and discipline them when necessary, but it is for their good. His message to be reconciled to God (5:20) is one of

---

[93] He is not apologizing for his boasting, which is incompatible with the meekness and gentleness of Christ as Leivestad ("Meekness," 164) argues.

[94] Barnett interprets it as one of many examples of understatement in this section (*The Second Epistle to the Corinthians,* 473).

[95] The implication is that the rivals' work has served to destroy the community, sowing seeds of discord and peddling a false gospel.

[96] The term "weighty" (βαρεῖαι) applied to Paul's letters refers to their severity and their reproachful tone. We have argued that in 2:14–7:3 Paul defends his frank criticism in the severe letter; and, after exhorting them about the collection for the saints in chaps. 8–9, he returns to the subject of his reproachful letter.

[97] See 1 Cor 3:9,14; 14:3,5,12,26; and 2 Cor 12:19.

salvation, not destruction.[98] They therefore should not perceive the frank criticism found in his letters to be some kind of verbal wrecking ball aimed their way to level them to the ground. He exercised his authority in his letters to build them up not to build himself up.[99]

Paul uses the term authority *(exousia)* to refer to his position of influence over the churches he established sparingly, only here in 10:8 and 13:10, when this authority has been challenged. Banks reasons that since the term was widespread in the ancient world, Paul's reticence in using it is intentional. He writes:

> At Corinth he certainly wishes to reestablish his unique relationship with the church as its founder (2 Cor 10–13), but he wants to disassociate himself from the authoritarian way the 'false apostles' conduct themselves. He does not seek to influence the members by improper means (2 Cor 10:3), boast to them of his preeminence (2 Cor 10:12–15), dazzle the church with rhetoric (2 Cor 11:5–6), or manipulate and control his converts (2 Cor 11:16–19; cf. 2 Cor 1:24). The 'authority' God has given him is for 'building up' not 'tearing down,' and he does not wish to use it in a harsh way when he arrives. Indeed he gives the church an opportunity to correct their attitude beforehand so that there will be no conflict when he arrives. This type of authority is basically charismatic, and therefore different from that found in traditional societies or in modern organizations; it is the authority of an unusual founder figure, who does not normally assert his position.[100]

Banks concludes:

> Paul does not treat authority, then, as something official or sacral. He views it primarily in relational and functional terms. It does not result in the formation of a leadership elite, formally marked off from others in the church. Only Christ has this distinction and he is the ultimate criterion of who should be regarded as a fundamental role model for others. Aspiring to this is apparently open to a wide range of people, including those with lower social status, and can be embodied in a group as well as individuals.[101]

---

[98] The image may echo Jer 24:6: "My eyes will watch over them for their good, and I will bring them back to this land. I will build them up and not tear them down; I will plant them and not uproot them" (see also Jer 18:7–9; 31:4,28; 32:41; 42:10; 45:4). If so, Paul identifies his role as not parallel to that of Jeremiah's "to uproot and tear down, to destroy and overthrow, to build and to plant" (Jer 1:10) since he rejects the negative function of destroying. He identifies his role as closer to what God promises to do for the people.

[99] This was how a later generation understood Paul's letters. Polycarp wrote "For neither am I, nor is any other like me, able to follow the wisdom of the blessed and glorious Paul, who when he was among you in the presence of the men of that time taught accurately and steadfastly the word of truth, and also when he was absent wrote letters to you, from the study of which you will be able to build yourselves up into the faith given you" (*Phil.* 3:2).

[100] R. J. Banks, "Church Order and Government," *Dictionary of Paul and His Letters,* ed. G. F. Hawthorne, R. P. Martin, and D. G. Reid (Downers Grove/Leicester: IVP, 1993) 132.

[101] Ibid., 133.

Paul does not have divine authority for his own purposes so that he might enjoy the status it brings. Best notes that what "is more important than the claim to possess authority is the manner in which it is exercised."[102] Paul uses his authority in ways that make for peace and mutual upbuilding (Rom 14:19). Therefore, he seeks to please (Rom 15:2), to show love (1 Cor 8:1), and to encourage (1 Thess 5:11) and instructs others to do so because this mode of dealing with others is what "builds up" the church.

10:9–10 The NIV has omitted the problematic *hina mē,* "lest," that begins v. 9. Paul returns to the perception of the inconsistency between his boldness in his letters and his timidity when he is present. It is best to place a full stop after v. 8 and then to connect v. 9 to v. 11 and treat v. 10 as a parenthesis. It reads as follows: "Lest I should seem as it were to frighten you [into obedience] through letters (for this is what one is saying, 'His letters are weighty and forceful, but in person he is unimpressive and his speaking amounts to nothing') let such a one who thinks this take note that what we say through letters when we are absent we will carry out when we are present."[103]

The definite article with the letters indicates that he has specific letters in mind. If the weighty and forceful letters allude to the "severe letter" (2 Cor 2:4; 7:8), which seems most probable, then that severe letter could not be chaps. 10–13 as some have argued.[104] The NIV translates it that "some say" (plural) his letters do not match his presence, but the verb *phēsin* is third person singular and means someone is saying. Does Paul allude to the ringleader of the opposition? Can we infer from this that not everyone in Corinth would agree with this negative appraisal of Paul's presence? However we answer these questions, the key issue behind the allegation is the ostensible inconsistency between his powerful letters and his weak presence.

---

[102] E. Best, *Second Corinthians,* INT (Atlanta: John Knox, 1987) 95.

[103] A. E. Harvey, *Renewal through Suffering: A Study of 2 Corinthians, Studies of the New Testament and Its World* (Edinburgh: T & T Clark, 1996) 96, n. 13; and Martin, *2 Corinthians,* 310–11. See also H. Krämer, "Zum sprachlichen Duktus in 2 K 10, V. 9 und 12," in Das Wort und die Wörter, ed. H. Balz and S. Schulz (Stuttgart/Berlin/Köln/Mainz: W. Kohlhammer, 1973) 97–98. Plummer regards reading 10:10 as a parenthesis to be an "intolerable construction: and argues that 10:9 depends on 10:8 as a whole (*The Second Epistle of St. Paul to the Corinthians,* 281). Another option interprets the ἵνα μὴ as equivalent to an imperative: "Let me not seem to be frightening you!" (see C. F. D. Moule, *An Idiom Book of New Testament Greek* [Cambridge: University Press, 1953] 145). Or some also argue that Paul has left out the key thought that he would not appeal to his authority lest he seem to frighten them (so Barrett, *The Second Epistle to the Corinthians,* 258–59, who claims that "Paul was not the most careful of writers, especially when writing, as here, under emotional stress").

[104] F. Watson argues that 2 Cor 10–13 is the painful letter and suggests that Paul has 1 Cor 4:18–20 in view here ("2 Cor. x–xiii and Paul's Painful Letter to the Corinthians," *JTS* 35 (1984) 343–44). But the context in 1 Cor 4:14–16 clearly refers to the gentle spirit of a loving father, not the threatening bluster of a disciplinarian.

Paul cautions the Corinthians not to be fooled by his seeming frailty, nor to confuse his meekness and gentleness for weakness and inferiority. He accepts the judgment about his letters—they are weighty and strong—but he does not fully accept the judgment about the ineffectiveness of his presence.

In the last century scholars have begun to pay more attention to Paul as a skillful practitioner of rhetoric.[105] The supposed dichotomy between Hebrew and Hellenistic culture has melted away, and many now argue that the Greco-Roman rhetorical stylistic tradition exerted more influence on the New Testament than it was previously accorded. Sociological studies have also revealed that the early church was not composed only of the simple, lower classes, but served up a "richer social and economic mix."[106] Paul's quotation of what persons are saying about his letters attests that even his opponents recognize that they have rhetorical power. What they called into question was his physical presence and his public oratory. He seemed to make an unfavorable impression as one who was physically unpresentable and less than articulate.[107] An unpolished and halting oral performance would have given the impression that he was uneducated. Either some in the church would have liked him to be more like the other golden-tongued orators who were lionized in Corinth so that their association with him would boost their own prestige; or his opponents fastened on to this weakness to advance their bid for influence over the church. Perhaps, both were true.

What was unimpressive about Paul? The key problem seems to have been his speech. The ancient world placed a premium on rhetorical skills. Peterson succinctly describes the situation:

> In Hellenistic society the practice and expectations of rhetorical eloquence were pervasive. Not only were political leaders expected to speak persuasively and eloquently, but so also those who claimed authority in philosophy and religion. Among such people there was great competition, and success depended upon one's ability to express the power of the divine in his or her performance—not only through miracles, but also through rhetorical performances.[108]

---

[105] Augustine, a professional rhetorician before his conversion, recognized Paul's rhetorical skill as a true marriage of wisdom and eloquence.

[106] Peterson, *Eloquence and the Proclamation of the Gospel in Corinth,* 14–15. Malherbe maintains: "There can no longer be any doubt that Paul was thoroughly familiar with the teaching, methods of operation and style of argumentation of the philosophers of the period, all of which he adopted and adapted to his own purposes" ("Paul Hellenistic Philosopher or Christian Pastor?" in *Paul and the Popular Philosophers* [Minneapolis: Fortress, 1989] 68).

[107] This kind of attitude toward the preacher's dress, style, and background still prevails as church members may scan the preacher from head-to-toe to see if the attire and coiffure measure up to their standards.

[108] Peterson, *Eloquence and the Proclamation of the Gospel in Corinth,* 59. Litfin avers: "The Greco-Roman people thrived on eloquence and lionized its practitioners in a way that it is difficult for moderns even to conceive" (*St. Paul's Theology of Proclamation,* 14).

Debates may have raged about the merits of different styles of rhetoric, "but the value of rhetorical skill was unquestioned."[109] Winter argues convincingly that the judgment that his bodily presence was weak "was rendered according to the canons of rhetoric. It meant that his presence constituted such a liability as to all but guarantee his failure as an effective orator."[110] He cites Alcidamas who noted that being a clever writer was no guarantee that one could speak well. "He may be able to write 'with extreme care, rhythmically connecting phrases, perfecting style' but when compelled to speak extemporarily 'in every respect he makes an unfavourable impression, and differs not a whit from the voiceless.' "[111] Quintilian also maintained, "For a good delivery is undoubtedly impossible for one who cannot remember what he has written, or lacks the facility of speech required by sudden emergencies, or is hampered by incurable impediments of speech. Again, physical uncouthness may be such that no art can remedy it, while a weak voice is incompatible with first-rate excellence in delivery."[112]

While Paul is not describing an evaluation of his looks with this phrase, "the weak presence of his body" (NIV, "in person he is unimpressive"), physical appearance was also considered to be important to an audience.

---

[109] Peterson, *Eloquence and the Proclamation of the Gospel in Corinth,* 65.

[110] Winter, *Paul and Philo among the Sophists,* 212. C. E. Glad comments from Philodemus that "the wise man thus talks so wonderfully that he fascinates the soul of his audience ('bewitching the mind like the fabulous siren') and has particular prestige among his friends. But in spite of apparent similarities to a flattering discourse, the content of the wise man's speech is morally formative, not corrupting" ("Frank Speech, Flattery, and Friendship in Philodemus," in *Friendship, Flattery and Frankness of Speech: Studies on Friendship in the New Testament World,* ed. J. T. Fitzgerald, NovTSup 82 [Leiden: Brill, 1996] 27). P. Marshall cites Isocrates, who asserted that "the ability to speak is the clearest indication of understanding" (*Antidosis* 253–57; *Enmity in Corinth: Social Conventions and Paul's Relations to the Corinthians,* WUNT 2/23 [Tübingen: Mohr [Siebeck], 1987] 328). He concludes that "if Paul were perceived to be unskilled in rhetoric, then he would be written off as ignorant or uneducated." Philo would have concurred with this assessment since he considered eloquence essential to possessing wisdom. Philo contended that God bestows on those who obey him full and complete "logos-excellence" (εὐλογία), for "He holds it just that the recipient of His bounty should both conceive the noblest conceptions and give masterly expression to his ideas" (*Migration of Abraham* 70–73). He argues elsewhere that some who love virtue but have not "so much as dreamt of jugglery with words" are defeated in debate by the sophists, since they are "unaccustomed to quibbling arguments." But others are more successful because they have their mind "secured by wisdom in counsel and good deeds, their speech by the arts of eloquence. Now to encounter the wranglings in which some folk delight is eminently fitting for these latter, ready and equipped as they are with the means of withstanding their enemies, but for the former class it is not safe to do so. For who are there that unarmed could meet armed men, and fight on equal terms, seeing that, even were they fully equipped, the combat would be an unequal one?" (*The Worse Attacks the Better* 35–36).

[111] Alcidamas, *On the Writers of Written Discourse or On the Sophists* 9, 16, cited by Winter, *Paul and Philo among the Sophists,* 205.

[112] Quintilian, xi.3.12–13.

Some considered an attractive physical appearance to be absolutely necessary for making a good impression. Epictetus laid down requirements for
effective preaching in the public square:

> And such a man needs also a certain kind of body, since if a consumptive
> comes forward, thin and pale, his testimony no longer carries the same weight.
> For he must not merely, by exhibiting the qualities of his soul, prove to the lay-
> men that it is possible, without the help of the things which they admire, to be
> a good and excellent man, but he must also show, by the state of his body, that
> his plain and simple style of life in the open air does not injure even his body:
> "Look," he says, "both I and my body are witnesses to the truth of my conten-
> tion." That was the way of Diogenes, for he used to go about with a radiant
> complexion, and would attract the attention of the common people by the very
> appearance of his body. But a Cynic who excites pity is regarded as a beggar;
> everybody turns away from him, everybody takes offence at him.[113]

Paul apparently did not fit the bill when it came to these qualities. We
should be careful, however, *not* to interpret this statement in light of the
widely known account of Paul's physical description from the apocryphal
Acts of Paul and Thecla. It describes Paul as "small of stature, with a bald
head and crooked legs, in a good state of body, with eyebrows meeting and
nose somewhat hooked, full of friendliness; for now he appeared like a man
and now he had the face of an angel."

This portrait of Paul tends to conjure up for moderns an image of ugliness. Malherbe shows, however, that according to ancient physiognomy
this description was by no means unflattering.[114] Grant connected this
description to a passage from Archilocus that offers an ideal description
of a general as short and bowlegged.[115] Malherbe points to similar features, small stature, hooked nose, and meeting eyebrows, in the description of Augustus in Suetonius[116] and in depictions of Greek heroes such
as Heracles. He concludes that this apocryphal description of Paul derives
from these sources, depicting the ideal political leader where meeting
eyebrows were a sign of beauty, a hooked nose a sign of royalty or magnanimity, and small stature a sign of quickness. Paul's supposed "bald-
ness" may have been inferred from the reference to shaving his head in
Acts 18:18 and 21:24.[117] In my opinion, we have no reliable witness to

---

[113] Epictetus, *Dissertations* III.xxii.86–89.

[114] A. J. Malherbe, "A Physical Description of Paul," in *Christians among Jews and Gentiles,*
ed. G. W. E. Nickelsburg and G. W. MacRae (Philadelphia: Fortress, 1986) 170–75.

[115] R. M. Grant, "The Description of Paul in the Acts of Paul and Thecla," *VC* 36 [1982] 1–4).

[116] *Lives of the Caesars* 2.79.2.

[117] Malherbe, "A Physical Description of Paul," 173–75. Plummer uncritically thinks that the
description in the *Acts of Paul and Thecla* could be based on early tradition (*The Second Epistle of
Paul the Apostle to the Corinthians* [Cambridge: University Press, 1911] 136–37).

Paul's physical appearance and should avoid speculations about it.

Paul's allusions to the Corinthians' dissatisfaction with his work at a trade suggest that this may have been a contributing factor behind their disdain for his public face. Lucian contrasts the "sublime words" and "dignified appearance" of truly great teachers with the filthy clothes and unkempt appearance of the craftsman who does not pursue eloquence or learning, but who clutches his tools, "back bent over his work ... altogether demeaned [*tapeinos;* see 10:2]."[118] Philo reports that the sophists in Alexandria were "men of mark and wealth, holding leading positions, praised on all hands, recipients of honors, portly, healthy and robust, revelling in luxurious and riotous living, knowing nothing of labour, conversant with pleasures which carry the sweets of life to the all-welcoming soul by every channel of sense." They derided their philosophical adversaries as "destitute of the necessities of life ... filthy, sallow, reduced to skeletons, with a hungry look for want of food, the prey of disease, in training for dying."[119] This sophistic ideal and this sophistic disdain of rivals may be behind the criticisms leveled at Paul. Consequently, Paul must constantly remind the Corinthians, who apparently were seduced by the allure of these so-called paragons of elegant style, that "The power of the message lies not in the skill and style of the messenger but in the knowledge and power of God."[120]

10:11   Paul does not need to defend the power of his letters since they recognize their effectiveness, but he does need to convince them that he can be no less effective when present as he is in his letters. He continues to prepare for his future visit by contending that there is no discrepancy between what he writes and what he does. Paul is not the weak, wretched quack his adversaries make him out to be, and the Corinthians should take immediate steps to get their house in order in obedience to his instructions. His boldness may have taken the unexpected form of a humble spirit of gentleness when present because he does not want to tear them down. He has spared the rod because he is a loving father not a hanging judge (1 Cor 4:14–21). Even now he hopes that this letter will reinforce their repentance and lay the groundwork for a peaceful visit (13:10). They do not need an arrogant, overbearing preacher throwing his apostolic weight around. There were plenty of such characters in Corinth already. They need to see instead the example of Christ. He first preached to them the gospel in weakness and in fear and much trembling (1 Cor 2:2), and he continues to minister to them in this way.

Striking terror in the hearts of his readers (10:9) does not ultimately build them up. It might lead to a worldly sorrow, but worldly sorrow only leads to

---

[118] Lucian, *The Dream,* 13.

[119] Philo, *The Worse Attacks the Better,* 34; noted by Winter, *Paul and Philo among the Sophists,* 167.

[120] K. Quast, *Reading the Corinthian Correspondence* (New York/Mahwah: Paulist, 1994) 151.

death (7:10). He wants to create in them a "godly sorrow" (7:9), and berating people rarely creates deep converts and is liable to stunt any Christian growth. He does not want to bring them down but to bring them up to a new level of understanding. When they reach that level, they will understand Paul for the true minister of Christ that he is and will recognize his arrogant, boastful, domineering rivals for what they are—not ministers of Christ but minions of Satan. He can come like an army and lay siege to them, or he can come with gentleness and meekness—and seeming weakness. War is sometimes necessary; but it leaves in its wake casualties, bitterness, and sorrow. His preference is therefore to come in meekness. He wants peace (13:11), not war. He desires peace with them and peace among themselves.

2. Proper Commendation (10:12–18)

¹²We do not dare to classify or compare ourselves with some who commend themselves. When they measure themselves by themselves and compare themselves with themselves, they are not wise. ¹³We, however, will not boast beyond proper limits, but will confine our boasting to the field God has assigned to us, a field that reaches even to you. ¹⁴We are not going too far in our boasting, as would be the case if we had not come to you, for we did get as far as you with the gospel of Christ. ¹⁵Neither do we go beyond our limits by boasting of work done by others. Our hope is that, as your faith continues to grow, our area of activity among you will greatly expand, ¹⁶so that we can preach the gospel in the regions beyond you. For we do not want to boast about work already done in another man's territory. ¹⁷But, "Let him who boasts boast in the Lord." ¹⁸For it is not the one who commends himself who is approved, but the one whom the Lord commends.

Paul now establishes the proper ground rules for boasting as well as what constitutes valid commendation. In the process he also turns his attention to rivals who have invaded his ministry field and boasted inappropriately over the fruits of *his* labors. The crux of the matter is that they have commended themselves while denigrating Paul's authority. How are the Corinthians to validate what is true or false when faced with competing claims? Paul offers two criteria to evaluate the boisterous claims of his rivals: boasting within limits and commendation from the Lord. Boasting in one's own accomplishments is theologically misguided; boasting in another's as if they were one's own is even worse. Paul argues first that his boasting is within the proper limits because he has kept to the field of action God assigned him. That assignment is to preach in new frontiers, and even now he has his sights set on new territory (10:16, presumably to the west, see Rom 15:17–20,24,28). Since he was the first to "plant" the gospel in Corinth when it was still unplowed ground (1 Cor 3:6), the Corinthians belong within the limits of his jurisdiction. Their very existence is his letter of commendation written by Christ (3:2–3).

Second, his boasting is within bounds because he does not try to assert his superiority over others by comparing himself with them. He measures himself only by what God does in him (see 1:21; 4:7; 5:11). He does not crow over his own achievements or strut about in a grand procession of one. He does not boast about his personal merit because he knows that his power is not his, it is God's (10:3–6). Self-commendation proves nothing except a lack of understanding on the part of those who commend themselves. Only commendation from God deserves any notice (see 1 Cor 4:5). His rivals are devious careerists who are simply trying to advance themselves rather than the cause of God. Nothing means more to them than themselves. Their goal was to garner commendations from others and to gain fame. One has quipped that a boaster is one with whom is it no sooner done than said. But these are empty boasters who have done nothing and still boast. They will earn only God's wrath.

10:12 In their scheme to undermine Paul's influence in Corinth and promote their own, his rivals have accused him of having nerve in his letters but no boldness in person (10:10). Paul responds to this criticism with wry sarcasm that he lacks the nerve to classify or compare himself with those who commend themselves. "Daring" *(tolman)* is related to the assurance that leads one "to push oneself forward."[121] He plays on this perception that he lacked that obligatory assurance to undermine the presumption of these braggarts. He has warned them, however, that he will "dare" to oppose those who think that he operates according to the world's standards (10:2). He will also "dare" to join those others who "dare to boast" but admits that it is the daring of a fool (11:21), not because he cannot back up this boasting with performance equal to his words but because God does not back up such foolish boasting. God humbles the proud so they will not try to take credit for what God alone has done.

In the ancient world "comparison" *(sygkrisis)* was a common "rhetorical exercise practiced in schools," and comparing oneself with other teachers was a common tactic for a teacher to attract students and their fees.[122] Stansbury points out that in the political arena Greek *hybris,* pride, combines with Roman *inimicitia,* enmity, to produce vicious smear tactics against rivals. People in this society assumed that honors were as limited as material wealth. Since there was only a limited amount of honor to go around, one resented and envied others for having it. "Political enemies were targets of exaggerated character assassination designed

---

[121] Martin, *2 Corinthians,* 319.
[122] Marshall, *Enmity in Corinth,* 53.

to make them symbols of shame or of political subversion."[123] In the cut-throat competition for plaudits and pupils, one had to advertise oneself publicly with audacious praise while impugning the qualities of other contenders for honor. People were constantly vying with others to attain elusive glory and engaged in a constant game of one-upmanship. This race for honor "encouraged outward expressions of pride and arrogance."[124] Self-boasting was considered an act of honor. Savage observes that "an individual's worth and consequently his respect in the community was dependent on the status he was able to project."[125] Boasting about one's status and achievements and comparing oneself favorably against others were routine tactics for those who aimed at gaining a following for themselves.[126]

In a "comparison" one would amplify one's good deeds and another's bad deeds to show superiority. Such topics as a person's race, upbringing, education, status, physique, pursuits, and positions held were all fair game in sizing up their relative merits and standing.[127] Dio Chrysostom derides the sophists of Corinth for craving the esteem of the crowd, wanting "to be looked up to and thought that they knew more than other men."[128] Winter notes that sophists fanned strife and jealousy, and intense rivalry "seemed to

---

[123] Stansbury, *Corinthians Honor, Corinthian Conflict: A Social History of Early Roman Corinth and Its Pauline Community,* 278; noting also B. Malina, *The New Testament World: Insights from Cultural Anthropology* (Atlanta: John Knox, 1981) 71–93; and P. Walcot, "The Funeral Speech, A Study of Values," *Greece and Rome* 20 (1973) 117.

[124] Savage, *Power through Weakness,* 23.

[125] Ibid.

[126] Savage makes the following helpful observations about status in the ancient world: "All people belonged to one of two classes: the *honestiores* or the *humiliores,* the high or the low. The former was made up of the nobility—senators, equestrians and, away from Rome itself, the decurions. These were men who, together with their womenfolk, were esteemed for their *dignitas* and often possessed great power and fortune. The *humiliores*—plebs, freedmen and slaves—lacked *dignitas* and were held in no honour by the nobility. Since rank was hereditary, movement from one class to the other was virtually impossible" (*Power through Weakness,* 20; see further P. Garnsey, *Social Status and Legal Privilege in the Roman Empire* [Oxford: Clarendon, 1970] 221–280). The nobility comprised one percent of the population; slaves and indigents the bottom third. The middle two thirds were consumed with improving their status which was achieved primarily by attaining wealth. But even wealth did not always confer the honor that so many people craved (see the account of Trimalchio's dinner in Petronius' *Satyricon*). Since attaining wealth was impossible for most people, noble philosophers argued that one could also achieve honor through virtuous living. But most chose other routes and sought honor from their occupations, neighborhoods, talents, education, religion, or athletic accomplishments (Savage, *Power through Weakness,* 21–22). Paul's Corinthian rivals have chosen religion as the field in which they will compete for the honor and status they so covet.

[127] See the manual of rhetoric discussing the use of comparison by Aelius Theon, cited by Forbes, "Comparison, Self-Praise and Irony," 6. See also Marshall, *Enmity in Corinth,* 54.

[128] Dio Chrysostom, *Orations* 6.21.

arise wherever two or three were gathered together."[129] Lucian, the great satirist, pokes fun at the popular teachers who compared themselves with others to exalt themselves. In his *Professor of Public Speaking* a wily veteran instructs the novice on how to achieve popular success: "make marvelous assertions about yourself, be extravagant in your self-praise, and make yourself a nuisance to him. What was Demosthenes beside me?"[130] Such extravagant self-regard was considered characteristic of sham philosophers who were frequently lampooned by other more serious philosophers. By implication, then, Paul lumps his opponents in with this crowd of frauds who can be identified by their extravagant self-regard and self-commendation.

Paul deflates the boasts of his rivals as he insinuates, "Such a dwarf as I could not possibly compare with such giants." "I hardly rank with such luminaries." He therefore disparages their boasting with mock self-deprecation. Speaking tongue in cheek in this way also raises the question whether his rivals are comparable to him at all.[131] No comparison can be made where no similarity exists.[132] In all their boasting they presume to be Paul's equal, but in his view they are false apostles (11:12–13). If he is going to stoop to compare himself with them, it will be only as a fool (11:21–12:11). They claim to be in a different league than Paul; and Paul would readily agree—they are in league with Satan. They may have won status in the eyes of some Corinthians with their boastfulness, but they have won God's judgment in the process.

Second, he rules out this fundamental rhetorical tool of showing superiority through comparison as something completely illegitimate for ministers of God.[133] Only fools dare to use self-comparison with others to commend

---

[129] Winter, *Paul and Philo among the Sophists,* 132.

[130] Cited by Forbes, "Comparison, Self-Praise and Irony," 8.

[131] Dio Chrysostom uses a similar tack in his oration to the Alexandrians. He refuses "to range himself beside" others who have flattered them, "For they are clever persons, mighty sophists, wonder-workers; but I am quite ordinary and prosaic in my utterance, though not ordinary in my theme" (*Orations* 32.39, noted by Forbes, "Comparison, Self-Praise and Irony," 4).

[132] Forbes points out: "For Philo, comparisons require a basis of similarity before they can be legitimate comparisons. Comparisons can be made between things which are very different, such as kings and commoners, but only on the basis of their common humanity. Where there is no real similarity, no comparison can be made" ("Comparison, Self-Praise and Irony," 4). Theon's manual of rhetoric laid down the principle "that comparisons are not drawn between things which are vastly different from each other. It would be ridiculous to debate whether Achilles is more courageous than Thersites" ("Comparison, Self-Praise and Irony," 6). We can infer from this backdrop that if the rivals compared themselves to Paul to exalt themselves, then they *do not* question Paul's apostolic calling or legitimacy because they would not want to consider themselves equal to (11:12) or to compare themselves with someone whom they regarded as a fraud or as illegitimate. Marshall is correct. The issue in dispute is not apostolic status but who is the apostle of the Corinthians. "It is a question of authority rather than legitimacy" (Marshall, *Enmity in Corinth,* 335).

[133] Forbes, "Comparison, Self-Praise and Irony," 3.

themselves to others. Even when he so "foolishly" joins the fray of comparison, "Are they servants of Christ? (I am out of my mind to talk like this) I am more" (11:22), he ends up only boasting in his weakness, the very things that they think should oust him from the contest. He thereby changes the ground rules of how to play the boasting game.[134]

Third, he challenges their criteria: "They have set themselves up as the measure of their ministry." There were no clear-cut biblical criteria to decide the spiritual legitimacy of Paul or his rivals, and the opponents and the Corinthians apparently reverted to the standards they were accustomed to from their culture.[135] They judged themselves and Paul according to their commanding presence (10:1,10), concrete displays of power and authority (11:19–20), impressive speech (11:20–21), worthiness to accept full compensation (11:7–11), Jewish pedigree (11:21b–22), endurance of hardships (11:23–29), and mystical visions (12:1–6). According to these criteria, they passed with flying colors and Paul failed. But Paul would insist that they not only have usurped God's role as the one who appraises ministry (1 Cor 4:4), but they have used false criteria and ignored the only measure that counts—what God has done in and through the minister. The statement "they are not wise" is an understatement. In chap. 11 he will be more direct: they are fools who deceive themselves and others. He concludes in 10:18 that if one is not commended by the Lord using the Lord's standard of judgment then one is not approved.

10:13–15a Paul's insists that his boasting in his authority over them (10:8) is not out of bounds but is based on the work that he has done in Christ in the region that God assigned him. Corinth is God's field (1 Cor 3:9), and God assigned him to work there as God's servant. He planted; God gave the growth (1 Cor 3:6). Therefore, Paul appeals to the indisputable fact that he founded the church in Corinth. His rivals could not claim this. In fulfilling this divine assignment as apostle to the Gentiles he came to Corinth, "and the success there of his missionary work in calling a church into being was proof that God had approved of his work."[136] He writes in Rom 15:17–18 that in the things pertaining to God—his work—he has a boast in Christ Jesus. The NIV translates "have a boast" as "glory": "Therefore I glory in Christ Jesus

---

[134] Furnish finds lying behind this principle "the familiar Pauline distinction between one's own righteousness, based on personal achievements and credentials, and the righteousness from God "which is through faith in Christ" (Phil. 3:9)" (*II Corinthians,* 482).

[135] The church has always struggled with this problem of establishing standards for discerning spiritual leadership as seen in the attempt to ascertain whether or not an itinerant teacher was a bona fide prophet. In the *Didache* we find the criteria that the true apostle will not tarry more than two days, will not ask for money except enough to reach his next night's lodging, and will not order, when they claim to be speaking in the Spirit, a meal (11:1–9). A more helpful criterion is the assertion that a true prophet does what he teaches (*Did.* 11:10–11; see Matt 7:15–20).

[136] Barrett, *The Second Epistle to the Corinthians,* 266.

in my service to God. I will not venture to speak of anything except what Christ has accomplished through me in leading the Gentiles to obey God by what I have said and done." The reason he can boast is that his ministry to the Gentiles and its success is not his own doing but "the work of God's grace in his life."[137] The rivals might point to their letters of commendation and exhibitions of spiritual power and rhetorical wizardry to corroborate their claims to divine authority. Paul appeals to the incontrovertible existence of the church in Corinthians, a church founded by his missionary preaching.[138] Their boasts are based on evidence manufactured from their own fantasies about themselves. What objectivity is there when they simply cite their own accomplishments as the norm? Paul's boast is based on undeniable fact.

The NIV chooses to translate the phrase in 10:13 that reads literally "according to the measure of the canon *(kanōn)* which measure God assigned to us," as "the field God has assigned us." A *kanōn* was a measuring rod, authoritative standard, or norm (Gal 6:16; see also *4 Macc* 7:21); but it could also apply to a measured field or jurisdiction.[139] Martin claims it relates to the geographical area assigned to apostolic leaders.[140] But he goes beyond the evidence in saying that Paul's opponents have claimed that he has no jurisdiction at Corinth, that it was, for example, Peter's bailiwick.[141] Neither Paul nor the Corinthians are talking about some arbitrary division of territory. It is best to retain the meaning "standard of judgment" or "norm" for *kanōn*.

The proper norm for evaluating Paul's claims of authority is that he was the founder of the church.[142] He argues that Corinth belongs to the sphere assigned him by God by virtue of the fact that he got there first and God blessed his work with growth. His complaint with the rivals is not simply that they have wrongfully invaded turf assigned to him but that they have

---

[137] D. Moo, *The Epistle to the Romans,* NICNT (Grand Rapids: Eerdmans, 1996) 891.

[138] The phrase the "gospel of Christ" implies a well-articulated kerygma about Jesus (J. H. Neyrey, "Witchcraft Accusations in 2 Cor 10–13: Paul in Social Science Perspective," *Listening* 21 (1986) 165). See 11:4, "another Jesus ... a different gospel."

[139] See E. A. Judge, who cites evidence that the word is used to refer to a measured area or a limited domain of service ("The Regional *kanon* for the Requisitioned Transport, in New Documents Illustrating Early Christianity 1, ed. G. H. R. Horsley [North Ryde: Macquarie University, 1989] 36–45). See also J. F. Strange, "2 Corinthians 10:13–16 Illuminated by a Recently Published Inscription," *BA* 46 (1983) 167–68.

[140] Martin, *2 Corinthians,* 316.

[141] Ibid., 321. Paul's protest is unrelated to any imagined violation of some territorial agreement hammered out between Paul and the pillar apostles, James, Cephas, and John (Gal 2:6–10), as F. F. Bruce (*I and II Corinthians,* 34) and Martin (*2 Corinthians,* 316) contend.

[142] S. Hafemann argues that the "unexpressed premise" behind Paul's boast is that his function as the founder of the church "is the only appropriate, divinely appointed 'canon' according to which apostolic authority in a particular church can be determined" ("'Self-commendation' and Apostolic Legitimacy in 2 Corinthians: A Pauline Dialectic?" *NTS* 36 [1990] 80).

tried to discredit his influence where he rightfully deserves influence and to take credit for what God has done through him. Paul counters their criticism of him by saying that he does not "meddle in other people's territory and then compare our performance with theirs."[143] This, according to Lambrecht, explains why Paul can boast. His boast is the result of his fulfilling God's commission. The results, the founding of the church in Corinth, are God's work. His boasting is therefore boasting in the Lord: "Paul has not exceeded his legitimate measure and he has not taken credit for what others have done."[144]

What follows in 10:14–15a basically repeats what Paul says in 10:13 but takes it a step further by making it more specific.[145] He does not overextend himself because he was the first to come to them with the gospel (10:14). He does not boast beyond measure because he does not boast in the labors of others (10:15a).[146] What he boasts about is work that he did under God's commission.

10:15b–16   Paul does not boast in another's labors because he does not work in fields already tilled by others. He expresses his sensitivity about working where others have already established churches in Rom 15:20, "It has always been my ambition to preach the gospel where Christ was not known, so that I would not be building on someone else's foundation." His opponents, however, have no qualms about building on another's foundation or claiming an equal, if not greater authority over a congregation that they did not found.[147] They have conferred no benefits on the Corinthians and have done nothing to expand the field of God's work. This is hardly surprising. Heretics always make inroads among believers, not unbelievers.

Even now Paul has set his sights on new areas of mission. The text is difficult and reads literally "but having hope [that] as your faith increases to be magnified among you [or by you] according to our *kanōn* for abundance." The NIV translation suggests that Paul wants his work to expand among them. But he states in 10:16 that his goal is to preach the gospel in the regions beyond you.[148] In Rom 15:24 we learn that he intends to go to Rome and then on to Spain. Clearly, he wants to settle the problems with the Corinthians so that he can concentrate on missionary endeavors elsewhere

---

[143] F. W. Danker, *II Corinthians,* ACNT (Minneapolis: Augsburg, 1989) 158.

[144] Lambrecht, "Dangerous Boasting: Paul's Self-Commendation in 2 Corinthians 10–13," 332–33.

[145] Ibid., 333.

[146] The word "labors" (κόποι) implies that his missionary work was arduous, involving toil (see 1 Cor 3:8; 2 Cor 6:5; 11:23,27; 1 Thess 2:9; 3:5; see also 1 Cor 15:10).

[147] Aristotle states, "And to speak at great length about oneself and to make all kinds of professions, and to take the credit for what another has done; for this is a sign of boastfulness" (*Rhetoric* 1348a,7).

[148] Since Paul lived in a premap culture, one should not try to figure out where Paul is writing from the statement "beyond you."

with their support. If Paul constantly has to be putting out back fires, he cannot move on to new work. But he expresses confidence that the Corinthians' faith will indeed grow. This will allow his area of activity to expand, not in Corinth, but in territory beyond them.

10:17–18   For the second time in his correspondence with the Corinthians Paul alludes to an adaptation of Jer 9:23–24, "Let him who boasts boast in the Lord" (LXX Jer 9:22–23; see 1 Cor 1:31).[149] Paul boasts in the Lord, whose commendation is the only one that counts.[150] This boast in the Lord has nothing to do with Paul's own pedigree or prowess. It has to do with what the Lord has accomplished through him. Artificial comparisons with others based on human criteria hardly compare with the work that Christ has done in and through him. His boasting is not inappropriate because it is based on what God has done in his life. The results of his mission work are so self-evident that he need not trumpet his commendation as his rivals do. That is why he says that the Corinthians should be commending him (12:11); they are his letter of commendation, to be known and read by all (3:2).

All human boasting is groundless because it is based on appearances, not reality. It is also mercurial. When mortals die, their praise usually dies with them. By contrast, the Lord's glory is eternal. The Lord's scrutiny is also far more exacting. Paul knows that he might preach to others and find himself disqualified as unapproved by God (1 Cor 9:27). He constantly examines himself and urges the Corinthians to do the same (13:5). If they fall under the sway of chronic boasters, who self-assuredly commend themselves, they are liable to ignore God's measures and find themselves disqualified.

3. Paul's Defense (11:1–21a)

[1]I hope you will put up with a little of my foolishness; but you are already doing that. [2]I am jealous for you with a godly jealousy. I promised you to one husband, to Christ, so that I might present you as a pure virgin to him. [3]But I am afraid that just as Eve was deceived by the serpent's cunning, your minds may somehow be led astray from your sincere and pure devotion to Christ. [4]For if someone comes to you and preaches a Jesus other than the Jesus we preached, or if you receive a different spirit from the one you received, or a different gospel from the one you accepted, you put up with it easily enough. [5]But I do not think I am in the least inferior to those "super-apostles." [6]I may not be a trained speaker,

---

[149] In 1 Cor 1:31 he introduces the quotation with "it is written" to underline its authority. See J. Schreiner, "Jeremia 9,22.23 als Hintergrund des paulinischen 'Sich-Rühmens'," in *Neues Testament und Kirche,* ed. J. Gnilka (Freiburg/Basel/Vienna: Herder, 1974) 530–42. Paul could also be alluding to 1 Sam 2:10.

[150] Grundmann states that Paul "lifts the whole question of attestation out of the hands of men and sets it in those of God. God alone decides the issue, which is not subject to human categories of judgment. This means, however, that the question what constitutes true attestation is posed the more urgently" ("δόκιμος ...," *TDNT* 2:258).

but I do have knowledge. We have made this perfectly clear to you in every way.

⁷Was it a sin for me to lower myself in order to elevate you by preaching the gospel of God to you free of charge? ⁸I robbed other churches by receiving support from them so as to serve you. ⁹And when I was with you and needed something, I was not a burden to anyone, for the brothers who came from Macedonia supplied what I needed. I have kept myself from being a burden to you in any way, and will continue to do so. ¹⁰As surely as the truth of Christ is in me, nobody in the regions of Achaia will stop this boasting of mine. ¹¹Why? Because I do not love you? God knows I do! ¹²And I will keep on doing what I am doing in order to cut the ground from under those who want an opportunity to be considered equal with us in the things they boast about.

¹³For such men are false apostles, deceitful workmen, masquerading as apostles of Christ. ¹⁴And no wonder, for Satan himself masquerades as an angel of light. ¹⁵It is not surprising, then, if his servants masquerade as servants of righteousness. Their end will be what their actions deserve.

¹⁶I repeat: Let no one take me for a fool. But if you do, then receive me just as you would a fool, so that I may do a little boasting. ¹⁷In this self-confident boasting I am not talking as the Lord would, but as a fool. ¹⁸Since many are boasting in the way the world does, I too will boast. ¹⁹You gladly put up with fools since you are so wise! ²⁰In fact, you even put up with anyone who enslaves you or exploits you or takes advantage of you or pushes himself forward or slaps you in the face. ²¹To my shame I admit that we were too weak for that!

Paul has repudiated self-commendation and comparison (one-upmanship) as worthless. Scripture attests that God gives the only valid praise. But he now asks the Corinthians to bear with a little foolishness of his own. The circumstances have driven him to this extremity. Boasting is clearly unwise; but if he ignores the slurs of rivals who have maligned him, the church might be persuaded that they were on target. If he stoops to their level by boasting, he is a fool. But if he does not defend himself, he might lose the congregation to even greater fools.[151] Forced into a corner, Paul feels he must opt for this foolishness (12:11) and introduce his own so-called boasts. It is more than a case of trying to fight fire with fire. In the process he turns his foolish boasting into a sly and devastating attack on his opponents. By repeatedly insisting that he is playing the fool by boasting in the same way that his opponents have, he hopes to lead his auditors to recognize how foolish his boastful rivals are and how foolish they have been for being taken in by them.

---

[151] Barrett comments that Paul knows "it is not expedient to boast, but it might be even more inexpedient not to boast" (*The Second Epistle to the Corinthians*, 306). John Chrysostom, *Homilies on Second Corinthians* XXIV.3, justifies Paul's boasting from examples from the OT—Samuel, Amos, David—and not from appeals to Hellenistic rhetoric. Paul's boasting is valid because he does it for the advantage of others and for the sake of the truth (*Saint Chrysostom: Homilies on the Epistles of Epistles of Paul to the Corinthians*, NPNF 1st ser. XII [Grand Rapids: Eerdmans, 1969; the Oxford translation revised by T. W. Chambers] 392–93).

The difference between Paul and the rivals is that Paul admits that what he does is foolish; they do not. Paul undercuts the rivals' boasting further by using irony. He does not boast only about his glorious accomplishments, as they had, but recounts a string of humiliating experiences and boldly contends that he is a better servant of Christ because of them (11:23). The battle lines are drawn between Paul, the weak but true apostle authorized by God, and the super but false apostles working under Satan.[152]

11:1   The fool's discourse begins in 11:1, but Paul does not start speaking as a fool until 11:21. Paul first warns them about what he is going to do. He starts by asking them to bear with him in a little foolishness.[153] He does not immediately tell them what this foolishness might be. It is foolishness of a different order from the folly of the cross (1 Cor 1:25); it is foolish human vanity that glories in itself, instead of God.[154] "Foolishness," "foolish," and "fool" are key words repeated throughout this section (11:1,16,17,19,21; 12:6,11). Someone who cannot evaluate himself soberly is a fool.[155] Nietzsche said that egoism is the very essence of the noble soul. But egoism that leaves God out of the equation always gets out of hand. As one has cracked, the vain person who vaunts himself as the center of the universe suffers from "a case of mistaken nonentity." Paul understands himself, his ego, entirely in terms of Christ: "I have been crucified with Christ and I no longer live, but Christ lives in me. The life I live in the body, I live by faith in the Son of God, who loved me and gave himself for me" (Gal 2:20).

The NIV renders the second use of the verb "to bear" *(anexesthe)* as an indicative, which would mean that they are already bearing with him. Plummer takes it in a positive sense that the Corinthians are sympathetic toward his point of view and offers two options for understanding it: "'Well I ought not to speak like that; you *do* bear with me,' or '*But* there is no need to wish;

---

[152] Neyrey, "Witchcraft," 165–66.

[153] The word ὄφελον normally expresses a wish that is assumed to be unrealizable, "O would that." By using it here, Paul stresses the unusual nature of what he is doing (J. Héring, *The Second Epistle of Saint Paul to the Corinthians* [London: Epworth, 1967] 77–78).

[154] Paul's view of what constitutes foolishness differs considerably from his surrounding culture. We can compare, e.g., Dio Chrysostom's defense of Nestor's bragging in the *Iliad*. Nestor boasts of his prowess and skill to defuse the quarrel between Agamemnon and Achilles, and it evokes this comment from Dio: "Is it not the mark of a foolish person to be ashamed to praise himself when by praise he is likely to confer the greatest benefits; just as it is also, I fancy, to do the opposite—put on airs and talk about oneself a great deal, in case some risk or loss should be involved? Therefore, just as when a physician who wants a patient to submit to surgery or cautery or to the drinking of some pleasant drug, knowing the patient to be cowardly and foolish, mentions others who have been saved by him because they willingly submitted to his treatment, no one says the man who makes these statements is bragging, so it seems to me that Nestor could not justly be accused of bragging either" (*Orations* 57.5). By contrast, even if his boasting does confer benefits on the Corinthians and saves them from spiritual catastrophe, Paul still regards it as foolishness.

[155] Furnish, *II Corinthians*, 485.

of course you do bear with me."[156] This statement, however, could also be taken ironically. He wishes that they would put up with a little foolishness and then corrects himself; they already do bear with him as a fool. His comment in 11:16 reveals that some currently dismiss him as a fool, probably because his claim to authority over the congregation does not match his unimpressive appearance or demeanor. He does not have the aura of a leader who deserves admiration but that of a buffoon who deserves contempt.

The verb *anexesthe* can also be rendered as an imperative (so KJV, NRSV, REB). The context in which he gives his reasons for joining the braggarts in their foolish boasting suggests that we should read it as an imperative, "Indeed, do put up with me!"[157] No one wants to hear another go on about himself or herself, and Paul takes pains to ready his audience for his recital of boasts. The irony pervading these boasts in which he pretends to be less than he is, however, makes them entertaining, for they deftly lampoon the absurdity of his rivals' boasting. He plays the fool to help the Corinthians grasp more firmly the wisdom of the cross.

He begins by expressing a wish that they would put up with his foolishness and then says they must put up with him. In 11:2–6 he gives three reasons for this proposed foolishness and why they should at least humor him. (1) His zeal for the church whom he betrothed to Christ compels him to try to protect them from being seduced and defiled by double agents of Satan (11:2–3). (2) The community's readiness to put up with a false gospel from almost anyone who shows up should dispose them to listen again to him, fool that he is (11:4; see 11:19, "they gladly bear with fools"). (3) He is convinced that he is not in the least inferior to his opponents who so enamor them (11:5–6).

11:2 Paul puts the matter in the framework of betrothal and marriage. He sees himself as the father of the congregation (1 Cor 4:15), and as their father he has betrothed them to Christ—to one man, not a slew of husbands.[158] Among the Jews, betrothal was the first stage of marriage, and it took place at a very early age.[159] Unlike betrothal in the modern era, Jewish betrothal in the first century was not something that was entered into lightly, nor was it easily broken. The betrothal could be canceled only by an official

---

[156] Plummer, *The Second Epistle of St. Paul to the Corinthians*, 293.

[157] Ibid.

[158] The verb ἡρμοσάμην ("I betrothed") is in the middle voice with an active meaning and is used because of Paul's personal involvement and interest. Israel is likened to God's bride in Isa 54:4–8; 62:4–5; Jer 2:2; Ezek 16:1–63; and Hos 2:19–20. Christ is portrayed as a bridegroom in Mark 2:19 / Matt 9:15 / Luke 5:34–35; John 3:29; and Rev 19:7; 21:2,9; 22:17. The image of the mysterious union of Christ and the church using the metaphor of marriage is developed in Eph 5:21–32.

[159] See *b. Yebam.* 62b.

bill of divorce.[160] If a betrothed woman had sexual relations with any other man, it was treated as adultery.[161] The betrothed couple did not live together until the marriage ceremony when they entered the wedding canopy and the marriage blessings were recited. A year therefore normally passed before the woman moved to her husband's home where they would take up common residence.[162] The responsibility of safeguarding his daughter's virginity fell to the father (see Deut 22:13–21). This image of betrothal suggests that the Corinthians' marriage to Christ awaits consummation when Paul will present them to him at the Parousia.[163] In the meantime they keep the spiritual father of the bride on tenterhooks lest she be defiled and disqualified for the marriage.[164] He feels a divine jealousy, as any father would, to preserve the purity of the bride for her husband.[165] Unlike the Judaizers whom Paul accuses of having a dishonorable zeal for his Galatian converts (Gal 4:17), a divine zeal for the Corinthians motivates Paul.[166]

Barnett correctly attempts to check confusing Paul's zeal for the Corin-

---

[160] See *t. Ketub.* 8:1.

[161] The woman guilty of adultery is to make the confession, "I am unclean" (*m. Sota* 3:3; see Num 5:28).

[162] See *m. Ketub*; *m. Ned.* 10:5; *b. Ketub.* 57b.

[163] The image of waiting for the bridegroom is found in the parable of the foolish and wise maidens (Matt 25:1–13).

[164] *Sirach* captures the typical father's worries in this culture:

A daughter is a secret anxiety to her father,
   and worry over her robs him of sleep;
when she is young, for fear she may not marry,
   or if married, for fear she may be disliked;
while a virgin, for fear she may be seduced
   and become pregnant in her father's house;
or having a husband, for fear she may go astray,
   or, though married, for fear she may be barren.
Keep strict watch over a headstrong daughter,
   or she may make you a laughingstock to your enemies,
a byword in the city and the assembly of the people,
   and put you to shame in public gatherings.
See that there is no lattice in her room,
   no spot that overlooks the approaches to the house (42:9–11).

[165] See R. Batey, "Paul's Bride Image: A Symbol of Realistic Eschatology," *Int* 17 (1963) 176–82.

[166] The phrase θεοῦ ζῆλος could be a qualitative genitive, "divine jealousy," or a genitive of source, "jealousy from God." On God's jealousy see Exod 20:5; 34:14; Deut 4:24; 5:9; 6:15; Josh 24:19; and Nah 1:2). Since God tolerates no rivals, perhaps Paul implies that he also tolerates no rivals who would corrupt their faith. R. Bieringer shows how Paul's concern for the relationship with the Corinthians, expressed by his image of divine jealousy, was particularly crucial in this letter ("Paul's Divine Jealousy: The Apostle and His Communities in Relationship," *LouvSt* 17 [1992] 197–231 =*Studies on 2 Corinthians* ed. R. Bieringer and J. Lambrecht, BETL 112 [Leuven: University Press, 1994] 223–53).

thians with "the petty possessiveness that mars human relationships" by connecting it to the theme of God's covenantal care for his people (LXX Isa 9:6; 37:32; 63:15–16)."[167] Before his conversion, Paul zealously sought to preserve the purity of Israel by violently trying to purge Christians (Gal 1:16–17). His former zeal has now been converted by Christ's love. He no longer resorts to violence, and he zealously strives to preserve purity and devotion to Christ rather than to Jewish tribal traditions.

11:3 Undivided ("total") devotion and purity are prerequisites for a continuing relationship to Christ, and Paul expresses his fear that the Corinthians may already have been unfaithful, ravished by theological libertines.[168] He draws on the account of the cunning serpent's deception of Eve (Gen 3:13; 1 Tim 2:14), which had developed in some segments of Jewish tradition as a sexual seduction.[169] The verb "to be led astray" *(phtharein)* frequently applies to moral ruin or corruption (1 Cor 15:33; see also Gen 6:11; Hos 9:9).[170] But Paul has in mind a spiritual debauchery. As the serpent ensnared Eve with guileful arguments (see 4:2), so his smooth talking rivals have snaked their way into the Corinthians' affection and captured their minds with a more alluring gospel but a deadly one since it is no gospel. Harvey observes:

> The very first human betrothal that between Adam and Eve was vulnerable to the seduction of the serpent, and resulted in disloyalty of thoughts and intentions. Paul is afraid a similar corruption of the mind is in the church, causing disloyalty to Christ. The signs of it are those different versions of "Jesus" or Spirit" or "gospel" which have apparently been imported into the congregation and tolerated by it.[171]

Paul's reference to the serpent's deception serves to remind the Corinthians that Satan is the master of disguise, which prepares readers for his identification of his opponents, who seem so impressive and wonderful, as servants of Satan in 11:15. Paul sounds the alarm that the same tempter who flattered and deceived Eve has ensnared them. Satan always lies coiled ready

---

[167] Barnett, *The Second Epistle to the Corinthians*, 499–500.

[168] Some texts have shorter readings, either ἀπὸ τῆς ἁπλότητος ("sincere") or καὶ τῆς ἁγνότητος ("and pure"). While the shorter reading is usually preferred and "purity" could have been added to match the symbolism of the pure bride in 11:2, the longer reading has the best external support (p[46] ℵ* B 33). The same ending -οτητος may have played tricks on the scribes' eyes (homoeoteleuton), causing the omission of one of the phrases. The word ἁπλότης has the meaning "liberality" in 8:2; 9:11,13. Here it means "innocent," "irreproachable." Its root meaning is "singleness" or "simplicity," and the single-minded person is the opposite of the one with a divided heart. Christ requires whole-hearted devotion from his followers.

[169] See *b. ʿAbod. Zar.* 22b; *b. Šabb.* 145b–146a; *b. Yebam.* 103b; *b. Sota* 9b; *1 Enoch* 69:5–6; *2 Enoch* 31:6; *Apoc Abr* 23:5; and *4 Macc* 18:7–8.

[170] Furnish, *II Corinthians*, 487.

[171] Harvey, *Renewal through Suffering*, 97–98.

to strike at the first sign of weakness (see 2:11) and to exchange sugarcoated lies for the unvarnished truth.

Eve was not exonerated from her sin because she was taken in by the supreme trickster, and neither will the Corinthians be exonerated. It is not difficult to deceive those who wish to be deceived. Their desires already primed their own hearts to be disobedient. "Eve was deceived by exciting the unholy feelings in her heart."[172] The Corinthians' penchant for error and illusions of grandeur, believing themselves to be kings who already reigned (1 Cor 4:8), made them easy marks for grandiloquent opponents to inject their poisonous notions.

11:4 Paul never names his opponents but continually refers to them only indirectly, "if someone comes."[173] Barrett comments that these rivals merely come, while Paul, as an apostle, is sent (see 1 Cor 1:17).[174] But Paul also describes his first visit as "coming" but with a distinct difference:

> When I came to you, brothers, I did not come with eloquence or superior wisdom as I proclaimed to you the testimony about God. For I resolved to know nothing while I was with you except Jesus Christ and him crucified. I came to you in weakness and fear, and with much trembling. My message and my preaching were not with wise and persuasive words, but with a demonstration of the Spirit's power, so that your faith might not rest on men's wisdom, but on God's power (1 Cor 2:1–5).

The opponents came with eloquence, a swaggering boldness, and persuasive words that proclaimed a testimony about themselves rather than Christ. Not only did they trespass on Paul's allotted field, but they sowed that field with the tares of a false gospel. Their preaching is false—a different Jesus, Spirit, and gospel—that can only lead Christians away from Christ. Paul therefore asks that "the same measure of toleration should be

---

[172] C. Hodge, *An Exposition of the Second Epistle to the Corinthians* (1859; reprint, Grand Rapids: Baker, 1980) 253.

[173] Marshall argues that not naming one's opponents was a rhetorical device that could be employed to good advantage not only because the enemies were well known to the readers, but nameless "certain ones" made easier targets for caricature. Blameworthy conduct associated with the antagonists' behavior could be contrasted with Paul's praiseworthy conduct and bring shame to them more effectively than a direct attack. In addition, Marshall notes that when a person has been subject to public attack, as Paul had, "he could commend himself as a man of dignity and restraint by not retaliating in kind. By not naming his detractor, he does not enter into the same game, so to speak" (*Enmity in Corinth,* 344). For an example, see Dio Chrysostom, *Orations* 37.35–36. The textual variant with the imperfect ἀνείχεσθε ("you were putting up") in p[34] ℵ D[2] F G H and the Byzantine text instead of the present ἀνέχεσθε ("you are putting up") represented by p[46] B D* 33 probably marks an attempt by a scribe to make this situation more hypothetical and not present the church as actually welcoming such persons.

[174] Barrett, *The Second Epistle to the Corinthians*, 275.

granted to him as is accorded a teacher of error."[175]

Paul's summary of their preaching, "another Jesus," "another gospel," "another Spirit," provides nothing concrete to identify the opponents, though that has not stopped interpreters from trying.[176] The disparate reconstructions of their views merely confirm the ambiguity of these terms. The only thing about which we can be sure is that their gospel differed from Paul's, and we can only infer how it differed from what Paul emphasizes in response.[177] It is clear from his criticism that their gospel allows for self boasting and arrogance. It also gives them a warrant for assuming spiritual authority to lord it over others and to berate those who take the role of a humble servant. This gospel apparently places greater emphasis on human standards as valid criteria for evaluating others, on rhetorical showmanship, on racial heritage, and on ecstatic visions.

"Another Jesus" refers to a different interpretation of Jesus that is not congruent with the facts of Jesus' life and death. Paul's emphasis in 13:4, that Christ was "crucified in weakness," suggests the possibility that the rivals presented a Jesus who was not "weak, suffering or humiliated."[178] They may talk about Christ, but Christ crucified is not the heart of their gospel nor does it influence the way they live. In contrast to his attack on the Judaizers who infiltrated the Galatians, Paul does not single out any particular false doctrine in condemning these Corinthian rivals. We may infer from this that it is primarily their haughty manner and actions that expose their faulty theological doctrine.[179] They are

---

[175] Ibid., 277. Furnish avers: "Since the Corinthians already have put up with false teachings from Paul's rivals, they ought to put up with a little foolishness from their own apostle" (*II Corinthians*, 488).

[176] R. P. C. Hanson comments that the triad "Jesus, Spirit, gospel" reveals what is essential about the Christian faith. These are not abstract virtues like "Love, Joy, Peace," or "Liberty, Equality, Fraternity" (*II Corinthians*, TBC [London: SPCK, 1954] 81).

[177] The similarity to the language against the opponents in Gal 1:6–9 is only superficial and does not mean that the opponents are Judaizers. Paul makes no mention of the Jewish law, nationalism, or circumcision. The only correspondence between these two different opponents is that their gospel is defective in some way.

[178] J. Murphy-O'Connor, "Another Jesus (2 Cor 11:4)," *RB* 97 (1990) 248. We can see the upshot of this thinking is the docetic picture of Christ found in the later apocryphal gospels. G. D. Fee, argues, however, that false Christology is not at issue: "Paul does not follow up on this phrase, either here or later." He thinks that the key item in the list is the third, "another Spirit," and the first and second items should be interpreted in light of it ("'Another Gospel Which You Did Not Embrace': 2 Corinthians 11:4 and the Theology of 1 and 2 Corinthians," in *Gospel in Paul: Studies on Corinthians, Galatians and Romans for Richard N. Longenecker*, ed. L. A. Jervis and P. Richardson, JSNTSup 108 [Sheffield: Sheffield Academic Press, 1994] 119).

[179] Bultmann claims that the opponents' error does not require specific, dogmatic, Christological doctrines. Although false doctrine may be involved, Paul does not attack any particular false doctrine. "For him, the denial of his apostleship and the arrogance of a false apostolate (vv. 13–15) already spells a falsification of the gospel" (*The Second Letter to the Corinthians,* 203; see also Furnish, *II Corinthians*, 502). But we argue that the opponents have not denied Paul's apostleship. The key issue is their arrogance and false boasting and the sinful motives behind their invasion of this church and denigration of Paul.

self-seeking, not self-denying. Savage concludes:

> Their approach to 'ministry' speaks volumes of their 'Jesus.' It suggests to Paul
> that their grasp of Jesus is not only gravely inadequate, but almost nonexistent.
> Their doctrine is not just unsound, it is empty. They use the name 'Jesus' and
> claim to be his ministers, but only as a means by which to advance their inter-
> ests.[180]

The Jesus they champion "confers a showy status and honour" on them.[181]

"A different spirit" may refer to some kind of human attitude (see
12:18), as the NIV translates it, or it may refer to a misrepresentation of
the Holy Spirit. "Receiving the Spirit" is language used to refer to the
Holy Spirit in the New Testament and would be a more fitting counterpart
to the references to Christ and the gospel.[182] What is this "other spirit"
that they represent as the Spirit? The context gives no indication that Paul
is thinking of a spirit of legalism.[183] The problem seems to be the rivals'
misinterpretation of the Spirit. They promulgate a Spirit who "has nothing
at all to do with the Spirit."[184] Perhaps they view the Spirit primarily as
the inrush of heavenly power into their lives and emphasize a Spirit who
produces miracles, displays of power, ecstasy, and visions.[185] The Spirit
that one receives from these rivals allows claims of superiority over others
in the church and creates divisions. They fail to recognize that God gives
the Spirit to the church to build up a harmonious community, not to exalt
one over another.

In Gal 1:8 Paul says that anyone who preaches a different gospel
should be accursed. Paul does not go that far here, but the parallel leads
some to conclude that Paul is dealing with the same problem of Judaizing
intruders. The infinite number of ways that the gospel can be perverted

---

[180] Savage, *Power through Weakness*, 158.

[181] Ibid., 162. S. B. Andrews claims that "the driving force in the debate between Paul and his
opponents is not who has 'a better theology' but rather who is more worthy or more virtuous to
lead the Corinthians" ("Too Weak Not to Lead: The Form and Function of 2 Cor 11.23b–33," *NTS*
41 [1995] 273.

[182] John 7:39; 14:17; 20:22; Acts 2:38; 8:15–17; 10:47; 19:2; Rom 8:15; 1 Cor 2:12; and Gal
3:2. Fee asks, "How does one 'receive' some aspect of Christian lifestyle or attitude, one wonders?" ("Another Gospel Which You Did Not Embrace," 121).

[183] Plummer argues that Paul offered a spirit of freedom (3:17) and of joy and that the opponents, whom he assumes are Judaizers, offered a spirit of bondage and of fear (*The Second Epistle
of St. Paul to the Corinthians*, 297). See also P. E. Hughes, *Paul's Second Epistle to the Corinthians*, NICNT (Grand Rapids: Eerdmans, 1962) 378; and Martin, *2 Corinthians*, 336.

[184] Fee, "Another Gospel Which You Did Not Embrace," 122–23.

[185] Belleville comments: "While one aspect of the Spirit's role is the working of signs, wonders, and miracles, it is a role that serves to validate the gospel, not displace it. The core of the gospel, according to Paul, is Christ crucified, not Jesus the wonder-worker, which may well be what
is meant by ἄλλον Ἰησοῦν" ("Paul's Polemic and Theology of the Spirit in Second Corinthians,"
CBQ 58 [1996] 296–97).

should prevent us from accepting this assumption too quickly. Paul does not counter these rivals in the same way that he takes on the Judaizers in Galatians. Fee is correct that Paul "is less concerned about what these insurgents are teaching and more on *what is happening to the Corinthians* as a result of this teaching" which conflicts with "their first encounter with Christ and the Spirit through Paul's preaching of the gospel."[186] But what is it that is happening that has him so concerned? The only thing he says specifically is that there is "quarreling, jealousy, outbursts of anger, factions, slander, gossip, arrogance and disorder," and "impurity, sexual sin and debauchery" (12:20–21). This "other Jesus" and "other Spirit" add up to "another gospel" that fosters and condones these vices. It is a gospel that apparently gives Paul's rivals license to slander him, to boast beyond measure, to enslave others, to put on airs, to exploit others, to slap them around, and to live in boastful confidence in their racial heritage, religious achievements, and mystical experiences. It is not a gospel that requires converts to live by the cross of Christ.

What are the criteria for identifying that someone is preaching a false Jesus, Spirit, and gospel as opposed to the genuine Jesus, Spirit and gospel? For the Corinthians, the "other Jesus" is one Paul did not preach. The Jesus Paul preached is Jesus Christ crucified (1 Cor 1:23) and Jesus Christ as Lord (4:5). Jesus as Lord requires humble submission and makes absolute moral demands. Any gospel that has no moral core, fosters boasting, and soft-pedals sacrifice is no gospel.

11:5 Paul reintroduces the idea of comparison that he rejected in 10:12. He expresses his certainty that he is not the least inferior to those "super-apostles" which presents his third reason for adopting the persona of a fool to defend himself. This statement implies that some at Corinth do think he is inferior in some way, and Paul debunks this assumption with irony and parody and the plain statement of the facts. At the conclusion of his fool's speech in 12:11, he will repeat the phrase, "I consider myself in no way inferior to these super apostles."

The adjective *hyperlian* ("superlative," "superfine") only occurs here in the New Testament and infrequently elsewhere. It is conceivable that Paul himself coined the term to box the ears of his rivals who are so full of themselves, or that they, with their overinflated self-esteem, applied it to themselves, or that the hero worshiping Corinthians exalted them with such fulsome praise. It raises the question whether this term is ironic or straightforward? Does it mean "super apostles" or "highest of all apostles"? Who

[186] Fee, "'Another Gospel Which You Did Not Embrace," 119–20.

are these supreme apostles?[187]

Many have argued that the superapostles are different from Paul's rivals in Corinth.[188] The arguments run as follows:

1. Paul castigates his opponents as false apostles (11:13) and ministers of Satan (11:14–15) and could hardly wish to claim an equal status with such charlatans.

2. The term therefore applies to the original apostles with whom he claims an equal status. He is the least of all the apostles, but he worked harder than all of them (1 Cor 15:9–10; see "with far greater labors," 2 Cor 11:23).[189]

3. Paul's complaint over the encroachment on his apostolic jurisdiction (10:14–16) is said only to make sense in the context of the agreement with the pillar apostles of Jerusalem, James, John, and Cephas (Gal 2:9).

4. Paul follows his reference to the superapostles with mention of financial support for apostles (11:5,7–12; 12:11,13–15). He preaches the gospel of God to them free of charge, which is his boast in Achaia. This assertion is said to parallel 1 Cor 9:5, where he compares himself with "the other apostles and the Lord's brothers and Cephas" who receive financial support. He has the same right as they to receive support, but he does not exercise this right (1 Cor 9:3–23). Preaching without compensation is his boast (1 Cor 9:15).

5. The conclusion is that the intruders claimed that they were sent out or were backed by the apostles in Jerusalem whom they characterize as the superapostles.[190]

---

[187] The opponents have been identified as: (1) the Judaizers who were attacked in Galatians (F. C. Baur, *Paulus, Der Apostel Jesu Christi* [1866, reprint, Osnabrueck: Zeller, 1968] I:297, 309); (2) envoys from the Jerusalem church inclined to spiritual display (Käsemann, "Die Legitimität des Apostels," 41–48); (3) Judeo-Christian Gnostics (W. Schmithals, *Gnosis in Corinth*, trans. J. E. Steely [Nashville: Abingdon, 1971]; (4) Hellenistic Jewish Christian divine men (D. Georgi, *The Opponents of Paul in Second Corinthians* [Philadelphia: Fortress, 1986] 229–313); (5) Hellenistic Jewish Christians from the circle of Stephen (G. Friedrich, "Die Gegner des Paulus im II. Korintherbrief," in *Abraham unser Vater*, ed. by O. Betz, M. Hengel, and P. Schmidt [Leiden: Brill, 1963], 179–208). What we can know about these opponents can only be inferred from the text; but it seems safe to say that they are proud of their Jewish heritage (11:22), skillful in the rhetorical arts (11:6, and therefore strongly influenced by the Hellenistic environment), boastful of various accomplishments, visions, and revelations that they claimed proved that Christ spoke in them (13:3).

[188] Käsemann, "Die Legitimität des Apostels," 41–48; C. K. Barrett, "Paul's Opponents in 2 Corinthians," in *Essays on Paul* (Philadelphia: Westminster, 1982) 60–86; *The Second Epistle to the Corinthians*, 242–44, 249–53, 278; and "Christianity at Corinth," 289–91; and M. E. Thrall, "Super-Apostles, Servants of Christ, and Servants of Satan," *JSNT* 6 (1980) 42–57.

[189] Some contend that Paul would not claim to be on a par with those he dubs false apostles, but the Corinthians do not regard them so and have compared Paul negatively to them. Paul shows that, in truth, they are not equals. He is a true apostle; they are empty braggarts.

[190] Bruce writes that the term might conceivably go back to the intruders who use this phrase to invoke the authority of men whose commission was incomparably superior to Paul's, but the ironic flavor of the term makes it "more likely that it is Paul's way of summing up his opponents' portrayal of the Jerusalem leaders" (*I & II Corinthians*, 237).

There are major problems with this view.

1. If the super fine apostles refer to the original apostles, Paul makes a surprising leap from the reference to his Corinthian rivals in 11:4 to the sudden mention of these first apostles in 11:5. This problematic transition would be removed if he were referring to the same group in both verses.

2. The thought in 11:5 continues in 11:6, where Paul admits his lack of skill or training in public speaking, presumably in comparison to the superapostles. Such skill or training would hardly be applicable to the Jerusalem apostles who would have no better mastery of the rhetorical arts than Paul. Peter and John's boldness amazed the Sanhedrin because they took them to be unschooled *(agrammatoi)* and ordinary *(idiōtai)* men (Acts 4:13). This distinction would tend to rule out the likelihood that these rivals came from Palestine. The well educated Josephus, who had become at home in the Greek speaking world as a client of the ruling Flavian family in Rome, still needed the help of assistants to put his history of the Jewish War into acceptable Greek.[191] He admits "Jews do not favor those persons who have mastered the speech of many nations or who adorn their style with smoothness of diction."[192] If the rivals did not come from Palestine, and there is no indication in the text that they did, then it is unlikely that they invoked the support of the Jerusalem apostles.

3. The arguments that the intruders appealed to the authority of the Twelve or made exaggerated claims about them have to be read into the text. The mention of the superapostles in 12:11 concludes his fool's speech in 11:21–12:10 and looks back over his comparison with the intruders, not the Jerusalem apostles.[193]

4. It is also unlikely that Paul would call the original apostles false apostles, deceitful workers, disguised as apostles of Christ by Satan (11:13–15), or that he would claim that he is a better servant of Christ than they are (11:23).[194] His zeal to complete the collection for the saints in Jerusalem undermines any the-

---

[191] Josephus, *Ag. Ap.* 1.9 §50.

[192] Josephus, *Ant.* 20.12.1 §264. Barrett counters that speech and knowledge were "the criteria employed by the Corinthians" and are not a reference to the claims or the abilities of the rivals (*The Second Epistle to the Corinthians*, 278). But it is amazing to think that itinerant preachers from Palestine would be regarded as rhetorically better trained than Paul.

[193] Bultmann notes that if Paul were comparing himself to the original apostles he would have to "make his authority explicit by appealing to his calling, just as he does in Galatians" (*The Second Letter to the Corinthians*, 203).

[194] The arguments adduced by Thrall that Paul was confused about the exact identity of his opponents and therefore inconsistent in his criticism of them, or that he recollects the tradition later found in the gospels that the figure of Peter could be seen in both roles, as servant of Christ and servant of Satan (Matt 16:16–23; Luke 22:31–34), are not persuasive ("Super-Apostles, Servants of Christ, and Servants of Satan," 52–54). See the negative response of S. E. McClelland, "Super-Apostles, Servants of Christ, Servants of Satan," *JSNT* 14 (1982) 82–87). Furnish dismisses it as "rather far-fetched" (*II Corinthians*, 510). The epithets can only make sense if they apply to the actual opponents on the scene whom Paul regards as impostors and not representatives of anybody but themselves.

ory that some mutual hostility simmers between Paul and the mother church.

We conclude that the term "superapostles" refers to the rivals in Corinth, and the context suggests that it is "a highly ironic way to refer to his opponents, who are making pretentious claims in order to win the allegiance of the Corinthian Christians."[195] They think that as apostles go they are second to none. No true apostle of Christ, however, shouts, "We are number one!" This attitude exposes what makes them so evil in Paul's eyes. All apostles are second to One, Christ; and all are servants of Christ's church, not overlords. These rivals show themselves to be false apostles when they seek to glorify themselves instead of Christ.

11:6 Ironically, Paul begins his comparison with his rivals by admitting that he does not measure up to them in the skill that the Corinthians so prize, speaking. He says he is unskilled *(idiōtēs)* in word. This statement recalls the criticism that "his speaking amounts to nothing" (10:10). Some take it to mean that his speaking lacks spiritual power.[196] But how could Paul admit that he was a layman when it came to spiritual power or utterance? It is more likely that it relates to Paul's style and strategy of public speaking. He lacks the polish of a skilled rhetorician who waxes eloquently with compelling arguments. He is a layman when it comes to rhetorical flourishes and comes off as amateurish to the Corinthians, whom Paul notes are "rich in word" (8:7).[197]

We must be alert, however, for understatement by Paul.[198] DiCicco argues that Paul's statement should not be taken at face value but as modest irony: "Far from being [unskilled in speech] ... he was a rhetor of great persuasive power."[199] According to DiCicco, Paul did not reject outright the persuasive

---

[195] Furnish, *II Corinthians*, 503–5. H. D. Betz says that the term "super apostle" puts the finger on the rivals' *hybris* while at the same time meaning what Paul says: he does not compare to such fools (*Der Apostel Paulus und die sokratische Tradition. Eine exegetische Untersuchung zu seiner "Apologie" 2 Korinther 10–13*, BHT 45 [Tübingen: Mohr (Siebeck), 1972] 121). Barrett goes too far in saying that if Paul calls his opponents both servants of Christ and servants of Satan, superlative apostles and false apostles, then he is "lashing out blindly, and using language irresponsibly" ("Paul's Opponents in 2 Corinthians," 64). C. J. Schlueter argues in a different context that Paul's use of polemical exaggeration and discordant terms does not require us to propose that there were different groups (*Filling Up the Measure: Polemical Hyperbole in 1 Thessalonians 2:14–16*; JSNTSup 98 [Sheffield: JSOT, 1994] 130–31).

[196] Georgi, *The Opponents of Paul in Second Corinthians*, 235, 402. Bultmann claimed that it refers to Gnostic speculations, perhaps conveyed by Alexandrian allegory (*The Second Letter to the Corinthians*, 204).

[197] E. A. Judge, "Cultural Conformity and Innovation in Paul: Some Clues from Contemporary Documents," *TynBul* 35 (184) 12–14, 35.

[198] The NIV omits the "if" clause (εἰ δὲ καί, "even though") that introduces this sentence, and this omission conceals the possibility that Paul may not be conceding to their judgment entirely.

[199] DiCicco, *Paul's Use of Ethos, Pathos, and Logos in 2 Corinthians 10–13*, 15. See Witherington, who compares Paul to the professional politician "who begins a well-rehearsed speech with 'Unaccustomed as I am to public speaking,' Paul knows well how to use irony effectively" (*Conflict and Community in Corinth*, 433, n. 14).

methods of rhetoric but the arrogant speech of those who are puffed up (4:19).[200] By contrast, Paul mentions coming to them in "fear and trembling" (1 Cor 2:1), a phrase that in the Old Testament depicts a humble response to the awe-inspiring majesty of God (see Exod 15:16; Isa 19:16). As one entrusted with the word of the cross (1 Cor 1:17–24), "the power of God and the wisdom of God," Paul "would have been confronted daily by the awe-inspiring majesty of God." Consequently, he did not come "in haughtiness of speech (v. 1), but in profound humility and trepidation (v. 3)."[201]

Judge contends that the rhetoric Paul has in mind is not that of the great Attic orators but that of the "artificial, undisciplined, and highly flamboyant style known as 'Asianism,' immensely popular among the sophists of Paul's day, and precisely in areas where Paul was active."[202] Most reputable philosophers were suspicious of rhetorical flourishes that substituted style for substance or bombast for profundity. Lucian parodied street orators:

> The traits that you should possess in particular are these: you should be impudent and bold and should abuse all and each, both kings and commoners, for thus they will admire you and think you manly. Let your language be barbarous ... like the barking of a dog. ... In a word, let everything about you be bestial and savage. Put off modesty, decency and moderation, wipe away blushes from your face completely. ... But at all events it is easy, man, and no trouble for all to follow, for you will not need education and doctrine and drivel, but this road is a short cut to fame. Even if you are an unlettered man ... there will be nothing to hinder you from being wondered at, if only you have impudence and boldness and learn how to abuse people properly.[203]

---

[200] Savage, *Power through Weakness*, 72. Since the Corinthians commend his letters (10:10), they have no problem with the content of his word, which might not have differed greatly from his speech. Barrett believes that they fault his manner of delivery when he speaks: "Paul's writing so strongly resembles speech, that there is much force in the conclusion that either Paul suffered from an impediment in his speech (which could have been the physical weakness he appears to refer to in xii.7), or that he writes with undue modesty" (*The Second Epistle to the Corinthians*, 279). Paul's mode of delivery was unlike the more flamboyant style they thought was exemplary. If Paul failed to measure up to their standards of what was fitting for an apostle, he counters that their standards conform to the fashions of this present evil age and do not conform to the pattern of the cross of Christ.

[201] Ibid., 73.

[202] Furnish, *II Corinthians*, 490. Savage comments: "His critics may well be faulting Paul for refusing to indulge in the imposing and abusive rhetoric which ... had become popular in first-century Corinth. This was not the carefully cultivated speech of classical oratory. It was the 'vulgar rhetoric,' a speech characterised by showy and often meaningless monologues in which orators sought to dominate their audience through sheer force of delivery" (*Power through Weakness*, 71). See further E. Fantham, "Imitation and Decline: Rhetorical Theory and Practice in the First Century after Christ," *Classical Philology* 73 (1978) 102–16.

[203] Lucian, *Philosophies for Sale* 10–11. Savage quotes Dio Chrysostom (*Orations* 8.8–9), who complained that when the sage Diogenes proclaimed in Corinth "relief from folly, wickedness, and intemperance, not a man would listen"; instead they applauded "the wretched sophists around Poseidon's temple shouting and reviling one another," the "many writers reading aloud their stupid works ... jugglers showing their tricks ... fortune tellers interpreting fortunes, lawyers innumerable perverting judgment" (*Power through Weakness*, 30–31).

We can also compare Dio Chrysostom's reaction to sophists that is similar to Paul's: "For they are clever persons, mighty sophists, wonder workers; but I am quite ordinary and prosaic in my public speaking, though not ordinary in my theme."[204] Unlike Dio, however, Paul's theme determines his manner of speech.

Paul's forthright disparagement of the "wisdom of word" ("words of human wisdom," NIV) in 1 Cor 1:17, however, suggests that he may have disdained more than a certain style of rhetoric or "speech marked by a spirit of pride and arrogance." In 1 Cor 2:1–5 Paul disavows the very presuppositions behind rhetorical persuasion. In 1 Cor 2:13 he maintains, "This is what we speak, not in words taught us by human wisdom but in words taught by the Spirit, expressing spiritual truths in spiritual words."

Paul's deviations from conventional oratory stand out in 1 Corinthians. First, ancient orators would ask listeners to propose topics by which they could exhibit their nimble wit and persuasive skills whatever the topic or the audience. Paul proclaimed only Christ crucified and took the same message to every audience.

Second, Aristotle defined rhetoric "as the faculty of discovering the possible means of persuasion in reference to any subject whatsoever."[205] The basic presupposition of rhetoric is that the audience will yield to belief when the speaker proves the case. As Litfin states it: "The speaker's task is to marshal the logical, emotional, and ethical means of persuasion so effectively that he produces conviction within the audience, or comes as close to it as humanly possible."[206] Orators carefully chose and adapted their words, arguments, arrangement, and delivery for the greatest impact to win the audience's positive verdict. Paul may have shunned this approach for theological reasons. He had no intention of engineering an audience's favorable response with rhetorical devices because that may mean that they have been

---

[204] Dio Chrysostom, *Orations* 32.39. A noted orator, Dio referred ironically to his "inexperience in simply everything, but especially speaking, recognizing that I am only a layman" (ἰδιώτης) compared to so-called professional teachers and philosophers (*Orations* 42.3; see also 12.15–16). Harvey notes that Plato made a distinction between the goal of philosophy (wisdom and truth) and the means by which it was conveyed to others. He attacked the "sophists" for obscuring the distinction between the two by putting more emphasis on the skillful manner of argumentation than on whether their argument was true or false (trial lawyers who do not care for getting at the truth but in winning the case). They make weak cases seem plausible to the weak-minded who are easily taken in by elocutionary fireworks (*Renewal through Suffering*, 35; see also Litfin, *St. Paul's Theology of Proclamation*, 119–124). Barrett cites Plato, *Ion* 532D: "You rhapsodes and actors, and the poets whose verses you sing, are wise; and I am a common man (ἰδιώτην ἄνθρωπον), who only speaks the truth" (*The Second Epistle to the Corinthians*, 279).

[205] Aristotle *Rhetoric* 1.1.1.

[206] Litfin, *St Paul's Theology of Proclamation*, 81. Aristotle described these means of persuasion in his *Rhetoric* as *ēthos*, the moral character of the speaker; *pathos*, the manipulation the audience's feelings; and *logos*, logical arguments.

convinced by the power of his rhetoric rather than converted by the power of the cross. The listener's faith would rest upon the preacher's facility as a rhetorician and the artful use of persuasive ploys, namely, human wisdom, rather than upon the Spirit's power to create faith.[207] Litfin outlines the five steps of persuasion as (1) attention, (2) comprehension, (3) yielding, (4) retention, and (5) action.[208] Greco-Roman rhetoric stressed step three, getting the audience to yield. Paul stressed step two, comprehension, which explains why he emphasizes that he is not lacking in knowledge. He may grant that he is untrained in the rhetorical arts, but he vigorously denies that he lacks knowledge. The adversative "but" is repeated twice: "*But* I do have knowledge. *But* we have made this perfectly clear to you in every way." Paul left the third step, yielding, to the Spirit. He rejected the rhetorical strategies designed to promote yielding because they empty the cross of its power and put in its place human wisdom.[209]

Third, in rhetorical discourse the speaker is on trial and the audience serves as judge and jury. Litfin observes, "In the realm of rhetorical discourse the audience is always sovereign," and ancient audiences relished this role.[210] To be effective, the speaker must sway the audience. For Paul, the sovereignty does not reside in the audience but in the message. To some, the message of Christ crucified is foolishness; to others, it is scandalous (1 Cor 1:17–25). But this negative response does not alter the truth that the message being heralded is the power and wisdom of God unto salvation. The audience therefore is not the final arbiter of what is true. Their yielding to the clever word-spinning and crafty modulations of the rhetor, each calculated for its effect, does not make what is proclaimed true. Paul did not get people to believe by arguing that Christ crucified accords with the common principles of logic or that belief is in the long term best interests of the hearers. As a herald he simply announced what God has done in Christ. From his perspective his job as proclaimer is to make sure that each hears and understands. The Spirit will demonstrate to the believer the truth of the gospel (1 Cor 2:4,13).

Cicero praised eloquence

---

[207] Litfin argues: "Paul disavowed the task of inducing his listeners. He insisted that creating πίστις was the sole province of the Spirit of God working through the cross of Christ. This Spirit-powered creation of faith in the saving efficacy of the crucified Christ constituted for Paul the persuasive dynamic of the cross" (*St Paul's Theology of Proclamation*, 247).

[208] Ibid., 261.

[209] But he had no theological qualms about employing steps one and two, attention and comprehension. He tells the Galatians, e.g., that "before your very eyes Jesus Christ was clearly portrayed as crucified" (Gal 3:1).

[210] Liftin, *St Paul's Theology of Proclamation*, 86.

which rushes along with the roar of a might stream, which all look up to and admire, and which they despair of attaining. This eloquence has power to sway men's minds and move them in every possible way. Now it storms the feelings, now it creeps in; it implants new ideas and uproots the old.[211]

Dio Chrysostom spoke of "a power of persuasion that is keener and truly formidable, which you call rhetoric, a power that holds sway both in the forum and on the rostrum."[212] Hubbard astutely observes that in contrast to Cicero, Paul believed "it is not the words of the speaker that rush in, uprooting the old and implanting the new, but the words of the Spirit (2.5,12–14)." In contrast to Dio Chrysostom, Paul believed that uprooting the old and implanting the new does not come from the power of persuasion but from the power of the Spirit (2:4).[213]

Paul is therefore more interested in proclaiming the power of the cross that will summon faith than in turning a sparkling phrase that will rouse applause. He is not out to amuse or to induce faith with argument but to proclaim the death and resurrection of Christ that confronts his listeners with a life and death decision. He may grant their negative judgment about his eloquence, but their evaluation is based on presuppositions that he did not share. The reason he is not expert in rhetorical adornment is that such expertise inhibits rather than releases the power of the cross. He does not want to be the equal of his rival braggarts in speech. Their preaching is deceptive (11:3) and robs the cross of its power by making their brilliant eloquence the center of attention rather than what God has done in Christ. Paul "believes that unadorned speech is more appropriate for conveying the 'folly' of the cross, in the very weakness of which God's power is disclosed."[214]

Consequently, Paul is unfazed by his supposed failing in speech because his knowledge more than makes up for it. The kind of speech that characterized his rivals, in fact, was a sign of their foolishness and the absence of any knowledge of God. High flown speech comes from showmen who are swollen with pride and interested only in making a splash and grabbing the limelight and honor for themselves. From Paul's perspective such methods only serve to conceal their gaping ignorance of God. Knowledge of God refers to spiritual insight that shines from an intimate relationship to Christ crucified. In every way Paul manifests to everyone this knowledge of God that governs all that he does and says.[215] It compels him to adopt a certain manner of

---

[211] Cicero, *Orator* 97.

[212] Dio Chrysostom, *Orations* 33.1.

[213] M. Hubbard, "Was Paul Out of His Mind? Re-Reading 2 Corinthians 5.13," *JSNT* 70 (1998) 62.

[214] Furnish, *II Corinthians*, 505.

[215] The phrase ἐν παντί ("in everything") appears frequently in 2 Corinthians (4:8; 6:4; 7:5,16; 9:8,11; 11:6). The Corinthians themselves are a reflection of this knowledge since they are a letter of Christ that is known and read by all (3:2–3).

speech that carries far more spiritual power than the ornate oratorical flourishes of the jaunty phrasemongers who are so full of themselves. Paul is full of the Holy Spirit, and his humble speech accords with spiritual wisdom and power.[216] It was not without its effects. By it, he betrothed the Corinthians to Christ (11:2). The flashy rivals, on the other hand, lead them astray with clever eloquence in the same way that the serpent deceived Eve.

11:7–9 Paul continues the sardonic tone of responding to Corinthian fault finding with his ministry style by asking, "Was it a sin for me to lower myself in order to elevate you by preaching the gospel of God to you free of charge?"[217] He refers to his own code of preaching without cost to his hearers although he is entitled to receiving payment (1 Cor 9:4–18). To characterize this way of operating as "committing sin" (11:7) or as "robbing other churches" (11:8)[218] or as a sign of his lack of love for them (11:11) is rhetorical exaggeration.[219] He is not out to amass a fortune from his churches. His refusal to accept any subsidy from them is not intended to dishonor them in some way but to honor them and, we might add, Christ. It remains hard for the Corinthians to comprehend why he would voluntarily accept humiliation for their sake and how his humiliation leads to their exaltation. This failure to comprehend why he would do this reveals a failure to understand their apostle fully, but, more seriously, a failure to understand the gospel that exchanges self-exaltation for self-sacrifice in service to others. They also fail to understand the paradox that God's power becomes perfect in humiliation and weakness. Their basic problem is that they have allowed the values of their culture to shape their understanding of the faith and community practice, and they lack the knowledge of God that exposes those values as foolish.

---

[216] Every preacher knows the danger created by the rush of pride after a rousing sermon that listeners praise. The pride can infect them so that they begin to preach for this applause and even allow it to determine what and how they preach.

[217] Witherington takes "sin" to be "mistake," but this reading takes the bite out of Paul's sharp decrial (*Conflict and Community in Corinth*, 448). The aorist tense (ἁμαρτίαν ἐποίησα) looks back on his past conduct as a whole (constative use).

[218] The verb συλᾶν ("to rob") means "to plunder" as in war, "to pillage," and is used of military commanders who despoil those who have been conquered to continue their military campaign in other regions. Paul did accept money from others to support his work in new regions, but he does not regard it as pillaging them, but as granting them the grace of participating in a partnership to advance the gospel.

[219] D. L. Dungan contends that the Corinthians caught him in a deception. What he did was quite different from what he said he did in 1 Cor 9:15. He did accept money from the Macedonians. They throw this back into his face accusing him of inconsistency, deceitfulness, and jumbled thinking (*The Sayings of Jesus in the Churches of Paul* [Philadelphia: Fortress, 1971] 37–39). Marshall counters that the Corinthians would have been aware that he was receiving gifts from Philippi on his first visit. If they then offered him support on the Lord's command, it was because Paul informed them of that command (*Enmity in Corinth*, 253).

Paul did enjoy hospitality from the Corinthians (Rom 16:23), but his refusal to accept financial remuneration galled the Corinthians in many ways. Many have argued that Paul's refusal to accept support cast doubt on the legitimacy of his apostleship. Barrett, for example, states:

> The Corinthians, it seems, thought less of him because he refused to be a burden. Greek teachers in general would not work with their hands, and the Corinthians may well have thought of Paul as Antiphon did of Socrates: If you set any value on your society, you would insist on getting the proper price for that too. It may be that you are a just man because you do not cheat people through avarice *(pleonexia);* but wise you cannot be, since your knowledge is not worth anything (Xenophon, *Memorabilia* I vi. 12).[220]

The rivals accepted financial support from the Corinthians; and, so the hypothesis goes, they argued that because Paul made no claims for himself, he must have been an inferior apostle, if an apostle at all. As Martin frames the issue, they took Paul to task on this score by insinuating that "he did not claim his (rightful) due because he knew in his heart that he had no apostolic standing and so professed no entitlement to it."[221] Besides reading too much into the text, the problem with this view is that the Corinthians know that Paul *does* receive support from other churches, namely the Macedonians (11:9). The verb *propempein* ("to send on the way") is a technical term for providing goods (1 Cor 16:6; 2 Cor 1:16; see also Acts 15:3; Rom 15:24; Titus 3:13; 3 John 6), and Paul does accept provisions from the Corinthians to help him with his missionary journeys to other areas.[222] There is no link in this text between the amount of financial support and the legitimacy of apostleship, and we have argued that the validity of Paul's apostleship is not at stake anyway.[223] It is no less plausible

---

[220] Barrett, *The Second Epistle to the Corinthians*, 281–282. See also Barrett, "Opponents," 245–46; Betz, *Der Apostel Paulus*, 100–17; Georgi, *The Opponents of Paul in Second Corinthians*, 238–42; and Martin, *2 Corinthians*, 345, 438.

[221] Martin, *2 Corinthians*, 354.

[222] See A. J. Malherbe, *Social Aspects of Early Christianity*, 2d ed. (Philadelphia: Fortress, 1983) 96, n. 11.

[223] G. Theissen claims that the Corinthians were comparing Paul to itinerant, charismatic missionaries from Palestine (*The Social Setting of Pauline Christianity: Essays on Corinth* [Philadelphia: Fortress, 1982] 27–54). Jesus sent his disciples out on mission to Israel without money and charged them to accept hospitality from any who would offer it. They had to trust entirely upon God and the kindness of others. They followed Jesus' instructions (Mark 9:41) to the letter: living without possessions and accepting support and being able to devote themselves entirely to their preaching. Because Paul worked to earn money, one can imagine critics perhaps familiar with the Jesus tradition saying that Paul did not trust God. He relies on worldly means of supporting himself (see 2 Cor 10:2). We think it unlikely that the rivals came from Palestine. But more important, nowhere in the text is there any hint that the Corinthians are concerned that Paul does not conform to the teaching of Jesus. In fact, their knowledge of what Jesus taught on this matter came from Paul (1 Cor 9:14). The Corinthians also may not be comparing Paul negatively with others at all. On the contrary, the rivals seem to be vaunting themselves as equals to Paul (11:12).

that the competitors contended that Paul has other congregations to whom he is more closely attached because he accepts their support. They promise the Corinthians, "We will commit ourselves only to you out of our special love for you." All such hypotheses about what the rivals argued, however, go beyond the evidence in the text and should be treated skeptically.

Understanding the social expectations that guided relations in the Greco-Roman world is more fruitful for getting at the Corinthians' concerns. These social expectations exerted a strong influence on the Corinthians. The verb *tapeinoō,* "to lower oneself," expresses their concern (see 10:2; 1 Cor 4:11–12). They considered it demeaning for him to work, the very thing that enabled him to preach the gospel without charge (see 1 Thess 2:9).[224] Craftsmen were held in low regard by the leisured class in the ancient world.[225] Cicero remarked, "Also vulgar and unsuitable for gentlemen are the occupations of all hired workmen whom we pay for their labor, not for their artistic skills; for these men, their pay is itself a recompense for slavery. … All craftsmen, too are engaged in vulgar occupations, for a workshop or factory can have nothing genteel about it."[226] Lucian shares the negative estimate of workmen: A laborer is "personally inconspicuous getting meagre and illiberal returns, humble-witted, an insignificant figure in public, neither sought by your friends nor feared by your enemies nor envied by your fellow citizens—nothing but just a labourer, one of the swarming rabble, ever cringing to the man above … a man who has naught but his hands, a man who lives by his hands."[227] Hock cites four ways a philosopher could find support in the ancient world: (1) He could charge fees for his teaching. (2) He could enter into the household of a wealthy patron (teach-

---

[224] According to Acts 18:3, Paul worked in his tentmaker's trade. The elder Pliny writes that tentmakers made sailcloth awnings for temporary shelters, stalls, and shops in the forum area before permanent buildings were erected and to provide shade (*Natural History* 19.23–24). In seaports Paul could also have worked making and repairing sails. J. Murphy-O'Connor also suggests that as a leather worker Paul may have turned his hand at making thongs, gourds, harnesses, saddles, and shields (*St. Paul's Corinth: Text and Archaeology* [Wilmington, Del.: Michael Glazier, 1983] 168). Stansbury notes, "Although Paul's background made him socially on a par with those in the leisured classes, his sense of mission and method of support made him identify with those of relatively low social status" (*Corinthians Honor, Corinthian Conflict,* 469). Three inscriptions from Rome refer to the Tentmakers Association (*CIL* 6.5183b, 9053, 9053a).

[225] R. MacMullen, *Roman Social Relations 50* B.C. *to* A.D. *284* (New Haven/London: Yale University Press, 1974) 114–15.

[226] Cicero, *An Essay about Duties* 1.42; 2.225. He thought that working with one's hands was a dirty business that coarsened body, soul, and manners (*An Essay about Duties* 1.150). He called craftsmen "the dogs of the city" (*Against Flaccus* 18). Civilized existence, he thought, required leisure. Naturally, only those who belong to the propertied upper class with tenants and plenty of slaves to do all the work could hold this view. See further G. E. M. De Ste. Croix, *The Class Struggle in the Ancient Greek World* (Ithaca: Cornell University Press, 1981) 112–204.

[227] Lucian, *The Dream* 9.

ing the sons). (3) He could beg. (4) He could work. He concludes, "Among
the philosophers and itinerant teachers of Paul's day, continuing to work at a
craft was regarded as the least acceptable way of providing for life's necessities."[228] Working in some trade or hiring out to another would prevent one
from having the leisure to live a civilized life.

The contempt of the leisured class toward paid work was not universally
held. Otherwise, workers would not have proudly depicted their occupations
on their tombstones.[229] The problem for the Corinthians was the incongruous combination they saw in Paul—apostle of the glorious risen Lord and
toil weary laborer with dirt under his nails. As a common artisan hiring his
skill out to others, Paul lacked status and authority, power and prestige. His
situation was compounded because, "His labor was a bitter necessity, and
perhaps the earnings were not sufficient."[230] He was not financially
secure.[231] Paul says, "If I ran short I sponged on no one" (11:9, REB); but
this statement implies that he did run short and was in need (see Phil 4:12).
They would not have understood his voluntary acceptance of poverty as a
means by which spiritually he made many rich (6:10; cp. 8:9) but would
have considered it debasing and reflecting negatively on them. Affluence
was a sign of personal worth in the ancient world as it is today. Leaders
came from the ranks of those who were "financially sound and fit," never
from the "unfit and poor."[232] Savage concludes that "an impoverished leader
was a contradiction in terms."[233] This issue was particularly important in an
affluent city like Corinth, whose citizens took pride in its wealth and aspired
to upward mobility. "Here more than elsewhere, wealth was a prerequisite
for honour and poverty a badge of disgrace."[234] Since wealth was a sign of

---

[228] R. F. Hock, *The Social Context of Paul's Ministry: Tentmaking and Apostleship* (Philadelphia: Fortress, 1980) 54–59. Savage claims that the literary sources written by those belonging to
the upper crust belies the inscriptional evidence. Many tradesmen put their place of work on their
tombstone or had a relief made of themselves pictured at work. They obviously did not consider
their labor to be demeaning. Paul certainly did not consider work to be degrading since he exhorts
the Thessalonians to work with their hands (1 Thess 4:11). Savage concludes that Paul "follows a
long line of Jewish tradition by maintaining that while work can be exhausting it is never demeaning" (*Power through Weakness*, 85–86). See Gen 3:17–19; 5:29; Deut 11:10–15; 16:14–15; *Sir*
29:4; 31:22; *1 Macc* 10:15; 14:6–15; *m.* ʾAbot 1:10; *b.* Pesah. 118a; and *b. B. Qam.* 79b. The issue,
however, is not about the Corinthians' attitude toward work but toward teachers who work to support themselves rather than accept fees for their services. Since this issue is a point of contention
between Paul and the Corinthians, they must have regarded his labor as somehow undignified.

[229] MacMullen, *Roman Social Relations*, 120.

[230] Bultmann, *The Second Letter to the Corinthians*, 206.

[231] A. Burford writes, "Without a patron, the craftsman was literally and figuratively at a loss"
(*Craftsmen in Greek and Roman Society* [Ithaca: Cornell University Press, 1972] 124).

[232] POxy 3273, cited by Savage, *Power through Weakness*, 87; see also Pliny *Epistles* 1.14;
Juvenal, *Satires* 1.137–40.

[233] Savage, *Power through Weakness,* 87.

[234] Ibid., 88.

status, Paul's insistence on remaining poor would have rankled since it also would make them bear the shame of "being associated with an impoverished apostle." His poverty is not simply his private business; it reflects on them. Their attitude, however, reflects both the class tensions of the ancient world and their snobbery.[235] Many modern churches feel no differently in desiring their pastor to be somebody to whom they can point with pride—"That's our successful pastor."

To receive aid from the relatively poverty stricken Macedonians (8:2) and to turn it down from the relatively well off Corinthians also would have insulted them. They gladly would share what is theirs with him (12:13–14), but he refuses to accept. Marshall shows that in the ancient world, "The refusal of gifts and services was a refusal of friendship and dishonoured the donor."[236] They interpreted his refusal to accept their support as a sign that he did not love them (11:11) but desired instead to shame them.[237] He judged them less worthy than others, and they were therefore less favored (12:13) since they were excluded from the charmed circle of Paul's partners

---

[235] This wide gulf between rich and poor manifests itself in most cultures, and it is poignantly described in *Sir* 13:15–23:

Every creature loves its like,
    and every person the neighbor.
All living beings associate with their own kind,
    and people stick close to those like themselves.
What does a wolf have in common with a lamb?
    No more has a sinner with the devout.
What peace is there between a hyena and a dog?
    And what peace between the rich and the poor?
Wild asses in the wilderness are the prey of lions;
    likewise the poor are feeding grounds for the rich.
Humility is an abomination to the proud;
    likewise the poor are an abomination to the rich.

When the rich person totters, he is supported by friends,
    but when the humble falls, he is pushed away even by friends.
If the rich person slips, many come to the rescue;
    he speaks unseemly words, but they justify him.
If the humble person slips, they even criticize him;
    he talks sense, but is not given a hearing.
The rich person speaks and all are silent;
    they extol to the clouds what he says.
The poor person speaks and they say, "Who is this fellow?"
    And should he stumble, they even push him down.

[236] Marshall, *Enmity in Corinth*, 397. He shows how one's standing and influence in the Roman societal structure was effected by the number of clients one had and explains the protocol associated with the giving and receiving of benefactions. To refuse friendship based on benefaction "was an act of social enmity" (12–202; 242–247; see also Furnish, *II Corinthians*, 507–508).

[237] Marshall, *Enmity in Corinth*, 177.

in the gospel (see Phil 4:15).

Even in our culture, refusing to accept a gift from others can easily be construed as an insult. The narrow social conventions of Paul's time made his refusal to accept their gifts a major factor behind their hostility toward him. Their anger may have fed unjustified suspicions that Paul was using the collection as a sly means of getting support from them without having to acknowledge and thereby to incur any social obligations to them. It was "a subterfuge, a way of gaining support from the Corinthians without obligating himself to them as their client (see 12:16)."[238] Paul needs to set the record straight.

11:10–11 If it is a sin to preach the gospel free of charge, accepting no stipend (11:7), then it is one of which Paul is proud, and he will continue to boast about it. He explains that his practice is his boast (11:10) and that he does it because of his love for them (11:11).[239] His boast is that he proclaims the gospel free of charge (1 Cor 9:15–18), and their complaints will not cause him to modify his firm policy.[240] But we need to clarify what his policy was.

Paul asserts that he has the right to be supported (1 Cor 9:11–12) but has refused to exercise that right (2 Cor 11:9; 12:14). He did, however, accept travel expenses to go to the next place of mission (1 Cor 16:6; 2 Cor 1:16). He also accepted support when he was absent from a church to "advance the message of the gospel in other regions" (Phil 1:5).[241] According to Philippians 4:15, he received money from them "*after he went out* from Macedonia." The letter to the Philippians is occasioned by their sending him support again while he is in prison. What is important to note is that Paul accepted support that *was sent*. He apparently did not consider this form of support to be a "burden" (11:9; 12:13).

The term "burden" should be understood in terms of its social connotations and does not simply mean that he did not want to be a bother to them. It cannot simply refer to a financial burden, since the Macedonians were far less able financially to assist him. It has to do with the social obligations that accepting gifts entailed. Accepting support from the Macedonians after he

---

[238] Ibid., 508.

[239] In proclaiming his love for them he uses an oath formula. Other oath formulas appear in 1:18,23; 11:31; and 12:19. He swears that he loves them, that his actions were motivated by love and intended to spare them (1:23), and that he is writing to build them up rather than defend himself (12:19).

[240] His boast must be assumed to be a boast in the Lord (10:17) and is "directly related to Paul's missionary work in Corinth and is thus within the 'limits' assigned to him by God (10:13–16)" (Holland, "Speaking Like a Fool: Irony in 2 Corinthians 10–13," 255). His insistence that "he will continue" in this policy (11:9) points to his future visit. Things will not change when he comes.

[241] G. W. Peterman, *Paul's Gift from Philippi: Conventions of Gift Exchange and Christian Giving,* SNTSMS 92 (Cambridge: University Press, 1997) 166.

had left them was a quite different arrangement. He understands it to be a "partnership" in advancing the gospel. He did not regard this assistance as compensation for his preaching; it was help for furthering the gospel and founding new churches (partnership in the gospel).[242] They become equals in his mission enterprise. Peterman shows that Paul's response to the Philippians' gift in 4:10–20 corrects any possible misinterpretation of its meaning in light of normal Greco-Roman social expectations regarding giving and receiving. In this passage Paul makes clear to them that he

> has not become socially obligated, and thereby in a sense inferior, by accepting their gifts. Rather, because he has accepted their gifts, they have been elevated to the place of partners in the gospel. Though Paul is in receipt of their gift and can mention his own benefit from it (4:18a), in 4:17b he rather makes it appear that they are actually the ones benefited. Their gift does bring them a return. It is an investment that reaps spiritual dividends. But ultimately the responsibility to reward them rests not with Paul, but with God (4:19).[243]

The key idea for understanding Paul's policy about not accepting support from a church while present with them is his reference to "burden" (11:9; 12:13,16). The Corinthians were the ones who initiated the question of support, and there is no indication that they are financially strapped and that Paul wishes to spare them extra expense. He does not worry that the Macedonians, who are poverty stricken (8:2), chipped in to help supply his needs while he was in Corinth (11:9; see also Phil 4:16). He also does not worry about what it would cost them when he solicits travel expenses from them to go on to new territory (1 Cor 16:6; 2 Cor 1:16). Some members of the congregation apparently were wealthy and somewhat powerful.[244] Giving to Paul would not create a financial hardship for them. If Paul is not referring to a financial burden, what is his concern?

Seneca uses the Latin equivalent, *onus* ("burden") to refer to financial and social dependence.[245] Peterman shows that the word "to burden" *(barynein)* was used for the social obligations or responsibilities which are incurred by giving and receiving (see POxy 3057). He argues that Paul's language makes "a veiled reference to his desire to avoid social dependence." Paul has not pressured anyone for money and steadfastly refuses to become indebted to the Corinthians (or anyone else, for that matter), who would then become his patrons. He wants to be free from any confining social con-

---

[242] See V. D. Verbrugge, *Paul's Style of Church Leadership Illustrated by His Instructions to the Corinthians on the Collection* (San Francisco: Mellen Research University Press, 1992) 119.

[243] Peterman, *Paul's Gift*, 159.

[244] See D. Sänger, "Die dynatou in 1 Kor 1:26," *ZNW* 76 (1985) 285–91.

[245] Cited by Peterman, *Paul's Gift*, 169.

straints attached to patronage.[246]

Accepting gifts in the ancient world placed one under a social obligation to show gratitude.[247] A social quid pro quo dictated relationships. Anyone who received a gift or benefit was obligated to respond in kind.[248] Gifts and favors therefore could not be taken for granted but placed serious obligations upon the recipient that could not be discharged by a brief thank-you note. Receiving a gift consequently put one under considerable social and financial pressure.[249] When there was disparity in the giving, the one who outgave the other gained status as the superior while the other dropped in social standing. If one could not reciprocate in kind, one was expected at least to return the favor by bestowing honor and praise, and/or offering verbal thanks. Verbally expressing thanks for a gift was not done between equals, however, and would have been regarded as a solicitation for more assistance.[250] Gratitude to a superior was most frequently expressed by acknowledging the affection and goodwill received and professing a sense of debt. Many benefactors sought to exalt themselves over the recipients and gave to others only to display their nobility and to have it heralded publicly. Seneca says that the gifts that most please are those in which the bestower does not exalt his superiority in giving the gift (*On Benefits* 2.13.2). But those kinds of gifts were few and far between. Saller writes, "The most basic premise from which the Romans started was that honour and prestige derived from the power to give to others what they needed or wanted."[251] That is the reason people gave, not because they thought that compassion for

---

[246] Ibid. Plautus captures how patrons could exercise control over another by giving "him all he wants to eat and drink every day, and he will never try to run away. ... The bonds of food and drink are very elastic, you know; the more you stretch them, the tighter they hold you" (*Twin Menaechmi*, Act 1, Scene 1, lines 90–95).

[247] Ibid, 177. The relevant texts from Seneca have been conveniently collected by Peterman (*Paul's Gift*, 201–4). Seneca states, "The giving of a benefit is a social act, it wins the good will of someone, it lays someone under obligation" (*On Benefits* 5.11.5). "The ungrateful man tortures or torments himself; he hates the gifts which he has accepted, because he must make a return for them, and he tries to belittle their value" (*Epistles* 81:23).

[248] S. C. Mott notes that the rules of reciprocity set up a chain of obligations. The one benefitting from a gift had to reciprocate, and this mutual giving could appear to be some kind of contest to see who could give more ("The Power of Giving and Receiving: Reciprocity in Hellenistic Benevolence," in *Current Issues in Biblical and Patristic Interpretation*, ed. G. F. Hawthorne [Grand Rapids: Eerdmans, 1975] 60–61).

[249] As Seneca expressed it: "A man is an ingrate if he repays a favor without interest" (*Moral Epistles* 81:18).

[250] See Seneca, *On Benefits* 3.5.2.

[251] R. P. Saller, *Personal Patronage under the Early Empire* (Cambridge: University Press, 1982) 126. In the Roman societal structure "the extent of one's philanthropies and the number of one's clients were important measure of a person's social standing and influence." See also MacMullen, *Roman Social Relations*, 88–120.

those in need was a virtue that God would reward, but because honor would accrue to them.

As someone who was impoverished, Paul could not show gratitude to the Corinthians with counter gifts.[252] Given the elaborate social protocol regarding how gratitude was to be expressed, if Paul accepted the Corinthians' gifts, he could only return the favor by heaping honor and praise upon them. In the process he would clearly become their social inferior — something he was not prepared to do. He cannot be free to preach the gospel with boldness if he is having to run around kissing men's hands, sending them gifts, groveling before them, and slavishly flattering them. He is a slave of Christ, not a slave of fashion or of his sponsors. He understands himself as bound to all (12:14–15) and a slave to all (4:5; see 1 Cor 9:19), not just to the wealthy movers and shakers in the church who treat their impoverished brethren with contempt (1 Cor 11:17–22).[253] Consequently, "Paul tried to distance himself from a burdensome web of social obligations that would hinder his apostleship, smack of favoritism, and introduce among his communities volatile strife over honor and ambitious claims to authority."[254] If he were financially dependent upon them, it would mean that he was socially inferior to them and would also have a variety of obligations to them. He would be less independent and less free to teach what needed to be taught, to admonish those who needed it, and to do what God led him to do.[255] In a church riven by disputes, if he accepted gifts from one party, he would be socially obligated to become their advocate. He would no longer be viewed as an impartial arbiter.

We can also add other reasons why Paul refused to accept money from churches in which he was currently preaching the gospel. For Paul, the overwhelming sense of God's gracious offer of forgiveness, salvation and a sacred commission made it impossible for him ever to receive wages. He professed himself to be Christ's slave, not his hired hand. He understood that God did not use the free enterprise system in offering the salvation to the world: You can have the gospel if you pay for it. In our world everything and everyone seems to have a price. The gospel, however, is price-less. No monetary value can be attached to it. Therefore it is free. Fee observes, "In

---

[252] This is why Paul tells the Thessalonians to work with their hands "so that you will not be dependent on anybody" (1 Thess 4:11–12).

[253] See B. Winter, "The Lord's Supper at Corinth: An Alternate Reconstruction," *RTR* 37 (1978) 73–82.

[254] Stansbury, *Corinthians Honor, Corinthian Conflict*, 19. Like Socrates, Paul did not want to place himself in a position of obligation in which he is given gifts that he could not reciprocate in kind. It was akin to voluntary servitude and a cause for shame (Seneca *On Benefits* 5.6.2–7; cited by Marshall, *Enmity in Corinth*, 16).

[255] See Lucian *On Salaried Posts in Great Houses* on the restrictions of being financially dependent on the one who employs you to teach them.

offering the 'free' gospel 'free of charge' his own ministry becomes a living paradigm of the gospel itself."[256] As Christ became poor that others might become rich (8:9), so Paul depicts himself as "poor, yet enriching many" (6:10).

If Paul's refusal of support denies his converts "an opportunity to glory in their own munificence, it also forces them to identify with the poverty of their apostle and hence to feel inferior to churches whose apostles are better maintained."[257] It was therefore an act of love in an attempt to exalt them (11:7; 12:15).[258] They need to learn humility. If they can bask in the glory of being the patrons of an apostle, they will see themselves as the benefactors and will not comprehend the divine grace that comes to the weak, low, and despised in the world so that no one might boast in the presence of God (1 Cor 1:26–31).[259]

Paul also would have wanted to divorce himself from the variety of hucksters roaming the world with their hands always extended in hopes of getting donations (see Acts 20:33–35; 1 Thess 2:3–6; and contrast Acts 16:16,19). They taught for profit, and he castigates them as peddlers who hawk their wares and water down their goods to enhance profits (2:17; 4:2). Paul's overriding concern in all that he did was whether it helped or hindered the gospel's advance (1 Cor 9:12). Paul did whatever he thought might serve the missionary enterprise, and he refuses to accept support because he believed it would hinder the reception of the gospel.

11:12 Paul offers another motive for refusing their financial support. He wants to cut the ground out from under his opponents, who claim to be his equals.[260] He has only hinted that they are boasters in 10:13,15, and now he says so explicitly. "They boast that they are just like me." The opponents have set out to gain the support of the Corinthians at the expense of Paul. They wanted the Corinthians to withdraw their affection for Paul and exclude him from any support, which was how the nasty game of politics worked in this era. "Show your support for me by joining me against my enemies or rivals."

---

[256] G. D. Fee, *The First Epistle to the Corinthians*, NICNT (Grand Rapids: Eerdmans, 1987) 421.

[257] Savage, *Power through Weakness*, 92.

[258] Paul expresses his love for the Corinthians in 2:4; 8:7; and 12:15. We should note that it was Paul's decision, *not* the church's, to keep himself humble in order to humble them. But humbling them was entirely motivated by his desire to build them up in the faith—to teach them something about the nature of the gospel.

[259] The reference to the "friends from Macedonia" and to "regions of Achaia" serves to remind him that he is not simply the apostle to the Corinthians. His calling is to the Gentiles throughout the world.

[260] Literally the text reads "in order that I cut off the opportunity of those who want an opportunity that they be found just as we are in what they boast about."

The rivals have tried to hoist themselves to the same apostolic status as Paul. Paul undercuts their boast by serving the church without accepting their money. If they want to attain Paul's status, then they need to adopt his position on boasting. If they want to operate on his level of ministry, let them abandon their self-serving ways and take the humble role of a slave (4:5). Unless they adopt his practice of preaching for nothing, they cannot class themselves with him.[261] Barrett concludes, "The real point is that the requirement of self-sacrifice … marks out the true apostle from the false."[262] Would they be willing to give up financial support and humble themselves with work to further the gospel? Paul thinks it unlikely. Their conceited boasting and self-centered ministry style expose them as false apostles. They are not benefactors of the community as Paul is (12:15) but crawling parasites who expect payment for their services. They are not apostles living out their calling in service to others but self-absorbed careerists serving their own private ends.

11:13   Paul has driven home the point in this letter that appearances can be deceptive (4:18; 5:12), and this is particularly true when unscrupulous persons don a religious guise to further their selfish ambitions. The rivals' claim to apostleship has been so convincing that the Corinthians have been tricked. In 11:13–15 Paul launches a frontal assault on his rivals. These superapostles are in reality pseudo-apostles, perhaps a word coined by Paul (see "false brothers" 11:26; Gal 2:4). He cannot compare himself with these so-called luminaries because there is no comparison between a true apostle and a false apostle.

They are deceitful (crafty, crooked) workers (see 2:17; 4:2). "Workers" may be a term for missionaries (see Matt 9:37 / Luke 10:2,7; 1 Tim 5:18; 2 Tim 2:15; *Did* 13:2). These are not unbelievers who maliciously plot to infiltrate the church as undercover agents. They "are professing Christians, whom he roundly accuses of doing the Devil's work."[263] They may deceive themselves and others that they are doing God's work, but their narcissism and superior air reveals that they serve someone other than God. They only masquerade as apostles in the same way that Satan masquerades as an angel of light.

---

[261] This is a more straightforward explanation of what Paul means, and it is to be preferred over Machiavellian reconstructions of the rival's intentions, such as that they were trying "to induce him to claim his right to material support" to prove his apostolic legitimacy and they would then have stolen his advantage over them (so, e.g., N. Watson, *The Second Epistle to the Corinthians*, Epworth Commentaries [London: Epworth, 1993] 121). What the Corinthians question is Paul's humble demeanor and weakness, not whether he is a legitimate apostle.

[262] Barrett, *The Second Epistle to the Corinthians*, 284–85.

[263] R. H. Strachan, *The Second Epistle of Paul to the Corinthians*, MNTC (London: Hodder & Stoughton, 1935) 24–25.

11:14   Paul has referred to Satan's nefarious designs in 2:11 and 4:4. He now ties his opponents to the serpent who deceived Eve (11:3). Satan can pose as an angel of light. It should not be surprising then if satanic evil infiltrates a church and deludes it. The argument runs, if Satan disguises himself with the raiment of righteousness, then so will his minions. The rivals are no different from the master they serve.

Paul's uses a Hebraic idiom, "an angel of light," to refer to Satan as a shining angel.[264] The story in Genesis 3, however, does not explicitly mention Satan as an angel of light. Paul may allude to popular Jewish tradition. In the *Apocalypse of Moses,* Eve recalls her seduction: "Satan appeared in the form of an angel and sang hymns like the angels. And I bent over the wall and saw him, like an angel" (17:1–2).[265] What is important for Paul is that the shining stars dazzle and make the ones working in the trenches, like Paul, look frumpish and unspiritual by comparison. But Satan is more likely to take the guise of a shining star with glamorous appeal than a foot soldier. Satan is seductive, insidious.

The greatest weapon the devil has in his arsenal to test us is praise and flattery. The serpent offers the promise of special knowledge that will allow Adam and Eve to become like God. The Corinthians, who want to become rich and reign as kings (1 Cor 4:8), are particularly susceptible to a false gospel dispensed by jaunty, diamond-studded apostles that appeals to their innate human pride and desire to be special. Swollen with pride themselves, these rivals gull the Corinthians by stroking their vanity. C. à Lapide cites this account about the hermit Abraham:

> While he was singing psalms at midnight, a light like that of the sun suddenly shone in his cell and a voice was heard saying: "Blessed art thou, Abraham: none is like thee in fulfilling all my will." But the humility of the Saint recognized the fraud of the devil, and exclaimed: "Thy darkness perish with thee, thou full of all fraud and falsehood; for I am a sinful man; but the name of my Lord, Jesus Christ, whom I have loved and do love, is a wall to me, and in it I

---

[264] The danger of the recent upsurge of interest in angels is that Satan can take the guise of a bright, happy angel; but Satan never deigns to take the role of one who was crucified in weakness and sacrificial love.

[265] In the *Life of Adam and Eve* 9:1, Satan transforms himself into the brightness of angels (see also 12:7, an angel of Satan) and deceived Eve again. In the retelling of the story of Job in *T. Job* 6:4, Satan appears as a beggar, a bread seller, the king of the Persians, and speaks through Elihu, one of Job's friends. In *1 Enoch* 19:1, Enoch is shown the spirits of the angels who "in many different appearances" have united themselves with women. "They have defiled the people and will lead them into error so that they will offer sacrifice to the demons as unto gods." This may explain Paul's warning in Gal 1:8 that if even an "angel from heaven" came preaching a different gospel they should not be fooled. Shining angelic figures are not always harmless and should not always be trusted.

rebuke thee, thou unclean dog." And then the devil vanished from his sight as smoke.[266]

Paul, with his frank criticism of their sins and uncompromising stand against any partnership with idolatry, is less appealing as an apostle when compared with those who flatter them. But false flatterers are of the devil.

11:15   Paul next accuses these rivals of disguising themselves as "ministers of righteousness." In 3:9 he describes his own ministry as a "ministry of righteousness" (NIV, "the ministry that brings righteousness"). His gospel proclaims that God made Christ "who had no sin to be sin for us, so that in him we might become the righteousness of God" (5:21). The rivals pose as participants in this same ministry that leads to righteousness and is undergirded by the Spirit.[267] They are frauds. Paul does not pinpoint the particulars of their false theology but focuses more on their boasting beyond measure. It is their demeanor and behavior that reveal them to be ministers of Satan rather than of righteousness. "Ministers of righteousness" are those who live righteously, not those who purport to be righteous or to preach a righteous message.[268] "Ministers of righteousness" remove the veil of hardheartedness and by the Spirit lead God's new covenant people to be transformed into the image of Christ—to be Christlike (3:12–17). They renounce shameful things and deceitful practices (4:2). They also repudiate all fleshly boasting and boast only in the Lord.

These persons are therefore not simply deceitful rivals of Paul. As servants of Satan, they are rivals of God (cp. Acts 13:10). "To follow them is to risk damnation."[269] Such language may sound harsh, but Paul judges the situation to be perilous, calling for sharp warnings to jar the Corinthians awake. God will judge them according to their works (5:10) and not according to appearances that so easily fool humans. When God puts his refining fire to their work, it will burn up in a puff of smoke (1 Cor 3:12–15).

Paul next deals with the difficult issue of how they might discern the appearance of false righteousness from true righteousness, the false apostle from the true. Any minister who passes darkness off as light, lies as truth, or

---

[266] C. à Lapide, *The Great Commentary of Cornelius à Lapide: II Corinthians and Galatians*, trans. and ed. W. F. Cobb (London: John Hodges, 1897) 163.

[267] Paul does not say that they are really ministers of the dispensation of condemnation that leads to death. There is no hint in this text that they are sham apostles because they are still wedded to the law and seek to make Gentiles obedient to its ritual requirements to become acceptable to God.

[268] It is stretching matters to argue from the term "ministers of righteousness" that they represent a ministry associated with righteousness derived from the observance of the law, as Barnett does (*The Second Epistle to the Corinthians*, 527). The genitive is descriptive (qualitative, Hebraic). They claim to be righteous ministers.

[269] DiCicco, *Paul's Use of Ethos, Pathos, and Logos in 2 Corinthians 10–13*, 172.

sin as an alternative lifestyle choice must reckon with God's judgment. He argues that these nameless rivals are aligned with the forces of evil, are thoroughly evil themselves, and therefore should be expelled from the community. Their end will be destruction (see Rom 3:8; Phil 3:19), and the same will hold true for any who fall sway to them.

11:16–19   Paul returns to the thought of foolish boasting expressed in 11:1 as he prepares them again for his fool's speech. He does not want them to be fooled by his fool's disguise and mistake it for true apostolic speech. This boasting is all a fool's jest, so repeats his second justification for his own boasting (see 11:4–6). The Corinthians have put up with the foolish boasting of his rivals without demurring. They can probably endure a little boasting from their own apostle. "Many have boasted the way the world does" ("according to the flesh"), that is, their boasting accords with the world's corrupt standards (11:18). If that is what it takes to get the Corinthians to listen, then that is what Paul will do. He joins in the game reluctantly, however, because he has been driven to it (12:11). But he makes clear in 11:17 that this is not the stuff of apostolic discourse. It is that of a "worldly man" trying to outshine his rivals, "itself a 'foolish' ambition."[270] He is not normally self-congratulatory, does not normally act according to worldly standards (10:2), and does not normally evaluate himself or others according to these standards (5:16). But he adopts his rivals' ways to show how ultimately foolish they are. Wanting to be better than others in terms of status is foolish; wanting to show oneself better than others is even more foolish. Best comments:

> Most of those who boast do not realize they are doing it. It is a sign of grace on Paul's part that he did realize and that he saw its foolishness. Since a comparison with others is inherent in boating, it may involve belittling them. Since it is never far way from exaggeration, there is the continual danger of untruth.[271]

Paul speaks as a fool because it will allow him to boast about himself, which is foolish, and not something that the Lord would approve. It is not boasting in the Lord (10:17) and not boastworthy. By explicitly saying that this is what he is doing, he undermines the boasting of his rivals. It shows it to be foolish and contrary to what the Lord would have them do.[272] They are fools who engage in worldly discourse that has nothing to do with "speaking according to the Lord."[273]

---

[270] Holland, "Speaking Like a Fool: Irony in 2 Corinthians 10–13," 256.

[271] Best, *Second Corinthians*, 123.

[272] Best points out that Paul shows exceptional sensitivity to transgressing the Lord's authority (*Second Corinthians*, 111).

[273] The phrase ἐν ταύτῃ τῇ ὑποστάσει τῆς καυχήσεως is difficult and is rendered by the NIV, "in this self-confident boasting." The noun ὑπόστασις could have the same meaning as in 9:4 and refer to the matter, project, or undertaking of boasting. Furnish translates it "when it comes to this business of boasting," which seems a better option (Furnish, *II Corinthians,* 496).

The phrase *kata sarka* ("in the way the world does") in 11:18 may refer to the object of the boasting, their Jewish heritage. But it more likely refers to the attitude behind the boasting—a brash confidence.[274] It is this brash self-confidence that has captivated the Corinthians (11:20) because it was culturally accepted and something they engaged in themselves (see 1 Cor 1:12; 3:21; 4:6–7). The Corinthians have no trouble with those who glory in themselves because that is exactly what they expect them to do. By contrast, they have been put off by Paul's abject humility.

If they will not put up with him when he is wise and speaks according to the Lord, then, Paul gibes, perhaps they will put up with him when he acts the fool and boasts in the same manner as the rivals they so esteem. He ironically appeals to their extraordinary tolerance of fools, "You gladly put up with fools since you are so wise!" (11:19). This statement is similar to 1 Cor 4:10, "We are fools for Christ, but you are so wise in Christ!" Things have not changed much in Corinth since Paul wrote those words. But neither has God's response to the wisdom of the world. God will destroy the wisdom of the wise and make the wisdom of the world look foolish (1 Cor 1:19–20). In this section Paul destroys the so-called wisdom of the wise by embracing it himself and in the process showing it to be the folly of the fool.[275]

Even when he descends to the level of his rivals in boasting, he transcends them. Paul will boast about the visible things. What is visible, however, points to his weaknesses—part of the problem as far as the Corinthians were concerned. His boasting in his weakness allows him to expound on God's grace.

11:20 Paul's razor-edged comments grow even sharper as he lists the offenses the Corinthians have suffered. His expression of mock pity for them before listing his own real hardships is particularly ironic.[276] They appear to welcome those who enslave them and lead them around by the nose.[277] These rivals understand power as something one has when others become compliant slaves. It is the power of coercion, not the power of the cross.

The Corinthians, however, seem to welcome being exploited. The verb translated "exploit" *(katesthiei)* means "devour," and Barrett translates it, "If anyone eats you out of house and home."[278] It refers to the rivals' avarice

---

[274] Savage, *Power through Weakness*, 57.

[275] Savage comments, "The opponents are opportunists who are exploiting the self-exalting tastes of the Corinthians to win places of honour and esteem for themselves within the church." (*Power through Weakness*, 158).

[276] DiCicco, *Paul's Use of Ethos, Pathos, and Logos in 2 Corinthians 10–13*, 186.

[277] There is no reason to read this statement as a reference to Judaizers from the parallel in Gal 2:4. If Paul were thinking in terms of their being enslaved to the law, he would have said so. He is thinking here about the rivals making them their slaves (see 2 Cor 1:24; 4:5).

[278] Barrett, *The Second Epistle to the Corinthians*, 291. The verb is used for the scribes' devouring the resources of widows (Mark 12:40).

and suggests that it is they, not Paul, who plunders churches. To gather the fruit, they chop down the tree. They eat up the community's resources and will earn God's judgment who says, "Will evildoers never learn— / those who devour my people as men eat bread" (Ps 14:4).

The church has been taken in. Paul uses the same verb *(lambanō)* in 12:16, where he says, "Yet, crafty fellow that I am, I caught you by trickery!" The image is one of baiting a trap and catching the unsuspecting. This is what Satan does by guile. The difference is that the rivals took them in and took their money. Paul took them in, they think, but he refused to take their money and refused to take advantage of them in any way.

The rivals also "pushed themselves forward" which means that they put on airs and lifted themselves up. The Corinthians apparently preferred this approach to that of Paul who humbled himself so that they might be exalted. The Corinthians also seemed to endure, if not welcome, being slapped in the face. This may be a reference to actual physical violence or a metaphor for verbal insults and general browbeating. The rivals may well be so puffed up with themselves that they actually cuff anyone who crosses them (see the use of the verb *derō* in 1 Cor 9:26). This is how superiors in the ancient world often treated inferiors. Their behavior toward the Corinthians is the conclusive evidence that their gospel is false.

Paul paints a picture of rivals who are aggressive, acquisitive, and authoritarian. They also attack others to build up their own authority.[279] He has never acted this way, and some Corinthians apparently are proud of their new, more forceful authorities. The meekness and gentleness of Christ (10:1), which characterizes his demeanor toward them, are interpreted as a sign of weakness. The Corinthians would not be the first to prefer tyrants to more gentle leaders. The Israelites rejected Samuel for a self-willed and despotic king (1 Sam 8).[280]

11:21a With biting irony Paul confesses, "I am ashamed to say we did not do that." He owns up to his weakness (see 10:10). They are absolutely right. He has utterly failed in this regard. But the dishonor is really theirs, not his, as far as God is concerned. His confession becomes a painful rebuke. As far as the world's values are concerned, he lives in dishonor; but according to God, he has honor (6:8). If being "strong" means doing what his rivals have done, then he is unquestionably weak. Yet it is a weakness that God approves. God never condones the tyranny, pomposity, and mean-

---

[279] Barrett comments: "Human strength is known by its fruit: the acquisition of dignity and influence by those who possess and use it. Divine power also is known by its fruit: the conversion of men and their building up into the new Christian society" (*The Second Epistle to the Corinthians*, 292). The rivals have excelled in the first, acquiring acclaim and power; they have failed when it comes to the second, reaching out into unplowed fields to make converts to Christ and building up communities of faith. That is why Paul judges them to be false apostles.

[280] Noted by Winter, *Paul and Philo among the Sophists*, 230.

ness that church despots have inflicted on the church across the ages.[281]

Paul will show that his weakness allows God's power to work more powerfully in him (1 Cor 2:3; 2 Cor 12:9; 13:4). Who is of Christ? The boastful autocrat who ascends the throne of his own pride, coercing others to bow to his will and running roughshod over any opposition? Or the gentle and mild servant whose only badge of rule is his consideration of others and devotion to their spiritual welfare? Paul's answer can be found in Phil 2:6–8; Rom 15:3; and 2 Cor 8:9. He gladly shares the shame with Christ of unselfish service for others.

4. Foolish Boasting (11:21b–33)

What anyone else dares to boast about—I am speaking as a fool—I also dare to boast about. [22]Are they Hebrews? So am I. Are they Israelites? So am I. Are they Abraham's descendants? So am I. [23]Are they servants of Christ? (I am out of my mind to talk like this.) I am more. I have worked much harder, been in prison more frequently, been flogged more severely, and been exposed to death again and again. [24]Five times I received from the Jews the forty lashes minus one. [25]Three times I was beaten with rods, once I was stoned, three times I was shipwrecked, I spent a night and a day in the open sea, [26]I have been constantly on the move. I have been in danger from rivers, in danger from bandits, in danger from my own countrymen, in danger from Gentiles; in danger in the city, in danger in the country, in danger at sea; and in danger from false brothers. [27]I have labored and toiled and have often gone without sleep; I have known hunger and thirst and have often gone without food; I have been cold and naked. [28]Besides everything else, I face daily the pressure of my concern for all the churches. [29]Who is weak, and I do not feel weak? Who is led into sin, and I do not inwardly burn?

[30]If I must boast, I will boast of the things that show my weakness. [31]The God and Father of the Lord Jesus, who is to be praised forever, knows that I am not lying. [32]In Damascus the governor under King Aretas had the city of the Damascenes guarded in order to arrest me. [33]But I was lowered in a basket from a window in the wall and slipped through his hands.

Paul now is ready to launch into his own boasting to counteract the extravagant claims of the rivals. We may infer from Paul's speech that his rivals took pride in their Jewish heritage, vaunted their various accomplishments that ennobled their ministry for Christ, and trumpeted their wondrous visions and revelations. Paul also is a Hebrew (11:22), endured innumerable hardships in his ministry (11:23–29), and had extraordinary visionary experiences (12:1–4). The question, however, is whether Paul provides a spoof on the boasts of his counterparts, a straightforward list of his accomplishments, or a mixture of the two.

Forbes argues that Paul's fool's speech is "a ruthless parody of the preten-

---

[281] In Jeremiah the Lord says that the people's pride will cause him to "weep in secret ... my eyes will weep bitterly, overflowing with tears" because it will result in their captivity (Jer 13:17). Paul has anxiety for this church because its pride will lead to captivity to Satan.

sions of his opponents."[282] Furnish concurs; Paul is not really trying to match or outmatch his opponent's boasts but to caricature their claims:

> Over against the pretentious boasts of those who claim for themselves special apostolic powers and religious insights, Paul offers a long list of sufferings (11:23b–29) and the curious account of a journey to heaven which yielded no useful religious knowledge (12:1–4). This, as the apostle explicitly says in 11:30–33 and 12:5–10, is a boasting of weakness.[283]

Paul begins his speech, however, with a straightforward statement about his pedigree. They claim to be Hebrews, Israelites, descendants of Abraham; he is too! We might find it surprising that instead of next listing his achievements he lists his sufferings. This is the third list of hardships in the letter, and the first two in 4:8–10 and 6:4–10 were not parodies. Fitzgerald has shown that overcoming hardships made one noble and deserving of respect.[284] Epictetus, for example, contended that response to adversity was proof of one's rigorous training in philosophy.[285] The opponents not only boasted of their Jewish pedigree, they may also have boasted about their labors and the hardships that they successfully endured.[286] Paul does not say that he has suffered and his rivals have not (contrast Gal 6:12) but that he has suffered more than they have. To be sure, he differs in how he interprets what these sufferings mean.[287] But the comparatives in 11:23, "with far greater labors, far more imprisonments," do not sound as if he is engaged in parody.[288]

Holland interprets the register of travails to mean that "Paul demonstrates his superior status by means already chosen by his opponents: suffering for the sake

---

[282] Forbes, "Comparison, Self-Praise and Irony," 18; so also Judge, "Paul's Boasting" 47; Barnett, *The Second Epistle to the Corinthians*, 534.

[283] Furnish, *II Corinthians*, 533.

[284] J. T. Fitzgerald, *Cracks in an Earthen Vessel: An Examination of the Catalogue of Hardships in the Corinthian Correspondence*, SBLDS 99 (Atlanta: Scholars Press, 1988) 47–116.

[285] Epictetus, *Discourses* 3.10.8, 10–11. Seneca writes, "God hardens, reviews, and disciplines those whom he approves, whom he loves" (*On Providence* 4.7).

[286] Fitzgerald claims that the opponents also listed their hardships to prove themselves ministers of Christ since hardship catalogues were used to give evidence of the truth of the philosopher's philosophy and his status as a sage (*Cracks in an Earthen Vessel*, 44–51, 85–86). O. Wischmeyer also argues that the opponents boasted of their sufferings and struggles (*Der höchste Weg*, SNT 13 [Gütersloh: Mohn, 1981] 85–86). Against this view, see Wolff, *Die zweite Korintherbrief*, 232.

[287] Fitzgerald, *Cracks in an Earthen Vessel*, 25, n. 95.

[288] Many commentators think it remarkable that Paul does not start by listing his crowning successes in ministry but catalogs his hardships and sufferings instead, which are assumed to be handicaps. Recounting only his good fortune and success, however, would be more likely to elicit envy than sympathy. He shows that he lives out his calling through hard labor and suffering. Plummer's concludes that Paul is not comparing himself with his opponents. Instead, he means that he suffers "more abundantly than most men" (*The Second Epistle of St. Paul to the Corinthians*, 322). But Paul does not say this.

of the gospel."[289] It is not improbable that they have prated on about their suffering as heroic ordeals. Paul counters that he has suffered courageously too from even greater ordeals.[290] He can outboast them because he has outdone them. This is exactly how John Chrysostom read the text:

> These things are the part of an apostolic soul, to suffer so great things, and yet in nothing to veer about, but to bear nobly whatever befalls. ... And just as a spark of unquenchable fire, if it fell into the sea, would be merged as many waves swept over it, yet would again rise shining to the surface; even so surely the blessed Paul also would now be overwhelmed by perils, and now and again, having dived through them, would come up more radiant, overcoming by suffering evil.[291]

Paul appeals to indisputable facts. But because boasting about such things has nothing to do with his ministry in Corinth and only serves to show his superiority in comparison to others, it is boasting according to the flesh and therefore foolish speech. It leads to a triumphalistic interpretation (represented, for example, by John Chrysostom) that glorifies Paul's personal courage. These boasts do make the point, however, that Paul's endurance of hardships reveals that he is no weakling.[292] The conclusion Paul must want the Corinthians to draw from this recital of hardships is that he "is filled with endurance, courage and fortitude in the midst of tribulations, of all kinds of difficulties, labour and persecution."[293]

Paul therefore begins his foolish boasting with his strengths, matching and surpassing his rivals point by point. Only then does he switch to his weaknesses in 11:29. The strengths prove that he is equal to the superlative apostles.[294] The weaknesses, however, prove "the power of God evident in his ministry" (see 4:7; 12:9). The ironic references to weakness enclose the boasts about his lineage and hardships: "I am too weak" (11:21); "Who is weak?" (11:29).

11:21b   Paul stirs himself from the weakness that some Corinthians suppose afflicts him (11:21a) and "dares" to boast with the best of his rivals; although, as Paul understands it, it is with the worst of them.[295] He continues to remind the Corinthians that this kind of discourse is utter foolishness. The "anyone else who dares to boast" takes aim at those who "compare and classify themselves" (10:12) and who commend themselves as tested and approved (10:18) and as supreme apostles (11:5). The only valid Christian

---

[289] Holland, "Speaking Like a Fool: Irony in 2 Corinthians 10–13," 259. See also Andrews, who concludes that the difference between the opponents' hardships and Paul's is that he had more of them in more arduous circumstances ("Too Weak Not to Lead," 274), and Peterson, who writes: "This list should not be read as a parody; Paul is here boasting κατὰ σάρκα (11:18), as the world boasts" (*Eloquence and the Proclamation of the Gospel in Corinth*, 118).

[290] D. Georgi claims that Paul "boasted of his sufferings" while the opponents were "proud of their spiritual experiences and powerful deeds" (*The Opponents of Paul in Second Corinthians*, 280). He assumes that they regarded themselves as divine men who had transcended the limits of humanity. But one way to transcend these limits was to prove oneself triumphant in various ordeals.

[291] John Chrysostom, *Homilies on Second Corinthians*, XXV.2 (p. 396).

criteria to measure apostles have nothing to do with noble birth or personal accomplishments but relate to how they conform to the cross of Christ and what God has done in them. Before he begins his own boast, Paul underscores that he is boasting about things that are not boastworthy. It proves nothing. Paul does not legitimate his ministry by comparing himself with others. He would compare himself only with Christ and recognizes how far short he falls in that comparison. Nevertheless he also recognizes how God's power courses through his ministry in spite of his weakness.

11:22   Betz notes that one's good breeding was a standard topic of Hellenistic rhetoric.[296] In this world noble parentage, not rising from humble

---

[292] In Plutarch's *Lives*, Alexander boasts: "But my body bears many a token of an opposing Fortune and no ally of mine. First, among the Illyrians, my head was wounded by a stone and my neck by a cudgel. Then at the Granicus my head was cut open by an enemies dagger, at Issus my thigh was pierced by the sword. Next at Gaza my ankle was wounded by an arrow, my shoulder was dislocated, and I whirled heavily round and round. Then at Marathon the bone of my leg was split open by an arrow. There awaited me towards the last also the buffetings I received among the Indians and the violence of famines. Among the Aspasians my shoulder was wounded by an arrow, and among the Granridae my leg. Among the Mallians, the shaft of an arrow sank deep into my breast and buried its steel; and I was struck in the neck by a cudgel. … Moreover, there were the trials of the campaign itself: storms, droughts, deep rivers, the heights of the Birdless Rock, the monstrous shapes of savage beasts, an uncivilized manner of life, the constant succession of petty kings and their repeated treachery" (*On the Fortune of Alexander* 341 E–F; cited by R. Hodgson, "Paul the Apostle and First Century Tribulation Lists," *ZNW* 74 [1983] 79–80). Alexander audaciously perceived his tribulation as the path to his deification. Paul interprets such boasting to be utter foolishness, and his tribulations point to divine power working in his weakness that saves him from any attempt to deify himself. This is a more suitable parallel than the memorial chronicle, *res gestae*, of the deified Augustus, posted throughout the empire, which rehearses all of the emperors many accomplishments: "Twice I received triumphal ovations. Three times I celebrated curule triumphs. Twenty times and one did I receive the appellation of imperator." It is unlikely that Paul is consciously mimicking this form since listings of hardships are found in many other writers. This interpretation makes it less likely that Paul is adopting tactics on how to win over an audience's good will by mixing in his misfortunes with his accomplishments as Witherington argues. He cites Cicero (*De Invention* I.16.22) on how to win the audience good will "when under attack by an opponent who has at least in part swayed the audience": "We shall win goodwill for ourselves if we refer to our own acts and services without arrogance, if we weaken the effect of charges that have been brought or of some suspicion of less honorable dealing that has been cast on us, if we dilate on the misfortunes that have come to us or the difficulties that we still face, and if we use prayers and entreaties with a humble and submissive spirit" (*Conflict and Community in Corinth*, 433).

[293] J. Lambrecht, "Strength in Weakness: A Reply to Scott B. Andrews' Exegesis of 2 Cor 11:23b–33," *NTS* 43 (1997) 288.

[294] In 4:7–11 and 6:4–7 Paul associates the hardships with God's power sustaining him.

[295] On the use of the verb "to dare" (τολμᾶν, also in 10:2, 12) in debate between philosophers and sophists, see Betz, *Der Apostel Paulus*, 67–69. He describes it as the favorite term of abuse used against sophists who are dismissed as daring charlatans characterized by their brazen propaganda. The verb "to boast" is absent from the text and is to be understood.

[296] Betz, *Der Apostel Paulus*, 97.

beginnings, was an indispensable condition for real prestige. The popular prejudice was that nobility only surfaced in those who were well born (see 1 Cor 1:26).[297] The rivals apparently touted their Jewish heritage to prove their supreme qualifications as servants of Christ. "Hebrews" may refer to Jews who originated from Palestine or may simply denote those who speak Hebrew.[298] An inscription found in Corinth "[Syn]agogue of the Hebr[ews]" suggests that the term "Hebrews" would have been known as a dignified title for an ancient people and would not necessarily identify the members of this synagogue as of Palestinian descent. Paul probably uses the term as an archaic title of respect for his nation.[299] It recalls that God set this people apart from all other peoples of the earth in descent (see Gen 11:14), language, faith, and practice.

"Israelites" denotes "membership in a people and religion."[300] It was the name God conferred on Jacob (Gen 32:28). Paul confirms that the adoption as sons, the divine glory, the covenants, the receiving of the law, the temple worship and the promises, the patriarchs, and the Messiah belong to Israel (Rom 9:4–5). "Abraham's descendants" ("seed of Abraham") refers to the people of the promise (Gen 12:7; 13:15; 15:5; 17:7; 22:17–18; 24:7; 28:4) for whom the messianic blessings were destined (John 8:33,37; Heb 2:16). These terms affirm that Paul and his rivals are full-blooded Jews. Paul has attested to this truth elsewhere with different purposes: "I am an Israelite myself, a descendant of Abraham, from the tribe of Benjamin" (Rom 11:1); "If anyone else thinks he has reasons to put confidence in the flesh, I have more: circumcised on the eighth day, of the people of Israel, of the tribe of Benjamin, a Hebrew of Hebrews" (Phil 3:4–5; see also Gal 1:14; and Acts 22:3; 26:4–5).

Paul had redefined the ultimate significance of these categories in other letters. He refers to "the Israel of God" (Gal 6:16), which includes those Jews and Gentiles who believe in Christ and walk by this rule: "Neither circumcision nor uncircumcision means anything; what counts is a new creation" (Gal 6:15). Therefore, the Israel of God stands over against the "Israel according to the flesh" (1 Cor 10:18). This view challenges the Jewish pride expressed in a later rabbinic text: "I am God over all that come into the world, but I have joined my name only with you; I am not called the God of

[297] Josephus presents his genealogy as one of racial purity, from royal stock and a priestly heritage, to show his qualifications for writing about Jewish history (*Life* 1–6). Danker comments that referring to one's ancestry not only allows one to boast of higher status "but that one's behavior is in keeping with the high standards that have been set in time past" (*II Corinthians*, 179).

[298] Acts 6:1; see also Philo (*On Dreams* 2.250; *Migration of Abraham* 28).

[299] Bultmann, *The Second Letter to the Corinthians*, 214.

[300] Ibid. See 3:7,13 "sons of Israel," and the address "Israelites" in the speeches in Acts 2:22; 3:12; 5:35; 13:16; 21:28. See also *4 Macc* 18:1, "O Israelite children, offspring of the seed of Abraham, obey this law and exercise piety in every way."

the idolaters, but the God of Israel" (*Exod. Rab.* 29). God's chosen people, according to Paul, now includes Gentiles who believe in Christ and who become joint heirs with him of the glory to come (Rom 8:15–17).

Paul also redefines the meaning of "seed of Abraham" to include Gentiles who have faith as Abraham did (Gal 3:7; Rom 4:12). He tells the Philippians that he once placed his confidence in these boasts in his heritage but he does so no longer (Phil 3:4–6). Such ethnic and religious distinctions make no difference in light of the new creation in Christ. But if his rivals still find such things to be impressive, then he is no less Jewish than they.

11:23 The opponents also apparently claim to be "servants of Christ."[301] But not all who lay claim to this title are true servants of Christ. Jesus warned of false prophets who will come saying all the rights words, "Lord, Lord," but who are inwardly ravening wolves (Matt 7:15–21). Paul's rivals arrogated the title "servants of Christ" to themselves understanding it to confer on them a lofty status which made others their inferiors, if not their servants. They may think of themselves as men sent on mission. Yet their mission is not "to preach the gospel where Christ was not known" (Rom 15:20) but to enhance their own reputation and following by building on another's foundation. Their arrogant, boastful attitudes betray whom they really serve.

To use the word "more" *(hyper),* "I am more, " in the same way as the rival *hyperlian* (super) apostles do was probably painful to Paul; and he reminds the Corinthians that it is utter madness to speak like this. Even though it is God's truth—he *is* more—God's truth is not expressed by boastful comparisons. The language "out of my mind" *(paraphronōn)* is even stronger than the reference to foolishness *(aphrosynē):* he is totally deranged. This language serves to warn them: Do not follow my example with this kind of boasting!

Paul now enumerates how he eclipses his rivals. First, he has far greater labors.[302] This statement recalls what he told the Corinthians earlier. He worked harder than the first disciples, but he qualified this statement by saying that it was not he but the grace of God that is with him (1 Cor 15:10). Here he simply asserts that his labors are greater.

Next, he claims that he has far greater hardships, more imprisonments, more beatings, more scrapes with death.[303] His language reveals that these were typical, recurring situations. Acts reports only the Philippian imprisonment (Acts 16:23–40) before the time that this letter would have been written. Brown suggests that comparing Paul's account of his tribulations with what we read about him in Acts "shows that, if anything, Acts might lead us to underestimate the

---

[301] The term appears in Col 1:7, referring to Epaphras; see also Paul's use of "servants of God," referring to himself, in 2 Cor 6:4.

[302] Furnish notes that περισσοτέρως could imply "of greater difficulty, or perhaps, of extent" (*II Corinthians,* 515).

[303] Seven imprisonments of Paul are mentioned in *1 Clem* 5:6. J. D. Quinn has challenged the accuracy of this account in "'Seven Times He Wore Chains' (*1 Clem* 5.6)," *JBL* 97 (1978) 574–76.

apostle's extraordinary career."[304] Paul is not exulting in some kind of Christian masochism, however. According to Epictetus, a true philosopher does not boast about the office that has been given him by Zeus; he proves it by his conduct.[305] And the proof of one's God-ordained training and education was not a diploma or the ability to compose and deliver rousing speeches, but the proper response to adversity.[306]

Judge argues persuasively that Paul's "dreadful catalogues of personal disaster" would have had no impact if he were a lowly man who could expect no better. The list of hardships would have only hit home if he were recognized as a man of rank. This was not his expected lot but something he accepted and overcame.[307] Unlike the previous lists in 4:8–9 and 6:8–10, which are more general in character, the list of tribulations now become quite specific. Harvey believes that at this fleshly level of speech, Paul needed "to show his superiority by the sheer cumulative weight of his whole variety of sufferings" rather than in general terms.[308]

"Exposed to death again and again" reads literally "in deaths often." Ellingworth makes the case that this phrase may begin a new stage of his argument: "Many times near death, five times ..."[309] The period should be placed after beatings, and the new thought translated "often near death." It would mean that Paul has come close to death in the following dangerous situations.

11:24 Paul refers to synagogue discipline of scourging which Jesus had warned his disciples would have to face: "Be on your guard against men; they will hand you over to the local councils and flog you in their synagogues" (Matt 10:17).[310] Paul may have inflicted this punishment

---

[304] R. E. Brown, *Introduction to the New Testament* (New York: Doubleday, 1997) 557.

[305] Epictetus, *Discourses* 3.24.118.

[306] Fitzgerald, *Cracks in an Earthen Vessel*, 112.

[307] E. Judge, "St Paul as a Radical Critic of Society," *Interchange* 16 (1974) 192.

[308] Harvey, *Renewal through Suffering*, 100.

[309] P. Ellingworth, "Grammar, Meaning and Verse Divisions in 2 Cor 11.16–29," *BT* 43 (1992) 245–46.

[310] The tractate *Makkot* ("Stripes") in the *Mishna* deals with the topics of forty lashes (Deut 25:2–3), false witnesses (Deut 19:16–21), and cities of refuge (Num 35:10–15; Deut 19:2–10). The crimes deserving scourging are listed in *m. Mak.* 3:1–9, and the manner they are to be given is explained in 3:10–15. By the first century the maximum of forty lashes was reduced to thirty-nine, possibly as a precaution against miscounting and going over the number prescribed. The number of lashes administered were to be divisible by three (*m. Mak.* 3:11). This number may be attributable to the use of a scourge with three thongs. Thirteen lashes would be the equivalent of thirty-nine stripes. If *Makkot* reflects first century practice, the victim was stripped and bound to a pillar. One-third of the stripes were administered on the front, the rest on the back while an attendant repeatedly recited Deut 28:58–59: "If you do not carefully follow all the words of this law, which are written in this book, and do not revere this glorious and awesome name—the LORD your God— the LORD will send fearful plagues on you and your descendants, harsh and prolonged disasters, and severe and lingering illnesses." Paul cites this text in Gal 3:10 to support the point that all who rely on works of the law are under the law's curse.

himself on Jewish Christians before his conversion and call (Gal 1:13). The number of lashes prescribed depended on the severity of the crime. The forty lashes are prescribed in Deut 25:1–3 as the maximum number that may be given before the punishment degenerates into a cruel humiliation. Despite the concern expressed in Deuteronomy that your neighbor not be degraded in your sight, Josephus regarded flogging as a most disgraceful penalty.[311]

We cannot know exactly why the synagogue inflicted this punishment on Paul. The best guess is that it was for the serious offense of blasphemy when he proclaimed his faith in Christ, his altered understanding of Judaism with the inclusion of Gentiles in the people of God.[312] According to the *Mishna*, thirty-six sins, including blasphemy, warranted being cut off from the people without warning (*m. Ker.* 1:1). But flogging averted both a harsher punishment at the hands of God and being cut off from the people (Lev 18:29; Num 15:3). The key text reads: "When he is scourged then he is thy brother" (*m. Mak.* 3:15). This principle may help clarify what Paul means when he said, "To the Jews I became like a Jew, to win the Jews. To those under the law I became like one under the law (though I myself am not under the law), so as to win those under the law" (1 Cor 9:20). He allowed the synagogue to administer punishment on him "in order to maintain his Jewish connections."[313]

Harvey notes that Jews were given special privileges to settle their disputes in their own courts. If one wanted to stay a member of the Jewish community, one had to submit to its discipline.[314] For Paul to submit to this punishment five times testifies not only to his physical stamina but to his commitment to his people, which he proclaims in Rom 9:2–4: "I have great sorrow and unceasing anguish in my heart. For I could wish that I myself

---

[311] Josephus, *Ant.* 4.8.21 §238.

[312] S. Gallas rehearses the various proposals that might have precipitated the punishment from the list of offenses in *Mishna Makkot* and settles on eating unclean food ("'Fünfmal vierzig weniger einen …' Die an Paulus vollzogenen Synagogalstrafen nach 2 Kor 11,24," *ZNW* 81 [1990] 178–90). This proposal seems unlikely, however. If Paul said only half of what he said about the law in Galatians, let alone his Christological assertions, he would have roused the ire of most devout Jews whose hearts, according to Paul, were hardened to prevent them from seeing the glory of the Lord (3:12–18). C. G. Kruse offers five reasons behind Paul's persecution at the hands of his fellow Jews: (1) his preaching the "faith"; (2) his devaluation of cherished elements of Judaism as "rubbish"; (3) his neglect of purity issues that separated Jews from Gentiles; (4) his rejection of circumcision as a requirement for inclusion in the people of God; and (5) the judgment that his preaching caused an erosion of ethical standards ("The Price Paid for a Ministry among Gentiles: Paul's Persecution at the Hands of Jews," in *Worship, Theology and Ministry in the Early Church: Essays in Honor of Ralph P. Martin*, JSNTSup 87 [Sheffield: JSOT, 1992] 260–72).

[313] A. E. Harvey, "Forty Strokes Save One: Social Aspects of Judaizing and Apostasy," in *Alternative Approaches to New Testament Study*, ed. A. E. Harvey (London: SPCK, 1985) 93.

[314] Ibid., 80–81.

were cursed and cut off from Christ for the sake of my brothers, those of my own race, the people of Israel." Submitting to this discipline also may have allowed him continued access to Gentiles on the fringe of the synagogue who were more disposed to the gospel's message.[315]

11:25 "Beaten with rods" is a specifically Roman punishment meted out in public by a lictor. This punishment would have taken place in the Roman colonies where Paul spent time, such as Antioch of Pisidia, Lystra, Troas, Philippi, and Corinth. As a Roman citizen Paul was technically exempt from such punishment, but citizenship did not accord one an iron clad guarantee against injustice, only the right to certain formal procedures.

After Jews from Asia stirred up a tumult against Paul in Jerusalem, the Roman military officer in charge seized him and was about to interrogate him by flogging. Paul calmly announced, "You can't do this to me. I am a Roman citizen" (Acts 22:25–29). Either Paul did not appeal to his Roman citizenship when he was previously beaten, or overly zealous magistrates ignored his appeal and meted out the modern equivalent of the third degree. The evidence suggests that not all magistrates adhered to this rule in the provinces.[316] A heavy beating with rods was generally imposed by earnest officials on members of the lower classes who could not afford to pay a punitive fee.[317] It was, however, "considered an appropriate punishment for those causing civic disturbances."[318] Acts 16:22 records that Paul was beaten with rods in Philippi as a warning for supposedly subversive teaching that threatened to upset the Roman order. In 1 Thess 2:2 Paul refers to his experience in Philippi as "being shamefully treated" (NIV "insulted"). Paul's final blast in the letter to the Galatians is that he bears in his body the marks *(stigmata)* of Jesus (Gal 6:17). He may well have in mind the scars left by whippings he received. Josephus records that when Antipater was accused of being disloyal to Caesar, he "stripped off his clothes and exposed his numerous scars. He said, 'His loyalty to Caesar need no words from him; his body cried it aloud, were

[315] T. Still, *Thlipsis in Thessalonica: A Study of the Conflict Relations of Paul and the Thessalonian Christians and Outsiders* (Ph.D. diss., University of Glasgow, 1996) 168, n. 57.

[316] Cicero reports that a Gaius Servilius was beaten and killed in spite of his cries, "I am a Roman citizen" (*Against Verres* 2.5.139–142). Josephus tells that Gessius Florus, the governor of Judea A.D. 64–66, scourged and crucified Jews who were invested with Roman dignity as men of equestrian rank, but he cites it as an unprecedented action (*J. W.* 2.14.9 §308).

[317] P. Garnsey, *Social Status*, 138.

[318] B. Rapske, *The Book of Acts and Paul in Roman Custody*, The Book of Acts in Its First Century Setting (Grand Rapids: Eerdmans, 1994) 125. A savage beating could lead to death as Cicero's emotional account of Gaius Servilius's punishment reveals. He reports that the senior lictor "took the butt end of the stick, and began to strike the poor man violently across the eyes, so that he fell helpless to the ground, his face and eyes streaming with blood. Even then the assailants continued to rain blows on his prostrate body" (*Against Verres* 2.5.142).

he to hold his peace.' "[319]

Once, Paul says, he received a stoning; and Acts reports a stoning taking place in Lystra (Acts 14:9). This battering was a mob action, and its motivations were quite different from the stoning of Stephen, that Paul himself witnessed (Acts 7:58–59).[320]

Three times Paul was shipwrecked and once he spent a twenty-four hour period in the sea before being rescued.[321] Acts reports Paul's many sea voyages but only one shipwreck, and that occurs some time after Paul wrote this letter.[322] Harvey thinks that four shipwrecks, including the one on the way to Rome, "would have been exceptional, even for a professional sailor."[323] But life on the sea was perilous and was made even more so by the absence of lifeboats on ancient sailing vessels. Paul probably did not have the funds always to travel first-class on the queens of the Roman merchant marine and may have taken more than one journey on a coastal tub that was less than seaworthy. At sea the unexpected could always happen, even when sailing during the right season with favorable winds. Secundus, the silent philosopher, was asked in a dialogue with the emperor Hadrian, "What is a boat?" His response was that a boat is "a sea-tossed object, a foundationless home, a well-crafted tomb, a wooden cubicle, a flying prison, a confined fate, a plaything of the wind, sailing death, an open cage, uncertain safety, the prospect of death." "What is a sailor?" Secundus replies, "A neighbor of death." A modern defined the sea as a large body of water surrounded by trouble. Paul's shipwrecks in carrying the gospel to other lands testify to the truth of this statement.

11:26 Paul's movements across the empire exposed him to endless dangers and hardships.[324] He next lists dangers from having to ford rivers, pre-

---

[319] Josephus, *J. W.* 1.20.2 §197.

[320] Contemporary American idiom that now connects "being stoned" to taking drugs makes the NRSV "once I received a stoning" preferable to the NIV "once I was stoned."

[321] The rendering "in the open sea" in the NIV accurately captures the sense of ἐν τῷ βυθῷ ("in the depth"). Since Paul was adrift a night and a day, a twenty-four hour period, the shipwreck occurred far from shore. For an account of travel by sea and land in the ancient world, see L. Casson, *Travel in the Ancient World* (Baltimore/London: Johns Hopkins University Press, 1994) 149–96. He describes frightened travelers wrapping themselves with all their gold and valuables so that if their bodies washed up on shore, whoever found them would give them proper attention (p. 161).

[322] See Acts 13:4, from Seleucia to Cyprus; and trips from Paphos to Perga (13:13); Attalia to Antioch (14:26); Troas to Samothrace (16:11); Berea to Athens (17:15); Corinth to Ephesus to Syria (18:18); and Jerusalem to Rome and the shipwreck off Malta (27:14–44).

[323] Harvey, *Renewal through Suffering*, 102. Josephus reports surviving a shipwreck on the way to Rome and having to swim all night. Eighty outswam the other 520 passengers and were rescued by another ship (*Life* 14–15). See also Dio Chrysostom, *Orations* 7.2–10.

[324] Murphy-O'Connor offers a vivid account of the dangers and hardships of travel in the ancient world in "On the Road and on the Sea with St. Paul," *Bible Review* 1 (1985) 38–47.

sumably swollen by floods, to danger from bandits.[325] The picture obtained from reading Apuleius's novel *Metamorphosis (or the Golden Ass)* is that robbers dotted the countryside where the policing presence of the imperial army was rare.

The danger from kinsmen reflects Jewish hostility to Paul, and in Acts this hostility rears its ugly head in Damascus (9:23), Jerusalem (9:29), Antioch of Pisidia (13:50), Iconium (14:5), Lystra (14:19), Thessalonica (17:5), Berea (17:13), Corinth (18:12), and finally again in Jerusalem. The Corinthians would have firsthand knowledge of these attacks against Paul. He also faced danger from pagans. Acts states that Gentiles, threatened by the gospel's message, posed serious threats to Paul. They made false charges that Paul was a rabble rouser intent on causing social unrest throughout the world, and they branded him as an enemy of Roman law and order (Acts 14:15; 16:16–24; 19:23–41).

"In danger in the city, in danger in the country, in danger at sea" sums up almost everywhere Paul went. In the city he barely escaped an angry rabble in Ephesus and a dragnet to capture him in Damascus. In deserted areas and mountainous regions he faced dangers from robbers, kidnappers who sold their victims into slavery, and wild beasts.[326]

The "false brothers" (see Gal 2:5) is the most startling item in the list because it implies that his fellow Christians were intent on harming Paul. Paul does not expand on what they tried to do to him, but the context suggests some kind of betrayal and possibly direct physical violence.[327]

11:27   Paul now refers to physical deprivation he suffered from his devotion to his calling and the toil and moil that came from his arduous labor as a craftsman. The sleepless nights probably were voluntary and connected to his mission campaign. He probably was working all day and preaching all night (see 1 Thess 2:9; 2 Thess 3:8; Acts 20:7–12).[328] "In hunger (famine) and thirst" is followed by "going often without food," which seems redundant. This phrase translates *nēsteia* ("fasts"). Some suggest that the fasts may have been voluntary as a spiritual discipline, but Paul is not talking about his asceticism. The "nakedness" ("ill-clothed") which follows in the list was not caused by some elective spiritual exercise. It is more

---

[325] Murphy-O'Connor observes, "The element of risk, not struggle, is evidently uppermost in his mind" (*Paul: A Critical Life* [Oxford/New York: Oxford University Press, 1997] 97).

[326] F. F. Bruce notes, "He does not include (though he might have done so) hazards incurred spending the night at inns along the road: these were notoriously dangerous and unsavory places" ("Travel and Communication (NT World)," *ABD* 6:651).

[327] Barrett, *The Second Epistle to the Corinthians*, 300. Paul may also be alluding to the "false apostles" plaguing Corinth and undermining his work there (11:13).

[328] *Sir* 36:27 refers to the artisan who must labor day and night. It is unlikely that Paul has in mind sleepless nights from worry or fear as Martin suggests (*2 Corinthians*, 380).

likely, then, that the fasts were forced upon him by his poverty.[329] Paul talks about how he is held in contempt for being hungry and thirsty and poorly clothed in 1 Cor 4:11 (see Phil 4:12). Being cold and naked caps his list of exigencies (see Job 24:7) and probably occurred in places far from human habitation or in times when there were no fellow Christians to supply his needs (11:9) or when he refused to accept assistance.[330]

The catalog of woes portrays an apostle lacerated by beatings, shadowed by enemies, worn down by exposure and deprivation, in shreds and tatters, and with no place to lay his head.[331] It also shows an apostle unbent by all the hardships in his devotion to Christ's cause and his calling.[332]

11:28 The phrase "besides everything else" *(chōris tōn parektos)* in the NIV is rendered "apart from these external things" in the REB (see KJV). The latter translation distinguishes the external suffering from the internal suffering. This interpretation of the phrase is not well supported by the linguistic evidence, and so it is best to understand it to mean "not to mention other things."[333] Paul distinguishes what he has just recited from what he will omit and from what he is about to recite. He skips over all the other dangers and problems caused by preaching the gospel and his grinding poverty that he could also have mentioned. There is still more to tell, but Paul drops it to turn his attention to the psychological stress of worrying about the churches in his care. They place a daily pressure upon him.

The word translated "concern" *(merimna)* could mean "anxiety" or "worry." Paul has shared in this letter how he was so anxious to receive news from Titus about how things were going in Corinth that he was unable to take advantage of a mission opportunity in Troas (2:12–13). He also will

---

[329] In 6:5 the NIV translates *nēsteia* as "hunger" that follows "sleepless nights."

[330] See his request for a cloak in 2 Tim 4:13. The Hebrews considered "nakedness" an extremely shameful condition, characteristic of those taken captive and led off in shame (Deut 28:48; Isa 20:4).

[331] Hodge comments, "This passage, more perhaps than any other, makes even the most laborious of the modern ministers of Christ hide their face in shame. What have they ever done or suffered to compare with what this apostle did?" (*An Exposition of the Second Epistle to the Corinthians*, 275). Modern interpreters of Paul, however, have tended instead to object to Paul's supposed misinterpretation of this or that issue rather than to stand in awe of his devotion, vigor, and sacrifice. But Paul's ambivalence about his foolish boasting springs from a fear that he would be regarded as some kind of hero rather than a clay vessel in whom God's power worked. These are the perils that a noble philosopher could expect to endure—grappling with hunger and cold, withstanding thirst, enduring the lash, hazards from travel (see Dio Chrysostom, *Orations* 8:16; Epictetus, *Dissertations* 3.24.29, noted by Danker, *II Corinthians*, 185). Paul is more than simply a noble man. He knows himself to be totally dependent on God.

[332] Best observes that Paul omits any mention of the number of churches he founded, converts made, persons healed, his superb training in Scripture, or the story of his amazing conversion (*Second Corinthians*, 123–24).

[333] Furnish, *II Corinthians*, 519.

voice his "fear" that when he returns to Corinth things will not be well (12:20–21). In other letters he tells the Thessalonians that he could no longer bear the anxiety of not knowing how their faith was faring in the midst of suffering. He therefore decided to send Timothy to find out, though it meant leaving himself alone in Athens (1 Thess 3:1,5). He was responsible for preaching the gospel that has led to their persecution and tells them, "For we now live, if you continue to stand firm in the Lord" (1 Thess 3:8, NRSV; the NIV interprets "if," *ei,* to mean "since"). In a world so hostile to Christian faith, Paul could not help but worry that his charges would not stand firm, and their failure would kill him inside. He tells the Galatians, already bewitched by Judaizers, that he is "again in the pains of childbirth until Christ is formed in you, how I wish I could be with you now and change my tone, because I am perplexed about you!" (Gal 4:19–20).

Barrett points out that "pastoral care is relatively easy (even though it involves endless hard work) when it is done for those who love their pastor and value his ministry." It is a quite different story when friction and suspicion mar that relationship.[334] Paul does not exaggerate when he says that he prays constantly for his churches (Phil 1:3–4; Col 1:9; 1 Thess 1:2–3). Having founded a congregation, he did not forget it as he moved on to other territory but continued to feel responsibility for them. This sense of responsibility for the spiritual welfare of his churches stoked his anxiety for them.

11:29   Paul concludes his list with two examples of his anxieties for his churches: concern for the weak and for those who stumble. The "weak" may mean someone who is immature in faith, "conscience-ridden, dependent on laws and regulations."[335] If it denotes someone who has "needless scruples," Paul expresses "intense sympathy," feeling "the weakness, though he did not share the scruples."[336] In 1 Cor 8:1–13 the "weak" are those who do not have knowledge (8:7), have been "accustomed to idols" (8:7), and have weak consciences (8:7,12) that might lead them to emulate those with knowledge and eat food sacrificed to an idol not as something indifferent but as food offered to an idol. The so-called knowledge of the "knowers" (1 Cor 8:1) could lead the weak back into idolatry and cause the eternal ruin of one for whom Christ died (1 Cor 8:11). Paul will never do anything that might cause the weak to stumble (1 Cor 8:13), and he also will not sit idly by and watch those with knowledge steam roll over the consciences of the weak. His correction of those claiming to have "knowledge" and "rights" (8:1,9) and his refusal to bend to their will regarding food sacrificed to an idol probably contributed to bringing the controversy in Corinth to a boil.

---

[334] Barrett, *The Second Epistle to the Corinthians,* 301.

[335] Ibid., 301–2.

[336] Plummer, *The Second Epistle of St. Paul to the Corinthians,* 331. Paul expresses his dismay that some in Corinth would arrogantly run roughshod over the unenlightened consciences of others regarding food connected to idols (1 Cor 8:11–12; cp. Rom 14:1–15:13).

In his effort to share the blessings of the gospel with all people, he says, "To the weak I became weak, to win the weak" (1 Cor 9:22). "Though he himself is strong, he is willing to identify with the weak so that their weakness becomes his own."[337] If what he eats might cause a weak brother to fall into sin, he declares, "I will never eat meat again, so that I will not cause him to fall" (1 Cor 8:13; see Rom 14:14–21). He expounds this principle in Rom 15:1–3:

> We who are strong ought to bear with the failings of the weak and not to please ourselves. Each of us should please his neighbor for his good, to build him up. For even Christ did not please himself but, as it is written: "The insults of those who insult you have fallen on me."

Black concludes: *"Should one of them [the weak] stumble in his Christian walk, Paul treats it as though it were his own stumbling, enduring the same pain and feeling the same vexation."*[338]

"The weak" may also refer to those who are powerless.[339] In this context Paul stresses his weaknesses, humiliation, poverty, and unimpressive appearance. In accepting this weakness, Paul follows the model of Christ. His boasting in this unit takes an ironic turn. He began this unit by asking, "Who boasts?" that I cannot outboast, although he boasts as a complete fool (11:21). He draws a stark contrast with that boasting by saying "Who is weak?" that I am not also weak?

Paul knows that anyone might fall (1 Cor 10:12), but the "weak" are particularly vulnerable. His anxiety for his churches is an expression of his godly jealousy (11:2), which can flame into a divine fury. He does not casually accept a member of one of his churches falling into sin or being caused to stumble. It makes him burn inwardly.[340] This attitude parallels Jesus' warning: "And if anyone causes one of these little ones who believe in me to sin, it would be better for him to be thrown into the sea with a large millstone tied around his neck" (Mark 9:42; Matt 18:17; Luke 17:1). It is more likely, however, that the "weak" refers to the intellectually and morally immature who are "unstable in their convictions" and "easily give their assent to false judgments."[341] In other words, they are the ones prone to

---

[337] Black, *Paul, Apostle of Weakness*, 143.

[338] Ibid.

[339] Paul takes the side of the weak when he expresses his exasperation with the Corinthians for going ahead with their so-called Lord's Supper while allowing their brothers, who had nothing, to go hungry (1 Cor 11:21–22).

[340] Plummer thinks that "to burn" refers to Paul feeling "burning shame with the sinner rather than hot indignation against the seducer" (*The Second Epistle of St. Paul to the Corinthians*, 331).

[341] A. Cheung, *Idol Food in Corinth: Jewish Background and Pauline Legacy,* JSNTSup 176 (Sheffield: Academic Press, 1999) 125.

stumble and fall and the ones that the so-called strong are prone to ignore. This chapter in 2 Corinthians testifies to his burning indignation when he lashes out at the false apostles, deceitful workers, and Satan's henchmen, who would deceive and lead astray the Corinthians (11:3,13–15).

Paul, however, reflects the spirit of a saint since his indignation is directed against those who would harm the faith of others and not against those who have physically harmed him. This concern for his charges is one of the true signs of an apostle. He has already explained in the letter that overcoming hardships is a clear sign that God's power is at work in him (4:7–12). It is not a definitive sign, however. Other persons have suffered terrible hardships out of intense devotion to various causes. Suffering for a cause does not automatically make that cause just or godly. Consequently, Paul switches gears. He will no longer boast of his success in overcoming overwhelming hardships but will now boast only of his weaknesses.

11:30 Paul abandons his comparison with the "superlative" apostles and his catalog of endured hardships and moves on to demonstrations of his weakness in 11:30–12:10. The necessity of boasting, or boasting of weakness, is repeated at the beginning of each of the next three subsections (11:30–33; 12:1–5; 12:6–10).

It is odd to boast about one's weakness, but Paul's declaration in 12:10 becomes the key for unlocking the purpose of this peculiar tactic. His weakness has a "revelatory function."[342] He will therefore tell tales of battle skirmishes, heavenly journeys with divine revelations, and miraculous cures but turn them on their heads. They do not show how brave and wonderful he is, but how great and wonderful the grace of God is that sustains him in his weakness.

11:31 It may seem strange that Paul invokes God's name to verify what he is about to say: "The God and Father of the Lord Jesus, who is to be praised forever, knows that I am not lying." It is strange because he is not boasting about any great accomplishments but rather his weaknesses. According to Judge, the oath preceding the tale of an exploit is an "example of *horkou schema* or *figura iusiurandi,* a rhetorical ornament."[343] Garnishing what follows with an oath has an ironic effect and suggests that he is now turning to parody.

11:32 Paul moves from listing his suffering to narrating events. The account of his escape from Damascus should not be regarded as simply providing an example of one of the dangers he faced in the city (11:26).

---

[342] Holland, "Speaking Like a Fool: Irony in 2 Corinthians 10–13," 260.
[343] Judge, "Paul's Boasting," 47.

Paul relates it as an example of his weakness. He places the emphasis on the manner of his escape rather than on the seriousness of the threat.[344] Hiding in a basket is not something that someone with power would do, and the incident occurs at the very beginning of his ministry. It serves as a paradigm, as it were, for what was to come.

The ethnarch under King Aretas could refer to someone who was (1) governor of the whole city; (2) governor of a particular ethnic group in the city;[345] or (3) a sheik outside of the city, suggested by the phrase, "was guarding the city." Most likely the threat was inside the city since it would have been improvident to flee the relative safety inside the walls of the city and make oneself vulnerable to capture by some force encircling the city. The incident must then assume a time when Aretas had control of the city and had appointed an ethnarch.[346] Paul is silent about why he was being sought.[347] It probably occurred during his stint in Arabia (Gal 1:17) and had something to do with his preaching.

11:33   The ethnarch apparently had posted guards at the gates of the

---

[344] Furnish, *II Corinthians*, 540–41.

[345] The Jews in Alexandria were under an ethnarch. Barrett thinks Paul refers to the king's chargé d'affaires in the city who dealt with Arab concerns (*The Second Epistle to the Corinthians*, 304). E. A. Knauf, however, argues that the ethnarch was the chief of the Nabatean business colony in Damascus ("Zum *Ethnarchen* des Aretas 2 Kor 11 32," *ZNW* 74 [1983] 145–47). See also B. Schwank, "Neue Funde in Nabatäerstädten und ihre Bedeutung für die neutestamentliche Exegese," *NTS* 29 (1983) 429–35.

[346] Pompey brought Damascus under Roman rule in 65 B.C. (Josephus, *Ant.* 14:29; *J. W.* 1:127). Aretas is Aretas IV, a Nabatean client king of Rome who reigned from 9/8 B.C. to A.D. 40/41 (see Josephus *Ant.* 16.9.1–4 §§271–99). His daughter had married the tetrarch Herod Antipas, but he divorced her to marry Herodias, his niece and sister-in-law, the wife of Herod Philip. John the Baptist was imprisoned for his harsh denunciation of this marriage (Mark 6:14–29). Aretas later avenged this slight by attacking and defeating Antipas in A.D. 36 (Josephus *Ant.* 18.5.1–2 §109–16). The Roman reprisal for this unauthorized action was forestalled by the death of the emperor Tiberius. Aretas died in 40/41. Consequently, this event occurred sometime before 40. G. W. Bowersock argues that Paul's language is explicit, "in Damascus the ethnarch of Aretas the king was guardian of the city of the Damascenes"— he was in charge of the city as a whole (*Roman Arabia* [Cambridge: Harvard University Press, 1983] 68–69). He thinks that after the remarkable defeat of Herod Antipas, Aretas marched on Damascus and later withdrew, perhaps after less than a year, when it became known that Tiberius had ordered an expedition against him. See also J. Taylor, "The Ethnarch of King Aretas at Damascus: A Note on 2 Cor 11:32–33," *RB* 97 (1990) 238–51; and Plummer, *The Second Epistle of St. Paul to the Corinthians*, 333–34, for other possible explanations for how Aretas had authority in Damascus.

[347] Acts mentions that the Jews were watching the gates day and night to kill him (Acts 9:24), and it is not improbable that they joined forces with the ethnarch in trying to destroy Paul. Murphy-O'Connor, "Paul in Arabia," *CBQ* 55 (1993) 732–37.

city, which necessitated Paul's escape when sympathizers lowered him in a basket from a window in the wall.[348] Bruce interprets this event to be "a humiliating and undignified experience, in which he cut such a ridiculous figure that the mere thought of it killed any tendency to pride."[349] Judge makes the case that Paul offers a parody of the achievement of the first Roman soldier to scale a wall and earn a badge of courage.[350] The "wall crown" *(corona muralis)*, one of the highest Roman military honors, was presented to the first soldier to go up and over the wall of an enemy city. It was made of gold and fashioned to look like the turreted wall of a fortified city. Under the empire it was awarded to no one below the rank of centurion. Judge suggests that the contrast between Paul's cowering descent in a basket from the wall of the city and the daring ascent of the wall by a courageous soldier would not have been lost on the Corinthians. Paul therefore describes a reversal of military bravery and another token of his humiliation and weakness. Such an inglorious escape is hardly something about which one would choose to boast. Paul was not the first one up; he was the first one down. As Martin puts it, "Unlike the proud vainglory of military prowess, his apostolic career opened on the note of humiliation and disgrace."[351] One might wonder if Paul did not intend to evoke laughter at this picture.

We should not overlook, however, that Paul's escape parallels similar escapes in the Bible.[352] The Israelite spies were hidden by Rahab the prostitute and let down by a rope through a window in the wall (Josh 2:15), and David escaped Saul's soldiers with the help of Michal, who let him down through the window (1 Sam 19:12). The biblical parallels show a pattern in which an ignoble escape on one day led to victory on another (Josh 6:1–25; 1 Sam 23:1–14). Any reader familiar with these biblical echoes "might expect that what appeared at first to be a humiliating

---

[348] Acts 9:25 has the word σπύρις for basket, and Paul uses a hapax legomenon σαργάνη.

[349] Bruce, *I and II Corinthians*, 244. Barrett comments that these "verses are a crowning illustration of the weakness and humiliation of which Paul speaks and boasts" (*The Second Epistle to the Corinthians*, 303).

[350] E. A. Judge, "The Conflict of Educational Aims in NT Thought," *Journal of Christian Education* 9 (1966) 32–45. See Polybius, *Histories* 6.39.5; Livy, *History* 6.20.8; 10.46.3; 23.18.7; 26.48.5. According to Aulus Gellius, "the special distinction of a mural crown belonged to the man who had been first to climb the wall" (*Attic Nights* 5.6.16). A statue of the goddess Tyche (Fortuna), luck or fate, has a wall crown on its head. See Furnish, *II Corinthians*, plate VIII.

[351] Martin, *2 Corinthians*, 387.

[352] Holland, "Speaking Like a Fool: Irony in 2 Corinthians 10–13," 261.

escape would in fact lead to powerful works on God's behalf."[353] One such victory can be seen in 10:13–17. Paul was the first to assail and take captives for Christ in Corinth.[354]

We conclude that Paul is not simply engaging in self-mockery. His point would be that God's power has worked in him in such a way that his weakness becomes strength, the conclusion in 12:10. From the very outset of his ministry when he escaped the clutches of Aretas in Damascus, God has been working in him. Beasley-Murray aptly comments: "It is ironical that the city to which Paul was making his way to arrest Christians was the scene of this memorable attempt to cut short his career of witness for Christ. Yet the attempt to silence him was as fruitless as his attempt to destroy the church."[355]

(4) God's Power Is Made Perfect in Weakness (12:1–10)

¹I must go on boasting. Although there is nothing to be gained, I will go on to visions and revelations from the Lord. ²I know a man in Christ who fourteen years ago was caught up to the third heaven. Whether it was in the body or out of the body I do not know—God knows. ³And I know that this man—whether in the body or apart from the body I do not know, but God knows—⁴was caught up to paradise. He heard inexpressible things, things that man is not permitted to tell. ⁵I will boast about a man like that, but I will not boast about myself, except about my weaknesses. ⁶Even if I should choose to boast, I would not be a fool, because I would be speaking the truth. But I refrain, so no one will think more of me than is warranted by what I do or say.

⁷To keep me from becoming conceited because of these surpassingly great revelations, there was given me a thorn in my flesh, a messenger of Satan, to torment me. ⁸Three times I pleaded with the Lord to take it away from me. ⁹But he said to me, "My grace is sufficient for you, for my power is made perfect in weakness." Therefore I will boast all the more gladly about my weaknesses, so that Christ's power may rest on me. ¹⁰That is why, for Christ's sake, I delight in weaknesses, in insults, in hardships, in persecutions, in difficulties. For when I am weak, then I am strong.

In 12:1 Paul introduces a new topic of boasting, visions and revelations from the Lord. He describes a rapture to paradise that took place fourteen

---

[353] Ibid. Barrett assumes that the account in 2 Corinthians provides an "outstanding example of the humiliation and weakness to which Paul is exposed" while the one in Acts emphasizes that Paul is "God's chosen vessel" and that God will deliver him from the hand of his enemies (*The Second Epistle to the Corinthians*, 304). But the latter point is also implicit in Paul's account.

[354] Andrews, "Too Weak Not to Lead," 272, n. 41.

[355] G. R. Beasley-Murray, "2 Corinthians," BBC (Nashville: Broadman, 1971) 11:71.

years ago (12:2–4) and then the nature of boasting in such an experience (12:5–7a). Next, he narrates the results of the vision, the thorn in the flesh and its persistence and purpose (12:7b–9a). He concludes this unit by formulating the theological significance of his weaknesses (12:9b–10).

12:1 Paul moves on to visions and revelations with a similar introduction to those found in 11:30 and 12:6, "it is necessary for me to boast."[356] But he adds a crucial caveat that it is not expedient.[357] Paul keeps reminding the Corinthians that boasting is not only foolish and unbecoming an apostle of Christ, but it is unprofitable for them. It proves nothing except that one is a fool and may mislead the audience into thinking that boasting is an appropriate exercise for Christians. To dwell on our own excellence is dangerous because it causes us to turn our attention from God's glory to our own and stokes the sinful desire to create a circle of admirers for ourselves rather than disciples for Christ.[358]

So why boast if nothing is to be gained from it? Because much more could be lost if Paul does not somehow cancel out the seductive megalomania of his rivals. The rivals have set the agenda and have bedazzled some Corinthians with their boasts. Paul's deft use of irony in his own boasting helps the Corinthians to see the foolishness of all boasting and will help them see the rivals for what they really are.

"But I will come to visions and revelations" provides a transition that suggests that perhaps Paul is moving through a list of items the rivals used to captivate the Corinthians. Barrett thinks that "visions and revelations" might even be a slogan.[359] The Corinthians are enamored with the more electrifying displays of spiritual inspiration, and their worship service is marked by each one giving a revelation and a tongue (see 1 Cor 14:6,26). We can only guess, but it is not improbable that the rivals were quite ready to feed the Corinthians' appetite for spiritually thrilling visions. Their accounts of supernatural revelations gave a boost to their authority.[360] The rivals may even have gone into detail about the circumstances in which they received

---

[356] The reading δεῖ ("it is necessary") is widely attested (p[46] B D[2] F G H L P 0243 0278 6 33 81 614 1739) and is to be preferred as the original text over δέ (ℵ D* Ψ bo), represented by the KJV, "it is not expedient for me doubtless to glory," or δή, "indeed" (K 0121 945 1505). Some texts add εἰ ("if") from a scribal attempt to make it conform to 11:30 and to make sense of why Paul thinks it necessary to boast.

[357] Again the widely attested συμφέρον μέν is to be preferred over other readings συμφέρει and συμφέρον μοι, which appear to be attempts to improve the style.

[358] Calvin, *The Second Epistle of Paul the Apostle to the Corinthians*, 155.

[359] Barrett, *The Second Epistle to the Corinthians*, 306. The NIV renders "visions and revelations of the Lord" as a subjective genitive, "visions and revelations from the Lord." The Lord is the one who gives the visions, but they may also be about the Lord, objective genitive (see Gal 1:12,16). The visions come with an explanation, making plain what they are about.

[360] Barrett claims that it is more probable that "the insistence on 'spiritual' and ecstatic phenomena as the marks of apostleship originated in Corinth, though the visiting apostles, seeing that these marks were demanded, proceeded to provide them" (*The Second Epistle to the Corinthians*, 312).

their transcendent visions. Micaiah boosts the authority of his oracle to King Ahab by describing how he received it—as an observer of the heavenly court who overheard the discussion with the supernatural advisors, the host of heaven (1 Kgs 22:19–23). The rivals may have done likewise.

Visions were also part of the religious landscape of the Gentile world as an important element in magical rites and as part of initiations into mystery cults. A surviving fragment of a Mithras liturgy depicts a visionary ascent to heaven:

> You will see yourself being lifted up and ascending to the height, so that you seem to be in midair ... you will see all immortal things, for in that day and hour you will see the divine order of the skies: the presiding gods will appear through the disk of God. ... And you will see the gods staring intently at you and rushing at you. ... Then you will see the gods looking graciously upon you and no longer rushing at you, but rather going about in their own order of affairs. So when you see that the world above is clear and circling, and that none of the gods or angels is threatening you, expect to hear a great crash of thunder, so as to shock you ... and [after you have said the second prayer] you will see many five–pronged stars coming forth from the disk and filling all the air. Then say again: 'Silence! Silence!' And when the disk is open, you will see the fireless circle, and the fiery doors shut tight.[361]

We cannot assume that converted Gentiles made a clean break with their religious past. Some Corinthian converts may still have been unduly influenced by their former religious background concerning visionary experiences.

Paul is reticent to speak about such things because he does not believe that recounting one's extraordinary mystical visions will do anything to build up the community. It only serves to build up the teller's ego and therefore is perilous. It certainly offers no proof of apostleship. History is littered with the tales of frauds who have seduced and deluded followers by claiming to have some divine mission from some divine vision.[362] Consequently, Paul rehearses this extraordinary episode in a way that only stresses how useless it is to prove anything about him.[363] True apostleship is established by the building up of the community (1 Cor 14:3–5,26; 2 Cor 5:13), not by how many ecstatic experiences one can claim.

12:2–5   Paul moves from the "embarrassing descent to escape the hands

---

[361] *PGM* IV.539–85, cited by C. E. Arnold, *The Colossian Syncretism*, WUNT 2/77 (Tübingen: Mohr [Siebeck] 1995) 126. In Apuleius's novel, *Metamorphoses (The Golden Ass)*, when the hero of the story is initiated into the Isis mystery, he says: "I approached close to the gods above and the gods below and worshiped them face to face" (11.23).

[362] The Anabaptist movement was marked by the fanatical excesses of Jan van Leyden, among others, who placed great stress on private visions; and he was denounced by Menno Simons.

[363] Furnish, *II Corinthians*, 543. We might compare Paul's claim to have experienced speaking in tongues more than anyone else, which he then dismisses as unimportant compared to speaking five words with the mind (1 Cor 14:18–19).

of men" to "an exhilarating ascent into the presence of God."[364] But this rapture has a disappointing result. He does not know anything about the circumstances of his ascent and cannot tell anything about what he heard.

Telling this story in the third person, "I know a man in Christ," causes some to question whether Paul is recounting what happened to himself.[365] Paul's clear reference to himself in 12:1,5,7, however, reveals that he has chosen to relate this event by referring to himself only indirectly. Reporting what happened to someone else he may know would be completely irrelevant to his argument. The key question, then, is why does he choose to describe the vision in this manner.[366]

1. Paul may be falling back on the convention of pseudonymity in Jewish tradition concerning visionary accounts.[367] Later rabbinic tradition consid-

---

[364] M. J. Harris, "2 Corinthians," in *The Expositor's Bible Commentary* (Grand Rapids: Zondervan, 1976) 10:393.

[365] Some have contended that Paul uses the third person because he indeed is referring to the experience of someone else. L. Herrmann suggests that Paul refers to Apollos ("Apollos," *RSR* 50 [1976] 330–36). M. Smith claims that Paul refers to Jesus ("Ascent to the Heavens and the Beginning of Christianity," *Eranos* 50 (1981) 403–29). M. Goulder thinks that he refers to a Jewish Christian friend ("Vision and Knowledge," *JSNT* 56 [1994] 53–71).

[366] Of the many proposals the following merit mentioning. (1) Barrett suggests that Paul distinguishes between two men within himself: "There is *a man* who is a visionary, and this man is in fact Paul; but Paul would rather be thought of as the weak man, who has nothing to boast of but his weakness" (*The Second Epistle to the Corinthians*, 307). (2) Käsemann argues that Paul wanted to distance himself from the event he describes because such ecstasy has nothing to do with his apostolic services for the church ("Die Legitimität des Apostels," 64, 66–67). (3) W. Schmithals claims that Paul used the third person to designate his future existence as opposed to his so-called Gnostic opponents who boast of their present experience (*Gnosticism in Corinth* [Nashville: Abingdon, 1971] 212). (4) W. Baird argues that "Paul wants to prove that his ministry is not grounded in the sort of experience they claim as normative" ("Visions, Revelation, and Ministry: Reflections on 2 Cor. 12:1–5 and Gal. 1:11–17," *JBL* 104 [1985] 651–62, 654). Furnish concurs: Paul uses the third person because he is unwilling to claim this private religious experience as an apostolic credential (*II Corinthians,* 544). Martin also argues that Paul's use of the third person and his admission of ignorance about his state during the experience are "polemical devices to play down the opponents' claim to ecstatic experience as a validation of ministry" (*2 Corinthians,* 403).

[367] Harvey makes the point, "We cannot of course know what Paul experienced. The most we can do is enquire into the resources which his religion and his culture offered him for giving it some shape and enabling him to communicate it, however vaguely, to others." In other accounts of visionary experiences in Jewish literature, "the writer never allowed himself to appear as the subject, but either wrote anonymously and ascribed the experience to a figure of the past (e.g. 'The Ascension of Isaiah') or else wrote pseudonymously in the person of Daniel, Enoch or some other venerable seer" (*Renewal through Suffering,* 103). Some argue that Paul's experience has parallels with Jewish Merkabah mysticism; see J. Bowker, "'Merkabah' Visions and the Visions of Paul," *JJS* 16 (1971) 157–73; P. Schäfer, "New Testament and Hekhalot Literature: The Journey into Heaven in Paul and Merkavah Mysticism," *JJS* 35 (1984) 19–35; C. R. A. Morray-Jones, "Transformational Mysticism in the Apocalyptic Merkabah Tradition," *JJS* 43 (1992) 1–31; and "Paradise Revisited (2 Cor. 12:1–12): The Jewish Mystical Background of Paul's Apostolate," *HTR* 86 (1993) 177– 217; 265–92. Kruse comments that the various literary parallels show that what Paul is relating would have been "understandable to his contemporaries" (*2 Corinthians,* 202). They would not have looked at him as if he were crazy. See B. H. Young, "The Ascension Motif of II Cor 12 in Jewish, Christian and Gnostic Texts," *GTJ* 9 (1988) 73–103.

ered this subject dangerous and forbade public discussion of it, and Paul's reserve may be an early reflection of this attitude.[368]

2. The use of the third person may derive from the very nature of the experience itself. Such an overwhelming event—he is not sure if it was in the body or out of the body—resulted in him observing "himself undergoing the experience" as a kind of spectator.[369]

3. It may also be attributable to his desire not to boast. Only the greatest figures of Scripture were ever snatched up to the heavens. Paul has no interest in ranking himself with these saints; he simply wants to drive pompous rivals from the ranks of the Corinthians. He therefore avoids an egocentric form of expression since he is already acutely conscious of the foolishness of self-praise.[370] Paul's reticence to refer to himself directly fits his ambivalence toward boasting in this section. He can boast about such a person in Christ, but not about himself (12:5).[371] What happened happened to a man in Christ. The reference to the man in Christ may lead us back to 10:17, "But, 'Let him who boasts boast in the Lord.'" God did not grant Paul this awesome experience of paradise because he was so special, "but solely because of his relationship to Christ."

Betz argues that Paul is parodying the practice of his rivals and the motif of heavenly journeys to make their heavenly raptures and visions seem absurd.[372] But referring to this rapture as happening to "a man in Christ" does not suggest parody. Paul's statement about grace in 12:9 is something fundamental to his whole understanding of his existence, something he was unlikely to spoof.[373] The incident was a cherished, life changing event for Paul; but it was also highly personal and not something he freely shared with others nor something about which he would brag.

---

[368] According to *b. Hag.* 14b, four great scholars ascended to heaven and beheld the glory. All but one suffered calamities, death, or mental illness. Elisha ben Abuya "cut down plants," i.e., he became a heretic cutting down the plants of truth. Simeon ben Zoma lost his mind. Simon ben Azzai died. Only Akiba escaped unscathed. We should note that Paul is forbidden to recount the vision to others (12:4).

[369] J. D. G. Dunn, *Jesus and the Spirit* (Philadelphia: Westminster, 1975) 214–15. So also M. E. Thrall, "Paul's Journey to Paradise: Some Exegetical Issues in 2 Cor 12,2–4," in *The Corinthians Correspondence*, ed. R. Bieringer (Leuven: University Press, 1996) 352– 53. Cp. *3 Apoc. Bar.* 17:3: "And when I came to myself, I praised God."

[370] Héring, *The Second Epistle of Saint Paul to the Corinthians*, 89, n. 1; so also P. E. Hughes, *Paul's Second Epistle to the Corinthians*, NICNT (Grand Rapids: Eerdmans, 1962) 429–30.

[371] A. T. Lincoln contends, "One of the elements of the apology in the Socratic tradition was that one must not boast about oneself, but if necessary this may be done by someone else. Paul's use of the third person is his way of observing this sort of convention. He does not praise himself but another described as ἄνθρωπος ἐν Χριστῷ (v. 2), ὁ τοιοῦτος ἄνθρωπος (v. 3) and again ὁ τοιοῦτος (v. 5)" (" 'Paul the Visionary': The Setting and Significance of the Rapture to Paradise in II Corinthians XII. 1–10," *NTS* 25 [1978–79] 208–9).

[372] Betz, *Der Apostel Paulus*, 84–92. See also Furnish, *II Corinthians*, 543

[373] Wolff, *Die zweite Korintherbrief*, 241.

Another curious detail in this account is his choice of an incident that happened "fourteen years ago." If he had so many visions and revelations, why did he choose this particular one?[374] Some conclude that such visions were actually unusual for Paul since he does not refer to anything more recent.[375] Though Paul never mentions such visions elsewhere in his letters, that does not allow us to infer that they were rare or only a negligible part of his life.[376] Paul claims to speak in tongues "more than all of you" (1 Cor 14:18–19), and we would not know that unless tongues had surfaced as a problem in Corinth. Lincoln concludes, "Clearly lack of frequent reference does not necessarily mean lack of frequent experience."[377] Therefore Paul must have some other reason for choosing this particular vision.

We have already suggested that it was a life-changing event, and Paul will explain its repercussions in 12:7–8. But it also predates the establishment of the church in Corinth, which he claims validates his credentials as an apostle (3:1–3). It means that he had spent months with them and never mentioned this incident once. As far as he is concerned, his rapturous visions had nothing to do with their becoming Christians; therefore, visions have nothing to do with authenticating an apostle.[378] This particular vision also resulted in the thorn in his flesh that seems to have provoked some disparagement of Paul. He notifies them that the thorn in the flesh, the clearest evidence of his weakness, was the outcome of a spectacular vision, his entrance into paradise.

Paul describes himself as being "snatched," "caught up" *(harpagenta)* to the third heaven and to paradise.[379] This verb suggests that "Paul's experience was

---

[374] Baird, "Visions, Revelation, and Ministry," 653.

[375] Barrett suggests that he goes back fourteen years because "He was thus ordinarily anything but a visionary, though it is no doubt true that he picked out the most striking, and not the only, visionary experience that he could claim" (*The Second Epistle to the Corinthians,* 308).

[376] See H. Saake, "Paulus als Ekstatiker: Pneumatologische Beobachtung zu 2 Kor. xii 1–10," *NovT* 15 (1973) 152–60.

[377] Lincoln, "Paul the Visionary," 205. We know from Paul's letter to the Galatians that he received other revelations. He received the gospel he proclaims from a revelation of Christ (Gal 1:11–12); he also went up to Jerusalem to meet with the pillar apostles in response to a revelation (Gal 2:2). His understanding of "mysteries" can be presumed to come from revelations—the mystery of the hardening that has come upon Israel (Rom 11:25); the resurrection of the dead (1 Cor 15:51); and the return of Christ (1 Thess 4:15), although Paul never gives any details about how he came by these revelations. Acts recounts that Paul was the recipient of numerous visions. In Troas Paul saw the vision of the Macedonian beckoning him (Acts 16:9–10). He received assuring visions of the Lord in Corinth (Acts 18:9–10), in Jerusalem (Acts 23:11), and on the voyage to Rome (Acts 27:23–24). In Acts 22:17–21 he states that after the Damascus experience he was in Jerusalem, and as he was praying in the temple, "he fell into a trance" (ἐν ἐκστάσει) and was warned to leave the city and to go to the Gentiles.

[378] "Heavenly vision" is used in Acts 26:19 for Jesus' resurrection appearance to Paul on the Damascus road (Acts 9:1–9; 22:3–16; 26:9–18), but it was of a different order because it could be related. Paul describes that appearance to him as central to his identity as an apostle

[379] ἁρπαγέντα 12:2; ἡρπάγη 12:4; see *Apoc. Mos.* 37:3. The vocabulary of being snatched is conventional; Acts 8:39; 1 Thess 4:1; Rev 12:5; *Wis* 4:11; *1 Enoch* 39:3–4; 52:1–2; *2 Enoch* 7:1; 8:1.

an involuntary one in which God took the initiative rather than one brought about by preparation or special techniques."[380] The experience was not something he sought or initiated and therefore was not something that he could repeat whenever he wanted.[381] It is something God did, and something only God can explain. Bernard of Clairvaux said, "If the great Apostle had to be transported to that place which he could not know by his own learning or climb to by his own strength even with a guide, then I, so tiny compared to Paul, must never presume that I can climb to the third heaven by my own strength and effort."[382]

Paul does not present himself, however, as a great apostle but simply as "a man in Christ." As far as he is concerned, this incomparable experience does not set him apart from others as one who is now their incomparable superior. He will clarify that this episode conveyed that he remains no different from anyone else, a weak vessel of clay who can only be sustained by the grace of God.

Paul repeats twice that he does not know the circumstances of his ascent, whether it occurred in the body or out of the body (12:2–3). This admission of his ignorance implies that it is all quite unimportant and may have a polemical edge to it. He could be taking a swipe at those who only prize out of body experiences.[383] On the other hand, Paul genuinely may not know. He would be aware that there were both types of rapture in the Jewish tradition.[384] But why does he repeat himself? Thrall thinks

---

[380] Lincoln, "Paul the Visionary," 215.

[381] C. H. Talbert, *Reading Corinthians: A Literary and Theological Commentary on 1 and 2 Corinthians* (New York: Crossroad, 1987) 123.

[382] Bernard of Clairvaux, *On Humility* Sermon VIII.22 (p. 50).

[383] Furnish comments, "By emphasizing the uncertainty of the mode of his rapture, Paul seems to be saying that he does not really care; and this suggests that there are some in Corinth who really do" (*II Corinthians*, 545).

[384] See Gen 5:24; 2 Kgs 2:11; Rev 4:2; 17:3; 21:10; *4 Ezra* 14:49 (Syr.); *1 Enoch* 12:1; 14:8; 39:3–4; 71:1,5; *2 Enoch* 1:6–10; 7:1; 8:1; 38:1–2; *3 Apoc. Bar.* (Gk.) 11:1–2 ; *Apoc. Sed.* 2:4; *Mart. Isa.* 6:10; 7:5; *T. Abr.* (B) 8:1–3; and Philo *On Dreams* 1:36; *Questions and Answers on Exodus* 2.39 (2.27–29, 51). C. Rowland argues that Jewish apocalypses reflected real experiences and suggests they "may have been conscious, at one and the same time, of being outside the body and yet of experiencing physical sensations of various kinds" (*The Open Heaven: A Study of Apocalyptic Judaism and Early Christianity* [London: SPCK, 1982] 214–28). Thrall cites Rowland's view with approval: "It is probably such twofold effects which Paul is hinting at when he refers to his uncertainty about the precise nature of his experience" ("Paul's Journeys," 355). But Paul differs from other accounts of heavenly ascents in that they describe it as *either* in the body *or* out of the body. Paul does not know which it was and does not seem to care. Schmithals, with his pan-Gnostic interpretation of Paul, thought that Paul allows for the possibility of a bodiless experience and "*becomes a Gnostic to the Gnostics*" (see 1 Cor 9:19–23), conceding the possibility of existence outside the body. His point is that the Gnostics are mistaken by thinking that they are perfected by such experiences and they do not need God's grace (*Gnosticism in Corinth*, 216–17). While Schmithals may be correct about Paul's emphasis on grace, the Gnostic conception of the body is not at issue here. Nevertheless, Paul's statement assumes that the body is not completely incompatible with paradise. Barrett believes "the experience described in our passage may be thought of as an anticipation of the final transference of believers to heaven, or Paradise" (*The Second Epistle to the Corinthians*, 309).

that Paul "may be emphasizing his total lack of comprehension about how
the event occurred. It was a wonderful happening whose mode of operation was known only to God."[385] This conclusion makes the best sense of
Paul's repetition.

The reference to "being caught up to the third heaven" in 12:2 and "caught
up to paradise" in 12:4 presents another perplexing detail. "Paradise" was a Per-
sian loan word used in the Hebrew Old Testament to refer to a park.[386] In intertestamental literature it was used for the realm entered upon death or the realm
where God is.[387] Paul's account raises several questions. Is the third heaven
identical with paradise? If not, is paradise in a realm higher than the third
heaven and was his ascension a two stage process?

Some argue that Paul ascended to paradise in two stages.[388] It could perhaps explain the repetition, in the body or out of the body. In the Jewish tradition we can find the concept of seven heavens and even ten heavens. If
Paul adopted this schema, the third heaven may have been a lower level of
seven or more.[389] It is then on the highest level, paradise, where Paul hears
the unutterable words.

But what is the purpose of mentioning a stop in the third heaven if this
were not understood as the ultimate heaven? In other stories of trips to the
heavens, the seers give copious reports of what they observe in each celestial
region. Paul, however, does not recount passing through other regions or
seeing or hearing anything significant at this third level. The repetition of the
same verb "caught up" *(harpazo)* in 12:4 for being taken to the third heaven
and to paradise suggests that Paul refers to a single experience. A three-
heaven schema is the most well established view in Jewish writings, and the
"third heaven" would therefore be recognized as the highest.[390] Thrall
points out that Paul's use of the two terms can be explained by Semitic syn-

---

[385] Thrall, "Paul's Journeys," 356.

[386] See Neh 2:8; Eccl 2:5; and *Cant* 4:12. In the LXX the Greek word παραδείσος is used for
the Garden of Eden in the Genesis account.

[387] See *1 Enoch* 40:7–8, 23; 60:7,23; 61:12; 70:4; *2 Enoch* 9:1; 42:3; *Apoc. Abr.* 21:6–7; *T Abr.*
20; *2 Apoc. Bar.* 4:6; *Apoc. Mos.* 37:5; 40:2; and *T. Abr.* 20:14 (A). In Ezek 28:13 and 31:8 the garden of Eden is referred to as the garden of God.

[388] Plummer cites Clement of Alexandria, who said that the apostle was "caught up ... to the
third heaven, and thence into paradise" (*The Second Epistle of St. Paul to the Corinthians*, 344).

[389] In *2 Enoch* 3–22 the seer moves through six heavens, which climaxes in the seventh. The
concept of seven heavens also appears in *Asc. Isa.* 6:13; 7:13; *b. Hag.* 12b; *Pesiq. R.* 5; *'Abot Rab.
Nat.* 37; and *Midr. Ps.* 92.

[390] *Testament of Levi* 2:7–10; 3:1–4 conceives of the heavenly spheres as three in number (per-
haps deduced from 1 Kgs 8:27, "the heavens and the heavens of the heavens" (see also Neh. 9:6; 2
Chron 2:6; 6:18; Ps 68:33; and 148:4). The following works locate paradise in the third heaven: *2
Enoch* 8:1; *Apoc Mos.* 37:5; and *3 Apoc. Bar.* 4:8.

thetic parallelism "in which the second element takes up the first, carries it
further, and intensifies its effect." The second term, "paradise," either gives
"a more precise indication of the part of the third heaven to which Paul was
transported, or else serves to clarify its character."[391] Calvin argued that the
term "third heaven" is not literal but symbolic:

> The number three is used as a perfect number to indicate what is highest and
> most complete. Also the word heaven by itself means here God's blessed and
> glorious kingdom about all spheres and the firmament itself and all the frame-
> work of the world. But not content with the word heaven, Paul adds that he had
> reached the utmost height and its innermost chambers.[392]

Lincoln is probably correct that "Paul has simply taken over the term 'third
heaven' in a formal manner as a variant designation for Paradise."[393]

When all is said and done, Paul confides very little about what happened.
We learn only that he was caught up to the third heaven, paradise, how he
does not know, and what he heard he cannot divulge. Paul's account of his
journey to heaven differs from the tours of heaven and hell recorded by other
apocalyptic and mystical writers of the age. He does not say how he was
transported because he does not know (contrast *Apoc. Mos.* 37:3,5). He does
not visit a series of heavens. He is not let in on secrets that he can then disclose to others or put in a book to be sealed for a later time.[394] The meaning
of what he sees and hears is not interpreted by an angelic tour guide. In the
aftermath what he gets instead is an angel from Satan who plagues him with
a thorn that leads him to a deeper understanding of his ministry. Paul sets the
stage for some angelic vision and comes back with the image of an angel of
Satan. The vision of heaven rouses adversaries from hell.[395]

---

[391] Thrall, "Paul's Journeys," 356–57, citing J. Zmijewski, *Der Stil der paulinischen "Nar-
renrede." Analyse der Sprachgestaltung in 2 Kor 11,2–12,10 als Beitrag zur Methodik von Sti-
luntersuchungen neutestamentlicher Texte*, BBB 52 (Köln/Bonn: Hanstein, 1978) 335.

[392] Calvin, *The Second Epistle of Paul the Apostle to the Corinthians*, 156.

[393] Lincoln, "Paul the Visionary," 213. Jewish writings only agree that there were various levels
of the heavens but not on the precise number, whether there are three, five, seven, or ten. The Hb.
word for heaven is plural, *šāmayim,* and lends itself to this kind of speculation.

[394] If Paul's Corinthian audience were not familiar with Jewish apocalyptic literature in which
seers received revelations that were to be sealed for a time, they would be familiar with such a concept from the mystery religions (Euripides, *Bacchae* 471–72; Aristophanes, *Clouds* 302; Lucian,
Menippos 2; and Apuleius, *Metamorphoses (the Golden Ass)* 11:23). But Lincoln points out that
secret mysteries could be passed on to initiates. By contrast, Paul could communicate what he
heard to no one. "Herein lies the ironic twist he gives his account, for in order to boast about revelations he selects from his many experiences a visionary experience which involved that which
could not be revealed to any one else" (Lincoln, "Paul the Visionary," 216).

[395] DiCicco identifies this as an example of aposipopesis—beginning to say something and
stopping short, leaving the audience to hang in suspense, which serves to add emphasis (DiCicco,
Paul's Use of Ethos, Pathos, and Logos in 2 Corinthians 10–13, 100–101; noting Aristotle, *Rhetoric* 4.53.67).

Paul's assurance that he beheld the glory of the Lord (3:18) and the coming glory of the believers (4:17; cp. Rom 8:18) may be related to this incident, but that is merely a guess and ranges far afield from what Paul actually says. He does not say that he *saw* anything but reports only that he heard something. Normally seers tell about what they see, but Paul tells about what he heard, except that he cannot tell it.[396] He heard unutterable utterances (cp. 1 Cor 2:9). Was it impossible to express in human language or was he forbidden to express it because it was too holy or too horrible? His explanatory statement, "which things it is not lawful for a man to speak" (literal trans.), argues for the latter.[397] There are certain divine things that humans may not know, and if they are granted the privilege of learning of them, they may not tell. Paul offers no explanation for why he must remain silent. If he gave any more hints, he would have broken the prohibition.[398] Paul's peculiar description of his experience when he *was caught up* to paradise reveals that it was a mystical vision quite different from the visions the prophets in the Old Testament experienced and quite different from his own call when the resurrected Lord *came down* to him. His call commissioned him to service; this vision was simply a heavenly diversion.[399]

This leads us to summarize what Paul's account of this experience means:

1. The benefit for Paul was not soteriological or vocational but concerned only his private relationship to God as a man in Christ. Talbert observes, "Like tongues (1 Cor 14:18), such mystical experiences' benefits are for the private devotional life of the believer."[400]

2. Private mystical experiences have no value for the church because they cannot be adequately communicated to others. They are useless in trying to make arguments in a public forum that requires logical argument. The danger of basing teaching on private heavenly revelations is that it will create a division between those blessed with such visions and the rank and file who

---

[396] Contrast Levi, who enters succeeding heavens, each more glorious, until he stands near the Lord and is told: "You shall see his priest and you shall tell forth his mysteries" (*T. Levi* 2:7–11). Martin claims that the inexpressible words are "a counterblast to gnosticizing secrets putatively revealed to the opponents" (*2 Corinthians*, 405), but this conclusion reads too much into the text.

[397] Philo talks about those who would rather have their tongues cut out "than say anything that should not be divulged" (τῶν ἀρρήτων ἐκλαλῆσαι; *The Worse Attacks the Better* 175). When Asenath asks the name of the angel so that she might praise and glorify his name forever, he responded: "Why do you seek this, my name, Asenath? My name is in the heavens in the book of the Most High, written by the finger of God in the beginning of the book before all (the others), because I am chief of the house of the Most High, And all the names written in the book of the Most High are unspeakable, and man is not allowed to pronounce nor hear them in this world, because those names are exceedingly great and wonderful and laudable" (*Joseph and Asenath* 15:11–12).

[398] His silence is quite different from the account of Ezra's ascent when he is troubled by a vision he is unable to explain (*4 Ezra* 10:32). The angel then interprets it for him.

[399] Bultmann, *The Second Letter to the Corinthians*, 222.

[400] Talbert, *Reading Corinthians*, 124.

are not. Matthew 28:19–20 makes clear that the teaching of the church is based on what Jesus had already commanded on earth, not on the latest visions from paradise.

3. Private mystical experiences may lead to boasting and self-justification. It would naturally result in a sense of spiritual triumph. Visions can lead one to become inappropriately elated, and Paul's thorn was an effective cure for any mistaken euphoria. As Barnett puts it, "God ... brought the elated Paul down to earth and pinned him there with a 'thorn.' "[401] It also kept Paul pinned closer to the Lord.[402] His rapture to paradise was not an apotheosis; he remains a mere mortal. Paul therefore does not use this experience as proof of his endorsement by God. As Best notes, it was an exceptional event that he hardly expects others to experience, "not even church officials as a condition of their appointment."[403] Such experiences take their toll as Paul reveals in what follows. They are not something that he sought, nor something that others should seek.[404]

12:6 Paul will boast only of his weaknesses, like his craven flight from Damascus in which God delivered him from the hand of his enemies, so that the credit will be given to God and not to him. He argues, however, that if he did boast about the flight to paradise and the vision he received from God, it would not be the exaggerated boasting of the fool who cannot reliably assess his own merit before God. What happened in this transcendent vision was not his own doing but God's. Consequently, he can speak of its effects, because they are true, even if he cannot tell what exactly transpired or what he heard.

The Corinthians cannot gauge his apostleship based on his tales about ecstatic visions. They can only evaluate him from what they have witnessed from his ministry among them (see 10:7, "Look at what is before your very eyes"). On the one hand, he does not want them to think too much of him because of any boasting on his part. To flaunt his heavenly visions would create in them a "worldly-minded trust in him, the apostle, rather than in God (cf. 1 Cor 2:5)."[405] On the other hand, he does not want them to think

---

[401] P. Barnett, *The Message of 2 Corinthians*, The Bible Speaks Today (Leicester/Downers Grove: IVP, 1988) 177–78.

[402] Ibid., 178.

[403] Best, *Second Corinthians*, 117.

[404] Jacob's wrestling with an angel (Gen 33:25) and the rabbinic account of the scholars ascent to heaven (*b. Hag.* 14b) reveal that some believed that supernatural religious experiences were charged with danger. See J. Maier, "Das Gefährdungsmotiv bei der Himmelreise in der Jüdischen Apokalyptik und 'Gnosis,'" *Kairos* 5 (1963) 18–40; R. N. Price, "Punished in Paradise (An Exegetical Theory of II Corinthians 12:1–10," *JSNT* 7 (1980) 33–40; and R. P. Spittler, "The Limits of Ecstasy: An Exegesis of 2 Corinthians 12:1–10," in *Current Issues in Biblical and Patristic Interpretation: Studies in Honor of M. C. Tenney*, ed. G. F. Hawthorne (Grand Rapids: Eerdmans, 1975).

[405] Savage, *Power through Weakness*, 162.

too little of him because of the boasting of others. The verb *logizesthai* ("think") has appeared in 10:2,7 ("consider"), 11 ("realize"), and 11:5 and points to a key issue that Paul is dealing with in these chapters: how the Corinthians "reckon" or "appraise" their apostle. The word "more" *(hyper)* has also appeared throughout these chapters and is one of the problems besetting his opponents.[406] They think more of themselves than is warranted.

Validation as God's minister does not come from one's own self-endorsement or from otherworldly experiences. The problem is that the Corinthians do not understand him fully (1:14), and what they have seen of him they have misread (10:1,10; 11:21). He needs to bring them to understand that the life and power of God (13:4) pulse beneath his mask of death, weakness, and humiliation (4:7–12). What is important are not the transcendent moments when he has become spiritually airborne, but his obedience in the daily chore of preaching the gospel faithfully despite "weaknesses, insults, hardships, persecutions, and difficulties" (12:10).

12:7 Paul introduces "the thorn in his flesh" as stemming from the excessive number or exceptional nature of the revelations.[407] He could be referring to the quantity of the revelations and implying that he has received many others besides this one fourteen-year-old revelation. It is more likely, however, that he refers to the quality of the revelations as reflected in the NIV translation, "these surpassingly great revelations" (see also NRSV). Over elation from the incredible experience of being allowed entry into paradise could easily lead to an over inflation of one's ego so that one feels superior to others less blessed by supernal visions.[408] To prevent such spiritual pride from welling up in Paul, he was given a thorn in the flesh.[409] The

---

[406] The preposition ὑπέρ appears in 11:23, "Are they servants of Christ? I more."

[407] The Gk. phrase at the beginning of 12:7, καί τῇ ὑπερβολῇ τῶν ἀποκαλύψεων ("because of these surpassingly great revelations") is a pendent dative of cause that requires in this instance the insertion of the phrase "because of" before it. But the Gk. text could be punctuated differently so that this phrase is a continuation of the thought in 12:6: "But if I wish to boast, I will not be a fool, for I will be speaking the truth. But I refrain from it, so that no one may think better of me than what is seen in me or heard from me, even considering the exceptional character of the revelations" (NRSV).

[408] The verb ὑπεραίρωμαι is used as a reflexive middle, "to exalt myself" (see 2 Thess 2:4). The verb ἐπαίρω ("exalt") appears in 11:20 (see 10:5) as one of the characteristics of the rivals who exalt themselves. By contrast, the thorn in the flesh prevents Paul from being overly uplifted and elated with himself.

[409] "To keep me from being conceited" (ἵνα μὴ ὑπεραίρωμαι) is repeated twice in the Gk., although some texts omit the second occurrence (ℵ*A, D, F, and G) as does the NIV. The NRSV preserves the redundancy: "Therefore, to keep me from being too elated, a thorn was given me in the flesh, a messenger of Satan to torment me, to keep me from being too elated." Cp. Philo's explanation of Jacob's limp that was given to him that he might not become too conceited (Philo, *On Dreams I,* 130–31).

passive voice implies that God gave it to him.[410] Paul's "thorn" was an effective cure for any mistaken euphoria that visions might evoke. God wanted Paul to remain humble and fully aware of his own weakness. The thorn punctured any pride that might surge within him because of his grand entry into heaven, and the result was that he dealt with others with the meekness and gentleness of Christ (10:1) rather than with the arrogant puffery of Satan.

The exact nature of this "thorn in the flesh" has prompted much speculation.[411] Paul does not go into any detail in describing it because the Corinthians apparently were well familiar with what he meant. Some of their number or his competitors may have made it the object of their derision. The word translated "thorn" *(skolops)* occurs only here in the New Testament. It refers to something pointed such as a stake for impaling, a medical instrument, or a thorn. "Stake" would be a better translation, though "thorn" has dominated English renderings of the word.[412] The metaphor carries "the notion of something sharp and painful which sticks deeply in the flesh and in the will of God defies extracting."[413] In rabbinic literature the image is used to refer to something that causes pain, annoyance—something vexing—and does not especially refer to sickness or affliction.[414] In the Septuagint the noun is used to refer to some kind of opposition (Num 33:55; Hos 2:6; Ezek 28:24). The phrase "in the flesh" seems to imply, however, that this thorn afflicts his physical body (a local dative, see 4:11; 10:2).[415] It may be the problem behind the criticism of his physical presence.

Most interpreters through the years have assumed that Paul alludes to some bodily ailment. This view is reinforced by Paul's mention of a physical illness that detained him in Galatia and led to his preaching the gospel to

---

[410] Martin comments that the verb "to give" (διδόναι) is used to denote God's favor (see Gal 3:21; Eph 3:8; 5:19; 1 Tim 4:14; *2 Corinthians*, 412). Plummer suggests that if Satan were the agent, the verbs, "lay upon" (ἐπιτίθημι, Luke 10:30; 23:36; Acts 16:23), or "cast" (βάλλειν, Rev 2:24) or "put on" (ἐπιβάλλειν, 1 Cor 7:35) would have been more appropriate (*The Second Epistle of St. Paul to the Corinthians*, 348).

[411] See P. H. Menoud, "The Thorn in the Flesh and Satan's Angel (2 Cor 12.7)," in *Jesus Christ and the Faith: A Collection of Studies* (Pittsburgh: Pickwick, 1978) 19–30; and U. Heckel, "Der Dorn im Fleisch. Die Krankheit des Paulus in 2 Kor 12,7 und Gal 4, 13f," *ZNW* 84 (1993) 65–92.

[412] D. M. Park, "Paul's ΣΚΟΛΟΨ ΤΗ ΣΑΡΚΙ: Thorn or Stake? (2 Cor XII 7)," *NovT* 22 (1980) 179–83. In German it is consistently rendered as *Pfahl*, "stake."

[413] H. R. Minn, *The Thorn That Remained* (Auckland: Institute Press, 1972) 10.

[414] Bultmann, *The Second Letter to the Corinthians*, 224.

[415] Others have taken it as a dative of disadvantage, "for the flesh" (so Plummer, *The Second Epistle of St. Paul to the Corinthians*, 348). Calvin interpreted "flesh" to refer to "the part of the soul that was not regenerate" and renders it: "To me there has been given a goad to jab at my flesh for I am not ye so spiritual as to be exempt from temptations according to the flesh" (*The Second Epistle of Paul the Apostle to the Corinthians*, 159). The context makes this interpretation doubtful. Paul identifies it as a weakness, and says that he is content with his weakness (12:10). He would hardly be content with constant temptations to sin.

them. He writes that his physical condition was a trial to them (Gal 4:13–14).[416] Assuming that this affliction was something that persisted, the suggestions range from a pain in the ear or head, to malarial fever, epilepsy, and solar retinitus.[417] To do and suffer all that Paul lists in 11:24–27, however, would rule out some chronic debilitating disease.[418] Martin states it well:

> One wonders if a person who was so often on the "battlefield" could have been so physically weak and still have withstood the rigors of Paul's life. ... Paul is one who must be seen as in robust health and with a strong constitution.[419]

Others have claimed that Paul suffered from some psychological ailment or distress, some personal anxiety or torment. Less incapacitating problems have been suggested such as depression over his earlier persecution of the church, a tendency to despair and doubt (so Luther, *Table Talk,* 24.7), or even sexual temptation.[420] Still others interpret the stake to refer to persecution or adversaries—the rise of the Judaizers, for example—who have dogged him throughout his ministry and now supposedly plague him at Corinth.[421]

---

[416] We should not forget that in the ancient world illnesses were attributed to demons.

[417] Commentators frequently resort to more technical medical terminology or more pedantic language such as "ophthalmic disability" when discussing the proposals for Paul's ailments, as if this kind of scientific language gives their guesswork more credibility.

[418] A. Oepke speculates that this thorn might have "increased the tendency towards ecstatic experiences" ("ἔκστασις," *TDNT* 2:457–58).

[419] Martin, *2 Corinthians*, 415.

[420] So C. à Lapide, *The Great Commentary of Cornelius à Lapide: II Corinthians and Galatians*, 187–88. Plummer's sly observation is apropos, "In each case men supposed that St. Paul's special affliction was akin to what was a special trouble to themselves" (*The Second Epistle of St. Paul to the Corinthians*, 350).

[421] T. Y. Mullins, "Paul's Thorn in the Flesh," *JBL* 76 (1957) 299–303; see also John Chrysostom, who thought it referred to adversaries of the word like Alexander the coppersmith (*Homilies on Second Corinthians,* XXVI.7 [400]). The arguments mustered for this view contend that (1) Paul uses *aggelos* to refer to a person. (2) Paul has already identified the false apostles as agents of Satan (11:13–14). (3) The verb κολαφίζειν ("to batter," Mark 15:14,65; Matt 26:67; 1 Cor 4:11) is used to refer to being beaten or battered especially for blows to the head. (4) Abuse occurs in a hardship list (1 Cor 4:11) where it refers to the hostility that Paul faces in his ministry. (5) The word "stake" appears in the LXX for the enemies of Israel (Num 33:55; Ezek 23:24). (6) The longer list of hardships preceding his mention of the stake and the brief one that follows it in 12:10 focus on persecutions and opposition. Contra this view (1) Satan is associated with illness in the NT, and an angel of Satan may simply refer to some demonic agency. (2) It would also seem strange for Paul to pray that he be spared opposition or persecution (12:8). (3) If opponents such as the Judaizers were in mind, the letter to the Galatians reveals they were far more than simply a thorn in his side; they were a grave danger to the salvation of the Galatians. Paul did not quietly accept such opposition, and their threat to the faith of his charges did not convey to him the message, "The Lord's grace is sufficient, do not worry." (4) It is also unlikely that the opposition to his ministry can be equated with his weaknesses. In the Corinthian situation Paul's weaknesses have apparently given rise to the opposition. (5) Finally, "a stake or thorn in the flesh is not the same as a pain in the heart" (Witherington, *Conflict and Community in Corinth*, 462, n. 93). J. W. McCant claims that the thorn is a metaphor for the Corinthian church, which refuses to acknowledge the legitimacy of Paul's apostleship ("Paul's Thorn of Rejected Apostleship," *NTS* 34 [1988] 550–72). This view is wrong because they do acknowledge his legitimacy, as witnessed by their submitting questions to him in 1 Corinthians and the account of Titus's visit in 2 Cor 7:5–16. Some do question his style of ministry and do not always obey him, choosing instead to follow their own spiritual leading. Finally, Paul connects the stake to the heavenly vision that occurred long before his relationship with the Corinthians.

Since Paul prays so fervently to have the stake removed, it was probably something that he felt interfered with his ministry. Marshall identifies it as a "socially debilitating disease or disfigurement which was made the subject of ridicule and invidious comparison."[422] Paul's speech has been the subject of the Corinthians' criticism (10:10), and the stake could have been something that led to some kind of a speech handicap.[423] The "angel of Satan" could allude to the story of Balaam (Num 22:22–34) where the angel of the Lord gets in his way three times to prevent him from speaking and cursing the nation of Israel, against God's will.[424] In the end we must accept the fact that we will never know for certain what Paul's stake in the flesh was. We can only be certain that initially it caused him considerable annoyance.

The ambiguity about what Paul's stake in the flesh might be allows others to identify their own personal "thorns" with Paul's and to appropriate the theological lesson.[425] Stakes in the flesh are not good, but they also are not bad because they may convey a word from God if we are attuned to hear it. What is important to Paul is the theological word-to-the-wise that his stake in the flesh provided him. It was a constant reminder of God's grace and God's power working through him.

The phrase "angel of Satan" is in apposition to the stake. Satan comes to

---

[422] P. Marshall, "A Metaphor of Social Shame: *THRIAMBEUEIN* in 2 Cor. 2:14," *NovT* 25 (1983) 315–16. This view makes sense since Paul has been the target of invective which, as a matter of course, ridiculed "the opponent's social background, immorality, physical appearance, religious and philosophical belief, speech, avarice, personal activities" (Marshall, *Enmity in Corinth*, 62–64).

[423] Barrett, *The Second Epistle to the Corinthians*, 315. It could not have been congenital, however, since Paul says that it came after his vision.

[424] Cited by V. Jegher-Bucher, "'The Thorn in the Flesh'/ Der Pfahl im Fleisch': Considerations About 2 Corinthians 12.7–10 in Connection with 12.1–13," in *The Rhetorical Analysis of Scripture: Essays from the 1995 London Conference*, ed. S. E. Porter and T. H. Olbricht, JSNTSup 146 (Sheffield: Academic Press, 1997) 388–89. She argues that the stake is Paul's "weak presentation" and "dull delivery of speech." She connects it to Aristotle's reference to an orator "carrying a stake" (*Rhetoric* 1413b), but Aristotle uses the word δοκός ("beam"), not σκόλοψ ("stake"). The proposed parallel hardly applies.

[425] We might compare this description of Calvin's ill-health. "His afflictions read like a medical journal. He suffered from painful stomach cramps, intestinal influenza, and recurring migraine headaches. He was subject to a persistent onslaught of fevers that would often lay him up for weeks at a time. He experienced problems with his trachea, in addition to pleurisy, gout, and colic. He was especially susceptible to hemorrhoids, which were aggravated by an internal abscess that would not heal. He suffered from severe arthritis and acute pain in his knees, calves, and feet. Other maladies included nephritis (acute, chronic inflammation of the kidney caused by infection), gallstones, and kidney stones. He once passed a kidney stone so large that it tore the urinary canal and led to excessive bleeding. He contracted pulmonary tuberculosis at fifty-one, which led ultimately to his death. His health problems were aggravated by his demanding pace of preaching" (C. S. Storms, *Healing and Holiness: A Biblical Response to the Faith-Healing Phenomenon* [Phillipsburg, N.J.: Presbyterian & Reformed, 1990] 138–39).

bedevil him as an agent of testing. The verb "to torment" (*kolaphizein,* "abuse," "batter") implies humiliating violence—being slapped around; and the present tense suggests that it was persistent—something that happens over and over again. The same word is used for the abuse of Jesus in his passion (Mark 15:65; Matt 26:67), and by choosing this word Paul might connect his sufferings as an apostle with those of Christ.

Satan comes as God's adversary to lure people away from God's rule, or he comes as God's proxy to implement trials God authorizes. The story of Job provides the foremost example of the latter.[426] Does this Satanic angel try to hinder the advance of the gospel in some way (see 1 Thess 2:18)? If so, Satan's purposes are thwarted (see 2:11). What is sent to torment Paul is transformed by God into a means of proclaiming Christ's power and grace. This surprising twist reflects the paradoxical way God defeats Satan.[427] God permits Satan to strike the apostle, but God turns the stricken Paul into an even greater instrument of his power. A proud, arrogant Paul would have only hindered the gospel's advance. A humiliated, frail Paul, led as a captive in God's triumph, has accelerated the gospel's progress so that the fragrance of knowing God spreads everywhere (see 2:14).

12:8 Paul's initial prayer entreating the Lord to remove the stake (or perhaps the messenger of Satan, since the verb *aphistēmi* is always used of persons in the NT) indicates that he did not initially appreciate the significance of this affliction nor was it something easily borne. Few are able to value the onset of anything unpleasant or difficult, and they usually grasp its value only in retrospect. Paul may have thought at first that this stake would stymie the effectiveness of his ministry, so he desperately wanted it removed. The three times may signify "earnest and repeated prayer," time and time again.[428] Or Paul may be drawing a deliberate parallel to the threefold prayer of Jesus in Gethsemane. As Jesus accepted the cross through fervent prayer, so Paul has resigned himself to submit to God's will about his weakness and no longer makes this request. Times come in our lives when

---

[426] S. Garrett, *The Temptations of Jesus in Mark's Gospel* (Grand Rapids: Eerdmans, 1998) 4. Garrett shows from the *Testament of Job* that in Jewish circles it was believed that Satan only attacks those who are righteous and serve God faithfully. God gives Satan authority only over the righteous man's body and cannot gain authority over that man's soul unless he forfeits that authority by cursing God (p. 42).

[427] Irony is also involved in the defeat of Satan as seen in Paul's affirmation that the God of peace will shortly crush Satan under your feet (Rom 16:20).

[428] Barrett, *The Second Epistle to the Corinthians*, 316. Martin also thinks that three times may be a "stereotyped expression for urgency in praying" (*2 Corinthians*, 418). Other possibilities are that it reflects Jewish prayer patterns, in the morning, afternoon and evening (Ps 55:16–17; Dan 6:10, 13; 1QS 10:1–7; 1 QH 12:3–9) or a stereotyped threefold petition for assistance in Hellenistic accounts of divine healing (so H.Windisch, *Der zweite Korintherbrief*, MeyerK [Göttingen: Vandenhoeck & Ruprecht, 1924] 389–90) are less likely.

we must learn to accept what is inescapable and then listen for what God is saying to us through it. We might find that we are mistaken about what we think is best for us and for God's work.

The audition in paradise resulted in the stake that led to his pleading petition. We might expect, then, that a miracle would occur for one so divinely connected. The stake miraculously would be taken away, and Paul could live triumphantly, free of any nagging afflictions.[429] The answer he received, however, was quite different from what he expected. "Request denied," the stake would remain. There would be no quick fix miracle, but the prayer does not go unanswered. The answer is simply different from what Paul wished. The Lord's response was to give him "a richer endowment of strength to overcome his weakness."[430] This response was far greater and more profound than anything Paul knew to ask from the Lord.[431] God gives his pride a knockout blow that makes him completely dependent on divine power, not his own. As Bruce puts it, "His prayer was indeed answered, not by his deliverance from the affliction, but by his receiving the necessary grace to bear it."[432] But he received more than grace to bear a vexing affliction; he received the power of Christ.

12:9 It is difficult to decide whether Paul refers to God or Christ as the one to whom Paul prayed and who answers Paul. Paul identifies Christians as those who call upon the name of Christ (1 Cor 1:2; see Acts 9:14), and it reflects his high christology that "the Lord" who answers his prayer could be either Christ or God. The answer he received was, "My grace is sufficient for you, for my power is perfected in weakness." Paul does not give us the details about how he received this answer from the Lord. Did it come in another vision? "He said to me" is in the perfect tense *(eirēken moi)*, which

---

[429] Betz claims it is a parody of a healing miracle (*Der Apostel Paulus*, 92–93). Baird concurs and claims that Paul's anecdote of his experiences subverts the audience's normal expectations concerning vision and miracle stories. Paul gives an apocalypse that does not result in a revelation, and a miracle story that does not result in healing ("Visions, Revelation, and Ministry," 661). Barrett counters that "the theological drive and coherence in what Paul says" means that the element of parody can only be "peripheral and incidental" (*The Second Epistle to the Corinthians*, 317–18).

[430] C. J. Hemer, "A Note on 2 Corinthians 1:9," *TynBul* 23 (1972) 107.

[431] Calvin explains that there are two kinds of answers to prayer: "We ask without qualification for those things about which we have sure promise, such as the perfecting of God's kingdom and the hallowing of His name, the forgiveness of sins and everything profitable to us. But when we imagine that God's kingdom can and indeed must be furthered in such and such a way, or that this or that is necessary for the hallowing of His name, we are often mistaken, just as, in the same way, we are often deluded as to what in fact tends to our own welfare." We can ask with full confidence for what is certainly promised to us, but "we cannot prescribe the means." God may grant the end that we ask for in prayer, but God may use a means that we do not desire (*The Second Epistle of Paul the Apostle to the Corinthians*, 160–61).

[432] Bruce, *I and II Corinthians*, 249.

means that the answer he received still stands.[433] The response follows a chiastic pattern:

A is sufficient
  B for you
    C my grace
    C′ my power
  B′ in weakness
A′ is perfected

Paul learns that the stake will not hamper his calling. He can make do with the grace he has already received, and the power of Christ will become more visible as it works through his weakness.[434] We learn from the message given to Paul that God's grace is not just the unmerited favor that saves us but a force that also sustains us throughout our lives. The modifier "my" in "my power," is important. Paul is not speaking about power in general, but "the power of Christ" revealed in the crucifixion and resurrection: "For to be sure, he was crucified in weakness, yet he lives by God's power. Likewise, we are weak in him, yet by God's power we will live with him to serve you" (13:4). Paul has testified to this power in 1:8–10. In Asia he was utterly, unbearably crushed but he was rescued by God's power which raises the dead. The cracked clay vessel, buffeted and battered, is held together by the extraordinary power of God (4:7; see 6:7). When this earthly tent is destroyed, Paul exudes confidence that the power of God will raise him up and give him a house, not made with hands, eternal in the heavens (5:1). The miracle is that this same divine power that accomplishes all that God wills dwells in a frail, persecuted, and abased apostle.

The verb "perfected" *(teleitai)* means "brought to completion" or "is made fully present."[435] The present tense indicates that it is not yet a finished product but that it is still in process of being made perfect. This answer from the Lord helps Paul to regard the stake no longer as the vexing mischief of Satan; instead, he recognizes that through it the grace of God operates more effectively.[436] The stake makes him acutely aware of his own inadequacies and prevents him from thinking that he is equal to the task

---

[433] G. O'Collins notes that these are the only words of the risen Jesus recorded in Paul's letters ("Power Made Perfect in Weakness: 2 Cor 12:9–10," *CBQ* 33 [1971] 528).

[434] Paul refers to Christ in 1 Cor 1:24 as "the power of God." A rabbinic tradition has it that Moses had a request denied by God: "Be content that the evil impulse has no power over you, yea rather that I will not deliver you into the hand of the angel of death, but will Myself be with you."

[435] Furnish, *II Corinthians*, 531.

[436] Best cautions against turning this message into some trite bromide. Paul *did not* receive the message "you must take the rough with the smooth," "every cloud has a silver lining," "suffering … borne patiently … strengthens character" (*Second Corinthians*, 120).

alone. It prevents a bloated ego from crowding out the power of God in his life. Paul now reveals why he is so willing to boast in his weakness rather than to pray for its removal. His weakness becomes the vehicle by which God's grace and Christ's power is most fully manifested to himself and to others. Furnish correctly points out that Paul is not saying that weakness is power. Instead, he is saying that "the weaknesses that characterize his life as an apostle—of which the Corinthians are very much aware and from which he neither seeks nor expects relief—represent the effective working of the power of the crucified Christ in his ministry."[437] What makes Paul seem so weak to some paradoxically allows the power of Christ to work through him all the more.

The stake in the flesh, the angel from Satan, broadcasts his weakness both to himself and to others; but it does not mean that he is under Satan's dominion and not a true apostle. On the contrary, it makes the power of Christ working in him more transparent. The verb "rest" *(episkēnoun)* recalls the Old Testament imagery of God dwelling with the people (Num 35:34; see John 1:14). Christ's powerful presence has made Paul, fragile vessel of clay that he is, his home. "I have been crucified with Christ and I no longer live, but Christ lives in me" (Gal 2:20), Paul says. Again he would emphasize to the Corinthians that it is his weakness, not his enchanting heavenly visions, that allows the power of Christ to be perfected and to be revealed more clearly to others. Paul's weakness plus Christ's power equals perfect power. He does not glory in his weakness or incapacity as such, except that it makes clear that the extraordinary power displayed in him, in spite of the absence of any apparent glory and success according to the world's standards, does not come from him but from God. If Paul boasted in his own strength, thinking that by himself he was equal to any task or any calamity, he would then cancel out the power of God in his life. He is therefore most powerful when he is least reliant on his own resources.

Illusions of our own strength cause us to overlook divine power and results in our rebelliousness against God. For this reason God brings low the proud who lift themselves up and believe their own hype that they are special in and of themselves. God requires total, unconditional surrender of our pride. In Paul's situation God's grace did not come to him as "a prop for his failing strength, but as the decisive question: Will you surrender, utterly surrender, to God's dealing—will you know yourself to be a sinner before God?"[438] When we accept our own weakness, we then also learn that we must totally rely upon God. This is why the stake was not some temporary lesson that God would allow quickly to pass. Tannehill comments, "The

---

[437] Furnish, *II Corinthians*, 551–52.
[438] R. Bultmann, *New Testament Theology* (London: SCM, 1952) 1:285.

continuing weakness is necessary so that man might not confuse the power of God with his own power and lose God's power by attempting to rely on himself."[439]

We should not neglect that Paul is defending himself and his weakness to the Corinthians, but what he says about himself and his apostolic ministry does not apply only to himself. The principle that the power of God rests on the humble can be found throughout the Old Testament (Isa 57:15). Abraham confesses that he is "nothing but dust and ashes" (Gen 18:27). Moses asks God, "Who am I, that I should go to Pharaoh and bring the Israelites out of Egypt?" (Exod 3:11). Gideon asks, "How can I save Israel? My clan is the weakest in Manasseh, and I am the least in my family" (Judg 6:15). David says, "Do you think it is a small matter to become the king's son-in-law? I'm only a poor man and little known" (1 Sam 18:23). In all these cases we see God's basic way of operating in the world:

> But God chose the foolish things of the world to shame the wise; God chose the weak things of the world to shame the strong. He chose the lowly things of this world and the despised things—and the things that are not—to nullify the things that are, so that no one may boast before him (1 Cor 1:27–29).

This basic principle undermines the whole infrastructure of Corinthian wisdom and boasting and causes the strongholds and high battlements of his competitors' boasting to collapse (10:5).

The divine answer Paul received to his entreaty means that he now gladly boasts in his weaknesses because they show both God's grace and power most clearly. Fascination with visions and heavenly journeys are unimportant: it is how God works through his human weakness that is more significant and confirms his legitimacy as an apostle. Paul's whole apostolic ministry may be summed up in weakness. It does not denote God's disfavor, but quite the reverse. Lincoln drives home the point:

> The existence of the Corinthian church is evidence enough that Paul's weakness has not stood in the way of the working of God's power but rather has provided the very conditions in which it can be displayed. ... Where the gospel is believed and a church has been founded, there God is at work, and thus in Paul's apostleship the principle is upheld that 'it is not the man who commends himself is *dokimos* [approved], but the man whom the Lord commends (x. 18).[440]

12:10 Paul scores his point with a memorable aphorism, "when I am weak, then I am powerful," which is the key for interpreting all that he says in this section. The point is the same as in 4:7. The power working in Paul is

[439] Tannehill, *Dying and Rising with Christ*, 100.
[440] Lincoln, "Paul the Visionary," 210.

most clearly seen as coming from God when he appears to be weak.

"I delight in" means that he accepts the way Christ's power works in his life through his weaknesses. That does not mean that he does not groan under the load of suffering (5:2, 4) and long for the mortal to be swallowed up by life (5:4). But he knows that his suffering follows the precedent of Christ's suffering. It was something that God enables him to endure, not escape. What he endures, he endures for the sake of Christ, and the paradox of the power of God hidden in his apparent weakness parallels Christ's weakness and power demonstrated in the crucifixion. Leivestad rightly sees, "As the power of God was revealed through the weaknesses of the crucified Lord for the salvation of the world, so the life and power of the risen Christ are being revealed through his weak apostles in the midst of humiliations and afflictions."[441] The false apostles keep the Corinthians from seeing how Christ's power is at work in him and lead them away from the cross of Christ. Paul's goal is not simply to defend himself, but to help them "see things correctly" through the proper spiritual lens.[442]

Paul concludes with a brief summary of the hardship lists in the letter. He "delights in"(the word *eudokeō* can also mean "is pleased") with his "weaknesses, insults, catastrophes, persecutions, and pressures." If *en hybresin* is to be interpreted as "with insults" rather than "with mistreatments" (see 1 Thess 2:2), Paul may have added it because of the rivals' insolent slander against him as one who was weak, debased, and amateurish. "Catastrophes" refer to the "hardships" he has listed in 4:8–9; 6:4–5; 11:27–28. The "persecutions" are listed in 11:24–25a, and the "pressures" or difficulties (tight situations) are listed in 11:25b–26. The phrase *hyper Christou* ("for the sake of Christ") is interpreted by the NIV (RSV, REB) as connected to the phrase, "I delight in." Paul placed it at the end of the lists of hardships, however; so it is better to connect it to the weaknesses, insults, hardships, persecutions, and calamities for the sake of Christ (NRSV). This means that he is not pleased with them for Christ's sake but endures them for Christ's sake.

(5) Foolish Boasting and the Signs of a True Apostle (12:11–13)

[11]I have made a fool of myself, but you drove me to it. I ought to have been commended by you, for I am not in the least inferior to the "super-apostles," even though I am nothing. [12]The things that mark an apostle—signs, wonders and miracles—were done among you with great perseverance. [13]How were you

---

[441] R. Leivestad, "'The Meekness and Gentleness of Christ' II Cor X.1," *NTS* 12 (1966) 163. J. L. Sumney shows, using 1 Thessalonians, that weakness was an integral part of Paul's understanding of his ministry from very early on, against Martin, e.g., who claimed that the Corinthian crisis precipitated this new understanding ("Paul's 'Weakness': An Integral Part of His Conception of Apostleship," *JSNT* 52 [1993] 71–91).

[442] Holland, "Speaking Like a Fool: Irony in 2 Corinthians 10–13," 263

**inferior to the other churches, except that I was never a burden to you? Forgive
me this wrong!**

12:11   Paul admits to being a fool by adopting the boastful tactics of his
competitors, but by doing so he tars his opponents with the same brush.
They are fools as well (see 11:19–20), but, unlike Paul, they are not playing
the part of a fool. They take their boasting seriously. The Corinthians are
also made out to be fools for allowing themselves to be captivated and led
astray by foolish boasting. They have dishonored themselves by betraying
their apostle and failing to defend him.

Paul uses this failure as his final justification for his fool's speech (see
11:1–6). Since they have not defended him against his competitors, he must
defend himself. The truth had to be told, more to save the Corinthians from
such fools than to save Paul's reputation. They were swept off their feet by
these encroachers who pandered to their aspirations. They turned away in
shame from their own apostle who seemed too afflicted, too weak, and too
tongue-tied. Since the Corinthians are the seal of his apostleship (1 Cor 9:2)
and his letter of commendation to be known and read by all (3:2), they
should have jumped to his defense and acclaimed his accomplishments
among them. It is self-evident that the church was founded through his
preaching, but Paul also asserts that they received every apostolic demonstration of power and favor—except that he did not allow himself to become
financially dependent on them (12:13).

He repeats his sardonic affirmation from 11:5 with a play on the word
"nothing": "[With respect to] nothing was I inferior to these super apostles
even if I am nothing."[443] We need not read "I am nothing" as a charge leveled
against him by the rivals or the Corinthians.[444] It is Paul's honest evaluation
of his status before God (see 1 Cor 15:9–10; 2 Cor 3:5; Phil 3:12–16). Paul
would insist that his apostleship is second to none, though he is the least of
all the apostles, and he certainly does not take a back set to the flamboyant
buffoons who have overrun his church. But he knows that whatever he is
comes from God. If he is nothing, so are the other superlative apostles (see 1
Cor 3:5–9). The difference is that they do not recognize that they are nothing
before God and strut around as if they were the kingpins of the kingdom.

12:12   The Corinthians may have been influenced by their cultural
expectations about what qualified as the signs of an apostle. We get the
impression from Paul's response in this letter that they assume that apostles speak well, look good, and have an air of authority about them. Possibly, "the signs of an apostle" was a slogan brandished about by the

---

[443] Cp. 1 Cor 1:7, the Corinthians are lacking in no spiritual gift.

[444] A parallel in Epictetus has a casual inquirer say, "Epictetus was nothing at all, his language
was full of solecisms and barbarisms" (*Dissertations* III.9.14).

rivals,[445] or perhaps it came from the Corinthians.[446] But this need not be an enemy's slogan at all. Paul asserts that certain signs were accomplished that verified that the power of God was at work in a community and that authenticated his ministry as Christ's apostle. He reminds the Thessalonians that "our gospel came to you not simply with words, but also with power, with the Holy Spirit and with deep conviction" (1 Thess 1:5). To the Romans he sums up his ministry from Jerusalem to Illyricum by saying "I will not venture to speak of anything except what Christ has accomplished through me in leading the Gentiles to obey God by what I have said and done— by the power of signs and miracles, through the power of the Spirit" (Rom 15:18–19a). When it comes to everything that truly commends an apostle as an apostle, Paul has it, from his straightforward speaking, his morally upright behavior, and his perseverance (1:12; 4:2), to signs, wonders and miracles.[447]

The Corinthians remain confused about how to distinguish an authentic apostle from a false one. Lofty speech, loftier visions, and electrifying miracles are not the proper criteria by which to judge apostles. Paul reminds them that "the signs of an apostle" were worked among them—something they cannot deny. He leaves vague what these signs precisely are, defining them only as signs, wonders, and miracles (compare the ministry of Jesus in the Gospels, Acts 2:22, and see Acts 14:3; and 15:12). Paul does not intend to distinguish between three different types of miracles with these words but may have in mind three different effects: miracles that point beyond themselves to spiritual realities, miracles that evoke awe, and miracles that are seen as mighty acts.[448] These miracles could involve healings, glossolalia, and conversions surrounding dramatic events. Unlike his hardships, Paul chooses not to dwell on them in detail.[449]

He words his remarks quite carefully and *does not* say, "I performed signs, wonders, and miracles (deeds of power)." Paul makes no claims to any supernatural power in himself; and the passive voice intimates that these things were done by God. According to Heb 2:3–4, the salvation brought by Jesus was attested by those who heard him, and "God also testified to it by signs, wonders and various miracles." While Paul does not claim to be powerful himself, he does affirm that God's power is made perfect in his weakness. God's power has testified to his genuineness.

---

[445] Bultmann, *The Second Letter Old Testament the Corinthians,* 233.

[446] Barrett, *The Second Epistle to the Corinthians,* 321; and Martin, *2 Corinthians*, 435.

[447] This verse could also be rendered: "At least (μέν), the signs of an apostle were worked among you in all endurance, with signs, wonders, and miracles." The signs of an apostle would be differentiated from "signs, wonders, and miracles" and could involve other things as well.

[448] Hodge, *An Exposition of the Second Epistle to the Corinthians,* 291–92.

[449] We read in Acts that Paul performed miracles (13:11; 14:9–10; 16:16–18; 19:11–12).

Working wonders and miracles does not make one an apostle, however. In the list of gifts in 1 Cor 12:28–30, those who work miracles are distinguished from apostles, whose main task is proclamation. Christians must still discern the difference between wonders wrought by God and false wonders wrought by Satan. Paul cautions the Thessalonians that the coming of the lawless one will be in accordance with the work of Satan displayed in all kinds of counterfeit miracles, signs and wonders (2 Thess 2:9). But Paul trusts that the Corinthians can attest that it was the power of God at work in Paul's preaching and presence in Corinth (1 Cor 2:4–5; 2 Cor 6:7). He can say that he is not inferior to these super apostles because God worked the signs. It follows from this that since he did not work the signs, he is nothing (see 1 Cor 3:7). Nevertheless, Paul says these "signs, wonders and miracles" were done "with great perseverance" ("all endurance"), which suggests that they were done over a long period and in the context of his hardships and afflictions catalogued earlier.[450]

12:13   Paul continues to press his case with irony. He asks in what respect they were inferior to or worse off than other churches except that he did not weigh them down with financial obligations to him. They are disadvantaged compared with other churches only in Paul's refusal to take advantage of them. The "I" in "I was never a burden to you" is an emphatic *autos,* "I myself." It sets him apart from the opponents who have exploited them (11:20). Surely they do not believe that refusing to sponge off them somehow disqualifies him as an apostle? If they count this a wrong or sin, he mockingly begs their forgiveness (see 11:7). He is no peddler of the gospel and will not be put into a position where he must fawn over his benefactors to repay their support and keep the gifts coming. He lives out the gospel principle of not seeking his own advantage but that of another (1 Cor 10:17).

5. Paul's Return to Corinth (12:14–21)

14Now I am ready to visit you for the third time, and I will not be a burden to you, because what I want is not your possessions but you. After all, children should not have to save up for their parents, but parents for their children. 15So I will very gladly spend for you everything I have and expend myself as well. If I love you more, will you love me less? 16Be that as it may, I have not been a burden to you. Yet, crafty fellow that I am, I caught you by trickery! 17Did I exploit you through any of the men I sent you? 18I urged Titus to go to you and I sent our brother with him. Titus did not exploit you, did he? Did we not act in the same spirit and follow the same course?

19Have you been thinking all along that we have been defending ourselves to you? We have been speaking in the sight of God as those in Christ; and every-

---

[450] Furnish, *II Corinthians,* 555.

thing we do, dear friends, is for your strengthening. [20]For I am afraid that when I come I may not find you as I want you to be, and you may not find me as you want me to be. I fear that there may be quarreling, jealousy, outbursts of anger, factions, slander, gossip, arrogance and disorder. [21]I am afraid that when I come again my God will humble me before you, and I will be grieved over many who have sinned earlier and have not repented of the impurity, sexual sin and debauchery in which they have indulged.

Paul broaches again the touchy subject of the Corinthians' desire to support him while he is ministering among them (see 11:7–11). This leads him to the topic of his impending visit to Corinth, which is solemnly announced by "behold" (*idou*, NIV "now," see 5:17; 6:2,9; and 7:11). This unit (12:14–21) and the next (13:1–10) begin with a reference to Paul's coming to them for the third time. In this unit he repeats his adamant refusal to accept their financial support while with them. He does not want their money; he wants their moral reformation and renewed commitment to Christ. Furnish comments that Paul wants them to know that "it is the gift of their lives to Christ, not of their money to himself, that he covets."[451] John Chrysostom interprets Paul to mean, "I seek greater things; souls instead of goods; instead of gold, salvation."[452] The rivals apparently have no qualms about accepting whatever they can get from the Corinthians, and Paul may be hinting that, unlike him, they are after what belongs to others.

Paul writes this letter to prepare for his anticipated visit. He has offered a defense of the frank criticism that marked his severe letter (2:14–7:3) and now addresses critical issues to avert another painful experience (2:1) on his third visit. He has warned them again about the danger of association with idols (6:14–7:1), has urged them to be prepared with their contribution to the collection (8:1–9:15), and has warned them not to be fooled by his weak bodily presence or meek and gentle demeanor so that they think he will not punish every disobedience when he comes (10:1–11). What he threatens to do in his weighty letters, he *will do* when present (10:11). As the letter comes to a close, Paul becomes more specific. He reminds them that he will not alter his policy of refusing to accept their financial support when he arrives. He warns them again about his fears over their factional quarrels and their immorality (12:20–21; 13:2). Finally, he explains why he has written what he has. He wants to build them up in Christ and does not want to have to be severe in using the authority given him by Christ.

12:14 In 12:14–18 Paul offers another explanation for his policy about refusing their support, as well as a declaration that all that he and his coworkers do is above board. In 11:7–12 he explains that his refusal to

---

[451] Ibid., 564.

[452] John Chrysostom, *Homilies on Second Corinthians* XXVII.2 (p. 405).

accept their patronage did not mean that he did not love them and that he will continue his set policy to undermine the pretensions of false apostles who claim to be on the same level as he. He now submits a fuller explanation for that policy. He is their parent and is responsible for them, not vice versa. The image recalls his plea in 6:13, "As a fair exchange—I speak as to my children—open wide your hearts also." He has described his relationship to them as the father who cares for them (1 Cor 4:14) and who begot them (1 Cor 4:15; see Phlm 10). He brought them the gospel (10:14); arranged their marriage to Christ (11:2); exalted them at his own expense (11:7); loved them faithfully, as God can attest (11:11); sacrificed himself for them (12:15, poured himself out for them); devoted himself to their upbuilding (12:19; 13:10); and, like any good parent, pointed out their faults and reprimanded them (12:20). Paul therefore appeals to the widely held expectations regarding the relationship between parents and children.

Parents are the benefactors who give their children life, and, from infancy on, give them all that is needed for them to grow and survive.[453] Whatever capital they amass, they pass on to their children, not the reverse. Philo states the obvious order of the nature of things, "the sons are the heirs of their fathers and not fathers of their sons."[454] As the recipients of untold gifts, the children are obligated to repay their parents with love and honor. In the Greco-Roman world ingratitude for benefits received was considered an outrageous sin. Paul therefore appeals to the Greco-Roman social conventions about the relationship between parents and children to turn the tables on them.[455] He is their spiritual parent who has given his children all that they needed from their infancy, providing milk to solid food (1 Cor 3:2). He has not injured them by refusing to accept their support, and he will not allow them to turn the natural parent-child relationship into an unnatural client-patron relationship. They have injured him instead and are guilty of egregious sin by failing in their unconditional duty as his children to show him love and honor.

12:15 Paul continues the theme of being a loving parent (see 11:11) with emphatic expressions: *but I* will gladly spend everything I have and will be spent for your souls. Here is the best litmus test for the sign of an

---

[453] Seneca states, "Can there possibly be any greater benefits than those that a father bestows upon his child?" (*On Benefits* 2.11.4–5); "And so the greatest of all benefits are those that, while we are either unaware or unwilling, we receive from our parents" (*On Benefits* 6.24.2).

[454] Philo, *Life of Moses* 2.245.

[455] Plummer says that Paul "appeals to nature and common sense" (*The Second Epistle of St. Paul to the Corinthians*, 362), but it is common sense derived from social conventions. Marshall delineates these conventions: (1) parents should outdo their children in benefits and services; (2) they owe them these benefits and services; (3) children never repay in kind or equal value; (4) they can only repay with greater love and honor (*Enmity in Corinth*, 248).

apostle. A true apostle of the crucified Christ is one who is willing to spend and be spent on behalf of a congregation. He serves at great cost to himself for the great benefit of others. They should recognize the depth of his love for them from the magnitude of his sacrifices enumerated in 11:23–29. The least they can do is love and honor him in return. But their filial obligation to Paul *demands* that they love and honor him. The problem is the more he loves them and sacrifices for them, even trying to avoid painful visits, the less they seem to love him in return. The community does not love him when it listens to and tolerates slander and puts him in the awkward position of having to commend himself to them all over again as if he were a stranger.

12:16 The Corinthians must agree that he has never asked for nor taken any material support from them for himself (1 Cor 9:12,15,18; 2 Cor 11:7,9; 12:13). But someone apparently has twisted his actions and concocted a conspiracy theory that Paul had hatched some dark plan to deceive them by profiting from the collection for Jerusalem. They accuse him of being crafty and catching them with guile (see 4:2). To use financial intermediaries to appear unsullied by concern for financial matters was not without precedent in the ancient world. Isocrates mocked the hypocrisy of the sophists who did not trust the virtue of their students and insisted that their fees be paid in advance and deposited with a third party.[456] Possibly, someone claimed that the collection was all a ruse by which Paul would have associates gather up the money and he would covertly skim a portion off the top without them being any the wiser and without incurring any social debt to them.[457] It is also possible that no one has accused him of defrauding them at all and that Paul is making a preemptive strike, nipping any such conspiracy theories in the bud before they blossom and sow further seeds of discontent.

12:17–18 If someone has attacked Paul's reputation with rumors and innuendo, he now asks them to give specific evidence. Identify the supposed instances of trickery. Paul's best defense is to point to the probity of others involved in the collection project. He phrases the first question, "Did I exploit you?" in such a way in Greek that it expects the answer no! The NIV captures this construction better in the second question, "Titus did not exploit you, did he?" They know firsthand the character of Titus. Their godly

---

[456] Isocrates, *Against the Sophists* 5–6.

[457] Talbert argues, "The allegation was that all the while Paul had made a great show of asking for no money for himself, he had instituted a collection allegedly for the poor saints in Jerusalem and was likely to profit the proceeds for himself" (*Reading Corinthians* 128). Hughes suggested that this accusation was intended to scuttle the collection and leave that money available for themselves (*Paul's Second Epistle to the Corinthians*, 465), but such speculation goes well beyond the evidence. In an age of conspiracy theories and suspicion, people are willing to believe almost anything bad about others, but all too often their suspicions betray the scheming of their own evil minds, which they project onto the motives of others. This may also have been the case with the Corinthians.

repentance and warm reception of Titus on his last visit (7:6–7,13–15) show that they do not harbor suspicions of his integrity. "The brother" could be understood as anaphoric—the brother whom I mentioned before—and refer to the brother mentioned in 8:18–19, who was appointed by the churches, or to "our brother," who has such great confidence in the Corinthians (8:22).

Some interpreters take this reference as a clue that these chapters are part of a later letter written after 8:6,18. It is just as likely, however, that Paul looks back on a previous mission when Titus and a colleague helped in the preparations for the collection. Barnett argues that the use of the aorist tense in the references to Titus's trip to Corinth in 8:6,17 and the sending of the brothers in 8:18,22 are epistolary aorists in which the writer does not look at the event from the time of writing as lying in the future, but from the perspective of the recipient of the letter as something that has already happened.[458] Paul may not be looking back to some earlier mission to Corinth but may be referring to the current mission of Titus and the brother when this letter arrives with them. The distrustful cynics can check things out for themselves now. Is Titus taking advantage of them? Is the acclaimed brother from the churches part of some plot to bilk them out of the obligation Paul will owe them as his patron if he takes advantage of their financial support? Would such upstanding men with unblemished reputations be part of some conspiracy to defraud them in any way?

Paul phrases the last question in Greek so that it expects the answer yes: "Did we not act in the same spirit and follow the same course?" "The same spirit" could be the Spirit and mean that they were guided by God's Spirit in what they did. It is parallel to "in the same footsteps" (NIV "same course"), which implies that Paul is thinking of their attitude. If his coworkers are not guilty of some kind of financial intrigue, then how could they think that he was? Why, after preaching the gospel for free and refusing to become a burden to them, would he now try to take advantage of them in some underhanded way? He could have received their support openly and received their approbation of him. They have quite failed to understand the reasons behind his refusal of their support.[459]

12:19 Paul's words, "Have you been thinking all along that we have been defending ourselves to you?" may be surprising.[460] Most readers

---

[458] Barnett, *The Second Epistle to the Corinthians*, 589–90. Plummer considers this option to be "barely possible" and argues that Paul has reference to an earlier mission when Titus and a colleague started the collection (8:6) (*The Second Epistle of St. Paul to the Corinthians*, 365).

[459] DiCicco, *Paul's Use of Ethos, Pathos, and Logos in 2 Corinthians 10–13*, 248–49.

[460] The majority of texts read πάλιν ("again"), and a handful of texts read πάλαι ("all along"). The "all along" is taken as the harder reading. The difference could have arisen from the similarity between the two words ΠΑΛΙΝ - ΠΑΛΑΙ. The sentence could be read as a question (NIV, NRSV, KJV) or as a statement (NEB, GNB). Both convey much the same sense.

would think that it is obvious that he has been defending himself. But Paul is not being disingenuous with this question. He wants to make it clear to the Corinthians that he is not the prisoner at the bar having to submit to an embarrassing cross examination. He has committed no offense and need not exonerate himself. Besides that, they are not his judges (1 Cor 4:2–4; 2 Cor 5:10). It is God, not they, he must please. He is therefore speaking before God, not them.

1. Paul is not defending himself here because that would lend credibility to any charges. Defending himself would be the same as commending himself again and would concede that he was in some way responsible for the breach in the relationship. Therefore, he insists that he is not on the defensive, but writing as their apostle out of concern for them rather than out of a concern to save his reputation. He is not arguing his own case but confronting them with the gospel. His theological clarifications about boasting in the Lord (10:17–18), God's grace being sufficient, and God's power being made perfect in weakness (12:9) should lead to their upbuilding—the principle governing all of apostolic ministry (10:8; 13:10). If they fail to heed his letter, the consequences will be dire for them—exclusion from the kingdom of God—but only heartbreaking for him.

2. If he were defending himself, it would mean that he is using the rhetorical techniques of a formal apology.[461] Barrett remarks that "a defense is a self-regarding composition, designed to further the writer's own interests and to commend him to the person who appears to be in a position to pass judgment *(before you)*."[462] Paul is not doing this because the Corinthians are not Paul's judges.

3. The letter does resemble a trial; accusations have been made and answered. Harvey points out, however, that we need to understand this trial in a first century context.

> … there was one feature of the Jewish legal process which was totally unlike ours. If a defendant was found to be innocent, the matter might not rest there: an immediate reversal of roles was possible, the former defendant could become the accuser, and charges that had been leveled against him could be used to discredit and condemn his opponents.[463]

In our context we are accustomed to the state carrying out the prosecution. In the Greco-Roman world the prosecution was brought by private parties (see Luke 23:2; Acts 24:1–8). Paul has in mind "the reversal of roles" which becomes clear in 13:1 when he will be bringing charges against them. Paul is not defending himself; he is prosecuting his opponents and the Corinthians.

---

[461] Harvey, *Renewal through Suffering*, 107; see Aristotle, *Rhetoric* 3.15.1.

[462] Barrett, *The Second Epistle to the Corinthians*, 328.

[463] Harvey, *Renewal through Suffering*, 107–8.

He has left the role of the fool and is now "speaking in Christ" (12:19; see 2:17; 11:17). The fool who seems so debased and weak now begins his assault and puts the Corinthians on the defensive. He has insinuated that they have failed in their duty to love and honor him by entertaining slander against him and failing to defend him against his detractors. He now says that he fears that they will add insult to injury when he will be humiliated by his next visit. The feared humiliation will not come at the hands of any individual (see 2:1) but from the shabby state of affairs in Corinth.

12:20 Paul expresses his fear earlier that they have already been deceived as Eve was by the serpent (11:3). Now he expresses his fear that when he comes the Corinthians will be riven with disputes and ravaged by immorality. The NIV does not translate the *mē pōs* ("lest somehow," "perhaps"), but this phrase introduces an element of doubt and the possibility that not all the Corinthians are guilty of these sins.[464]

The first four sins in this list of vices, quarreling, jealousy, outbursts of anger, self-seeking (factions, party spirit), appear in the same order in the list of the works of the flesh in Gal 5:20. Paul rebuked the Corinthians about their quarreling and jealousy in 1 Cor 1:11 and 3:3; and the party spirit surfaced in their party slogans, "I belong to Paul," "I belong to Apollos," "I belong to Cephas," and "I belong to Christ" (1 Cor 1:12). "Quarreling" *(eris)* was used by Homer to refer to eagerness for combat. It was applied to those who are always ready for a fight. "Jealousy," or bitter zeal, fuels a sense of rivalry, and "outbursts of temper" vent the animosity that such rivalry and polemicizing nourishes.[465] Self-seeking *(eritheia)* derives from the verb to work for hire, and it became associated with paid work that "is done solely for interested motives ('What's in it for me?')." It then is applied to intrigues to gain advantage over others and to "personal ambition, the exclusive pursuit of one's own interests."[466] These are the "fruit of paganism, the deeds of people not yet spiritualized by grace."[467] In such situations truth, fairness, and harmony lose out.

The next four vices in the list seem specific to the more recent problems at Corinth: slander, gossip, arrogance and disorder. Slanders and gossiping directly relate to the recent situation with all the backbiting and insinuations. Paul has been the victim of a politically motivated smear campaign by arrogant rivals. Arrogance is a continuing problem at Corinth. Paul uses the verb "to puff up," "to be arrogant" *(physioun),* only in the Corinthian correspon-

---

[464] The same expression μή πως occurs in 11:3 (see 2:7; 9:4).

[465] Spicq recounts that the Greeks had "divinized Dispute or Emulation, which they considered the energizing spirit of the world and one of the primordial forces. They had a cult of rivalry" *(Theological Lexicon of the New Testament,* 2:71).

[466] Ibid., 2:70.

[467] Ibid., 2:71.

dence (1 Cor 4:6,18–19; 5:2; 8:1; 13:4). It "denotes that arrogant behaviour which results from a failure in self-knowledge, a delusion in regard to sophia, which has led to the violation of accepted norms of behavior."[468] The mix of all these vices created a disordered church that was bound to split into several unholy fragments unless they were checked.[469]

12:21 If the congregation's life is marked by disharmony and immorality, it will be humiliating to Paul. The NIV takes the "again" with the verb "humiliate," "lest God humiliate me again." But it could also be read with the participle "coming"; "when I come again, lest God humiliate me." Both are possible, and both make sense. The latter option seems best, however. The "again" in 13:2 is connected to his coming, and it is questionable whether Paul understood his previous humiliation as coming from God.[470] In that earlier painful visit a nasty confrontation with someone so disturbed Paul that he made a swift exit. He does not attribute that painful experience to God. Now Paul fears a different level of humiliation on his next visit when he comes again. It will not result from any human barbs or unpleasantries but from the sinful plight of the church he founded and was charged by God to build up into spiritual maturity. Paul believes that the proof that Christ is speaking in him—something the Corinthians are so interested in (13:3)—derives from the founding of the congregation and its faithfulness to the gospel, not from such peripheral things as revelatory visions or magisterial bearing. If the congregation's life is still plagued by impurity, immorality, and licentiousness (12:21), he fears that God will rule that he has run in vain, and he will be chastened *before God,* who tests each one's work by fire (see 1 Cor 3:10–15). That is something far more serious than any humiliation caused by any one of them. Their disobedience to God's will is as humbling to him as his stake in the flesh.

While he is afraid that he will not find them as he might want, he also concedes that they will not find him as they might want. They have already expressed their disdain of his humbleness when face to face with them (10:1). But it will be a different kind of humiliation. It will not come from being demeaned and abased according to the world's standards but from being spiritually humbled before God for their moral disgrace. Most fear being judged by other humans; Paul feared God more. Most are only willing to take responsibility for their own conduct and, even then, will try to pin any blame on someone or something else. Paul accepted responsibility before God for the Corinthians' conduct. No wonder he spent many a sleepless night burdened by anxiety over his churches (11:28).

---

[468] Marshall, *Enmity in Corinth*, 205.

[469] Disorder had earlier poisoned their worship (1 Cor 14:33).

[470] On the other hand, "again" is not used with "I come" in 12:20.

Paul adds to the list of sins that he fears that the "many" may be guilty of continuing to do: indulge in impurity, immorality, and licentiousness. These same sins open the list works of the flesh in Gal 5:19 in a slightly different order and were rampant in the bankrupt moral climate of the Gentile world. We should not suppose that Paul believes that passions are running riot in Corinth, but this morally lax seaport city provided ample opportunities to gratify sexual sins. Paul's fear is that an embarrassing number of Corinthian Christians have not been fully reformed from their past sexual conduct to bring it in line with the new creation in Christ, "washed, sanctified, and justified in the name of the Lord Jesus and the Spirit of our God" (1 Cor 6:9–11).[471] The immorality may be related to some kind of continued associations with idolatry. They may excel in faith, speech, knowledge, and complete earnestness (8:7); but if they fail basic Christian ethics, they will be excluded from the kingdom of God (1 Cor 6:9). They need to heed his call to holiness (7:1).

Paul does not lash out against their sins with righteous indignation but with mourning (see 1 Cor 5:2). They remain his "beloved ones"; and like a loving, responsible parent, he feels guilt and shame for the sins that his children commit. Paul hopes that in sharing such misgivings the Corinthians will be chastened and seek to put their house in order to present themselves as spiritually mature to both Paul and God. This verse recalls what Paul wrote earlier, "I wrote as I did so that when I came I should not be distressed by those who ought to make me rejoice" (2:3). He therefore hopes that when he comes again he will not be humiliated by their failure to have their contribution for Jerusalem ready (9:4) nor be humiliated by their moral wretchedness.

In the context of chaps. 10–11 Paul may imply that such a moral collapse could be expected after the Corinthians have been flirting with false apostles, the deputies of Satan, who peddle a false gospel. He wants them to get rid of the vices and get rid of the agitators. Paul replicates the kind of frank criticism that might have been in the severe letter. Some think this ringing denunciation against their vices to be a strange finale to a letter that earlier had praised them for their godly repentance (7:9–11), and therefore it would seem to make more sense if it belonged to a separate letter. But the Corinthians would have taken this admonishment quite differently in their context. Plummer lists statements in the first nine chapters that he deems inconsistent with the fears expressed here.[472] He asks, "What would the Corinthians think of one who could thus blow hot and cold in successive breaths?"[473] Danker cites Plutarch to help explain how the Corinthians

---

[471] The participle προημαρτηκότων ("have continued in their former sins") is in the perfect tense, emphasizing the continuance of their past sinful state.
[472] See 1:24; 2:3; 3:3; 7:4,11,15,6; 8:7; 9:2.
[473] Plummer, *The Second Epistle of Paul the Apostle to the Corinthians,* 128.

might have understood this combination of warm affirmation and stern warning: "When blame is mingled with praise, and is expressed with complete frankness, yet devoid of disdain, and induces repentance rather than ire, it appears well-disposed and remedial."[474] This frank criticism is fitting for Paul's role as their apostle and guardian who must preserve their purity for Christ (11:2). Paul still has qualms about whether they have completely submitted to Christ and writes again in this reproachful vein to insure their obedience. His goal is to build them up in Christ.

6. Warning: Paul May Have to Be Severe in Using His Authority When Present (13:1–10)

[1]This will be my third visit to you. "Every matter must be established by the testimony of two or three witnesses." [2]I already gave you a warning when I was with you the second time. I now repeat it while absent: On my return I will not spare those who sinned earlier or any of the others, [3]since you are demanding proof that Christ is speaking through me. He is not weak in dealing with you, but is powerful among you. [4]For to be sure, he was crucified in weakness, yet he lives by God's power. Likewise, we are weak in him, yet by God's power we will live with him to serve you.

[5]Examine yourselves to see whether you are in the faith; test yourselves. Do you not realize that Christ Jesus is in you—unless, of course, you fail the test? [6]And I trust that you will discover that we have not failed the test. [7]Now we pray to God that you will not do anything wrong. Not that people will see that we have stood the test but that you will do what is right even though we may seem to have failed. [8]For we cannot do anything against the truth, but only for the truth. [9]We are glad whenever we are weak but you are strong; and our prayer is for your perfection. [10]This is why I write these things when I am absent, that when I come I may not have to be harsh in my use of authority—the authority the Lord gave me for building you up, not for tearing you down.

13:1 Paul warns the Corinthians that on his next visit he will be putting them on trial. "This will be my third visit to you" translates "the third time I am coming to you" (see 12:14). To make it fit certain chronological theories, some have tried to interpret this phrase to mean the third time I have *planned* to come to you. But the plain sense of the text is that Paul's next visit to Corinth will be his third, and his reference in the next verse to when he was with them a second time confirms this reading.[475]

According to Acts 18:1–17, Paul had an extended mission in Corinth

---

[474] Danker, *II Corinthians,* 208

[475] This statement provides further proof that chaps. 10–13 cannot be the sorrowful letter because he wrote that letter *to avoid making a visit* and sent Titus with it to confront them with their disobedience.

when he founded the church. The second visit was painful and short. It was unplanned and undertaken to quell rebellion in Corinth. Paul's grievous confrontation with an individual in the church caused him to cut the visit short. Though he sounds annoyed and disturbed in this section of the letter and paints an alarming picture of a church infested with strife and immorality, he has been successful enough through the severe letter and the personal intervention of Titus, and, he trusts, through this letter, to reestablish his authority over the church. He therefore warns them that he comes ready to punish every disobedience and to purge all pockets of resistance. But he will not be acting alone because he cannot act without some base of support. Those who are obedient in the church will act in concert with him (10:6; see 1 Cor 5:3–5).

Paul abruptly cites Deut 19:15 in a slightly abbreviated form: "Every matter must be established by the testimony of two or three witnesses" (see also Num 35:30; Deut 17:6). The assumption behind the law is that it is better for someone who is guilty to go unpunished because of a lack of the requisite number of witnesses than to harm an innocent person's reputation with reckless charges. This principle is applied elsewhere in the New Testament (see Matt 18:16; John 8:17; 1 Tim 5:19; Heb 10:28). But how does Paul's third visit relate to the rules of evidence? By saying that no one can be condemned without the testimony of two to three witnesses, Paul tips his hand that he has every intention to bring charges against them on this next visit (see 12:19).

What are the two or three witnesses? Some argue for a literal understanding of the text so that Paul warns the Corinthians that he will open a court of inquiry that will evaluate the misconduct of wrongdoers and that due process will be used.[476] Others, from ancient times to modern, take the reference to the rules of evidence in a figurative sense and understand Paul to be referring to his visits. His next visit will be the third and decisive witness against the troublemakers.[477] Although widely held, this view fails to explain why Paul would regard his first visit in which he founded the church as constituting a witness against them. He did not work in their midst to gather evidence against them but to evangelize them. The third visit also is not to gather evidence but to confront them. Paul would also be taking strange liberties with the text of Deut 15:19 that clearly refers to persons and not events if this view were accurate.

[476] Hughes, *Paul's Second Epistle to the Corinthians*, 475.

[477] John Chrysostom, *Homilies on Second Corinthians* XXVII.2 (411–12); Calvin, *The Second Epistle of Paul the Apostle to the Corinthians*, 169; and Plummer, *The Second Epistle of St. Paul to the Corinthians*, 372.

Others argue that Paul applies the law of the witnesses to the threefold warnings issued to them, for example, those found in 1 Cor 4:21, the second visit and the severe letter, and 2 Cor 13:2. Van Vliet contends that the rule of the two or three witnesses was used in Palestinian Judaism to support the requirement that person suspected of wrongdoing should be carefully forewarned of the possibility of punitive action against them.[478] The text becomes a kind of proverb. Furnish accepts this conclusion and writes, "In this context Paul's quotation of the rule makes good sense: he will have given them the requisite *two or three warnings,* to Corinth."[479] But would the Corinthians have been aware of such a recherché usage of the text?

Harvey points to the citation of the rule elsewhere in the New Testament (Matt 18:16; 1 Tim 5:19; John 8:17) and claims that it "marks the point at which a private dispute becomes a matter for public arbitration: from now on strict rules of evidence will apply."[480] This is how Paul uses it here. Paul is saying: "My next visit will be the occasion for our dispute to be settled publicly." Paul will take disciplinary action according to the biblical principles governing a judicial proceeding (see 1 Cor 6:1–6). He can call three witnesses against them—Titus and Timothy, for example, and even God. Can they call three legitimate witnesses against him? They should remember that the law also warns that malicious, dishonest witnesses will be punished in the way they intended for the falsely accused to be punished (Deut 19:16–19).

13:2 Paul reminds them that he is not suddenly springing this threat on them; he has warned them before. "The second" *(to deuteron)* can be connected to being present with them a second time or to forewarning them a second time. The natural order of the words argues for it being related to when he was with them. He gave this warning when he was present the second time. Paul's use of the perfect tense for the two verbs, "I warned *(proeirēka)* those who sinned previously *(proēmartēkosin),*" implies that the warning from that second visit still stands and that those who sinned have not fully repented because their sin still stands. Has the warning gone unheeded? Did his rivals meddle in some way and forestall their repentance?

The ones who have sinned could include a variety of persons: those causing the disruption in the church, those involved in sexual sins, and those involved in associations with idolatry, though none of these categories is mutually exclusive. Paul also warns "any of the others" (literally, "all the rest"). This category could include those whom he may find guilty of sin when he comes for the third time. The construction of this verse (translated

---

[478] H. van Vliet, *No Single Testimony: A Study on the Adoption of the Law of Deut. 19:15 Par. into the New Testament* (Utrecht: Kemink & Zoon, 1958) 53–62.

[479] Furnish, *II Corinthians*, 575.

[480] Harvey, *Renewal through Suffering*, 108.

literally) consists of a series of three parallel phrases linked by "and."[481]

I have said beforehand	and	I do say beforehand
when I was present the second time	and	now being absent
to them that have sinned before	and	to all the rest

In this structure "all the rest" would embrace those who have also sinned.

But "all the rest" might also include those "who by their indifference to or leniency toward immoral conduct on the part of church members have tacitly condoned it."[482] To Paul's mind there are no "innocent bystanders" in what has happened at Corinth. "Standing by" implies toleration and makes one a party to the sin. Paul's aggravation with the Corinthians' tolerance of even outrageous sins bursts forth in 1 Cor 5:1–2 when he expresses dismay and surprise that they are not mourning about the man living with his father's wife. He fully expects Christians to be active in disciplining fellow members who have sinned (1 Cor 5:5) as well as merciful in forgiving those who repent (2 Cor 2:5–11). They are not to ignore sin or to sit back and wait for some member of an ecclesiastical hierarchy to handle matters. The church can only maintain its holiness if its members discipline the fallen believer with spiritual discernment and Christian love.

Paul has acted with gentleness in dealing with the Corinthians and once even retreated rather than force a showdown. Now, he has given sufficient warning and has sufficient support to act firmly. He will not spare them. What punishment he will inflict is not specified, but a precedent appears in 1 Cor 5:5, where the sinner is to be handed over to Satan, which is then defined as dissociation in 5:11 (cp. 2 Thess 3:6). The command not to eat with those who bear the name of Christ but are "sexually immoral, greedy, idolaters, slanderers, drunkards or swindlers" (1 Cor 5:11) implies that they are barred from participation in the Lord's Supper. If Paul implies that they will be subject to divine judgment if he does not spare them, then it may involve sickness and even death (1 Cor 11:29–32).

13:3 Paul rebuts a demand on someone's part in Corinth for proof that Christ is speaking through him. It is a grievous insult to him to imply that he needs to go through another "trial" period to prove whether or not he satisfactorily meets the conditions of being a genuine apostle. Why do they demand such proof? Besides their complete confusion about what makes an apostle sufficient, Paul's earlier restraint in dealing with wrongdoers may have fanned their doubt. Perhaps they expected him to be more heavy-handed in dealing with the rebels and mistakenly inferred from his forbear-

---

[481] Hughes, *Paul's Second Epistle to the Corinthians*, 476.
[482] Furnish, *II Corinthians*, 570.

ance that he either lacked sufficient authority or lacked the courage to use it. Some may have attributed his meekness and gentleness to his being a weak-kneed flatterer, which caused them to question his suitability as an apostle.

Meekness and gentleness were not virtues in a Corinthian culture marked by pitched battles for social supremacy over others. Ruthlessly bludgeoning one's social rivals was the rule. The Corinthians therefore may have expected some miracle of power from Paul against adversaries who so boldly opposed him. They may have thought that an apostle would be a lot tougher, louder, bolder, and more fiery. He would unleash shafts of lightning, hailstones of wrath, and raging tempests to lay waste the opposition. Something along the order of what happened to Elymas, who was struck blind for trying to thwart Paul (Acts 13:11), would have provided convincing proof that Christ's power was indeed working in him. The Corinthians' confusion about Paul comes from their failure to see proof that the crucified and resurrected Christ is working in him in his weaknesses (5:20; Rom 15:18). They find his weakness distasteful. But Paul's weakness fits the paradigm of Christ's crucifixion. If this displeases or mystifies them, then there is some serious flaw in their faith. They do not understand the full implications of the cross and resurrection.

They have demanded proof that Paul is sufficient for his task as an apostle, but Paul will turn the tables on them and demand proof that they are truly in the faith. The important question is not whether Christ is speaking in Paul but whether Christ is living in them. When Paul does not spare those who have sinned, they will get all the proof that they want that Christ speaks in him; but it will not be something to welcome. Yet they already have plenty of proof that Christ speaks through him if they would only reflect on what Christ has done among them already. They need to "look at what is before your eyes" (10:7). "He is not weak in dealing with you, but is powerful among you." It is a miracle of God that a church was planted and grows in such a city as Corinth, and they cannot deny that they have experienced the power of Christ in their midst through signs, wonders, and mighty works (12:21; 1 Cor 12:4–11). How did this experience of Christ's power come to pass? Paul was the first to come to them with the gospel of Christ (10:14). The proof that Christ is speaking in Paul is in the pudding, unless they would exclude the pudding as evidence.

13:4   Paul gives further proof that Christ speaks by showing the parallels between himself, as a man in Christ, and Christ. "For to be sure *(kai gar)* he was crucified in weakness" parallels "likewise *(kai gar)* we are weak in him." "Yet *(alla)* he lives by God's power" parallels "yet *(alla)* by God's power we will live with him."[483] Paul does not use the future "will

---

[483] Lambrecht, "Paul's Boasting," 344.

live" elsewhere to refer to the resurrection life, so the future tense here does not imply some eschatological scenario—that we will live with him in the resurrection. He is talking about his future relations with the Corinthians. In the last clause Paul adds "unto you." The verb "to serve" is not in the Greek text; and the NRSV translation "in dealing with you" better captures Paul's thought (see GNB "in our relations with you"). Paul asserts that weakness covers all of his relations with the Corinthians. But weakness does not mean impotence. As God's power overcomes weakness in raising the seemingly vanquished Jesus from the dead and making him victorious over all, so God's power works in Paul's weakness in his dealings with the Corinthians, thus overcoming this weakness with divine power.

This verse exposes the key difference between Paul and the Corinthians: they do not perceive power in the same way.[484] The Corinthians understand power as something exerted by assertive, domineering, forceful personalities who boisterously and tyrannically wield authority. The apostle sees divine power perfected in weakness. Barrett comments, "Since Paul, like all his fellow-Christians, lives in this age, on the side of death, it is to be expected that the main sign of Christian existence will be weakness—that is, the same kind of vulnerability that Christ himself chose to adopt."[485] The Corinthians need to see the whole picture and look at things the way Paul does: "So we fix our eyes not on what is seen, but on what is unseen. For what is seen is temporary, but what is unseen is eternal" (4:18). The crucifixion displayed an apparent helplessness that caused the spectators to taunt Jesus to show them some miraculous display of power or to pull off some miraculous escape that would finally convince them that he was the Son of God. A spectacular show of worldly power on the cross—the kind they wanted to see—would have proven only that Jesus was some kind of superman, but not the Messiah, the Son of God. Just as his tormentors suspected, nothing happened. His eyes closed, his head went limp, the breathing spasms stopped. The bystanders could not see that his weakness came from his voluntary sacrifice to give his life for others in absolute obedience to God. They also could not believe that God would deliver one whom they dismissed as so contemptible. The resurrection showed the power of God working in the most abject human weakness—death, even death on a cross. It also revealed that "the weakness of God is stronger than man's strength" (1 Cor 1:25) and that God has chosen the weak things of the world to shame the strong (1 Cor 1:27).

Unlike the Corinthians, Paul recognizes that God does not allow Christ's followers, and especially apostles, to bypass Christ's way of weakness that seems so foolish to the world. As Christ's ambassador, he will continue to be

---

[484] Martin, *2 Corinthians*, 476.
[485] Barrett, *The Second Epistle to the Corinthians*, 337.

given up to death for Jesus' sake, so that the life of Jesus may be manifested
(4:11). The Corinthians still fail to grasp that, with God, weakness and
power are two sides of the same coin. Some Corinthians have dismissed Paul
because he is weak, and they think that they are strong (1 Cor 4:10). Paul
admits to his weakness and glories in it because he knows that he is weak *in
Christ* and that it continually proclaims his saving death and the power of
God (4:11). His weakness is "a reflection of his fellowship with the Lord
and of his participation in his death and resurrection."[486] What he knows
and they do not is that "Christians do not merely imitate, follow or feel
inspired by Christ, but actually live in him, are part of him, dwell supernaturally in a new world where the air they breathe is his Spirit."[487] By sharing
Christ's weakness, he shares the same divinely ordained paradox that constituted the life and destiny of Jesus Christ: comfort from suffering, life from
death, strength from weakness, wisdom from foolishness. Divine power
transforms the opposites from one to the other. If he is weak in Christ, he is
powerful, because God's power is made perfect in weakness and because
God has already shown that power in Christ. Consequently, Paul wears his
weakness as "a badge of honor" because it becomes "the platform from
which the power of God is exhibited in the world."[488]

13:5 If some in Corinth are asking what proof Paul can provide that
Christ speaks in him, he turns the question around and challenges them to
conduct a spiritual audit on themselves to see how they check out as
Christians: "Test yourselves"; "Prove yourselves."[489] They should be
examining themselves, not cross examining him. Paul plays on the verb
"to prove" (*dokimazō*, 13:5; see 8:9; 25) and the adjectives "proven"
("approved," *dokimos,* 13:7; see 10:18) and "unproven" ("fail the proof,"
"unapproved," "counterfeit," *adokimos,* 13:5,6,7). He tells the Galatians
that each one should test *(dokimazō)* his own work, then he might have a
boast, but only in himself, not by comparing himself to someone else (Gal
6:4). Paul uses the adjective *dokimos* to refer to Apelles who is "tested
and approved in Christ" (Rom 16:10, NIV). He tells the Corinthians that
he beats his body to make it his slave "so that after I have preached to
others, I myself will not be disqualified *(adokimos)* for the prize" to warn
them that no one can slide by God's judgment (1 Cor 9:27; see 3:13).
Hebrews 6:8 contains a vivid picture of what "failing the proof" entails:
"But land that produces thorns and thistles is worthless *(adokimos)* and is

---

[486] Black, *Paul, Apostle of Weakness,* 164.

[487] Hanson, *II Corinthians,* 32.

[488] D. A. Black, "Weakness," in *Dictionary of Paul and His Letters,* ed. G. F. Hawthorne, R. P.
Martin and D. G. Reid (Downers Grove: IVP, 1993) 966.

[489] "Yourselves" is in the emphatic position in Greek: ἑαυτοὺς πειράζετε ... ἑαυτοὺς
δοκιμάζετε.

in danger of being cursed. In the end it will be burned."

Betz ties the parallel challenge in Gal 6:4, "Each one should test his own actions," to the famous Delphic maxim, "know yourself." He comments that "self-examination meant the scrutinizing of one's own conduct of life … exclusively, not a comparison with others."[490] This is Paul's answer to those who dare to commend themselves by comparing themselves to others. They are to know themselves in Christ and to examine themselves by the faith.

"To see whether you are in the faith" may also be translated "to see whether you are holding the faith" (RSV). "Faith" here does not refer simply to trust in Christ, which is its primary meaning in Paul's usage, but to the whole Christian way and truth (see Titus 1:13; 2:2). It is not a matter of examining their doctrines, however, but of bringing their conduct and thinking into conformity with their belief in Christ.

We have interpreted Paul's statement in 1:24 to mean that they stand firm by faith, but others take it to be an affirmation that they stand firm in the faith. Even if this latter interpretation is correct, this challenge at the end of the letter, "see whether you are in the faith," does not mean that his former confidence in them is now shaken. If it were, he could hardly expect them even to want to administer such a test, let alone to grade it responsibly.[491] The suggestion of doubt, "to see whether" is part of his exhortation for them to shape up before he arrives so that he can be pleasantly surprised by their moral reform and their good order.

Paul does not give them a checklist of items to inspect to ascertain whether they are approved or in the faith. We might assume that such a list would involve theological, ethical, and social criteria. For example, he has told them in 1 Corinthians, "no one who is speaking by the Spirit of God says, 'Jesus be cursed,' and no one can say, 'Jesus is Lord,' except by the Holy Spirit." (1 Cor 12:2). He warned, "Flee from sexual immorality" (1 Cor 6:18), and, "Flee from idolatry" (1 Cor 10:14). He berated them for ignoring and mortifying the poor at their Lord's supper, "Do you despise the church of God and humiliate those who have nothing?" (1 Cor 11:22). But given the Corinthians' high opinions of themselves as "spiritual ones," (1 Cor 3:1), Paul may be taking for granted that they will conclude that Christ is indeed in them (Rom 8:9–11; Gal 2:20).[492] He does not think that they will fail themselves on the test. The jeopardy is real (see 1 Cor 10:12); their conduct has been unseemly for those who are in Christ. But they could not test themselves unless they were true Christians.

---

[490] H. D. Betz, *Galatians*, Her (Philadelphia: Fortress, 1979) 302.

[491] Contra Furnish, *II Corinthians*, 577.

[492] The question, "Do you not know?" appears three times in 1 Corinthians (1 Cor 3:6; 5:6; 6:2–3; see Rom 6:3,16) and introduces a well-known fact. "In you" may also be translated "among you" (REB).

The summons to test themselves will therefore authenticate Paul's ministry to them when they conclude that Christ is in them. This conclusion should lead them to recognize that just as they belong to Christ, so does Paul (10:7). Barnett is correct, "their verdict about themselves will likewise be their verdict about him."[493] If they approve themselves, they must also approve Paul who brought the gospel to them. If Christ is in them, it was Paul who first preached Christ crucified to them. But Paul has spelled out another criterion earlier in the letter for determining if one is approved: "The reason I wrote you was to see if you would stand the test *[hē dokimē]* and be obedient in everything" (2:9). If they are to pass as those who are approved, they will be obedient to Paul, particularly in his commands about appropriate Christian conduct. Christian behavior is the touchstone for determining whether those who claim to be Christians really are. Hanson comments, "A Christian's conduct, then, is a very good ready reckoner for determining his relationship to Christ, and a much better one than his religious experience."[494]

13:6 The interpretation of the previous verse is confirmed by what Paul says in 13:6. It may seem a puzzling jump in logic to write "Test yourselves to see if you are living in the faith" and then to conclude "I trust [lit., "I hope"] you will discover that we have not failed the test." How does testing themselves relate to Paul passing the test? The two are obviously intertwined in his mind. If they pass the test and know that Christ is in them; then their apostle passes the test as well (see 10:15). Paul is the one who betrothed them to Christ (11:2), and they are the seal of his apostleship in the Lord (1 Cor 9:2) and his letter of commendation in Christ for all the world to read (3:1–3). If they fail the test, then all Paul's work among them has been in vain (1 Cor 3:12–15). If they pass the test, it confirms that he is a genuine apostle.

"I hope that you will know" (*gnōsesthe,* NIV, "I trust that you will discover") takes us back to the theme statement of the letter: "And I hope that, as you have understood ("knew" *epegnōte*) us in part, you will come to understand fully ("know fully," *epignōsesthe*) that you can boast of us just as we will boast of you in the day of the Lord Jesus" (1:13b–14). They should now know that he is genuine and not counterfeit. If they recognize his genuineness, they will respond accordingly to what he demands. If they do not, they call into question their genuineness and their own spiritual discernment.

13:7 Paul *hopes* that the Corinthians will come to know that he has not failed the proof, but he *prays* to God for their ethical rectitude (see 12:20–21). This complicated sentence may be graphed as follows.

---

[493] Barnett, *The Second Epistle to the Corinthians,* 607. He also scores the point, "If the Corinthians reject Paul as Christ's apostle, they reject themselves as apostolic" (p. 609).

[494] R. P. C. Hanson, *II Corinthians,* TBC (London: SPCK, 1954) 95.

> We pray to God
>> that you not do anything bad
>>> not that we might appear approved
>>>> but that you might do the good
>>>>> and [even though] we might be as unapproved.

This statement means that if this letter stimulates their moral reformation, he will have no opportunity to prove his authority through some external display of apostolic power when he returns to Corinth. He will therefore still lack proof, in the eyes of some, that he can be bold in person. All he wants, however, is their obedience. He has no desire to demonstrate through some kind of apostolic showdown that Christ speaks in him. Therefore, he corrects what he says in 13:6, "And I trust that you will discover that we have not failed the test." His passing or failing the test is not at issue, and he does not want them to get the wrong impression that it is uppermost in his mind. His goal as an apostle is not to maintain his own reputation or to set himself up on a pedestal for all to revere but to make others worthy for Christ.

Paul is therefore less concerned to appear as a tried and true apostle than that the Corinthians prove to be tried and true Christians by resisting all evil. He does not have any need to display his power or to show that he can be just as severe in person as he is in his letters. If the Corinthians submit to the truth of the gospel, he will maintain his usual "weak" presence among them. The result of their obedience, therefore, may mean that he will still appear to some to be a failure as an apostle.[495] He will not be putting on airs, or slapping them in the face (11:20–21), the kind of things that some wrongly believe demonstrates the proper authority of an apostle. They may yet be tempted to regard him as too humble when face to face with them (10:2). But God judges realities not appearances, and Paul is indifferent about proving his own merit as long as the church remains obedient to Christ (10:6). To be vindicated as a forceful and dynamic apostle through visible demonstrations of power before a church that fails in its basic Christian calling does not even qualify as a hollow victory. It instead would mean abject failure. Their faithfulness to Christ is a living testimony of his genuineness as an apostle; but, more important, they are to be ambassadors of Christ to a strife-torn, egocentric, power hungry, and immoral world. If they are the mirror image of the pagan world surrounding them, what good are they to God? A church riddled by factions and chasing after falsehood is hardly fit for ministry to the world. Like worthless *(adokimos)* land that produces only thorns

---

[495] Fitzgerald writes: "Their restoration to wholeness (13:9) is more crucial than his self-vindication, and for that reason he is even willing to keep his authority in abeyance and appear ὡς ἀδόκιμοι (as though we were counterfeit [13:7])" ("Paul, The Ancient Epistolary Theorists, and 2 Corinthians 10–13," 200).

and thistles, it will be scorched (Heb 6:8).

13:8   The truth is expressed in 13:4. Christ "was crucified in weakness, yet he lives by God's power; likewise we are weak in him, yet by God's power we live with him."[496] This truth cannot be changed even if it may be unpalatable to the Corinthians' tastes. Paul will not tamper with the truth (2:17; 4:2; 6:7) to make things easier for himself (see Gal 2:5,14) or easier for his congregations.[497] He cannot change his spots as a weak apostle and will not change his mode of working or preaching to please them. He also cannot adjust the truth to excuse the Corinthians' sins and errors. This parenthetical statement makes clear that true apostles are controlled by the truth and not preoccupied with themselves.[498]

13:9   The Corinthians regard Paul as weak and boast of their own strength (see 1 Cor 4:10). Paul may be repeating in this verse a Corinthian slogan and bending it around the gospel so that it comes out meaning something quite different from what they intended.[499] In 12:10 he reports the lesson he learned from the stake in the flesh: when I am weak, then I am powerful because God's power is perfected in my weakness. In 13:4 he lays down the principle that Christ's weakness in his death and resurrection by the power of God strengthens us. Here Paul draws out the implications of his weakness for the Corinthians, something he has already explained in 4:10–12. He rejoices when he is weak because that is how God's power works in him most powerfully and has the most powerful effect on his converts. This verse therefore complements what Paul has said earlier: "Death is at work in us, but life is at work in you" (4:12).

Paul continues to explain why he will not be disappointed that he will not get to use his heavy artillery to destroy opposing battlements, thereby showing himself to be a mighty apostle if they are obedient. Rather than pick a fight, he sends this letter hoping that there will be no frenzied battle at all. In his mind a "weighty" letter that creates godly repentance beats a "weighty" face-to-face confrontation any day.

Paul therefore prays that they not do wrong (13:7) and for their "perfection." The noun translated "perfection" *(katartisis)* appears only here in the New Testament. The verb form *(katartizō)* is more common and is used for restoring something to its original condition or to make it fit for its purpose.

---

[496] Others interpret the truth to refer to "that revelation which God has made in his word as the rule of our faith and practice" (Hodge, *An Exposition of the Second Epistle to the Corinthians*, 308–09); or the right order of things (K. Schelkle, *The Second Epistle to the Corinthians* [New York: Herder & Herder, 1969] 209).

[497] Best writes, "He can … neither deviate in his expression of it [the truth] nor moderate its consequences for the Corinthians" (*2 Corinthians*, 131).

[498] Héring, *The Second Epistle of Saint Paul to the Corinthians*, 102.

[499] Bultmann, *The Second Letter to the Corinthians*, 248.

It is used to refer to restoring the walls of a city, preparing fabric so that it is ready to wear, preparing a remedy, preparing a vessel (Rom 9:22), or preparing a body for sacrifice (Heb 10:5). It is also used for resetting a dislocated bone, outfitting a boat, equipping a child for adulthood with a solid education, or fully training a disciple to reach his teacher's level (Luke 6:40).[500] The noun *katartismos* appears in Eph 4:12 for equipping the saints for the work of ministry. The verb form also appears in the New Testament with the sense of restoring something that is damaged, such as fishing nets (Matt 4:21; Mark 1:19), supplying what is lacking in a church's faith (1 Thess 3:10), restoring those who have suffered from persecution in this world (1 Pet 5:10), and restoring a church member who is caught in a sin (Gal 6:1). This last usage best fits the context of Corinthians. Paul is not talking about their "perfection" but their "reclamation." The use of this word here assumes that something is not right. The Corinthians need reconditioning, restoring (see the use of the verb in 13:11, "mend your ways" REB). They need to re-knit their relationship with Paul, their relationship with one another, and their relationship with the crucified and resurrected Christ.

The image of their "restoration" best ties into Paul's task of upbuilding or edifying them. Paul wants to make them fit for their task as God's people in Corinth. Hebrews closes with the prayer that the God of peace may "equip ("perfect," *katartizō*) you with everything good for doing his will" (Heb 13:20–21). The goal of the Corinthians' restoration is that they will do what is pleasing to God (5:9).

13:10 Paul hopes (13:6) and prays (13:7,9) for the Corinthians' amendment, but the warning in 10:11 and 12:19–13:4 still stands in case they fail to change their ways. The warning serves the interest of the community. He will exercise the authority that God gave to him (10:8), but he does not relish having to be harsh with them. The adverb "harshly" *(apotomōs)* appears in a noun form in Rom 11:22 *(apotomia)* and refers to God's severity in lopping off the natural branches of the olive tree. Paul can and will take punitive measures. If destroying strongholds and demolishing arguments raised up against the knowledge of God (10:4–5) means destroying a church gravitating toward sham apostles and living lives steeped in vice, then so be it. He offers a final defense for the frank criticism of his letters (see 10:10). He writes sharply so that he will not have to act sharply.[501] He would gladly come in the meekness and gentleness of Christ rather than as a disciplinarian with a rod in his hand. If they take offense at anything that seems harsh in his letters, they should remember that he does not want his return to provoke another painful clash that reopens the raw wounds of the past. He wants it to

---

[500] Spicq, *Theological Lexicon of the New Testament*, 2:271.
[501] Plummer, *The Second Epistle of St. Paul to the Corinthians*, 378.

be a happy reunion that finally heals the rift between them.

Furnish identifies chaps. 10–13 as a separate letter and asserts that 13:10 articulates the purpose of that letter. Paul writes, he says, "to urge their recommitment and their obedience to the gospel they have received from him." Furnish then claims that this statement "is ill-suited as a description of the purpose of chaps. 1–9."[502] He bases this conclusion on the following arguments:

1. Nothing in chaps. 1–9 suggests that Paul is planning a visit to Corinth in the near future. But Paul does mention his coming visit in 9:4–5, and this argument assumes that Paul's travel plans would be laced throughout the letter rather than appearing, more appropriately, at the end, as they do in 1 Cor 16:5–12.

2. According to Furnish, nothing in chaps. 1–9 "suggests that he would find it necessary to *deal harshly* with the congregation if he were to come."[503] Paul does say that he wrote the severe letter to spare them a painful visit (1:23). He wrote to test them, and Titus reported that they responded well. But until Paul returns to Corinth again in person, he cannot assume that all is well at Corinth, in spite of the promising news from Titus. The admonition to be reconciled to God (5:20) and the harsh challenge to break completely with all associations with idols and cleanse themselves from bodily and spiritual defilement (6:14–7:1) reveals that Paul still has some serious reservations about their behavior. His defense of his sufficiency as an apostle and his weakness as an earthen vessel also reveals that Paul is not fully assured that all is well between them. He must still make the case that Christ speaks through him.

3. Furnish contends it "is unthinkable that Paul would sum up the purpose of any letter which included the kind of appeal found in chaps. 8; 9 (on behalf of the collection for Jerusalem) without the slightest further reference to that request."[504] This argument wrongly assumes that 13:10 sums up the purpose of the letter. No other Pauline epistle has a closing verse that sums up every issue in the letter. Nothing comparable to a purpose statement appears at the end of 1 Corinthians. Rather than being a purpose statement, this verse actually functions to conclude the section that began in 10:1–2 and restates the premise in 10:8. The purpose statement for the letter is to be found at the beginning of the letter in 1:12–14, not at the end. To expect Paul to recapitulate everything he said in a long letter in a final verse and then to argue that his failure to do so indicates that chaps. 10–13 belong to a separate letter is arbitrary. First Corinthians reveals that Paul has a tendency to deal

---

[502] Furnish, *II Corinthians*, 580.
[503] Ibid.
[504] Ibid.

with issues seriatim. Assuming that he does the same thing in 2 Corinthians would explain why mention of the collection (which, he says, he did not need to write about, 9:1) was not restated in the closing lines of the letter.

7. Benediction (13:11–14)

11Finally, brothers, good-by. Aim for perfection, listen to my appeal, be of one mind, live in peace. And the God of love and peace will be with you.
12Greet one another with a holy kiss. 13All the saints send their greetings.
14May the grace of the Lord Jesus Christ, and the love of God, and the fellowship of the Holy Spirit be with you all.

13:11 The final lines of the letter shift from stern scoldings to a more affectionate tone. The shift in tone is no less sudden than the one between chap. 9 and chap. 10. Those who claim that 2 Corinthians consists of more than one letter must decide to which letter this closing originally belonged. Some commentators claim that such a mild, gentle, and loving conclusion following such a menacing onslaught in 13:1–10 does not fit, so it must have been originally the salutation to chaps. 1–9.[505] But we can see a similar switch in mood in 2 Thess 3:10–15 and 3:16–18.[506] We reject the premise that a shift in tone and subject matter is a reliable indicator that a letter has been doctored by a later editor.

The NIV translation, "Finally, brothers, good-by," interprets the verb *chairete* as a word of farewell. It appears frequently in secular letters as a word of greeting (in the NT, see Acts 15:23; 23:26; Jas 1:1, which have the infinitive *chairein*). But the word could also mean "rejoice." After "expressions of anxiety, self-defense, castigation of opponents and sarcasm," some commentators think that an exhortation to rejoice would be incongruous.[507] But the weight of evidence argues for the translation "rejoice."[508] Paul has used this verb to mean "rejoice" in 13:9. First Thessalonians 5:16 provides a parallel in which *chairete* ("rejoice") heads the list of final exhortations. This exhortation would recall Paul's summary of his apostolic work in Corinth, "but we work with you for your joy" (1:24; see 2:3).[509]

The verb translated "aim for perfection" *(katartizesthe)* is a cognate of the noun "restoration" *(katartismos,* NIV "perfection") in 13:9. It could be passive or middle voice. If it is middle, Paul is telling them, "Mend your

505 So Strachan, *The Second Epistle of Paul to the Corinthians*, 145.
506 Plummer, *The Second Epistle of St. Paul to the Corinthians*, 379–80.
507 Kruse, *2 Corinthians*, 222; Watson, *The Second Epistle to the Corinthians*, 149–50.
508 Furnish, *II Corinthians*, 581; Witherington, *Conflict and Community in Corinth*, 474 n. 2; Barnett, *The Second Epistle to the Corinthians*, 615.
509 See also Rom 12:12,15; Phil 2:18; 3:1; 4:4; 1 Thess 5:16.

ways"; if passive, "May your ways be mended" or "Be restored."

"Listen to my appeal" *(parakaleisthe)* could also mean "exhort one another" (see 1 Thess 4:18; 5:11), but the reciprocal pronoun is absent. If it means exhort here, then the passive is more appropriate to what precedes, "be exhorted." But this is the same word that Paul uses to open the letter by talking about the comfort that he has received from God and with which he comforts others (1:3–7). It may mean "be comforted." The NIV translation, "listen to my appeal," assumes that it means basically the same thing as Heb 13:22, "Brothers, I urge you to bear with my word of exhortation."[510] But of the eighteen times the verb *parakalein* appears in 2 Corinthians, nine times it means "to comfort" (1:4,6; 2:7; 7:6,7,13), and eight times it means "to beseech" or "entreat" (2:8; 5:20; 6:1; 8:6; 9:5; 10:1; 12:8; 18). If *parakaleisthe* is rendered as a middle voice in 13:11, it would be the only time that the verb appears in the middle voice in the letter. If it is rendered as a passive, the four other times the verb appears in the passive it means "comfort" (1:4,6; 7:7,13). This evidence suggests that the word means "be comforted" and repeats the theme with which Paul opened the letter. It makes this an astonishing appeal. They have recently mutinied against him, and he suspects that they continue to engage in flagrant sin. He must trust that the living and merciful God who has comforted him so many times in the past will work in their midst to bring about the needed reformation and comfort them as well. Paul's hope for the congregation is that as they share in his sufferings, so they will also share in his comfort.

"Be of one mind" (see also Rom 12:16; 15:5; and Phil 2:2; 4:2) recalls the dissension alluded to in 12:20, "quarreling, jealousy, outbursts of anger, factions, slander, gossip, arrogance and disorder." It does not mean that they need to agree in everything, but they do need to be intent on the same purpose (see 1 Cor 1:10).

"Live in peace" echoes the command of Jesus in Mark 9:50: "Be at peace with each other." That command concludes a discourse that began with the disciples disputing among themselves about their status (9:33–37) and included Jesus' warning about causing other believers to stumble (9:42–48). It presents "peaceful fellowship as the model for disciples' relations."[511] Paul applies the exhortation to live in peace to Christians' relationships with outsiders ("Make every effort to keep the unity of the Spirit through the bond of peace," Rom 12:18; see 1 Cor 7:15) and fellow Christians ("Live in peace with each other," 1 Thess 5:13; see Rom 14:19). These five imperatives, "rejoice," "be restored," "be comforted," "be of one mind," and "live in peace," sum up Paul's aspirations for the church.

---

[510] See also Furnish, who translates it "pay attention to my appeal" (*II Corinthians*, 581),

[511] D. E. Garland, *Mark,* NIVAC (Grand Rapids: Zondervan, 1996) 370–71.

Paul concludes these admonitions with a blessing, "and the God of love and peace will be with you." This blessing is similar to one Jesus commanded his disciples to use when they went out on their tour of Israel: "When you enter a house, first say, 'Peace to this house.' If a man of peace is there, your peace will rest on him; if not, it will return to you" (Luke 10:5–6; see Matt 10:12–13). The phrase "God of love" appears only here in the New Testament. "The God of peace" is frequent (Rom 15:33; 16:20; 1 Cor 14:33; Phil 4:9; and 1 Thess 5:23).[512] God shows inconceivable love to humans and makes peace through an incredible sacrifice (Rom 5:1; Eph 2:14–18).

13:12–13 The command to greet one another with a holy kiss appears elsewhere in Rom 16:16; 1 Cor 16:20; 1 Thess 5:26; and 1 Pet 5:14. Why does such a kiss need to be commanded?[513] Is it a new practice that needs encouragement?[514] Is it to be restricted only to worship, or does it apply wherever Christians meet?[515] Klassen argues that the kiss "is to be seen in a living context of people who are building a new sociological reality rather than in restrictive eucharistic or liturgical terms."[516] He thinks that it is "the kiss which 'saints' give each other when they meet."[517]

A kiss appears in the New Testament as a sign of respect and greeting (Luke 7:45), of love and reverence (Luke 7:38,45), and of reconciliation and family fellowship (Luke 15:20). We find a parting kiss in Acts 20:37. But a "*holy* kiss" represents something more than a social custom. It is a sign of mutual fellowship among persons of mixed social background, nationality, race, and gender who are joined together as a new family in Christ.[518] The

---

[512] See G. Delling, "Die Bezeichnung 'Gott des Friedens' und ähnliche Wendungen in den Paulusbriefen," in *Jesus und Paulus*, ed. E. E. Ellis and E. Grässer (Göttingen: Vandenhoeck & Ruprecht, 1978) 76–84.

[513] W. Klassen, "The Sacred Kiss in the New Testament: An Example of Social Boundary Lines," *NTS* 39 (1993) 122.

[514] Ibid., 130.

[515] Ibid., 131.

[516] Ibid., 132.

[517] Witherington contends that the command shows that "Paul expects his letter to be read in worship and to lead up to the climax of the service and final benediction" (*Conflict and Community in Corinthians*, 475). Most commentators assume that it is associated with a cultic act. E.g., Stählin comments: "The kiss and the Supper point forward to the eschatological consummation of salvation, to the future fellowship of the perfected" ("φιλέω ...," *TDNT* 9:140). Tertullian maintained that no public prayer was complete without members of a congregation kissing each other but was sensitive to the pagan husband who would not have his wife kissing other men in public (*De oratione* 18), and Justin spoke of it occurring between intercessory prayers and offertory (*I Apology* 65.2). Barrett recognizes the possibility that the kiss of peace as a liturgical rite was secondary, "derived from the connection between the kiss of peace and the triadic formula in the epistle" (*The Second Epistle to the Corinthians*, 343).

[518] Talbert (*Reading Corinthians*, 130) notes that it is a sign of reception in a closed group such as in an initiation (see Apuleius, *Metamorphoses* 7.9; 11.25). See also S. Benko, "The Kiss," in *Pagan Rome and the Early Christians* (Bloomington: Indiana University Press, 1984) 79–102.

holy kiss becomes a token of the joy, love, reconciliation, peace, and communion that Christians know in Christ and with one another.

There is no reason to think that in the early churches genders were separated from one another, and the holy kiss would have been extended to male and female alike. Qualifying it as "holy" removes any dimension of erotic kissing. But something holy can easily be perverted into something unholy (see the kiss of Judas), and a holy sign can become an unholy sin. Concern for any impropriety with the kiss is expressed by Athenagoras who quotes a lost apocryphal text claiming that if it is made with the slightest ulterior motive it excludes one from eternal life.[519] Many modern Christian living in a highly sexualized culture would be uncomfortable with the kiss as part of worship or greeting. Hodge comments that "the spirit of the command is that Christians should express their mutual love in the way sanctioned by the age and community in which they live."[520] The key is that it must express mutual love in a tangible way.

Paul also relays the greetings of "all the saints" to the Corinthians.[521] He may have in mind the Christians in Macedonia where he writes the letter, but its general character implies that it is more sweeping. Christians throughout the world are bound together in Christ and have an uncommon relationship to one another. The reference to "all the saints" makes clear that Paul is not some loner apostle but part of an expanding network of Christians.

13:14 The final greeting mentions all three persons of the Trinity according to their "roles in relationship to believers."[522] The emphasis falls on grace, love, and fellowship experienced by believers rather than on Trinitarian theology. "The grace of the Lord Jesus Christ" appears in the final greeting in 1 Cor 16:23; Phil 4:23; and Philemon 25.[523] According to Calvin, "grace" "by metonymy stands for the whole blessing of redemption."[524] It is summarized in 8:9: "For you know the grace of our Lord Jesus Christ, that though he was rich, yet for your sakes he became poor, so that

---

[519] Athenagoras *Legatio pro Christianis* 32; cited by Héring, *The Second Epistle to the Corinthians*, 103.

[520] Hodge, *An Exposition of the Second Epistle to the Corinthians*, 312.

[521] The NIV (KJV, NASB, NRSV, REB) numbers this greeting as v. 13 and the benediction as v. 14. The Nestle-Aland Greek text numbers it as part of v. 12 as do all Roman Catholic translations. The renumbering of the passage to make fourteen verses can be traced to the second edition of the Bishops' Bible published in 1572.

[522] Witherington, *Community and Conflict in Corinth*, 476. A similar triune reference appears in 1:21–22: "Now it is God who makes both us and you stand firm in Christ. He anointed us, set his seal of ownership on us, and put his Spirit in our hearts as a deposit, guaranteeing what is to come." Others occur in Rom 8:9–11; Gal 4:4–6; 1 Cor 6:11; 12:4–6; Eph 1:3,13–14; 2:18; 3:14–17; and 4:4–6.

[523] The grace wish is found in Rom 16:20; Gal 6:18; 1 Thess 5:28; and Col 4:18,

[524] Calvin, *The Second Epistle of Paul the Apostle to the Corinthians*, 176.

you through his poverty might become rich."

"The love of God" is expressed and seen most clearly in Christ's sacrificial death. "The fellowship of the Holy Spirit" is sometimes interpreted as an objective genitive, meaning our participation in the Spirit and in the spiritual gifts, or as a subjective genitive, referring to the fellowship created by the Spirit. The other two genitival constructions are subjective, and the context emphasizes unity and harmony, which would argue for the second meaning (see Eph 4:3). But posing this as an either / or question may fail "to do justice to the richness of Paul's thought."[525] It may best be understood as a "plenary" genitive which incorporates both ideas.[526] Paul wishes for the Corinthians a deepening of their participation in the Holy Spirit; he also wishes for the unity which the Holy Spirit gives to the community.

Paul calls down God's blessings upon *all* of them, including those who have given him so much trouble in Corinth. The letter seems to have met with success.[527] According to Acts 20:2–3, Paul spent three months in Greece and we may assume that most of that time was spent in Corinth. The letter to the Romans was probably written from Corinth on the eve of his departure for Jerusalem with the collection to which the Achaians contributed (Rom 15:26). Clement, a leader of the Roman church, wrote to the Corinthians at the end of the first century, referring to 1 Corinthians (*1 Clem* 47:1) and praising Paul as an example (*1 Clem* 5:5–7). Best comments: "He would hardly have done this unless Paul and his writings were held in honor in Corinth. We may then assume that Paul's pleas were successful and that when he came to Corinth he did not have to tear down but was able to build up."[528]

---

[525] Watson, *The Second Epistle to the Corinthians*, 151.

[526] D. B. Wallace, *Greek Grammar Beyond the Basics* (Grand Rapids: Zondervan, 1996) 119–21.

[527] Barnett, *The Second Epistle to the Corinthians*, 619.

[528] Best, *2 Corinthians*, 139.

1:1–2 Greeting
1:3–7 Blessing for God's Provision of Comfort
I. THE PAINFUL VISIT AND TEARFUL LETTER: PAUL'S DEFENSE OF HIS EXCEPTIONAL CANDOR (1:8–7:16)
    A 1:8–2:13 The Issue of Paul's Love for the Church and His Dependability
        1:8–11 Paul's Afflictions in Asia
        1:12–14 Theme Statement of the Letter: Rightly Understanding Paul's Ministry
        1:15–22 Paul's Changes in Travel Plans and the Faithfulness of God
        1:23–2:4 The Sorrowful Visit and the Explanation for his Decision Not to Return
        2:5–11 Forgiveness of the Offender
        2:12–13 Paul's Afflictions in Macedonia and Waiting for Titus
    B 2:14–7:3 Paul's Defense of His Frank Criticism
      A 2:14–3:6 Christian Ministry
        A 2:14–17 Paul's Sufficiency for a Ministry That Results in Life or Death
        B 3:1–3 The Corinthians as Paul's Letter
        A′ 3:4–6 Paul's Sufficiency as Minister of the New Covenant
      B 3:7–18 The Old and the New Ministries
        A 3:7–9 The Glory of the Ministry Now Set Aside
        B 3:10 The Greater Glory of the New Eclipses the Old
        A′ 3:11 The Glory of the Ministry Now Set Aside
        A 3:12–13 The Unveiled Paul (We, Apostles)
        B 3:14–17 Veiled Israel (They, Israelites)
        A′ 3:18 Unveiled Christians (We, Christians)
      A′ 4:1–6 Christian Ministry
        A 4:1–2 Commending Himself through the Open Statement of the Truth
        B 4:3–4 The Spiritual Condition of Those Blinded to the Glory of Christ in "Our Gospel"
        A^1 4:5–6 The Basic Thrust of Paul's Preaching: Christ as Lord; Ourselves as Your Slaves
      A 4:7–15 Self-Defense: Catalog of Afflictions: Always Being Given Over to Death
      B 4:16–5:10 The Resurrection Hope
        4:16–18 Our Inner Nature Prepared by God for an Eternal Weight of Glory
        5:1–5 The Eternal Building from God
        5:6–10 Our Eternal Destiny before the Judgment Seat of Christ
      B′ 5:11–21 Persuading Others to Be Reconciled to God
        5:11–13 Self-Defense: Reiteration of the Letter's Theme Statement (1:12–14)
        5:14–21 An Emissary of Christ for Reconciliation
      A′ 6:1–10 Self-Defense: Catalog of Afflictions: Why the Corinthians Should Honor His Appeals
      A 6:11–13 Plea for Them to Open Their Hearts
      B 6:14–7:1 Frank Appeal: Separate Yourselves

Selected Bibliography of Works in English

Commentaries

Barnett, P. *The Message of 2 Corinthians*. The Bible Speaks Today. Downers Grove: IVP, 1988.

———. *The Second Epistle to the Corinthians*. NICNT. Grand Rapids: Eerdmans, 1997.

Barrett, C. K. *The Second Epistle to the Corinthians*. HNTC. New York: Harper & Row, 1973.

Belleville, L. L. *2 Corinthians*. IVPNTC. Downers Grove/Leicester: IVP, 1995.

Best, E. *Second Corinthians*. Interpretation. Atlanta: John Knox, 1987.

Betz, H. D. *2 Corinthians 8 and 9: A Commentary on Two Administrative Letters of the Apostle Paul*. Hermeneia. Philadelphia: Fortress, 1985.

Bruce, F. F. *I & II Corinthians*. NCB. Grand Rapids: Eerdmans, 1971.

Bultmann, R. *The Second Letter to the Corinthians*. Edited by E. Dinkler. Translated by R. A. Harrisville. Minneapolis: Augsburg, 1976.

Calvin, J. *The Second Epistle of Paul the Apostle to the Corinthians and the Epistles to Timothy, Titus and Philemon*. Calvin's Commentaries. Translated by T. A. Small. Edited by D. W. Torrence and T. F. Torrance. Grand Rapids: Eerdmans, 1964.

Danker, F. W. *II Corinthians*. ACNT. Minneapolis: Augsburg, 1989.

Furnish, V. P. *II Corinthians*. AB. Garden City: Doubleday, 1984.

Hanson, R. P. C. *II Corinthians*. TBC. London: SPCK, 1954.

Harris, M. J. "2 Corinthians." In *The Expositor's Bible Commentary*. Grand Rapids: Zondervan, 1976, 10:301–406.

Héring, J. *The Second Epistle of Saint Paul to the Corinthians*. London: Epworth, 1967.

Hughes, P. E. *Paul's Second Epistle to the Corinthians*. NICNT. Grand Rapids: Eerdmans, 1962.

Kruse, C. *2 Corinthians*. TNTC. Grand Rapids: Eerdmans, 1987.

Lambrecht, J. *2 Corinthians*. Sacra Pagina. Collegeville: Liturgical, 1999.

Martin, R. P. *2 Corinthians*. WBC. Waco: Word, 1986.

Plummer, A. *The Second Epistle of Paul the Apostle to the Corinthians*. Cambridge: Cambridge University Press, 1911.

———. *A Critical and Exegetical Commentary on the Second Epistle of St. Paul to the Corinthians*. ICC. New York: Charles Scribner's Sons, 1915.

Scott, J. M. *2 Corinthians*. NIBC. Peabody: Hendrickson, 1998.

Strachan, R. H. *The Second Epistle of Paul to the Corinthians*. MNTC. London: Hodder & Stoughton, 1935.

Talbert, C. H. *Reading Corinthians: A Literary and Theological Commentary on 1 and 2 Corinthians*. New York: Crossroad, 1987.

Thrall, M. E. *A Critical and Exegetical Commentary on the Second Epistle to the Corinthians. Volume 1*. ICC. Edinburgh: T & T Clark, 1994.

Watson, N. *The Second Epistle to the Corinthians*. Epworth Commentaries. London: Epworth, 1993.

Witherington, B. III. *Conflict and Community in Corinth: A Socio-Rhetorical Commentary on 1 and 2 Corinthians*. Grand Rapids: Eerdmans, 1994.

Monographs and Collected Essays

Barrett, C. K. *Essays on Paul.* Philadelphia: Westminster, 1982.

Bieringer, R., ed. *The Corinthian Correspondence.* BETL 125. Leuven: Leuven University Press, 1996.

———., and J. Lambrecht. *Studies in 2 Corinthians.* BETL 112. Leuven: Leuven University Press, 1994.

Belleville, L. L. *Reflections of Glory: Paul's Polemical Use of the Moses-Doxa Tradition in 2 Corinthians 3.1–18.* JSNTSup 52. Sheffield: JSOT, 1991.

Black, D. A. *Paul, Apostle of Weakness: Astheneia and Its Cognates in the Pauline Literature.* American University Studies. New York/Berne/Frankfurt on the Main/Nancy: Peter Lang, 1984.

Carson, D. A. *From Triumphalism to Maturity: An Exposition of 2 Corinthians 10–13.* Grand Rapids: Baker, 1984.

Crafton, J. A. *The Agency of the Apostle. A Dramatic Analysis of Paul's Responses to Conflict 2 Corinthians.* JSNTSup 51. Sheffield: JSOT, 1991.

Fitzgerald, J. T. *Cracks in an Earthen Vessel: An Examination of the Catalogues of Hardships in the Corinthian Correspondence.* SBLDS, 99. Atlanta: Scholars Press, 1988.

Georgi, D. *The Opponents of Paul in Second Corinthians.* Philadelphia: Fortress, 1986.

Hafemann, S. J. *Suffering and Ministry in the Spirit: Paul's Defense of His Ministry in II Corinthians 2:14–3:3.* Grand Rapids: Eerdmans, 1990.

———. *Paul, Moses, and the History of Israel: The Letter/Spirit Contrast and the Argument from Scripture in 2 Corinthians 3.* Peabody: Hendrickson, 1996.

Harvey, A. E. *Renewal through Suffering: A Study of 2 Corinthians.* Studies of the New Testament and Its World. Edinburgh: T & T Clark, 1996.

Hay, D. M., ed. *Pauline Theology. Vol. II: 1 & 2 Corinthians.* Minneapolis: Fortress, 1993.

Horrell, D. *The Social Ethos of the Corinthian Correspondence: Interests and Ideology from 1 Corinthians to 1 Clement.* Studies of the New Testament and Its World. Edinburgh: T & T Clark, 1996.

Kreitzer, L. *2 Corinthians.* New Testament Guides. Sheffield: Academic Press, 1996.

Lorenzi, L. de. *The Diakonia of the Spirit (2 Co 4:7–7:4).* Monographic Series of "Benedictina": Biblical Ecumenical Section 10. Rome: Benedictina, 1989.

Marshall, P. *Enmity in Corinth: Social Conventions in Paul's Relation with the Corinthians.* WUNT II/23. Tübingen: Mohr (Siebeck), 1987.

Murphy-O'Connor, J. *St. Paul's Corinth. Texts and Archaeology.* Good News Studies, 6. Wilmington: Michael Glazier, 1983.

———. *The Theology of the Second Letter to the Corinthians.* Cambridge: Cambridge University Press, 1991.

Pate, C. M. *Adam Christology as the Exegetical and Theological Substructure of 2 Corinthians 4:7–5:21.* Lanham/New York: University Press of America, 1991.

Peterson, B. K. *Eloquence and the Proclamation of the Gospel in Corinth.* SBLDS 163. Atlanta: Scholars Press, 1998.

Savage, T. B. *Power through Weakness: Paul's Understanding of the Christian Ministry in 2 Corinthians.* SNTSMS 86. Cambridge: University Press, 1996.

Stockhausen, C. K. *Moses' Veil and the Glory of the New Covenant: The Exegetical Substructure of II Cor. 3,1–4,6.* AnBib 116. Rome: Pontifical Biblical Institute, 1989.

Sumney, J. L. *Identifying Paul's Opponents. The Question of Method in 2 Corinthians.* JSNTSup 40. Sheffield: JSOT, 1990.

Tabor, J. D. *Things Unutterable: Paul's Ascent to Paradise in Its Greco-Roman, Judaic, and Early Christian Contexts.* Lanham: University Press of America, 1986.

Theissen, G. *Essays on Corinth. The Social Setting of Pauline Christianity.* Philadelphia: Fortress, 1982.

Verbrugge, V. D. *Paul's Style of Church Leadership Illustrated by His Instructions to the Corinthians on the Collection.* San Francisco: Mellen Research University Press, 1992.

Webb, W. J. *Returning Home: New Covenant and Second Exodus as the Context for 2 Corinthians 6.14–7.1.* JSNTSup 85. Sheffield: JSOT, 1993.

Wellborn, L. L. *Politics & Rhetoric in the Corinthian Epistles.* Macon: Mercer University Press, 1997.

Young, F., and D. F. Ford. *Meaning and Truth in 2 Corinthians.* Biblical Foundations in Theology. London: SPCK, 1987.

Articles

Andrews, S. B. "Too Weak Not to Lead: The Form and Function of 2 Cor 11,23b–33." *NTS* 41 (1995) 263–76.

Ascough, R. S. "The Completion of a Religious Duty: The Background of 2 Cor 8.1–15." *NTS* 42 (1996) 584–99.

Baird, W. "Letters of Recommendation: A Study of II Cor 3:1–3." *JBL* 80 (1961) 166–72.

———. "Visions, Revelation, and Ministry. Reflections on 2 Cor 12:1–5 and Gal 1:11–17." *JBL* 104 (1985) 651–62.

Bates, W. H. "The Integrity of II Corinthians." *NTS* 12 (1965–66) 56–69.

Beale, G. K. "The Old Testament Background of Reconciliation in 2 Corinthians 5–7 and Its Bearing on the Literary Problem of 2 Corinthians 6.14–7,1." *NTS* 35 (1989) 550–81.

Belleville, L. L. "A Letter of Apologetic Self-Commendation: 2 Cor. 1:8–7:16." *NovT* 31 (1989) 142–63.

———. "Tradition or Creation? Paul's Use of the Exodus 34 Tradition in 2 Corinthians 3.7–18." In *Paul and the Scriptures of Israel.* Edited by C. A. Evans and J. A. Sanders. JSNTSup 83. Sheffield, Academic Press, 1993, 165–86.

———. "Gospel and Kerygma in 2 Corinthians." In *Gospel in Paul.* Edited by L. A. Jervis and P. Richardson. JSNTSup 108. Sheffield: Academic Press, 1994, 134–64.

———. "Paul's Polemic and Theology of the Spirit in Second Corinthians." *CBQ* 58 (1996) 281–304.

Berry, R. "Death and Life in Christ: The Meaning of 2 Corinthians 5.1–10." *SJT* 14 (1961) 60–76.

Best, E. "II Corinthians 4.7–15: Life through Death." *IBS* 8 (1986) 2–7.

Betz, H. D. "2 Cor 6:14–7:1: An Anti-Pauline Fragment?" *JBL* 92 (1973) 88–108.

———. The Problem of Rhetoric and Theology According to the Apostle Paul." In *L'apôtre Paul. Personnalité, style et conception du ministère.* Edited by A. Vanhoye. BETL 73. Leuven: Leuven University Press, 1986, 16–48.

Blomberg, C. "The Structure of 2 Corinthians 1–7." *CTR* 4 (1989–90) 3–20.

Borchert, G. L. "Introduction to 2 Corinthians." *RevExp* 86 (1989) 313–24.

Bornkamm, G. "The History of the Origin of the So-Called Second Letter to the Corinthians." *NTS* 8 (1961–62) 258–64.

Bowker, J. W. "'Merkabah' Visions and the Visions of Paul." *JSS* 16 (1971) 157–73.

Breytenbach, C. "Paul's Proclamation and God's 'THRIAMBOS.' Notes on 2 Corinthians 2:14–16b." *Neotestamentica* 24 (1990) 257–71.

Bruce, F. F. "Paul on Immortality." *SJT* 24 (1971) 457–72.

Cassidy, R. "Paul's Attitude to Death in II Corinthians 5:1–10." *EvQ* 43 (1971) 210–17.

Collins, J. N. "Georgi's 'Envoys' in 2 Cor 11:23." *JBL* 93 (1974) 88–96.

Craddock, F. B. "The Poverty of Christ. An Investigation of II Corinthians 8:9." *Int* 22 (1968) 158–70.

Craig, W. L. "Paul's Dilemma in 2 Corinthians 5.1–10: A 'Catch–22.'" *NTS* 34 (1988) 145–47.

Cranfield, C. E. B. "Minister and Congregation in the Light of II Corinthians 4:5–7. An Exposition." *Int* 19 (1965) 163–67.

———. "The Grace of Our Lord Jesus Christ. 2 Corinthians 8:1–9." *Communio viatorum* 32 (1989) 105–9.

Dahl, N. A. "A Fragment and Its Context. 2 Corinthians 6:14–7:1." In *Studies in Paul.* Minneapolis: Augsburg, 1977, 62–69.

Danker, F. W. "Paul's Debt to the *De Corona* of Demosthenes: A Study of Rhetorical Techniques in Second Corinthians." In *Persuasive Artistry: Studies in New Testament Rhetoric in Honor of George A. Kennedy.* Edited by D. F. Watson. Sheffield: Academic Press, 1991, 262–80.

Derrett, J. D. M. "2 Cor 6,14ff. A Midrash on Dt 22,10." *Bib* 59 (1978) 231–50.

———. "*Nai* (2 Cor 1:19–20)." *Filologia neotestamentaria* 4 (1991) 205–9.

DeSilva, D. A. "Measuring Penultimate against Ultimate Reality: An Investigation of the Integrity and Argumentation of 2 Corinthians." *JSNT* 52 (1993) 41–70.

———. "Recasting the Moment of Decision: 2 Corinthians 6:14–7:1 in Its Literary Context." *Andrews University Seminary Studies* 31 (1993) 3–16.

Dewey, A. J. "A Matter of Honor: A Social-Historical Analysis of 2 Corinthians 10." *HTR* 78 (1985) 209–17.

Duff, P. "Metaphor, Motif, and Meaning. The Rhetorical Strategy behind the Image 'Led in Triumph' in 2 Corinthians 2:14." *CBQ* 53 (1991) 79–92.

———. "Apostolic Suffering and the Language of Processions in 2 Corinthians 4:7–10." *BTB* 21 (1991) 158–65.

———. "The Mind of the Redactor: 2 Cor. 6:14–7:1 in Its Secondary Context." *NovT* 35 (1993) 160–80.

———. "2 Corinthians 1–7: Sidestepping the Division Hypothesis Dilemma." *BTB* 24 (1994) 16–26.

Dumbrell, W. J. "Paul's Use of Exodus 34 in 2 Corinthians 3." In *God Who Is Rich in Mercy.* Edited by P. T. O'Brien and D. G. Peterson. Homebush, Australia: Lancer Books, 1986, 179–94.

Dunn, J. D. G. "2 Corinthians III.17—'The Lord Is the Spirit.'" *JTS* 21 (1970) 309–20.

Egan, R. B. "Lexical Evidence on Two Pauline Passages." *NovT* 19 (1977) 34–62.

Ellis, E. E. "II Corinthians V.1–10 in Pauline Eschatology." *NTS* 6 (1959–60) 211–24.

Fallon, F. T. "Self-Sufficiency or God's Sufficiency: 2 Corinthians 2:16." *HTR* 76 (1983) 369–74.

Fee, G. D. "II Corinthians vi.14–vii.1 and Food Offered to Idols." *NTS* 23 (1976–77) 140–61.

———. "ΧΑΡΙΣ in II Corinthians 1.15: Apostolic Parousia and Paul-Corinth Chronology." *NTS* 24 (1977–78) 533–38.

———. "'Another gospel which you did not embrace: 2 Corinthians 11.4 and the Theology of 1 and 2 Corinthians." In *Gospel in Paul.* Edited by L. A. Jervis and P. Richardson. JSNTSup 108. Sheffield: Academic Press, 1994, 111–33.

Fitzgerald, J. T. "Paul, the Ancient Epistolary Theorists, and 2 Corinthians 10–13." In *Greeks, Romans, and Christians.* Edited by D. L. Balch, E. Ferguson, and W. A. Meeks. Minneapolis: Fortress, 1990, 190–200.

Fitzmyer, J. A. "Qumran and the Interpolated Paragraph in 2 Cor 6:14–7:1." *CBQ* 23 (1961) 271–80.

―――. "Glory Reflected on the Face of Christ (2 Cor 3: 7–4:6) and a Palestinian Jewish Motif." *TS* 42 (1981) 630–44.

Forbes, C. "Comparison, Self-Praise and Irony. Paul's Boasting and the Conventions of Hellenistic Rhetoric." *NTS* 32 (1986) 1–30.

Fraser, J. W. "Paul's Knowledge of Jesus. II Corinthians 5:16 Once More." *NTS* 17 (1970–71) 293–313.

Fredrickson, D. E. "ΠΑΡΡΗΣΙΑ in the Pauline Epistles." In *Friendship, Flattery and Frankness of Speech: Studies on Friendship in the New Testament World.* Edited by J. T. Fitzgerald. NovTSup 82. Leiden: Brill, 1996, 163–83.

Furnish, V. P. "Corinth in Paul's Time." *BAR* 15 (1988) 14–27.

Garland, D. E. "Paul's Apostolic Authority: The Power of Christ Sustaining Weakness (2 Corinthians 10–13)." *RevExp* 86 (1989) 371–89.

Garrett, S. R. "The God of This World and the Affliction of Paul: 2 Cor 4:1–12." In *Greeks, Romans, and Christians.* Edited by D. L. Balch, E. Ferguson, and W. A. Meeks. Minneapolis: Fortress, 1990.

Gillman, J. "A Thematic Comparison: 1 Cor 15:50–57 and 2 Cor 5:1–5." *JBL* 107 (1988) 439–54.

Glasson, T. F. "2 Corinthians v. 1–10 versus Platonism." *SJT* 43 (1990) 145–55.

Gnilka, J. "2 Cor 6:14–7:1 in the Light of the Qumran Texts and the Testament of the Twelve Patriarchs." In *Paul and Qumran. Studies in New Testament Exegesis.* Edited by J. Murphy-O'Connor. Chicago: The Priory Press, 1968, 48–68.

Goulder, M. "2 Cor. 6:14–7:1 as an Integral Part of 2 Corinthians." *NovT* 36 (1994) 47–57.

―――. "Vision and Knowledge." *JSNT* 56 (1994) 53–71.

Grech, P. "2 Corinthians 3:17 and the Pauline Doctrine of Conversion to the Holy Spirit." *CBQ* 17 (1955) 420–37.

Greenwood, D. "The Lord Is Spirit: Some Considerations of 2 Cor 3:17." *CBQ* 34 (1972) 467–72.

Hafemann, S. J. "The Comfort and Power of the Gospel: The Argument of 2 Corinthians 13." *RevExp* 86 (1989) 325–44.

―――. "'Self-Commendation' and Apostolic Legitimacy in 2 Corinthians: A Pauline Dialectic?" *NTS* 36 (1990) 66–88.

―――. "The Glory and Veil of Moses in 2 Cor 3:7–14: An Example of Paul's Contextual Exegesis of the Old Testament—A Proposal." *HBT* 14 (1992) 31–49.

Hanson, A. T. "The Midrash in II Corinthians 3: A Reconsideration." *JSNT* 9 (1980) 2–28.

Harris, M. J. "2 Corinthians 5:1–10: A Watershed in Paul's Theology?" *TynBul* 22 (1971) 32–57.

Harvey, A. E. "Forty Strokes Save One: Social Aspects of Judaizing and Apostasy." In *Alternative Approaches to New Testament Study.* Edited by A. E. Harvey. London: SPCK, 1985, 79–96.

Hemer, C. J. "A Note on 2 Corinthians 1:9." *TynBul* 23 (1972) 103–7.

Hettlinger, R. F. "2 Corinthians 5:1–10." *SJT* 10 (1957) 174–94.

Hickling, C. J. A. "The Sequence of Thought in II Corinthians, Chapter Three." *NTS* 21 (1974–75) 380–95.

Hodgson, R. "Paul the Apostle and First Century Tribulation Lists." *ZNW* 74 (1983) 59–80.

Holland, G. "Speaking Like a Fool: Irony in 2 Corinthians 10–13." In *Rhetoric and the New Testament: Essays from the Heidelberg Conference.* Edited by S. E. Porter and T. H. Olbricht. JSNTSup 90. Sheffield: Academic Press, 1993, 250–64.

Hooker, M. D. "Interchange in Christ." *JTS* 22 (1971) 349–61.

Horrell, D. "Paul's Collection: Resources for a Materialist Theology." *Epworth Review* 22 (1995) 74–83.

Hubbard, M. "Was Paul Out of His Mind? Re-Reading 2 Corinthians 5.13." *JSNT* 70 (1998) 39–64.

Hughes, F. W. "The Rhetoric of Reconciliation: 2 Corinthians 1.1–2.13 and 7.5–8.24." In *Persuasive Artistry.* Edited by D. F. Watson. JSNTSup 50. Sheffield: JSOT, 1991, 246–61.

Jegher-Bucher, V. "'The Thorn in the Flesh'/ Der Pfahl im Fleisch': Considerations About 2 Corinthians 12.7–10 in Connection with 12.1–13." In *The Rhetorical Analysis of Scripture: Essays from the 1995 London Conference.* Edited by S. E. Porter and T. H. Olbricht. JSNTSup 146. Sheffield: Academic Press, 1997, 388–97.

Johnson, S. E. "A New Analysis of Second Corinthians." *ATR* 47 (1965) 436–45.

Judge, E. A. "Paul's Boasting in Relation to Contemporary Professional Practice." *Aus-BR* 16 (1968) 37–50.

Kee, D. "Who Were the 'Super-Apostles' of 2 Cor 10–13." *Restoration Quarterly* 23 (1980) 65–76.

Kennedy, J. H. "Are There Two Epistles in 2 Corinthians?" *The Expositor* 5th series, 6 (1897) 231–38, 285–304.

———. "St. Paul's Correspondence with Corinth." *The Expositor* 5th series, 10 (1899) 182–95.

Kent, H. A. "The Glory of Christian Ministry. An Analysis of 2 Corinthians 2.14–4.18." *Grace Theological Journal* 2 (1981) 171–89.

Kune, J. J. "We, Us and Our in I and II Corinthians." *NovT* 8 (1966) 171–79.

Kim, S. "2 Cor 5:11–21 and the Origin of Paul's Concept of 'Reconciliation.'" *NovT* 39 (1997) 360–84.

Kolenkow, A. B. "Paul and Opponents in 2 Cor 10–13—*Theoi Andres* and Spiritual Guides." In *Religious Propaganda and Missionary Competition in the New Testament World.* Edited by L. Bormann, K. Del Tredici, and A. Standhartinger. Leiden/ New York/Köln: E. J. Brill, 1997, 351–74.

Kruse, C. G. "The Offender and the Offence in 2 Corinthians 2:5 and 7:12." *EvQ* 60 (1988) 129–39.

———. "The Relationship between the Opposition to Paul Reflected in 2 Corinthians 1–7 and 10–13." *EvQ* 61 (1989) 195–202.

Lambrecht, J. "Strength in Weakness. A Reply to Scott B. Andrews' Exegesis of 2 Cor 11:23b–33." *NTS* 43 (1997) 285–90.

———. "Paul's Boasting about the Corinthians: A Study of 2 Cor. 8:24–9:5." *NovT* 40 (1998) 352–68.

Leary, T. J. "'A Thorn in the Flesh'—2 Corinthians 12:7." *JTS* 43 (1992) 520–22.

Leivestad, R. "'The Meekness and Gentleness of Christ' II Cor. X.1." *NTS* 12 (1965–66) 156–64.

Lillie, W. "An Approach to 2 Corinthians 5.1–10." *SJT* 30 (1977) 59–70.

Lincoln, A. T. "'Paul the Visionary': The Setting and Significance of the Rapture to Paradise in II Corinthians XII.1–10." *NTS* 25 (1978–79) 204–20.

Lodge, J. G. "The Apostle's Appeal and Readers' Response: 2 Corinthians 8 and 9." *Chicago Studies* 30 (1991) 59–75.

Loubser, J. A. "Winning the Struggle (or: How to Treat Heretics) (2 Corinthians 12:1–10)." *Journal of Theology for Southern Africa* 75 (1991) 75–83.

———. "A New Look at Paradox and Irony in 2 Corinthians 10–13." *Neotestamentica* 26 (1992) 507–21.

McCant, J. W. "Paul's Thorn of Rejected Apostleship." *NTS* 34 (1988) 550–72.

McClelland, S. E. "'Super-Apostles, Servants of Christ, Servants of Satan.'" *JSNT* 14 (1982) 82–87.

McDonald, J. I. H. "Paul and the Preaching Ministry: A Reconsideration of 2 Cor. 2:14–17 in Its Context." *JSNT* 17 (1983) 35–50.

Malherbe, A. J. "Antisthenes and Odysseus and Paul at War." In *Paul and the Popular Philosophers*. Philadelphia: Westminster, 1989, 91–119.

Manson, T. W. "St. Paul in Ephesus (3) and (4): The Corinthian Correspondence." In *Studies in the Gospels and Epistles*. Edited by M. Black. Philadelphia: Westminster, 1962, 190–224.

———. "2 Cor. 2:14–17: Suggestions Toward an Exegesis." In *Studia Paulina*. Edited by J. N. Sevenster and W. C. Van Unnik. Haarlem: Bohm, 1953, 155–62.

Manus, C. U. "Apostolic Suffering (2 Cor 6:4–10): The Sign of Christian Existence and Identity." *Asia Journal of Theology* 1 (1987) 41–54.

Marguerat, D. "2 Corinthiens 10–13. Paul et l'expérience de Dieu." *ETR* 63 (1988) 497–519.

Marshall, P. "A Metaphor of Social Shame: θριαμβεύειν in 2 Cor. 2:14." *NovT* 25 (1983) 302–17.

———. "Hybrists Not Gnostics in Corinth." *SBLSP* (1984) 275–87.

———. "Invective: Paul and His Enemies in Corinth." In *Perspectives on Language and Text*. Edited by E. W. Conrad and E. G. Newing. Winona Lake: Eisenbrauns, 1987, 359–73.

Martin, R. P. "The Setting of 2 Corinthians." *TynBul* 37 (1986) 3–19.

———. "The Opponents of Paul in 2 Corinthians: An Old Issue Revisited." *Tradition and Interpretation in the New Testament*. Edited by G. F. Hawthorne and O. Betz. Grand Rapids Eerdmans, 1987, 279–89.

———. "The Spirit in 2 Corinthians in Light of the 'Fellowship of the Holy Spirit' in 2 Corinthians 13:14." In *Eschatology and the New Testament*. Edited by W. H. Gloer. Peabody: Hendrickson, 1988, 113–28.

Martyn, J. L. "Epistemology at the Turn of the Ages: 2 Corinthians 5:16." In *Christian History and Interpretation*. Edited by W. R. Farmer, C. F. D. Moule, and R. R. Niebuhr. Cambridge: Cambridge University Press, 1967, 269–87.

Mealand, D. L. "'As having nothing and yet possessing everything,' 2 Cor 6:10c." *ZNW* 67 (1976) 277–79.

Melick, R .R. Jr. "The Collection for the Saints: 2 Corinthians 8–9." *CTR* 4 (1989–90) 97–117.

Menoud, P. H. "The Thorn in the Flesh and Satan's Angel (2 Cor. 12.7)." In *Jesus Christ and the Faith: A Collection of Studies*. PTMS 18. Pittsburgh: Pickwick, 1978, 19–30.

Metts, R. "Death, Discipleship, and Discourse Strategies: 2 Cor 5:1–10 Once Again." *CTR* 4 (1989–90) 57–76.

Minear, P. S. "Some Pauline Thoughts on Dying: A Study of 2 Corinthians." In *From Faith to Faith*. Edited by D. Y. Hadidian. Pittsburgh: Pickwick, 1979, 91–106.

Mitchell, M. M. "New Testament Envoys in the Context of Greco-Roman Diplomatic and Epistolary Conventions: The Example of Timothy and Titus." *JBL* 111 (1992) 641–62.

Mitton, C. L. "Paul's Certainties. V. The Gift of the Spirit and Life beyond Death—2 Corinthians v.1–5." *ExpT* 69 (1957–58) 260–63.

Morray-Jones, C. R. A. "Paradise Revisited (2 Cor 12:1–12): The Jewish Mystical Background of Paul's Apostolate. Part 1: The Jewish Sources." *HTR* 86 (1993) 177–217.

———. "Paradise Revisited (2 Cor 12:1–12): The Jewish Mystical Background of

Paul's Apostolate. Part 2: Paul's Heavenly Ascent and Its Significance." *HTR* 86 (1993) 265–92.

Moule, C. F. D. "St Paul and Dualism: The Pauline Conception of Resurrection." *NTS* 12 (1965–66) 106–23.

———. "2 Cor 3,18b." In *Neues Testament und Geschichte*. Edited by H. Baltensweiler and B. Reicke. Tübingen: Mohr (Siebeck), 1972, 231–37.

———. "Peculiarities in the Language of 2 Corinthians." *Essays in New Testament Interpretation*. Cambridge: Cambridge University Press, 1982, 158–61.

———. "Reflections on So-called 'Triumphalism.'" In *The Glory of Christ in the New Testament. Studies in Christology*. Edited by L. D. Hurst and N. T. Wright. Oxford, Oxford University Press, 1987, 219–28.

Mullins, T. Y. "Paul's Thorn in the Flesh." *JBL* 76 (1957) 299–303.

Murphy-O'Connor, J. "The Corinth That Saint Paul Saw." *BA* 47 (1984) 147–59.

———. "Paul and Macedonia: The Connection Between 2 Corinthians 2.13 and 2.14." *JSNT* 25 (1985) 99–103.

———. "'Being at home in the body we are in exile from the Lord' (2 Cor 5:6b)." *RB* 93 (1986) 214–21.

———. "Pneumatikoi and Judaizers in 2 Cor 2:14–4:6." *AusBR* 34 (1986) 42–58.

———. "Relating 2 Corinthians 6.14–7.1 to its Context." *NTS* 33 (1987) 272–275.

———. "Faith and Resurrection in 2 Cor 4:13–14." *RB* 95 (1988) 543–550.

———. "Philo and 2 Cor 6:14–7:1." *RB* 95 (1988) 55–69.

———. "Pneumatikoi in 2 Corinthians." *Proceedings of the Irish Biblical Association* 11 (1988) 59–66.

———. "'Another Jesus' (2 Cor 11:4)." *RB* 97 (1990) 238–51.

———. "The Date of 2 Corinthians 10–13." *AusBR* 39 (1991) 31–43.

———. "Co-Authorship in the Corinthian Correspondence." *RB* 100 (1993) 562–79.

Myrick, A. A. "'Father' Imagery in 2 Corinthians 1–9 and Jewish Paternal Tradition." *TynBul* 47 (1996) 163–71.

Neyrey, J. H. "Witchcraft Accusations in 2 Cor 10–13: Paul in Social Science Perspective." *Listening* 21 (1986) 160–70.

O'Collins, G. G. "Power Made Perfect in Weakness: 2 Cor 12:9–10." *CBQ* 33 (1971) 528–37.

Olley, J. W. "A Precursor of the NRSV? 'Sons and Daughters in 2 Cor 6:18." *NTS* 44 (1998) 204–12.

Olson, S. N. "Epistolary Uses of Expressions of Self-confidence." *JBL* 103 (1984) 585–97.

———. "Pauline Expressions of Confidence in His Addressees." *CBQ* 47 (1985) 282–295

Osei–Bonsu, J. "Does 2 Cor. 5.1–10 Teach the Reception of the Resurrection Body at the Moment of Death?" *JSNT* 28 (1986) 81–101.

———. "The Intermediate State in the New Testament." *SJT* 44 (1991) 169–94.

Park, D. M. "Paul's ΣΚΟΛΟΨ ΤΗ ΣΑΡΚΙ Thorn or Stake? (2 Cor. Xl1.7)." *NovT* 22 (1980) 179–83.

Perriman, A. C. "Paul and the Parousia. 1 Corinthians 15.50–57 and 2 Corinthians 5.1–5." *NTS* 35 (1989) 512–21.

———. "Between Troas and Macedonia: 2 Cor 2:13–14." *ExpT* 101 (1989–90) 39–41.

Polhill, J. B. "Reconciliation at Corinth: 2 Corinthians 4–7." *RevExp* 86 (1989) 345–57.

Price, J. L. "Aspects of Paul's Theology and Their Bearing on Literary Problems of Second Corinthians." In *Studies in the History and Text of the New Testament*. Edited by B. L. Daniels and M. J. Suggs. Studies and Documents 29. Grand Rapids: Eerdmans, 1967, 95–106.

Price, R. M. "Punished in Paradise (An Exegetical Theory on II Corinthians 12:1–10)." *JSNT* 7 (1980) 33–40.

Provence, T. E. "'Who Is Sufficient for These Things'? An Exegesis of 2 Corinthians ii 15–iii 18." *NovT* 24 (1982) 54–81.

Rensberger, D. "2 Corinthians 6:14–7:1: A Fresh Examination." *SBT* 8 (1978) 25–49.

Richard, E. "Polemics, Old Testament, and Theology. A Study of II Cor. III,1–IV,6." *RB* 88 (1981) 340–67.

Roetzel, J. C. "'As Dying, and Behold We Live.' Death and Resurrection in Paul's Theology." *Int* 46 (1992) 5–18.

Sabourin, L. "Christ Made 'Sin' (2 Cor 5:21): Sacrifice and Redemption in the History of a Formula." In *Sin, Redemption and Sacrifice. A Biblical and Patristic Study.* Edited by S. Lyonnet and L. Sabourin. AnBib 48. Rome: Pontifical Biblical Institute, 1970, 185–296.

Sampley, J. P. "Paul, His Opponents in 2 Corinthians 10–13, and the Rhetorical Handbooks." In *The Social World of Formative Christianity and Judaism.* Edited by J. Neusner. Philadelphia: Fortress 1988, 162–77.

Scott, J. M. "The Use of Scripture in 2 Corinthians 6:16c–18 and Paul's Restoration Theology." *JSNT* 56 (1994) 73–99.

———. "The Triumph of God in 2 Cor. 2:14: Another Example of Merkabah Mysticism." *NTS* 37 (1991) 573–91.

Schäfer, P. "New Testament and Hekhalot Literature: The Journey into Heaven in Paul and in Merkavah Mysticism." *JJS* 36 (1984) 19–35.

Sevenster, J. N. "Some Remarks on the ΓΥΜΝΟΣ in II Cor. V.3, *Studia Paulina*. Edited by J. N. Sevenster and W. C. Van Unnik. Haarlem: Bohm, 1953, 202–14.

Sloan, Jr., R. B. "2 Corinthians 2:14–4:6 and 'New Covenant Hermeneutics' — A Response to Richard Hays." *BBR* 5 (1995) 129–54.

Spittler, R. P. "The Limits of Ecstasy: An Exegesis of 2 Corinthians 12:1–10." In *Current Issues in Biblical and Patristic Interpretation.* Edited by G. F. Hawthorne. Grand Rapids: Eerdmans, 1975, 259–66.

Stephenson, A. M. G. "A Defence of the Integrity of 2 Corinthians." In *The Authorship and Integrity of the New Testament.* Edited by K. Aland. London: SPCK, 1965, 82–97.

Steward–Sykes, A. "Ancient Editors and Copyists and Modern Partition Theories: The Case of the Corinthian Correspondence." *JSNT* 61 (1996) 53–64.

Stockhausen C. K. "2 Corinthians 3 and the Principles of Pauline Exegesis." In *Paul and the Scriptures of Israel.* Edited by C. A. Evans and J. A. Sanders. JSNTSup 83. Sheffield: Sheffield Academic Press, 1993, 143–64.

Story, C. I. K. "The Nature of Paul's Stewardship with Special Reference to I and II Corinthians." *EvQ* 48 (1976) 212–29.

Stowers, S. K. "ΠΕΡΙ ΜΕΝ ΓΑΡ and the Integrity of 2 Cor. 8 and 9." *NovT* 32 (1990) 340–48.

Sumney, J. L. "The Role of Historical Reconstruction of Early Christianity in Identifying Paul's Opponents." *Perspectives in Religious Studies* 16 (1989) 45–53.

———. "Paul's 'Weakness': An Integral Part of His Conception of Apostleship." *JSNT* 52 (1993) 71–91.

Talbert, C. H. "Money Management in Early Mediterranean Christianity: 2 Corinthians 8 and 9." *RevExp* 86 (1989) 359–70.

Taylor, N. H. "The Composition and Chronology of Second Corinthians." *JSNT* 44 (1991) 67–87.

Thrall, M. E. "2 Corinthians 1:12: ΑΓΙΟΤΗΤΙ or ΑΠΛΟΤΗΤΙ?" In *Studies in New Testament Language and Text.* Edited by J. K. Elliott. NovTSup 44. Leiden: Brill,

1976, 366–72.

_____. "The Problem of II Cor. vi.14–vii.1 in Some Recent Discussions." *NTS* 24 (1977–78) 132–48.

_____. "Super-Apostles, Servants of Christ, and Servants of Satan." *JSNT* 6 (1980) 42–57.

_____. "Salvation Proclaimed. 2 Corinthians 5:18–21: Reconciliation with God." *ExpT* 93 (1982) 227–31.

_____. "A Second Thanksgiving Period in II Corinthians." *JSNT* 16 (1982) 101–24.

_____. "The Offender and the Offence: A Problem of Detection in 2 Corinthians." In *Scripture. Meaning and Method.* Edited by B. P. Thompson. Hull: Hull University Press, 1987, 65–78.

Turner, D. L. "Paul and the Ministry of Reconciliation in 2 Cor 5:11–6:2." *CTR* 4 (1989–90) 77–95.

van Unnik, W. C. "'With Unveiled Face': An Exegesis of 2 Corinthians iii 12–18." *NovT* 6 (1963) 153–69.

Wagner, G. "The Tabernacle and Life 'in Christ.' Exegesis of 2 Corinthians 5.1–10." *IBS* 3 (1981) 145–65.

Watson, F. "2 Cor. x–xiii and Paul's Painful Letter to the Corinthians." *JTS* 35 (1984) 324–46.

Watson, N. "'...To make us rely not on ourselves but God who raises the dead': 2 Cor. 1,9b as the Heart of Paul's Theology." In *Die Mitte des Neuen Testaments.* Edited by U. Luz and H. Weder. Göttingen: Vandenhoeck & Ruprecht, 1983, 384–98.

Wenham, D. "2 Corinthians 1:17,18: Echo of a Dominical Logion." *NovT* 28 (1986) 271–79.

Williamson, L., Jr. "Led in Triumph: Paul's Use of *Thriambeuō*." *Int* 22 (1968) 317–32.

Wolff, C. "True Apostolic Knowledge of Christ: Exegetical Reflections on 2 Corinthians 5.14ff." In *Paul and Jesus. Collected Essays.* Edited by A. J. M. Wedderburn. JSNTSup 37. Sheffield: JSOT, 1989, 81–98.

Wong, E. "The Lord Is the Spirit (2 Cor 3:1 7a)." *ETL* 61 (1985) 48–72.

Wong, K. "'Lord' in 2 Corinthians 10:17." *Louvain Studies* 17 (1992) 243–53.

Woods, L. "Opposition to a Man and His Message: Paul's 'Thorn in the Flesh' (2 Cor 12:7)." *AusBR* 39 (1991) 44–53.

Wright, N. T. "Reflected Glory: 2 Corinthians 3:18." In *The Glory of Christ in the New Testament: Studies in Christology.* Edited by L. D. Hurst and N. T. Wright. Oxford: Oxford University Press, 1987, 139–50.

Yates, R. "Paul's Affliction in Asia: 2 Corinthians 1:8." *EvQ* 53 (1981) 241–45.

Young, F. "Note on 2 Corinthians 1:17b." *JTS* 37 (1986) 404–15.

Selected Subject Index

Person Index

Selected Scripture Index